WORD
BIBLICAL
COMMENTARY

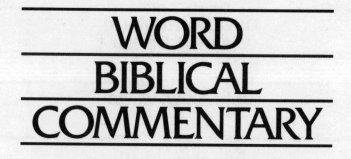

WORD
BIBLICAL
COMMENTARY

General Editors
David A. Hubbard
Glenn W. Barker †

Old Testament Editor
John D. W. Watts

New Testament Editor
Ralph P. Martin

WORD
BIBLICAL
COMMENTARY

VOLUME 7

Joshua

TRENT C. BUTLER

THOMAS NELSON PUBLISHERS

Nashville

Word Biblical Commentary:
JOSHUA
Copyright © 1983 by Word, Incorporated

Library of Congress Cataloging in Publication Data
Main entry under title:

Word biblical commentary.

    Includes bibliographies.
    1. Bible—Commentaries—Collected works.
BS491.2.W67   220.7′7   81–71768
ISBN 0–8499–0206–1 (v. 7)   AACR2

Printed in Colombia

03 04 05 06 07 08 09 QWB 15 14 13 12 11

Contents

Author's Preface   ix
Editorial Preface   xi
Abbreviations   xiii

Introduction   xvii
  The Text   xvii
  The Formation of the Book   xx
  The Meaning of the Material   xxiii
  Review of Critical Research   xxvii
  Literary (Source) Criticism   xxviii
  Form Criticism   xxx
  "The Amphictyony"   xxxiii
  Archaeology and Joshua   xxxvi
  Bibliography   xxxviii
  Summary   xxxix
I. POSSESSING THE PROMISE (JOSHUA 1–12)   1
  Divine Marching Orders   (1:1–9)   2
  Chain of Command Organized   (1:10–11)   15
  Lesson in Leadership   (1:12–18)   18
  A Prostitute's Profession   (2:1–24)   24
  Crossing to Conquer   (3:1—5:1)   36
  Cultically Correct for Conquest   (5:2–15)   53
  Faith Fells Fortifications   (6:1–27)   63
  Consequence of Covenant Curse   (7:1—8:29)   73
  Fulfilling Moses' Orders   (8:30–35)   89
  Covenant Compromise   (9:1–27)   95
  The Southern Sweep   (10:1–43)   105
  Northern Annihilation   (11:1–23)   120
  Victory's Victims   (12:1–24)   131
  God's Geographical Guidance   (13–19)   141
II. LOTS FOR THE LAND (JOSHUA 13:1—19:51)   141
  Divide What You Have   (13:1–7)   145
  Reviewing Moses' Allotments   (13:8–33)   153

CONTENTS

Beginning with Caleb   (14:1–15)   167
Judah and Joseph   (15:1—17:18)   175
The Shiloh Selections   (18:1—19:51)   193

III. LIFE IN THE LAND   (JOSHUA 20—24)   209
Setting Up Sanctuaries   (20:1–9)   210
The Levitical Cities   (21:1–42)   218
Gifts from God's Goodness   (21:43–45)   233
Authority and Aim of an Altar   (22:1–34)   236
The Commander's Concluding Charge   (23:1–16)   250
Commitment to the Covenant   (24:1–28)   257

INDEXES   285

Author's Preface

What type person would devote years in Switzerland to a study of the conflicts and conquests of the Book of Joshua? Why would one look down from the majesty of the Swiss mountains to the horror of Hebrew "holy war" *cherem?*

The answer lies, I suppose, in the "accidents" of human history under God. I drove out of the dusty heat of West Texas into the classrooms of Southern Baptist Seminary in Louisville, Kentucky, ready to put aside the pat answers of childhood because they no longer seemed to have meaning in face of questions brought to the fore by the recent death of my adopted hemophiliac brother and a near-fatal accident which had forced me to spend University graduation night unconscious in the hospital.

I began looking for answers in the normal places. Strangely, exegesis of Genesis, Galatians, John, seemed to join Systematic Theology in raising new questions rather than solving the old ones. Finally, Professor Don Williams offered a seminar course in Deuteronomy and the Deuteronomic history. I joined a team including my roommate Paul Redditt, who also later joined the ranks of Old Testament professors. We explored the Hebrew Passover in enough depth to develop wild new theories on the most varied aspects of Hebrew worship, faith, and the origin of the Hebrew Scriptures. Actually, I learned few real answers here, but I learned something much more important. I learned how to ask significant questions of the biblical materials. I lost my preoccupation with the standard "unanswerable questions" and devoted my life to the excitement of biblical exegesis.

Then God introduced a new excitement into my life. Mary Burnett of Nashville, Tennessee, entered Southern Seminary. Soon she occupied more of my time than did the classroom excitement I had just discovered. The marvelous mystery of trusting, loving personal relationship began to supply answers to many of the questions, whose answers I had sought for in vain in my many books. After sixteen years of marriage and two exciting, loving sons, the excitement keeps increasing, and the answers continue to appear mysteriously when they are most needed.

The academic quest continued in Vanderbilt University with a seminar on Methods in Biblical Scholarship demanding research on historical method as illustrated in the study of Joshua 1–12. Exploring the history of historical research revealed the flood of questions I had never asked, questions to which I would devote the next ten years of my life. Archaeological results, literary studies, sociological theories, textual investigations, linguistic developments, and a flood of other information all had to be sorted out and fitted into theological presuppositions to form a new theological perspective. The more study I devoted to Joshua, the more I became convinced that a solution to its problems would yield a solid foundation for constructing a literary and theological history of the Old Testament, if not of the entire Bible. Joshua offered the keys to understanding the time-honored Pentateuch/Hexateuch debate, the origin and nature of Israel's worship prior to the Temple, the nature of pre-monarchical government, and the home and meaning of covenant theology. What was more, Joshua presented both the fulfillment of the promises to the patriarchs and the establishment of the promises to the Exiles.

Sad to report, the present commentary, as all others, cannot provide keys to open the locks to all these tantilizing subjects. We must suffice with a report along the scholarly way. We can report that the years devoted to the venture have raised not only new questions but have also raised new levels of personal faith for the author.

For this faith-provoking venture, I want to express personal thanks to the many compatriots who have helped and encouraged me along the way: Church members at Hopewell Baptist Church, Springfield, Tennessee; Calvary Baptist Church, Lilburn, Georgia; Ruschlikon Baptist Church, Ruschlikon, Switzerland; and the several congregations of the European Baptist Convention, English Language. Further thanks are due the constantly questioning, yet supporting, students at Atlanta Baptist College (now Mercer University, Atlanta); Baptist Theological Seminary, Ruschlikon, Switzerland; Southern Baptist Theological Seminary, Louisville, Kentucky, and the many others at guest lectures throughout Israel, Yugoslavia, Germany, Poland, Portugal.

The greatest gratitude goes to Mary, Curt, and Kevin who have endured the lonely days while Daddy wrote "the Book." Their support and love have made the endeavor worthwhile.

A final word must be directed to John Watts and his editorial staff for enduring with me to the end.

Nashville, Tennessee
September 21, 1982   TRENT BUTLER

Editorial Preface

The launching of the *Word Biblical Commentary* brings to fulfillment an enterprise of several years' planning. The publishers and the members of the editorial board met in 1977 to explore the possibility of a new commentary on the books of the Bible that would incorporate several distinctive features. Prospective readers of these volumes are entitled to know what such features were intended to be; whether the aims of the commentary have been fully achieved time alone will tell.

First, we have tried to cast a wide net to include as contributors a number of scholars from around the world who not only share our aims, but are in the main engaged in the ministry of teaching in university, college and seminary. They represent a rich diversity of denominational allegiance. The broad stance of our contributors can rightly be called evangelical, and this term is to be understood in its positive, historic sense of a commitment to scripture as divine revelation, and to the truth and power of the Christian gospel.

Then, the commentaries in our series are all commissioned and written for the purpose of inclusion in the *Word Biblical Commentary*. Unlike several of our distinguished counterparts in the field of commentary writing, there are no translated works, originally written in a non-English language. Also, each commentator was asked to prepare his own rendering of the original biblical text and to use those languages as the basis of his own comments and exegesis. What may be claimed as distinctive with this series is that it is based on the biblical languages, yet it seeks to make the technical and scholarly approach to a theological understanding of scripture understandable by—and useful to—the fledgling student, the working minister as well as to colleagues in the guild of professional scholars and teachers.

Finally, a word must be said about the format of the series. The layout in clearly defined sections has been consciously devised to assist readers at different levels. Those wishing to learn about the textual witnesses on which the translation is offered are invited to consult the section headed "Notes." If the readers' concern is with the state of modern scholarship on any given portion of scripture, then they should turn to the sections on "Bibliography" and "Form/Structure/Setting." For a clear exposition of the passage's meaning and its relevance to the ongoing biblical revelation, the concluding "Explanation" is designed expressly to meet that need. There is therefore something for everyone who may pick up and use these volumes.

If these aims come anywhere near realization, the intention of the editors will have been met, and the labor of our team of contributors rewarded.

General Editors: *David A. Hubbard*
Glenn W. Barker †
Old Testament: *John D. W. Watts*
New Testament: *Ralph P. Martin*

Abbreviations

Abbreviations of Biblical Books and Apocrypha

Gen	1–2–3–4 Kgdms
Exod	Add Esth
Lev	Bar
Num	Bel
Deut	1–2 Esdr
Josh	4 Ezra
Judg	Jdt
1–2 Sam	Ep Jer
1–2 Kgs	1–2–3–4 Mace
Isa	Pr Azar
Jer	Pr Man
Ezek	Sir
Hos	Sus
Joel	Tob
Amos	Wis
Obad	Matt
Jonah	Mark
Mic	Luke
Nah	John
Hab	Acts
Zeph	Rom
Hag	1–2 Cor
Zech	Gal
Mal	Eph
Ps (*pl.*: Pss)	Phil
Job	Col
Prov	1–2 Thess
Ruth	1–2 Tim
Cant	Titus
Eccl	Phlm
Lam	Heb
Esth	Jas
Dan	1–2 Pet
Ezra	1–2–3 John
Neh	Jude
1–2 Chr	Rev

Texts, Versions and Ancient Works

B. Bat.	*Baba Batra*	Syr	Syriac
Frg. Tg.	Fragmentary Targums	Tg	Targum
LXX	Septuagint	Vg	Vulgate
MT	Masoretic Text		

Modern Translations

JB	*Jerusalem Bible*	NIV	*New International Version*
NEB	*New English Bible*	RSV	*Revised Standard Version*

Periodicals, Reference Works and Serials

AASOR	Annual of the American Schools of Oriental Research
AB	Anchor Bible
AEHL	*Archaeological Encyclopedia of the Holy Land*, ed. A. Negev
AER	*American Ecclesiastical Review*
AfO	*Archiv für Orientforschung*
AJBI	*Annual of the Japanese Bible Institute*
AJSL	*American Journal of Semitic Languages and Literature*
AnBIb	Analecta Biblica
ANEP	*Ancient Near East in Pictures*, ed. J. B. Pritchard
ANET	*Ancient Near Eastern Texts*, ed. J. B. Pritchard
AOAT	Alter Orient und Altes Testament
ArOr	*Archiv Orientalni*
ASTI	*Annual of the Swedish Theological Institute*
ATANT	Abhandlungen zur Theologie des Alten und Neuen Testaments
BA	*Biblical Archaeologist*
BASOR	*Bulletin of the American Schools of Oriental Research*
BBB	Bonner biblische Beiträge
BDB	F. Brown, S. R. Driver and C. A. Briggs, *Hebrew and English Lexicon of the Old Testament*
BeO	*Bibbia e oriente*
BHH	*Biblisch-Historisches Handwörterbuch*, ed. B. Reicke and L. Rost
BHK	*Biblia hebraica*, ed. R. Kittel
BHS	*Biblia hebraica stuttgartensia*
Bib	*Biblica*
BibS(N)	Biblische Studien (Neukirchen, 1951–)
BKAT	Biblischer Kommentar: Altes Testament
BN	*Biblische Notizen*
BTS	Bible et terre sainte
BWANT	Beiträge zur Wissenschaft vom Alten und Neuen Testament
BZ	*Biblische Zeitschrift*
BZAW	Beihefte zur *ZAW*
CAH	*Cambridge Ancient History*
CahRB	Cahiers de la *Revue Biblique*
CBQ	*Catholic Biblical Quarterly*
DBlatt	*Dielheimer Blätter zum Alten Testament*
DOTT	*Documents from Old Testament Times*, ed. D. W. Thomas
DTT	Dansk teologisk tidsskrift
EAEHL	*Encyclopedia of Archaeological Excavations in the Holy Land*, ed. M. Avi-Yonah and E. Stern
EncJud	*Encyclopedia Judaica* (1971)
EvT	*Evangelische Theologie*
ExpTim	*Expository Times*
FRLANT	Forschungen zur Religion und Literatur des Alten und Neuen Testaments
GKC	*Gesenius' Hebrew Grammar*, ed. E. Kautsch, tr. A. E. Cowley
GS	*Gesammelte Studien*
HAT	Handbuch zum Alten Testament
HDR	Harvard Dissertations in Religion
HKAT	Handkommentar zum Alten Testament
HSM	Harvard Semitic Monographs
HTR	*Harvard Theological Review*
HUCA	*Hebrew Union College Annual*

IDB	*Interpreter's Dictionary of the Bible,* ed. G. A. Buttrick
IDBSup	Supplementary volume to *IDB*
IEJ	*Israel Exploration Journal*
Int	*Interpretation*
JAOS	*Journal of the American Oriental Society*
JBL	*Journal of Biblical Literature*
JNES	*Journal of Near Eastern Studies*
JPOS	*Journal of the Palestine Oriental Society*
JQR	*Jewish Quarterly Review*
JSOT	*Journal for the Study of the Old Testament*
JSOTSup	*Journal for the Study of the Old Testament,* Supplement Series
JSS	*Journal of Semitic Studies*
KAT	Kommentar zum Alten Testament, ed. E. Sellin
KB	*Lexicon in Veteris Testamenti libros,* ed. L. Koehler and W. Baumbartner (KB³, Third Edition)
KS	*Kleine Schriften*
NCB	New Century Bible
NICOT	New International Commentary on the Old Testament
NRT	La nouvelle revue théologique
OLZ	*Orientalische Literaturzeitung*
OTL	Old Testament Library
OTS	*Oudtestamentische Studiën*
PEFQS	*Palestine Exploration Fund, Quarterly Statement*
PEQ	*Palestine Exploration Quarterly*
PJ	*Palästina-Jahrbuch*
RB	*Revue biblique*
RevExp	*Review and Expositor*
RGG	*Religion in Geschichte und Gegenwart*
RHR	*Revue de l'histoire des religions*
RTP	*Revue de théologie et de philosophie*
SANT	Studien zum Alten und Neuen Testament
SBLMS	SBL Monograph Series
SBS	Stuttgarter Bibelstudien
SBT	Studies in Biblical Theology
SEÅ	Svensk exegetisk årsbok
ST	*Studia theologica*
TBu	Theologische Bücherei
TDOT	*Theological Dictionary of the Old Testament*
TGl	*Theologie und Glaube*
THAT	*Theologisches Handwörterbuch zum Alten Testament,* ed. E. Jenni and C. Westermann
TLZ	*Theologische Literaturzeitung*
TP	*Theologie und Philosophie*
TRu	*Theologische Rundschau*
TWAT	*Theologisches Wörterbuch zum Alten Testament,* ed. G. J. Botterweck and H. Ringgren
TZ	*Theologische Zeitschrift*
UF	*Ugaritische Forschungen*
VD	*Verbum domini*
VF	*Verkündigung und Forschung*
VT	*Vetus Testamentum*
VTSup	Vetus Testamentum, Supplements
WMANT	Wissenschaftliche Monographien zum Alten und Neuen Testament

WTJ	Westminster Theological Journal
ZAW	Zeitschrift für die alttestamentliche Wissenschaft
ZDPV	Zeitschrift des deutschen Palästina-Vereins
ZKT	Zeitschrift für katholische Theologie
ZTK	Zeitschrift für Theologie und Kirche

Introduction

Bibliography

Texts and Versions

Brook, A. E. and **McLean, N.** *The Old Testament in Greek.* Vol. 1, Part IV. *Joshua, Judges and Ruth.* Cambridge: University Press, 1917. **Elliger, K.** and **Rudolph, W.** *Biblia Hebraica Stuttgartensia.* Stuttgart: Deutsche Bibelstiftung, 1976/77. **Field, F.** *Origenis Hexaplorum.* Vol. I. *Prolegomena Genesis-Esther.* Hildesheim: Georg Olms Verlagsbuchhandlung, 1964 (original, 1875). **Kittel, R.** *Biblia Hebraica.* Stuttgart: Württembergische Bibelanstalt, 1937. **Macdonald, J.** *The Samaritan Chronicle No. II* (or: *Sepher Ha-Yamim*) *From Joshua to Nebuchadnezzar.* BZAW 107. Berlin: Walter de Gruyter, 1969. **Margolis, M. L.** *The Book of Joshua in Greek.* Publications of the Alexander Kohut Memorial Foundation. Paris: Librairie Orientaliste Paul Geuthner, 1931. **Rahlfs, A.** *Septuaginta.* Vol. 1. *Leges et historiae.* Stuttgart: Württembergische Bibelanstalt, 1935. **Sperber, A.** *The Bible in Aramaic.* Vol. II. *The Former Prophets according to Targum Jonathan.* Leiden: E. J. Brill, 1959. **Weber, R.** et al. *Biblia Sacra Iuxta Vulgatam Versionem.* Stuttgart: Württembergische Bibelanstalt, 1969.

Studies of the Text of Joshua

Auld, A. G. *Studies in Joshua: Text and Literary Relationships.* Dissertation, University of Edinburgh, 1976. ———. "Judges 1 and History: a Reconsideration." *VT* 25 (1975) 261–85. ———. "A Judean Sanctuary of 'Anat (Josh. 15:5)?" *Tel Aviv* 4 (1977) 85–86. ———. "Textual and Literary Studies in the Book of Joshua." *ZAW* 90 (1978) 412–417. ———. "The 'Levitical Cities': Texts and History." *ZAW* 91 (1979) 194–206. ———. "Joshua: the Hebrew and Greek Texts." VTSup 30 (1979) 1–14. **Benjamin, C. D.** *The Variations between the Hebrew and Greek Texts of Joshua: Chapters 1–12.* Thesis, University of Pennsylvania. Leipzig: W. Drugulin, 1921. **Greenspoon, L.** "Theodotion, Aquila, Symmachus, and the Old Greek of Joshua." Unpublished paper read to the one hundred fifteenth annual meeting of the Society of Biblical Literature in New York, Nov. 15, 1979. **Holmes, S.** *Joshua, the Hebrew and Greek Texts.* Cambridge: University Press, 1914. **Margolis, M. L.** "The Groupings of the Codices in the Greek Joshua." *JQR* New Series 1 (1910) 259–63. ———. "The K Text of Joshua." *AJSL* 28 (1911) 1–55. ———. "The Washington MS of Joshua." *JAOS* 31 (1911) 365–67. ———. "Specimen of a New Edition of the Greek Joshua." *Jewish Studies in Memory of Israel Abrahams.* New York: 1927, 307–23. *Preliminary and Interim Report on the Hebrew Old Testament Text Project.* Vol. 2. *Historical Books.* Stuttgart: United Bible Societies, 1976. **Rofé, A.** "The End of the Book of Joshua According to the Septuagint." *Shnaton* 2 (1977) 217–27.

The Text of the Book of Joshua

The first step in interpretation is to determine the basic text. As of this writing, critical editions of the earliest texts of Joshua have not yet been published. Joshua material remains unpublished in the Hebrew University Bible Project, the Göttingen Septuagint, the Leiden Peshitta, and the Dead Sea Scrolls publication. Margolis' critical edition of the Joshua Septuagint remained unfinished at his death. Thus the history of the text of Joshua remains a future goal for scholarship.

The present work can only hope to show the necessity of the goal and the nature of the textual process. The work, as all current work on Joshua, is based on the Leningrad Codex B 19ᴬ published in a new critical edition *Biblia Hebraica Stuttgartensia* ed. R. Meyer (1972). The manuscript itself dates from A.D. 1008. We have limited our text critical work to a rather thorough comparison of the Hebrew text with the earliest Greek translation, dating back to about the second century B.C., but preserved only in manuscripts dating from the fourth Christian century (*Septuaginta.* Ed. A. Rahlfs [1935]). The comparison leads to several interesting conclusions. The Greek shows numerous divergences from the Hebrew text in every chapter, at times in every verse of a chapter. Many of these divergences can be explained as simple mechanical errors which occur when a text must be copied by hand. The majority of the differences cannot, however, be explained in this manner. A few of the changes result from translators who did not understand the precise nuance of Hebrew words, forms, or syntax. A greater number of the differences rest on attempts of the Greek translator to improve the style or continuity of the narrative itself. Here it becomes clear that the earliest translator did not feel himself obliged to reproduce an original text word for word. Critical evaluation of such changes leads a step further. The changes are not limited to the Greek translator. Indeed, at points the Greek translation represents a better preserved text than our Hebrew manuscripts. Comparison shows that the Hebrew manuscript behind our Greek text was different from the Hebrew manuscripts we presently possess. This means that such literary changes do not reflect simply a change caused by going from one language and culture to another. Such changes were already occurring in the transmission of the Hebrew text. The discovery of the Dead Sea Scrolls has proved this point beyond a shadow of a doubt.

A frequent cause of distinction between the two text forms comes in the use of idiomatic phrases, particularly those which appear in variant forms. Thus at 1:11 the Hebrew speaks of "Yahweh your God," while the Greek reads "Yahweh, the God of your fathers." Similarly, titles such as "servant of Yahweh" are often used at different places by the traditions, without a pattern being visible in either (e.g. 1:1, 15).

The most interesting changes are those with practical and theological relevance to the communities for which the Bible was preserved and translated. Here we see the copyists often bringing in material from other biblical texts or interpreting the material in a way to make it more relevant for their own time. This shows us that the Bible was not simply a book to be copied by the community. It remained a dynamic text to be preached and applied within the community. Such preaching and application was not confined to the teaching situation or the cultic worship. It took place even within the copying of the text itself.

A final category that must be noted is that of obvious theological change made to avoid language which could be misinterpreted and thus dangerous for the new generation, thus the elimination of Baal in the Hebrew text of 18:15.

The following table seeks to summarize the most obvious of such changes discovered in the preparation of the commentary and to categorize them in the general classes named above. It is clear that such categorization is too simple, each example being open to being placed in a different category. The purpose is to present in tabular form the quantity of the textual evidence involved and to provide quick reference for those who would like to study further the interesting question of how the textual evidence leads to a history of the interpretation as well as the transmission of the text.

The material is arranged according to the tradition in which the textual differences appear to have arisen, either the Greek Septuagint (LXX) with the Hebrew tradition on which it is based or the Massoretic tradition (MT) which resulted in the present Hebrew text.

Tendencies in Textual Transmission of Joshua

	MT	LXX
1. Mechanical Errors in Copying	2:1, 3, 4; 6:13, 20; 7:17; 8:6, 13, 29, 33, 9:2, 27; 10:3, 10, 13; 11:6, 7; 12:5; 13:7–8, 9, 29–30; 14:12; 15:1, 12, 18, 23, 28, 32, 36, 47, 59; 17:7, 9, 11; 18:16, 18–19, 24, 28; 19:2, 4–5, 7, 10, 13, 14, 21, 28, 29, 34, 42, 45, 46; 21:8, 15, 16, 22, 25, 27, 31, 34, 36–37, 42; 22:7, 12, 16, 19; 23:5, 11, 12, 13; 24:6, 30, 32.	1:11; 2:5, 13, 15, 21; 3:8; 6:10, 13; 7:2, 6, 17–18, 19; 8:15–16, 26, 29; 9:2, 10, 14, 18; 10:3, 10; 11:2, 4, 7, 10, 22; 12:1, 2, 3, 7, 13–14, 16, 20; 13:5, 9, 17–19, 26, 27, 29–30; 31; 14:2, 9, 15; 15:3, 5, 9–10, 14, 25, 59; 16:3; 17:7, 11; 18:4, 5, 15, 16, 18–19; 19:15, 19, 22, 29, 30, 35–36, 41, 50; 21:18, 20, 22, 29, 32, 40; 23:5, 14; 24:1, 14, 30, 33
2. Misunderstanding of Meaning, Forms, or Syntax	21:42	2:1, 4; 3:12; 4:3; 6:4; 7:5, 7, 21; 9:2, 7, 20; 10:25; 12:5; 13:3, 4, 9, 21, 22, 26; 14:4; 15:18; 17:14; 18:4; 19:8, 11; 21:42; 22:3, 8, 10, 14, 19, 20, 23; 23:11, 16; 24:6, 17, 20, 32
3. Literary Improvements	1:2; 2:4, 5, 22; 3:13; 5:9; 6:1, 2, 5, 15, 20; 7:2, 11, 15, 25–26; 8:1, 2, 9, 18, 20, 24, 28, 31, 32, 34; 9:6, 9, 12, 21; 10:1, 2, 11, 13, 15, 18, 26, 27, 28, 36, 43; 12:16, 18, 20, 23; 13:1, 10–11, 24; 15:20; 18:9; 19:1; 22:25; 24:30	1:1, 2, 4; 2:2–3, 4, 12, 13, 14, 15, 16; 3:10; 4:1–3, 5, 7, 11; 5:1, 10, 11, 14; 6:3, 12, 15, 20; 7:1, 13, 16–18; 8:1, 5, 11–14, 16, 21, 24, 32, 34, 35; 9:1, 5, 6, 9, 11, 20, 24, 25; 10:6, 11, 28, 30, 32, 33, 35, 37, 39; 11:2–3, 19; 12:4, 9, 18, 22, 24; 13:1, 2, 6, 12, 14, 16, 17, 23, 31, 33; 14:1, 4, 11, 12, 15; 15:4, 15, 18, 20; 16:1, 6–7, 10; 17:5, 14; 18:2, 6, 8, 9, 26–28; 19:8, 16, 25, 27, 31; 20:3; 22:9, 19, 22, 28, 33, 34; 23:3; 24:1, 4, 18, 19, 26, 33
4. Free Use of Familiar Phrases	6:1, 2; 8:7, 34; 12:6; 16:10; 17:15; 18:3, 11, 21; 19:41; 21:1, 5–6, 11, 13, 19, 20; 22:1, 4, 13, 16, 18, 29, 31–32; 23:13, 15; 24:3, 9, 17, 24	1:1, 11, 15; 2:10; 3:13; 4:8, 10; 6:17; 14:13; 18:7; 19:1, 8, 12, 16, 24, 32, 39, 40; 21:45; 22:1, 23; 23:2; 24:6, 7, 10, 11, 15, 33
5. Homiletic Interpretation & Exegesis	1:4, 7, 15; 2:3, 9, 14, 18; 3:1, 16; 4:3; 5:2; 6:3, 5, 8, *11*, 20, 22; 7:11, 24, 25, 26; 8:1, 8, 9, 17, 18, 24, 31; 9:1, 5, 19; 10:2, 5, 13, *22–23*, *24*, *28*, 35, 40, *41*; 11:*13*, 14, 15; 13:1, 14, 21; 14:1–2; 15:14, 32, 36, 63; 17:2, 3, 4, 5; 18:10, 13, 28; 19:6;	1:7, 14; 2:10, 12, 15, 17, 19, 20; 3:3, 9; 4:7, 8, *10*; 5:1, 4, 6; 6:3, 9, *21*, 26; 7:22, 23; 8:30–35, 34, 35; 9:2, 18, *22*, 23, 27; 10:*1*, 5, 10, 20, 21; 11:11, 19, 21, 22; 13:13, 14, 25, 26, 28; 14:2; 15:1, 5, *13*, 14; 16:10; 17:6, 11, 16, 17, 18; 18:*4–5*, 9, 11,

Tendencies in Textual Transmission of Joshua *(Continued)*

MT	LXX
20:3, 4–6, 8, 9; 21:10, 11, 21; 22:5, 30, 33; 23:5, 7, 12, 14, 16; 24:5, 8, 12, 13, 17, 22, 24, 27, 28–31, 32	17, 18, 28; 19:15, 22, 30, 38, 42–48; 20:3, 7, 9; 21:9, *12*, 34–35, 42; 22:4, 8, 10, 13, 15, 19, 30, 32–34, *34*; 23:4, 14; 24:1, 4, 5, 6, *13*, 15, 18, 25, *27*, 28–31, 30, 31, 32, 33
6. Avoid Unacceptable Language	13:5; 18:15; 24:30	9:17; 10:14, 32; 17:9; 19:11; 24:10, 11, 26

References in italics reflect a tendency of the tradition to emphasize the role and significance of Joshua.

Such a quantity of evidence raises problems for the biblical student. Should he work with the oldest manuscript, thus basing his work on the Septuagint, which served as the Bible of the Christian church for much of its history? Or should he work with the text representing the language in which the book was originally written, thus choosing the Hebrew text? Or should he attempt to remove the copyists' errors and work with the text which he reconstructs as being closest to the source used by the Massoretic or Septuagint tradition? Or should he be audacious enough to believe that he can remove all the interpretation of the later tradition and find the text which was first written down, thus removing from his text the earliest interpretation and exegesis? The arbitrary choice here is to take the Massoretic Text of the Hebrew tradition, translate it and interpret it as well as possible, while showing awareness of the problems into which this leads.

The Formation of the Book

The long period of interpretation and exegesis which text-critical work reveals leads one to suppose that such work did not have its beginning with the first copyists of the book. Such a process began long before the material was reduced to a text. This was the method by which Israel received the Word of God and passed it on to the ensuing generations. The purpose of this section is thus to seek to outline the process by which the present book received its present shape. This involves an attempt to study the history of the materials as they were used within Israel to celebrate the work of God and to proclaim the Word of God.

We can establish one clear point as we seek to understand the formation of Joshua. The language of Deuteronomy reappears at many points within the book. This has led Martin Noth to suggest that Joshua is part of a larger historical work, reaching from Deut 1 through 2 Kgs 25. Noth named this the Deuteronomistic history. The history itself may not be the product of one man, at one time. R. Smend and his students W. Dietrich and T. Veijola have attempted to demonstrate at least three stages in the Deuteronomistic writings, all written in Jerusalem after 580; that is, during the Exile. A. D. H. Mayes is more cautious, and rightly so, as he speaks of the editing of Deuteronomy as "a process rather than an event or events" (*Deuteronomy*,

NCB [1979] 29). He also notes that "there is no doubt but that the work of the deuteronomistic circle represents a process or movement which was not completed in the context of a single editing even incorporating Deuteronomy into the deuteronomistic history" (*Deuteronomy*, 43). Such a process of editing is precisely what text-critical study reveals. Israelite theologians were continually at work under the leadership of God seeking to interpret the holy traditions for the people of God. Still, we are justified in speaking of a Deuteronomistic editing which gave the book of Joshua its basic form and meaning. Such editing is most obvious in 1:1–18; 2:9b–11; 3:7, 10; 4:10, 12, 14, 24; 5:1, 5–6; 6:21, 26; 7:7–9, 11*, 15*; 8:18, 26, 29, 30–35; 9:9b–10, 24aB, 27bB; 10:25, 40; 11:3, 11–12, 14b–15, 20b–23; 12:1–13; 13:1–14, 32–33; 14:1–5, 14–15; 15:13–15; 17:3–6; 18:1, 7; 19:51; 20:8–9; 21:1–3, 43–45; 22:1–6; 23:1–16; 24:1, 11aB, 12b–13, 24, 31–32.

Noting such editorial interpretation is extremely important theologically. Here we find how the inspired canonical writer understood and interpreted the sacred traditions transmitted to him by the community of faith. These verses unite the book into a theological whole. They tie the book to the biblical works which precede and follow. They provide the major theological perspective of the book.

The interpreter cannot be satisfied at this point. Was this the first interpretation given the material? Or can we discover still earlier ones? Admittedly, the work here becomes ever more subjective. Verse divisions attributed to tradition and interpretation are even more tentative. Still, an effort must be made and tentative results reported. An early editing of chaps. 2–11 appears quite evident. Such editing may even have extended into chaps. 14–17. It is most apparent in 2:1, 17–21, 24; 3:1; 4:9; 5:4, 7, 9, 10–12; 6:17–19, 22–25, 27; 7:1a, 10–12, 26; 8:2, 8, 9aB, 12–13, 23–25, 27–28; 9:1–3, 6–7, 15b, 22–23, 25–27abA; 10:1–2, 7, 9b, 10b–11a, 12a, 13aB–15, 19–20, 23, 26b–28, 29–39*, 41–43; 11:1–2, 10, 13–14a, 16–20a.

The editorial work of this Compiler, to use Noth's term, was not the first effort to gather Israel's traditions. Indeed, it was only the continuation of a process which the cult at Gilgal had been carrying on for a long time. The activity of this cult is particularly obvious in the cultic additions to chaps. 3 through 6: 3:5, 8, 15–16aAB; 4:1–3, 8, 15–23; 6:3b, 4, 6b, 8aB, b, 9*, 13a, 14–16a, 20a. The work of the Gilgal cult probably extended far beyond what we are able to isolate. The Compiler has had reason to make Gilgal the center of activity in 5:9–10; 9:6; 10:6, 7, 9, 15, 43 (cf. 14:6 and the *Comment* on chap. 22). Though we cannot describe the Gilgal cultic celebrations in as concrete terms as H. J. Kraus (*Gottesdienst in Israel* Munich: Kaiser Verlag, 1962, 179–193 = *Worship in Israel* Oxford: Blackwell, 1966, 152–165) or E. Otto (*Das Mazzotfest in Gilgal* BWANT 107. Stuttgart: W. Kohlhammer, 1975) would like, we do get enough evidence to show that this Benjaminite sanctuary played a primary role in gathering and celebrating the traditions which eventually became the heart of the book of Joshua. This teaches us that the heart of God's Word began not in the isolation of the scribe's study but in the active worship of the people of God. This means that one element in the mighty mystery of divine inspiration comprehends not just a lone individual, but extends to the entire community in its joyous celebration of worship.

Gilgal had no monopoly on Israelite tradition nor on divine inspiration. Gibeon (chaps. 9–10), Shechem (chap. 24; cf. 8:30–35), and Shilo (chaps. 18–22) also used their traditions to celebrate the greatness of Yahweh, eventually contributing their materials to the word of God.

Even worship in all its solemn greatness was not the beginning point for the book of Joshua. We can grope our way even beyond the Deuteronomistic historian, the Compiler, and the early worship of Israel to an earlier stage of the tradition. This stage shows great variety: ancient war poetry (10:12b–13aA); a spy narrative report (2:1–9, 12–16, 22–23); holy war catechesis (3:2–4, 6, 9, 11–14, 16b; 4:4–7, 11, 13); a popular anecdote about circumcision (5:2–3, 8); a divine test narrative (5:13–15); a story of military ruse (6:1–3a, 7, 8aA, 9*, 10–12, 13b, 16b, 20b); an ironical spy narrative introducing a story of military ambush (7:2–6; 8:1, 3–7, 9*, 10–11, 14–17, 19*, 20–22); a polemical narrative of sacral procedure used in face of divine anger (7:13–14, 16–25); a polemical etiology defending a social position (9:4–5, 8–9a, 11–15a), whose function has been reversed within the tradition (9:15b–21); a holy war miracle story (10:3–6, 8, 9a, 10a, 11b); a popular story of the defeat of five kings at Makkedah (10:16–18, 21–22, 24, 26a); a conquest itinerary (10:31–39*); another narrative of military ruse (11:4–9); and a political list of cities (12:14–24). Common to all of these materials is their roots in the political and military struggles of Israel and her tribes. Holy war theology, which Israel shared with her Near Eastern neighbors, is the common bond holding the traditions together. Here we see another dimension to the process by which God taught his people and directed the formation of his word.

The latter half of the book also contains traditional materials used in Israel long before they were incorporated into the Deuteronomistic history. The major elements comprise three types:

(a) Narratives: 14:6–13; 15:16–19; 17:14–18; 18:3–6, 8–10; 19:47, 49–50; 22:9–34.

(b) Political boundary and city lists: 13:15–31; 15:1–12, 20–62; 16:1–9; 17:1–2, 7–11; 18:11–28; 19:1–46, 48; 21:4–42.

(c) Notes on Canaanites remaining in the land: 13:13; 15:63; 16:10; 17:12–13.

Two other forms of literature must be noted, the law of the cities of refuge in 20:1–7 and the report of the covenant ceremony in 24:1–28. Appended to the book are the burial notices of 24:29–30, 32–33.

These traditions also have roots in the political and military struggles of early Israel. This gives us an important clue as to the earliest formation of the traditions. Such traditions had their origins amidst the struggles of Israel itself to gain her land, to gain peace with her neighbors, and quite importantly to gain a sense of unity among her own various tribes and clans. Such traditions are peculiarly at home among the tribe of Benjamin and its attempts to gain territory from the inhabitants of the land and to live in harmony with its tribal colleagues to the northwest, to the south, and across the Jordan to the east. Many of these traditions found a home in the cultic celebration, catechetical teaching, and even legal claims of the sanctuary of the Benjaminites in Gilgal. The sanctity of the holy place was not enough to insure peace even for the traditions. Other sanctuaries had other traditions with other claims. Thus Benjamin and its trans-Jordan allies faced the claims of Shiloh (Josh 22). Benjamin faced the land claims of an expanding Ephraim (Josh 17:14–18; Judg 12:1–6; 8:1–3; cf. 19–21; Deut 32:17). And the relationships to the south (cf. Josh 7:13–26) eventually burst into the fierce competition between the Benjaminite Saul and the Judean David (1 Sam 16–2 Sam 5). Such fightings within and without gave roots to the Joshua traditions. God used even the wars and squabblings of his people to prepare the foundation of his word. If we are to understand this word in its depths, we must seek to understand how that word functioned in this earliest setting, as well as within the later literary settings which provide the present form. This understanding sets out our methodology for understanding the meaning of the book of Joshua. The meaning cannot be limited to one level of the story. Rather, the history of the formation of tradition must be understood, a history which leads from ancient military traditions in the earliest history of Israel and her tribes and cults to a compiler seeking to unite the traditions to the final Deuteronomistic edition, which itself was probably the product of a literary process and which gave rise to continued literary activity as seen in the textual history.

The Meaning of the Material

The oral stage of the traditions center on certain life and death questions for God's people as they seek to settle in the land and establish their grip on its territory. These illustrate the weakness of the enemy kings (chap. 2); the miraculous power of Israel's God (chaps. 3–4, 6, 10, 11), the inability even of clever enemy kings to outsmart Israel (chap. 9), and the demand for obedience from Israel herself (chap. 5, 7–8). Political tensions lie behind the surface within these narratives, particularly chaps. 7, 9 and 10.

Cultic celebration has transformed the materials. Now they illustrate the mighty acts of God in continuing the work he began at the Exodus (4:23–24). Now the role of the priests are underscored. Gilgal assumes center stage. Motifs of polemic and ridicule are sublimated to the praise and adoration of the great acts of Yahweh for his people.

The first literary work is that of the Compiler, who continued the process of centering the materials on Gilgal (5:9; 9:6; 10:7, 9, 15, 43; cf. 14:6). He ties all the materials together explicitly into a continuous narrative emphasizing the conquest of the land. To do so, he uses the theme of pursuit. But past conquest is not his major emphasis. He brings this up to date, showing its present relevance through the use of etiological notations (4:9; 5:9, 12; 6:25; 7:26; 8:28; 9:27). Israel not only conquered the land, she gained a control over it which had results and effects still visible in the Compiler's day, so that no one could dispute Israel's claim to the land.

For the compiler, however, conquest and control were not the only themes. He showed conquest and control by a committed leader and his committed people. Thus the role of Joshua is emphasized with his obedience (4:9; 5:7; 6:25, 27; 8:1, 27, 28; 9:3, 22–27; 10:1, 14, 26, 41–42; 11:9, 16). Over against this stands the disobedience of the people (7:1; 9:16–21). We do not know the name of the Compiler chosen by God to collect and edit the traditions

of his people. We do know that the center of his life was the house of God
with its altar (6:24; 9:23, 27). The location of this house of God is likewise
unknown. In the present context, it appears to be at Gilgal. For the Compiler
it could have been Bethel (7:2; 8:9, 12, 17) or less probably Gibeon, the
center of the climactic battle (9–10). It may well have already been Jerusalem.
Here, we see that in the process of divine inspiration, the human agent and
geographical location are not important. What is important is the message
God has for his people. That message is summarized in the theological formula
of transference: "The Lord has given you the land" (2:9, 14, 24; 6:2, 16;
8:1, 7; 10:8, 12, 19, 30, 32; 11:6, 8). Both sides of the formula are important
for the Compiler. Speaking to Israel, he underlines the identity of the giver
of the land. Yahweh, not one of the gods of the land, gave the land to Israel.
Thus Israel's only allegiance is to Yahweh, the God of Israel. Over against
political enemies, the Compiler says the land belongs to Israel, being given
to her by Yahweh through the acts of Joshua. The importance of this "legal
claim" of Israel has been described recently by Martin Rose (*Deuteronomist
und Jahwist* Zurich: Theologischer Verlag, 1980). We have seen how the traditions themselves played a major part in the land claims between tribes, particularly in Benjamin's troubles with Judah to the south and with Ephraim to
the north. Rose claims that the written materials would not have found a
function within Israel until the land claim was a matter of major dispute,
having already been lost. Thus Rose dates the first written compilation of
the narratives to the period after 722. It is doubtful if one must look so
late in Israel's history to find a setting for such a writing. Rather, the period
of Saul and David already presents a moment of bitter dispute over land
claims, a dispute that was prolonged after the death of Saul. Precisely, Hebron,
the center of David's activities (1 Sam 26:31; 2 Sam 2:1–3), is the place where
Gilgal and the south are brought into confrontation in Joshua (cf. 14:6).
David's kingship was troubled by revolt centering again in Hebron (2 Sam
15:7–12). Opposition from Saul and the north had not vanished either (2
Sam 16:5–14; 20:1–22). The great division of the kingdom at Solomon's death
brought renewed crisis in the land claims of Israel, with Benjamin the dividing
point (1 Kgs 12). It was precisely at this period that Egypt once again threatened Judah (1 Kgs 14:25–27). Thus the early years of monarchy in Israel
proved to be a time of crisis in which tribes and then kingdoms fought over
the land which Yahweh had given Israel. It may well have been in the earliest
part of this era that a Benjaminite Compiler sought to set forth the claims
of Benjamin over against the Judean monarchy of David. The division of
the monarchy then saw Benjamin joined to the south, so that the southern
kingdom could now use the Benjaminite traditions as its base of land claim
over against the north. But such inner rivalry was not the ultimate meaning
of these traditions. God simply used the processes of men to maintain the
traditions of the people for the use to which God had intended them. Thus
the Deuteronomistic school took over the Jerusalem traditions and gave them
their canonical interpretation. Here again, God used anonymous men to teach
his people the divine word.

The final, canonical message of the Joshua traditions is made clear by
the Deuteronomistic structural markers:

   I. Theological prologue: Qualification for occupying the land (1:1–18).
  II. Cultic composition: Directions for a sinful people occupying the land (8:30–35).
 III. Theological summary: The results of meeting the qualifications (11:23).
  IV. Theological review: Program in face of unfinished task (13:1–7).
   V. Theological acclamation: God has been faithful in everything (21:43–45).
  VI. Theological program: A life of obedience beyond the Jordan (21:1–6).
 VII. Theological justification: Leaving the Lord loses the land (23:1–16).
VIII. Theological hope: A covenant with God (24:1–28).

This structure reveals both the setting and the message of the Deuteronomistic interpretation of the traditions of Joshua. It is a program for a life beyond the Jordan for a people who have lost the land and seek new hope. The final edition of Joshua thus speaks to the exiles beyond the Jordan in Babylon. It makes several points perfectly clear to them. These points can be discerned in two ways. First, one can observe the structure of the book, as we have just done. Secondly, one can seek recurring themes in the book, specifically in those parts which can be recognized as theological interpretations of the tradition. These can be considered in four major categories: the land, the leadership, the law, and the Lord.

The land is the most obvious subject. First, the book's structure shows that the land has been conquered (1–12) even though Israel has not been totally obedient (chaps. 7; 9). The land has also been divided among the people (chaps. 13–21). More specifically, the land is that which was promised to the fathers (1:6; 21:43; cf. 1:3). It is the land given by God (1:2, 3, 11, 13, 15; 9:24; 22:4; 24:11, 13). It is the land which Joshua was told to divide as an inheritance to the people (1:6; 13:6–7). It is the land which Joshua actually divided as an inheritance for the people (11:23; 14:5; 19:51; 21:43; 23:4). It was a land closely connected to the land east of the Jordan (1:12–18; 12:1–6; 13:8–33; 20:8; 21:6–7; 22:1–9, 10–34; 24:8–10). It was a land whose inhabitants proved no military problem, because God had caused them to tremble with fear (2:9, 11; 5:1; 9:9b–10, 24). It was a land, however, whose ancient gods tempted Israel (23:7, 12, 16; 24:15, 20, 23). This was possible because Israel had not possessed all the land or defeated all the peoples (13:1–6; 13:13; 15:63; 16:10; 17:12–13, 18; 19:47; 23:4, 12–13). But the promise remained that God would give this land himself (13:6; 23:5; cf. 17:18), but only if Israel obeyed (5:5–6; 7:7–9; 23:13, 15, 16; 24:20).

Israelite leadership presented a chronic problem and was in many ways the central problem for the Deuteronomists. Placed in Joshua's time, the problem was that of a successor for Moses. In the monarchy, the problem was that of a proper king. In the exilic day of the Deuteronomists, the problem was hope for new leadership (cf. 2 Kgs 25:27–30). The book of Joshua sets up an example of the perfect leader after Moses. The primary requisite for leadership proves not to be military but religious. The leader must be loyal to the law of Moses and his example (1:1, 5, 13–16; 3:7; 4:10, 14; 8:18, 26, 30–35; 11:11–12, 15, 20, 23; 17:3–6; 21:2–3; 22:2, 5–6; 24:25). Thus the entire book from first to last is a call for a leader and people to follow the law (1:7–8; 22:5; 23:6–8, 11, 16; cf. chap. 24). The leader who follows the law of Moses enjoys the presence of Yahweh, which was with Moses (1:5, 9, 17; 3:7, 10). This is grounds for a call to courage in leadership (1:6, 9, 18; 10:25). The leader who follows the law can expect to be followed by the people (1:10, 16–18; 4:10; 24:31).

The land is the reward. Leadership is the means. The law is the focus of attention. The essential theme remains. That is, naturally, God himself. This is the God of all the earth (2:11; 4:24)—the God of the revered name Yahweh (7:9; 9:9b). It is the God of the Exodus, who led Israel to conquer the kings east of the Jordan (2:10; 4:23; 9:9–10; 24:1–10, 17). It is the God who allowed Israel to conquer the entire land, thus fulfilling all his promises (10:40; 11:23; 21:43–45; 23:3, 9, 14; 24:11–13, 18).

These are the components of the Deuteronomistic theology of Joshua: a conquered land, which could be lost; a model for leadership, which was never again followed; a law given to Israel as her covenant, but repeatedly disobeyed; and a God of the universe, who had chosen and helped Israel, fulfilling all his promises and blessings, but who remained the God holy and jealous (24:19), ready to fulfill all his curses (6:26; 23:15–16; 24:20). For the exilic audience, the Deuteronomist sketched a picture loud with meaning. Those curses had been fulfilled. Israel had lost her land. Israel had not been faithful to her pledge to the covenant law. God had been faithful to his pledge to curse an unfaithful people. The remainder of Judges, Samuel, and Kings is used by the Deuteronomist to sketch Israel's history of unfaithful leadership and rebellious people. But the book of Joshua remains the central focus. For here is not only the historical explanation of why Israel was punished. Here is also a paradigm of hope. Israel must become as the east Jordan tribes (22:2–3). She must listen again to the law as Israel had done after her first defeat at Ai (8:30–35). She must pledge anew her obedience to God's covenant, even if God's leader was now old and weak and the chances of future military action appeared hopeless (chap. 24). She must remain totally faithful to Yahweh, the God of Israel and of all the earth, rather than following the temptation of the gods of the fathers beyond the River or of the ancestors in the land (chap. 23–24). A faithful Israel, even an Israel who had once made a covenant with the foreigners (chap. 9), could hope for victory once more. The promise to the fathers could once again be fulfilled. The land which remained, no matter how large, no matter how mighty its inhabitants and rulers, that land could once again be Israel's. But it depended on faithful leadership, loyal to the covenant law.

Israel in exile was thus called to renew its covenant, even if this had to be done without sacrifices (chap. 24). Only when Israel renewed its pledges, could Israel expect God to raise up a new judge or a new king to give the people the land again. But the ultimate goal was not the land itself. The ultimate goal was rest from war so Israel could serve Yahweh (1:13, 15; 11:23; 14:15; 21:44; 22:4; 23:1).

In such a light, the book of Joshua continues to speak to the people of God with its call for leadership, obedience to the divine will, and loyalty to the God of all the earth who fulfills all his promises. As the people in exile, the people of God today remain waiting for the promises to be fulfilled. We, too, await the day of rest. As we await the day of rest, we are given the same program as was Joshua, the program of studying the Word of God to search out its depths and embody them in our lives.

Review of Critical Research: Major Twentieth Century Commentaries

Keil and Delitzsch (1893) presents a strongly conservative orientation, while thoroughly conscious of critical work up to its time. This remains the most thorough linguistic study available, without losing the theological dimension (C. F. Keil and F. Delitzsch, *Joshua, Judges, Ruth.* Translated by J. Martin from *Biblischer Kommentar* [Leipzig, 1863]. Grand Rapids, Michigan: Wm. B. Eerdmans Publishing Company, 1950).

Holzinger (1901) emphasizes literary source delineation (H. Holzinger, *Das Buch Josua.* KAT II 6. Tübingen: J. C. B. Mohr [Paul Siebeck] Verlag, 1901).

Steuernagel (1900) wrote the most thorough commentary from the early part of the century with close attention to critical matters and language (C. Steuernagel, *Deuteronomium, Josua, Einleitung zum Hexateuch.* HAT I, 3. Göttingen: Vandenhoeck & Ruprecht, 1900).

Gressmann (1922) introduces form critical methodology to Joshua with thorough analysis of strata in tradition and literary activity (H. Gressmann, *Die Anfange Israels.* I *Die Sagen des Alten Testaments.* Vol 2. *Die Schriften des Alten Testaments.* 2nd ed. Göttingen: Vandenhoeck & Ruprecht, 1922).

Noth (1938) has become the standard German commentary with detailed attention to matters of geography, literary analysis, and form criticism but little interest in theology (M. Noth. *Das Buch Josua.* HAT I, 7. Tübingen: J. C. B. Mohr [Paul Siebeck], 1938, 1952 [2]).

Hertzberg (1965 [3]) presents more theological concern with the text than any of the other major commentaries, while still explaining the critical issues which arise (H. W. Hertzberg, *Die Bucher Josua, Richter, Ruth.* ATD 9. Göttingen: Vandenhoeck & Ruprecht, 1965 [3]).

Abel (1950) has the most up-to-date French commentary (F. M. Abel, *Le Livre de Josué. La sainte Bible.* Paris: Editions du Cerf, 1950, 1958 [2]).

Gray (1967) centers attention on sifting out the historical nucleus of the biblical traditions and illuminating details from the author's vast knowledge of the Ancient Near East. Only brief attention is paid to theological concerns (J. Gray, *Joshua, Judges and Ruth. The New Century Bible.* London: Thomas Nelson Ltd., 1967).

Kroeze (1968) has the most recent full Dutch commentary (J. H. Kroeze, *Het Boek Jozua. Commentaar op het Oude Testament.* Kampen: N. V. Uitgeversmaatschappij J. H. Kok, 1968).

Soggin (1970) gives massive details on literary, geographical, archaeological, and history of tradition matters but seldom ties his information together into a theological whole (J. A. Soggin, *Le Livre de Josué.* CAT 5a. Neuchatel: Éditions Delachaux et Niestlé, 1970; *Joshua.* OTL. Tr. R. A. Wilson. Philadelphia: Westminster Press, 1972).

Woudstra (1981) presents a massive contribution from the conservative side, aware of the problems raised by more critical scholars but intent to show the reliability of the Joshua narrative while identifying with the "German school" in the use of archaeological materials (M. H. Woudstra, *The Book of Joshua.* NICOT. Grand Rapids, MI: Wm. B. Eerdmans Publishing Company, 1981).

Literary (Source) Criticism

The history of Joshua and the Joshua of history have occupied biblical students at least since the early rabbis admitted that Joshua could not have reported his own death (see *B. Bat.* 14b, 15a). In 1564, John Calvin stressed the insignificance of the issue: "Let us not hesitate, therefore, to pass over a matter which we are unable to determine, or the knowledge of which is not very necessary, while we are in no doubt as to the essential point—that the doctrine herein contained was dictated by the Holy Spirit for our use, and confers benefits of no ordinary kind on those who attentively peruse it" (J. Calvin, *Commentarius in Librum Iosue.* Corpus Reformatorum. Brunsvigae: Schwetschke, 1882 [Calvina Opera 25] 421. Reprinted New York: Johnson Reprint Co., 1964. *Commentaries on The Book of Joshua.* Tr. Henry Beveridge. Edinburgh: Calvin Translation Society, 1854, xvii–xviii).

Calvin recognized the probability that Eleazar, the high priest, has compiled a summary of events which provided the materials for the composition of the book (xvii). His translator was uneasy with Calvin at this point and sought to underline the reasons for accepting the traditional view that Joshua wrote the book. The translator did note that "the authorship, however, is so uncertain that there is scarcely a writer of eminence from the period of the history itself down to the time of Ezra, for whom the honor has not been claimed. Among others may be mentioned Phinehas, Samuel, and Isaiah. The obvious inference is, that the question of authorship is one of those destined only to be agitated but never satisfactorily determined" (xviii, n. 1).

The sixteenth century Catholic jurist Andreas Masius (*Josuae imperatoris historia illustrata atquea explicata,* Antwerp [1574] noted the similarity between literary problems in Joshua and those in the Pentateuch, speaking of compilation and redaction for the first time. In the seventeenth century Benedict Spinoza (*Tractatus theologico-politicus* [1670]. Opera philosophica omnia, ed. A. Gfroerer, 164) attributed compilation to Ezra.

Friedrich Bleek (*De libri Geneseos,* 1836) and Friedrich Tuch (*Commentar über die Genesis,* 1858), fathers of the supplementary hypothesis, drew Joshua into the Pentateuchal documentary theories. Julius Wellhausen's climactic synthesis remained ambiguous in its analysis of Joshua. While finding evidence in chap. 24 that E formed the basic source in Joshua, Wellhausen noted in the same chapter, basic characteristics of Deuteronomistic editing, which, in turn, proved distinct from that in Deuteronomy (J. Wellhausen, *Die Composition des Hexateuchs und der historischen Bücher des Alten Testament.* [Berlin: Georg Reimer, 1889]). Rudolph later tried to bury E and claim all for J (W. Rudolph, *Der 'Elohist' von Exodus bis Josua.* [BZAW 68. Berlin: Alfred Töpelmann Verlag, 1938]). Möhlenbrink, on the other hand, traced separate traditions back to Shilo and Gilgal. For him, these proved to be older literarily, tradition-historically, and thematically than those of the Pentateuch. Indeed, Möhlenbrink claimed that many of the Pentateuchal materials had first crystalized around those of Joshua. (K. Möhlenbrink, "Die Landnahmesagen des Buches Joshua," *ZAW* 15 [1936] 236–68). See the recent discussion by Martin Rose noted below.

Martin Noth's writings illustrate the progression of literary studies in Joshua in this century. In 1930 he saw no reason to debate the basic E source (M. Noth, *Das System der zwölf Stämme Israels.* [BWANT 4. Heft 1. Stuttgart: W. Kohlhammer Verlag, 1930. Reproduced by Darmstadt: Wissenschaftliche Buchgesellschaft, 1966]). By 1937 with the first edition of his commentary, Noth had begun to speak of glosses and expansions of a basic narrative which could not be identified with any Pentateuchal source. He remained content to speak generally of a Gilgal collection of etiological narratives formed into a conquest narrative by a collector about 900 B.C. He described the lists in the middle of the book with Alt as a combination of a pre-monarchical list of tribal borders with a Josianic list of Judean cities divided into twelve districts. Exilic additions, Deuteronomistic redactions, and final Priestly supplementation closed the book for Noth (A. Alt, "Judas Gaue unter Josia." *PJ* 21 [1925] 100–116 [=*KS* 2, 1953, 276–288]; "Das System der Stämmesgrenzen im Buche Josua." *Beiträge zur Religionsgeschichte und Archaeologie Palästinas.* Sellin Festschrift. Leipzig: A. Deichert, 1927, 13–24 [=*KS* 1, 1953, 193–202]).

Noth opened a new epoch in Old Testament scholarship in 1943, birthing the Deuteronomist as compiler of a history work encompassing Deuteronomy, Joshua, Judges, Samuel, and Kings (M. Noth *Ueberlieferungsgeschichtliche Studien.* Tübingen: Max Niemeyer, 1943. Reprinted Darmstadt: Wissenschaftliche Buchgesellschaft, 1957 [= *The Deuteronomistic History.* JSOTSup 15. Sheffield, 1981]).

The second edition of Noth's commentary in 1952 officially buried the Priestly source as far as Joshua was concerned and made Deuteronomistic hands responsible ultimately for the basic narrative, for the later incorporation of 13:1–21:42, and for the final addition of chap. 24. A few priestly elements, but no priestly strata, were gradually assimilated into the book.

Major commentaries have followed the Nothian perspective with slight alterations of elements and dates. Only recently have steps been taken to refine or make significant shifts away from Noth.

Smend, Dietrich, and Veijola have sought to define more precisely three exilic editions of the Deuteronomistic history (R. Smend Jr. "Das Gesetz und die Völker." *Probleme biblischer Theologie.* von Rad Festschrift ed. H. W. Wolff. Munich: Chr. Kaiser Verlag 1971, 494–509. W. Dietrich, *Prophetie und Geschichte.* FRLANT 108. Göttingen: Vandenhoeck & Ruprecht, 1972. T. Veijola, *Die ewige Dynastie.* Annales Academiae Scientiarum Fennicae 193. Helsinki: Suomalainen Tiedeakatemia, 1975). Otto has attempted anew to demonstrate a Jahwistic strand in Joshua 1–11 alongside the Deuteronomistic, both based on ancient celebrations of the Feast of Unleavened Bread at Gilgal during the second half of the twelfth century (E. Otto, *Das Mazzotfest in Gilgal.* BWANT 107. Stuttgart: W. Kohlhammer Verlag, 1975). Tengström returned to a supplementary hypothesis, speaking of a Hexateuch which was the work of a premonarchical editor at Shechem in its basic constituents. For him, only such a hypothesis can explain the important role of Shechem at major narrative turning points. Deuteronomistic and Priestly supplementation produced first the Deuteronomistic and then Priestly history, though the latter is scarcely evident after Moses (S. Tengström, *Die Hexateucherzählung*. Coniectanea Biblica OT Series 7. Gleerup:CWK, 1976).

Finally, Woudstra's new commentary seeks to place the writing in the first generation or so after Joshua. Occasionally, he refers to possibilities of later redactors without really being willing to affirm their existence or work. In contrast stands the recent Zurich *Habilitationschrift* of Rose. He wants to understand the Pentateuch/Hexateuch question from the end, not the beginning. He starts his analysis with Joshua, not Genesis, searching for materials parallel to or related to Tetrateuchal materials. He finds the Joshua materials to be in an older form than the corresponding material in the Tetrateuch. Indeed, for Rose, the Deuteronomistic history with its exclusive focus on existence in the land, proved to be older than the earliest Tetrateuchal strand. Rose concludes that the conquest narrative was the established tradition for which the post-Deuteronomistic Jahwist wrote a *pre-history*. (Rose, M. *Deuteronomist und Jahwist*. Zurich: Theologischer Verlag, 1980).

The literary history of the first books of the Bible continues to intrigue and yet defy scholarship. We have many more theories but hardly any more certainty than did Calvin. We may be only in the beginning stages of understanding the way in which God worked with men to produce his word. It may be that old traditional understandings may eventually be vindicated. The present work can only hope to note a few clues for further research and to emphasize the note raised in Joshua studies at least since the time of Wellhausen, namely the contribution of theologians using language akin to that of Deuteronomy to interpret the work of Joshua.

Form Criticism

Herman Gunkel taught scholarship to seek not only the literary history of a book but also the forms of the tradition used in its oral stage of development (H. Gunkel, "Die israelitische Literatur." *Die orientalischen Literaturen*, ed. P. Hinneberg. KdG 1/7. Leipzig/Stuttgart: B. G. Teubner, 1906. 2nd ed. 1925. Reprinted separately in Darmstadt: Wissenschaftliche Buchgesellschaft, 1963). Hugo Gressmann applied the work of Gunkel on etiological sagas in Genesis to the book of Joshua in his 1922 commentary. Albrecht Alt (A. Alt, "Josua." *Werden und Wesen des Alten Testaments*. BZAW 66. Berlin: A. Töppelmann, 1936, 13–29 [= *KS* I, 1953, 176–192]) and Martin Noth then carried the work further, isolating a series of narratives featuring the formula "unto this day" which seemed to have developed in the territory of Benjamin. Biblical authors, according to Alt and Noth, could thus explain various types of noteworthy phenomena in the "present" through narratives of the past. They noted that when the Joshua narrative retreats from the Gilgal area, the etiological formula also fades.

John Bright opened fire on Alt and Noth with his reverse claim that etiology was not a creative factor in the formation of tradition, being secondary rather than primary in the development of the tradition (J. Bright, *Early Israel in Recent History Writing*. SBT 19. London: SCM Press, 1956). Noth later backed down somewhat to leave open a whole scale of possibilities in the relationship between historical event, developing tradition concerning the event, and the etiological form (M. Noth, "Hat die Bibel doch Recht?" *Festschrift für Günther Dehn.* Neukirchen: Neukirchener Verlag, 1957, 7–22 [=Aufsätze I, 1971, 489–543]; "Der Beitrag der Archaologie zur Geschichte Israels." *VTSup* 7, 1960, 262–282 [=*Aufsätze* I, 1971, 34–51]).

Subsequent research has further analyzed the components of etiological narrative. Fichtner separated two forms of name-giving etiologies, which he shows to be at home in Israel's old saga material, not her later historical works. Etiology is again seen as sometimes primary, sometimes secondary within the tradition. (J. Fichtner, "Die etymologische Aetiologie in den Namengebungen der geschichtlichen Bücher des Alten Testaments." *VT* 6 [1956] 372–396).

Soggin analyzed the etiologies formed as children's questions and connected these to liturgical catechesis rather than family conversations. Having some relationship to the early sanctuaries at Gilgal and Shechem, the form is seen to be at home in the early stages of the Deuteronomic movement (J. A. Soggin, "Kultätiologische Sagen und Katachese im Hexateuch." *VT* 10 [1960] 341–347).

Childs returned to the basic "until this day" formula. The complete and pure form occurs only rarely (Josh 7:26; Judg 18:21; 2 Chr 20:26). In the great majority of the cases the formula represents a redactional commentary on the tradition, giving personal testimony confirming the received tradition (B. Childs, "A Study of the Formula 'Until this Day.'" *JBL* 82 [1963] 279–292). In his second study of the problem, Childs sought to clarify definitions and functions by showing that Gunkel's discovery involved a mythical conception of cause and effect not present in the narratives of Joshua first analyzed by Gressmann. Childs pleads for the distinction between the mythical act which alters the structure of reality and a non-mythical story establishing a precedent for the present. He warns against unwarranted mythologizing of Israel's historical tradition (B. Childs, "The Etiological Tale Re-examined." *VT* 24 [1974] 387–397).

Long studied the formal structure of various etiological clauses, finding them rarely related to a story. He concluded that rarely in Israel did etiological interest play a strong role in building extensive narrative material. Only in studying narrative function could one safely discuss and isolate etiological narrative (B. O. Long, *The Problem of Etiological Narrative in the Old Testament.* BZAW 108. Berlin: A. Töppelmann, 1968).

Smend undertook the examination of etiological function rather than form. He showed that narrative continued to be used both etiologically and paradigmatically. Basic etiology had to grow beyond itself to survive. As narratives were assimilated into larger complexes, the complexes could also become etiological. In the book of Joshua, original narratives picturing the settlement of the land as a military operation were fed by the ideology of Yahweh War which bound together the narratives into a larger complex. They then functioned etiologically to justify Israel's possession of the land, or at least the piece of land under discussion in the individual narrative. Together they produce a paradigm of Yahweh as the glorious warrior who fights for Israel. The etiological function, however, did not disappear. The narrative complex demonstrated how Israel occupied Palestine. Even the original boundary documents of chaps. 13–21 functioned in this etiological fashion. Both when possession was not self-evident and when it was no longer self-evident, the stories fulfilled this etiological role (R. Smend, Jr., *Elemente alttestamentlichen Geschichtsdenkens*. Theologische Studien 95. Zurich: EVZ-Verlag, 1968).

Westermann carefully studied the basic structure of narrative which runs from tension to resolution. He distinguished between an etiological story in which the line of tension is identical with the line of the etiology on the one hand and an etiological notice concluding a story in a brief sentence or two at the end without a necessary connection to the line of narrative tension. The true etiological narrative answers real questions reliably rather than inventing answers to obscure questions (C. Westermann, "Arten der Erzahlung in der Genesis." *Forschung am Alten Testament*. Theologische Bücherei 24. Munich: Chr. Kaiser Verlag, 1964, 9–91 [=*Die Verheissungen an die Väter. FRLANT* 116. Göttingen: Vandenhoeck & Ruprecht, 1976. =*The Promises to the Fathers*. Tr. by D. Green. Philadelphia: Fortress Press, 1980]).

Golka attempted to apply Westermann's criteria to OT historical narratives. In Joshua he found true narratives in the story in chapters 2 and 6, 7:1, 5b–26; 7:2–5a; 8:1–29; 9:1–27. Only a narrative torso could be isolated in 5:2–9, while 6:25 represented an etiological motif. Etiological notes appear in 13:12; 15:63; and 16:10. Golka apparently ignored his own distinctions along with many of the issues and cautions raised by Long and Childs when he turned to find a historical period for the etiologies. He found that the etiology was alive among the tribes, not among the families nor in Israel's history writing. It began to disappear at the organization of the national state, to be artificially revived in an "unreal existence" later (F. Golka, "Zur Erforschung der Aetiologien im Alten Testament." *VT* 20 [1970] 90–98. "The Aetiologies in the Old Testament." Part I, *VT* 26 [1976] 410–428; Part 2, *VT* 27 [1977] 36–47).

Reviewing recent study of etiological narrative in Joshua, Ramsey has concluded that the appearance of etiological narrative does not automatically prove the narrative to be lacking in historical value, determination of genre or form being incapable of answering the historical question (G. W. Ramsey, *The Quest for the Historical Israel*. Atlanta: John Knox Press, 1981, 77–81).

Polzin has turned in an entirely different direction, examining the book from the perspective of classical study of literature and its structural elements and devices. He finds the book seeking to witness to the method of interpreting the word of God in general and the law in particular (p. 144). The themes of God's mercy and justice on the one hand and Israel's identity as both citizen and alien connect the narratives, all pointing back to God's decision in Deuteronomy 10:11 (R. Polzin, *Moses and the Deuteronomist*. New York: The Seabury Press, 1980).

This brief study has revealed that a study of Joshua must be ready to confront the complex problem of etiological narrative/etiological motif/etiological note in the examination of almost every chapter of Joshua. Such confrontation will involve an analysis of narrative structure following the arc of tension to its resolution. It will involve study of the function of narrative units rather than simply the appearance of isolated forms. It will seek to determine if a pattern exists within the larger complexes which allows us to speak of the etiological function of the complex and of the redactional function of etiological notes. No unified preconception can cover all etiological elements. The exegetical task is to seek to determine the point of entry of the etiological motifs into the narrative complex(es) and the function of these motifs both at the time of entry into the complex and within the final composition. Ultimately, one must ask if the entire book of Joshua fulfilled an etiological function for an Israel which had lost control of her land and her destiny. The recent work of Martin Rose is important at this point. Was the first conquest narrative formed at Dan on the basis of earlier narrative legitimating the cult? Was such a narrative formulated only on the border territories when they became threatened by outside invaders? Do conquest narratives function as legal claims to land threatened or lost? Is this theme of legal claim to the land the interpretative key for Josh 2–6? Does this point specifically to a time when the entire land is unstable or has been lost?

Can one go further with Rose and isolate an oldest traditional layer comprising a relatively unspecific war narrative with spy story, siege, oracle of encouragement, and conquest? Is any historical memory of an event concerning the actual conquest of a city fully secondary at this oldest traditional level? Does the basic literary level then try to demilitarize this narrative? Or must one apply form criticism to a much smaller narrative scope with concrete details and narrative structure to determine the oldest level of tradition?

The commentary must seek to find answers to form critical questions dealing with etiological narratives and with each individual narrative tradition in the book. Are these literary units from the historical era of a generation after Joshua (see Woudstra)? Or are there marks of older traditions which have been preserved and interpreted through the long history of Israel's worship before reaching the form God chose to use to teach his people over the succeeding millennia? Could this mean that God used the validating experiences of generations of his people listening to, responding to, and interpreting the ancient stories of his people to give theological and experiential depth to the word he wished to communicate to his people through the many succeeding centuries?

Research into the particular detailed questions will be noted at proper spots in the commentary. The special problems of Josh 13–21 will be reviewed in an introductory section to that complex.

"The Amphictyony"

Solution to the form critical questions can help us delve beneath the narrative materials of Joshua and their theological perspectives to the historical events. Other questions also arise as we seek the historical setting for Joshua. A major question deals with the nature of Israel's government in the early stages of her life in the Promised Land. Again Martin Noth has formulated the hypothesis against which modern scholarship reacts. Using analogies from Greece and Italy as well as the biblical materials, Noth reconstructed the institution of the amphictyony in which the twelve-tribe system of Israel was supposed to have found concrete expression.

Such an amphictyony had its historical beginnings in a six-tribe Leah amphictyony with a central sanctuary at Shechem prior to the introduction of Yahwistic worship. Benjamin and the four "concubine" tribes established themselves in Palestine but did not gain entrance into the amphictyony. The Joseph tribes coming from Egypt and Sinai introduced Yahwistic worship to a group already beginning to be formulated only on historical traditions, since Levi, Reuben, and Simeon were quickly becoming mere remnants. The rise of the monarchy spelled doom for the tribal system. Amphictyonic life had centered around the central sanctuary with the ark as its central cult object. *Nasim* or cultic representatives conducted tribal business, based on a form of the Book of the Covenant. The annual cultic festival brought the tribes together.

A complicating factor was the membership of Judah and Simeon in yet another amphictyony centering in Mamre and comprising Caleb, Othniel, Jerahmeel, and the Kennites. This brought split loyalties which plagued Israel throughout her history (Noth, M. *Das System der zwölf Stämme Israels*. BWANT 4. Heft 1. Stuttgart: W. Kohlhammer Verlag, 1930. Reproduced by Darmstadt: Wissenschaftliche Buchgesellschaft, 1966).

Adamant opposition to the amphictyonic theory has come from Fohrer, de Geuss, Herrmann, Mayes, and Anderson, among others. They have trouble finding evidence for one central sanctuary and close tribal cooperation. The twelve-tribe system is seen to be based on genealogical developments reflecting changing political alliances. No political office really joins the tribes, the only abiding feature being common worship of Yahweh, though this was practiced at separate sanctuaries (G. Fohrer, "Altes Testament—'Amphiktyonie und 'Bund'?" *ThL* 91 [1966] 801–816 [=BZAW 115 (1969) 84–119]; C. H. J. de Geuss. *The Tribes of Israel*. Studia Semitica Neerlandica 18. Assen: Koninklijke Van Gorcum & Comp., B. V., 1976; S. Hermann, "Autonome Entwicklungen in den Konigreichen Israel und Juda" VTS 17 [1969] 139–58; A. D. H. Mayes, *Israel in the Period of the Judges*. SBT 2nd Series, 29. London: SCM Press, 1974; G. W. Anderson, "Am Kahal; Èdah." *Translating and Understanding the Old Testament. May Festschrift*. Nashville: Abingdon Press, 1970, 135–51).

The new literary theories of Tengström and Otto have produced alternate understandings of the amphictyony, a term Tengström would rather avoid. He speaks, rather, of a twelve-tribe ideology centering in Shechem and the Rachel tribes. Joshua 24 shows the rise of such ideology in the covenant understanding in which Joshua played a central role. The only outward manifestations produced by the ideology were the Shechemite Passover, occasional meetings of the tribal representatives, and the foundation of the Hexateuchal narrative. Otto shifts the focus to Gilgal as the only shrine able to involve Judah. Cultic reality became political reality under Saul (1 Sam 15:1–9).

Mendenhall, de Geuss, and especially Gottwald have argued for a new sociological understanding of Israel, emphasizing the sociological split between rural farmers and the city-state establishment rather than that between landed Canaanites and immigrating nomadic shepherds. The twelve-tribe system represents, for Gottwald, a political compromise achieved by David in administering his newly established kingdom. Solomon, however, replaced the system with one imposed from above. Prior to David, Israelite society had formed a confederacy of extended families and tribes cooperating in worship, war, and justice, but "twelve" was not an essential element of the confederacy (G. E. Mendenhall, *Law and Covenant in Israel and the Ancient Near East.* Pittsburgh: Bible Collogquium, 1955; "Social Organization in Early Israel." *Magnalia Dei, The Mighty Acts of God.* Wright *Festschrift.* Garden City, New York: Doubleday & Company, Inc., 1976, 132–51; *The Tenth Generation.* Baltimore: Johns Hopkins, 1973; N. Gottwald, *The Tribes of Yahweh.* Maryknoll, New York: Orbis Books, 1979).

Support for Noth has come recently from two directions. Smend underlines the radical distinction between tribal systems and political reality under the monarchy. Thus twelve-tribe Israel must have originated at Shechem when the Leah tribes with an amphictyonic tradition merged with the Rachel tribes with a war of Yahweh tradition. The amphictyony must be defined as a sacral institution which does not produce historical narrative. The war of Yahweh tradition results in narrative (R. Smend, Jr., *Jahwekrieg und Stämmebund.* Göttingen: Vandenhoeck & Ruprecht, 1963; *Yahweh War and Tribal Federation.* Tr. by Max Gray Rogers. Nashville: Abingdon Press, 1970).

Bächli demonstrates the necessity for conclusions by analogy and pleads for a replacement theory before total abandonment of Noth's hypothesis. He admits that Noth's hypothesis must be updated, particularly in eliminating six or twelve as an essential number and in correlating the theory of a Deuteronomistic history with the exegesis of texts crucial to the amphictyonic hypothesis, particularly Joshua 24 (O. Bächli, *Amphiktyonie im Alten Testament.* TZ Sonderband 6. Basel: Friedrich Reinhardt Verlag, 1977).

Reflection on the history of research forces on us the radical necessity for identifying and defining Israel. How does a people with the name "El" in its own name become identified with the radical devotees of the one God Yahweh? Why do lists and genealogies of tribal units differ both in contents and genealogical relationships? Why do the narratives of the judges depict isolated tribal actions and intertribal battles? Why are Israelite judges named Othni*el* and Jerub*baal*? Why is Shechem, the "amphictyonic center," so closely associated with a temple of Baal-berith? What are the relationships among Shechem, Gilgal, Tabor, Shiloh, Beersheba, and so on, as far as the worship practices of early Israel are concerned? Did Philistine and continued Canaanite or Jebusite occupation of the major valleys allow communication and joint operations between the tribal groups north and south in Palestine? Did the north-south split under Rehoboam have antecedents in the early history of Israel? Did a separate northern Exodus theology stand over against a southern Zion theology? Where would an amphictyony have had its early political and cultic roots?

All such questions demand explanation before we can confidently describe the political and religious organization of early Israel. Yet, as Ramsey has shown recently, "the ambiguity of biblical texts and external evidence make it impossible for one to be categorical in his judgments or interpretations" (*The Quest* 98). Fortunately for our task, such questions become more exegetically acute in the book of Judges.

Archaeology and Joshua

Archaeology and its discoveries have provided primary evidence for exegesis of Joshua during the twentieth century. It has been used to prove and disprove the biblical accounts of the conquest. The major issues have been raised in the debate between Martin Noth and John Bright. Noth argued that the nature of the literary traditions must be assessed in and of themselves before archaeological information could be introduced to support a historical character of the traditions. He noted that archaeological findings must be fitted into a larger historical context, and so historical synthesis was necessarily involved. Historians are prone to search too quickly and improperly for direct biblical connections. Noth cautioned that archaeology does not give evidence of particular historical events unless it yields written documents. Instead, archaeology illuminates the environment and life style of the times. Archaeology may show an event to have been possible but cannot prove it actually occurred.

Bright retorted that Noth had asked the wrong question. We cannot seek absolute proof but must ask where the balance of probability lies. For the conquest, archaeology can distinguish dates and occupants of the various sites. The row of towns taken in the thirteenth century place the balance of probability on the side of the Joshua narrative (J. Bright, *Early Israel;* M. Noth, "Grundsätzliches zur geschichtlichen Deutung archäologischer Befunde auf dem Boden Palästinas," *PJ* 34 [1938] 7–22. [*Aufsätze*, I, 1971, 3–16]. See the more mediating position of Noth in *VTS* 7 [1960] 262–282).

John Bimson has recently introduced another way of handling the archaeological materials. He has questioned the basic presuppositions of archaeologists in comparative pottery dating of sites and in identifying archaeological sites with biblical ones. He pushes the dating of the conquest from the thirteenth century back to the second half of the fifteenth, which he interprets as the end of the Middle Bronze Age (J. J. Bimson, *Redating the Exodus and Conquest.* JSOTSup 5. Sheffield: JOTS Press, 1978). Reviewers have criticized Bimson strongly for his disregard for literary criticism of the biblical sources but have not levied significant criticisms of his archaeological explanations (see J. Maxwell Miller, *JBL* 99 [1980] 133–135; J. Alberto Soggin, *VT* 31 [1981] 98–99; with more hesitation, William H. Shea, *CBQ* 42 [1980] 88–90). The most extensive and valuable critique of Bimson has been provided by Ramsey (*The Quest*, 73–77). He concludes: "Although Bimson's method of establishing a biblical chronology as the norm for adjusting the dates of archaeological periods is highly questionable and the particular arguments from the Bible which he employs to re-date the end of the Middle Bronze Age are very weak, his work merits attention. He has summarized well the problem which others have recognized, namely, that the Palestinian cities whose remains from the Late Bronze Age create problems for the theory of a thirteenth century conquest outnumber the cities which do not, and he has given a reasonable alternative archaeological context for consideration" (p 77).

Alternative solutions to the archaeological questions have been offered.

Callaway used the Ai evidence to lower the dating to the twelfth century (J. A. Callaway, "New Evidence on the Conquest of Ai." *JBL* 87 [1968] 312–320). Aharoni has rewritten the conquest with "Nothing Early and Nothing Late," thus returning in most essentials to Noth's position (Y. Aharoni, "Problems of the Israelite Conquest in Light of Archaeological Discoveries." *Antiquity and Survival* 2 [1957] 131–150; "Nothing Early and Nothing Late: Re-writing Israel's Conquest." *BA* 39 [1976] 55–76).

Manfred Weippert has nuanced the Nothian arguments somewhat, identifying the patriarchs with Late Bronze Age nomadic settlers in the Palestinian mountains related to the Shoshu known in other texts. Only later did this Shoshu population of Canaan called Israel form a twelve-tribe system and still later adopt the Yahwistic religion of the Exodus group. Overpopulation forced some to migrate into Trans-jordan, while others settled down to agricultural lives (M. Weippert, *Die Landnahme der israelitischen Stämme in der neuren wissenschaftlichen Diskussion.* FRLANT 92. Göttingen: Vandenhoeck & Ruprecht, 1967; *The Settlement of the Israelite Tribes in Palestine.* SBT 2nd Series, 21. Translated by J. D. Martin. London: SCM Press, 1971; "The Israelite 'Conquest' and the Evidence from Transjordan." *Symposia Celebrating the Seventy-Fifth Anniversary of the Founding of the American Schools of Oriental Research* (1900–1975). Zion Research Foundation Occasional Publications. Ed. by Frank Moore Cross. Cambridge, Ma.: American Schools of Oriental Research, 1979, 15–34).

In the same forum as Weippert, Yigael Yadin has forcefully reasserted the Albright/Bright position: "I believe everyone will agree that results of thorough archeological excavations in the last fifty years prove clearly that a certain culture—which we may call the Late Bronze Age culture—based on fortified city-states, had come to a sudden, abrupt end; cities were destroyed, with many of them showing indications of conflagrations and destructions which could not be attributed to famine or earthquakes. Sometime later—stratigraphically speaking—either on the same site or elsewhere, a new, completely different culture developed, having a rather poor architectural concept which could hardly be called urban and which seems most like the first efforts of settlement of a semi-nomadic people. Notwithstanding this remark, some sites—although destroyed in the previous period—were immediately rebuilt and could definitely be regarded as proper cities with fortifications and all the necessary attributes and elements" (58). Yadin sees the excavations at Hazor supporting his conclusions that the Egyptian pharaohs of the fourteenth and thirteenth centuries so weakened the Palestinian city-state system that the seminomadic Israelites could apply the *"coup de grace"* (Y. Yadin, "The Transition from a Semi-Nomadic to a Sedentary Society in the Twelfth Century B.C.E." *Symposia,* 1979, 57–68).

Lawrence Toombs adds one other piece of evidence in examining the Shechem excavations, concluding that "there was a hitherto unrecognized conquest of Shechem during the Late Bronze Age, probably in the late fourteenth or early thirteenth century. This conquest, which may have come about as a reaction by other city-states to the expansionist policies of the dynasty of Lab'ayu, greatly weakened and impoverished the city and, thus, became an important factor in the subsequent peaceful passage of Shechem into Israelite political control" (L. Toombs, "Shechem: Problems of the Early Israelite Era." *Symposia,* 1979, 69–83).

Ramsey has reminded us of the problem of using archaeological results in dealing with the conquest. He notes that such materials can sometimes falsify the biblical account, at other times show that no known conditions exclude the possibility of the biblical account, but seldom explicitly confirm the biblical account. He notes in conclusion that "the reliability of the biblical witness for the period prior to the monarchy *is itself an hypothesis* which has not been proved" (104, Ramsey's italics).

Archaeological research thus leaves confusion and unanswered questions for the present generation. This does not lead us to abandon archaeological research. It reminds us of the great difficulties which stand in our way when we seek to utilize archaeological discoveries for historical reconstruction. Archaeology can rarely name sites. Seldom, if ever, can it determine precisely who destroyed a site. It often cannot tell who occupied a site; it can place only relative dates on sites. Only rarely can it excavate an entire site and secure all the evidence.

Still, we must acknowledge our deep appreciation for the detailed work archaeologists have accomplished through long hours of hot, sweaty labor. We must not ignore the large amounts of negative evidence, periods when the biblical sites were unoccupied. We must not be too quick to identify every destruction layer with the Israelite conquest. Nor can we too rapidly set aside the tradition that Israel was involved in military conquest. Perhaps refined work in pottery chronology and further excavation and analysis will provide more data for use in exegeting the conquest literary materials. It appears certain that Ai will continue to present the major stumbling block, since it has no signs of occupation during any period which can realistically be set forward as a conquest date.

For detailed accounts of the various sites, see the work of Bimson, the appropriate places in this commentary, and Miller, J. M. "Archaeology and the Israelite Conquest of Canaan: Some Methodological Observations." *PEQ* 109 (1977) 87–93.

Bibliography

Historical Atlases, Geographies, and Histories
Aharoni, Y. and **Avi-Yonah, M.** *The Macmillan Bible Atlas.* New York: The MacMillan Company, 1968. **Avi-Yonah, M.** and **Stern, E.,** eds. *Encyclopedia of Archaeological Excavations in the Holy Land.* 4 vols. London: Oxford University Press, 1975–1978. **Baly, D.** *The Geography of the Bible.* New York: Harper and Brothers Publishers, 1957. **Negev, A.,** ed. *Archaeological Encyclopedia of the Holy Land.* Jerusalem/London: Weidenfeld and Nicolson, 1972. **Noth, M.** *Die Welt des Alten Testaments.* 4th ed. Berlin: Alfred Topelmann, 1964. (=*The Old Testament World.* Tr. V. I. Gruhn. Philadelphia: Fortress Press, 1966). **Smith, G. A.** *The Historical Geography of the Holy Land.* 25th ed. London: Hodder & Stoughton, 1931; reprinted London: Collins Clear-Type Press, 1966 (original edition, 1894). **de Vaux, R.** *Les Institutions de l'Ancien Testament.* Paris: Les Editions du Cerf, 1960. (=*Ancient Israel. Its Life and Institutions.* Tr. J. McHugh. London: Darton, Longman

& Todd, Ltd., 1961). **Wiseman, D. J.,** ed. *Peoples of Old Testament Times.* Oxford: Clarendon Press, 1973.

Ancient Texts

Pritchard, J. B. *Ancient Near Eastern Texts Relating to the Old Testament.* Princeton, N. J.: Princeton University Press, 1969. ————. *The Ancient Near East. Supplementary Texts and Pictures Relating to the Old Testament.* Princeton, N. J.: Princeton University Press, 1969. **Thomas, D. W.,** ed. *Documents from Old Testament Times.* New York: Harper & Row, Publishers, 1961 (original edition, London: Thomas Nelson and Sons, Ltd., 1958). ————. *Archaeology and Old Testament Study.* Jubilee Volume of the Society for Old Testament Study 1917–1967. Oxford: Clarendon Press, 1967.

Histories of Israel

Bright, J. *A History of Israel.* 3rd ed. Philadelphia/London: Westminster/SCM Press, 1981. **Edwards, I. E. S.; Gadd, C. J.; Hammond, N. G. L.;** and **Sollberger, E.** eds. *The Cambridge Ancient History.* Vol. 2, Parts 1 and 2. Cambridge: The University Press, 1973, 1975. **Garstang, J.** *The Foundations of Bible History. Joshua, Judges.* London: Constable, 1931. **Gunneweg, A. H. J.** *Geschichte Israels bis Bar Kochba.* Theologische Wissenschaft 2. Stuttgart: Verlag W. Kohlhammer, 1972. **Hayes, J. H.** and **Miller, J. M.,** eds. *Israelite and Judean History. Old Testament Library.* Philadelphia: Westminster Press, 1977. **Herrmann, S.** *Geschichte Israels in alttestamentlicher Zeit.* Munich: Chr. Kaiser Verlag, 1973 (=*A History of Israel in Old Testament Times.* Tr. J. Bowden. London: SCM Press, 1975). **Netanyahu, B.** and **Mazar, B.,** eds. *The World History of the Jewish People.* First Series, Ancient Times. Vols. 1–4. London/Jerusalem: W. H. Allen/Masada Press, Ltd., 1964–1979. **Noth, M.** *Geshichte Israel.* 2nd ed. Gottingen: Vandenhoeck & Ruprecht, 1954 (=*The History of Israel.* 2nd ed. New York: Harper & Row, Publishers, 1960). **de Vaux, R.** *Histoire ancienne d'Israel.* 2 vols. Paris: J. Gabalda et Cie Editeurs, 1971, 1973 (=*The Early History of Israel.* 2 vols. Tr. D. Smith. London/Philadelphia: Darton, Longman & Todd/Westminster Press, 1978).

Summary

Review of the literary, form critical, and archaeological research has revealed the complexity of describing the history of the conquest. The problem begins, however, with none of these areas of study but rather with one's theological and faith presuppositions. To what degree must biblical narrative mirror historical events in order for the truth quality of the narrative to be validated? This is the basic question lying behind all historical research into biblical narratives. Yet, in itself, it represents an improper question. The believer does not go to the narratives to validate their truth quality. Rather, the narratives have proved themselves true for the life of faith long before the believer learns to raise the historical issue. The historical question becomes a means to buttress one's faith or to validate one's doctrine. The issue at hand revolves around a different type of question. Can one objectively raise the historical issue, determine the balance of probability, and then incorporate that balance of probability answer into one's growing and maturing faith? Can one truly seek an answer to the historical question without a dominating prior determination already lurking in his soul?

The historical problem lies in several directions. The literary problem is illustrated by a comparison of Josh 11:23; 21:43–45 with 13:1–7; 15:63; 16:10; 17:12–13; 19:47; Judg 1:27–36 or by a comparison of Josh 10:36–39 with 14:13–15; 15:13–19; Judg 1:10–15.

The form-critical problem lies not only in the solution to the question of etiology. It lies in the deeper determination of the nature and function of the materials within Israelite society prior to their compilation and incorporation into the theologically dominated whole. Was the basic narrative material originally intended to convey brute historical fact, whatever that may be? Did the material attempt to entertain? To provide material for worship ritual and praise? To defend the political claims of one group against another?

To raise such questions risks theological consequences. Was God limited to one methodology in his work to preserve his Word for his people? Or was God willing to take the risk of using the processes which his people instituted for preserving tradition in order to prepare his Word for them? Was revelation limited to the interplay between God and one author at one specific moment in history? Or was God able to reveal his Word to his people in a protracted period of tradition formation and preservation?

Archaeological results have forced biblical students to raise such theological questions. No one archaeological solution to the conquest has satisfied everybody. No matter how many of the cities of Joshua have provided destruction remains in the thirteenth century, the twelfth century, or the fifteenth century, not all of the cities have provided the needed remains in any one century. The greatest problems lie precisely with those cities which play the most prominent roles in the Joshua narrative—Jericho, Ai, Gibeon. Proper methodology would force these cities at the center of their investigation and not those which appear more on the periphery of the narrative. This has brought varied scholars to a variety of answers to the basic historical questions in Joshua. Men of faith dedicated to the study of God's holy word have understood the nature of the material within the book in different ways.

W. F. Albright readily admitted, "It is no easy task to reconstruct the details of the Conquest, since the extant Israelite tradition is not uniform and our biblical sources vary considerably. . . . The results of excavations are ambiguous and sometimes in apparent conflict with the tradition" (*The Biblical Period from Abraham to Ezra*, 1963, 27). He then used the appearance of the name Israel on the Merneptah stele about 1219 in correlation with archaeological destruction layers at Tell Beit Mirsim, Bethel, Lachish, and Hazor to date the conquest in the thirteenth century. Still Albright admitted that Joshua's military feats were "somewhat exaggerated" by the tradition (*Biblical Period*, 30) and that Hebrews already in Palestine joined those coming out of Egypt. Albright's student John Bright spoke of Israel as "surely not a race" but a people, "a mixture from the beginning and in no essential distinct from her neighbors" (*Early Israel in Recent History Writing*, 1956, 113).

Albrecht Alt and Martin Noth analyzed the patterns of commerce and settlement in Palestine during the second millenium and concluded that "Israelite occupation did not ensue from a warlike encounter between the newcomers and the previous owners of the land" (Noth, *The History of Israel*, 68). Instead, over a period of years Israelite tribes settled areas in the hill country previously not occupied by the Canaanites. The narratives of Joshua represent only

the traditions of one tribe—Benjamin. "In time . . . the specific and historically accurate memories of the occupation of the land by the important central
Palestinian tribes were imposed on all the tribes of Israel" (75).

Even the most conservative writers temper their discussions when they
come to the historical problem of the conquest. Bimson wants to follow the
major picture of the OT but admits that the whole group was not necessarily
involved in the conquest of every area, Judg 1 being a truer picture than
the Joshua narratives (*Redating*, 30–32). Woudstra says that the purpose of
the story does not depend upon solution of chronological or compositional
matters. While maintaining historical accuracy, he recognizes that biblical
narrative performs a function "beyond that of the chronological recording
of history," i.e. it teaches (*Joshua*, 146–47). He leaves open the possibilities
of both oral tradition (159) and later redaction (195) without ever drawing
consequences from such statements, though he does say, "one cannot always
reconstruct the exact course of events from the biblical record" (195).

Recent sociological study has produced a new approach. De Geuss, and
particularly Mendenhall and Gottwald have proposed an entirely different
model of Israel, namely that of a peasant's revolt against a repressive city-
state governing system. Gottwald thus speaks of "revolutionary Israel: a Canaanite coalition" (*The Tribes of Yahweh*, 491). Resorting to his technical jargon,
Gottwald concludes: "Consequently, Israel is most appropriately conceived
as an eclectic composite in which various underclass and outlaw elements
of society joined their diffused antifeudal experiences, sentiments, and interests, thereby forming a single movement that, through trial and error, became
an effective autonomous social system. . . . Israel's vehement and tenacious
identity as one people under one God has its indisputable axis around an
antifeudal egalitarian social commitment" (491).

Each of the views sketched above—peaceful settlement, wars of conquest,
and peasant rebellion—is gradually being weighed in ongoing research. As
of yet, none is totally convincing to the "scholarly consensus." Further study
must bear in mind basic understandings. The biblical tradition was not invented from thin air. The experience of conquest of the land under divine
leadership pervades Israel's entire tradition and must be accounted for by
any specific theory. The role of Joshua as the lieutenant of Moses and the
human agent in Israel's gaining possession of the land is equally pervasive
and cannot be ignored. The "El" component of Israel's name and of the
patriarchal divine titles points to a complex pre-history of the people Israel
prior to their conquest and settlement in the land. The name of the judge
Jerubbaal and the sanctuary of El-berith at Shechem point to a continued
complexity, as does the unique tribal listing in Judges 5. Archaeological data
cannot be fitted into a simplified picture and must be understood as both
concrete data and human interpretation of such data. Thus we must continue
to investigate the literary nature and the "traditional" nature of the Joshua
narratives, as the commentary will seek to do. Such study reveals a complexity
at this level, as well as at the others. Simplified chronological and reportorial
conclusions are ruled out for the present state of research, if we follow the
rules of the objective historian in reaching conclusions. Our theological presuppositions may incline us to go beyond such rules to a statement of faith

concerning the historical situation. If this is the case, we must be consciously aware of the nature of the statements we are making.

More important is that we be consciously aware of the nature of the book of Joshua. It is not only a book based on the historical traditions of Israel. It is a book based on the use of those traditions in the everyday life, the worship, and the scholarly study and meditation upon those traditions through many generations of the life of Israel. As such, it represents the mature reflection of Israel upon her own identity. It contains that which God had revealed to Israel as who she had been, who she was supposed to be, and who she could become. She was one people, formed by one covenant, under one God, destined to live in and control one land. She was also a people for whom much remained to be done because she had, even in her best days, refused to follow God completely and carry out his instructions, preferring to argue and feud among her own individual components and to follow the paths of the gods of the land along with the God of the Exodus and Conquest. Thus Israel had to look forward to a new Joshua, who would bring the people to follow God all his days and to confess once and for all that this God fulfilled all his promises to his people.

I. Possessing the Promise (*Joshua 1–12*)

Josh 1–12 demonstrates as well as any other portion of Holy Scripture the complex nature of the process in which God worked with and through man to produce his inspired word for all future generations. Word of God did not begin as a book. It began as a story told by men reacting in faith to actions they interpreted as the work of God. Such stories took various forms: spy stories, stories of Holy War, cultic catechism, divine call and testing, sacral judgment, tribal etiology, and so on. It did not remain as simple story. Instead the stories were adopted and adapted by the Israelite cult, particularly the cult at Gilgal. Story of divine action became the center of cultic celebration. As such it received a new form and function, but continued to give dynamic life and faith to the people of God through many generations. Here each new generation learned of the faith of the fathers and was incorporated into the people of God.

Finally, after Israel developed its own political and cultural organizations, liturgy became literature, used to give identity and hope to the people of God. Still, it was not complete. Each new generation read, listened, and applied the word of God to its own situation. In so doing it incorporated its own experience with the word of God and with the continued leadership of God in daily life into the text.

Then, in 587, major crises confronted Israel—exile, loss of self-government, loss of land, apparent loss of the promise and gift of God celebrated so enthusiastically in the sacred text. Now how would Israel react? At least a portion of Israel was true to her tradition! In time of exile and loss, she turned to word of God for direction. Experiencing new hope and challenge, she incorporated the new experiences and new elements of faith into the holy tradition. She collected a wide range of traditions and used them to proclaim God's new word based on his old actions for a new people of God. The Deuteronomistic history spanning Deuteronomy through 2 Kings resulted.

Still the process of God speaking his word to Israel was not finished. Study of the textual history, particularly the Septuagint (LXX), shows that God continued to let his people understand more of his word for their own generation and incorporate such understanding into the ancient text. Ultimately, near the time of the first Christian century, the text was stabilized. It is the stabilized form of the Hebrew or Massoretic tradition which we have found to be inspired by God because it has given divine direction to our lives. Thus we interpret the Massoretic text and seek to proclaim its Word to our generation. In so doing, we follow a long tradition which has produced the Jewish Talmud and a multitude of Christian commentaries. Even with a stabilized text, the people of God is constantly confronted with a call for a contemporanized interpretation, so that the ancient tradition will still be heard, understood, and applied by the new generation.

The following commentary tries to demonstrate the dynamic character

of the action and word of God in its development and application within
the community of his people. Just as such growth and use within the community of God revealed the authoritative character of the word for Israel, it is
the prayer of the present commentator that the commentary will be used
by God to bring forth contemporary confession and testimony to the dynamic
power of God to work through his people and his word to give hope and
identity to his people.

Divine Marching Orders   (1:1–9)

Bibliography

Hölscher, G. *Geschichtsschreibung in Israel.* Lund: C. W. K. Gleerup, 1952, 259–61,
336. **Lohfink, N.** "Die deuteronomistische Darstellung des Übergangs der Führung
Israels von Moses auf Josue." *Scholastik* 37 (1962) 32–44. **Noth, M.** *Überlieferungsgeschichtliche Studien.* Tübingen: Max Niemeyer Verlag, 1943, 40–41. **Otto, E.** *Das Mazzotfest in Gilgal.* BWANT 107. Stuttgart: W. Kohlhammer Verlag, 1975, 22–23, 57, 86–
88, 135–46. **Porter, J. R.** "The Succession of Joshua." *Proclamation and Presence,* ed.
J. I. Durham and J. R. Porter. London: SCM, 1970, 102–32. **Rudolph, W.** *Der "Elohist"
von Exodus bis Josua.* BZAW 68. Berlin: Alfred Töpelmann, 1938, 164–65. **Schmitt,
G.** *Du sollst keinen Frieden schliessen mit den Bewohnern des Landes.* BWANT 91. Stuttgart:
W. Kohlhammer Verlag, 1970, 146–47. **Simpson, C. A.** *The Early Traditions of Israel.*
Oxford: Basil Blackwell, 1948, 280. **Smend, R.** "Das Gesetz und die Völker." *Probleme
Biblischer Theologie,* ed. H. W. Wolff. München: Chr. Kaiser Verlag, 1971, 494–509.
Tengström, S. *Die Hexateucherzählung.* Coniectanea Biblica, OT Series 7. Lund:
C. W. K. Gleerup, 1976, 143–54. **Veijola, T.** *Die ewige Dynastie.* SARJA-Series B, 193.
Helsinki: Suomalainen Tiedeakatemia, 1975, 28–29, 128–29, 141. **Wellhausen, J.** *Die
Composition des Hexateuchs und der historischen Bücher des Alten Testaments.* 2nd ed. Berlin:
Georg Reimer, 1889, 119.

Translation

[1] *After* [a] *the death of Moses, the servant of Yahweh,* [b] *Yahweh said to Joshua,
the son of Nun, the official of Moses,* [2] *"Moses, my servant,* [a] *is dead. Therefore,* [b]
you are now to get up and cross over this [c] *Jordan—you along with all this people—
to the land which I am giving to them, to the sons of Israel.* [d] [3] *Every place where
the sole of you all's* [a] *foot steps, to you all I have given it, precisely as I told Moses.*
[4a] *From the wilderness and this Lebanon unto the major river, the River Euphrates,
all the land of the Hittites,* [b] *and across to the Mediterranean Sea in the west shall
be the territory for you all.* [5] *No man shall be able to stand his ground before you* [a]
*all the days of your life. Just as I was with Moses, so I will be with you. I will not
forsake you, nor will I abandon you.* [6] *Have conviction and courage because it is
you who will cause this people to inherit the land* [a] *which I made an oath with
their fathers* [b] *to give to them.* [7] *Just have great* [a] *conviction and courage to obey
carefully* [b] *the whole Torah* [c] *which* [d] *Moses, my servant, commanded you. Do not*

turn away from it to the right nor to the left so that you may prudently prosper [e] *everywhere you go.* [8] *This book of the Torah shall not depart from your lips. You shall meditate upon it day and night in order that you may obey carefully according to* [a] *everything which is written in it, because* [b] *then you shall make your paths* [c] *successful, and then you will be prudently prosperous.* [9] *Have I not commanded you, 'Have conviction and courage. Do not tremble or get all shook up, for with you is Yahweh your God everywhere you go'?"*

Notes

1.a. The book begins with a consecutive form of the verb, as do Leviticus, Numbers, Judges, 1 Samuel, 2 Samuel, 2 Kings, Ezekiel, Ruth, Esther, Nehemiah, and 2 Chronicles. GKC § 49b, n. 1 attributes this to an attempt to show the close connection of the books to the preceding book. Cf. the discussion of Heb. tenses by W. Schneider, *Grammatik des biblischen Hebräisch* (München; Claudius Verlag, 1974) § 48. The consecutive form of היה introduces a temporal clause (cf. discussion of T. O. Lambdin, *Introduction to Biblical Hebrew* [New York: Charles Scribner's Sons, 1971] § 110.)

1.b. The LXX omits "servant of Yahweh." This may be a conscious effort to avoid repetition with v 2 or a later insertion of a familiar biblical idiom into v 1. At no point in chap. 1 does the LXX represent a longer text (See Auld, VTSup 30 [1979]3).

2.a. ועתה functions as a transitional formula leading to the main point of the dialog and should be translated "therefore" rather than as a simple temporal adverb "and now" (Cf. Schneider, *Grammatik*, § 54.1).

The imperatives are sing., but the subject is made plur. by adding "and all this people." This is expressed in English translation by subordinating the "people" to Joshua by means of the preposition "along with."

2.b. LXX does include the reference to Moses as servant here, employing the word ϑεράπων, implying free and honorable service, instead of δοῦλος. Cf. 9:4, 6 (= 8:31, 33 MT).

2.c. LXX omits "this," but retains it in v 11.

2.d. LXX omits "to the sons of Israel," a phrase as unnecessary in the original Heb. construction as it is in the English translation.

2–9. The divine speech is carefully formulated without consecutive tenses or the use of ו to connect sentences.

V 3, with the direct object opening the sentence, is appositional, specifying the claim of v 2 (cf. F. I. Andersen, *The Sentence in Biblical Hebrew* [The Hague: Mouton, 1974] 47). V 4 continues the specific apposition. V 5a represents a somewhat extended form of what Andersen (*Sentence*, 43) calls "antithesis in apposition," repeating the positive statement of v 3 in a negative form. V 5b is in the form of a comparative clause (cf. GKC 161), but its function in the context is causal (cf. P. Joüon, *Grammaire de l'Hébreu biblique* [2nd ed. Rome: Institut biblique pontifical, 1947] 170k). The concluding negative clauses again form an "antithesis in apposition." V 6 changes moods and perspective, forming an "apposition in another perspective" (Andersen, *Sentence*, 44), namely that of Joshua rather than God. V 7 is an "exclusive clause" limiting the comprehensive statement of the previous clause (Andersen, *Sentence*, 168–77). The meaning is "you cause them to inherit. . . , only just be sure to . . . ." The sentiment is again repeated in a clause of "antithesis in opposition," concluding with a purpose clause which functions similarly to the preceding "exclusive clause." V 8 brings yet another appositional clause, this time from the perspective of the book of Torah, then again from the perspective of Joshua, again ending in a purpose clause. This is all summarized in v 9 through means of a rhetorical question.

3.a. The pronouns change from third pers. plur. to second pers. plur. The frequent change of pronouns in the Hebrew will be reflected in the translation through use of the dialectal "you all" for the second pers. plur.

4.a. The text of v 4 represents a variant of Deut 11:24 and has provided material for scholarly comment throughout the ages. The most honest approach simply states: "It is impossible to tell how this textual corruption came about" (Soggin, 26). Both verses have been transmitted in various forms by the early versions. The MT of the Deuteronomy passage reads: "Every place where the sole of you all's foot steps will belong to you all, from the wilderness and the Lebanon, from the river, the river Euphrates and across to the western sea will be you all's territory." Compared to Josh 1:4, the Deuteronomy text omits the "this" modifying Lebanon; reads "from the river" rather than "and unto the great river"; omits "all the land of the Hittites"; and refers simply to "the western sea" rather than the "great sea at the setting of the sun," the literal reading in Joshua. The LXX in Joshua reads v 4 as the direct object of "I will give" in v 3 (read as future rather than the perfect of the Hebrew). This necessitates the omission of the opening preposition of the Heb. text. The LXX reads: "the wilderness and the Antilebanon unto the great river, the river Euphrates, and unto the far sea, from the setting of the sun will be your territory." This represents a quite literalistic translation of the Hebrew, but omits "this" modifying Antilebanon, with which LXX always translates Lebanon, and "all the land of the Hittites." The "this" does not make sense in the context. It should point to territory near at hand in the view of the speaker. Such would not be the case for a speaker east of the Jordan. Lebanon appears to be of particular interest to at least some part of the late Israelite community (cf. Deut 3:25; Josh 9:1; 11:17; 12:7; 13:5; Zech 10:1). "This" may represent a late gloss into the text attempting to underline Lebanon as a vital part of the promised land. *"Unto* the major river" in the present context "would in fact include the whole desert region east of Jordan" (Soggin, 26). The idiom is used more logically in Deut 1:7 and may have been taken up into the Joshua tradition due to familiarity with the usage there. Otherwise, it is an attempt to lay claim to the Transjordanian desert regions.

4.b. "All the land of the Hittites" derives from the early Hittite empire in Asia Minor, ca. 1680–1190, but the geographical reference during Israel's history was to the land of Syria-Palestine, as shown by its frequent use in Assyrian inscriptions. LXX omission of the term here may show that this, too, is a later gloss added to the Hebrew text to insure that the land promised by Joshua would be understood as including the land north of that actually controlled by Israel during most of her history. This was made necessary by the fact that Joshua is not credited with conquering nor with apportioning this land.

5.a. The Hebrew returns to the second per. sing. in direct address to Joshua. The early versions seek to achieve grammatical continuity with the preceding verses by reading the second pers. plur.

6.a. *BHS* notes, where *BH* did not, that more than twenty Heb. mss read the preposition אל rather than the sign of the direct object before the land. This goes against all other biblical usage of the hiph'il of נחל, which regularly has a double object following as here. The use of אל does not appear to conform to Rabbinic practice either. Indeed, one might more appropriately expect את before the "people." Perhaps the later tradition read the promise in the light of the incomplete conquest of Josh 13; Judg 1, etc., and interpreted it to mean "to inherit in the land" thus a portion of the land. Cf. GKC § 119g for the use of אל to answer the question "Where?"

6.b. Consistent with its previous readings, the LXX has the second pers. plur. suffix rather than the third person.

7.a. The LXX has no equivalent for the Heb. adverb מאד. No reason for the addition or omission of the particle is apparent, unless it is another attempt to maintain consistency by reproducing exactly the formula of v 6.

7.b. MT has two consecutive infinitives, which the Greek reproduces by joining them with a conjunction. In the similar construction in Deut 15:5, 28:1, 15, and 32:46, the LXX has a similar "addition" of the conjunction, but in Deut 24:8 the LXX does not have the conjunction where MT does. (In the latter passage the Heb. מאד appears after לשמר and is translated by the LXX with σφόδρα.) MT joins the pair with the conjunction in Deut 28:13 and Josh 23:6. The evidence points again to a tendency of the Greek to use a uniform formulation, whereas the Hebrew has various formulations.

7.c. "Torah" of MT is called into question in two ways. LXX does not witness it, and the following preposition ממנו has a masculine suffix, whereas a feminine suffix would be needed to agree with Torah. The latter may be explained as a weakening of the gender distinction in Hebrew (GKC § 135o). The omission of Torah is frequently used as evidence that it is a later interpolation into the Hebrew tradition (Noth; Gray, 50). The case can be argued both directions. The reference to the whole Torah may have entered from the succeeding verse or may have been omitted in the tradition to avoid repetition.

7.d. LXX omits the אשר because of the omission of its antecedent, "Torah."

7.e. The Heb. root שכל means "to be wise, clever, to understand, to have success." The translation attempts to incorporate the breadth of the semantic field of the Hebrew.

8.a. The MT uses the same formulation as in 7a. As there, some mss read the preposition ב rather than כ. The Greek tradition is not uniform at this point, with the result that Rahlfs reads ἵνα συνῇς ποιεῖν πάντα τὰ γεγραμμένα while Margolis reads ἵνα εἰδῇς. . . . The former picks up the wording of 7b, while the latter repeats that of 7a. Neither reading contains a preposition with "all." The MT is preferable here, representing the traditional Deuteronomic idiom (cf. M. Weinfeld, *Deuteronomy and the Deuteronomic School.* [Oxford: Clarendon, 1972] 336:17, 17a, 17b; 346:6).

8.b. LXX does not witness the causal conjunction of the MT, expressing the interclausal relationship with the temporal adverb alone. This does not necessarily reflect a different text.

8.c. Whether a sing. or plur. reading is intended by the Massoretic pointing is debatable (GKC § 91k). Among the versions, *Vg* reads the sing. while LXX and *Syr* read the plur.

Form/Structure/Setting

Chapter 1 serves as the transition between Deuteronomy and Joshua, picking up the narrative themes of the first half of Joshua. The chapter itself has two sections. The first nine verses are given in the form of divine speech addressed to the new leader. They set the theological tone for Josh 1–12. The remaining verses then pick up the narrative sequence from Deuteronomy and give the first illustration of the theological themes of 1:1–9 being actualized.

Form-critical inquiry has led to different perspectives from which to view the section. Lohfink (*Scholastik* 37 [1962] 32–44) sees the section as the conclusion of the series of narratives found in Deut 1:37–38; 3:21–22, 28; 31:2–8, 14–15, 23; Josh 1:2–9. He describes Josh 1 as the Prologue or Overture to the book introducing important motifs, joining the volume to the first volume of the work (i.e. Deuteronomy), and pointing to the arrangement of the book being introduced. Lohfink assigns this last function to 1:1–9, which introduces the two major themes of the book: occupation of the land west of the Jordan (chaps. 1–12) and distribution of the land among the tribes (chaps. 13–21). Each theme has its own vocabulary. Distribution of the land is noted through the hiphil of the verb נחל (Deut 1:38; 3:28; 31:7; Josh 1:6). Occupation of the land utilizes either עבר or בוא (Deut 1:38; 3:21, 28; 31:3, 7, 23; Josh 1:2). Lohfink then isolates within Josh 1:1–9 two distinct forms correlating with the two major themes. A legal command to assume the office of commander of the army, an office in which Joshua was installed in Deut 31:23, appears in 1:2–5. This consists of a sentence establishing a fact (2a), a command (2b), and the necessary basis for implementation of the command (3–5). Such a form is rooted in the legal language of Israel (cf. N. Lohfink, "Darstellungskunst und Theologie in Dtn 1:6–3:29" *Bib* 41 [1960] 124–26, esp. 125, n. 2). An actual installation in the office of land distributor appears in 1:6, 9b. This consists of the formula of encouragement, the naming of the task, and the promise of divine presence, a form also found in Deut 31:7–8; 31:23; 2 Sam 10:12; Hag 2:4; 2 Chr 19:11b. Inserted within the installation form is the true interest of the Deuteronomist, the paraenetic formula used in a concentric structure to interpret all that has preceded.

H. G. Reventlow (*Liturgie und prophetisches Ich bei Jeremia* [Gütersloh: Gütersloher Verlagshaus, 1963] 24–77) brings the prophetic call, the installation in office, and the oracle of salvation together into a single form consisting of a) epiphany of Yahweh, b) lament, c) introduction of the oracle of salvation through the messenger formula and its basis in the nature of Yahweh, d) the oracle of salvation introduced by "Fear not," e) the commission centering on the key words, "Go, I send you," f) the objection raised by the one installed, g) the renewal of the call by Yahweh, h) the symbolic act, and i) the word interpreting the symbolic act. Reventlow sees his results verified by the work of Lohfink (*Liturgie*, 68, n. 206).

Weinfeld (*Deuteronomy*, 45, n. 5) rejects the conclusions of Lohfink and Reventlow, claiming the key formulas "Fear not" and "Have conviction and courage" do not belong to a ceremony of appointment to office but rather to "the occasion of war and confrontation with a difficult task that must be performed." Weinfeld thus discusses "The Military Oration" (*Deuteronomy* 45–51), finding that early examples have a variety of styles, while those in Deuteronomy are more general and stylized.

The present passage cannot be forced into the wide-ranging "form" of Reventlow. Too few of the elements are present. The theory of Lohfink depends on a technical meaning of the formula חזק ואמץ. The expression occurs precisely in the Deuteronomistic contexts introducing Joshua into the narrative (Deut 3:28; 31:6, 7, 23; Josh 1:6, 7, 9, 18). Otherwise it occurs only in the speech of Joshua in 10:25, in two Psalms of mixed *Gattung* (27:14; 31:25) and in three passages introduced by the Chronicler (1 Chr 22:13; 28:20; 2 Chr 32:7). Josh 10:25, Ps 27:14, and 2 Chr 32:7 definitely reflect the oracle of salvation given by the commander in battle. Deut 31:6 reflects the same background, with the possibility being that Ps 31:25 is also oracular. Josh 1:7, 18 reflect a peculiar adaptation by the Deuteronomist for his paraenetic interests. The same usage appears in 1 Chr 22:13. Only Deut 3:28; 31:7, 23; Josh 1:6, and perhaps 1 Chr 28:20 remain for an installation formula. The first four of these do not represent different witnesses to the form; rather they represent one witness repeated four times. The basic conclusion must be that both in Deuteronomistic literature and in the Chronicler specific language has been so generalized that any form in which it has been imbedded no longer plays a role in the extant literature.

This means that no oral form plays an effective role in the formulation of Josh 1:1–9. Rather, this is a piece of Deuteronomistic literature composed specifically as an introduction to the book of Joshua.

The tradition history behind this chapter cannot be written until the entire book has been exegeted, for the tradition behind this chapter is the tradition behind the entire history of Moses and Joshua. This chapter shows connection with at least two Pentateuchal traditions:

1. The Pentateuchal tradition of Joshua as minister of the prophet Moses, wherein Moses is exalted and Joshua abased (see *Comment* section).

2. The Pentateuchal tradition of the appointment of Joshua as successor to Moses. Josh 1 is a recapitulation of the Deuteronomistic report in Deut 1:38; 3:21–28; 31:1–8, 14–15, 23; 34:9. This, in turn, is related to the tradition which found written expression in Num 27:12–23. Literary criticism has not been productive at this point. The Numbers account and Deut 34:9 appear to be related to the Priestly literature in vocabulary but to reflect much older

tradition (M. Noth, *Überlieferungsgeschichte des Pentateuch,* [Stuttgart: W. Kohlhammer Verlag, 1948] 193; K. Baltzer, *Die Biographie der Propheten* [Neukirchen-Vluyn: Neukirchener Verlag, 1975] 55).

Likewise the content of Deut 31:14–15, 23 is unique in form and vocabulary and more closely related to early Pentateuchal sources than to Deuteronomistic literature (von Rad, *Deuteronomy.* tr. by D. Barton, [Philadelphia: Westminster, 1966]; M. Görg, *Das Zelt der Begegnung.* BBB 27. [Bonn: Peter Hanstein Verlag, 1967] 149). Vv 1–8, on the other hand, represent typical Deuteronomic paraenesis. The older tradition reflects some prophetic elements: possession of the spirit (Num 27:18); emphasis upon listening to and obeying the word of the leader (Num 27:20–21); the tent of meeting (Deut 31:14; cf. M. Haran, "The Nature of the *'ōhel mô'edh'* in Pentateuchal Sources," *JSS* 5 [1960] 50–65); oracular form (Deut 31:23). The tradition may have its origin in prophetic circles concerned about the continuation of the prophetic office, sharing a concern with the tradition behind 2 Kgs 2:9–15. Such tradition has received its formulation in terms of the language of war, so that both the Deuteronomistic and Priestly forms emphasize the role of Moses as leader of war (Num 27:17; Deut 31:2). Joshua 1:1–9 takes up the military element and expands it. Joshua is the military successor to Moses, but still dependent upon the commands of Moses as well as those of Yahweh.

The solution to the literary-critical problems of Joshua are based on somewhat different criteria than those of the Pentateuch. There doublets, contradictions, distinctions in divine names, and so on are used to separate literary strata. Only occasionally are such criteria apparent in Joshua. Here the problem is one of literary style (e.g., shifts from singular to plural address), shifts of content and perspective, theological shifts, and so on. The answers emanating from such study are anything but unanimous. The present section illustrates the problem. It repeats much of the language of Deuteronomy but is not a "doublet" to any section of Deuteronomy nor to Num 27. Still, scholars have uncovered abundant evidence of a literary "history" within the passage. Moses is called "servant of Yahweh" three times (vv 1, 2, 7). The audience addressed shifts from singular (vv 2, 5–9) to plural (vv 3–4). The statement of v 3 makes that of v 5 unnecessary. Verses 7–9 are separated grammatically from the preceding by the particle רק; formally by the variation in the use of the encouragement formula; and contextually by the placing of a condition on the previous promises (cf. Holzinger, 2). How does one describe such a literary history? A variety of solutions are possible:

1. A continuation of Pentateuchal sources in 1–2 with various Deuteronomistic layers added (e.g. Holzinger, 2, xvii; Gressmann, 134; Eissfeldt, *Introduction,* 248–57; Tengström *Die Hexateucherzählung,* 143–54).

2. A Deuteronomic compiler's adaptation of older liturgical narrative tradition (Gray, 48).

3. A unified introduction of the Deuteronomist with a few glosses (Noth, *Überlieferungsgeschichtliche Studien,* 40–41).

4. A succession of Deuteronomistic editors (e.g. Smend, *Probleme,* 494–97; Otto, *Mazzotfest,* 86; Veijola *Die ewige Dynastie,* 28–29).

One thing is clear. The larger part of the material is Deuteronomistic. V 1 takes up the narrative from Deut 34:5, 10–12. The only evidence for an

older source might be the expansion משרת משה, but its use in the earlier
literary sources is doubtful (see *Comment*). The participial נתן formula in v 2
is likewise Deuteronomistic and the application of the "servant" title to Moses
is beloved by Deuteronomistic circles (see *Comment*) though not confined to
them. Vv 3–5a are closely related to Deut 11:24–25a, adding a formula closely
related to the Deuteronomic *"Promulgationssatz"* (cf. N. Lohfink, *Das Hauptgebot*
[AnBib 20. Romae: Pontificio Institutio Biblico, 1963] 59–63; 297–98). The
motif of divine presence (5b) rests ultimately on the tradition of the call of
Moses (Exod 3:12), but is taken up in Joshua directly from the Deuteronomistic
context of Deut 31:8, 23. Indeed, Deuteronomy never explicitly uses the
formula to express the divine presence with Moses, but it is typical of Deuteronomistic argument to refer back to the divine presence with the fathers or
with predecessor(s) (H. D. Preuss, ". . . ich will mit dir sein!" *ZAW* 80 [1968]
146, 148).

The Hiph'il of נחל, the encouragement formula, and the oath formula
combine to show that v 6 is Deuteronomistic. Every phrase of v 7 is Deutero-
noministic (cf. Weinfeld, *Deuteronomy*, 336, 339, 343, 346). V 8 has Deuteronomic tints (Weinfeld, *Deuteronomy*, 336, 339), but הגה (cf. Ps 1:2) and צלח
(Ps 1:3; 1 Chr 22:13; 2 Chr 20:20; 24:20; 31:21) may join it to a later strand
of legalistic piety in Israel. V 9 then returns to Deuteronomic vocabulary
(Weinfeld, *Deuteronomy*, 343, 344) and the promise of presence.

Josh 1:1–9 is thus Deuteronomistic in vocabulary and literary connections.
It represents one of the many orations by which the Deuteronomistic writer(s)
bring theological interpretations to bear on historical materials (Noth, *Überlieferungsgeschichtliche Studien*, 5). Only in v 8 do we have reason to suspect a
later literary hand (contrast Deut 17:18–19). The only question that remains
is the number of Deuteronomists who have been at work. Verses 3–4 represent
an insertion on the basis of Deut 11:24–25. The plural address does not
necessarily make it a part of the later redaction (Lohfink, *Das Hauptgebot*,
248). The other point in question comes at v 7 with the variation of the
encouragement formula. This finds its counterpart in 1 Kgs 2:1–4. Both are
speeches to new leaders following the death of the leader beyond compare
and contain similar structural elements: external presuppositions for the following speech, followed by the speech composed of introduction, paraenesis,
and practical instructions (cf. Veijola, *Die ewige Dynastie*, 28–29). In both cases
a portion of the admonition involves loyalty to the law, a portion Veijola,
following Smend, would attribute to a secondary "nomistic," Deuteronomist.
This fails to note the structure of the Deuteronomistic work which is determined by the commands to obey the law and commandments given Israel
through Moses (the key passages are Deut 1:5; 4:44; 28:69; 31:9; Josh 1:7;
22:2, 4, 5; 23:6; Judg 2:20; 1 Sam 12:14–15; 2 Sam 8:10–11; 1 Kgs 2:3–4;
8:24–25, 56–57; 9:4–7; 11:9–13, 31–39; 14:7–11; 2 Kgs 17:7–20; 18:6–7; 21:2–
15; 22:11–20). From beginning to end, the history has one theme and one
measuring rod—the book of the law given to Moses. Obedience to it brought
rest for Joshua, following Moses, and for Solomon, following David. Rebellion
against it brought destruction on the generations following Joshua and Solomon and ultimately on both kingdoms. Neither Moses nor David were enjoined
to follow the law; both are pictured as doing so. Their successors had to

be admonished to follow the law in the second generation. Joshua was able to and gained the land. Solomon was not and lost the kingdom.

The admonition to keep the law in v 7 is thus necessary for the structure of the Deuteronomistic history. It also follows the form used by the Deuteronomist, that of the covenant (cf. K. Baltzer, *Das Bundesformular* WMANT 4. [Neukirchen-Vluyn: Neukirchener Verlag, 1960] 79). Language, structure, and purpose join to attest the literary unity of the unit with the possible exception of v 8.

Repetition and contradiction combine to underline the theological thought of the section. The entire section is repetition, yet elaboration of the commission of Joshua in Deut 31. Key words constantly resound: *Moses* (1a, 1b, 2, 3, 5, 7); *give* (2, 3, 6); *all* (2, 3, 4, 5, 7a, 7b, 8, 9); *will be with you* (5, 9); the encouragement formula (6, 7, 9). Different words repeat the same thought: *success in conquest* (3a, 4, 5, 6, 7b, 8b, 9b); *freedom from fear* (5b, 9a, the encouragement formula). The constant repetition does not express a straightforward, unambiguous statement. Rather, it unfolds a theological dialectic. Moses, the receiver and mediator of promise, is dead; so now promise can be fulfilled (1–3). Moses is dead, yet continues to speak through his officer and his law (1, 7). Everything is done to fulfill the words spoken to Moses (3), yet the promise was ultimately to the fathers (6). Victory is repeatedly promised (3–9), yet must be won through human action (2, 3, 5) and obedience (7–9). The promised land can be described explicitly (4), yet only what is precisely touched is won (3). Victory is certain, but the human leader must be repeatedly admonished to have courage and not to fear (5–9).

The intention of the section is clarified when one further contrast is noted, namely the formal one. The section is dominated by divine imperative (2b, 5b, 6, 7, 8). The climatic summary is not imperative. It is interrogative. The rhetorical question forces the human leader addressed by God to respond. Divine imperative is not so overwhelming that response is automatic. Divine imperative remains dialogue addressed to the human partner, eliciting but not intimidating.

Comment

¹ The book opens with a contrast between Moses as the עבד "servant" of Yahweh and Joshua as the משרת "official," of Moses. This is not unique to the Joshua narratives. Moses is called the servant of Yahweh in Exod 4:10; 14:31; Num 11:11; 12:7–8. The first two of these form a theological arc joining Exod 1–14 into a larger theological unit (cf. R. Rendtorff, *Das überlieferungsgeschichtliche Problem des Pentateuch* BZAW 147. [Berlin: Walter de Gruyter, 1977] 71, 155). The origin of the Pentateuch is again up for grabs in scholarly circles, but certainly the central theme of the larger unit Exod 1–14 has been formulated prior to a final incorporation into a "Deuteronomistic" tetrateuchal source or pentateuchal redaction. Perhaps the incorporation into the Pentateuch occurred with a Jehovistic redaction during the time of Hezekiah (cf. P. Weimar, *Untersuchungen zur Redaktionsgeschichte des Pentateuch* BZAW 146. [Berlin: Walter de Gruyter, 1977] 53–55; 168–69). The theme itself may have been formulated within or in conversation with disciples of Isaiah, since this

would explain the formal similarities between Isa 7 and Exod 14 as well as
the theme of belief on the prophetic word (cf. H. H. Schmid, *Der sogenannte
Jahwist* [Zürich: Theologischer Verlag, 1976] 54–55). The prophetic call form
of Exod 4 would also fit into this pattern. Similarly, Num 11–12 centers around
the prophetic office of Moses (cf. Num 11:23; 12:6–8). The motif of Moses
as the servant of Yahweh appears to have arisen in prophetic circles at least
as early as Hezekiah. It was one element used to define the Mosaic office
as prophetic and thus to help authenticate contemporary prophecy. The Deuteronomistic historian took up the motif and formed it into a dominant element
in his presentation of Israel's history. By means of it honor was given to
Moses and thus authenticity and authority to the words of Moses (Deut 34:5;
Josh 1:1, 2, 7, 13, 15; 8:31, 33; 11:12, 15; 12:6; 13:8; 14:7; 18:7; 22:2; 4–5;
1 Kgs 8:53, 56; 2 Kgs 18:12; 21:8; cf. I. Riesener, *Der Stamm* עבד *im Alten
Testament* BZAW 149. [Berlin: Walter de Gruyter, 1979] 184–91). Only occasionally is the motif used in the later literature (Ps 105:26; Neh 1:7–8; 9:14;
10:30; 1 Chr 6:34; 2 Chr 1:3; 24:6; Mal 3:22; Isa 63:11; Dan 9:11).

Over against the great "servant" of the deity, stands Joshua as the "minister" of Moses. The tradition appears only here and three times in the Pentateuch: Exod 24:13; 33:11; Num 11:28. It utilizes a well-chosen term. משרת
represents a youthful page serving his master freely and never implies slavery
(C. Westermann, "שרת—dienen," *THAT* 2 [1976] 1019–20). Joshua is thus
introduced as the young page waiting on Moses. Where did such a picture
develop? Exod 24:13 is a literary bridge to Exod 32, where in vv 17–18,
Joshua abruptly appears to announce the sound of war in the camp to Moses,
and is just as abruptly shut up by the superior knowledge of the master. In
Exod 33:11, Joshua's role switches to that of a minister at the oracular Tent
of Meeting in the absence of master Moses. In Num 11:26–30, a narrative
likewise centering on the Tent of Meeting, Joshua is again introduced abruptly
as he pleads with Moses to punish unauthorized prophets. Once again he
is abruptly shut up by the master. To discover a literary origin for the motif
is impossible. None of the texts may be shown to belong to the original
literary context (R. Schmitt, *Zelt und Lade als Thema alttestamentlicher Wissenschaft*
[Gütersloh: Gütersloher Verlagshaus, 1972] 186). Outside Josh 1, the term
is applied to Joshua in cultic contexts, twice in connection with the Tent of
Meeting. Deut 31:14 also connects Joshua with the tent. Num 11 makes the
context a little more specific. The tradition is at home among "circles of
ecstatic 'prophecy' " (Noth, *Numbers* [Tr. J. D. Martin, Philadelphia: Westminster, 1968] 89). The understanding of Joshua as minister of Moses as well
as that of Moses as servant of God has arisen in prophetic circles. The repeated
emphasis on Moses' superiority and Joshua's inferiority, if not downright
stupidity, lends credence to the theory that such tradition arose in circles
seeking to demonstrate the superiority of Moses as a prophet of God over
against the tradition of Joshua, who appears to be pictured as an ignorant
warrior ready to condemn and destroy. As we shall see, the Deuteronomistic
historian has used the term in quite a different manner. Joshua is subordinate
but not stupid. His willing submission to Moses is the mark of greatness.

2 Central to the thought of the book of Joshua is the land given by God, inherited by Israel, and conquered by Joshua. In contrast to the superpowers of her environment, Israel did not claim possession of her land from primeval times on. Her land belonged originally to the Canaanites (Gen 11:31; 12:5; Deut 1:7; etc.) or to a long list of former inhabitants (e.g. Exod 3:17). Israel claimed the land only because Yahweh chose to punish the original inhabitants (Gen 15:16; Deut 9:4–5). He thus promised the land to Abraham. The motif of the promise of land to the patriarchs may rest on a nomadic tradition of divine direction during the change of pasture land (V. Maag, "Der Hirte Israels," *Schweizer Theologische Umschau* 28 [1958] 2–28; "Malkût YHWH," VTSup 7 [1960] 129–53). It has been applied specifically to the land of Canaan as early as the settlement (C. Westermann, *Die Verheissungen an die Väter* [FRLANT 116. Göttingen: Vandenhoeck & Ruprecht, 1976] 133–38). It is used to link the various sections of the Pentateuch together theologically (Gen 50:24; Exod 3:8; 6:4; 13:5, 11; 32:13; 33:1; Num 11:12; 14:16, 23–24; 32:11–12; Deut 1:8; 4:38; 6:3, 10, etc.). The language of such theological editing is closely related to that of the Deuteronomic school (cf. Rendtorff, *Das überlieferungsgeschichtliche Problem*, 40–45, 51–70, 75–79). The book of Joshua takes up the land theme in dependence upon Deuteronomy and brings the theme to its completion. The promise to the fathers is realized; the punishment of the inhabitants carried through; the hope of the Pentateuch fulfilled; the inheritance from Yahweh is received.

⁴ Israel has two sets of borders, that in which her own people live and that which is the land of promise. The first can be described simply as from Dan to Beersheba (2 Sam 24:2–8, 15; 2 Kgs 4:25; cf. Deut 34:1–3), including land beyond the Jordan (2 Sam 24:5–6). The land of promise stretches from the Brook of Egypt to the Euphrates and from the Jordan River to the Mediterranean (Gen 15:18; Exod 23:21; Num 13:21; 34:1–12; Deut 1:7; 11:24, 1 Kgs 5:1 (Engl. 4:21); 8:65; 2 Kgs 14:25; Amos 6:14; 1 Chr 13:5; 2 Chr 7:8). The book of Joshua knows both types of boundaries. The conquest covered only the first (10:41; 11:17, 22; 13:2–7), but the promise was for more. Behind each of the border descriptions stood a specific historical reality. Dan to Beersheba represented the land actually occupied by Israelites and governed directly by the Israelite kings. The second represented the traditional description of the land of Canaan by Egyptian sources of the fourteenth and thirteenth centuries as adopted by the Israelite tradition (cf. Y. Aharoni, 58–72). The use of the latter system results in the land of the Trans-Jordan tribes being viewed as not belonging to the land of the Lord (Josh 22:9–34). On the few occasions that Israel controlled the territory described by the second system, she governed territory outside the Dan to Beersheba limits through a system of tributary states (1 Kgs 5:1).

The motif of land as נחלה is central for Deuteronomy (G. von Rad, "Promised Land," in *The Problem of the Hexateuch and other Essays* [Tr. E. W. T. Dicken; Edinburgh: Oliver & Boyd, 1966] 91). This has normally been translated "inheritance" and used as the basis of a theology. G. Gerleman ("Nutzrecht und Wohnrecht," *ZAW* 89 [1977] 313–25) has recently called such theologizing into question by showing that the term means "home, place of residence, security of home." The verb means "to settle, to cause to occupy a territory."

Deuteronomy uses the term in a unique way, referring to the home of all Israel, whereas earlier sources spoke of the homestead of individuals or individual tribes (e.g. Mic 2:2; 1 Kgs 21:3; Num 16:14). The term thus unifies the nation into a homeland for Deuteronomic theology, a homeland never before experienced by the wandering, landless, homeless Israelites. At the same time the term limits the claim of Israel, for it shows that the homeland comes from God, not from natural rights nor from human claims of possession or power (see P. Diepold, *Israels Land* [BWANT 95. Stuttgart: W. Kohlhammer Verlag, 1972] 81–84).

Still another theological motif of importance to the Deuteronomic movement appears in v 3b: the fulfillment of prophecy given through Moses (cf. G. von Rad, *Studies in Deuteronomy* [Tr. D. Stalker, London: SCM, 1953] 83–91). The force of the prophetic word is nothing created by the Deuteronomic theologian(s). It is implicit in the patriarchal promises of Genesis and explicit in the work of the prophets at least from Nathan onward. "The Deuteronomist's innovation was to make this prophetic word of God the focal point of his history" (Weinfeld, *Deuteronomy,* 21).

Josh 1:3 is the first reference to fulfillment of prophecy given to Moses. It refers back to the specific commissions given Joshua by Moses, commands which appear only in Deuteronomy and not in the Tetrateuch (Deut 3:21, 28; 31:3–8; cf. 1:38; 31:23). The motif appears to be another element in the picture of Moses as the great prophet painted by the Deuteronomist on the basis of earlier traditions (cf. L. Perlitt, "Mose als Prophet," *EvT* 31 [1971] 588–608).

[5] The motif of divine presence frames the second half of our section (vv 5, 9, cf. v 17). This motif has its roots in the nomadic lives of the patriarchs, particularly in the Isaac, Jacob and Joseph narratives (Preuss, *ZAW* 80 [1968] 139–73; "עם, את" *TWAT* 1 [1971] 485–500; C. Westermann, *Verheissungen,* 130–32; D. Vetter, "עם-mit," *THAT* 2 [1976] 325–28). The motif expresses the divine promise to accompany the patriarch on a fearful journey (e.g. Gen 28:15; 31:3; Exod 3:12). The formula is taken up into the holy war ideology of Israel (Judg 6:11–16; Num 14:43; 1 Sam 17:37; 2 Sam 7:9). The law corpus of Deuteronomy uses the theme only in the laws for battle (Deut 20:1–4), while the Deuteronomistic framework of the book uses the theme in reference to guidance through the wilderness (2:7) and in Joshua's preparation for conquest (31:6, 8, 23). The motif thus expresses one of the basic roots of Israelite faith, the belief that Yahweh is the God of Israel who accompanies, leads, protects, fights and goes with the men he has chosen for his work (cf. Preuss, *ZAW* 80 [1968] 157).

The book of Joshua takes up the ancient motif and claims it for Joshua, but again a characteristic modification is made. The presence with Joshua is the presence which was with Moses (vv 5, 17).

[7] The final motif which underlines Joshua 1 is Torah, specifically the Torah commanded by Moses. Torah designated the teaching of the priests (Jer 18:18; Ezek 7:26; Hos 4:6). Particularly important here was the information given members of the community who asked questions of the priests (e.g. Hag 2:11–13). Torah was not confined to the priests. The teaching of Isaiah

was Torah for his disciples (8:16). The wise man also produced Torah (Prov 13:14), a task which may have ultimately had its roots in the family (Prov 1:8; 4:4, 11).

Hosea chaps. 4 and 8 introduce the idea of a collected body of traditions called Torah. This may rest on a similar tradition as that found infrequently in the Tetrateuch (Gen 26:5; Exod 13:9; 16:4, 28). Torah is attributed to Moses in the earlier sources only in Exod 18:16–20; 24:12. Even the basic core of Deuteronomy does not appear to make use of the term (for the appearances in chaps. 17, 27, 28, cf. Lohfink, *Das Hauptgebot,* 58). Torah, particularly Torah written in a book, becomes a central theological motif for the Deuteronomistic historian (Deut 1:5; 4:8, 44; 29:20, 28; 30:10; 31:9–12, 24–26; 32:46; 33:4, 10; Josh 1; 8:31–35; chaps. 22–24; 1 Kgs 2:3; 2 Kgs 10:31; 14:6; 17:13, 34, 37; 21:8, 11; 23:24, 25). The Deuteronomist defines precisely which book of Torah he means, that one given to Moses after he defeated Sihon and Og (Deut 1:1–5) and written down by Moses to be placed in the ark of the covenant entrusted to the Levitical priests (31:24–26). It was this Torah by which the kings of Israel and Judah were judged (e.g. 2 Kgs 17:37) and which sparked the Josianic reformation (2 Kgs 22–23). Again in Josh 1 a motif with primary Mosaic connections, but only secondary Joshua connections, surfaces.

Explanation

At the narrative level, Josh 1:1–9 introduces the narrative of the conquest of the land. At this level the threefold task given to Joshua corresponds to the three major sections of the book: a) Conquer the land, chaps. 1–12; b) distribute the land, chaps. 13–19); c) obey the law, chaps. 20–24. The section thus functions as a formal introduction to the book, giving in summary fashion a brief survey of the contents. More than that, it sets the tone for the book, a tone dominated by the divine imperative, directing, demanding and yet encouraging his people into action. Behind all that follows stands word and will of God, not man.

The Israelite historian was not content to remain at the narrative level. He used the introduction of this portion of his history to make an important theological statement. Deuteronomy portrayed *the* leader of Israel's history— Moses, the prophet without parallel. The remainder of the history centered likewise around the great leaders of Israel—Joshua, Samuel, David, Solomon, Hezekiah, Josiah, and so on. What did one expect of such leaders? Deuteronomy 17:14–20 gave a legal standard by which to measure Israel's leaders. Joshua 1:1–9 gives a corresponding paradigm. The remainder of the book then gives flesh and blood to that paradigm in the figure of Joshua.

The paradigm of Israelite leadership has five major components. The first is the context of leadership. All leadership in Israel occurs in the shadow of Moses. He has died, but his example and teaching stand before every successor. The Israelite leader must be an official, a minister of Moses. The remaining elements of the paradigm point to what this means.

The second component is the divine command to fulfill the promise. Lead-

ership in Israel stands tied to the gift of the land. The leader may not multiply
emblems of power for himself, but must remain on equal footing with his
fellow Israelites (Deut 17:16, 17, 20). His task is to maintain the land for
himself and his fellows. In so doing, he maintains the true identity of Israel,
the people of the promise to Moses (v 3) and to the fathers (v 6). The explicit
command to each generation may be different. For Joshua, it was the conquest
of the whole land. For a later editor, the emphasis seems to have been on
Lebanon and the land of the Hittites, the northern territory beyond Dan,
so that the editor inserted these territorial names into the border description
(see *Notes*). No matter what the specific command, it was simply a specification
of the general command to Moses. Israelite leadership fulfilled the command
to Moses to possess the land for Israel.

The third component is the divine consolation. The biblical historian is
well aware of the consequences of obedience to the divine command. The
command, in human perspective, leads to danger and risk. The danger is
counterbalanced by the promise of divine presence. Again, this is not something new. It is as old as the patriarchs. For the Deuteronomist, however, it
is based on the promise to Moses (v 5). The Israelite leader stands not only
in the shadow of Moses but also in the shadow of that presence which led
Moses from Egypt into the wilderness to the plains of Moab. Such presence
guarantees fulfillment of the command. It stands as the basis of the call to
courage and certainty (v 6).

One condition modifies the word of consolation. Divine gift has a human
corollary, the call to obedience. For the Deuteronomist the path was clearly
marked. It had been given to Moses. It was the Torah of Moses. The leader
of Israel, whether king (Deut 17) or conqueror (Joshua), had no claim to
new revelation. The word to Moses sufficed. Only he who obeyed Moses,
the leader of Israel, could expect success in his leadership endeavors.

The final component of the Deuteronomistic theology of leadership took
up into itself all the others. This was the call to response. In a rhetorical
question, God summarized all that he had said and called upon the leader
to reflect upon and respond to the divine word. Was the leader willing to
walk in the shadow of Moses beneath the larger shadow of divine presence,
fulfilling both the promise and the Torah? The Deuteronomist saw a positive
response in the person of Joshua. He sought similar responses among his
people beyond the Great River, the River Euphrates. Could the promise once
again be fulfilled, the land once again received as gift by a people once again
walking in the shadow of Moses and his larger Shadow?

People of God have constantly been plagued by the Deuteronomistic dialectic: fulfill the promise through fulfilling the condition. The tendency is ever
to place the emphasis on one side or other of the dialectic and thus destroy
the delicate balance achieved here. Promise and presence frame the section
and its thought. Yet they are offered only to a people willing to hide itself
in the shadow of the divine and his human representative. Deuteronomist,
prophet, priest, and sage form a great biblical chorus calling forth volunteers
to accept the divine gift through human obedience. The NT witnesses point
to an even greater representative who completed the task given him in total
obedience and called men to follow him in similar obedience.

Chain of Command Organized (1:10-11)

Bibliography

See 1:1–9.

Translation

¹⁰ *Joshua gave orders to the national officials,* ¹¹ *"Pass through the midst of the camp* ^a *and order the people, 'Prepare provisions for yourselves,* ^b *because within three days you all* ^c *will be crossing over this Jordan to enter in order to possess the land which Yahweh your God* ^d *is giving you to possess it.* ^e *' "*

Notes

11.a. LXX reads the camp "of the people." Such a phrase never occurs in MT. LXX has copied the addition from the previous or succeeding verse, where "the people" are mentioned.

11.b. "For yourselves" is not stated expressly in LXX but is implicit in the use of the middle voice.

11.c. LXX reads the conjunction following the temporal clause, a characteristic of Semitic grammar, not Greek. An original Heb. conjunction may underlie the reading.

11.d. LXX reads "the God of your fathers." Auld has noted the MT preference of the second plur. pronoun attached to "God" (VTSup 30 [1979] 11–12). Deuteronomy uses the divine title "God of your fathers" eight times, but the Deuteronomistic history has the title only in Josh 18:3; Judg 2:12; 2 Kgs 21:22. The title is connected with the giving of the land formula in Deut 12:1 and 27:3 and may have entered our text tradition from there. The LXX thus may be a witness to the fluidity of the text tradition in the use of pious idioms.

11.e. "To possess it" is a characteristic Deuteronomistic idiom (Weinfeld, *Deuteronomy*, 342, n. 2) but is missing in the LXX here and in v 15. Both times the expression is redundant and may represent again the fluidity of pious idioms.

Form/Structure/Setting

Form and content isolate these two verses from their present context. Vv 1–9 have employed divine speech to set the theological stage for the conquest. Vv 12–18 use a speech of Joshua directed to the Trans-Jordan tribes to complete that theological context. Vv 10–11 represent a speech of Joshua directed to the officers of the people, introducing the conquest itself. The verses serve a narrative function rather than a theological function in that they set the narrative stage for chapter three.

The section represents a narrative fragment. Both the setting and the execution of the command are lacking. Both are preserved elsewhere: the setting in 1:1–2; the execution in 3:2–17. Further comments will be made in chap. 3.

These two verses form the center of argument for an earlier or Pentateuchal source in Josh 1 (most recently, Otto, *Mazzotfest*, 86–87; for attribution to E, see Simpson, *Early Traditions*, 280). They also provide evidence for the Deuteronomistic character of the whole chapter (Wellhausen, *Composition*, 119; Noth). The problematic was aptly described by J. Hollenberg "Die deuteronomischen Bestandtheile des Buches Josua," *Theologische Studien und Kritiken* 1 [1874] 476–77). V 11b closely parallels Deut 11:31 and contains Deuteronomic phraseology (Weinfeld, *Deuteronomy*, 342g n. 2, 3). שטרים, "officials," does appear in Exod 5 and Num 11:16 (addition to J?), but is typical for Deuteronomy. צידה, "provisions," occurs only three times in the Pentateuch (Gen 42:25; 45:21; Exod 12:39, all either J or E), but also appears in the sources peculiar to the Deuteronomistic history (Josh 9:11; Judg 7:8; 20:10; 1 Sam 22:10). The word appears to be archaic, but that does not prove that the "literary source" is. The most we can deduce is that the Deuteronomist may be relying upon tradition at this point (cf. chap. 3). Such tradition has been reworked by the Deuteronomist. The conclusion that the section represents an old source rests on conclusions drawn from studies of the succeeding chapters of the book not on internal evidence from the section itself (e.g. Otto, *Mazzotfest*, 86–88).

The section plays on terminology picked up from the previous section and carried further. V 9 has summarized the previous section as a divine command. This, in turn, centered on obedience to the command of Moses (v 7). V 10 describes Joshua obediently commanding the officers to command the people. The section introducing the military occupation of the land (see *Comment*) does so through a "divine chain of command."

In similar manner, the divine command opened with the call to pass over (v 2). The officers now pass over the camp (v 11) to command the people to pass over (v 11).

The divine command to Joshua involved "passing over this Jordan to the land which I am giving" (v 2). The entire section centered around the promises and provision of God in giving the land as well as the encouragement of the leader of the people. Joshua's command centers on human provisions needed for the hard march of conquest to take possession of the land God is giving. Thus v 11 places the reference to the land in a subordinate clause and introduces into it the unnecessary repetition of the root ירש, "possess," emphasizing the military participation of the people. (For an understanding of עם "people," as showing dependence upon Yahweh, see Waltraut Schulz, *Stilkritische Untersuchungen zur deuteronomistischen Literatur* [dissertation, Tübingen, 1974] 45–68).

Comment

10 שטרים, "officials," reflects the tradition of Exod 18:24–25, Num 11:16; and Deut 1:15, wherein Moses appointed tribal officials to assume part of the responsibility which had become burdensome for him. The tradition is closely tied to the reorganization of the military and legal system by Jehoshaphat (2 Chr 19:5–11; cf. R. Knierim, "Exodus 18 und die Neuordnung der mosaischen Gerichtsbarkeit," *ZAW* 73 [1961] 146–71; G. Macholz, "Zur Geschichte der Justizorganisation in Juda," *ZAW* 84 [1972] 314–40). For the Chronicler the term is tied closely to the legal duties of the Levites (1 Chr 23:4; 26:29; 27:1; 2 Chr 19:11; 26:11; 34:13). Deuteronomy assumes the Tetrateuchal tradition of civil administration set up by Moses and sees their duties closely connected to the military (Deut 20:5–9) in addition to legal duties (16:18). The one appearance in wisdom appears to presuppose a position

of some political power (Prov 6:7). The Deuteronomist takes up the term in a stereotyped fashion to speak of administrators of the people prior to the monarchy (Deut 1:15; 29:9; 31:28; Josh 8:33; 23:2; 24:1). This may well reflect tribal organization and terminology later adapted into the monarchical system, but the details remain unclear.

11 A new element of Deuteronomistic theology emerges in v 11 expressed by the root ירש. The precise meaning of the term is broad and its basic meaning disputed. L. A. Snijders ("Genesis XV. The Covenant with Abram," *OTS* 12 [1958] 267–71) begins with Mic 6:15; Deut 28:42; and Isa 63:18, concluding that the basic meaning is "to tread upon." H. H. Schmid, ("ירש-beerben," *THAT* 1 [1971] 780–81) starts from Gen 15:3–4; 21:10; 2 Sam 14:7; Jer 49:1–2, concluding that the original meaning was "inherit." J. G. Plöger (*Literarkritische, formgeschichtliche und stilkritische Untersuchungen zum Deuteronomium* [BBB 26; Bonn: Peter Hanstein, 1967] 83) speaks of a technical military term. The usage underlying our passage has its apparent roots in a traditional popular blessing formula transmitted in Gen 24:60 (cf. H. W. Wolff, "Das Kerygma des Jahwisten," *EvT* 24 [1964] 84–85). The Deuteronomic meaning becomes clear in Deut 2:12, 21, 22, 24, 31; 4:47; 6:18. It is the action of Israel in taking by force the territory of nations living in the "promised" land. A similar meaning is confirmed in Num 13:30; 21:24, 32, 35; 33:53. Israel's military possession of the land becomes the basis of Deuteronomic paraenesis (e.g. chap. 4; 5:31; 6:1; 18; 28:21, 63; 30:5, 16, 18; 31:13; 32:47; almost fifty times in all). It also becomes a link between the patriarchal promises and the conquest narratives (Gen 15:7; 22:17; 28:4; Num 33:53; Deut 1:8, 21, 39; 3:12, 18, 20; 31:3; Josh 1:11). Our text is thus the final link in the fulfillment of the land promise to the patriarchs, a fulfillment that includes the gift from God but also the military participation of men. (See Plöger, *Untersuchungen*, 83–87; P. Diepold, *Israels Land*, [BWANT 95; Stuttgart: W. Kohlhammer Verlag, 1972] 88–89).

11 The Jordan River wanders about two hundred miles to cover the sixty-five mile distance from the Lake of Galilee to the Dead Sea, dropping an additional six hundred feet below sea level as it goes. The river itself is generally quite shallow and narrow with numerous places where it can be forded, but the spring thaw brings flood waters down from Mount Hermon in the north. Still, the river forms a major geographical barrier because it is bordered by the jungle-like זור in the river bed itself and the desolate, infertile קתתה—or desolate hills—just above. It offered no opportunity for navigation and little for settlement. It simply separated the land of Canaan from Trans-Jordan and made control of the fords a military necessity (Cf. D. Baly, *The Geography of the Bible* [New York: Harper & Brothers, 1957] 193–210; Y. Aharoni, *Land*, 29–32; S. Cohen, "Jordan," *IDB* 2 [1962] 973–78; E. G. Kraeling, *Rand McNally Bible Atlas* [New York: Rand McNally, 1956] 25–29; N. Glueck, *The River Jordan* [Philadelphia: Westminster, 1946]).

Explanation

The opening section of the book introduced a specific understanding of Israelite leadership. The remainder of the book repeatedly plays on the theme of Joshua as the example of Israelite leadership in the shadow of Moses.

This first section transposes traditions and interrupts chronology to show that Joshua obeyed the divine command immediately without question. The motif of "within three days" belongs to chap. 3, introducing the need to cleanse the camp prior to the great cultic procession through the Jordan (cf. 3:2). It totally ignores the tradition of the spies sent out (chap. 2). It also transforms the cultic tradition into a battle tradition through the insertion of יֹרֵשׁ, "possess" and the emphasis upon preparation of provisions for a long journey. Joshua thus interprets the divine command as a command to lead the nation into battle and responds accordingly. He is the military commander *par excellence* in Israel by the very fact that he carries out the command of the heavenly general.

Lesson in Leadership   *(1:12–18)*

Bibliography

See 1:1–9 and:
Barth, C. "Die Antwort Israels." *Probleme biblischer Theologie,* ed. H. W. Wolff. München: Chr. Kaiser Verlag, 1971, 44–56. **Mittmann, S.** *Deuteronomium 1:1–6:3.* BZAW 139. Berlin: Walter de Gruytar, 1975. **Wüst, M.** *Untersuchungen zu den siedlungsgeographischen Texten des Alten Testaments.* Beihefte zum Tübinger Atlas des vorderen Orients B9. Wiesbaden: Ludwig Reichert Verlag, 1975.

Translation

[12] *Meanwhile* [a] *to the Reubenites, Gaddites, and half the tribe of Manasseh, Joshua said,* [13] *"Remember the word which Moses, the servant of Yahweh, commanded you all: 'Yahweh, your God, is giving you rest in that he has given you all this land.'* [14a] *Your women, children, and herds are to remain in the land which Moses gave to you all beyond the Jordan,* [b] *but* [c] *you all are to pass over armed before your brothers, all the warriors, so that you all may help them* [15] *until Yahweh gives rest to your brothers just as to you all. They also are to possess the land which Yahweh your God is giving to them. Then you all may return to the land you all possess so that you all may possess that which Moses, the servant of Yahweh,* [a] *has given you all beyond the Jordan at the rising of the sun."*
[16] *They answered Joshua, "Everything which you have commanded us, we will do; everywhere you send us, we will go.* [17] *According to all the way in which we have obeyed Moses, so we will obey you. Only* [a] *let Yahweh your God be with you just as he was with Moses.* [18] *Every man who rebels against your order and does not obey your words, to the last detail which you command us, shall be put to death. Only may you have conviction and courage."*

Notes

12.a. The section does not begin with a consecutive verb form which would indicate action subsequent to the preceding. Rather it begins with a nominal form. This introduces an episode-initial circumstantial clause contemporaneous to the preceding (Andersen, *Sentence,* 77–80). New actors are thus issued onto the scene.

13.a. זכור is an infinitive absolute used for the emphatic imperative (GKC § 113bb). The Mosaic command employs a participle followed by a perfect verb with the copula. This construction does not appear to have received adequate attention. The present context refers to the command of Moses in Deut 3:18 which presupposes the possession of Trans-Jordan. It must therefore refer to past or present possession and rest, not a future promise. D. Michel in reference to the Psalms says when the perfect appears after an imperfect or a participle, it does not carry the action further but rather introduces beside it an explanatory fact (*Tempora und Satzstellung in den Psalmen* [Bonn: Bouvier, 1960] 99; cf. A. B. Davidson, *Hebrew Syntax,* 3rd ed. [Edinburgh: T. & T. Clark, 1901] §§ 55c, 56; Joüon, *Grammaire,* § 119r, v).

14.a. It is not clear where the Mosaic "quotation" ends. The language of v 14 comes from Deut 3:19 but speaks of Moses in the third person, unless one omits the reference to Moses on the basis of the LXX.

14.b. The LXX retains God as the giver of the land rather than Moses and omits the anachronistic localization "beyond the Jordan." However, LXX itself is not consistent at this point, for in 15 it too speaks of land given by Moses beyond the Jordan. Here is one of many examples of a shorter LXX which may represent a text tradition which avoided repetition of pious terminology.

14.c. ואתם introduces a contrast sentence (Andersen, *Sentence,* 150–52). The expectations for the men are contrasted to those of their family and flocks.

15.a. The MT is repetitive and difficult. The LXX omits וירשתם אותה as do many modern commentators (e.g. Holzinger, 2; Soggin, 27). LXX apparently read איש לירשתו, "each to his own possession"(Margolis, 13); however, this may be an attempt to translate a difficult MT. Either the original text or a later reader sought to underline the fact that the Trans-Jordan tribes would actually possess their land, another example of the textual tradition noted in v 4. The possession of territory outside the strict land of Canaan was important to this tradition.

The LXX also omits "servant of Yahweh," which is repetitious. Again the tradition of avoiding superfluous pious language is evidenced.

17.a. The particle רק "only" in vv 17–18 introduces an exclusive sentence (Andersen, *Sentence,* 168–77) placing limits on the total commitment of the people. Such obedience is given to Joshua when God is present with him and Joshua is courageous.

Form/Structure/Setting

This section has in common with the previous one the fact that Joshua is giving orders. The previous section, however, stands isolated in its context, pointing forward to chap. 3. The present section is a unit with command (vv 12–15) and response (vv 16–18). Chap. 2 then turns to an entirely new subject, the sending out of spies.

The section concludes the introductory theological narrative of the Deuteronomist. As such its genre remains a literary theological narrative. It is not, however, independent literature. Rather, it repeatedly quotes other literature. As such it can be classified as a collection of quotations. The quotations themselves are not simply strung together loosely. They are imbedded in a particular form. Christoph Barth has called this the "Answer of Israel" or "Declaration of Readiness" ("Die Antwort Israels," 52–56). From examples in Exod 19:7–8; Exod 24:1–7; Ezra 10:10–12; Neh 8:2–6, joined with Deut 27:11–26; 1 Kgs 18:17–40; Josh 24:14–28; 2 Kgs 23:1–3; Num 32:28–32; Deut 31:9–13 and the present section, Barth has isolated elements of the structure of Israel's answer ("Die Antwort Israels," 48–53). The entire people speak unanimously in true dialogue with God. The answer is to follow definite directions given by God. Such directions are issued through a mediator to the people. The people pledge themselves to obey the divine directions through the use of a verb of action in the first person plur. imperfect. This represents a declaration of readiness to follow God's directions. The place of such an event is the cultic liturgy, says Barth, but it is not any specific festival. It is rather a celebration *sui generis,* wherein the congregation was confronted with the expressed will of God. This ritual grew out of the Deuteronomic paraenesis, particularly in the seventh century B.C. ("Die Antwort Israels," 53, 55).

Barth's suggestion bears some problems within it, particularly in light of the restriction to Deuteronomic theology at such a late date. As so many questions, this one hangs together with the question of the liturgical practices, apparently in northern Israel, which lay behind the Deuteronomic paraenesis. Still, the suggestion is illuminating for our passage. The form of the passage rests on liturgy between man and God. The content of the passage reports vows between man and men. The leaders of Israel pledge to Joshua what men normally pledge to God. This is not absolute, however. Two exclusions are made. These lay requirements upon Joshua. He must show the two basic requirements of Israelite leadership (see 1:1–9). God must be with him. He must be a man of great conviction and courage.

The problem of Israelite tribes choosing to live in Trans-Jordan rather than in the land of Canaan forms the basis of Num 32 and Deut 3. The tradition history behind these may never be known, but it is generally agreed that the early settlement of Reuben and probably of Gad is reflected in the narrative. Deuteronomistic and Priestly redactors have incorporated the narrative into the Israelite conquest tradition to underline the unity of all Israel and the joint responsibility shared by all the tribes (cf. Num 32:20–23). Our passage reflects the tradition after it has reached a written stage in the Deuteronomistic school and presupposes the incorporation into the all-Israel context. Similar material has been used, however, for distinct purposes. Deut 3 seeks to remind the Trans-Jordan tribes of their responsibility while encouraging Joshua in his. Num 32 seeks to justify the separation of Israel into Cisjordan and Trans-Jordan parts and to underline the common loyalty of both groups to Yahweh and to one another. Josh 1:12–18 uses the same tradition to demonstrate the total obedience of all Israel to Joshua.

Josh 1:12–15 virtually quotes Deut 3:18–20. The few distinctions can be explained from the new historical context given the tradition and from particular theological interests in the Joshua narrative. Thus v 12 sets the context for what follows even if this involved an abrupt shift in the Joshua narrative. The call to remembrance sets the stage for the quotation from Deut 3. Significant changes occur in v 13, where Joshua adds "is giving you all rest" to introduce the key word of promise for this section. The "servant of Yahweh" attribution again takes up a theological refrain of the chapter (see 1:1–9). In v 14 Joshua substitutes "in the land" for Deuteronomy's "in your cities." This must be viewed in light of the change in v 15 from Deuteronomy's picture of each man returning to his possession (3:20) to all the tribes returning to their collective possession. Here Joshua is consistent in introducing Joshua as the leader of the conquest of united Israel seeking a united land. This is also seen in the addition of "to help them" in v 14. The Joshua text goes its own way in introducing חמשים, "in battle array" (v 14) for חלוצים, "armed" (v 18) and substituting גבורי, "warriors" (v 14) for בני, "sons" (v 18). The significance of the changes is uncertain if they are not an attempt to make the military tone of the passage even stronger. They do not give reason for making source distinctions.

Verses 16–17 are related to content but not the phraseology of Num 32. The language itself may rather be that of liturgy. The final verse stems certainly from the author of the chapter and ties it together.

The entire section is thus Deuteronomistic, dependent upon Deut 3:18–20, but going its own way to make specific points.

Comment

Repetition of key terms continues to demonstrate the emphasis of the text. Themes repeated in vv 1–9 reappear: *Moses* (vv 13, 14, 15, 17a, b); *give* (13, 14, 15a); *land* (13, 14, 15a, b). Each section then has its own emphasis. Verse 13 introduces the new theme of rest (cf. v 15). Verse 14 uses repeated references to military preparations. Verse 15 speaks of possessing the land. Verses 16–17a underline the obedience of the people, while 18a speaks of the consequences of disobedience. Enumeration of these themes points to the typical Deuteronomistic emphasis on the divine gift of the land to an obedient people through the mediation of Moses. A shift in form and context has introduced the familiar themes into service for a radically distinct Deuteronomistic point. The context is a call to battle, not worship, issued by Joshua, not Moses. The form indicates call to obedience to divine command, but is utilized for oath of allegiance to Joshua, which in turn is modified by the final exclusive clauses in vv 17, 18, calling for obedience by Joshua.

נוח, "rest," is the new word of promise in this section. The term has a variety of contexts within the OT. The cult speaks of "divine deliverance" to the individual as bringing rest (Ps 116:7; 23:2; Jer 45:3; Job 3:13, 26; cf. Exod 33:14). It also speaks of the cult as the place of divine resting (Ps 132:8, 14; 1 Chr 28:2; cf. the earlier ark tradition of Num 10:33, 36; contrast the later prophecy Isa 66:1). The early Sabbath commandments spoke of human rest (Exod 23:12; cf. Deut 5:14), which the priests reinterpreted to speak of divine rest (Exod 20:11; cf. Gen 2:2–4, שבת). The term appears also to have roots in early legal language (2 Sam 14:17).

Isaiah used the term to apply to the life God desired for his people, who rejected it (28:12). Prophecy then eschatologized the term (Isa 14:3, 7; 11:20; 32:18; cf. Dan 12:13). Prophetic schools also used the term to speak of the gift of the divine spirit (Num 11:25–26; 2 Kgs 2:15), a usage that also became eschatologized (Isa 11:2; 63:14; Zech 6:8).

The Deuteronomistic school took up the term so widely used to speak of peace and rest from the problems of life and gave it a specific theological meaning: rest from war and enemies (Deut 3:20; 12:9–10; 25:19). Our passage takes precisely this line from Deut 3:20 and points it a step forward to its eventual realization (Josh 21:44; 22:4; 23:1). But realization is not a static thing. It can be lost (Judges) and regained (2 Sam 7:1, 11; 1 Kgs 5:18; 8:56). The exile of 597–586 is precisely the time when Israel through her disobedience lost her rest (Deut 28:65; Lam 1:3). The line of thinking connecting rest with salvation history is also taken up by other schools of thought in Israel (Ps 95:11; Isa 63:14; 1 Chr 22:9, 18; 23:25; 2 Chr 14:5; 15:15; 20:30; Neh 9:28). Rest can be a reality for Israel. It can be a goal lost and looked forward to again. It can even be a goal regained. Whatever stage Israel finds herself in, rest is a term with concrete content. It represents freedom from enemy oppression and deadly war. It represents life lived with God by the gift of God. (See G. von Rad, "Es ist noch eine Ruhe vorhanden dem Volke Gottes," *Zwischen den Zeiten* 11 [1933] 104–11=*Gesammelte Studien zum Alten Testament I* [München: Chr. Kaiser Verlag, 1958] 101–8=*The Problem of the Hexateuch and Other Essays,* [Tr. E. W. T. Dicken; Edinburgh; Oliver & Boyd, 1966] 94–102). Josh 1 thus pictures Israel in Trans-Jordan looking across the river into the promised land. Surrounded by the memory of the difficult years in the wilderness and by the knowledge of the giants in the land, Israel must choose to enter and fight or to turn back to the wilderness (cf. 7:7). Motivation to fight comes from the divine promise of rest first uttered by Moses and now repeated by Joshua. Such rest may be the possession of a part of Israel in East Jordan, but that is not enough. Guarantee of that rest depends upon the conquest of the whole of the gift of God so that the whole of the people of God have rest. Rest, not war, is the ultimate goal of Israel for the Deuteronomist. But he sees the dialectic that rest could be won only through war. The dialectic style points then to a dialectical intention. This is best seen in the outline.

I. Call to remember the Mosaic marching orders (vv 12–15)
II. Response of loyalty to loyal Joshua (vv 16–18)

Explanation

The text shifts abruptly from preparations to march to an admonition to fulfill a former pledge to fight. Here it becomes most evident that the text is not simply interested in relating pure historical narrative. Rather, specific pieces of tradition have been joined without logical consistency or narrative harmony to illustrate a theological teaching.

The earlier sections of the chapter have demonstrated the nature of Israelite response to that leadership. The present section then illustrates the nature of Israel which makes that response and sets Israel under oath to make such response perpetually.

Israel is defined as a unified body. The Jordan rift does not divide Israel. Threat to Israelite unity does not lie in geography but in loyalty. Israelites outside the narrow confines of the land promised by Yahweh must be loyal and contribute to Israelites within the land. Despite geographical separation, Israel must remain one body dedicated to one land.

Such a definition of Israel is based on one word, that of Moses given to Israel outside the land. Obedience to that law was once expressed by direct cultic statement through use of the cultic form "Answer of Israel." When such direct response is not available, another type of response is made available. This is response to the man who has taken over the Mosaic office. This manner of telling the ancient story has far-reaching consequences within the setting of the Deuteronomistic movement. If the movement has pre-exilic roots, the story would speak to the Josianic situation wherein northern Israel, or its remnants, is called back to loyalty to the leader of God in the land of God. In the exilic period, even more relevance can be seen. The exilic community in Babylon with its Priestly element seeking to compile and transmit the Torah of Moses is reminded of the central identifying characteristic of Israel. Israel is the people of the law of Moses living in the land promised to Moses. Any part of Israel living outside the land must help those in the land. Rest, peace, security can exist for Israel only when Israel has the land given by Moses. Exiles in Babylon cannot simply rest on the Mosaic law and in the comfort of living in the center of the world empire. They, too, must find a way to help the tribes living in the land to find peace and security in that land. Such peace and security appears to rest on loyalty to the occupant of the Mosaic office. For Deut 17:18–20, this appears to be the Israelite king. The Deuteronomistic history ends with reference to an Israelite king in Babylon (2 Kgs 25:27–30). Is this loosely constructed narrative at the beginning of the story a pointer to the hope of the Deuteronomistic historian? This would point to a newly unified Israel, obedient to a new king, dedicated to the old Mosaic law, seeking to find rest in the land which God would again give his loyal people.

The first chapter of Joshua centers on the identity of the people of God and its relationship to its human leader. The Christian church has taken up much of this identity for itself. The leadership has changed from Moses and Joshua to Jesus and his present-day interpreters. The geography has changed from one small piece of land to the universe. The intention of the text still points to the identity of the people of God. People of God must have strong leadership from men loyal to the incomparable pioneer of the faith. Such leadership must face the task given by God with strong conviction and courage. Such leadership can find its authority only in the presence of God. Only then can such leadership expect a declaration of readiness to follow from the congregation.

The book of Joshua set this out in dialectical terms. Leader and congregation look for the free gift of God; yet they must be prepared to go to war to win that gift. God is giving, but he gives only to an obedient people. This dialectic remains in the NT call to accept justification by faith without any works of the law coupled with the call to follow after Christ in perfect obedience demonstrating faith through works.

The book of Joshua dealt extensively with the dialectic of unity in geographical divergence. The Christian church may face this as its biggest hurdle. Released from identity with one geographical spot, the church continues to struggle with the problem of expressing its loyalty to the one body when it is separated by so many different conditions produced by its historical development.

A Prostitute's Profession (2:1–24)

Bibliography

Abel, F. M. "L'anathème de Jéricho et la maison de Rahab." *RB* 57 (1950) 321–30. ————. "Les stratagèmes dans le Livre de Josué." *RB* 56 (1949) 321–39. **Astour, M.** "Bené-lamina et Jéricho." *Semitica* 9 (1959) 5–18. **Bächli, O.** "Zur Aufnahme von Fremden in die altisraelitische Kultgemeinde." *Wort-Gebot-Glaube*, ed. H. J. Stoebe. ATANT 59. Zürich: Zwingli Verlag, 1970, 21–26. **Campbell, K. M.** "Rahab's Covenant." *VT* 22 (1972) 243–44. **Heller, J.** "Die Priesterin Raab." *Communio Viatorum* 8 (1965) 113–17. **Hölscher, G.** "Zum Ursprung der Rahabsage." *ZAW* 38 (1919–20) 54–57. **Langlamet, F.** "Josué II et les traditions de l'Hexateuque." *RB* 78 (1971) 5–17, 161–83, 321–54. **McCarthy, D. J.** "Some Holy War Vocabulary in Joshua 2." *CBQ* 33 (1971) 228–30. ————. "The Theology of Leadership in Joshua 1–9." *Bib* 52 (1971) 165–75. **Moran, W. L.** "The Repose of Rahab's Israelite Guests." *Studi sull'Oriente e la Bibbia offerti al P. Giovanni Rinaldi.* Genoa: Editrice Studio e Vita, 1967, 273–84. **Mowinckel, S.** *Tetrateuch-Pentateuch-Hexateuch.* BZAW 90. Berlin: Alfred Töpelmann, 1964, 13–15. **Otto, E.** *Das Mazzotfest in Gilgal.* BWANT 107. Stuttgart: W. Kohlhammer Verlag, 1975, 86–88. **Rudolph, W.** *Der "Elohist" von Exodus bis Josua.* BZAW 68. Berlin: Alfred Töpelmann, 1938, 165–69. **Simpson, C. A.** *The Early Traditions of Israel.* Oxford: Basil Blackwell, 1948, 280–83. **Soggin, J. A.** "Gerico: anatomia di una conquista." *Protestantesimo* 29 (1974) 193–213. **Stolz, F.** *Jahwes und Israels Kriege.* ATANT 60. Zürich: Theologischer Verlag, 1972, 80–81. **Tucker, G. M.** "The Rahab Saga (Joshua 2): Some Form-Critical and Traditio-Historical Observations." *The Use of the Old Testament in the New and Other Essays*, ed. J. M. Efird. Durham, NC: Duke University Press, 1972, 66–86. **Vincent, A.** "Jéricho, une hypothèse." *Mélanges de l'Université Saint Joseph* 37 (1960–61) 81–90. **Wagner, S.** "Die Kundschaftergeschichten im Alten Testament." *ZAW* 76 (1964) 255–69. **Weippert, M.** *Die Landnahme der israelitischen Stämme in der neueren wissenschaftlichen Diskussion.* FRLANT 92. Göttingen: Vandenhoeck & Ruprecht, 1967, 32–34. **Wellhausen, J.** *Die Composition des Hexateuchs und der historischen Bücher des Alten Testaments.* 2nd ed. Berlin: Georg Reimer, 1889, 119–20. **Wilcoxen, J. A.** "Narrative Structure and Cult Legend: A Study of Joshua 1–6." *Transitions in Biblical Scholarship*, ed. J. C. Rylaarsdam. Chicago: University of Chicago Press, 1968, 43–70. **Windisch, D. H.** "Zur Rahabgeschichte." *ZAW* 37 (1917–18) 188–98.

Translation

[1] *Then Joshua, the son of Nun, sent out from Shittim two men for secret spying,*[a] *saying, "Go, see the land and Jericho."*[b] *So they went and came*[c] *to the house of a woman, a prostitute. Her name was Rahab. They bedded down there.* [2] *It was then reported to the king of Jericho, "Two men have just come here tonight*[a] *from the Israelites to spy out the land."* [3] *So the king of Jericho sent to Rahab, "Bring out the men who have come to you, who have come*[a] *to your house,*[b] *for they have come to spy out all*[c] *the land."* [4] *The woman took the two*[a] *men and hid them.*[b] *She said,*[c] *"Certainly you are right.*[d] *The men came to me, but I did not know from where they came.*[e] [5] *When the gate was to close at dark, the men went out. I do not know where the men*[a] *went. Pursue quickly*[b] *after them because you can overtake them."*

[6] *Then she brought them up to the roof and concealed them in the flax stalks*

arranged by her on the roof. [7] *Meanwhile, the men pursued after them the way of
the Jordan upon* [a] *the crossings, but they had closed the gate just as* [b] *the pursuers
went out after them.* [8] *But they were still not bedded down when she came up to
them upon the roof.* [9] *She said to the men, "I know that Yahweh has given to you
all the land and that* [a] *the dread of you all has fallen upon us and that all the
inhabitants of the land melt away before you all,* [b] [10] *for we have heard that Yahweh* [a]
dried up the waters [b] *of the Reed Sea before you when you came out of Egypt* [c] *and
what you all did* [d] *to the two kings of the Amorites who were beyond the Jordan, to
Sihon and to Og whom you committed to the ban.* [11] *We heard and our heart melted.
Spirit remains in no one because of you all, for Yahweh your God it is who is God
in heaven above and upon the earth below.* [12] *Now make an oath with me in the
name of Yahweh. Since I have treated you graciously, you, yes you all, shall deal
graciously with the house of my father. You shall give me a true sign.* [a] [13] *You shall
save alive my father* [a] *and my mother and my brothers and my sisters* [b] *and all
that belongs to them.* [c] *You shall deliver our lives from death."*

[14] *The men said to her, "Our lives are in place of yours even to death! If you
all* [a] *do not report this business of ours,* [b] *then* [c] *when Yahweh gives us the land,* [d]
we will treat you with kindness and faithfulness."

[15] *Then she let them down with rope* [a] *through the window because her house
was in the city wall. Thus she was living in the wall.* [b] [16] *She said to them, "Go to
the mountain lest the pursuers encounter you. Hide yourselves there three days until
the pursuers* [a] *return. Afterwards you may go your way."*

[17] *The men said to her, "We are exempt from this oath of yours which you have
caused us to swear.* [a] [18] *Right as we are entering the land,* [a] *this cord of scarlet thread
you shall tie in the window from which you let us down. Your father, mother, brothers,
and all the house of your father you shall gather to yourself to the house.* [19] *Everyone
who shall go out from the doors of your house to the outside shall have his blood on
his own head. We shall be exempt.* [a] *But everyone who is with you in the house, his
blood shall be on our head if a hand should be laid upon him.* [b] [20] *But if you report
this business of ours, then we will be exempt from your oath* [a] *which you caused us
to swear."* [b]

[21] *She said, "According to your words, thus it shall be." Then she sent them
away, and they left. And she tied the scarlet cord in the window.* [a] [22] *So they left
and came to the mountain. They remained there three days until the pursuers had
returned.* [a] *The pursuers searched in all the way, but found nothing.* [23] *The two men
returned and came down from the mountain. They passed over and came to Joshua,
the son of Nun, and reported to him all their findings.* [24] *They told Joshua that
Yahweh had given into our hand* [a] *the whole land. All the inhabitants of the land
even melt before us."*

Notes

1.a. MT has a participle and adverb. It is not clear whether the adverb relates to Joshua's
action or to that of the spies. LXX and *Syr* omit the adverb. The Massoretic accents have actually
connected it with לאמר, the Hebrew quotation marks. Benjamin (*Variations*) describes it as a
later corruption from an original הארץ "the land," admitting that other Greek evidence represents
a guess. It is more probable that the corruption resulted in the more common word הארצה,
while the earlier Greek tradition may have refused to guess at the meaning of the *hapax*.

1.b. "And Jericho" is awkward in the context. *Syr, Frg. Tg.,* and *Vg* give evidence for reading "the region of Jericho," but this is most likely an attempt to interpret the present MT in a less awkward fashion. Text criticism cannot solve the problem.

1.c. LXX adds "the two men came into Jericho." This probably represents an original reading which has fallen from the Hebrew tradition through homoioteleuton (cf. Benjamin, *Variations*).

2.a. LXX does not witness "tonight" here but does in v 3. This represents a smoothing out of narrative style within the tradition.

3.a. LXX and *Syr* represent separate traditions here. LXX omits "to you," while *Syr* omits "who have come to your house." MT probably represents a conflation of traditions.

3.b. LXX adds "tonight." See note 2.a. above.

3.c. A few Heb. mss., LXX, *Syr* omit "all." This is a traditional idiom which may easily have worked its way into the textual tradition as a theological heightening. It does not fit the original context well.

4.a. "Two" is redundant and omitted by LXX and *Vg*. The form is different here than that in v 1. The numeral does not reappear until the close of the narrative (v 23). It may here represent a gloss from the tradition.

4.b. The versions read the expected plur. suffix here. MT may represent dittography of the following *waw* (Delitzsch) or a scribal error in copying the suffix.

4.c. LXX adds "to them" unnecessarily. For כן LXX reads the difficult λέγουσα, "saying."

4.d. The sentence attempts to reproduce the Heb. כן, "right, true" either omitted or misunderstood by LXX.

4.e. "But I did . . ." is omitted by LXX, possibly in view of the explanation following in v 5. There is no apparent reason for its being added later to the Hebrew.

5.a. "Men" does not appear in the versions and may represent a growth in the textual tradition seeking to make the subject explicit.

5.b. "Quickly" does not appear in LXX, which may represent a loss due to the similarity of the following word (*Variations*).

7.a. That Ugaritic usage can prove a meaning of "as far as" for the Heb. על is at best doubtful (*contra* Soggin, 36–37). The logical meaning of the text is that the men were upon the crossings of the Jordan. It may be a simple confusion with אל (cf. Noth).

7.b. The construction אחרי כאשר is "singulär" (Noth) but not impossible (C. Brockelmann, *Hebräische Syntax* [Neukirchen: Verlag der Buchhandlung des Erziehungsvereins, 1956] § 163b). LXX apparently read the more usual temporal construction with ויהי. The more complicated theory of abbreviations and variant textual traditions proposed by Benjamin is at least worthy of further study.

9.a. LXX has gone its own way with the end of the verse, reading γαρ for the Heb. וכי, thus transforming the relative clause into a result clause.

9.b. LXX could make the interpretation noted in 9.a. because it did not have the parallel result clause with which MT concludes the verse. This expression occurs also in v 24, which served either as the basis for addition to MT or for omission from the LXX tradition. Again traditional phrases are easily added to the tradition.

10.a. LXX adds God. Auld VTSup 30 [1979] 12–13) implies the originality of the LXX reading in all ten cases of such LXX addition. Such is hard to prove in view of the fluidity of the text particularly in the use of such traditional pious phrases.

10.b. LXX omits "waters." The expression ים-סוף "Reed Sea" appears twenty-four times in the MT, only here and Deut 11:4 with "waters." LXX reads "waters" in Deut 11:4. It is possible that textual corruption has changed an original אלוהים into את-מי.

10.c. LXX adds "from the land" before Egypt. Benjamin (*Variations*) is right in calling this a "tendency to full phrase" within the ongoing textual tradition.

10.d. LXX reads third masculine sing. attributing the action to God, a much easier reading than the MT and so probably secondary. Actually the theological statement is implicit in either reading.

12.a. LXX omits "You shall give. . . ." LXX does mention a "sign" in v 18, where MT does not. LXX is the easier reading, since the red thread in the window is more easily interpreted as a sign for saving alive of Rahab's family. The same problem is apparent in Exod 3:11–12. "Sign" may cover a broader semantic and temporal field than in our western culture.

13.a. LXX expands to "house of my father," copying v 12. The expression is not apt for the present list of relatives.

13.b. The traditional Heb. text reads "my sister." The Massoretic pointing suggested "my sisters." LXX referred to "all my house," reflecting the reading of v 18. The plur. corresponding to "brothers" would be expected. That the Greek reading is to be preferred because it would make the list correspond to that of v 18 is doubtful (*contra* Benjamin *Variations*).

13.c. Heb. אשר can mean either "all which" or "everyone who." Perhaps both readings are comprehended here.

14.a. There exists strong Heb. evidence in addition to Origen and the *Vg* for reading the second pers. feminine sing. This is the easier reading. MT tradition is to be retained and applied to the entire family of Rahab just mentioned.

14.b. LXX omits the entire clause "If . . . ours." This avoids the duplication with v 20, but it also misses the subtle change of direction given the conversation over against the woman's statement of the agreement in v 12.

14.c. LXX changes the subject to Rahab. Soggin (37) characterizes this as meaningless repetition. It could be original, showing Rahab's acceptance of the agreement as stated by the men. In the textual transmission, this was misunderstood and changed to continue the speech of the spies.

14.d. LXX reads "city" rather than land. Again, this fits the story itself more aptly. Rahab's concern is with the city and its walls in which she lives. "The land" represents the ongoing theological interpretation of the story.

15.a. LXX omits "rope," probably an accident in textual transmission.

15.b. LXX omits "because . . . in the wall." *Vg* also omits the final sentence. The sentence is problematic in light of chap. 6. This has caused the tradition to omit the clause.

16.a. LXX adds "after you" following the expression "those pursuing." Hebrew also has the prepositional phrase in vv 5, 7. However, participial forms are not used there. Here it is an explanatory addition on the basis of the pattern of vv 5, 7.

17.a. The verse contains problems in its grammatical forms. The masculine זה "this" does not agree with the feminine noun "oath." Also the noun has a pronominal suffix. The demonstrative pronoun following such nouns does not ordinarily take the article (see R. J. Williams, *Hebrew Syntax: An Outline* [2nd ed. Toronto: University of Toronto Press, 1976] § 74). The form for the second pers. sing. feminine verb is slightly irregular (Note GKC § 59h). The LXX simply omits the last clause "which . . . swear" here and v 20.

18.a. LXX reads "Outskirts of the city" for land. This again (see 14.d.) fits the story better. MT represents a theologizing of the tradition.

19.a. LXX mentions "this oath of yours" here as in vv 17 and 20. Again familiar language has intruded into the textual tradition.

19.b. LXX transfers the concluding condition to the next verse, changing the object of injury to the spies: "If anyone should wrong us. . . ." This is done in the textual transmission to relieve the spies of any shadow of blame.

20.a. The versions read "this" as in v 17 (also v 19 LXX). The originality of such "familiar" language cannot be decided.

20.b. LXX omits last clause "which . . . swear" as in 17. The phrase agrees with the tenor of tradition in attributing initiative to Rahab but control of situation to spies. Cf. notes 14.b, c.

21.a. LXX lacks "and she . . . window." This is a rather clear case of homoeoteleuton (cf. Benjamin, *Variations*, 27).

22.a. LXX omits "until . . . returned," a duplication of the command in v 16. This may reflect later expansion in MT.

24.a. Some Heb. mss, *Syr, Frg. Tg.*, and *Vg* change hand into the plural. MT, witnessed by LXX, is more difficult reading.

Form/Structure/Setting

The setting changes to Shittim (v 1). The interest shifts from crossing the Jordan (e.g. 1:11) to spying out Jericho (e.g. 2:1). Chapter 2 then carries out a complete narrative from the commission of Joshua (v 1) to the report back to Joshua (vv 23–24). Chapter 3 then returns to the narrative of the Jordan crossing. Thus chap. 2 must be handled as a complete unit within itself.

Gunkel (*RGG* [1], vol. 4, 2019) described the story of Rahab as typical of a common type of saga characterized by foreign travelers finding hospitality and protection from a compassionate woman. Greek and Latin parallels led Hölscher (*ZAW* 38 [1919–20] 54–57) to narrow the category to an etiological saga of a Jericho cult served by cult prostitutes descended from Rahab. This presupposed an original ending describing the fall of Jericho through betrayal in 6:25.

A new direction was given by Wagner, even while he maintained the etiological character of the narrative. He included the story among his spy narratives, whose form he described as having six elements (*ZAW* 76 [1964] 261–62): 1) Selection or naming of the spies; 2) Dispatching of the spies with specific instructions; 3) Report of the execution of the mission, along with confirmation through an oracle or reference to the context of salvation history; 4) Notice of return and results; 5) A perfect tense formula confirming the gift of the land by Yahweh; 6) Conclusions derived from 1–5, namely action of entering or conquering the land. The form, Wagner found, appeared in Num 13–14; Deut 1:19–46; Josh 14:7–8; Judg 18; Num 21:32, 33–35 (*ZAW* 76 [1964] 255–62). Wagner found the *Sitz im Leben* of the spy narratives in the ritual surrounding holy war (*ZAW* 76 [1964] 263–67). It served as the basis for the proclamation that Yahweh had given the land to Israel (*ZAW* 76 [1964] 267–69; cf. G. von Rad, *Der Heilige Krieg im alten Israel* [ATANT 20. Zürich: Zwingli Verlag, 1952] 7, 9). In a study independent of Wagner, Wilcoxen also placed Josh 2 into the Israelite cult, but in a more elaborate fashion, as part of the Gilgal Passover-Feast of Unleavened Bread celebration involving all of Josh 1–6 as a cultic legend ("Narrative Structure," 64).

The enthusiasm for etiological explanations was seriously dampened by B. O. Long, *The Problem of Etiological Narrative in the Old Testament*, BZAW 108 (Berlin: Alfred Töpelmann, 1968), B. Childs, "A Study of the Formula, 'Until This Day,'" *JBL* 82 (1963) 279–92, and C. Westermann, "Arten der Erzählung in der Genesis" in *Forschung am Alten Testament* vol. 1 [T Bü 24. München: Chr. Kaiser Verlag, 1964] 39–47. F. Langlamet (*RB* 78 [1971] 323–28, 353) then applied this specifically to Josh 2, finding that Josh 6:25 provided a narrative epilogue but not an etiological conclusion to the story and perhaps in connection with 2:12ff. allows us to catch a glimpse of the original etiology of the legend. Langlamet agrees with Wagner that it is a spy story (*RB* 78 [1971] 330–33). He notes that it is related to Judg 18 in being very regional (*RB* 78 [1971] 337).

At the same time, D. J. McCarthy (*Bib* 52 [1971] 165–75) worked in a slightly different direction, claiming that what is of interest in stories is not the etiology but the story itself and the general social attitudes revealed. McCarthy shows that the vocabulary in 6:17, 22–23, 25 is decisively distinct from that of chap. 2 (*Bib* 52 [1971] 169–70). The story in chap. 2 reveals for McCarthy all the elements of the popular folktale (*Bib* 52 [1971] 171–72).

Without reference to Langlamet, McCarthy, or Wagner, G. Tucker ("Rahab Saga," 71–83) shows that chap. 2 had its own conclusion in v 24 and owed its existence to the theological conception and cultic institution of holy war.

The literary form given by the pre-Deuteronomistic redactor, however, was etiological.

This brief survey of the history of research shows the complication involved in the form critical study of the chapter. Several stages of work are called for. First, the form of the present written narrative must be determined. Second, editorial elements or other additions in the growth of the tradition must be removed to determine if earlier oral forms served as sources for the present literary product. Thirdly, the nature and function of such earlier forms must be described where possible. At each stage, we must remember the lessons of C. Westermann (*The Promises to the Fathers.* [Tr. D. Green. Philadelphia: Fortress, 1980] 1–94) that narrative material must lead from the opening through narrative tension to a resolution. Where possible, we can test the insights of W. Dommershausen (*Die Estherrolle,* 1968) that narrative begins with a statement in perfect tense or noun clause, building tension through imperfect consecutive clauses, climaxing with speech or dialogue, leading to a denouement in imperfect consecutive clauses ending in a formulaic construction.

The present piece of literature is an Israelite spy story as outlined by Wagner (*ZAW* 76 [1964] 261–62). The selection of the spies is not mentioned. Rather the narrative begins with the sending out of the spies with specific instructions (v 1). The basic part of the narrative is devoted to the execution of the mission, confirmation being found in the actions and confession of Rahab (particularly vv 9–11). The final three elements of Wagner's form are concentrated in the final two verses with the return and report of results (v 23) and the perfect tense formulation of the gift of the land (v 24). The conclusion to enter or conquer the land comes only in the following chapters.

The outline of Wagner fits our text. It is not, however, an outline of narrative. It contains no dramatic tension within it. It outlines a report, not a narrative. At the present stage, it is a literary report. The opening verse, the middle verses (9–11) and the concluding verses give the report its form along with the following chapters. This is a large form which has its home either in literature or in the cult. The standardized formulations in vv 9–10 and 24 may well point to cultic usage as Wagner (*ZAW* 76 [1964] 268–69) and Wilcoxen ("Narrative Structure," 56) insist. With such a story Israel celebrated and reaffirmed Yahweh's gift of the land. But what lay behind the present report?

Tucker ("Rahab Saga," 82) is certainly correct in pointing to the diversity of traditions which finally contributed to the narrative. What is interesting is that the elements which form the story into a cultic spy report can be removed with the narrative form still in view. Here we have a true spy story complete with folklore elements (McCarthy, *Bib* 52 [1971] 171–72), humor, and narrative tension. The literary opening has probably destroyed the original opening. What remains is the brief series of imperfects (1b–2) building to the climatic dialogue (3–5). A resolution appears to come as the soldiers are persuaded to join a wild goose chase (6–8), but the plot is complicated by the demands of the prostitute (v 12). These are met with the counterproposal of the spies (v 14). Finally, the denouement arrives, as she lets the

spies down through the window (v 15). Vv 16 and 22 may also belong to
the original denouement. Here is a narrative unit built around the intrigue
and conspiracy of betrayal, similar to Judg 1:22–26. Such a story would be
told among the military campfires or at the city well accompanied by snickers
and sneers and laughter. Perhaps it was called "The Harlot Helped Us Do
It."

The etiological form in 6:25 has gained the most notice in discussion of
the text. F. Golka ("The Aetiologies in the Old Testament," *VT* 26 [1976]
416) still classifies Josh 2 and 6 as an etiological narrative in which the etiology
is identical with the arc of tension. Yet he goes on to admit that 6:25 represents
an etiological motif not identical with the arc of tension (419). Rather the
motif is based on old clan tradition. The motif is much more a theological
epilogue to the story (cf. Langlamet *RB* 78 [1971] 323–28). It encompasses
both chaps. 2 and 6, resulting in some expansion in 2:12–21. That which
gives rise to etiological speculation is rather the red cord in the window.
This, however, appears and disappears without explanation. Etiology represents editorial comment and connections, not the original narrative form.

Formal analysis has revealed a complex tradition behind the present narrative. The narrative is now an introduction to the complex procedure leading
to the conquest of Jericho. Originally, the narrative elements arose in popular
folklore. The popular story has been taken up by the cult to explain its procedure in conquering the entire land. This has transformed the popular folk
narrative into an Israelite spy story. The center of interest was no longer
Jericho, but the land. The central figure was Joshua. The conclusion came
to be found only in chap. 6. The initiative came to rest with the spies, who
spelled the conditions of the oath (vv 18–21a) and with Joshua, who faithfully
fulfilled his promises (6:17, 22–23, 25). Finally with the Deuteronomistic interpretation, the story becomes an illustration of holy war theology.

The chapter is a critical battleground for the entire question of a "hexateuch." Langlamet (*RB* 78 [1971] 5–17, 161–83) has given an extensive history
of research with appropriate charts. He has also provided detailed word statistics. Evidence of literary unevenness is self-evident. Shittim (v 1) is at home
in the Tetrateuch (Num 25:1; 33:49; cf. Mic 6:5), not in Deuteronomic literature. Doublets appear in vv 4 and 6; 1b and 8 with reference to שׁכב; 17
and 19–20. Contradictions appear in emphasis on the location of the house
on the wall (15) and the later total destruction of the walls (6:20); the chronology of vv 16 and 22 with 1:11 and 3:1; and in the unconditional and conditional
oaths of vv 14 and 19. The narrative sequence of vv 15–21 leaves questions,
since the men are depicted as entering in long haggling over details of the
agreement while dangling from the end of a rope. Finally, one may infer a
double interpretation of the scarlet cord as the rope on which the men are
swinging (v 18) with a smaller string (v 21). Such evidence has led to repeated
efforts to isolate two narrative strands in the material. Such evidence does
not necessarily, however, lead to the conclusion of parallel narratives. In
fact, most recent discussion assumes a rather unified narrative with some
secondary accretions (cf. Rudolph, *Elohist*, 165–69; Langlamet, *RB* 78 [1971]
353–54; Otto, *Mazzotfest*, 87–88). Narrative technique explains most of the
difficulties (Moran, "Repose," 273–84). The geographical and chronological

difficulties do point to a different literary origin from that of chaps. 1 and 3. Reinterpretation within tradition, whether oral or literary, accounts for the sequential problems of vv 15–21 as well as the problem of the house on the wall. The basic narrative unit is thus explicable without reference to differing literary parallel narratives. This does not, however, answer the question of the literary origin itself. The one major clue is the geographical reference. This reappears in 3:1, where it is used by the redactor to tie chaps. 3–6 with chap. 2. The origin of the Shittim reference lies in Josh 2. This, in turn, uses Shittim as knowledge presupposed by the listener or reader. This may be explained as a part of a larger oral tradition or, more likely, as a conscious literary reference back to Num 25. There Israel became harlots (25:1). Here Israel is saved by a harlot. Num 25 is the launching point of the conquest narrative in the Tetrateuch. Josh 2 is the launching pad of the actual conquest. Num 25 points to the narrative of holy war carried out in disobedience (25:16–18; 31). Josh 2 points to the perfect example of holy war (Josh 6). Shittim appears to form a literary bridge spanning the Deuteronomic materials. As such it may well point to an early literary source of the materials, a source which incorporated Joshua and the conquest of Jericho into the Tetrateuchal tradition, or at least into the wilderness tradition. The exact nature and dating of such a source remains open until new light is shed upon the nature of the Pentateuchal sources themselves. The linguistic evidence of Langlamet (*RB* 78 [1971] 61–83, 353–54) simply proves that the story represents typical Israelite narrative language, not that it represents vocabulary which is exclusively J.

The one thing that does appear to be clear is that the Deuteronomist has introduced his own theological conception into the mouth of Rahab in vv 9–11. The tradition of the fear of the nations, the drying up of the waters (יבשׁ, *hi.*), the two kings of the Amorites, and the divine title (12b) all bear Deuteronomic stamp. Verse 24 stems from the same source. Here then is pre-Deuteronomic literature given a Deuteronomic stamp.

The present narrative is dominated by ironic humor. The setting in the house of prostitution lends itself to such a style. Repeatedly the spies do just what one expects in such a house: they bed down (vv 1, 8, cf. v 6). But each time the lady of the house has other business. The king's intelligence system is so thorough it knows when strange men enter a prostitute's house, but so ignorant that it follows the advice of the prostitute without even searching the house or watching the window to discover the spies, who dangle tantalizingly within reach for such a long time (vv 15–21). When the lady of the house finally has time to come to the men in their beds, her bedtime story for them is just what is expected in such an establishment: a confession of religious faith, an act of religious conversion (vv 8–11). This leads to the prolonged bargaining between the woman and spies. She appears to gain the advantage from them (vv 12–16). Suddenly the tables are turned. Jericho's intelligence agents may fall for Rahab's tricks, not Israel's spies. They are innocent. They set the conditions of the agreement (vv 17–21). The burden of proof is upon Rahab and her family for their future actions, not upon the spies because of the past graces of Rahab. Such irony is built into the speech forms chosen. The report to the king uses the impersonal passive,

subtly underlining the inevitability of such a report (v 2). Over against this
is the emphatic naming of the prostitute (v 1). Rahab is able to run back
and forth between the spies and the royal messengers without arousing suspicion (vv 4, 6). Whatever the original role of the sign in the tradition, it now
occupies an ironically mysterious place. The prostitute demands it of the
spies (v 12). She appears to define the sign as a future event, the rescue of
her family (v 13). The spies then subtly change the nature of the sign. It is
a cord which *she* must tie in her window (v 18). Her family can be saved
only if she obeys their commands (vv 18–20). The very form of Rahab's
speech to the messengers mimics the legal defense speech (Moran, "Repose,"
280–81), as Rahab claims to tell the truth while in reality telling the biggest
lie possible (vv 4–5). She is so persuasive the royal messengers are transformed
into "pursuers" though the game they pursue lies behind them at the starting
gate (cf. M. Weiss, "Einiges über die Bauformen des Erzählens in der Bibel,"
VT 13 [1963] 462–63).

All of this ridicules the enemies of Israel represented by the king and
his messengers. It also ridicules Canaanite enclaves remaining within Israel,
as represented by the clever prostitute tricked by the spies (For other rhetorical
tricks, see Moran; Langlamet, *RB* 78 [1971] 338–43).

Comment

The present narrative centers on Jericho. The city has been excavated as
extensively as any in Palestine. It has several distinctions. It is the lowest
town on the globe, 250 meters or about 750 feet below sea level. It is the
earliest fortified town known to scholarship, being settled ca. 8,000 B.C. and
fortified by 7,000. The 70-foot high Tell es-Sultan, six miles north of the
Dead Sea, first felt the excavator's shovel in 1867. Major excavations were
carried out by Sellin and Watzinger between 1907 and 1909. J. Garstang
dug there from 1930–1936 and thought he had found Late Bronze Age walls
destroyed by Joshua. Finally, Dame Kathleen Kenyon (*The Bible and Recent
Archaeology* [Atlanta: John Knox Press, 1978] 36–40) led the expedition to
Jericho from 1952 to 1958. She demonstrated that the large Early Bronze
Age walls represented settlement between 2900 and 2300 B.C. Middle Bronze
Age walls reflect a series of building stages. The final stage was marked by
a new type of rampart wall defense system. This was destroyed, according
to Kenyon, ca. 1560. The site was abandoned during most of the sixteenth
and fifteenth centuries. Scanty evidence shows some occupation but no walls
for a few decades after 1400. From before 1300 until the eighth or even
seventh century, the site was again abandoned.

J. J. Bimson (*Redating*) has tried to reinterpret the archaeological evidence.
He associates the Israelite entrance into Palestine with the destruction of
cities between 1450 and 1400. To do so, he rejects any association with the
so-called Hyksos movement, moves the destruction date from the sixteenth
century dates proposed by archaeologists to the fifteenth century, and revolu-
tionizes the pottery chronology, the basic tool of archaeological dating.

The most one can conclude is that the interpretation of the archaeological
evidence from Jericho is an open question, requiring an immense amount

of new examination and interpretation in light of current archaeological knowledge and theories. The other option, expressed recently by J. M. Miller ("The Israelite Occupation of Canaan," *Israelite and Judean History,* ed. J. H. Hayes and J. M. Miller [London: SCM, 1977] 260), is that "archaeological evidence from Jericho, Ai, and Gibeon conflicts with the narratives in Joshua 1–9."

Archaeological and form critical evidence bring the historical question of the Rahab narrative into sharp focus. At the basis of the account is an entertaining folk narrative concerning the spies in Jericho. It presupposes the city at the height of its power and strength. The purpose of the story in its present setting is not so much to reconstruct history as to ridicule the original inhabitants of the land. From the perspective of a people settled in the land which does not belong to them, Israel looks back and draws an intentionally one-sided portrait of her enemies in order to glorify her God. The question of when is simply ignored.

Shittim is pictured by the Old Testament as a site in Trans-Jordan in Moab across from Jericho (Num 33:48–49). The precise site is not known. It has been identified traditionally with Tell el-Kefrein seven miles east of the Jordan and six miles north of the Dead Sea. Most modern commentators, however, accept the identification made by N. Glueck ("Some Ancient Towns in the Plains of Moab," *BASOR* 91 [1943] 13–18). He argues that Shittim was located at present-day Tell el-Hammam es Samrī, located one and a half miles (two and a half kilometers) east of Tell el-Kefrein. Tell el-Hammam is a much larger site and more important militarily and economically.

[10] This monotheistic confession occurs also in Deut 4:39, with quite similar language in 1 Kgs 8:23. Here, as in the other two passages, the Deuteronomistic editor seeks to emphasize the unique authority of Yahweh when compared to the other gods. Israel's neighbors had high gods with functions in the heavens and other gods whose chief functions were on earth. Israel had one God, who exercised authority over all spheres of existence. In the exilic period, when the Deuteronomistic message became vital for Israel, this claim for Yahweh became expressly important (cf. Isa 40–55). The Deuteronomist wants to say that such clarification should not have been needed. From the experience in Egypt onwards, Yahweh had proved himself more powerful than any other claimants to deity. The irony of the situation existed in the fact that Israel's enemies recognized this when Israel did not.

Israel's hope lay in the divinely caused חרם "ban" (10b). This term is central to the Deuteronomistic theory of holy war (see N. Lohfink, חרם *TWAT* 3 [1978] 192–213). Such war was permitted only for the cities in the Promised Land (Deut 20:15–18) and explained for the Deuteronomists how Yahweh had fulfilled his promises to the patriarchs and why many peoples of the lists of nations no longer existed. Again the irony of Josh 2 is apparent. The foreign harlot knows the Israelite laws and reacts accordingly. She is clever enough to make herself an exception to the Israelite law. Her exceptional status is important for the Israelite identity. It was obvious to later generations that Israel included a "mixed multitude" (Exod 12:38). The introduction to the conquest narrative explains this part of Israel's population. Israel included those Canaanites who had treated Israel with grace and helped

her conquer the land. Even such Canaanites could not appeal to their great
social status. They were descended from a prostitute.

¹² The precise nature of the Israelite-remaining Canaanite relationship is
described in a clever bargaining session. The prostitute claims that Israel is
indebted to her because she has done חסד for Israel (v 12), that is she has
preserved and enriched Israel's life as a community with enduring results
(cf. H.-J. Zobel, "חסד," *TWAT* 3 [1978] 48–71). Thus she wants a sign with
enduring quality, that is a promise which will be confirmed as a true sign
in the future fulfillment (cf. A. Jepsen, "אמן," *TWAT* 1 [1971] 334). The
spies lay at her feet. They must accept her terms. But dangling from her
window on a rope, they turn the tables. They set out the conditions. The
Canaanite must carry out חסד in the future. She must put out the sign (v
18). She must be responsible for gathering her family to safety. She must
prove trustworthy (v 20). In the end she capitulates to their terms (21a).
Israel claims that certain "foreigners" dwell among her because they have
met Israel's demands, not because Israel has met theirs. The basic requirement
is not listed, however. It had already been fulfilled. Any foreigner who lived
among Israel had to adopt Israel's creed.

²⁴ Safely back at camp, the spies report to Joshua. Their report sounds
like a prophetic oracle. But it has not come from the mouth of an Israelite
prophet. It has come from experiences with a Canaanite prostitute. The prostitute had to give Israel evidence for her basic conviction. Just as the Canaanites
had no right to lay claims upon Israel, so Israel could not make claims
for itself. Israel had, in the final analysis, to confess her own lack of faith.
She, too, had learned in the process of history to believe Yahweh. Part
of the knowledge came from most unlikely sources. A prophetic prostitute gave Israel courage to carry out the divine command and conquer the
land.

Explanation

Israel has taken up a popular story centering around the ability of a prostitute to trick a king and gain freedom for two men. Israel has transformed
this into a story preparing for the conquest of Jericho. The two men are
spies sent out by Israel to conquer the land, that is the city-state ruled by
the king of Jericho. The story has then been placed at the front of the conquest
narratives as a whole to introduce the theology of conquest. The Deuteronomist has then made the story the basis for his theological creed. The growth
of the story thus represents a manifold theological interpretation. Each generation of Israelites has learned something new about itself and its God through
telling and retelling the story of Jericho's favorite prostitute.

Conquest narratives begin in Israel with the dispatch of spies (Num 13–
14; Judg 1:22–26; 18, etc.). Only in the conquest do spy stories play a role
for Israel. This must be set beside the fact that the intent of spy stories is
to show that God has given the land into the hands of his people. Human
spying and divine gift are not self-exclusive realities. God sends human spies.
Why? The obvious explanation would be that spies should help develop military strategy. That is not the case with the biblical materials, in every case.

Rather, the biblical spies convince Israel that God can and will give the land to Israel. God uses human spies to convince his people to do what he has called them to do. This is very evident in the present context. The first chapter has demonstrated the need for strong, courageous leadership through both divine (vv 1–9) and human (vv 16–18) exhortation. The second chapter gives a concrete example showing how God is fulfilling his promises and how weak Israel's opposition is. A common prostitute is more intelligent than the intelligence agents of the king. Yet even she is no match for Israel's spies. Israel can easily get its opponents to chase shadows while she occupies the enemy fortresses. Israel behind strong, courageous leadership will face an enemy king without intelligence and an enemy people scared stiff in the face of Israel and her mighty God.

The basis for Jericho's fear lies in common gossip. The grapevine has brought news of God's mighty deeds for Israel to Jericho. No prophet or preacher has been there. God has simply used that mysterious manner of human beings in which they learn the important events of the day from sources they can no longer identify. The source is not important. The message and the response are.

The message itself is couched in terms of holy war theology, which has become a Yahwistic creed. The full form of the creed is found in Deut 26:5–9; 6:21–23; Josh 24:2–13. This particular version centers on the action at the Egyptian sea (cf. Exod 14) and on the battles with the Amorite kings (Deut 3:8; 4:47; 31:4: Josh 5:1; 9:10; 10:5–6; 24:12; cf. Deut 1:4; 2:26–3:11; Ps 135:11; 136:19–20. In Num 21:21–35 only Sihon is called king of the Amorites.) God's mighty acts in the history of his people have two immediate results. Future opponents are afraid. Intelligent ones confess Yahweh, the God of Israel, as God of heaven and earth.

The NT takes the example of Rahab as an example of faith. She is one of three women, all with tarnished reputations, included in the ancestors of the Messiah (Matt 1:5–6). She is enshrined in the faith hall of fame (Heb 11:31). James 2:25 praises Rahab as the prime example, alongside Abraham, of justification through works. Both of these emphasize the role and significance of Rahab in the narrative. In so doing, they turn to the intention of the original narrative rather than to the present biblical context. The present OT context uses the narrative to give identity and courage to Israel, particularly to Israel without land and power. That Israelite identity includes the ironic fact that God uses not only his own prophets and leaders to bring faith and courage to disconsolate Israel. God uses the most unexpected and immoral persons to further his purposes in the world. The leadership of Joshua dependent upon Moses is one side of the picture. The power of God to convince even the enemy is the other side. People of God must be open to learn from all sources which God would use. They must always be aware of their own prejudiced tendencies to look to powerful leaders for direction and to fear powerful enemy leaders. Throughout the Bible and church history, God has opened new doors and new opportunities for his people through the most unlikely people. Through it all, God has shown himself able to fulfill the promises he made. He has indeed proved to be the God of heaven above and earth below without competition.

Crossing to Conquer (3:1–5:1)

Bibliography

Abel, F. M. "Les stratagèmes dans le Livre de Josué." *RB* 56 (1949) 323–25. **Auzou, G.** *Le don d'une conquête.* Paris: Éditions de l'Orante, 1964. 70–79. **Cross, F. M.** "The Divine Warrior." *Canaanite Myth and Hebrew Epic.* Cambridge, MA: Harvard University Press, 1973, 91–111. **DeVries, S. J.** "The Time Word *maḥar* as a Key to Tradition Development." *ZAW* 87 (1975) 65–79. **Dus, J.** "Die Analyse zweier Ladeerzählungen des Josuabuches (Jos. 3–4 und 6)." *ZAW* 72 (1960) 107–34. **Fernández, A.** "Critica historico-leteraria de Jos. 3, 1–5, 1." *Bib* 12 (1931) 93–98. **Fohrer, G.** "Altes Testament-'Amphiktyonie' und 'Bund'?" *TLZ* 91 (1966) 801–16, 893–904. (= *Studien zur alttestamentlichen Theologie und Geschichte (1949–66).* BZAW 115. Berlin: Walter de Gruyter, 1969, 84–119.) **George, A.** "Les récits de Gilgal en Josué (5:2–15)." *Mémorial J. Chaine.* Lyon: Facultés Catholiques, 1950, 169–86. **Gressmann, H.** *Die Anfänge Israels.* Göttingen: Vandenhoeck & Ruprecht, 1922, 137–40. **Hulst, A. R.** "Der Jordan in den alttestamentlichen Überlieferungen." *OTS* 14 (1965) 162–88. **Kaiser, O.** *Die mythische Bedeutung des Meeres in Ägypten, Ugarit und Israel.* BZAW 78. Berlin: Alfred Töpelmann, 1959, 135–40. **Keller, C. A.** "Über einige alttestamentliche Heiligtumslegenden II." *ZAW* 68 (1956) 85–97. **Kraus, H. J.** "Gilgal." *VT* 1 (1951) 181–99. "Zur Geschichte des Passah-Massot-Festes im Alten Testament." *EvT* 18 (1958) 47–67. **Langlamet, F.** *Gilgal et les récits de la traversée du Jourdan.* CahRB 11. Paris: J. Gabalda, 1969. **Long, B. O.** *The Problem of Etiological Narrative in the Old Testament.* BZAW 108. Berlin: Alfred Töpelmann, 1968, 78–86. **Maier, J.** *Das altisraelitische Ladeheiligtum.* BZAW 93. Berlin: Alfred Töpelmann, 1965, 18–32, 76–80. **Mann, T. W.** *Divine Presence and Guidance in Israelite Traditions: The Typology of Exaltation.* Baltimore: Johns Hopkins University Press, 1977, 196–212. **Mayes, A. D. H.** *Israel in the Period of the Judges.* SBT 2nd Series 29. London: SCM, 1974, 47–53. **Möhlenbrink, K.** "Die Landnahmensagen des Buches Josua." *ZAW* 56 (1938) 254–58. **Mowinckel, S.** *Tetrateuch-Pentateuch-Hexateuch.* BZAW 90. Berlin: Alfred Töpelmann, 1964, 33–43. **Otto, E.** *Das Mazzotfest in Gilgal.* BWANT 107. Stuttgart: W. Kohlhammer Verlag, 1975, 4–57, 104–75, 186–91, 306–11, 323–65. **Porter, J. R.** "The Background of Joshua 3–5." *SEA* 36 (1971) 5–23. **Rudolph, W.** *Der "Elohist" von Exodus bis Josua.* BZAW 68. Berlin: Alfred Töpelmann, 1938, 169–78. **Saydon, P. P.** "The Crossing of the Jordan." *CBQ* 12 (1950) 194–207. **Schmid, R.** "Meerwunder- und Landnahme-Traditionen." *TZ* 21 (1965) 260–68. **Schmitt, R.** *Zelt und Lade als Thema alttestamentlicher Wissenschaft.* Gütersloh: Gütersloher Verlagshaus Gerd Mohn, 1972, 60–65, 76–78, 91, 133, 161, 166, 280–81. **Schunck, K. D.** *Benjamin.* BZAW 86. Berlin: Alfred Töpelmann, 1963, 39–48. **Simpson, C. A.** *The Early Traditions of Israel.* Oxford: Basil Blackwell, 1948, 283–86. **Soggin, J. A.** "Gilgal, Passah und Landnahme," VTSup 15 (1965) 263–77. ———. "Kultätiologische Sagen und Katechese im Hexateuch." *VT* 10 (1960) 341–47. **Stolz, F.** *Jahwes und Israels Kriege.* ATANT 60. Zürich: Theologischer Verlag, 1972, 60–62. **Tengström, S.** *Die Hexateucherzählung.* Lund: C. W. K. Gleerup, 1976, 58–65. **de Vaux, R.** *Histoire ancienne d'Israël.* vol. 1. Paris: J. Gabalda, 1971, 552–59. (= *The Early History of Israel.* Tr. D. Smith. London: Darton, Longman & Todd, 1978, 598–608.) **Vogt, E.** "Die Erzählung von Jordanübergang. Josue 3–4." *Bib* 46 (1965) 125–48. **Wellhausen, J.** *Die Composition des Hexateuchs und der historischen Bücher des Alten Testaments.* 2nd ed. Berlin: Georg Reimer, 1889, 120–22. **Wiesmann, H.** "Israels Einzug in Kanaan." *Bib* 11 (1930) 216–30 and *Bib* 12 (1931) 90–92. **Wijngaards, J. N. M.** *The Dramatization of Salvific History in the Deuter-*

onomic Schools. OTS 16 (1969). **Wilcoxen, J. A.** "Narrative Structure and Cult Legend: A Study of Joshua 1–6." *Transitions in Biblical Scholarship,* ed. J. C. Rylaarsdam. Chicago: University of Chicago Press, 1968, 43–70. **Wildberger, H.** *Jahwes Eigentumsvolk.* ATANT 37. Zürich: Zwingli Verlag, 1960, 40–62. **Woudstra, M. H.** *The Ark of the Covenant from Conquest to Kingship.* Philadelphia: Presbyterian and Reformed Publishing Co., 1965, 103–33.

Translation

¹ *Joshua got up early in the morning. They set out from Shittim and came to the Jordan, he and all the sons of Israel.*ᵃ *They spent the night there before they passed over.* ² *At the end of three days the officials passed through the midst of the camp.* ³ *They commanded the people, "When you see the ark of the covenant of Yahweh your God with the Levitical priests* ᵇ *carrying it, then you shall set out from your place and march after it.* ⁴ *Still, there shall be some distance between you and it, about a thousand yards in length.*ᵃ *You shall not approach it in order that you may know the way which you are to follow, since you have never passed over in the way."* ᵇ

⁵ *Then Joshua told the people, "Sanctify yourselves, for tomorrow Yahweh will perform wonders among you."* ⁶ *Then Joshua told the priests, "Carry the ark of the covenant and pass over before the people." Then they carried the ark of the covenant and marched before the people.* ⁷ *Then Yahweh told Joshua, "Today I will begin to make you great in the eyes of all Israel that they may know that just as I was with Moses, I am with you.* ⁸ *As for you,*ᵃ *command the priests who carry the ark of the covenant, 'When you come to the edge of the waters of the Jordan, in the Jordan you shall take your stand.' "* ⁹ *Then Joshua told the sons of Israel, "Come over here and listen to the words* ᵃ *of Yahweh your God."* ¹⁰ *Then Joshua said,*ᵃ *"By this you shall know that the living God is among you* ᵇ *and that he will certainly drive out from before you the Canaanites, the Hittites, the Hivites, the Perizzites, the Girgashites, the Amorites, and the Jebusites.* ¹¹ *Right now* ᵃ *the ark of the covenant of* ᵇ *the Lord of all the earth is passing over before you into the Jordan.* ¹² *Therefore,*ᵃ *take for yourselves twelve men from the tribes of Israel, one man per tribe.* ¹³ *As the soles of the feet of the priests, who bear the ark of Yahweh, the Lord of all the earth, rest in the waters of the Jordan, then the waters of the Jordan will be cut off, that is the waters going down from above, so that they will stand as one heap."* ᵃ

¹⁴ *When the people set out from their tents to pass over the Jordan, with the priests who carry the ark of the covenant in front of the people,* ¹⁵ *and while the ones carrying the ark came to the Jordan, the feet of the priests who carry the ark having dipped in the edge of the waters, the Jordan being full over all its banks all the days of harvest,* ¹⁶ *then* ᵃ *the waters going down from above stood up; they formed one heap a great distance at Adam,*ᵃ *the city which is at the side of Zarethan, while those waters going down into the Sea of Arabah,*ᵇ *the Sea of Salt, were completely cut off. During all this the people passed over opposite Jericho.* ¹⁷ *The priests who carry the ark of the covenant of Yahweh stood firmly* ᵃ *on dry ground in the middle of the Jordan while all Israel was passing over on dry ground until all the nation had completed passing over the Jordan.*

⁴:¹ *When all the nation had completed passing over the Jordan, Yahweh told Joshua,* ² *"You all take for yourselves from the people twelve* ᵃ *men, one per tribe.* ³ *You all*

command them, 'Carry for yourselves from this place, from the midst of the Jordan, from the place where the feet of the priests stood firm,ᵃ twelve stones. You shall cause them to pass over with you and shall cause them to rest in the camp where you camp tonight.'" ⁴ Then Joshua called to the twelve men whom he had appointed from the sons of Israel, one man per tribe, ⁵ and Joshua told them, "Pass over before the ark of Yahweh your God ᵃ to the middle of the Jordan. Each man shall hoist a stone upon his shoulder according to the number of the tribes of the sons of Israel, ⁶ in order that this may be a sign in your midst when your children ask on the morrow, 'What do these stones represent for you?' ⁷ You shall tell them that the waters of the Jordan were cut off before the ark of the covenant of Jahweh: when it passed over the Jordan, the waters of the Jordan were cut off.ᵃ These stones shall be an eternal memorial to the sons of Israel." ⁸ The sons of Israel acted just as Joshua had commanded. They carried twelve stones from the middle of the Jordan just as Yahweh had spoken to Joshua, according to the number of the tribes of the sons of Israel. They passed them over with them to the camp and caused them to rest there.ᵃ ⁹ Meanwhile Joshua raised up twelve stones in the middle of the Jordan ᵛ in the place of the standing place ᵘ of the feet of the priests who carry the ark of the covenant. They have been there until this day. ¹⁰ But the priests who carry the ark were standing in the middle of the Jordan until everything was complete which Yahweh commanded Joshua to speak to the people according to all which Moses commanded Joshua. The people hurried and passed over.ᵃ ¹¹ As all the people completed passing over, the ark of Yahweh and the priests ᵃ passed over before the people. ¹² The sons of Rueben and the sons of Gad and half the tribe of Manasseh passed over armed before the sons of Israel just as Moses had spoken to them. ¹³ Approximately forty thousand armed for battle passed over before Yahweh for battle to the plains of Jericho.

¹⁴ In that day Yahweh made Joshua great in the eyes of all Israel. They stood in respectful awe of him just as they had stood in respectful awe of Moses all the days of his life.

¹⁵ Yahweh told Joshua, ¹⁶ "Command the priests who carry the ark of testimony ᵃ so that they may come up from the Jordan." ¹⁷ Joshua commanded the priests, "Go up out of the Jordan." ¹⁸ When the priests who carry the ark of the covenant of Yahweh went up from the middle of the Jordan, the soles of the feet of the priests having been drawn up to the dry ground, then the waters of the Jordan returned to their place. They flowed as always over all its banks. ¹⁹ Now it was on the tenth day of the first month when the people went up from the Jordan. They camped at Gilgal on the eastern edge of Jericho. ²⁰ It was precisely these twelve stones which they had taken from the Jordan that Joshua raised up in Gilgal. ²¹ He told the sons of Israel, "When your sons ask their fathers on the morrow, 'What are these stones?' ²² you shall instruct your sons, 'On dry ground Israel passed over this Jordan, ²³ when Yahweh your God dried up the waters of the Jordan before you all until you passed over just as Yahweh your God did to the Reed Sea which he dried up before us until we passed over, ²⁴ so that all the peoples of the earth might know the hand of Yahweh that it is strong in order that you may have ᵃ respectful awe before Yahweh all the days. ⁵:¹ When all the kings of the Amorites, who were beyond the Jordan to the west ᵃ and all the Kings of the Canaanites who were beside the sea heard that Yahweh had dried up the waters of the Jordan before the sons of Israel until we ᵇ had passed over, their heart melted. Spirit was no longer in them because of the sons of Israel.

Notes

3:1.a. The Hebrew syntax is a bit awkward with the shift from the singular "he got up early" to the plural "they set out. . . ." Hebrew manages the shift by inserting "he and all the sons of Israel" after "to the Jordan." LXX omits the inserted subject and reads "he set out," but then adapts the plural verbs for the remainder. Langlamet (*Gilgal*, 44–45) is correct here in seeing an attempt at harmonization on part of the Greek changing the verb to singular *and* a glossator's insertion in the Hebrew.

3:3.a. Strong textual support is found for dividing the priesthood into two branches—priests and Levitical servants. This represents a later understanding than that of Deuteronomy and the Deuteronomistic History, wherein priests are Levites (cf. Deut 18:1–8; 21:5; 1 Kgs 12:31).

3:4.a. The Jerusalem Bible and Soggin (47) transpose the two halves of v 4. Without textual support this is precarious. For the Qere-Kethib problem with the preposition בין cf. GKC103o.

3:4.b. The Hebrew reads literally: "because you have not passed over in the way yesterday or the day before," an idiom meaning any time previous to the present.

3:8.a. LXX read the logical connective ועתה, "now, therefore," instead of the MT second masculine plural pronoun. The two terms sound alike, so that an error could have occurred in copying from dictation. MT represents a contrast sentence (cf. Andersen, *Sentence*, 150–53; Lambdin, *Introduction to Biblical Hebrew* [New York: Charles Scribner's Sons, 1971] § 132).

3:9.a. The versions give strong support to reading sing. "word." Soggin (48) argues for LXX as reflecting early use of י as abbreviation for the divine name later incorporated into the word דבר as plur. const. ending. Langlamet (*Gilgal*, 45–46) argues that LXX is the easier reading following the prophetic formula, admitting that no criteria are decisive here.

3:10.a. The repetition "And Joshua said" is unnecessary in the context and does not appear in LXX. No reason appears why it would be added to Hebrew, so LXX has omitted it on stylistic grounds.

3:10.b. The syntax of vv 10–11 is not clear. To what does "by this" refer? A conditional particle usually follows (Gen 42:15; Num 16:28; Mal 3:10; cf. Ps 41:12). Exod 7:17 uses the construction with the הנה clause introducing the apodosis (see Langlamet, *Gilgal*, 111). It is probable that the הנה clause opening v 11 introduces the apodosis here, but one could read v 10b as the apodosis.

3:11.a. The הנה clause expresses the immediate presence of an object or idea. Cf. Lambdin, *Biblical Hebrew*, §§ 125, 135; Joüon, *Grammaire*, § 177i.

3:11.b. The Massoretes placed a strong disjunctive accent (*Zāqēp̄ parvum*) on הברית, "covenant," thus separating it from the divine title which follows. Soggin (48) prefers the *Syr* insertion of Yahweh after ברית as in v 13. Langlamet (*Gilgal*, 46–47) notes that this still contains a grammatical irregularity with the article before the *nomen regens* and that the Syriac may represent a correction based on v 13. Gray (62) explains MT as "an obvious Deuteronomic interpolation." Langlamet is certainly correct in seeing here "a unification of terminology." His further conjecture that a glossator sought to create series of seven uses of different formulas is more open to question but worthy of further study. Text criticism cannot solve the issue. Only study of the sources, forms, and redaction can do so.

3:12.a. LXX read vv 10 and 11 together and could not see a logical connection with v 12. Thus it omitted the "before you" of v 11 as well as reading a long genitive construction there, while it omitted the opening conjunction of v 12. The "therefore" of MT is certainly preferable.

3:13.a. This verse concludes the quotation begun in v 10, though the Hebrew has no means of denoting this fact. LXX includes "of the covenant" after ark, but omits "from above" and the following conjunction. "One heap" also lacks a LXX equivalent. The textual tradition has attempted to make the prophecy of v 13 correspond exactly to the fulfillment of v 16. The LXX parallelism may represent a close proximity to the original text.

3:15.a. The syntax of vv 14–16 is overloaded. V 14 begins with a temporal clause followed by a disjunctive clause indicating contemporaneous action, in effect continuing the temporal clause. V 15 then adds another temporal clause followed by two contemporaneous disjunctive clauses. Only with v 16 does a main clause appear. This is then followed by an apposition sentence (Andersen, *Sentence*, 36–60). The following disjunctive clauses again give contemporaneous action. The Hebrew consecution of tenses finally takes up again in v 17, but there the subject matter repeats that of 14–16.

3:16.a. Neither the Massoretic tradition nor the versions were agreed on the precise readings of v 16's geographical descriptions. Langlamet (*Gilgal*, 48–50) has ingeniously restored a primitive text: הרחק מאד מאדם (ו)עד קצה צרתן, translating "at a very great distance from Adam to the edge of Zarethan." The textual diversities reflect two early problems: a) the geographical location of Adam and b) the need to intensify the miraculous. Here as often textual history is exegetical history.

3:16.b. The Arabah is the depression running from the Sea of Galilee to the Gulf of Aqabah. The sea of Arabah and the Salt Sea are both biblical names for what we call the Dead Sea.

3:17.a. The Hebrew word הכן, "firmly" appears to be the Hiph'il infinitive absolute of כון. Noth and Soggin (49) see it as meaningless in the context, being a composite of כן, "here," and the article used in a demonstrative sense. *KB* (427) is more likely correct in seeing the infinitive used as an adverb. Again, as in v 11, the formulation of "the carriers of the ark" contains a grammatical anomoly. Here textual observation may lead to the literary decision that a later gloss has entered the text in the words "covenant of Yahweh" (see Langlamet, *Gilgal*, 50).

4:2.a. The LXX renders the command of v 2 in singular, as appropriate to the context of v 1, i.e., God speaking to Joshua. MT retains the plural in the imperative in vv 2–3a as well as the dative pronoun. The LXX is clearly harmonizing. The reason for the MT reading does not result from textual criticism. LXX also omits the number 12 in v 2 and the phrase "place where the feet of the priests stood" in v 3. The number may have been omitted in the LXX tradition as redundant or supplied by the Hebrew tradition for explicitness. The latter phrase may be a gloss seeking to underline the prophetic element (cf. v 9) or a Greek simplification. Again we see that transmitting the text involved interpreting the text.

4:3.a. הכין presents a problem similar to that of 3:17. Here the infinitive construct form appears but seems to function similarly to the infinitive absolute here. LXX omitted the word in 3:17 but refers it here to the stones as "prepared stones," having omitted the priestly reference of MT. Steurnagel referred to the term as meaningless.

4:5.a. Greek omits the repetition of Joshua's name, adds "before me" while omitting reference to the ark, and specifies twelve as the number of tribes, an item it omitted in v 2. Here the Greek tries to simplify the tradition (cf. Soggin, 49–50). Textual transmission is textual interpretation.

4:7.a. Again LXX has simplified and interpreted a complicated text changing sons into singular in vv 6–7 with corresponding grammatical changes; adding "river" to Jordan and "of all the earth" to Lord, omitting the second mention of Jordan and of the waters of the Jordan being cut off. Syntactically, one may ask where the words of the fathers to the sons ends and where the instructions of Joshua to the children of Israel take up.

4:8.a. LXX reads "just as the Lord commanded Joshua," again a different theological interpretation of the text within the transmission tradition. Instead of "according to the number of the tribes" LXX reads "at the completion of the passing over," again an interpolation of a different traditional formula within the transmission of the text.

4:10.a. LXX adds the traditional "of the covenant" to ark, and says Joshua finished all which the Lord had commanded to announce to the people. LXX omits the reference to all which Moses commanded Joshua. Langlamet (*Gilgal*, 51) explains the latter as an Hebraic gloss in an attempt to have exactly forty uses of the word צוה, command. This misses, however, the theological ordering of Yahweh—Moses—Joshua made explicitly in the book (see *Explanation*). LXX and MT have gone different ways in their interpretation of the text.

The syntax of the verse also deserves comment. The verse begins with a disjunctive clause pointing to contemporary action or explanation of what has preceded. The imperfect consecutive then refers to the continuation of the action, the priests crossing only after everything else has been completed.

4:11.a. MT has a sing. verb for ark of Yahweh and the priests "passed over." LXX omits priests. This may be explained grammatically (GKC § 146f). It may be combined with the LXX reading "and the stones were before them" instead of "before the people" to see the later correction of a partially erased text (Langlamet, *Gilgal*, 51). The latter may be explained as a LXX interpretation of a contradiction in content (Steuernagel). See *Comment*.

4:16.a. עדות has waved a red flag for source critics to find the priestly source here. Langlamet (*Gilgal*, 52) sees it as an attempt of a late editor to mark the sixteenth of thirty occurrences of the word "ark" in Joshua, an attempt which replaces an original ברית, "covenant." Whatever the case, we see again the textual tradition interpreting the text.

4:24.a. The MT change of persons is cause for pause. Langlamet (*Gilgal*, 54) follows a host of witnesses in reading the infinitive with third plur. suffix without textual support. Soggin (50) is correct in saying: "the remedy is no better than the malady, which is not very great in any case."

5:1.a. LXX omits "westwards." The Hebrew most often employs some phrase to indicate "westwards" with "beyond the Jordan," when this is meant, since the term is most often used to refer to the territory east of the Jordan (BDB, 719). LXX may also show its own historical setting in interpreting the Canaanites by the sea as Phoenicians.

5:1.b. The textual tradition witnesses a confusion between first plur. and third plur. suffix on the infinitive. Grammar in the context would demand third plur. Cultic usage of the text would give rise to first plur.

Form/Structure/Setting

This passage gives primary evidence for the necessity of historical critical study of the OT. No reading of the narrative can overlook duplications and chronological contradictions. The three days' wait of 1:11 occurs twice (2:22; 3:2) plus two more nights, one camping (3:1) and one in cultic purification (3:5), though the latter is never actualized (cf. v 6). Structural elements of the narrative recur: crossing the river (3:16b; 4:10); the priests leaving the river (4:11, 18); the selection of men to carry the stones (3:12; 4:2); the setting up of the stones at the camping place (4:8), in the middle of the Jordan (4:9), and at Gilgal (4:20); and the command to teach the children (4:6–7; 4:21–24). Such duplication of structural elements leads to the suspicion of duplicate sources rather than simply duplicate motifs and traditions. The reconstruction of such sources has long occupied and entranced scholars without consensus being attained (see the lists by Langlamet, *Gilgal,* 21–38, along with his own unique solutions and later ones by Otto *Mazzotfest,* 26–57, and Mann, *Divine Presence,* 196–212). Certain markers are given. 3:1 connects to chap. 2, while 3:2 reaches back to 1:11. One narrative appears to point toward a camping place near Jericho (3:16), while the other points to Gilgal (4:19–20). One version is painted in terms used in Exod 14–15 to describe the crossing of the sea and climaxes in a catechetical statement (4:21–23) explicitly connecting the two events. The other version describes only the crossing of the river by the ark, again climaxing in a catechetical statement using these terms (4:6–7). Precise distinction of the sources is made difficult by the lack of vocabulary evidence to connect the accounts to traditional "hexateuchal sources" (note that Simpson's extensive lists affect only five verses, two of which he attributes to sources in direct contradiction to his own vocabulary evidence and two of which he refers to redactors [*Early Traditions,* 283–86], while Weinfeld's Deuteronomic vocabulary [*Deuteronomy,* 320–59] appears only in 4:24–5:1.). We are left with only internal consistency as criteria for source division. This is then complicated by the fact that later hands have sought to expand the many references to priests and ark with conventional terminology. The climactic catechetical statements give clues of content. The first (4:6–7) centers upon the ark cutting off the waters and the memorial stones. The second (4:21–23) centers upon the miracle that Israel crossed on dry ground. We would expect the other narrative material to point toward these climactic statements. Closer observation proves that it does.

The ark cutting off the waters of the Jordan is the central emphasis of 3:2–4, 6, 9, (10?), 11–14, 16b; 4:4–7, 11. The basic identifying vocabulary is נסע, "to set out," כרת, "be cut off." The second version centers on the action of the priests with the ark allowing Israel to cross on dry ground and appears in 3:1b, (5?), 7aA, 8–10, 15–16aA, 17; 4:1–3, 8, 15–22. The central vocabulary here includes בוא, "to come," עמד, "to stand," עלה, "to go up," along with "dry ground" and "edge of the waters."

The first narrative cannot be classified in any category of popular stories and sagas. It does not have an arc of tension with which the narrator could hold the attention of the audience. Instead, it has a quite different function. It seeks to teach the audience the nature of the ark. It is a catechetical example showing how the divine presence in the ark led the people when they followed obediently.

Such a description of the narrative has several consequences. It means the narrative stands at a distance removed from the event and from attempts to describe the event itself. Rather, the event has become a subject of reflection. It can be used as an example from history to help the present generation. This nature of the story as an example based upon historical reflection is shown by several details. The change of leaders from the officials (3:2) to Joshua (3:6, etc.) shows a long growth in the tradition. The picture of Joshua as both prophet (3:9–11) and military commander (3:6; 4:4–5) shows a development within the understanding of the office of Joshua. The narrative of the crossing of the ark has been supplemented with a traditional catechism of the ark. Gressmann (140) noted long ago that a military crossing of the river does not allow time for stopping to carry heavy rocks and dedicate them. The rocks themselves may well have represented an altar or an open air sanctuary in their original context. The present context reduces them to a roadside monument. This first narrative source behind Josh 3:1–5:1 thus reveals itself to be a composite of many motifs bound together into a catechetical example reflecting upon the history of Israel.

Where would such a teaching task arise in Israel? This involves the entire question of Israel's "holy war" or "Yahweh war" theology and its development which has been the object of much recent research. Certainly the fullblown schema set out by von Rad (*Der Heilige Krieg im alten Israel*, ATANT 20, [Zürich: Zwingli Verlag, 1951] 6–14) represents a rather late development, but the understanding of Jahweh as a warrior fighting for Israel with his ark as battle emblem has deeper roots (G. H. Jones, " 'Holy War' or 'Yahweh War'?" *VT* 25 [1975] 642–58). Where in that history of development the present story originated is at present impossible to pinpoint. It could have developed and served many different eras of Israel's history to remind them of the nature of warfare with Yahweh.

The second narrative is of a quite different nature. The cult dominates it. Cultic sanctification is the first order of business (3:5). The entire story is a narration of God's wonders (3:5b), a cultic expression reappearing in Ps 9:2, 26:7; 40:6; 72:18; 86:20; 98:1; 106:22; 111:4, altogether fifteen times in Psalms and nine more in psalmic literature in Chronicles. Narrative uses in Exodus 3:20 and 34:10 may witness an earlier usage in the traditions of Israel, but not necessarily a place in the Gilgal cultus of the magnitude imagined by Otto (*Mazzotfest*, see especially 133–34). The emphasis is now on the priests standing in the edge of the water (vv 8, 15) bringing dry ground (v 17), and going up out of the water onto dry ground (4:16–18). The emphasis is an entirely different type of catechetical statement, one filled with cultic confession. The site is an explicitly-named sanctuary at an explicit time of festival (4:19–20).

Again this narrative is not to be classified in any category of popular story or saga, having no arc of tension. Instead it is cultic teaching or proclamation. Several details show that the proclamation is itself a developed piece of tradition within Israel's cultic history. The catechetical piece (4:21–23) uses different Hebrew terminology for dry ground than the narrative. The theme has tied two originally different motifs together. The very development of a catechetical statement linking the experiences at the sea with those at the river represents a period of cultic reflection. This is shown further by the development of the catechetical statement into personal confession involving you and we. Development within the material is revealed in the explicit etiological nature of the stone materials. No set phrase marks this as etiology. Rather, the climax of the narrative itself is the setting up of the stones in the cultic place of Gilgal at the cultic festival time. A cultic legend of the founding of Gilgal lies at the roots of this narrative. Such a legend cannot, however, be isolated in full form from the present narrative. Otto is correct in arguing against the attempts of Keller, Dus, Vogt, Maier, and Langlamet to isolate a number of early oral traditions within the material (*Mazzotfest*, 104–18). None of the proposed traditions meet form critical criteria. This does not mean such traditions did not exist. The signs of development within both narrative sources show that earlier material must have been at hand for both sources. However, the present combination of these materials into two narrative complexes has destroyed the possibility of isolating the precise nature of the earlier materials. They have been reshaped for communication of the word of God to a different age.

This has left unanswered the question of the origin of the present form of the second narrative. The obvious answer is that Gilgal and its cult have played the dominant role in the formation of the cultic legend adapted into the present cultic cathechetical confession. The heyday of the sanctuary was the reign of King Saul (cf. 1 Sam 7:16; 10:8; 11:14–15; 13:4–15; 15:12–33). Even then Gibeah, not Gilgal, was Saul's headquarters (1 Sam 10:26; 13:2, 15; 14:16; 15:34; 26:1). Gilgal was only one of many important sanctuaries (cf. 1 Sam 7:16–17).

The developed state of the present narrative and its relation to the sea narrative make it possible that any of the cultic centers of Israel could have taken up and reflected upon earlier material, formalizing it into the present shape. The central role of the ark might indicate that Shiloh or even Jerusalem has influenced the material.

The literary narratives did not become items for Israelite archives. Rather they functioned within the community as instruments to teach what God had done for his people. As such, they became the object of continuing study and exegesis. The community continually sought to explain what the verses meant to the new generations and in new contexts. This is evident at several

points within the text. The editor who inserted the tradition into the larger
literary context joined it to chap. 2 by means of the itinerary item of Shittim
(3:1), which itself was based on tradition now found in Mic 6:5 and Num
22:1; 25:1; 33:48–49. This gave geographical staging and continuity to the
tradition. The editor of Joshua in its basic form took up the theological and
thematic motifs of chap. 1 and gave them a further formulation here. Thus
he showed the greatness of Joshua based on the divine presence begun with
Moses (3:7; 4:10aB, 14). The greatness of Joshua was reinforced by showing
that the Trans-Jordan tribes kept their word and obeyed his command (4:12–
13). The holy war theology of 2:9–11 is extended further in the concluding
verses of this section (4:24–5:1). The entire composition then becomes something quite distinct from its original components. It becomes a narrative given
parallel theological construction. First, God promises to make Joshua great
(3:1–7). Then he promises to reveal his own greatness (3:8–17). He then
makes Joshua great (4:1–14) before bringing greatness to himself before all
the kings (4:15–5:1).

Comment

3:1 The problems begin in the first verse with the change from singular
"Joshua got up" to the plural "they set out." Here the final editor seeks to
emphasize two points. First he seeks to show that Joshua is the leader, who
initiates all action. He begins building toward his summary statement in v
7. Secondly he shows that Joshua acted immediately upon the return of the
spies. When God opened the opportunity, Joshua acted. He moved immediately to the goal, the Jordan River. Except in flood season, the Jordan has
never served as a real political or communications barrier. It is much more
a theological symbol defining for Israel the promise of God. The Jordan
was the last obstacle Israel had to cross to escape the wilderness and enter
the land of promise. As so often, God intervened in a marvelous fashion to
help her cross her obstacles.

The first verse ends with the term עבר, "cross over." This becomes the
chorus for the following passage, appearing twenty-two times (Hertzberg,
24). The emphasis is not, however, on the simple fact of crossing. The emphasis in the present text is on the subjects making the crossing possible.

3:2 The שטרים, "officials" appear unexpectedly in v 2. This may rest in
the history of the tradition, but it serves an explicit theological purpose in
our text. This brings to mind their appearance in 1:10 and shows that the
command of Joshua issued there is carried out. Joshua's leadership is effective.
His time schedule (1:11) works. His commands are obeyed.

3:3 The ark surprises us here. We are not really prepared for its appearance.
Joshua has said nothing about it. Deuteronomy mentioned it as the home
of the Decalogue (10:1–5) and the Deuteronomic law (31:26) and as the identifying mark of the Levitical priests (10:8; 31:9, 25). The ark had appeared
first in the Exodus account of the construction of the wilderness sanctuary
(chaps. 25–31; 35–40), where it is set up in the holiest place where God
met Moses (25:22; 30:6; cf. Num 7:89). Later Aaron was allowed to enter
but only on the Day of Atonement (Lev 16). Among the priests the Kohathites

were set apart to care for the ark and sanctuary (Num 3:31), particularly during travel (4:5–15).

A different role for the ark appears in Num 10:33–35, that of leading Israel in her wilderness journeys and wars. Such a role is described only once in Numbers and then negatively (14:44). Josh 3 is the first time the ark actually leads Israel explicitly in the biblical narratives.

The titles given the ark in Josh 3–4 represent a sample of the many titles given the ark throughout the biblical literature. "The ark of the covenant" is basically restricted to Deuteronomistic literature (Deut 10:8; 31:9, 25, 26; Josh 6:6, 8; 8:33; Judg 20:27; 1 Sam 4:3–5; 2 Sam 15:24; 1 Kgs 3:15; 6:19; 8:1, 6; Jer 3:16) taken over later by the Chronicler. The only possible exceptions appear to be Num 10:33; 14:44, and any traditions which lay behind Josh 3–4. To use these as a basis for a wide-ranging theory of covenant theology at Gilgal, as does Otto (*Mazzotfest*, 199–202), is going beyond what the evidence allows.

A second title given the ark is that of the "ark of the Testimony" (4:16), which is not to be wiped away through text critical procedures as would Langlamet (*Gilgal*, 51–54). This title is at home in priestly, cultic literature, based on the understanding that the testimony of God, that is his law, was placed in the ark (Exod 25:16, 21; cf. 25:22; 26:33, 34; 30:6, 26; 31:7; 39:35; 40:3, 5, 21; Num 4:5; 7:89).

Finally, the ark is called the ark of Yahweh (e.g. 3:13), a title also found frequently in the narrative of the ark in 1 Sam 4–6 and 2 Sam 6.

These different titles of the ark appear to reflect different stages in its history and function within Israel and her theological reflections. They give another indication of the history of theological reflection which lies behind the present passage. Each of the narratives in our section show a stage of the reflection. The first narrative shows the ark as the divine symbol leading the armies of Israel into battle, performing miracles, and promising victory over the enemies. In the second narrative the ark has been reduced to a secondary role. Its role is simply that of a cultic object carried by the priests. It is the feet of the priests, the standing place of the priests, the actions of the priests which are significant. The ark has become a customary cult object which one presupposes but whose role is no longer a matter of reflection or real significance.

The final editor adds nothing about the ark. His interests lie elsewhere, in the question of the leadership of Israel.

Verse 3 also introduces the Levitical priests for the only time in the section. The role of the Levites has been much discussed by scholarship. They play a significant role in Deuteronomic literature (von Rad, *Studies in Deuteronomy*, 66–69; E. W. Nicholson, *Deuteronomy and Tradition*, [Philadelphia: Fortress, 1967] 73–76; R. Abba, "Priests and Levites in Deuteronomy," *VT* 27 [1977] 257–67). The introduction of the Levites into this narrative is usually taken as a mark of Deuteronomic editing. What is important in the context is that the emphasis of the verse is upon the ark. The priests are placed in a quite secondary position in the grammar of the sentence and in the view of the writer. The people are to look for the ark and follow it.

3:4 Follow, but not too closely is the message of v 4. We expect this to be given theological reasoning. The ark could be explained as the symbol of divine presence. Israel would be warned to keep its distance from the danger of the divine holiness (e.g. Exod 33:17–23). This is not the case here. Here the problem is one of transportation. Israel is entering foreign territory. She must have a guide. That is the ark. She must not get too close. The actual distance, however, is rather significant, the length of a pasture (Num 35:4). Such great distance does not derive from the need to follow the ark to find one's way. Again we have signs of theological reflection. The concept of keeping a distance from divine holiness has entered the passage. Our text thus gives two emphases to the ark. It shows God's people God's way into the Promised Land, but it also represents a holy presence from which the people must keep their distance.

3:5 The same concept of divine holiness carries over to v 5. Israel is to sanctify herself, literally "make yourselves holy." This involves purification ritual which prepares a person to enter the divine presence (e.g. Exod 19:22; 1 Sam 16:5; cf. Exod 22:30 = Engl. 22:31). Such a ritual required time, so that it was often done for the morrow. (cf. Num 11:18; Josh 7:13; cf. S. De Vries, *ZAW* 87 [1975] 65–79). This explains why the extra day appears to enter the narrative at this point though it is not mentioned in the remainder of the narrative. The introduction of the purification ritual brought with it the traditional motif of preparing for the morrow. This purification is not pictured as simply cultic. It is purification for battle, in accord with the law of Deut 23:15(=Engl. 14). When God leads his people into the land of the enemy, her camp must be purified.

3:6 Having made all necessary preparations, Joshua issued the long-awaited order: Forward. The priests obeyed immediately. The picture of Joshua the leader following Moses is thus complete. God's order to Joshua (1:2) has been carried out. Joshua is leading the people over Jordan. Joshua in purifying the camp has followed the rules set up by Moses (cf. 1:7–8). The officials and priests have responded to Joshua's leadership. The ground is laid for the first divine Word of our section.

3:7 The divine Word is closely related to chap. 1. God promises to validate the leadership of Joshua for the people and thus to fulfill his promise to Joshua (1:5). The miracle at the Jordan becomes the basis of Joshua's claim for divine authority and divine presence. Joshua's claim to power does not rest on anything he has accomplished. It rests on what God has accomplished at the Jordan and on the obedience of Joshua to the words and example of Moses. Joshua thus inherits the Mosaic presence and the Mosaic office through obedience to the divine word and the Mosaic word.

3:8 Joshua again takes the speaking role. Now the goal is different. All that follows points to what God is going to do while the priests are standing (v 8), the people listening (v 9), and Joshua explaining (v 10).

3:10 God's actions will reveal God's power and person. The living God is in the midst of Israel. This designation for God appears in Hos 2:1; Ps 42:3; 84:3. Slightly different formulations occur in 1 Sam 17:26; Deut 5:23; Jer 10:10; 23:36; Dan 6:21, 27; 2 Kgs 19:4, 26. The acclamation, "Yahweh lives," appears in Ps 18:47. Israel's God is thus contrasted to the other claimants to the title. Only Yahweh is active and alive. Only Yahweh intervenes in the affairs of his people. God's actions for his people prove his power and demonstrate the nature of his person. (Cf. H. Ringgren, "חיה," *TWAT* 2 [1977] 891–93).

In our context the actions are quite specific. He will drive out the inhabitants of the Promised Land and give the land to his chosen people, Israel. The order of the peoples in v 10 is distinctive within the OT (Langlamet, *Gilgal,* 109–11). The list of the peoples inhabiting the Promised Land reflects a long tradition. Details about each of the peoples named are difficult to establish. The Amarna Letters demonstrate clearly that the political and cultural makeup of Palestine was exceedingly diverse and lacking in unity long before Israel entered. She did not face a common foe. She faced a number of different small city-states, each with its own tradition, people, culture, and god. None of these were any match for the living God of Israel.

3:11 Israel can know the living God is active for her, driving out her enemies, because she can see his present action. He is present in the ark of the covenant. He is present as Lord of all the earth. This further divine epithet is yet another indication of the theological reflection and development within even the first of the narratives used as sources for this section. The Hebrew term ארץ means either "land" or "earth" depending upon the context. Its meaning in the present context is debated, basically because its original context is debated. The divine epithet appears also in Mic 4:13; Zech 4:14; 6:5; Ps 97:5; 114:7 (the latter following the emendation of Kraus). The epithet may have been at home in the Gilgal cult (H.-J. Kraus, *Psalmen.* vol. 2 [BKAT XV. 2nd ed. Neukirchen: Neukirchener Verlag, 1961] 781; Otto, *Mazzotfest,* 150, 187–88). Kraus (*Psalmen,* vol. 1, 199) speaks of the Jebusite or Canaanite origin of the epithet. Langlamet (*Gilgal,* 112–15) working on the Ugaritic parallels drawn by Maier (*Ladeheiligtum*) and biblical studies of E. Lipinski (*La royauté de Yahwé dans la poésie et le culte de l'ancien Israël,* [Brussels: Paleis der Academiën, 1965] 173–275) sought to demonstrate that the material taken over from a Canaanite cult has been shorn of mythical elements and reduced to the concerns of Israel, namely the possession of the land of Canaan. Gray (62) takes the other extreme and views the phrase as a late Deuteronomistic elaboration of Deuteronomy 10:14.

The earliest history of the phrase in Israel is perhaps hidden to us. It apparently represents one of the many items appropriated by Israel from its Canaanite heritage and baptized into service to proclaim the greatness of Yahweh, the God of Israel. A limitation of its meaning to the land which Israel sought to possess is possible within an early framework, but such is not strongly witnessed in the present text. Rather, here we may well have the appropriation of the material within the Jerusalem cult, from which spring all other uses of the epithet. At any rate, we have evidence in the several divine idioms of a growth of tradition and a reflection upon the theological significance of the material. When the terminology was read and used by the late Israelite community as it was threatened and finally captured by the nations of the world, the confession of Josh 3:11 would certainly have been seen in a universalistic context, giving hope that Yahweh would once more lead Israel out of the wilderness of the east over the Jordan into the Promised Land.

3:12 The transition to 3:12 is abrupt and unexpected, giving rise to many theories of textual disruption. Certainly, one can debate where the reference stood in earlier tradition. Within the present context, the material represents a part of the divine command preparing Israel for its great moment and testing the leadership of Joshua. Thus it is placed in the section where Joshua is acting as a prophet and relaying to Israel the words of Yahweh (cf. v 9).

3:13–17 With 3:13 a complicated Hebrew sentence structure is introduced. This makes all the action described in vv 13–15 contemporary with and subordinate to the great action of v 16, the formation of a great heap of waters. The waters, the Jordan and waters going down to the sea, are mentioned ten times in the context. They are the center of attention. Everything and everyone else is subordinate to the miracle at the waters. Whereas the opening section of the chapter centered on the person and office of Joshua, these final verses center on the words and actions of Yahweh for Israel at the waters. The living God, the Lord of all the earth, moves before his people and makes good his claims to universal dominion.

3:15 The miracle of the Jordan is heightened in the last half of v 15. At many seasons of the year, the Jordan is a mere trickle of water which could easily be forded. During the spring harvest, melting snows from the northern mountains flooded the riverbed. Only resulting landslides or divine miracles allow crossing in this time of year (cf. 4:19).

3:16 The tradition has tried to locate the miracle quite exactly in 3:16 though this has not always resulted in a clear understanding even for the early versions (see Notes, 3:16.a. b). The MT tradition gives two cities and two names for what we call the Dead Sea. The first of the cities is Adam, associated by scholarship with *Tell ed-Dāmiyeh*, on the eastern shore of the Jordan, a mile south of the junction of the Jordan with the Jabbok and about sixteen miles north of Jericho. The location of Zarethan is greatly disputed. Recent excavations at Tell *es-Sa'idiyeh* have not confirmed nor denied Glueck's identification with Zarethan (J. B. Pritchard, "Tell es-Sa'idiyeh," *EAEHL* 4 [1978] 1028).

The early tradition appears to have connected the miracle with Jericho, rather than with Gilgal. Again we can see a development within the tradition. This may indicate that the narrative of the conquest of Jericho was later taken up in a Gilgal cultic celebration. Israel is here identified as a גוי, a nation. In the late history of Israel and Judaism, the word took on a negative character and was applied only to the foreign nations. The biblical witness, however, shows that Israel knew herself as one nation among many, a status she owed to the greatness of her god (cf. Exod 19:6; Gen 12:2; Deut 32:8–9; R. E. Clements, "גוי," *TWAT* 1 [1973] 965–73). Our text testifies that Israel crossing the Jordan under Joshua had achieved unified nationhood. She was the גוי which God had promised she would become.

4:1–3 Chap. 4 introduces a new speech form. God has been talking through the prophet Joshua announcing his great act. The predicted miracle has occurred. Now we return to the sequence of divine command and human execution pointing to the greatness of Joshua. This has been imposed on an older tradition, as can be seen by the plural imperatives in vv 2–3. What was once addressed to the entire nation or a group of its leaders is now addressed only to the leader Joshua. The tradition presupposes Israel as a league of twelve tribes and interprets the stone monument in this light. The stones are taken from the midst of the Jordan. This is interpreted as the standing place of the priests. Vv 8 and 15 have emphasized the edge of the waters as the standing place of the priests. Only v 17 has placed them in the middle of the Jordan. In 4:9 the stones are set up in the middle of the Jordan. Again, a development of and reflection upon the tradition is seen. The original tradition appears to have associated the priests with the edge of the waters, emphasizing the miracle that ensued. Another tradition associated the stones with the middle of the waters, either as the place of their collection or of their deposit. Combining the traditions has enhanced the role of the priests. The memorial stones not only memorialize what Yahweh has done, they also show precisely where the sacred priests have stood. The exact location of the stones remains obscure in 4:1–3, being simply the camping place for the night.

4:4–5 Joshua responds immediately to the divine command and proves himself an obedient leader. But he is something more. He is also an interpreter of the divine will and the founder of later teaching practice, just as Moses had been. **4:6–7** The section is given in the form of an answer to a question posed by a son for his father. This form appears also in Exod 12:26–27; 13:14–15; Deut 6:20–21; Josh 4:6–7, 21–23, always in connection with cultic materials to which a young child would not have access (Soggin, *VT* 10 [1960] 341–47). It represents the cultic practice of teaching the adults specific formulas to teach their children the meaning of God's history with his people (see Otto, *Mazzotfest*, 131–33). Joshua thus instituted the later practice of the priests, who must look to him as their founding father. The teaching itself is confined strictly to the Jordan event interpreted as a miracle of God without mention of priests.

4:8 The people follow their leader precisely, doing just what Joshua commanded. This is the theological point of the present context. God has rasied up for himself and his people a leader who listens to the divine word and to whom the people listen obediently.

4:9 The role of Joshua is shown in a different light in 4:9. He acts rather than speaks. He honors the priests rather than serving as their founding father. He establishes a permanent memorial to the priests in the middle of the Jordan, rather than commanding others to establish a memorial to the acts of God in the camping place across the Jordan. This verse plays its own theological role in the tradition. It establishes the fundamental role of the priests, giving them an eternal monument. Here we see how the tradition spoke to each new generation and gave authority to varying groups of leaders within Israel.

4:10 V 10 brings a narrative and theological climax. Here it is made specifically clear that the people crossed the Jordan. As narrative material, this duplicates 3:17–4:1. Tradition-historically the material may have referred originally to the crossing of the priests, who are the subjects of the opening disjunctive clause. As theological material, the verse climaxes all that has gone before. Joshua had commanded the priests to stand in the water while the people crossed (3:8). This command is obeyed in 4:10. The people of Israel gained victory when they accepted the life style given by God. They obeyed in every detail what God commanded their leader. This, in turn, corresponded precisely to that which Moses had commanded their leader. When Israel followed the Mosaic commandment mediated through their God-given leader, Israel experienced the miraculous leadership of God. This was realized through the presence of the ark, the symbol of divine presence.

4:12 Quite unexpectedly the tradition from 1:12–18 appears. Again the word of Joshua based on the word of Moses is totally obeyed (cf. 1:13). The Trans-Jordan tribes had kept their promise (1:16–18). The unity of Israel was preserved. The authority of Joshua was proven.

4:13 Verse 13 summarizes the preceding, but how much of it? Does it relate only to v 12 and the Trans-Jordan tribes? Its vocabulary is closely related to that of Num 32, particularly v 27, another tradition of the Trans-Jordan tribes (see Langlamet, *Gilgal,* 136–37). The vocabulary is, however, distinct from that of Josh 4:12. If related only to v 12, the verse would simply repeat the information of v 12. The disjunctive sentence structure may indicate that v 13 forms the conclusion of the entire preceding narrative. The verse would then indicate that the Israelite army marched across the Jordan forty thousand strong to fight Jericho. This would point forward to the narratives of chap. 5. It could represent the original conclusion of an early tradition of the crossing of the Jordan. As such it would be a good conclusion to the first narrative source of this chapter. In the present context it underlines the obedience of Israel preparing to fight the wars of Yahweh.

4:14 Verse 14 concludes the first half of the chapter. The divine command (1–3) has resulted in perfect obedience by Joshua (4–7) and by the people. The actions of Joshua (9), the priests (10a), the people (10b) have brought forth the sign of the divine presence (11). Finally the tribes least affected by the action have demonstrated their loyalty to Joshua and Moses (12). Israel is prepared to fight for her land (13). The great event of the Jordan under Joshua thus has the same ending as the great event at the sea under Moses (Exod 14:31). The people held in awe the divinely appointed leader. Joshua has become the new Moses (cf. D. J. McCarthy, "The Theology of Leadership in Joshua 1–9," *Bib* 52 [1971] 175). The promise of 3:7 is realized. But the story does not end. Only half the purpose has been realized. The greatness of Yahweh must also be underlined. This follows.

4:15-18 Again the divine command is followed by human command. The result is human obedience (18a), but now this is only expressed in a temporal clause. The major result is miracle (18b). The situation of 3:15b is restored. God's action, rather than human obedience, is again in the center of focus.

4:19-20 The cultic, priestly interest finds its climax in v 19. The date would be in April and is given according to a calendar beginning the year in the spring according to Babylonian practice (cf. D. J. A. Clines, "New Year," *IDBSup* [1976] 625–29), a practice connected with observance of the Exodus passover ritual in Exod 12, the tenth day being the day for selection of lambs (Exod 12:3). Jordan crossing and sea crossing thus converge in the cultic calendar. The cultic site also becomes clear. Gilgal is mentioned for the first time in the book, being located even here in reference to Jericho. The stones become a cultic memorial to the deeds of God leading Israel across the Jordan to Gilgal. Theological reflection again shines through. The story of the Jordan crossing has been used to authorize the cult practices of Gilgal.

4:21–23 The cultic teaching form reappears (see 4:6–7). The point of emphasis is no longer the cutting off of the waters before the ark but the appearance of dry ground allowing Israel to pass over. This provides a basis for comparison with the Exodus event (see A. R. Hulst, *OTS* 14 [1965] 162–88; R. Schmid, *TZ* 21 [1965] 260–68). The teaching is now the climax of the second narrative, but its distinctive vocabulary shows that it had a separate origin from the Jordan crossing tradition. A parallel vocabulary distinction also appears in the crossing of the sea tradition (Exod 14–15). There also the early narrative tradition uses חרב, while the cultic, priestly tradition uses יבש to describe the drying up of the sea.

The present context uses the drying of the waters motif to underline the mighty acts of God for Israel. In so doing it uses an interesting device to define Israel. "You all"—the sons—are the Israel who crossed the Jordan. "We"—the fathers—are the Israel who crossed the sea. Liturgical teaching dramatizes the events and transforms it into personal confession and involvement. The church has done a similar thing in singing together, "Were you there when they crucified my Lord?" Such cultic language brings each generation back to the point where its faith originated and forces it to relate personally to the God of the beginnings. In this the greatness of God is recognized again.

4:24–5:1 The final two verses of the section present grammatical problems. The sentence appears to end smoothly in 4:22, but it is continued by means of a temporal clause in 4:23 and a result clause in 4:24. This demonstrates the reflection of later generations on the meaning of cultic teaching. The content of the result clause is precisely the teaching of the Deuteronomic school concerning holy war. The teaching is aimed on the surface level to two audiences. First, it seeks to demonstrate to all the enemies of Israel that Israel's God controls the military power to win any battle for Israel and thus is truly Lord of all the earth. Such reaction by the nations should then teach Israel to stand in worshipful awe of her God forever, no matter what happens. The material is not written and given to the nations. It is written and taught only to Israel. Thus the actual purpose of the writer is to bring Israel to reflect upon her history as he had done and to respond with reverence and awe to Yahweh, the God who has brought the nations to their knees. The knowledge about God results not in pride and dogmatism but in worship and service.

The final verse of the section demonstrates that God had done his part. The nations whom Israel faced in the Promised Land hear the report of Yahweh's action and fear for their lives, unable to react in any way. They have lost all spirit. Before Israel has fought a single battle, the entire land is hers for the taking. This is the message of the book of Joshua (cf. the "giving" motif of chap. 1; the confession of 2:9–11). Later generations of Israelites heard the story and applied the message to their own day. If God gave his people the land once, he could do it again, if the people had leaders and obedience as in the day of Joshua.

Explanation

The experience at the Jordan River proved theologically fruitful to the long generations of Israelites. Two cultic sources eventually expressed Israel's understanding of what the miracle at the river had meant and what it continued to mean to the worshiping community. These sources had incorporated many Israelite traditions to express the total meaning of the event. The sources were in turn incorporated into an even greater literary context to continue proclaiming the meaning of the Jordan event long centuries after the event itself.

The central focus of both sources and the final biblical context is the action of God and its meaning for Israel. The presence of God, symbolized by his ark, cut off the waters and allowed Israel to enter the Promised Land. Israel passed on dry land across the Jordan. It was another Exodus miracle. The God of the Exodus was also the God of the land. In the land of a great international power and in the land of the numerous kingdoms vying for possession of Israel's promised territory, Yahweh proved himself to be Lord of all the earth. No matter where Israel found herself, she could depend upon her God to deliver her. He controlled the natural powers of the universe. He could control any enemy facing Israel.

One qualification must be made. Israel must be identified. The people of God must realize that God does not help them automatically. God helps them when they obey his commands given through his leader. The final context makes certain of these commands important. Israel must follow the symbol of divine presence among her. Only God could lead the way Israel was to walk. They must sanctify themselves, for the holy God did miracles only for a holy people. Israel must remember her tradition and devise means to teach it to her children. Israel was responsible that the reputation of God live on. God did not do miracles of the proportion of the Exodus or the Jordan in every generation. Yet every generation could devise teaching and ritual situations in which Israel could experience anew what God had done for them. For the people who followed, sanctified, remembered, and taught, God would raise up leaders in the Mosaic tradition who would teach the people the things to do to be the people of God. When miracle was again needed by such a people, God could again prove that his hand was still strong, that he could still bring fear upon the nations, and that he was still worthy of the reverential awe of his people.

Such teaching troubles the contemporary people of God. We in Jesus Christ have been stripped of national identity. We do not look for a warrior God to freeze our enemies with fear and give us a land. Our hero won the victory through self-giving and suffering. Still, we can learn from the story of the Jordan the nature of the people of God. Whatever the historical setting, the people of God still face a life confronted with opposition and are tempted to find other gods who can please for the moment. We are called again to confess that there is only one Lord of all the earth. We need not seek out new gods. We do need to renew our quest for the identity God would give us as his people and for the leaders God raises up to lead his people in the way of Moses and in the way of Jesus through our modern difficulties.

Cultically Correct for Conquest   (5:2–15)

Bibliography

Abel, F. M. "L'apparition du chef de l'armée de Yahveh à Josué (Jos. V, 13–15)." *Miscellanea Biblica et Orientalia R. P. Athanasio Miller Oblata.* Studia Anselmiana 27–28 (1951) 109–13. **Deurloo, K. A.** "Om Pesach te kunnen vieren in het land (Joz. 5, 2–9)." *Verkenningen in een Stroomgebied.* Amsterdam: University of Amsterdam, 1974, 41–50. **Elder, W. H.** "The Passover." *RevExp* 74 (1977) 511–22. **Finkel, J.** "The Case of the Repeated Circumcision in Jos 5, 2–7: An Historical and Comparative Study." *Annals of the Jewish Academy of Arts and Sciences.* New York: 1974, 177–213. **Füglister, N.** *Die Heilsbedeutung des Pascha.* SANT 8. München: Kösel–Verlag, 1963, 27–28, 67, 87, 112, 202, 216, 244. **George, A.** "Les récits de Gilgal en Josué (5:2–15)." *Mémorial J. Chaine.* Lyon: Facultés Catholiques, 1950, 169–86. **Gradwohl, R.** "Der 'Hügel der Vorhäute' (Josua V,3)." *VT* 26 (1976) 235–40. **Gressman, H.** *Die Anfänge Israels.* Göttingen: Vandenhoeck & Ruprecht, 1922, 140–41, 143–44. **Haag, H.** *Vom alten zum neuen Pascha.* SBS 49. Stuttgart: K. B. W. Verlag, 1971, 67–71. **Halbe, J.** "Erwägungen zu Ursprung und Wesen des Massotfestes." *ZAW* 87 (1975) 324–45. **Hermisson, H. J.** *Sprache und Ritus im altisraelitischen Kult.* WMANT 19. Neukirchen-Vluyn: Neukirchener Verlag, 1965, 66–67. **Hölscher, G.** *Geschichtsschreibung in Israel.* Lund: C. W. K. Gleerup, 1952, 338–39. **Keel, O.** *Wirkmächtige Siegeszeichen im Alten Testament.* Orbis Biblicus et Orientalis 5. Freiburg: Universitätsverlag, 1974, 82–88. **Keller, C. A.** "Über einige alttestamentliche Heiligtumslegenden II." *ZAW* 68 (1956) 85–97. **Kraus, H. J.** "Gilgal." *VT* 1 (1951) 181–99. ———. *Gottesdienst in Israel.* 2nd ed. München: Chr. Kaiser Verlag, 1962, 64–67, 179–93. ———. "Zur Geschichte des Passah-Massot-Festes im Alten Testament." *EvT* 18 (1958) 47–67. **Kutsch, E.** "Erwägungen zur Geschichte des Passafeier und des Massotfestes." *ZTK* 55 (1958) 20–21. **Laaf, P.** *Die Pascha-Feier Israels.* BBB 36. Bonn: Peter Hanstein Verlag, 1970, 86–91, 103–15, 131, 167. **Long, B. O.** *The Problem of Etiological Narrative in the Old Testament.* BZAW 108. Berlin: Alfred Töpelmann, 1968, 54–55. **Lubsczyk, H.** *Der Auszug Israels aus Ägypten.* Erfurter Theologische Studien 11. Leipzig: St. Benno-Verlag, 1963, 135–37. **Maier, J.** *Das altisraelitische Ladeheiligtum.* BZAW 93. Berlin: Alfred Töpelmann, 1965, 24, 33–39. **Miller, P. D.** *The Divine Warrior in Early Israel.* HSM 5. Cambridge, MA: Harvard University Press, 1973, 128–31. **Möhlenbrink, K.** "Die Landnahmensagen des Buches Josua." *ZAW* 56 (1938) 262–68 **Mowinckel, S.** *Tetrateuch-Pentateuch-Hexateuch.* BZAW 90. Berlin: Alfred Töpelmann, 1964, 36. **Otto, E.** *Das Mazzotfest in Gilgal.* BWANT 107. Stuttgart: W. Kohlhammer Verlag, 1975, 57–65, 158–59, 175–86, 189–91, 195–98, 311. **Porter, J. R.** "The Background of Joshua 3–5." *SEA* 36 (1971) 5–23. **Rudolph, W.** *Der "Elohist" von Exodus bis Josua.* BZAW 68. Berlin: Alfred Töpelmann, 1938, 178–82. **Schmitt, R.** *Exodus und Passah: ihr Zusammenhang im Alten Testament.* Orbis Biblicus et Orientalis 7. Freiburg: Universitätsverlag, 1975, 51–53. **Segal, J. B.** *The Hebrew Passover.* London Oriental Series 12. London: Oxford University Press, 1963, 3–4. **Simpson, C. A.** *The Early Traditions of Israel.* Oxford: Basil Blackwell, 1948, 286–88. **Soggin, J. A.** "Gilgal, Passah und Landnahme." VTSup 15 (1965) 263–77. ———. "La 'negazione' in Gios. 5:14." *BeO* 7 (1965) 75 (= *Old Testament and Oriental Studies.* Rome: Biblical Institute Press, 1975, 219–20.) **de Vaux, R.** *Histoire ancienne d'Israël.* vol. 1. Paris: J. Gabalda, 1971, 557–59. (= *The Early History of Israel.* Tr. D. Smith. London: Darton, Longman & Todd, 1978, 605–8.) **Wambacq, B. N.** "Les origines de la *Pesah* israélite." *Bib* 57 (1976) 216, 223. **Wellhausen, J.** *Die Composition des Hexateuchs und der historischen Bücher des Alten Testaments.* 2nd ed. Berlin: Georg Reimer, 1889, 122–23. **Westermann, C.** "Arten der Erzählung in der Genesis." *For-*

schung am Alten Testament. TBü 24. München: Chr. Kaiser Verlag, 1964, 84–85. **Wijngaards, J. N. M.** *The Dramatization of Salvific History in the Deuteronomic Schools. OTS* 16 (1969) 60, 104–5, 120. **Wilcoxen J. A.** "Narrative Structure and Cult Legend: A Study of Joshua, 1–6." *Transitions in Biblical Scholarship,* ed. J. C. Rylaarsdam. Chicago: University of Chicago Press, 1968, 43–70. **Wildberger, H.** *Jahwes Eigentumsvolk.* ATANT 37. Zürich: Zwingli Verlag, 1960, 40–62. **Zenger, E.** *Die Sinaitheophanie.* Forschung zur Bibel 3. Würzburg: Echter Verlag, 1961, 136–47.

Translation

² *At that time Yahweh said to Joshua, "Make for yourself flint knives and circumcise again* ª *the sons of Israel a second time."* ᵇ ³ *Joshua then made for himself flint knives and circumcised the sons of Israel on* ª *the hill of the foreskins.* ⁴ *This is the reason for Joshua's circumcising: all the people* ª *coming out from Egypt, the males, all the warriors had died in the wilderness on the way when they came out from Egypt.* ⁵ *Indeed, all the people coming out were circumcised, but all the people who were born in the wilderness on the way when they came out from Egypt they had not circumcised.* ⁶ *Because forty years* ª *the Israelites were on the move in the wilderness until all the nation, the men of war coming out from Egypt, were finished off* ᵇ *who did not listen obediently to the voice of Yahweh when Yahweh swore to them that they would not see the land which Yahweh had sworn to their fathers to give to us, a land flowing with milk and honey.* ⁷ *But it was their sons whom he set up in their stead that Joshua circumcised, since uncircumcised were they because they did not circumcise them in the way.* ⁸ *When all the nation was finished being circumcised, they remained in their stead in the camp until they recovered.* ⁹ *Then Yahweh said to Joshua, "Today I have rolled the disgrace of Egypt away from you." So he called the name of that place Gilgal until this day.* ª

¹⁰ *Then the sons of Israel camped in Gilgal.* ª *They kept the Passover on the fourteenth day of the month in the evening in the plains of Jericho.* ¹¹ *They ate from the produce of the land on the day after Passover* ª—*unleavened bread and parched grain—on that very same day. Then the manna stopped from the day when they ate from the produce of the land.* ¹² *Manna was never again available for the sons of Israel. They ate the crops of the land of Canaan that year.*

¹³ *When Joshua was in Jericho, he lifted his eyes and watched. Right before his face a man was standing with his sword drawn in his hand. Joshua went to him and said to him, "Do you belong to us or to our enemies?"* ¹⁴ *He said, "No!* ª *Because I am the prince of the host of Yahweh, I have now come." Joshua fell on his face to the ground and worshiped him.* ¹⁵ *He said to him, "What will my lord say to his servant?" Then the prince of the host of Yahweh said to Joshua, "Loosen your sandal from upon your foot for the place upon which you are now standing is holy." Joshua obeyed.*

Notes

LXX forces the interpreter of this section, particularly vv 4–6, to consider the implications of textual variants and textual criticism. LXX offers not only a much shorter text, but a different interpretation of the events. Clear evidence appears that textual transmission involved interpretation as late as the translation into Greek and beyond as each new generation explained the meaning of the cultic practices for its own worship, teaching, and self-identity as heirs of the tradition.

2.a. LXX read וֹשֻׁב, "sit down," rather than וֹשׁוּב, "again." For the MT double imperative, see GKC 120g. LXX may reflect an older circumcision practice wherein youth were circumcised at puberty in community ritual (cf. *ANEP*, no. 629).

2.b. The best Greek witnesses omit שֵׁנִית, "a second time" (*contra* Otto, *Mazzotfest*, 58). MT represents interpretation of the tradition in light of Gen 17 and Exod 12:43–49.

3.a. Here and v 14, MT reads אֶל, "towards," in the sense of the עַל, "upon."

4.a. LXX omits 4b referring to the death of generation in the wilderness and 5a stating that all people leaving Egypt were circumcised. LXX thus reports the circumcision of those born in the wilderness and those not circumcised in Egypt. MT again is more in line with tradition of Gen 17 and Exod 12 (cf. Auld, VTSup [1979] 9).

6.a. LXX reads forty-two years, interpreting the tradition in Num 10:11–12; 12:16; 13:3; 14:33–34. MT follows the chronology of Deut 1:3; 2:14 (cf. Margolis, 69–70).

6.b. LXX reads "therefore many of them were uncircumcised" instead of "until all the nation were finished off," consistent in both text traditions with the interpretations of vv 4–5.

9.a. LXX does not record the formulaic "until this day," again perhaps reflecting continued interpretation in the Hebrew tradition.

10.a. LXX does not record the encampment in Gilgal, which is repetitious of 4:19. MT specifically connects Gilgal and Passover. LXX expands the identification of the locale with Jericho.

11.a. LXX appears to reflect a differing chronological order, omitting "on the day after Passover," and placing "on that day" at the end of v 11, where it may have been understood either as closing the previous sentence or opening the following. MT makes clear that the regulations of Deut 3:1 were followed. There is no indication, however, that the feast of unleavened bread was celebrated (*contra* Otto, *Mazzotfest*, 62–63, 185).

14.a. MT לֹא, "No," represents the most difficult reading and should be retained against the evidence of Hebrew manuscripts, LXX, Syr, which translated the Hebrew homonymn לוֹ, "to him."

Form/Structure/Setting

Chapter 5 unites three traditional reports into a liturgical unit qualifying the people and their leader cultically for the task ahead. The transition to the unit is marked by 5:1, showing how Israel had time and security for such cultic activities. Transition from the unit is marked by 6:1 which shows the reaction of the city marked out as Israel's first military objective.

The three stories have been essential to Israel's identity, so that generations of scribes, priests, and teachers have labored over the precise interpretation of the text (cf. *Notes*). The first narrative simply affirms that Joshua carried out the divine command to circumcise the nation (vv 2, 3, 8). This is located on the Hill of Foreskins (v 3) and involved a painful healing process (v 8; cf. Gen 34:25). Its chronological setting is simply "once upon a time" (v 2). It is a time when iron knives are known, so that flint knives have to be specifically prescribed if they are to be used. Formally, the ancient narrative is simply an anecdote about Joshua and the problems resulting from circumcision (thus its conclusion in v 8). It could well have been used in Israel's cultic and/or teaching tradition to encourage the faithful to keep up the tradition of circumcision despite the pain. The anecdote has become part of a larger literary setting. LXX reflects a setting in which the anecdote is used to explain how Joshua had to purify the disobedient wilderness generation, with possibly a few exceptions such as Joshua himself and Caleb. MT represents a different literary setting. Circumcision had once been universal for Israel as exemplified by the Exodus generation (5a), but that generation had disobeyed (6b) and died (4b, 6a). A new people had come of age, but they were not Israel, for they were uncircumcised (5b, 7b). Thus Israel had to be circumcised again, a second time (v 2; cf. *Notes*). Only a circumcised Israel could become a conquering Israel. This is the present literary setting. Textual notes have given clues that this may not have been the original literary setting. Verses 5b and 7b are doublets, as are 4b and 6a. The narrative continuation of 4 comes in v 7, the necessary answer to the question of v 4. The original *literary* piece may have encompassed vv 2–4, 7–8. Later interpreters gradually made the picture more explicit and tied it closer to the Pentateuchal narrative.

One section has not yet been discussed. Verse 9 forms the etiological conclusion on which Noth laid so much emphasis. Even here Noth had to speak of the Compiler who omitted the original ending of the geographical etiology, replacing it with the story of circumcision. B. S. Childs ("A Study of the Formula, 'Until This Day,' " *JBL* 82 [1963] 285) has shown form critically that the present etiology is only a fragment originally unconnected with the preceding. The LXX even omits the etiological formula. Verse 9 thus does not belong to the original anecdote. It does belong to the original literary piece (with Noth), for the etiology connects the narrative to Gilgal rather than to the anonymous "camp" of v 8. We see, then, that an original anecdote about Joshua bringing soreness upon the men of Israel has been taken up by the theological tradition to show that Israel under Joshua was theologically and cultically correct in its camp at Gilgal as it prepared to begin the conquest of Jericho. Later interpretation made explicit that the people in Egypt had followed the command to Abraham and had been circumcised, only those in the wilderness had not been, for obvious reasons. That courageous generation corrected this as soon as they entered the Promised Land. Thus they saw the land which God did not allow their fathers to see.

The second narrative encompasses vv 10–12, describing the first Passover in the land. Again literary problems arise. The opening reference to Gilgal is missing in LXX (see *Notes*), duplicates, if not contradicts, 4:19, and stands in tension with the end of v 10: "in the plains of Jericho." In v 11 the phrase "on the day after Passover" stands in tension with the concluding notice "on that very same day." and is lacking in LXX. The notice can be explained in light of a later generation's reading the text and seeing two festivals celebrated, Passover and Unleavened Bread (cf. Lev 23:6; Num 28:17; Exod 12:14–20). The Joshua text knows nothing of a seven–day celebration (cf. Halbe, *ZAW* 87 [1975] 332). The dating of the Passover reflects later tradition also (Ezek 45:21; Num 28:16; Lev 23:6) and could be interpreted in light of later celebration, though this is not certain (cf. Soggin, 74). The interesting point here is the climax of the narrative. No further remark is made about festival celebration. The conclusion centers on life in the land. This has consequences for understanding the type of narrative under discussion. Verses 10–12 are not a unit preserved from oral literature of any type. It is a literary production presupposing a much larger context, namely the context of the entire saving history. In a real way, this is the literary climax to the entire Exodus-wilderness narrative. The people who celebrated Passover in Egypt prior to experiencing the Exodus celebrate Passover again prior to taking over control of the fertility of the land. Wars of conquest may lie ahead to bring political control, but the produce of the land lies in the hands of those who celebrate Passover.

The narrative of 13–15 shifts subjects and locale in a startling fashion. Whereas Joshua was not mentioned in the preceding notice about Passover, he alone is the subject here "in Jericho" (v 13). Chronological data is conspicuous through its absence. The form of the narrative is connected to that of Exod 3 (note particularly 5:15 and Exod 3:5) but has caused trouble for all commentators, since it appears to be incomplete. Here a closer examination of the structure of the individual narrative rather than a too-quick comparison with other narratives may help. The story centers on Joshua and his actions. He is surprised to see a mysterious figure standing before him with a sword. As Moses went to investigate the bush (Exod 3:3), so Joshua goes to investigate the mysterious figure confronting him (5:13b). Joshua goes so far as to speak first (13b). The figure refuses to answer Joshua's question (14a; see *Notes*) but does identify himself. In fact he starts to tell his mission (14aB; cf. the same form in 2 Sam 14:15). He does not finish his sentence. This has led commentators repeatedly to speak of a broken form and an original ending which was quite distinct. We must ask if this is not precisely the intended reaction. Joshua, not the figure, has the center of the stage. He acts so quickly that the sentence is not finished. Joshua does not wait to see the messenger's mission. He knows the proper reaction, and falls upon his face in awe (note that Moses allowed Yahweh to identify himself fully before covering his face [Exod 3:6]). Having expressed proper reverence, Joshua then asks the figure before him to continue his introduction. The answer is both a demand for yet another sign of reverence and a revelation that the spot of ground is holy. The expected conclusion is instruction for establishing or changing the cultic practice (Noth, 23). That is not the case here. One might expect the instruction to the man chosen by God as follows in the Moses narrative. That is unnecessary here, having been given in chap. 1 and in Deut 31. The conclusion is simply the obedience of Joshua. Whatever the original form of the narrative, the present form is that of divine test. The divine messenger appears and places demands upon the human recipient. Such a story can end with a detailed account of the obedience (cf. Gen 17:22–27). Here the ending is a simple statement of fact—Joshua obeyed.

Three independent units have served the biblical editor well as he has interpreted Israel's origins in the land as the basic identity of Israel through the ages. He has joined them together without any transitional material. The subject matter is important to him, as he writes a Deuteronomistic history. Passover occupies a central place in his conception (Deut 16; 2 Kgs 23:21–23). Though not mentioned in the Deuteronomic law, circumcision does play an important role in the early narratives distinguishing Israel from other nations aspiring to dominate the land (Judg 14:3; 15:18; 1 Sam 14:6; 17:26, 36; 31:4; 2 Sam 1:20, cf. Gen 34:14). And the authority and obedience of Joshua has consistently been the subject for the book of Joshua. Geography, subject, and possibly even chronology separate the material. The biblical theologian discovers an amazing connecting link. All three narratives point to the cultic correctness of Israel and her leader as she views the conquest of the land. That Israel was actually cultically correct was never self-evident within her history, as the Deuteronomist takes pains to prove in the remainder of his work. But the period of Joshua and then later of each of the Judges are painted as examples of cultic correctness.

Comment

[2] The book of Joshua continues as a dialogue between the divine and human commander. The command this time is to obtain flint knives and use them to circumcise the people. The use of flint knives represents a common ritual phenomenon. Time-honored, old-fashioned materials are used in the cult even when more "modern" equipment is available. Such utensils yield an awesome aura to the cultic event. Exodus 4:25 shows a similar connection to circumcision. Metal knives were also forbidden in the construction of altars (Exod 20:25; Deut 27:5; Josh 8:31). Circumcision is performed on adult males, as is also the case in Egypt. It may have once been a rite of passage into puberty for Israel, but the biblical record knows it only as a religious ritual by which Israel shows her loyalty to Yahweh (Gen 17; 21:4; Exod 12:43–49; Lev 12:3). Many of Israel's neighbors may have been physically circumcised (cf. Jer 9:24–25). This was not the point. God sought a people who obediently carried out what he commanded, even Abraham at age ninety-nine (Gen 17:24). Circumcision and the Israelite(s) became identical (Gen 17:13–14). In the time of the Deuteronomistic historian, this became essential, for the Babylonian overlords were not circumcised. Thus physical rite helped man identify his own flesh, his own children, as belonging to his God and not to the culture and gods of his environment. The Deuteronomic school realized, too, that the ritual was not enough in itself. It demanded more—a circumcised heart (Deut 10:16; 30:6; cf. Lev 26:41; Jer 9:4).

Israel's interpreters made clear that Joshua had not initiated circumcision into Israel. He was only restoring Israel to her previous state. The present text takes this state back to Egypt (v 5a). The Pentateuchal tradition takes it clear back to Abraham (Gen 17), while affirming the circumcision of those in Egypt (Exod 12:43–49).

[3] True to his promise in chap. 1, Joshua is obedient to the divine command. He accomplishes the task at the "hill of foreskins." No location is given this in the immediate context, though v 9 attaches the whole scene to Gilgal. The hill itself originally represented the site, probably cultic in nature (cf. Soggin, 69–70; Bright, 573; Gradwohl, *VT* 26 [1976] 235–40), where the community practiced circumcision. It is now identified with the area of Gilgal. The story itself was not, however, an etiology of this hill, for the conclusion does not come in v 3. The story was an anecdote concerning the healing of the circumcision (v 8).

[4] The story is no longer simply an anecdote. It now is an important part of sacred history. It describes Israel's atonement (cf. LXX) for a whole generation's neglect, a neglect caused in part at least by the sins of the previous generation. The fathers went out circumcised, identified as people of God, experiencing the saving act of God.

⁵ But going out of Egypt they went out from God. The years in the way were years of disobedience. The mark of the people of God was not passed to the next generation. ⁶ Thus forty years were spent until the entire generation was spent.

The Hebrew text makes an interesting play on two words. The older generation left Egypt as an עַם, a people of God (v 4), indeed a circumcised עַם (v 5a). It died, however, as a גּוֹי, a nation of God's enemies (v 6; cf. R. E. Clements, "גּוֹי," *TWAT* 1 [1973] 972). The younger generation was born an עַם in the wilderness (v 5b). It became a גּוֹי (v 8) until it was circumcised. Both גּוֹיִם were finished off (Heb. תֹּם) by God, the first by death (v 6), the second by circumcision (v 8). Turning from a nation to a people is the goal of Israel for the Deuteronomist (Deut 4:6). But Israel sought to be like the גּוֹיִם (e.g. Deut 17:14–20; 1 Sam 8:5; Waltraut Schulz, *Stilkritische Untersuchungen zur deuteronomistischen Literatur,* [Tübingen dissertation, 1974] 45–68).

The writer makes clear how the circumcised people of God came to be a nation opposed to God. Here is the Deuteronomistic theme. God has clearly revealed his will to his people in the Deuteronomic law. They have refused to listen and act. This brings immediate action from God. He swears an oath that the disobedient generation will not have part of the oath he has sworn to the fathers. Here is an important statement about the nature of God's promises to his people. He has made a promise which directs the history of his people, but that promise is realized only by an obedient people. A disobedient generation finds themselves under an oath counteracting for a time the promise of God (cf. the blessings and cursings of Deut 27–28). The promise itself is maintained and transmitted among the people in the first person plural. It is an oath sworn to *us.*

⁸ The new generation receives new life. Originally the story referred to the problems suffered by grown men undergoing a children's operation (cf. Gen 34). It may have been told tongue in cheek to get a good laugh at the sufferers' expense. In the biblical context it has taken on new meaning. The root חיה has the basic meaning "to live, be alive." But biblical man did not consider himself fully alive when he was ill. Thus the Psalmists often describe themselves as dead (33:19; 56:14; cf. C. Barth, *Einführung in die Psalmen,* BibS(N) 32, [Neukirchen: Neukirchener Verlag, 1961] 56–62). In a real sense Israel the nation had to let her God make her sick before she could be healed. This proved to be true not only in the ritual of circumcision but also on the plain of history.

⁹ Circumcision delivered Israel from the reproach of Egypt. The text assumes that the readers know precisely what is meant. Such precise knowledge eludes modern commentators, giving rise to many theories. The present context would appear to connect it with circumcision. Genesis 34:14 calls uncircumcision "a reproach." The present biblical context makes this impossible, for the Israelites were circumcised while in Egypt (5:5). The term refers rather to the insulting social position to which Israel was degraded in Egypt (cf. Gray, 69–71; Hertzberg, 33; and the uncertainty of Soggin, 72). Such social reproach is not relieved through political or military maneuvers, however. Cultic ritual in obedience to Yahweh removes social disgrace.

The theological conclusion is transformed into an etymological wordplay and etiology in 9b: גלותי "I have rolled away," is connected to Gilgal. This insures that the narrative is understood in the context of chaps. 3–4. Circumcision stands in continuity with the cultic traditions of the crossing of the Jordan and the teaching of what God has done for Israel. At Gilgal Israel both learned the catechism and endured the circumcision. This has sanctified Gilgal as an important cultic place for Israel throughout the generations, clear "until this day."

[10] The connection to Gilgal came to be repeated by the interpreters of vv 10–12, assuring again the explicit unity of the context. This also transforms the circumcision narrative into a ritual prelude for Passover, meeting the requirements of Exod 12:43–49. Passover itself is celebrated on the proper day of the calendar (Deut 16:1; Exod 12:4; Num 9:3; Lev 23:5; for general orientation on the biblical calendar, see S. J. De Vries, "Calendar," *IDB* 1 [1962], 483–88). The expression עשה את-הפסח "keep the Passover" appears only in the "Priestly" strata of the Pentateuch (Num 9:2, 5) and in the Chronicler's work (2 Chr 35:17; Ezra 6:19; cf. Exod 12:47; Num 9:3, 11, 12; Laaf, *Pascha-Feier*, 87–89). Laaf is surely correct in arguing that late priestly circles did not invent such vocabulary (*contra* Otto, *Mazzotfest*, 184). Whatever the original language of the tradition, Passover is the festival of interest here (Halbe, *ZAW* 87 [1975] 330–31; *contra* Wildberger, *Jahwes Eigentumsvolk*, 52). This represents the practice of the wandering Israelites joining a feast from their (semi-?) nomadic background with new cultural and religious realities (cf. L. Rost, "Weidewechsel und altisraelitischer Festkalender," *ZDPV* 66 [1943] 205–16= *Das kleine Credo und andere Studien zum Alten Testament*, [Heidelberg: Quelle & Meyer, 1965] 101–12). This took place in Jericho and its surrounding territory, which the tradition has connected with Gilgal.

[11] The point of interest for the original tradition is not the Passover as such, but the transition in life style. Israel can now eat the produce of the land rather than the manna of the desert (cf. Segal, *Hebrew Passover*, 237). The language used to express this requires attention. מעבור "produce," occurs only in this passage (vv 11–12) in the entire Hebrew Bible. The root קלה appears nine times in the Bible, being related to roasted grain only in Lev 2:14; 23:14; Josh 5:11; 1 Sam 17:17; 25:18; 2 Sam 17:28; Ruth 2:14. The biblical texts do not seem to support the claim that this represented a delicacy (G. Dalman, *Arbeit und Sitte in Palästina*, vol. 3 [Gütersloh: C. Bertelsmann, 1933] 265; Halbe, *ZAW* 87 [1975] 333). Rather it represents food able to be sent easily to those away from home from a supply readily available. For newcomers from the wilderness, it would be a delicacy, in any case. The Israelites are not pictured as eating it in relation to a harvest festival, but simply eating grain ready to hand, growing wild in fields they had not planted. The same applies to מצות, "unleavened bread." This is the typical bread for a journey, that to which a wandering people would be accustomed. The point is not that Israel denied themselves the use of yeast for festival regulations. Rather, the point is one of joy. They could eat their normal diet with the prospect of much more to come because the whole land lay before them.

Joshua 5:10–12 shows one stage in the development of Israel's cultic history, a stage when Passover was celebrated on one day and included the eating of the crops of the new land in celebration of God's gift of the land. The seven-day festival of Unleavened Bread is unknown. The separate history of the two festivals is revealed in the early cultic calendars, where only Unleavened Bread is mentioned (Exod 23:15; 34:18) and in the Exodus narrative where each of the festivals is given a separate origin (Exod 12:21–27; 13:3–9). At some point in its history, Israel's cultic calendar united the two festivals (Deut 16:1–8; Lev 23:5–8). Israelites celebrating Passover under these new cultic conditions did not read our text in the same way it had been composed. For them the reference to מצות could mean nothing else than their seven-day festival immediately following Passover. Thus they interpreted the text by adding "on the day after Passover" (see *Notes*).

[12] The manna tradition is taken up from the Pentateuchal traditions, if not the finished literary product (Exod 16:13–35; cf. Num 11: 4–9; Deut 8:1–20). Israel has not conquered the land, but she can live off its bounty and no longer needs special divine provision. Yahweh proved himself to be the giver of the fruit of the land before he gave the fortifications of the land to Israel.

[13] The Bible consistently pictures Joshua as a rather brash young man asking questions and giving opinions in the most unlikely circumstances (Exod 32:17; Num 11:28). Here he boldly confronts the visitor and demands proper identification before permitting him to enter the camp. The camp is located "in Jericho" if one takes the most natural reading of the text. This ties in both to the previous location "in the plains of Jericho" and to the site of the following chapter, though it is unlikely that the present context means to place Joshua inside the walls of the city. Unlike the previous sections (9b, 10a), no attempt is made to tie the material here to Gilgal.

[15] "The prince of the host of Yahweh" appears only here and Dan 8:11, where the reference is to God himself. Our passage is more closely akin to the figure of the messenger of Yahweh who appears fifty-eight times in the OT, with eleven further occurrences of "messenger of God." Such a messenger commissions Gideon (Judg 6:11) and even appears briefly in the narrative of Moses' commissioning (Exod 3:2). Another brief appearance comes in the deliverance at the sea (Exod 14:19; cf. Num 20:16). Seeing the messenger can be equated with seeing God (Judg 13:22). As a military figure, the messenger destroys God's enemies (Num 22:23; 2 Sam 24:16–17; 2 Kgs 19:35). O. Keel (*Wirkmächtige Siegeszeichen*, 85–88) argues on the basis of Near Eastern art that the scene here is one of commissioning in which the messenger hands the javelin in his hand to Joshua, noting the javelin in his hand in 8:18, 26, as well as the "rod" of Moses in Exod 4:17; 17:9. Whatever the scene imagined here, the present narrative has drastically altered it. The prince is never given opportunity to commission Joshua or hand over anything to him. Joshua continues talking and acting. The scene thus pictures Joshua as the totally obedient servant doing precisely what the divine messenger requires. He needs no further commission. Chapter 1 has given that. What he does need is a) personal confrontation with deity that confirms his commission and b) personal devotion to deity which confirms his readiness for the task ahead. These are provided here.

[15] The messenger's words may have their ultimate origin in the stories of the founding of sanctuaries (Noth), but the present literary function is distinct.

The words are borrowed from the experience of Moses to attest once more
the dependence of Joshua upon Moses. Even his "call experience" with the
divine messenger is simply a replica of the Mosaic one. Wherever he turns,
Joshua cannot escape the Mosaic shadow.

Explanation

A theological depth funds this, as most biblical passages. The first level
comprises three isolated incidents. The example of Joshua's generation stands
as testimony that people of God undergo even the pain and inconvenience
of ritual, perhaps enduring gentle ridicule from their friends, to demonstrate
their loyalty to their God. Celebration of Passover provides opportunity to
enjoy the fruits of the land and look in anticipation to the fuller bounty
God will provide. Experience of the prince of God's armies assures the leader
of his role in leading God's people into battle.

Set into a literary context the materials charge one another theologically.
Circumcision is proper preparation for the observance of Passover. God's
people show themselves to be responsible in their preparations to celebrate
what God has done. In turn the act of circumcision testifies that their God
is active among them, rolling away their reproach and shame and establishing
them as at least equals in the councils of the nations. The action also provides
a name and a basis of authenticity for the sanctuary where Israel's history
of worship in the land began. Passover is the end of the story of God's saving
history with his people, an end which repeats the beginning of that story.
History has come full circle. The people who escaped the deadly visit of
God in Egypt through observance of the Passover, now observe the Passover
to celebrate the bountiful gifts of God's presence in the new land. The miracle
of manna is replaced by the miracle of fertility provided by God in the as
yet unconquered land. The land will be conquered, however, for the prince
of the divine host has appeared to the commander of the host of Israel,
and the human commander has proved himself worthy of the task given him.

For the exiles reading the history of the Deuteronomistic editors, the story
takes on still new meaning. Circumcision was not unique in Canaan, but it
is in the land of captivity. In Babylon the ritual of circumcision is certainly
cause for ridicule and physical suffering. Passover is once more celebrated
in hope rather than celebration of a gift already given. The prince of the
heavenly host appears to be the only hope, unless God might send him to
the king in exile (cf. 2 Kgs 25:27–30). The story can be read as a call for
obedient worship on the part of the king.

After the return from exile, the narrative continues to speak to the people
of God. Their own cultic celebration is now undergirded. To be circumcised
again may be a call to portions of the community who had, like the wilderness
generation, neglected the rituals of their people in a foreign land or under
persecution and hopelessness. It is certainly a prerequisite for participation
in the new rituals of the new temple. The Passover at God's chosen sanctuary
on the proper date followed by eating unleavened bread on the day after
Passover is an example for the second temple community to celebrate again
God's gift of the land, this time the return to the land after a journey across

a different wilderness. Such celebration for the second temple community would involve both the Feast of Passover and of Unleavened Bread. After such proper worship, Israel could expect renewed opportunity to enjoy the fruits of the land. Perhaps then the prince of the heavenly hosts would again appear, this time even to a new Joshua (cf. Hag 1:1, 12; 2:2, 4; Zech 3; etc.).

Joshua 5 thus stood through many generations as a testimony to God's greatness in enduring the unfaithfulness of one generation of Israelites and stirring new hopes in a new generation. It stood as a call to each generation to cultic faithfulness even when the result might be shame, reproach, or suffering. It stood as a call to remember God's gift of fertility, a gift given to a faithful people. It stood as a promise of divine appearance and divine protection for a leader ready to worship and obey.

Faith Fells Fortifications (6:1-27)

Bibliography

Abel, F. M. "Les stratagèmes dans le Livre de Josué." *RB* 56 (1949) 321–39. **Baars, W.** *New Syro-Hexaplaric Texts.* Leiden: E. J. Brill, 1968, 101–3. **Bimson, J. J.** *Redating the Exodus and Conquest.* JSOTSup 5. Sheffield: University of Sheffield, 1978, esp. 115–45. **Brekelmans, C. H. W.** *De Ḥerem in het Oude Testament.* Nijmegen: Centrale Drukkerij, 1959, 86–92. **Burgmann, H.** "Der Josuafluch zur Zeit des Makkabäers Simon (143–34 v. Chr.)." *BZ* 19 (1975) 26–40. **Delcor, M.** "Le trésor de la maison de Yahweh des origines à l'exil." *VT* 12 (1962) 353–77. **Dus, J.** "Die Analyse zweier Ladeerzählungen des Josuabuches (Jos 3–4 und 6)." *ZAW* 72 (1960) 107–34. **Franken, H. J.** "Tell es-Sultan and Old Testament Jericho." *OTS* 14 (1965) 189–200. **Gevirtz, S.** "Jericho and Shechem: A Religio-Literary Aspect of City Destruction." *VT* 13 (1963) 52–62. **Kenyon, K. M.** *Digging Up Jericho.* London: Ernest Benn, 1957. ———. "Jericho." *EAEHL* 2 (1976) 550–64, 575. **Kraus, H. J.** *Gottesdienst in Israel.* 2nd ed. München: Chr. Kaiser Verlag, 1962, 185–89. **Maier, J.** *Das altisraelitische Ladeheiligtum.* BZAW 93. Berlin: Alfred Töpelmann, 1965, 32–39. **McKenzie, J. L.** *The World of the Judges.* Englewood Cliffs, N.J.: Prentice-Hall, 1966, 52–54. **Möhlenbrink, K.** "Die Landnahmensagen des Buches Josua." *ZAW* 56 (1938) 258–59. **Noth, M.** "Der Beitrag der Archäologie zur Geschichte Israels." VTSup 7 (1960) 262–82. (=*Aufsätze zur biblischen Landes- und Altertumskunde.* vol. 1. Neukirchen-Vluyn: Neukirchener Verlag, 1971, 34–51.) ———. "Grundsätzliches zur geschichtlichen Deutung archälogischer Befunde auf dem Boden Palästinas." *PJ* 34 (1938) 7–22. (=*Aufsätze* 1, 3–16.) ———. "Hat die Bibel doch recht?" *Festschrift für Günter Dehn,* ed. W. Schneemelcher. Neukirchen: Neukirchener Verlag, 1957, 7–22. (=*Aufsätze* 1, 17–33.) **Otto, E.** *Das Mazzotfest in Gilgal.* BWANT 107. Stuttgart: W. Kohlhammer Verlag, 1975, 65–86, 191–98. **Rudolph, W.** *Der "Elohist" von Exodus bis Josua.* BZAW 68. Berlin: Alfred Töpelmann, 1938, 182–88. **Schottroff, W.** *Der altisraelitische Fluchspruch.* WMANT 30. Neukirchen-Vluyn: Neukirchener Verlag, 1969, 150–52, 212–14. **Soggin, J. A.** "Gerico: anatomia di una conquista." *Protestantesimo* 29 (1974) 193–213. ———. "Gilgal, Passah und Landnahme." VTSup 15 (1965) 263–77. **Stolz, F.** *Jahwes und Israels Kriege.* ATANT 60. Zürich: Theologischer Verlag, 1972, 66–68. **de Vaux, R.** *Histoire ancienne d'Israël.* vol. 1. Paris: J. Gabalda, 1971, 560–63. (=*The Early History of Israel.* Tr. D. Smith. London:

Darton, Longman & Todd, 1978, 608–12.) **Vincent, A.** "Jéricho, une hypothèse." *Mélanges de l'Université Saint Joseph* 37 (1960–61) 81–90. **Wellhausen, J.** *Die Composition des Hexateuchs und der historischen Bücher des Alten Testaments.* 2nd ed. Berlin: Georg Reimer, 1889, 122–25. **Wendel, A.** *Das freie Laiengebet im vorexilischen Israel.* Leipzig: Pfeiffer, 1931. **Wilcoxen, J. A.** "Narrative Structure and Cult Legend: A Study of Joshua 1–6." *Transitions in Biblical Scholarship*, ed. J. C. Rylaarsdam. Chicago: University of Chicago Press, 1968, 43–70. **Wright, G. E.** *Biblical Archaeology.* 2nd ed. Philadelphia: Westminster, 1962, 76–80.

Translation

[1] *Now Jericho was totally sealed off* [a] *in face of the sons of Israel.* [b] *No one could leave or enter.* [2] *Then Yahweh said to Joshua, "Look, I have given into your hand Jericho and her king, valiant warriors.* [a]

[3] *You all shall encircle the city, all the warriors marching around the city one time. So you shall do six days.* [a] [4] *Seven priests shall carry seven trumpets of rams'* [a] *horns before the ark. But on the seventh day you all shall encircle the city seven times while the priests blow on their trumpets.* [5] *With the prolonging of the ram's horn, when you all hear the sound of the trumpet,* [a] *all the people shall shout the great war cry. Then the walls of the city will fall down under it. The people will go up, each straight ahead."* [6] *Joshua, the son of Nun, called to the priests and said to them, "Lift the ark of the covenant while seven priests lift seven trumpets of rams' horns before the ark of Yahweh."* [a] [7] *They said to the people, "Pass over and encircle the city, while the armed men pass over before the ark of Yahweh."* [8] *As Joshua spoke to the people,* [a] *the seven priests carrying seven trumpets of rams' horns before Yahweh passed over and blew in the trumpets. All the while the ark of the covenant of Yahweh was moving along behind them.* [9] *Meanwhile, the armed men were moving along before the priests, who were blowing the trumpets, while the rear guard* [a] *was moving along after the ark, blowing the trumpets continuously.* [10] *But as for the people, Joshua commanded them, "Do not shout nor cause your voices to be heard. Do not let a word go out from your mouth until the day when I* [a] *tell you all to shout. Then you shall* SHOUT!*"* [11] *Then he made* [a] *the ark of Yahweh encircle the city, marching around one time. They came to the camp and spent the night in the camp.*

[12] *Joshua rose up early in the morning.* [a] [13] *The priests carried the ark of Yahweh, while seven priests carrying seven trumpets of rams' horns before the ark of Yahweh were moving along. They blew on the trumpets continuously.* [a] *But the armed men were moving before them, while the rear guard was marching behind the ark of Yahweh, blowing continuously on the trumpets.* [14] *They encircled the city on the second day one time, and then they returned to camp. So they did six days.*

[15] *On the seventh day, they rose up early as the dawn came up. They encircled the city according to this procedure seven times.* [a] [16] *Only on the seventh time, the priests blew on the trumpets. Then Joshua said to the people, "*SHOUT! *for Yahweh has given to you the city.* [17] *The city shall be put under the ban, it and all that is in it, to Yahweh.* [a] *Only Rahab, the harlot, shall live, she and all that is with her in the house, for she hid the messengers whom we sent out.* [b] [18] *Only you all be sure to keep away from the banned goods lest you all should set up the ban and then you would take something from the banned goods. You would then set up the camp of Israel for the ban and would make it taboo.* [19] *Indeed, all the silver and gold and*

the vessels of bronze and iron are sanctified for Yahweh. The treasury of Yahweh it shall enter."

²⁰ *Then the people shouted.*ᵃ *They blew on the trumpets. When the people heard the sound of the trumpet, the people shouted out the great cry. Then the wall fell under it, and the people went up to the city, each straight ahead, and they captured the city.*ᵃ ²¹ *They set everything in the city under the ban, male and female, young and old, cattle, sheep, and donkey were devoted to the sword.* ²² *But to the two men who had spied out the land, Joshua said, "Enter the house of the woman, the prostitute, and bring out from there the woman and all that belongs to her just as you swore to her."*ᵃ ²³ *The young spies entered and brought out Rahab and her father and her mother and her brother and all that belonged to her. All her clan they brought out. They let them rest outside the camp of Israel.* ²⁴ *But the city they burned with fire and everything which was in it. Only the silver and the gold and the utensils of bronze and iron they gave to the treasury house of Yahweh.* ²⁵ *As for Rahab the harlot and her father's house and all that belonged to her, Joshua saved them all alive. She has dwelt in the midst of Israel until this day, because she hid the messengers whom Joshua sent to spy out Jericho.*

²⁶ *Joshua swore at that time, "Cursed be the man before Yahweh who should raise and build this city, namely Jericho. With his first born shall he lay its foundation, and with his youngest shall he establish its gates."*ᵃ ²⁷ *Yahweh was with Joshua, and his reputation was in all the land.*

Notes

1.a. Two items in the text of chap. 6 are of particular interest. The LXX is considerably shorter than MT, and the Hebrew syntax appears to go to great lengths to avoid the normal consecution of tenses. The basis of the first problem must be examined in individual detail. (cf. Steuernagel). The second points anew to the pressing need for renewed study of Hebrew word order in relationship to syntactical meaning. The present translation relies heavily on principles set out by T. O. Lambdin (*Introduction to Biblical Hebrew;* [*New York: Charles Scribner's Sons, 1981*]) *and F. I. Andersen* (*Sentence*). Often the narrator is attempting to present several scenes with contemporaneous action rather than the more normal Hebrew manner of describing events in succession.

1.b. "In face of the sons of Israel" is lacking in the LXX. It may well be an "explanatory" plus in the later Hebrew tradition (cf. Benjamin, 34).

2.a. The concluding phrase "valiant warriors" fits the Hebrew syntax no better than the English, there being no conjunction nor possessive pronoun. The expression appears only in the Deuteronomistic history (Josh 1:14; 6:2; 10:7; 2 Kgs 15:20; 24:14) and often in the Chronicler. In the singular the phrase appears only in Ruth 2:1 outside the two histories. It is a synonym for "warriors" in v 3 and may originally have been placed there as a marginal gloss on the text (cf. Noth, Benjamin).

3.a. The two major verbs are both second person, but the first is plural and the second singular. The text thus switches from speech to Joshua (v 2) to speech to the warriors (v 3) to speech to Joshua (3b). LXX reads singular throughout, but represents a much shorter text in vv 3–5, lacking any equivalent to 3aB, b, 4. This heightens both the military and the miraculous (cf. walls fall αὐτόματα "by themselves, of their own accord," v 5). LXX preserves narrative tension, while MT describes minute divine commandment precisely followed. The latter may represent later scribal interpretation and expansion. The expansion of the miraculous element in LXX may represent similar expansion.

4.a. The Hebrew root יובל, translated "ram" throughout this chapter, has that meaning only here and Exod 19:13. Otherwise it refers to the year of release or jubilee (cf. Lev chaps. 25, 27; Num 36:4). LXX never translates the term (cf. Benjamin, 35). The horns here are short instruments for signaling rather than musical trumpets (Hertzberg, 40).

5.a. "When you hear the sound of the trumpet" is lacking in LXX and may represent expansion on the basis of v 20.

6.a. Joshua's statement in 6b is lacking in LXX, while MT (*Kethib*) has the speaker of v 7 in the plural, perhaps representing a tradition where the priests mediated between Joshua and the people. MT of 6 again represents the tendency to have Joshua spell out every detail prior to execution (cf. vv 8, 13).

8.a. LXX lacks reference to Joshua's speaking, a statement in tension with the plural verb of v 7 (*Kethib*) but in accord with the singular tradition of *Qere*, mss, and versions. LXX presents further instructions, while MT describes the beginning of the action. MT thus initiates action before the conclusion of the instructions. This is further evidence of the ongoing scribal interpretation of the tradition as command and immediate fulfillment (cf v. 4).

9.a. LXX continues v 9 as instruction, but knows only two groups: warriors in the lead followed by a rear guard of priests with the ark in the middle. This contradicts the LXX order in v 8. MT leaves the subject of "blowing the trumpets continuously" ambiguous. The Targum variant noted by Soggin (81) identifies the house of Dan as the rearguard. The original tradition apparently sought to surround the holy place with military guard. LXX sought rather to underline the role of the priests and the ark.

10.a. LXX has the third person subject with redundant subject pronoun, based on a misreading of the unpointed text and later interpretation awaiting direct command from God.

11.a. The causative form is not represented by the versions, where the ark is subject. MT represents continued emphasis on the role of Joshua.

12.a. LXX adds "second day" here, while MT waits until v 14. MT is probably original. V 11 is unprepared for in LXX so that reference to second day in v 12 makes clear that v 11 depicts day one.

13.a. LXX changes the marching order, the priests being in front of the warriors, contradicting its own order in v 9 and probably representing a scribal mistake. MT repeats the trumpet blowing, the second being without clear subject. LXX omits the first reference and makes the priests clearly the subject of the second. MT may reflect scribal mistake.

15.a. LXX omits "according to this procedure" and mentions only six times, leaving the seventh for the next verse. It lacks 15b, probably a later expansion, making explicit reference to obedience to command.

17.a. LXX adds "Sabbaoth" transliterating the divine title "lord of hosts." This is one of several examples where titles of divine objects and of deity are expanded in the written as well as the oral tradition. Compare references to the ark in this chapter.

ᴾ LXX lacks "for she . . . sent out," preserving it for v 25, from which it has probably entered MT at this point.

20.a. "The people shouted" is premature in the context and missing from LXX. It probably represents a copyist's error based on the second half of the verse. Explicit reference to the priests as the ones blowing the trumpet (LXX) is not essential to the context. Simultaneity of the war cry (LXX) also reflects expansion.

21.a. LXX lacks the final clause which may be expansion. Margolis (95) suggests the possibility of homoeoteleuton.

21.a. LXX makes Joshua the subject, joining the tradition of expanding his role.

22.a. LXX lacks reference to the oath, another example of MT expansion emphasizing precise fulfillment of command.

26.a. LXX adds explicit reference to the fulfillment of the curse, taken from 1 Kgs 16:34, another example of scribal interpretation of the text to show explicit fulfillment.

Form/Structure/Setting

The *Notes* have shown again the extensive interpretation given the material in its use in Israel prior to the written fixation of the canon. Closer literary study reveals further stages in that interpretation process. Several elements of the narrative demand explanation. How does the total silence of the people (v 10) relate to the constant blaring of the horns (vv 8, 9, 13)? Do not vv 4–5 presuppose that the priests will blow the horns only on the seventh day? What is the relationship in duty and in marching order of the men of war (v 3), the armed men (vv 7, 9, 13), the rear guard (vv 9, 13), and the priests? Do the various conversations reflect a chain of command, or are various groups and individuals recipients of divine command? Why is the final Priestly signal recorded twice (vv 16, 20)? Why is the destruction of the city reported twice (vv 21, 24)?

Scholars have formulated various theories to answer these questions. Eissfeldt (*Introduction*, 252–53) found three literary sources, while Otto (*Mazzotfest*, 84–86; cf Wellhausen, *Composition*, 122–25) reduced this to two. Noth spoke of a growth of tradition and final redaction. Dus (*ZAW* 72 [1960] 119–20) and Kraus (*Gottesdienst*, 187–89) seek to reconstruct a cultic ritual which gave rise to the tradition. Wilcoxen ("Narrative Structure," 52–53) has opted for three slightly different forms of cultic ritual as the basis for the story.

Certainly the strict literary theory is difficult to sustain in its traditional form, for it assumes that different sources differed only on points of cultic acts, the basic narrative of the fall of the city being the same in all sources and thus not producing doublets in the final redaction. Still, the LXX reveals that literary interpretation continued to produce differences in the material until a quite late date. Such new interpretation is, in the final analysis, only a continuation of the growth of tradition posited by Noth. Our task is to determine as closely as possible how that growth of tradition occurred and why. In so doing, we are aware of the cultic interests which are so evident in the material and must constantly ask what role the cult played both in preserving and in interpreting the traditions.

Analysis of the growth of tradition can best begin with isolation of the important traditional elements involved. Of primary importance here are Joshua, the holy war scheme, Rahab, the ark, the treasury house of God, the seige of Jericho, and the Priestly celebration. The role of Joshua may well be the most elusive element in the text. The story is now told to celebrate the fame of Joshua (v 27). The switches between singular and plural address (vv 3, 6–7); the LXX wherein Joshua is not the subject of action (vv 10, 11), the double introduction of Joshua into the narrative (vv 2, 6), the doublet of the climactic shout (vv 16, 20), one of which (v 20) does not mention Joshua, may all point to a stage of the tradition which did not include Joshua.

The scheme of holy war is based on Deuteronomic theology (Deut chaps. 7, 20). It is also a part of Near Eastern warfare (Moabite Stone, *Anet*, 320–21). Here holy war does not form part of the basic narrative but represents a theological appendix (vv 17–19, 21), which causes doublets in the narrative.

The Rahab tradition forms a conclusion to chap. 2. Her house on the wall is basically incompatible with the chap. 6 tradition where the walls come tumbling down before she is rescued. Yet chap. 2 is complete in itself, and the vocabulary distinctions of 6:17, 22–23, 25 (D. J. McCarthy, "The Theology of Leadership in Joshua 1–9," *Bib* 52 [1971] 169–70) show that these verses represent a later interpretation (cf. B. S. Childs, "A Study of the Formula, 'Until This Day,'" *JBL* 82 [1963] 286). In fact, these verses function in the same way as much of the interpretation discovered in textual analysis (see *Notes*). They seek to make explicit the connection between original command or promise and final execution.

The ark tradition presents an element of mystery and intrigue to the study. It is connected with the encircling of the city (v 11), the armed men (v 6), the priests (vv 7, 12), but it disappears at the climax of the story. Elsewhere it is directly connected with war tradition (Num 10:35; 14:44; 1 Sam 4:3), but for Deuteronomy it is simply the container of the law (chaps. 10, 31). Here we may have a rather early element of the tradition, connecting the ark with battle. This was one role in which the ark symbolized Yahweh's leadership of Israel (cf. H.-J. Zobel, "אָרוֹן," *TWAT* 1 [1973] 391–404). The interesting element here is that in our narrative the ark does not lead. It follows.

The house of God tradition (v 24) is peripheral here, but quite important, even though LXX has ignored it. It is part of the holy war tradition and indicates the later date of that tradition, since certainly the Israelites had no house of God ready as they sought to gain a foothold in the land. Here again we see a clue that Israel updated her tradition as she told it, making it fit the circumstances and practices of the generation telling the story. For later Israel, spoils of war were to be taken to the house of God.

The siege of Jericho offers a possible clue to the earliest tradition. This is introduced in v 1. The city defends itself against siege in typical Near Eastern fashion. Other elements of siege warfare also appear. The army surrounds the city (vv 3, 14). An attack signal is planned (v 5). Men armed for war lead the divine symbol into battle (7b, 13bA). A rear guard followed (9b, 13bB), blowing horns of war (9bB, cf. *Notes,* 13bC). The troops have a base camp to which they return (v 14). Finally, the signal is given and the city taken (v 20). Behind such a tradition of military siege and capture may lie a story of military ruse and strategem such as hinted at in the story of Rahab (chap. 2) or narrated concerning the Romans (Y. Yadin, *The Art of Warfare in Biblical Lands in the Light of Archaeological Study* vol 1; [New York: McGraw-Hill, 1963] 99–100). Such a narrative is specifically tied to Jericho and would have originated among elements whose descendants identified themselves with Israel. It would from the first have religious elements within it but not yet be clothed in full cultic dress. The form of the narrative would not be etiological saga but popular war narrative, ridiculing the enemy, while encouraging the local populace by reporting how easy victory had been won with God's help.

Priestly celebration dominates the present text. Four basic elements compose the festive atmosphere. First are the priests. They may belong to the original story as bearers of the divine symbol. In the main stream of the present text, they, not the rear guard, carry and blow the trumpets. They play no essential element in the narrative. If they were totally removed from the story, the narrative would still be complete and even easier to comprehend. Addition of the priests is not due, however, to a literary editor. Rather, the priests have played an important role in the development of the narrative itself. Their role has been to transform the narrative from battle story to cultic drama. Preservation of the story has moved from the popular narrators of the community to the cult. There the story has not remained narrative. It has become cult drama, a means of remembering the great acts of God and of worshiping that God. The narrative now includes not only the original battle elements but also the description of the ritual elements used to remember and retell the battle.

The trumpets constitute the second festive element. They belong to the original battle narrative in the hands of the rear guard. Cult drama transforms them into cultic trumpets accompanying the drama and lending fanfare and excitement to it. No longer can they remain simply instruments to relay battle signals. Now they must be blown constantly, as occurs in cultic drama.

The third cultic element is the shout of the people. This may well have its basis in the war narrative as a signal of attack and an attempt to frighten the unsuspecting enemy. The cult has heightened and transformed the element. The shout of the people serves simultaneously to mark the cultic moment of victory and to raise the cultic shout of praise.

The fourth element of celebration is the seven-day scheme. It could possibly have a basis in the battle narrative as part of the ruse (cf. Yadin, *The Art of Warfare,* 100). It is most probable that the description of the second day's activities goes back to the original narrative, since it is somewhat disruptive in the present context (v 14; LXX 12). The present seven-day scheme reflects something entirely different—the week of cultic festival. But which festival originally? And where? The present narrative has linked the material to Passover (5:10) at Gilgal. This presents the problem of a seven-day Passover, something not apparently known in early Israel, unless this is our only clue. It also presents the problem of the relation of Gilgal to the tradition. We saw above that Gilgal is connected to Passover only at a secondary stage of the tradition. We also saw that a secondary stage of tradition also interpreted the festival as a combination of the Feast of Passover and Unleavened Bread. Such connection could come about in one of two ways. Either the literary tradition chose Gilgal as the center of the early traditions on the basis of geography and some early tradition, or Gilgal actually played such a cultic role in early Israel. The latter is the much more likely alternative. Early in the history of Israel, then, the cult of Gilgal celebrated the greatness of Yahweh and his gift of the land during a seven-day festival. Along with the Exodus Passover (Exod chaps. 12–13), this became the example for later Israel's cultic celebration.

At some point cultic celebration was reduced to writing, probably in connection with the collection of the basic conquest tradition. Here began a process which would not be complete for centuries, as LXX witnesses. What had once been popular narrative and then cultic drama became sacred, written tradition from which the community gained its identity. Several stages in such written interpretation are evident in the text. The earliest collector added the Rahab ending to demonstrate that faithful Israel fulfilled her promises and kept her treaties (vv 22–23). The collector may well have inaugurated the ongoing process of underlining every element as commandment and obedience. The MT reflects this in several places. Cultic celebration was reflected in the Priestly activities of v 13. This became command and fulfillment in the literary version (vv 4, 6, 8). The silence motif (5, 20) became total prohibition, faithfully observed (vv 10, 16, 20aA). The ark is now carried by the priests obeying Joshua (vv 6a, 12).

The Deuteronomistic historians also added their own special touches. This is particularly evident in the motif of the ban on all war booty (vv 17–19, 24). This also brought a further introduction to and interpretation of the

Rahab narrative (vv 17b, 25). Finally the Deuteronomist prepared for his story of the rebuilding of Jericho (1 Kgs 16:34) by reciting the ancient tradition of the curse on Jericho (v 26). The Deuteronomist also interpreted the whole narrative as one giving glory to Joshua by proving God's presence with Joshua (v 27; cf. chap. 1).

The long traditional process has produced a literary creation with its own characteristics and purposes. It is a paradigm of victory for the nation and especially for its leader. The paradigm is carefully constructed. The divine command is given (1–5), but then nothing else is heard from the deity. All is in the hands of the leader. He issues the battle plans (5–7), which are immediately (8aA) obeyed (8–9). A final command (v 10) closes the opening section of the narrative and silences the people prior to the battle itself (11–16). This is executed precisely as planned with Joshua as the causative agent. At the precise moment when victory is at hand, the action is halted. Victory plans must be given (17–19) in a tone of warning, demanding obedience. The section is then closed with the brief statement of victory itself (v 20). The final section illustrates obedience in victory as well as in battle (vv 21–25). The section is closed with an example of the curse of disobedience (v 26) and the blessing of obedience (v 27).

Comment

[1] Jericho is a crux for archaeological interpretation, the discussion of which has been opened anew by Bimson (*Redating*, 52–53, 115–45), who fails, however, to discuss the literary and tradition history problems involved (See the discussion in chap 2).

[2] "Given in your hand . . ."—See 2:24.

[3] The horns carried by the priests are variously named in the Hebrew text: שופרות היובלים, (vv 3, 6, 8, 13); השופרות, (vv 4, 8, 9, 9, 13, 13, 16, 20); קרן היובל, (v 5); השופר, (vv 5, 20). For יובל, see *Notes*. קרן is used to refer to an animal horn often (e.g. Gen 22:13), but as a musical instrument only here and possibly in 1 Chron 25:5; cf. Aramaic קרנא in Dan 3:5, 7, 10, 15. The term קרן may be archaic and derive from the original military version of the story. The שופר is the most frequently named biblical instrument and was basically used for signaling (E. Werner, "Musical Instruments," IDB 3[1962], 473). It was more of a noise maker than a music maker. (Cf. further, A. L. Lewis, "Shofar," *Enc Jud* 14 [1971] 1442–47; 12, 565; G. Cornfeld, *Pictorial Biblical Encyclopedia*, 537–42; M. Weippert, " 'Heiliger Krieg' in Israel und Assyrien," *ZAW* 84 [1972], 486).

[5] The shout of the people (יריעו תרועה) has a double meaning, as does much of the vocabulary here. It refers to the call to battle in war (Jer 20:16; Amos 1:14; 2:2; Zeph 1:16; Num 23:21; 31:6) and to the shout of religious joy (1 Sam 4:5–6; 2 Sam 6:15; Ezra 3:11–13; Ps 33:3). Both overtones are meant to be heard in the final form of the narrative.

[7] The Hebrew term עבר, "to cross over, to pass over," is often used in contexts connected with the celebration of Passover (Exod 12:12, 23) and is the key verb in Josh 3–4. It is not related to the Hebrew name for Passover (פסח).

[11] Any army besieging a walled city established a camp as a base of supplies

and as a base of defense against surprise attacks from allies of their enemies. Our narrative never states where the camp was located. The collector of the Joshua narratives understands it to be at Gilgal.

12 The information that Joshua rose serves two functions. It introduces the second day (cf. LXX, v 14), but more importantly underlines the commanding role of Joshua in all that follows even though he does not specifically appear until 16b.

16 Joshua confesses what God has already promised him (compare vv 2, 16), even when the victory is not yet clearly in hand. This is part of the paradigm of the divinely blessed leader.

17 The city is set under the ban (חרם). This has two roots. It rests on Ancient Near Eastern military practice, as evidenced for Moab by the Moabite Stone. But it is also a strong part of Deuteronomistic theology (Deut 7:20). That certain elements might be rescued from the ban and devoted to the treasury of God (v 19) is a specification not mentioned in Deuteronomy and represents one stage in Israel's interpretation of the ban. חרם in 6:17 is the only instance in the OT where men and goods are included. Everywhere else the verb, not the noun, is used in reference to men (N. Lohfink, *TWAT* 3, 199). It refers to the cultic dedication of these men and things, so that God, not man, receives glory and profit. How often Israel actually practiced the חרם is questionable (cf. Lohfink, "חרם," *TWAT* 3, 207). What is of importance for the present text is that חרם is understood as the goal of the entire conquest operation (cf. Josh 11:14, 20). Jericho's conquest is set up as the prime example of obedience to divine command (cf. the negative example of Ai that follows).

חרם is not carried out totally. Rahab and her family escape. The importance of this is underlined by the etiological formula placed at the conclusion (v 25). Israel understands its own identity to be that of mixed blood (cf. Exod 12:38). At least implicitly Israel's theologians understood that foreigners were welcome in Israel when they confessed the God of Israel (2:9–11) and helped the people of Israel (cf. 6:25).

18 חרם was not only a program for Israel to accomplish. It was a temptation in Israel's way. She could be placed under חרם if she violated the program of חרם set out for her by her leader. The danger was not only individual. The individual's act endangered the entire community. This is seen clearly in the next narrative.

21 Implementation of חרם follows the prescriptions of Deuteronomy 20 (cf. Deut 2:34; 3:6).

23 Israel did nothing to threaten the holiness of her war operations and bring חרם upon herself. She kept the foreign heroes outside the camp so that they would not bring cultic impurity upon the people. This is not the final word, however. Rahab and her family came to live in the midst of Israel (v 25).

26 חרם is depicted as complete, not only for Joshua's day, but forever. Whoever seeks to rebuild the city placed under חרם by Joshua will find his own family placed under חרם. An ancient curse formula, alive among the inhabitants of the region, is incorporated by the historian to illustrate his theological point. This is then made perfectly clear in 1 Kgs 16:34, another indication of the unity of authorship of the books Joshua-Kings.

Explanation

The story of Jericho entertained and instructed Israel for long generations. Each new historical situation added another dimension of meaning to the narrative. Throughout the long history of telling and interpretation, one message continued to ring out loud and clear: God fights for his people. The people of God testified repeatedly that what they possessed came from the hand of God, not the strength of men. Israelite audiences never lost the captivating awe and mystery of the lesson. The most ancient city of the land with its seemingly impregnable fortifications fell easily before Joshua and his God.

Such a wonderful testimony could not be left in the domain of the popular storytellers. It became part of worship, in fact the central part of the main worship experience of the year. The very identity of the worshiping community derived from the victory of God over the enemy. The audience no longer simply listened, laughed, and learned. Now they marched, made music, and marveled at the miracle. They remembered anew that the food they ate depended on the victory God had given and the protection he continued to give. The trumpets—calling the Israelites to battle and to worship—guaranteed Israel that she had never again to cower in fright before such foreboding sounds. Her God protected her just as surely as he had given her the land.

Liturgy became literature, expanding again the audience to whom it could speak the word of God. Now an Israel again embattled in international politics turned back to her roots for help. Again she found her identity. The identity still rested in the God who gave victory to his people. Now the people were called on to see that being people of God meant obeying the word of God. Battle plans and life plans were laid out not by man but by God. Even the general of the army had to get his battle plans from his Commander-in-Chief. This lesson became even more profound when Israel lost her land and marched into exile. Were the odds now more overwhelming than those faced by Joshua? Had God failed his people? Or had the people failed God? Might not a new obedient commander with an obedient people find anew that God would give the land into their hand? Was not the curse of God still upon those who rebuilt what he had destroyed?

Yet not every foreigner stood under the curse! Long ago Rahab had seen the deeds of God and confessed him as her God. Her reward lasts to this day. Was it not still possible for Israel to do mighty deeds in the power of her God which would win the nations to her God? Rahab stood beside Joshua as examples of the blessing of God upon an obedient person, no matter what the racial origin. Over against them stood the warning of a curse to whomever would dare disobey.

The Jericho story provided an illustration of God's promises fulfilled. He had promised to Joshua that he would receive the gift of the land and the presence of God if he were obedient to the command of God (chap. 1). Chapter 6 shows that Joshua listened to the command of God, carried out the command of God, received the land of God, experienced the presence of God, and enjoyed the acclaim of the people. What God said, he did.

Consequence of Covenant Curse (7:1–8:29)

Bibliography

A. *Archaeology and Geography*

Albright, W. F. "The Israelite Conquest of Canaan in the Light of Archaeology." *BASOR* 74 (1939) 11–23. **Bimson, J. J.** *Redating the Exodus and Conquest.* JSOTSup 5. Sheffield: University of Sheffield, 1978, 60–65, 215–25. **Callaway, J. A.** "Ai." *EAEHL* 1 (1975) 36–52 (bibliography). ———. *The Early Bronze Age Citadel and Lower City at Ai (et-Tell).* No. 2. Cambridge, MA: ASOR, 1979. ———. "New Evidence on the Conquest of Ai." *JBL* 87 (1968) 312–20. **Cross, F. M.** "A Footnote to Biblical History." *BA* 19 (1956) 12–17. **Dussaud, R.** "Le nom ancien de la ville de ʿAy en Palestine." *RHR* 115 (1937) 125–41. **Grintz, J. M.** " 'Ai Which Is Beside Beth-Aven.' " *Bib* 42 (1961) 201–16. **Kuschke, A.** "Hiwwiter in ha ʿAi?" *Wort und Geschichte,* ed. H. Gese and H. P. Rüger. Neukirchen-Vluyn: Neukirchener Verlag, 1973, 115–19. **Livingston, D.** "Location of Biblical Bethel and Ai Reconsidered." *WTJ* 33 (1970) 20–44. ———. "Traditional Site of Bethel Questioned." *WTJ* 34 (1971) 39–50. **Lods, A.** "Les fouilles d'Aï et l'époque de entrée des Israélites en Palestine." *Mélanges F. Cumont.* Brussels: Secretariat de l'Inst., 1936, 847–57. **Marquet-Krause, J.** *Les fouilles d'Ai (et-Tell) 1933–35.* Paris: Geuthner, 1949. **Noth, M.** "Bethel und Ai." *PJ* 31 (1935) 7–29. (= *Aufsätze zur biblischen Landes- und Altertumskunde,* Vol. 1. Neukirchen-Vluyn: Neukirchener Verlag, 1971, 210–28.) ———. "Grundsätzliches zur geschichtlichen Deutung archäologischer Befunde auf dem Boden Palästinas." *PJ* 34 (1938) 7–22. (= *Aufätze* 1, 3–16.) **Rainey, A. F.** "Bethel Is Still *Beitîn.*" *WTJ* 33 (1971) 175–88. **Vincent, L. H.** "Les fouilles d'et-Tell-Ai." *RB* 36 (1937) 231–66. **Weippert, M.** *Die Landnahme der israelitischen Stämme.* FRLANT 93. Göttingen: Vandenhoeck & Ruprecht, 1967, 28–36.

B. *Exegesis*

Abel, F. M. "Les stratagèmes dans le Livre de Josué." *RB* 56 (1949) 329–32. **Baltzer, K.** *Das Bundesformular.* WMANT 4. 2nd ed. Neukirchen-Vluyn: Neukirchener Verlag, 1964, 66–67. **Boecker, H. J.** *Redeformen des Rechtslebens im Alten Testament.* WMANT 14. Neukirchen-Vluyn: Neukirchener Verlag, 1964, 115–16, 141–42, 147–48. **Briend, J.** "Le récit biblique face à l'archéologie." *BTS* 151 (1973) 16–17. **DeVries, S. J.** "The Time Word *maḥar* as a Key to Tradition Development." *ZAW* 87 (1975) 73–79. **Hermisson, H. J.** *Sprache und Ritus im altisraelitischen Kult.* WMANT 19. Neukirchen-Vluyn: Neukirchener Verlag, 1965, 39–42. **Hölscher, G.** *Geschichtsschreibung in Israel.* Lund: C. W. K. Gleerup, 1952, 340–42. **Keel, O.** *Wirkmächtige Siegeszeichen im Alten Testament.* Freiburg: Universitätsverlag, 1974, 13–34, 77–88. **Knierim, R.** *Die Hauptbegriffe für Sünde im Alten Testament.* Gütersloh: Gütersloher Verlagshaus Gerd Mohn, 1965, 21–22, 27, 38–41, 106. **Long, B. O.** *The Problem of Etiological Narrative in the Old Testament.* BZAW 108. Berlin: Alfred Töpelmann, 1968, 6–7, 25–26. **Macholz, G. C.** "Gerichtsdoxologie und israelitisches Rechtsverfahren." *Dielheimer Blätter zum Alten Testament* 9 (1975) 52–69. **McKenzie, J. L.** *The World of the Judges.* Englewood Cliffs, NJ: Prentice-Hall, 1966, 54–58. **Möhlenbrink, K.** "Die Landnahmesagen des Buches Josua." *ZAW* 56 (1938) 259–62. **Mowinckel, S.** *Tetrateuch-Pentateuch-Hexateuch.* BZAW 90. Berlin: Alfred Töpelmann, 1964, 37–38. **Otto, E.** *Das Mazzotfest in Gilgal.* BWANT 107. Stuttgart: W. Kohlhammer Verlag, 1975, 89, 193. **Roth, W.** "Hinterhalt und Scheinflucht." *ZAW* 75 (1963) 296–304. **Rudolph, W.** *Der "Elohist" von Exodus bis Josua.* BZAW 68. Berlin: Alfred Töpelmann, 1938, 189–98. **Scharbert, J.** *Solidarität*

in Segen und Fluch im AT und in seiner Umwelt. BBB 14. Bonn: Hanstein, 1958, 115–
19, 249. **Schmitt, G.** *Du sollst keinen Frieden schliessen mit den Bewohnern des Landes.* BWANT
91. Stuttgart: Verlag W. Kohlhammer, 1970, 144–47. **Simpson, C. A.** *The Early Traditions of Israel.* Oxford: Basil Blackwell, 1948, 293–301. **Stolz, F.** *Jahwes und Israels Kriege.*
ATANT 60. Zürich: Theologischer Verlag, 1972, 81–84. **Tricot, A.** "La prise d'Ai
(Josh 7,1–8, 29)." *Bib* 3 (1922) 273–300. **de Vaux, R.** *Histoire ancienne d'Israël.* vol.
1. Paris: J. Gabalda, 1971, 563–70. (= *The Early History of Israel.* Tr. D. Smith. London:
Darton, Longman & Todd, 1978, 612–20.) **Wagner, S.** "Die Kundschaftergeschichten
im Alten Testament." *ZAW* 76 (1964) 255–69. **Wellhausen, J.** *Die Composition des Hexa-
tuechs und der historischen Bücher des Alten Testaments.* 2nd ed. Berlin: Georg Reimer,
1889, 125–26.

Translation

¹ *The sons of Israel disregarded the ban. Achan,* ᵃ *the son of Carmi, the son of
Zabdi, the son of Zerah of the tribe of Judah, took part of the banned goods. Then
the anger of Yahweh burned against the sons of Israel.*

² *Joshua sent men from Jericho* ᵃ *to The Ruin* ᵇ *which is beside Bethaven,* ᶜ *east
of Bethel. He told them, "Go up and spy out the land." The men went up and
spied out The Ruin.* ³ *They returned to Joshua and told him, "Do not make all the
people go up. About two or three thousand men should go up to attack The Ruin.
Do not make all the people exert themselves there, since they are insignificant."* ⁴ *So
about three thousand of the people went up there, and they fled before the inhabitants
of The Ruin.* ⁵ *The inhabitants of The Ruin killed about thirty-six of them and
chased them away from the gate clear to The Breaking Points.* ᵃ *They smote them at
the Descent. The heart of the people melted and became water.* ⁶ *Then Joshua tore
his clothes and fell on his face to the ground in front of the ark* ᵃ *of Yahweh until
evening, he and the elders of Israel. And they placed dust on their head.* ⁷ *Then
Joshua said, "Alas, O Lord Yahweh, why have you so certainly caused* ᵃ *this people
to pass over the Jordan to give us into the hand of the Amorities to bring about our
destruction? If only* ᵇ *we had been content to live beyond the Jordan!* ⁸ *With your
permission,* ᵃ *my Lord! Oh, what can I say after Israel has turned its back before its
enemies,* ⁹ *so that the Canaanites and all the inhabitants of the land will hear and
turn themselves about against us and cut our name off from the earth. Then what
will you do for your great name!"*

¹⁰ *Yahweh said to Joshua, "Get up! What is the reason that you are falling on
your face?* ¹¹ *Israel has sinned. They* ᵃ *have transgressed my covenant which I commanded them. They have taken from the banned goods, stolen, deceived, and put
them among their own things.* ¹² *Unable to stand before their enemies, the sons of
Israel turn their backs to their enemies, because they have become banned goods. Never
again will I be with you all if you all do not banish the banned goods from your
midst.* ¹³ *Get up, sanctify the people, and say, 'Sanctify yourselves for tomorrow, for
thus says Yahweh, the God of Israel, "Banned goods are in your* ᵃ *midst, O Israel.
Thus you are not able to stand before your enemies until you have removed the banned
goods from your midst.* ¹⁴ *You all must appear in the morning by your tribes. Then* ᵃ
*the tribe which Yahweh captures must draw near by clans, while the clan which
Yahweh captures must appear by houses, and the house which Yahweh captures must
appear individually.* ¹⁵ *The one captured with the banned goods* ᵃ *will be burned*

with fire, he and everything which belongs to him, for he has transgressed the covenant of Yahweh and because he has committed a sacrilege in Israel.' "

¹⁶ Then Joshua rose early in the morning and caused Israel to approach by tribes.ᵃ The tribe of Judah was taken. ¹⁷ He caused the clan ᵃ of Judah to approach, and he captured ᵇ the clan of the Zerahites. He caused to approach the Zerahite clan individually, and Zabdi was captured. ¹⁸ He caused his house to approach individually, and Achan, son of Carmi, son of Zabdi, son of Zerah of the tribe of Judah, was captured. ¹⁹ Then Joshua said to Achan, "My son,ᵃ set forth glory to Yahweh, the God of Israel, and give him praise. Then tell me what you have done. Do not hide anything from me!"

²⁰ Achan answered Joshua, "Truly I have sinned against Yahweh, the God of Israel. Here are the details of what I have done. ²¹ I saw among the spoils a lovely robe from Shirar,ᵃ two hundred shekels of silver, a bar of gold weighing fifty shekels, then I coveted them and took them; they are right there hidden in the ground in the center of my tent.ᵇ The silver is underneath."

²² Joshua sent messengers. They ran to the tent.ᵃ It was right there hidden in his tent with the silver underneath. ²³ They took them from the center of the tent and brought them to Joshua and to all the sons ᵃ of Israel and poured them out before Yahweh. ²⁴ Then Joshua took Achan, the son of Zerah, and the silver ᵃ and the robe and the bar of gold, and his sons and his daughters and his oxen and his donkey, and his sheep and his tent, and everything which belonged to him. All Israel was with Joshua. They brought them up to the Valley of Aching.

²⁵ Joshua said, "For what reason have you made us ache? ᵃ May Yahweh make you ache today!" Then all Israel stoned him with stones and burned ᵇ them in the fire and threw rocks at them. ²⁶ They raised upon him a great heap of stones until this day.ᵃ Then Yahweh repented of his burning rage. Therefore he called the name of that place the Valley of Aching until this day.

⁸:¹ Yahweh said to Joshua, "Do not fear nor be terrified. Take with you all the warriors, and get up and go to The Ruin. See, I have given into your hand the king of The Ruin and his people ᵃ and his city and his land. ² Treat the Ruin and its king ᵃ just as you treated Jericho and its king, with the exception that its booty and its animals you shall plunder for yourselves. Set up for yourselves an ambush behind the city." ³ Joshua and all the warriors got up to go to The Ruin. Joshua chose thirty thousand men, valiant heroes, and sent them by night. ⁴ He commanded them, "You are setting an ambush for the city behind the city. Don't move exceedingly far away from the city so that you, all of you, may be prepared. ⁵ But I and all the people with me will approach the city. When they ᵃ come out to meet us, just like the first time we will flee before them, ⁶ so that they will come out after us until we have lured them from the city, because they will say, 'They're fleeing before us just like the first time.' We will flee before them,ᵃ ⁷ but you all shall rise up from ambush and take possession ᵃ of the city, and Yahweh ᵇ your God will give it into your hand. ⁸ As you seize the city, you shall set the city on fire. According to the word of Yahweh,ᵃ you shall act. See, I have commanded you."

⁹ Joshua sent them, and they went to the ambush and settled down between Bethel and The Ruin, west of The Ruin. And Joshua ᵃ lodged that night in the midst of the people.

¹⁰ Joshua rose early in the morning and summoned the people. Then he and the

elders of Israel went up at the head of the people to The Ruin. [11] *Indeed all the army which was with him went up and drew up and entered near the city. They camped* [a] *north of The Ruin with the valley between it and The Ruin.* [12] *He took about five thousand men and set them as an ambush between Bethel and The Ruin, west of the city.* [13] *Then the people set up the camp which was north of the city and its "heel" west of the city.* [14] *Joshua went* [a] *that night into the midst of the Valley. When the king of The Ruin took notice, the men of the city* [a] *hurriedly got out of bed and went out to meet Israel in battle, he and all those with him going to the Assembly Point in front of the Arabah. But he did not know that there was an ambush for him behind the city.* [15] *Joshua* [a] *and all Israel feigned defeat before them and fled* [b] *the way of the wilderness.* [16] *Then all the people who were in the city were called out to pursue them. They pursued Joshua* [a] *and were lured away from the city.* [17] *Not a man was left in The Ruin or in Bethel* [a] *who did not go out after Israel. They left the city open and pursued after Israel.*

[18] *Yahweh said to Joshua, "Stretch out the sword* [a] *which is in your hand toward The Ruin, for into your hand I will give it."* [b] [19] *Joshua stretched out the sword in his hand to the city, whereupon the ambush arose hurriedly from its place and ran just when he stretched out his hand. They entered the city and captured it. They hurriedly set the city afire.* [20] *Then the men of The Ruin made an about face and saw right in front of them smoke from the city went up toward heaven. But they did not possess strength to flee in any direction. Meanwhile* [a] *the people fleeing to the wilderness turned back to the pursuit.* [21] *When Joshua and all Israel saw that the ambush had captured the city and that smoke from the city ascended,* [a] *then they turned and smote the men of The Ruin.* [22] *At the same time this group came out from the city to meet them. They were thus in the midst of Israel, one group on one side and the other on the other side. They smote them until there remained nothing for them, neither survivor nor remnant,* [23] *but the king of The Ruin they seized alive. They brought him before Joshua.*

[24] *When Israel completed killing all the inhabitants of the Ruin in the field, in the wilderness,* [a] *into which they pursued them, all of them fell* [b] *before the sword until their total extermination. Then all Israel* [c] *returned to The Ruin. They smote it with the sword.* [25] *Now all who fell that day both men and women numbered twelve thousand, all the people of The Ruin.* [26] *But* [a] *Joshua did not return his hand which he had stretched out with the sword until he had put to the ban all the inhabitants of The Ruin.* [27] *The only exceptions were the animals and the booty of that city. Israel plundered them for themselves, according to the word of Yahweh, which he commanded Joshua.* [28] *Then Joshua burned* [a] *The Ruin. He set it up as a Tell forever, desolate until this day.* [29] *But the king of The Ruin he hung on the tree until evening time. As the sunset, Joshua commanded and they brought his corpse down from the tree and cast it out to the opening of the gate* [a] *of the city. Then they set up over it a circle of boulders until this day.*

Notes

7:1.a. Achan is read as "Achar" in 1 Chr 2:7. LXX consistently reads "Achar" in all occurrences. This makes the play on the name of the Valley (v 26) more exact (cf. L. Koehler, "Hebräische Etymologien," *JBL* 59 [1940] 38–39), but MT is the more difficult reading.

7:2.a. LXX lacks "from Jericho," which demonstrates how one tradition has made explicit that which was implicit.

7:2.b. The city name Ai *means* "The Ruin" and is so translated throughout here to give the proper "color" of the narrative.

7:2.c. LXX lacks "Beth-aven, east of." Hosea uses the term Beth-aven, literally translated "house of iniquity," as a derogatory reference to the royal sanctuary at Bethel (4:15, 5:8, 10:5, cf. Josh 18:12). In 1 Sam 13:5, 14:23, it may represent actual geography, but this is uncertain (cf. H. J. Stoebe, *Das erste Buch Samuelis*. [KAT 8. Gütersloh: Gütersloher Verlagshaus, 1973] 244). Our text may also represent geography (Albright, *BASOR* 74 [1939] 15–17; Grintz, *Bib* 42 [1961] 210–16), LXX representing scribal homoearchton.

7:5.a. The meaning of the geographical term is uncertain. LXX appears to have read it as a military term meaning total destruction (cf. 2 Chr 14:12). RSV simply transliterates the MT; NEB translates "quarries," while Soggin (93) suggests "ravines." We have tried to retain the ambiguity of the MT based on the root שׁבר, "to break in pieces." The connotation of מורד, "descent," is equally ambiguous and might be rendered "the dropping off point."

7:6.a. LXX lacks "ark," and probably is based on a text in which ארון, "ark," had become אדון, "Lord."

7:7.a LXX reads "your servant caused . . . to give him (=people)," for the rare infinitive form (GK§113x) of MT. The double "correction" represents a theological interpretation of the tradition, avoiding any judicial charges lodged by man against God.

7:7.b. For לו, "if only, would that" cf. T. O. Lambdin *Biblical Hebrew*, 278. Lambdin (238) notes the use of יאל in verbal hendiadys. Cf. GK§120e.

7:8.a. בי, "with your permission," is an idiom used in addressing a superior and accepting responsibility for the result of the conversation (cf. KB³, 117; W. Schneider, *Grammatik des biblischen Hebräisch* [München: Claudius Verlag, 1974] 265).

7:11.a. The series of וגם clauses defies English translation. They form an "inclusive sentence" (Anderson, *Sentence*, 154) joining the parts into a whole. LXX lacks "stolen, deceived," later liturgical amplification of the text (cf. Josh 24:7; Hos 4:2).

7:13.a. MT fluctuates between sing. and plur. "you(r)." The versions harmonize.

7:14.a. The Heb. disjunctive clauses (Lambdin, *Biblical Hebrew*, 162–65) present the process as one continuous act with its parts rather than a series of acts in temporal sequence.

7:15.a. LXX lacks "with the banned goods," which the tradition added to make explicit what the original text implied.

7:16.a. Vv 16–18 do not carry out exactly the instructions of v 14. LXX has achieved grammatical harmony but lacks reference to 17bB, 18aA, processing of the house of Zabdi, as a result of scribal homoioteleuton, skipping from the first to the second "individually." This proves, however, that it read the MT "inconsistent" tradition of bringing both clan and house "individually" over against the instructions of v 14. Syr and Vg show that tradition tried to harmonize completely, reading "by houses" for the first "individually."

7:17.a. "Clan" of Judah is an anomaly. LXX reads the plural. Total consistency would require "tribe." The reading may represent a tendency of the narrative itself to polemicize, reducing the tribe of Judah to clan status.

7:17.b. "He captured" represents the more common verb form and is probably a scribal error for the passive form used elsewhere in the sequence. Cf. LXX, Syr., Tg.

7:19.a. LXX read Heb. כיום, "today," rather than בני, "my son" due to scribal confusion of letters (Benjamin).

7:21.a. LXX and Vg show that early translators were not sure of the meaning, resulting in a tradition of a coat of many colors here (cf. Gen 37:3).

7:21.b. MT article + personal suffix causes grammatical purists to change the text, but the tradition followed its rules and habits, not ours.

7:22.a. LXX adds "into the camp," an example of later exegesis explaining why the entire community was polluted (cf. reference to camp in 6:18).

7:23.a. LXX reads "elders" for "sons" perhaps in light of later practice and of other references in the context (7:6, 8:10).

7:24.a. LXX lacks list of banned goods, including only his other possessions. MT is later expansion in light of v 21. LXX repeats the leading into the valley at beginning and end of verse. The first reference may point to earlier text tradition without any list at all.

7:25.a. The verb used is a play on the name Achan and the Valley of Achor, using the root of the latter. The meaning is to trouble, to make taboo, bring destruction upon. The translation seeks to imitate the wordplay.

7:25.b. The versions omit redundancy, ending the verse after stoning (LXX) or burning (Vg, Syr). MT represents expansion to bring total agreement with command of v 15 and prepare for stone heap of v 26, thus understanding sequence of burning, covering of remains by stoning, and setting up of stone heap (cf. Soggin, 94).

7:26.a. LXX lacks first "until this day," a MT expansion making explicit that both the heap and the name survived.

8:1.a. LXX lacks "and his people and his city." MT represents amplification for completeness.

8:2.a. LXX lacks "and its king," an amplification in light of the following reference to Jericho. The LXX plurals for MT singulars are harmonizations to the context.

8:5.a. LXX adds "inhabitants of Ai" as explicit subject.

8:6.a. LXX lacks "we will flee before them," possibly dittography from 5b (Margolis, 126), or possibly a clause placed in contrast to 7a but not understood by later tradition (cf. *Preliminary and Interim Report on the Hebrew Old Testament Text Project* [Vol. 2; Stuttgart: UBS, 1976] 15).

8:7.a. LXX lacks 7b, 8aA, the first a later insertion of a traditional formula and the latter harmonization with v 19.

8:8.a. For MT "word of Yahweh," LXX reads "this word," representing the more original tradition. MT reflects prophetic tradition.

8:9.a. LXX lacks 9b which gives narrative preparation to 10a and narrative contrast to 13b, but still may be the product of the ongoing tradition seeking to harmonize and make explicit every detail.

8:11.a. LXX simplifies the geography and contextual contradictions in vv 11–13 by reading: "on the east side with the ambush west of the city." Auld (VTSup 30 [1979] 4–5) argues that "small is beautiful" and earlier, but the tendency of the ongoing tradition is to harmonize, which is precisely what LXX has done, omitting the contradiction in numbers between vv 3 and 12 and placing the two companies exactly opposite of one another, while MT sets one to north and the other to the west.

8:13.a. Several Hebrew MSS read ילן for MT ילך, thus "he spent the night" rather than "he went." This makes the contrast to 9b exact. An easy interchange of letters is involved and another explicit example of different Hebrew traditions becomes evident. Syr. makes the parallelism complete reading "people" for "Valley."

8:14.a. LXX reads all verbs in the singular, omitting "got out of bed," "men of the city," and the geographical details. The latter reflects the tendency seen in 11–13. The verbal changes and omission of the men of the city as co-subjects is "more logical" (Soggin, 95), which may show its character as later simplification and harmonization.

8:15.a. LXX adds "saw," making the obvious explicit.

8:15.b. Lacks 15b–16a, "and fled . . . to pursue them," due to homoioteleuton (Holmes; Margolis, 131).

8:16.a. LXX reads "sons of Israel" for Joshua, harmonizing with the context.

8:17.a. LXX lacks Bethel, an amplification making the conquest complete in light of contextual references to Bethel (7:2; 8:9, 12), the notices in 12:9, 16, and the greater importance of Bethel in later tradition. (But see Albright, *BASOR* 74 [1939] 15–17.)

8:18.a. LXX reference to "sword" is gramatically awkward and may reflect late addition (Benjamin; cf. Keel, Siegeszeichen 20–21).

8:18.b. LXX adds, "and the men in ambush will rise quickly from their place," an expansion in light of v 19 underlining the theme of prediction and fulfillment.

8:20.a. LXX lacks the last part of the verse, an expansion making the obvious explicit and dependent upon 15b, which may itself be an expansion.

8:21.a. LXX adds "into heaven," from v 20.

8:24.a. For "in the wilderness," LXX reads "in the mountain, at the descent." All may be later explication of "in the field" (Noth; Soggin, 96), but LXX at least reflects Hebrew tradition reading בהר במורד based on 7:5 (Margolis, 138).

8:24.b. LXX lacks "all of them fell before the sword," a later explication duplicating the end of the verse.

8:24.c. LXX may be original in reading Joshua instead of all Israel as the subject of the final action, thus giving prominence to Joshua at the conclusion of the narrative as in v 28 and the other narratives in this section. MT represents a harmonization to the context.

8:26.a. LXX lacks entire verse either due to inner-Greek homoioteleuton (Margolis, 140) or because it was doublet to 24b.

8:28.a. LXX adds the obvious "with fire."

8:29.a. LXX reflects Hebrew פחת, "pit," a transposition of פתח, "gate," showing two early Hebrew variants later expanded to "the opening of the gate of the city." This may find Qumran verification, according to Callaway (*JBL* 87 [1968] 319–20).

Form/Structure/Setting

The opening of the section is well marked by the concluding formula in 6:27 and the opening transition in 7:1. The ending is open to debate. A concluding formula appears in 7:26, but concludes only the episode of Achan, not the fate of defeated Israel and Ai. The latter is ended only with the concluding etiological formula of 8:29. At this narrative conclusion we break off the current section. Yet it is not theologically complete. Theological completion occurs only with the section 8:30–35. That section, however, completes not only our present section, but the first major division of the book as a whole. It also represents a totally independent tradition so that we will consider it in a separate section of the commentary.

The structure of the present section is clear and interesting. It is introduced by a general theological problem (7:1a): Israel has been unfaithful to divine prohibition. All that follows must be understood in light of the introductory theological problem. Verse 1b sets the specific details to the general introduction and gives the divine reaction. The problem is addressed through six narrative scenes: self-confident attack and defeat at Ai (7:2–5), national lamentation (7:6–12), public trial (7:13–26), salvation oracle (8:1–2), obedient battle against Ai (8:3–23), destruction of Ai (8:24–29). Each of the component narratives contains its own form and its own tradition. These must be understood if the present unit as a whole is to be fully appreciated.

The defeat at Ai is presented as a spy narrative (cf. Wagner, *ZAW* 76 [1964] 258) much more than as a battle report. Elements of such a narrative include the sending of the spies (7:2), the commissioning with a specific task (7:2aB), the report of the mission itself (7:2b), the return and report of the spies (7:3), and the attack (7:4). Such a form with much the same vocabulary is found also in Num 13–14; Josh 2; Judg 18; cf. Num 21:32–35; Deut 1:19–25. Certain important elements are absent. The spies are neither named nor given specific qualifying credentials (cf. Num 13:2; Judg 18:2, Deut 1:23). Nothing is done to establish certainty that the task will succeed (Josh 2:9–11; Judg 18:5–6; cf. Num 13:30; 14:6–9; 21:34). Most important the climactic formula of transference: "Yahweh has given them into our hand" is missing (Num 14:8; 21:34; Deut 1:25; Josh 2:24; Judg 18:10). Our narrative has unexpected additions to the spy narrative form. The spies plot battle strategy without reference to the Deity or his appointed leader (7:3). The battle plan is unsuccessful (7:4b–5a), and the concluding formula (5b) belongs in the mouths of Yahweh's enemies (Josh 2:11; 5:1; cf. Is. 13:7; 19:1; Ezek 21:12; Nah 2:11; Deut 1:28). An Israelite spy narrative has been ironically transformed into an explanation of how people of God become defeated enemies of God. It is set in exact contrast to Josh 2.

The liturgical element dominates vv 6–12. Defeated Israel falls to the ground in national lamentation. Joshua tears his clothes and puts dust on his head expressing both that he has been humiliated and that he is humbling himself before God (cf. E. Kutsch, " 'Trauerbräuche' und 'Selbsminderungsri-ten' im Alten Testament," *Drei Wiener Antrittsreden* [Zürich: EVZ-Verlag, 1965] 25–42). His prayer follows the typical lament pattern (cf. C. Westermann, *Das Loben Gottes in den Psalmen* [4th ed., Göttingen: Vandenhoeck & Ruprecht, 1968] 39–48), beginning with the address and introductory cry for help to God, the reference to God's earlier saving deeds, the lament proper with regard to the people, the foes, and God himself. But here, too, subtle changes are noticeable and informative. The reference to God's earlier saving deeds is not a motif "which should move God to intervene" (Westermann, *Loben*, 41). Rather it is part of the introductory cry for help. The history of God's salvation for his people is pictured as the reason for lamentation, not the basis of future hope. The confession of trust is absent entirely, but so is the petition, "the most constant of all parts" (Westermann, *Loben*, 39). Lamentation has been transformed from trusting pleas to God for intervention into hopeless complaint against the saving acts of God.

The lament can include or allude to an oracle of salvation (Westermann, *Loben*, 46–48) within "prophetic liturgy." V 10 introduces that here, but again a dramatic shift occurs. Salvation is not announced. Rather, a lawsuit ensues. Joshua is called to court to plead his case (cf. Mic 6:1; Ezra 10:4) rather than lay on the floor complaining (v 10). Yahweh makes the specific accusation against Israel (v 11). The accusation is justified by the evidence of history: Israel lost the battle (v 12). This gives the basis for the legal decision: They have become banned (חרם). That is, they are guilty (cf. Boecker, *Redeformen*, 141–42, 147–48; Knierim, *Hauptbegriffe*, 21–22).

Speech forms change again in 12b. Words of a cultic prophet address Israel directly in second person describing the process of ridding Israel of the guilt. The prophetic messenger formula of v 13 reveals the prophetic nature of the speech. The suggested procedure is concluded in 15b with a renewed double pronouncement of guilt.

The procedure of the sacred lot is carried out (vv 16–18), concluding with the call for the doxology of judgment (cf. G. von Rad, "Gerichtsdoxologie," in *Schalom*. [ed. K. H. Bernhardt, Stuttgart: Calwer Verlag, 1971] 28–37 = *Gesammelte Studien zum AT*. [vol. 2: München: Chr. Kaiser Verlag, 1973] 245–54; Macholz, *Dielheimer Blätter zum AT* 9 [1975] 52–69). This ends the court proceedings by letting the defendant admit his guilt while, at the same time, confessing the justice of the divine judge and of the announced punishment (cf. F. Horst, "Die Doxologien im Amosbuch," *ZAW* 47 [1929] 50–51 = *Gottes Recht* [München: Chr. Kaiser Verlag, 1961] 162–64). The confession is substantiated by the messengers (vv 22–23). The sentence is then carried out (vv 24–26). An etiological interpretation concludes the narrative (v 26).

Chapter 8 begins where 7:10 left off. Here we have the salvation oracle belonging to the prophetic liturgy. The liturgy had been interrupted by the long public trial. Only after the trial was complete, could the word of salvation be delivered. Over against the spy narrative, the salvation oracle leaves the directions for battle precisely in the mouth of God. The battle is presented in the form of a pretended flight leading to ambush (Abel, *RB* 56 [1949] 329–32; Roth, *ZAW* 75 [1963] 296–97). An almost exact parallel appears in

Judg 20:18–48: salvation oracle (Josh 8:1–2//Judg 20:18, 23, 28); preparation of ambush (8:3–9//20:29); attack and flight before the enemy (8:10–17//20:30–36); signal to ambush (8:18//—); attack from ambush (8:19//20:37); signal of smoke from city (8:20–21//20:38–41); victory accomplished (8:21b–23//20:42–48). The lamentation in 20:23, 26–27 is paralleled in the Joshua context by 7:6–9. Further this larger context includes the initial defeat prior to the ambush tactics (7:2–5//20:19–25). This suggests that the narrative of Ai represents a separate unit which has now been divided by the Achan materials. Such an assumption is strengthened by the fact that the Achan material is divided from its introduction (7:1) by the rather abrupt transition to the Ai battle in 7:2. Form critically then we have two major units: a) the story of Ai given in the form of a spy narrative introducing a battle of pretended flight leading to ambush and b) the sacral procedure against Achan. The two are joined by the lamentation liturgy, which is a component of the pretended flight and ambush narrative.

Other considerations point to the separate nature of the two narratives. The first is topographical and geographical. The Achan narrative is localized in the tribe of Judah at Achor (cf. F. M. Cross, "El-Buqeiᶜa'" *EAEHL* 1 [1975] 267–270). The Ai narrative points to a site near Bethel about thirty kilometers or eighteen miles across rugged hill country from Achor. Literary criteria include the fact that each narrative has its own concluding etiology pointing to a pile of stones over a man's body (7:26; 8:29). Further, Joshua's lamentation presupposes only the defeat of Ai and is answered by the salvation oracle of 8:1–2. Verses 10–12 consciously tie the two units together.

The questions then arise as to how the two narratives have arisen individually, how they have come to be joined, and how they are seen to function in the present context. The Achan narrative is Noth's classic example of etiological narrative. It is one of the few "pure, unbroken" forms found by B. Childs ("A Study of the Formula 'Until This Day,' " *JBL* 82 [1963] 281–82), but even he is reluctant to see etiology as the primary focus of tradition here (285, n. 18). Long (*Etiological Narrative,* 25–26) has shown how the etiology differs from primary etiological material: a) the valley, not the pile of stones, is named; b) the narrative points to burning (v 15), not stoning which is central to the etiology (v 26); c) the etiology relates to a minor theme, not the major narrative tension; d) the etiological form is disturbed and does not comprise an integrated unit; e) the name of the etiology is not essential to the narrative. Etiology, then, is not the primary setting for the Achan narrative. Instead, the narrative proceeds from the anger of God (v 1) to the discovery of the reason for that anger (v 13), to the removal of the anger (v 26a).

It is an example narrative teaching Israel how to deal with divine anger. The earliest form we can discover is at home in Israel's cult, where such sacral processes were carried out. This has been transformed into an etiology. Why? The content of the etiology offers the best clue. Rather than being a direct play upon the name Achan, the etiology plays on the root עכר, "trouble." Such a name is not given with patriotic feeling to one's homeland. Rather it represents a negative reaction. Similarly the narrative would not

be told by members of the family of Achan or of the tribe of Judah. It is a
narrative told by Judah's enemies. On both counts we are most likely in
the realm of tribal polemic. Study of the Ai narrative will amplify the point.

The Ai narrative represents narrative mastery. Every element is chosen
with the proper touch of sarcasm. Forms are transformed to give them the
ironic note. Israel has forsaken her dependence on God's oracles and her
trust in his salvation history to fight her own battles. In so doing she cannot
even conquer The Ruin, with its few inhabitants. This has incredible results.
The name of God himself may be cut off from the face of the earth (7:9).
All this because thirty-six Israelites were killed (7:5). But this story, too, stands
in etiological form (8:28–29). Childs (*JBL* 82 [1963] 283–84) has shown the
breakdown in form here. The complex narrative arc moves from self-confident
prediction of victory (7:3), to defeat and lamentation (7:4–9), to salvation
oracle with instruction for battle (8:1–2), to victory following the explicit
instruction of the oracle (8:22–27). The etiological elements are secondary
to the narrative arc. The narrative itself centers around the elements of the
wars of Yahweh (cf. R. Smend, *Jahwekrieg und Stämmebund,* FRLANT 84, Göttingen: Vandenhoeck & Ruprecht, 1963). The questions raised are Israel's dependence on Yahweh for victory, Israel's gratitude for her salvation history, and
Israel's willingness to follow the battle plan of Yahweh rather than that of
man. The story is at home in those circles which instructed Israel of her
basic identity as people of Yahweh, dependent upon him for their very existence as a nation. But it is at home where the identity as people of Yahweh
comes from the crossing of the Jordan (7:7). Thus it is akin to one strata
of Josh 3–4 (cf. 4:7). This is evidently the cult at Gilgal. The narrative has
been combined with two elements. It has become an etiology and has become
the finale to the Achan episode. The etiological element shows the long range
effects of Joshua's action. Ai is nothing but two heaps of stones. Why is
this significant? It stands over against the narratives of Judg 19–21. There
Israel, particularly Judah (20:18), had practically destroyed Benjamin, but
Benjamin survived with its towns and inheritance (21:23). In Josh 8, the action
is on Benjaminite soil. Benjamin's major sanctuary stands behind the tradition.
Ultimately the tribe of Benjamin stands behind the tradition. Benjamin has
used the same tactics as those in Judg 20 but with more lasting effect. This
is seen when the results of the study of Josh 7 are included. The etiology
there is polemic against a piece of land in Judah. The story there is about
a traitor from the tribe of Judah. The union of the Achan tradition with
the Ai tradition forms a narrative showing the superiority of Benjamin to
Judah. It could point to the time of the conflict between the Judean David
and the Benjaminite Saul (but see K.-D. Schunck, *Benjamin.* BZAW 86; Berlin:
Alfred Töpelman, 1963).

The two narratives joined into a new whole did not remain part of an
intertribal polemic. They were introduced into the larger conquest narratives
of Israel. Here they played a new role. They gave Israel claim to the territory
of Ai and Bethel "until this day," while demonstrating over against Josh 6
what happens when God's people seek to conduct war without his leadership.
For the Deuteronomistic historian such narratives then spoke to an exilic

audience without land and home. For them the narrative exemplified hope for a landless people seeking once more the leadership of God in giving into their hands the land. Such hope rested not on their own numbers or those of the enemies, but upon leadership and people obedient to the directions of God.

Comment

7:1 Israel's sin lies in disregarding (מעל) the חרם. The term appears only in the exilic/postexilic literature and appears to be the work of the Deuteronomistic redactors in our passage. It refers to the trust relationship between persons or with God and signifies a break in that relationship. Josh 7:1 is the only passage where the linguistic reference is to a thing (the ban) rather than to persons. Here the ban represents the divine-human relationship which stands behind it (cf. R. Knierim, "מעל-treulos sein," *THAT* 1 [1971] 920–22).

Divine anger dominates the opening narrative (cf. v 26). It represents the divine reaction to the human breach of trust and threatens the very existence of the nation. A basic theme of the Deuteronomistic history is taken up (cf. Deut 6:15; 7:4; 11:17; 29:26; 31:17; Josh 23:16; Judg 2:14, 20; 3:8; 10:7; 2 Sam 6:7; 24:1; 2 Kgs 13:3: 23:26). Israel cannot take her position as people of God or her possession of the land of God for granted. She is constantly under obligation to God. When she disregards that, his anger burns, and her position and possessions are threatened.

2 The geography ignores the destruction of Jericho and the camp at Gilgal (cf. 5:10). Joshua sends spies from Jericho to the city of Ai. Modern archaeologists (Marquet-Krause and Callaway, *EAEHL* 1 [1975] 36–52) have searched the ruins of Et-Tell for traces of Joshua's Ai. They found a city covering twenty-seven and a half acres dating from 3100 to 2400 B.C. and a two and a half acre village without fortifications occupied from 1220 until 1050. This has led to the conclusion that "at the time when the Israelites arrived in Canaan, there was certainly no town at Ai, nor was there a king of Ai. All that existed there was an ancient ruin of a town destroyed about 1200 years before" (de Vaux, *Histoire ancienne,* 565; *Early History,* 614). Or it has led to attempts to show that Bethel, not Ai, was the town really involved (Vincent, *RB* 46 [1937] 231–66; Albright, *BASOR* 74 [1939] 15–17). Or it has dismissed the narrative as another etiological invention (Noth). Two new suggestions have appeared recently. Callaway (*JBL* 87 [1968] 312–20) has suggested that the narrative refers really to the late stage of the Iron Age village of Ai, but this has been brusquely dismissed by de Vaux (*Histoire ancienne,* 568; *Early History,* 617); Bimson (Redating, 60–65), and Kuschke ("Hiwwiter," 115–19). Grintz (*Bib* 42 [1961] 208–16) has sought to locate Ai away from Et-Tell, which he wishes to identify with Beth-Aven. Soggin (99) has hinted at a relocation of Bethel. Livingston (*WTJ* 33 [1970] 20–44; *WTJ* 34 [1971] 39–50) then seeks to show that Bethel should be located at modern el-Bireh, Ai being at an unnamed tell nearby. Despite Rainey's objections (*WTJ* 33 [1970] 175–88), Bimson (*Redating,* 215–25) seeks to keep this option open.

Whatever view one holds, the fact remains that archeology has not clarified the background of our narrative. As yet, we cannot locate it in time nor space.

[3] The numbers in the narrative require comment. The spies suggest that two or three thousand men should go up. In fact, three thousand are sent (v 4). Great alarm breaks out when thirty-six are killed (v 5). The second time around Joshua takes ten times as many soldiers (8:3), just for the ambush. Later, only five thousand are set in ambush (v 12). The battle destroyed twelve thousand citizens of The Ruin (v 25). Several factors are at work here. The contrast between Israelites sent and Israelites killed is part of the narrative art seeking to ridicule the self-confident, self-reliant Israel. The five thousand in ambush may represent a traditional narrative, while the thirty thousand is set in contrast over against the three thousand when the Achan story was joined to the Ai battle narrative. The original battle narrative may well have shown the faith of Israel enabling the five thousand in ambush to destroy the city of twelve thousand. The twelve thousand also stands over against the spies' ridiculing of the city as having only a very few (7:3). In actuality, the narrator says, one city proved to have a population equal to more than a fourth of Israel's army (cf. 4:13). The task of taking the land was no small one. Self-reliant Israel could not do it.

[5] "The heart . . . melted" represents Deuteronomic vocabulary (Weinfeld, *Deuteronomy*, 344, No. 15). It represents one of the few Deuteronomistic flourishes in the narrative. It vividly expresses the fact that Israel has become the enemy rather than the people of God (cf. 2:11; 5:1).

[6] Joshua had fallen on his face once before, when he confronted the divine messenger (5:14). That was in the humility of worship. This is in the humility of defeat and shame.

[7] The ark plays no subsequent role in the narrative and may represent an element which entered the tradition when the ark was the central sanctuary symbol for Israel.

The "elders of Israel" have not appeared earlier in the book. They are included here to show that national lamentation rather than individual is meant. The elders represented tribal, then city, political leaders at different periods of Israel's development with fairly wide-ranging functions (cf. Ruth 4:1–12; Judg 8:14, 16; 11:5–11; 1 Sam 11:3; 16:4; 2 Sam 3:17; 5:3; 17:4; 19:12–13; J. Conrad, "זקן," *TWAT* 2 [1975] 644–50). The elders reappear in 8:10. Such cameo appearances do not represent sufficient evidence to reconstruct a history of tradition without Joshua.

[7] אהה is a cry of shock and hopelessness (Judg 11:35; 2 Kgs 3:10; 6:5, 15). It is most often used in addressing God (Judg 6:22; Jer 1:6; 4:10; 14:13; Ezek 4:14; 9:8; 11:13). The lamentation ritual contrasts sharply with the festal rites of chaps. 3–5.

[9] Joshua fears that the name of Israel and of Yahweh will disappear from the land. Here name refers to the fame, the reputation. Behind it lies an important theological development in Deuteronomy and the Deuteronomic literature, where God chooses to reveal his name, not his glory or his person to men. He chooses to allow his name to dwell in the temple, while he dwells in heaven (Deut 12:5–28; 1 Kgs 8; cf. Deut 26:15; 4:12; 2 Kgs 23:27; cf. G.

von Rad, *Studies in Deuteronomy* [Tr. D. Stalker; London: SCM, 1953] 37–44; Weinfeld, *Deuteronomy* 193–209; and the opposing view of A. S. van der Woude, "שם-Name," *THAT* 2 [1976] 953–55). The temptation of Israel was to see the name of Yahweh connected to her, her temple, and her power. The Deuteronomistic historian writes to show that Yahweh's power is not diminished even though his temple, where he has *chosen* to put his name, disappears. Israel depends for its name on Yahweh. Yahweh does not depend for his name upon Israel.

11 Israel's sin lies first and foremost in transgressing God's covenant. The verb used here is the same as used to refer to Israel passing over the Jordan (cf. chaps. 3–4; 7:7). Israel does not want to pass over the Jordan. She wants to pass over the covenant. The origin and meaning of covenant theology is the center of contemporary scholarship (cf. L. Perlitt, *Bundestheologie im Alten Testament,* WMANT 36, Neukirchen-Vluyn: Neukirchener Verlag, 1969]; E. Kutsch, *Verheissung und Gesetz,* BZAW 131; Berlin: Walter de Gruyter, 1972]; *idem,* "ברית/Verpflichtung," *THAT* 1 [1971] 339–52; M. Weinfeld, "ברית," *TWAT* 1 [1972] 781–808; D. J. McCarthy, *Treaty and Covenant,* 2nd ed. [An Bib 21A; Rome: Pontifical Biblical Institute, 1978]; J. Barr, "Some Semantic Notes on Covenant," *Beiträge zur Alttestamentlichen Theologie,* ed. H. Donner, R. Hanhart, and R. Smend [Göttingen: Vandenhoeck & Ruprecht, 1977] 23–38). A fully developed covenant theology is the work of the Deuteronomistic school, but the pattern is developed over long centuries of cultic worship (McCarthy, *Treaty and Covenant,* 15–16). According to the canonical pattern, God made a covenant with Noah (Gen 9) and with Abraham (Gen 15, 17). Both involved a promise of God, while the latter enjoined circumcision on man. Sinai represented the climax, where God set his covenental obligations upon his people, while promising to continue the special relationship with them (Exod 19; 24; 34). The Deuteronomist sees the covenant based on the ten commandments (Deut 4:13; 5:2; 9:11), particularly the first two commandments (4:23; 17:2). God is thus pictured as the loving God who keeps covenant (4:31; 7:9), but also as the God who remembers to punish those who break covenant (7:10–11; 8:19–20; 29:15–28). Joshua 7 then presents the first example of Israel—in the land—breaking the covenant. Immediately they discover the consequences: death. Israel becomes banned goods before God (7:12).

12 The key promise to Joshua in the book is the presence of God (1:5, 9; 3:7). Divine presence is the prayer of the people for Joshua (1:17), the basis of Joshua's exaltation (3:7) and the hope of possessing the land (3:10). Passing over the covenant has let all this pass away. All is not totally hopeless. There is a big "if." Obedient people will destroy the banned goods in their midst and again experience divine presence. Israel must choose between the presence of God (v 12) and the presence of חרם (v 13).

14 Criminal investigation is not left to men. God captures the thief. The process involved the casting of the sacred lot (cf. 1 Sam. 10:20–21; 14:42).

19 The culprit discovered in the sacral process is called upon to confess his guilt, which gives praise and glory to God by showing that the divine judgment has been just.

20 The confession is in general terms. The details are added only in the

following verse, causing many scholars to regard it as a secondary insertion
into the narrative (cf. Noth).

21 The first item which caught Achan's eye was "one fine luxury mantle
from Shinar." This could be a piece of clothing imported from lower Mesopo-
tamia, the area of the city of Babylon (Cf. D. Kellermann, "Überlieferungsprobleme alttestamentlicher Ortsnamen," *VT* 28 [1978] 424–25). The shekel
represented part of the Ancient Near Eastern weight system. Israel seems
to have had at least two systems (cf. O. R. Sellers, "Weights and Measures,"
IDB 4 [1962] 828–33). A shekel weighed approximately four ounces or eleven
and one half grams.

24 The Lord instructed that all which belonged to the guilty party must
be destroyed (v 15). This is now interpreted as meaning his family and possessions. Interestingly, his wife is never mentioned. The principle of community
solidarity may be involved here, so that the social focus is on the group
rather than the individual, the sins of the individual being seen as involving
the group (cf. H. Robinson, "The Hebrew Conception of Corporate Personality," *Werden und Wesen des Alten Testament,* ed. P. Volz, F. Stummer, J. Hempel
[BZAW 66; Berlin: Alfred Töpelmann, 1936] 49–62 = idem, *Corporate Personality in Ancient Israel* [Philadelphia: Fortress Press, 1964] 1–20). A more likely
explanation is to be seen in the conception of holiness. The spoils of war
are devoted to God and are holy (cf. Josh 6:19). As such they must be given
over to God. Their holiness contaminates man. If they are brought into the
camp they contaminate the entire camp, so that it must be sanctified, made
holy (7:13). Anyone who had come into contact with the goods was contaminated and had to be removed from the community to protect the community
(see J. R. Porter, "The Legal Aspects of the Concept of 'Corporate Personality'
in the Old Testament," *VT* 15 [1965] 361–380).

26 The point of the narrative lies in the action of Yahweh. He has turned
aside or returned from his anger. The relationship Israel did not regard (v
1) has been restored by obedience to the divine directions and removal of
the contaminating sin from Israel's midst. With the חרם no longer in her
midst (v 13), Yahweh can once more move in her midst without destructive
anger. Only as a holy people can Israel have the holy God with her. The
relationship restored must not lead to forgetfulness. The example must never
leave Israel's memory. Therefore it is memorialized in a geographical name.
Every time Israel approaches the Valley of Achor, she remembers the example
of Achan and dedicates herself once more to be the holy, obedient people
of God.

8:2 The king of Jericho is not mentioned in chap. 6. He is introduced here
to underline the total obedience of Israel in light of the large role played
by the king of Ai in this narrative. Specific regulations are given for the
ban here. Deuteronomy 20 lists only people to be destroyed, since the aim
of Deuteronomy is to prevent disobedience of the first commandment, not
to be specific in all details. War itself brought various vows and various interpretations of the ban as can be seen in Num 21:2; 1 Sam 15:3, 9–10. The
present oath is known in Deut 2:35, 3:7. The present narrative sets forth a
definite understanding of the banned goods so that it can be demonstrated
that Israel was totally obedient (v 27).

[7] The war strategy of man may work. He may possess the city, but the praise goes to God, not man. The ultimate cause is the Divine Warrior who gives the city into the hands of his obedient people.

[8] Such obedience is shown in that the people do everything according to the word of Yahweh (v 8). Such a word comes only through the divinely chosen spokesman. Joshua has commanded the word of Yahweh. Here again we see the emphasis on the person and role of Joshua.

[17] For the textual problem of Bethel, see *Notes*. The present Hebrew text underscores the understanding that Joshua defeated not only Ai but also Bethel at this time.

[18] The role of the sword in the narrative is not clear. Certainly it was not large enough to be seen by the ambush on the other side of the city. V 19 refers to the outstretched hand, not sword. V 26 (see *Notes*) sees the function to be one similar to the hands of Moses in Exod 17:8–13. There, too, the rod of Moses is mentioned in the context (v 9). Keel (*Siegeszeichen*, 51–76) has demonstrated the motif in Egyptian art, where the sword is raised in the hand of the victorious god. The OT places the sword in the hand of the general appointed by the deity. This demonstrates the power of the Deity working on behalf of his warring people. The motif may well be given to Joshua here to show yet another way in which he continued the work and ways of Moses. Keel (*Siegeszeichen*, 34) has shown the sword itself to be a curving sickle-shaped sword used in the Ancient Near East between 2400 and 1150 B.C. Thus it would not have been familiar except as a literary item to the first readers of the book of Joshua.

[29] Israel carries out the execution of the king according to the letter of the law in Deut 21:22–23. She has learned her lesson. She will not defile the land Yahweh is giving her. She knows the consequences.

Explanation

The two chapters show the reverse sides of warfare led by Yahweh. Warfare carried out in thoughtless self-confidence leads to disaster. Warfare carried out in obedience to each of God's commands leads to victory and possession of the land forever. The narrative of a sacred process has illustrated to Israel how she must act when she brings the anger of God upon herself.

These two chapters play a key role in defining the identity of the people of God. In so doing they stand in stark contrast to the preceding chapters. There the people of God were pictured in all their festal gaiety and victorious jubilation. Here people of God return to the reality of life, learning to deal with defeat. They learn that even people of God face the anger of God when they act in self-confidence, refusing to look to God for direction or give him the glory for victory. The lesson learned by the fathers in the wilderness had no effect on the sons in the Promised Land. They had to learn it all over again. From their experiences with the anger of God, they developed rituals to deal with such times of defeat. One such ritual was that of the sacral lot, whereby God captured the guilty party and demanded from him a confession of guilt and of the justice of God. The Psalms and the book of Lamentations show us that Israel incorporated this lesson into her worship.

She recognized the signs of God's anger upon her and learned to express her own anger to God. The NT continues this picture as it shows Jesus in Gethsemane and at Golgotha declaring his deepest feelings and even his sense of being forsaken to the heavenly Father. People of God cannot always be the people marching through the Jordan and around Jericho. Often they are the people in utter defeat falling before the Father with pleas for mercy and renewal.

People of God do not only have problems relating to God. They often have problems relating to one another. They feel slighted by other groups of the people of God. Tribal warfare can be the result. Tribal polemic is the literary result. Amazingly, even this can be taken up by the community and used as the word of God. As it is, the tribal polemic recedes into the background, but it stays clear enough to remind us hauntingly that even people of God have their struggles for power and need to learn from them.

Through the agonies of defeat and intertribal polemic, the people of god learned one major lesson. They learned what it meant to be the covenant people of God. Covenant meant more than simply accepting promises of God to multiply the nation and extend her power in the land. It meant more than going through the ritual of circumcision and the celebration of the yearly festivals. Being people of God meant accepting certain obligations set down by God. It meant adopting the divinely ordered life style. It meant making each decision of life in the light of divine leadership, not in the light of personal self-confidence. Even the Ruin could not be captured by a few of God's people relying on their own power and marching forth with no thought of divine leadership. Being covenant people of God meant looking back at salvation history with gratitude, not regret. It meant recognizing that God could undo the elements of the saving history, but he did it when he chose to punish his people, not when his people chose to retreat from hardship and setback.

In summary, the elements of chaps. 7–8 taught Israel the meaning of life in the divine presence. Only the covenant people could expect that divine presence, but even they had to learn that divine presence was demanding as well as promising. They had to learn how to react to a punishing as well as a promising God. They had to learn to value the divine presence above material prosperity. And they had to learn that the acts of man were only temporary, whereas the acts of God gave results lasting to this day. Through such results God assured the greatness of the name of his people and of his own name. This was important for the readers of the Deuteronomistic history in exile. These people were in the midst of defeat and wondered why the divine anger had replaced the divine presence. They worried that the destruction of the temple, where God had chosen to make his name dwell, meant the destruction of the reputation of God. Thus they were tempted to turn to worship the victorious gods. Joshua 7–8 told them to remember their covenant with God and their ways of admitting their own guilt and God's justice. Victory could lie just around the corner for them, just as it had for Joshua. God's anger was not his last word. He waited for the people's word of lamentation, confession, and petition. Then the salvation oracle would again resound among the people of God.

Fulfilling Moses' Orders   (8:30–35)

Bibliography

Eissfeldt, O. "Gilgal or Shechem?" *Proclamation and Presence,* ed. J. I. Durham and J. R. Porter. London: SCM, 1970, 90–101. **Hollenberg, J.** "Die deuteronomischen Bestandtheile des Buches Josua." *Theologische Studien und Kritiken* 1 (1874) 478–81. **L'Hour, J.** "L'Alliance de Sichem." *RB* 69 (1962) 178–81. **Keller, C. A.** "Über einige alttestamentliche Heiligtumslegenden." *ZAW* 67 (1955) 143–48. **McCarthy, D. J.** *Treaty and Covenant.* 2nd ed. AnBib 21A. Rome: Pontifical Biblical Institute, 1978, 197–99. **Möhlenbrink, K.** "Die Landnahmensagen des Buches Josua." *ZAW* 56 (1938) 241–45. **Mowinckel, S.** *Psalmenstudien* 5. Oslo: Dybwad,1924, 97–107. **Nielsen, E.** *Shechem.* Copenhagen: G. E. C. Gad, 1955, 74–85. **Noth, M.** *Das System der zwölf Stämme Israels.* Stuttgart: W. Kohlhammer Verlag, 1930, 140–51. **Rudolph, W.** *Der "Elohist" von Exodus bis Josua.* BZAW 68. Berlin: Alfred Töpelmann, 1938, 198–99. **Sellin, E.** *Gilgal.* Leipzig: A. Deicherische Verlagsbuchhandlung Werner Scholl, 1917, 40–41, 50–53. **Soggin, J. A.** "Zwei umstrittene Stellen aus dem Überlieferungskreis um Schechem." *ZAW* 73 (1961) 82–87. **Tengström, S.** *Die Hexateucherzählung.* Lund: C. W. K. Gleerup, 1976, 153–54. **de Vaux, R.** *Histoire ancienne d'Israël.* Vol. 1. Paris: J. Gabalda, 1971, 570. (= *The Early History of Israel.* Tr. D. Smith. London: Darton, Longman & Todd, 1978, 620.) **Vink, J. G.** "The Date and Origin of the Priestly Code in the Old Testament." *OTS* 15 (1969) 77–80. **von Rad, G.** *Das formgeschichtliche Problem des Hexateuch.* Stuttgart: W. Kohlhammer Verlag, 1938, 33–34. (= *Gesammelte Studien zum Alten Testament.* Vol. 1. TBü 8. München: Chr. Kaiser Verlag, 1958, 44–45.)

Translation

[30][a] *Next Joshua builds* [b] *an altar to Yahweh, God of Israel in Mount Ebal,* [31] *just as Moses, the servant of Yahweh, commanded the sons of Israel as it is written in the book* [a] *of the law of Moses, "An altar of stones which are intact, on which no one has wielded* [a] *an iron tool." They sent up burnt offerings to Yahweh and sacrificed peace offerings.* [32] *He* [a] *wrote there upon the stones a duplicate* [b] *of the Torah of Moses which he wrote* [c] *before the sons of Israel.* [33] *Meanwhile all Israel, including its elders, officers and judges, were standing* [a] *on each side of the ark in front of the Levitical priests,* [b] *who carry the ark of the covenant of Yahweh. Both citizens and aliens were there, half before Mount Gerizim and half before Mount Ebal, just as Moses, the servant of Yahweh, had commanded to bless the people of Israel* [c] *formerly.* [34] *Afterwards he* [a] *read out all the words of the* [b] *Torah, the blessing and the curse, according to all which was written in the book of the Torah.* [c] [35] *There was not a word from all which Moses commanded* [a] *that Joshua did not read out before all the assembly of Israel, including* [b] *women and children, and the aliens active among them.* [c]

Notes

30.a. LXX places the section after 9:2, where it disrupts the narrative sequence even more than in MT. Sellin (40–41, 50–53), Soggin (241–42), and others seek to connect it with chap. 24 due to the similar subject matter. We will try to demonstrate below the theological purpose in its present context.

30.b. The use of the imperfect after אז, "then," has often been noted (e.g. C. Brockelmann, *Hebräische Syntax* [Neukirchen: Kreis Moers, 1956] 42a; P. Joüon, *Grammaire*, §113i; W. Schneider, *Grammatik des biblischen Hebräisch* [München: Claudios Verlag, 1974] 197–98), but never adequately explained.

31.a. Here and in v 34, LXX lacks "book," which the MT tradition added to bring the text "up-to-date" with their practice.

31.b. The Heb. verb הניף, "wielded," has no explicit subject.

32.a. LXX adds the explicit subject "Joshua."

32.b. LXX translates משנה, "duplicate," as Deuteronomy, which literally means "second law."

32.c. "Which he wrote" is missing in the best Greek tradition. Its subject is not clear in the Hebrew. The immediate antecedent is Moses, but the intention appears to be to emphasize the work of Joshua.

33.a. LXX appears to have read עבר, "pass over," instead of the similar appearing עמד, "standing." LXX may represent an original cultic procession.

33.b. LXX read the text to refer to priests and Levites, reflecting the post-exilic cult. Deuteronomic literature repeatedly speaks of Levitical priests.

33.c. LXX omits Israel, an addition in MT tradition representing traditional vocabulary and concern to make the definition of people of God explicit.

34.a. LXX makes Joshua the explicit subject.

34.b. LXX reads "this" law, again pointing to explicitness.

34.c. Rather than "book of the Torah," LXX reads "law of Moses," repeating its reading of v 31.

35.a. LXX limits the commandments to that which was commanded "to Joshua."

35.b. LXX completes the list by adding "men." Originally, the "assembly of Israel" was probably understood as being composed of men. In the postexilic period women were admitted (Ezra 10:1; Neh 8:2), so the tradition added men to this text.

35.c. LXX makes "Israel" explicit here as MT tradition did in v 33.

Form/Structure/Setting

The section is a literary accumulation of citations from Deuteronomy:

v 30 = Deut 27:4–5.
31a = Deut 30:10 (cf. 31:24; 17:18; 28:58, 61; 29:19–20; 26; 31:24, 26(!); Josh 1:8.
31aB = Deut 27:5; cf. Exod 20:25.
31b = Deut 27:6–7; cf. 12:13–14, 27.
32a = Deut 17:18; cf. 27:8; Josh 24:26.
32b = Deut 31:9; cf. 4:13; 5:22; 10:2, 4; 17:18; 31:24.
33 = periphrastic combination of Deut 29:9–14 and 27:12–13; cf. 11:29; 31:9–13; Josh 23:2; 24:1; Lev 19:34; 24:22; Exod 12:49; Num 9:14; 15:29.
34 = Deut 31:11; cf. 17:19; 11:26–29; 27:13; 28:2, 15, 45; 29:26; 30:1, 19; Josh 8:31.
35 = Deuteronomistic summary of 8:30–34 based on Deut 4:2; 12:32; cf. 26:16–19; 27:1, 10; 17:18–20; 28:13–14, 58; 30:1, 8; 32:46, Josh 1:7.

The citations from the Deuteronomic imperatives have been transformed into narrative. Joshua has fulfilled each of the commandments of Moses, building an altar, offering sacrifices, writing down the Mosaic law on stones, assembling the people and reading the law to them, showing them both the blessing and the curse which lay before them. The section itself does not represent oral narrative. It is a literary composition of the final Deuteronomistic editor(s) of the book. It may well point back to cultic traditions of Shechem, but only the study of chap 24 will permit definite conclusions on that point. The major question for the present context does not concern the traditions behind the passage but rather the function of the passage in the present literary context.

The passage interrupts the narrative, moving the action suddenly and unexpectedly from the newly conquered Ai to the previously unmentioned Shechem. In the midst of warfare, the narrative switches to construction and cult. Why? The question has consistently baffled interpreters. Already in the middle of the last century, commentators had noted the fragmentary nature of the material and its unsuitability for the present context (e.g. Hauff [1843] 142–143; Knobel [1861] 388–390). In 1874, Hollenberg (478–81) could assume as generally recognized the fact that the unit did not fit the present context. The unit has been seen as so problematical that Soggin (222) simply moves it from its present context to chap 24 without manuscript warrant of any type.

If we ignore the geographical and chronological difficulties to look for theological explanations, the present passage can be more easily understood. The preceding section has contrasted the experiences of a disobedient people of God and of an obedient people of God. It has introduced the covenant terminology into the book for the first time and demonstrated what must be done for the individual clan which brought such trouble upon Israel. One theological question remained unanswered. How did the congregation (cf. v 35) which had transgressed the divine covenant restore that relationship? This theological question is so vital that the biblical editor ignored problems of geography, unconquered territory, chronology, and even literary unity to supply the vital theological answer. A people of God who have transgressed the divine covenant goes to the place where God has chosen and renews its commitment to all the law which Moses has set out for them. This involves participation in the specific cultic directions of the book of Deuteronomy. This shows us that 8:30–35 was inserted by the Deuteronomistic editor to answer what he considered to be the burning theological issue for his audience. It calls the reader to attention. He must not skip over the section as a literary problem whose original tradition cannot be restored and whose original context must be restored by scholarly ingenuity. Instead, the section closes the first major section of the book of Joshua, tying back through Josh 1 to the book of Deuteronomy, especially chaps 17, 27–31.

Comment

[30] Altars play only a minor role in the book, this being the first mention. Aside from the passing reference in 9:27, altars reappear only in the tradition of chap 22. The Deuteronomist recognizes the legitimacy of the sacrificial worship and of Israel's worship in various places prior to David's establishment of Jerusalem as the central sanctuary. He faces the problem that for his own time the altars of Yahweh have been destroyed, so that the complex sacrifical worship is not a possibility. What is possible is adherence to the law of Moses.

The particular altar is built on Mount Ebal, which is mentioned only in Deut 11:29; 27:4, 13; and here. The Deuteronomic literature thus portrays Mount Ebal as the place of the altar but also as the place of the curse. The

Samaritan Pentateuch places the altar on Mount Gerizim in Deut 27:4. This would be more consistent, but it also represents the regard of the Samaritans for their major sanctuary on Mount Gerizim. Polemic between postexilic Jews and Samaritans has most likely influenced the text tradition, but the original reading cannot be ascertained. In any case, Ebal, the great northern mountain overlooking the crucial east-west trade route is pictured as an important point of early Israelite worship.

31 As was seen clearly in Josh 1, authority for Israel is based on the law of Moses. Joshua gains his authority only as he follows that law. This section underlines the authority of Joshua by showing how he carried out the Mosaic commands.

Joshua's care to obey the Mosaic command is shown in that he follows primitive construction techniques rather than following the trends of modern architecture. The law shows that it originated among an Iron Age people. Normally, Joshua himself is dated to the Late Bronze Age, so that the passage is anachronistic in attributing to Joshua the possibility of utilizing instruments of iron. In any case, the law is not an invention of the Deuteronomist, for it appears in the Covenant Code (Exod 20:25), possibly Israel's earliest collection of laws. Similar altars appear in 1 Sam 14:33–35, 1 Kgs 18:31–32.

Two types of sacrifices are mentioned. עלות represents the offering of a whole animal in fire (cf. Exod 29:18; R. Rendtorff, *Studien zur Geschichte des Opfers im alten Israel.* [WMANT 24; Neukirchen-Vluyn: Neukirchener Verlag, 1967] 74–118; L. Rost, "Erwägungen zum israelitischen Brandopfer," *Von Ugarit nach Qumran.* [BZAW 77; Berlin: Alfred Töpelmann, 1958] 177–83). שלמים are always mentioned in connection with the עלות. They are offered on the altar at occasions of particular public significance (Rendtorff, *Studien,* 123–26). The precise meaning of the Hebrew term is debated. From the time of the early versions on, various translations have been made: salvation offering, peace offering, thanksgiving offering, welfare offering, offering of friendship or alliance. L. Köhler (*Theologie des Alten Testaments* [Tübingen: J. C. B. Mohr (Paul Siebeck), 1935] 178) suggests concluding or final sacrifice and is followed by Rendtorff (*Studien,* 133). G. Gerleman suggests a derivation from a verbal meaning to "pay," the sacrifice consisting of the fat pieces brought as a substitution for the entire animal ("שלם—genug haben," *THAT* 2 [1976] 932).

Whatever the derivation, Joshua is pictured as bringing the two major types of sacrifices on a special occasion and thus fulfilling the teaching of Moses. Such an offering may present Joshua in a kingly role (cf. 2 Sam 6:17–18; 24:25; 1 Kgs 3:15; 8:64; 9:25; Rendtorff, *Studien,* 78–81).

32 The function of the stones suddenly changes from altar to writing tablet. This results from the easily misunderstood base text in Deut 27:1–8, where plaster stones are set up for writing the law (vv 2–4), an altar is built for sacrifice (vv 5–7), and the command to write the law on the stones is given in the summary conclusion (v 8). The author of Joshua has summarized the material and in so doing has described only one set of stones, serving both for altar and for writing. In so doing, he reveals his own point of emphasis. He underlines the importance of preserving and obeying the law much more than building an altar and offering sacrifices.

The reference to the duplicate copy of the law has its literary base in Deut 17:18, the Deuteronomic description of the role of the king. The two passages have several points of contact which reveal another side to the image being painted of Joshua. He is a royal figure. Thus Weinfeld (*Deuteronomy*, 170–71) speaks of a "quasi-regal figure" and notes that David was the first ruler after Joshua to implement the Deuteronomic laws. Joshua thus becomes a paradigm of monarchy not only in the manner he leads Israel into battle, but also in his worship and his reaction to the sin of the people.

The final words of v 32 are ambiguous and lack a real basis in Deuteronomy. They represent another emphasis of the author. The actions of the regal representative are not only in seclusion, as might be inferred from Deut 17, but are also to be done publicly before the people. The leader of Israel is not only an example, he is also a teacher of the people.

33 Verse 33 goes to great length to list the participants. Still the list is not exhaustive, as comparison with Deut 29:9–10 shows. The first words, "all Israel," are the important ones. No member of the people of God is exempt from the worship service which outlines the duties of the people of God.

The worship service meets all Deuteronomistic requirements, having the ark and the Levitical priests at its center. The inclusion of aliens rests on a particular Deuteronomic concern. The alien included anyone living outside his own clan and thus not protected by clan law. Thus the patriarchs were "aliens" in the Promised Land (Gen 12:10; 19:9; 20:1; 21:23, 34; 26:3; 32:5; 47:4, 9). The Deuteronomic law viewed such aliens as economically underprivileged and provided special means of support for them (14:29; 16:11, 14; 24:17, 19–21; 26:12–13; 27:19; cf, 24:14). Special protection (Deut 1:16; 5:14; 24:17; 27:19) and even privilege (14:21; cf. Lev 17:15) were granted them. Their presence in the cult was assumed and commanded (Deut 16:11, 14; cf. Lev 23:42), based on Yahweh's love for them (10:18–19). Still, one of the curses facing a disobedient Israel was that the tables would be turned so that citizens depended upon aliens for livelihood (Deut 28:43–44). (See further D. Kellermann, "גור," *TWAT* 1 [1973] 979–91 with bibliography.) Joshua 8:33 builds on the Deuteronomic understanding to assure the aliens a place within the cultic life of Israel (cf. Deut 31:12).

The immediate purpose of the assembly is to bless the people of Israel. This is based on the cultic instructions of Deut 27:12–13. A significant shift of emphasis occurs. In Deuteronomy, the emphasis is on the curse (cf. vv 16–26). The Joshua context makes clear that the blessings are to be given first. The focus of the section is thus shifted from threat to promise. Israel, which has transgressed the covenant, is still the subject of divine promise and blessing before any mention of curse (v 34) appears. The promise of Deuteronomy (cf. 7:13; 12:7; 14:22–27; 15:4–18; 16:9–17; 24:19; 26:15; 28:1–14; 30:16) is secured for Israel through the ritual ceremony even after their transgression. The people who respond properly to the call of Yahweh to worship and to renewal of the covenant are accepted and blessed by him.

No other OT passage connects the ark with Shechem. This has led Eissfeldt ("Gilgal or Shechem," 96) to suggest that the present passage was originally a Gilgal tradition seeking to join the Book of the Covenant with a pre-Deutero-

nomic Hexateuch. A later editor, on the basis of the Shechem traditions of
Deut 11:29–32 and 27:11–13 interpreted Josh 8:30–35 as the fulfillment of
the Deuteronomistic commands. The ark motif here does not, however, identify our passage as a Gilgal tradition. Rather it shows the constant Deuteronomic concern for the ark as the divine symbol from the wilderness period
until the time of the dedication of the Solomonic temple (1 Kgs 8). The
presence of the ark is only one more sign of the Deuteronomistic character
and of the theological importance of this passage. Joshua included the proper
priests and the proper divine symbol in his major act of dedicating the people
of Yahweh in the Promised Land. The Shechemite location derives from Deut
27 in its present literary form, as is seen by the retention of the confusion
of the function of the stones.

[34] Only after the emphasis on blessing, does the text return to follow the
ritual of Deut 27. Joshua reads the law to the people. Here another shift is
made. Moses spoke to the people and taught the people. Moses had the
direct word for the people from their God. Joshua's word is second-hand.
It comes through Moses. Here is the paradigm for Israelite leadership (cf.
Josh 1). Joshua acts as the Israelite king was supposed to act (Deut 17:18–
20).

[35] The total obedience of Joshua concludes the section. The original context
of Deut 27 referred only to a small number of blessings and cursings. The
context in Deut 4:13; 5:22 referred only to the Ten Commandments as being
written down. Deuteronomy 31:24–26 expanded the writing to include all
the book of Deuteronomy. The canonical tradition then expanded this to
include the entire Pentateuch. Joshua 8 takes the process one step further.
Not only is the entire material to be written down for Israel, it is to be
read to them in an annual ceremony and is to be written on the altar. Here
is the extreme to which the biblical writer felt impelled to go to enforce his
teachings upon the community. The community must know the entire law.
They must be reminded of the entire law. They must be brought to pledge
themselves to observance of the entire law. Why? Because to be people of
God meant to be an obedient people, following the divinely given life style.

Explanation

Joshua 8:30–35 does not fit the present geographical, chronological, or
narrative context. It was not supposed to. Rather, it gives a theological summary of the first major division of the book of Joshua. This summary reveals
the nature of the literature preserved for us in the book. It also underscores
the major teachings of the book to this point.

The final editor of Joshua inserted this section to speak directly to his
contemporaries. He saw them standing in the same confused condition as
Israel after the battle of Ai. They had suddenly faced the faith-shaking fact
that victory was not automatic for the people of Yahweh. An identity based
on possession of the land as fulfillment of the promises of God was not
enough. Another element was necessary. This element had been given in
the imperative mode in chap. 1. It is given in the paradigm of historical
narrative in chap. 8. Here Israel sees the real meaning of the command to

obey, to live the divine life style. She learns an even deeper lesson, the way back to the identity as people of God once that identity is lost.

Chapters 3 through 6 outlined the victorious identity of the people of God in cultic terms. Chapter 7 caricatured cultic terms to show the loss of such identity. The concluding verses of chap. 8 continue in the cultic framework to show that identity regained. The people who transgressed the divine covenant, disregarding the divine will, must return to the place of God's choice. As Deut 11:29; 27:1–26; and Josh 24 show, that place was Shechem with a tradition of a ceremony of blessing and cursing understood in the Deuteronomic school as covenant theology. The sinful nation must again stand under the blessing and the cursing, must again hear the whole law of Moses, must again renew their pledge to Yahweh by bringing him the proper sacrifices. For such a cultically obedient people, the blessing would again ring out loud and clear, drowning out the cursing. The fight for the land could be taken up anew, in the assurance that the identity of people of God had been restored and so the oracle of salvation would again come to their armies. Israel was again the people of the covenant. Yahweh was again in her midst to bless rather than to express anger. All of this was possible because God had given to Israel two gifts. The first was the Torah of Moses showing the proper life style with God. The second was a new leader, one who was certainly no Moses, speaking face to face with God, but one who followed the law for leaders by reading the Torah of Moses, teaching it to his people, and embodying it in his own personal life as an example to all the people. With the law of Moses and the leadership of Joshua, Israel could again pass over into the covenant, be the people of God, and enjoy the blessings of God. This was gospel for a people who had lost their land and its temple, the symbol of God's presence with them. Having experienced the curse, they needed desperately to hear the directions to blessing.

Covenant Compromise (9:1–27)

Bibliography

Bächli, O. "Zur Aufnahme von Fremden in die altisraelitische Kultgemeinde." *Wort-Gebot-Glaube*, ed. H. J. Stoebe. ATANT 59. Zürich: Zwingli Verlag, 1970 21–26. **Blenkinsopp, J.** "Are There Traces of the Gibeonite Covenant in Deuteronomy?" *CBQ* 28 (1966) 207–19. ———. *Gibeon and Israel.* Cambridge: Cambridge University Press, 1972, 28–40. **Coats, G. W.** *Rebellion in the Wilderness.* Nashville: Abingdon, 1968, 40–43. **Culley, R. C.** "Structural Analysis: Is It Done with Mirrors?" *Int* 28 (1974) 176–77. ———. "Themes and Variations in Three Groups of OT Narratives." *Semeia* 3 (1975) 3–13. **Dus, J.** "Gibeon—eine Kultstätte des Šmš und die Stadt des benjaminitischen Schicksals." *VT* 10 (1960) 353–74. **Fensham, F. C.** "The Treaty between Israel and the Gibeonites." *BA* 27 (1964) 96–100. **Grintz, J. M.** "The Treaty of Joshua with the Gibeonites." *JAOS* 86 (1966) 113–26. **Halbe, J.** "Gibeon und Israel." *VT* 25 (1975) 613–41. ———. *Das Privilegrecht Jahwes.* FRLANT 114. Göttingen: Vandenhoeck & Ruprecht, 1975, 247–50, 341–46. **Halpern, B.** "Gibeon: Israelite Diplomacy in the Conquest Era." *CBQ* 37 (1975) 303–16. **Haran, M.** "The Gibeonites, the Nethinim, and the Sons of Solomon's Servants." *VT* 11 (1961) 159–69. **Kearney, P. J.** "The Role of the Gibeonites in the Deuteronomic History." *CBQ* 35 (1973) 1–19. **Liver, J.** "The Literary History of Joshua IX." *JSS* 8 (1963) 227–43. **Möhlenbrink, K.** "Die Landnahmensagen des Buches Josua." *ZAW* 56 (1938) 241–45. **Mowinckel, S.** *Tetrateuch-Pentateuch-Hexateuch.* BZAW 90. Berlin: Alfred Töpelmann, 1964, 38. **Otto, E.** *Das Mazzotfest in Gilgal.* BWANT 107. Stuttgart: W. Kohlhammer Verlag, 1975, 89–92, 96–97, 309–11, 318–22. **Pritchard, J. B.** "Gibeon's History in the Light of Excavation." VTSup 7 (1960) 1–12. **Rösel, H.** "Wer kämpfte auf kanaanäischer Seite in der Schlacht bei Gibeon, Jos. 10?" *VT* 26 (1976) 505–8. **Rudolph, W.** *Der "Elohist" von Exodus bis Josua.* BZAW 68. Berlin: Alfred Töpelmann, 1938, 200–204. **Schmitt, G.** *Du sollst keinen Frieden schliessen mit den Bewohnern des Landes.* BWANT 91. Stuttgart: W. Kohlhammer Verlag, 1970, 30–45. **Schottroff, W.** *Der altisraelitische Fluchspruch.* WMANT 30. Neukirchen-Vluyn: Neukirchener Verlag, 1969, 80–84. **Schunck, K. D.** *Benjamin.* BZAW 86. Berlin: Alfred Töpelmann, 1963, 38–39. **Stolz, F.** *Jahwes und Israels Kriege.* ATANT 60. Zürich: Theologischer Verlag, 1972, 84–85. **de Vaux, R.** *Histoire ancienne d'Israël.* vol. 1. Paris: J. Gabalda, 1971, 571–76. (= *The Early History of Israel.* Tr. D. Smith. London: Darton, Longman & Todd, 1978, 621–26.) **Yeivin, S.** *The Israelite Conquest of Canaan.* Istanbul: Nederlands Historisch-Archaeologisch Instituut in het Nabije Oosten, 1971, 80–81.

Translation

   ¹ *When all* [a] *the kings* [b] *who were beyond the Jordan in the hill country and in the Shephelah and on all the Mediterranean coast in front of the Lebanon mountains, namely the Hittites, Amorites, Canaanites, Perizzites, Hivites, and Jebusites heard,* ² *they assembled together to make war with Joshua and with Israel in complete accord.* [a] ³ *But the inhabitants of Gibeon, having heard what Joshua* [a] *had done to Jericho and to Ai,* ⁴ *were the very ones who acted with cunning. They went and prepared supplies.* [a] *Then they took dilapidated sacks for their donkeys* [b] *and dilapidated wineskins which had been cracked and mended.* ⁵ *They put dilapidated sandals* [a] *which they had patched up on their feet and dressed in dilapidated clothing. All* [b] *their bread supply was dried out and crumbling.* ⁶ *So they came to Joshua to the camp at Gilgal and said to him and to the man* [a] *of Israel, "From a far distant land we have come. Therefore, sign a covenant agreement with us."* ⁷ *And they* [a] *said, that is the men of Israel, to the Hivites, "It could just be the case that you live nearby. How then could I sign a covenant agreement with you?"* ⁸ *They replied to Joshua, "We are your servants." Joshua said to them, "Who are you? From where do you come?"* ⁹ *They said to him,* [a] *"From an extremely distant land your servants have come due to the name of Yahweh your God, for we have heard his reputation* [b] *and all that he had done in Egypt,* ¹⁰ *and all that he did to the two* [a] *kings of the Amorites who were beyond the Jordan, that is to Sihon, king of Heshbon,* [b] *and to Og, king of Bashan, which is in Ashtaroth.* [c] ¹¹ᵃ *Our elders and all the inhabitants of our land said to us, 'Take supplies in your hands for the way and go to call on them and say to them, "We are your servants; therefore sign a covenant agreement with us."'* ¹² *This is our bread. It was piping hot when we packed it among our supplies at our homes* [a] *the day of our leaving to come to you. Right here it is, all dried out. It has become crumbly.* ¹³ *These are the wineskins which we filled when they were new. But look here, they are split open. This is our clothing and our sandals. They have become dilapidated from the great distance of our journey."*

14 *The men* ᵃ *accepted* ᵇ *the evidence of the supplies, but of Yahweh* ᶜ *they did not inquire.* 15 *So Joshua made peace with them and signed a covenant agreement with them to let them live. The chiefs of the congregation swore an oath with them.*

16 *Three days after signing the covenant agreement with them, they heard that they were from the vicinity, that in fact they were living quite near to them.* 17 *Then the sons of Israel set out and came to their cities on the third day.* ᵃ *Their cities included Gibeon, Cephirah, Beeroth, and Kiriath-Jearim.* 18 *But the sons of Israel did not kill them because the chiefs of the congregation* ᵃ *had sworn an oath to them in the name of Yahweh, the God of Israel. Then all the congregation grumbled against the chiefs.* 19 *All the chiefs explained to all the congregation, "We have sworn to them by Yahweh, the God of Israel; therefore we are not able to touch them.* 20 *But this we will do to them, preserving them alive* ᵃ *without the wrath coming upon us due to the oath which we have sworn to them."* 21 *The leaders said to them,* ᵃ *"Let them live." Then they became gatherers of firewood and drawers of water for all the congregation,* ᵇ *just as the chiefs said to them.*

22 *Joshua called to them and spoke to them, "Why have you deceived us,* ᵃ *saying, 'We are a long way away from you all,'* ᵇ *when you all live right in the vicinity?* 23 *Therefore, you are accursed! Servitude shall never be eliminated from you all. Rather, you will be gathers of firewood and drawers of water for the house* ᵃ *of my God."* 24 *They answered Joshua and said, "Since it was clearly reported to your servants that Yahweh your God had commanded Moses, his servant, to give to you all the whole land and to destroy* ᵃ *all the inhabitants of the land from your presence, we feared greatly for our lives before you all so that we have done this thing.* 25 *Now here we are in your* ᵃ *hands. Whatever is good and right in your eyes to do to us, do."*

26 *Then he acted accordingly and rescued them from the hand of the sons of Israel and did not kill them.* 27 *Joshua appointed them that day gatherers of firewood and drawers of water for the congregation* ᵃ *and for the altar of Yahweh* ᵇ *until this day to the place which he chose.*

Notes

1.a. LXX lacks "all," possibly an interpretation in the MT tradition in light of the all-inclusive conquest.

1.b. LXX adds "of the Amorites," using the term for all pre-Israelite occupants. They are then listed after the Hivites as one among many inhabitants at the end of the verse. Here the LXX adds Girgashites (cf. Gen 10:16; 15:21; Deut 7:1; Josh 3:10; 24:11).

2.a. LXX understood the Hebrew idiom "with one mouth" in a temporal sense. It transposed 8:30–35 here, thus showing Israelite devotion to divine law even in the face of mounting danger.

3.a. LXX reads "Lord" for "Joshua," refusing to give a man credit for divine actions. MT is the superior reading in line with the consistent aim of the book to define Joshua's role and underline his achievement. LXX, Vg, and a few MSS underscore the divine achievement by noting that *all* that had been done was heard.

4.a. MT has the Hithpa'el of ציר, which occurs nowhere else. The noun derivative is "messenger," so that the verbal root could mean "disguise oneself as a messenger" (Abel; Soggin, 108). LXX translates with two terms meaning "to prepare" or more specifically "to prepare food." This appears to witness, with many MSS and versions, to the verb ציד, "to go hunting, to prepare provisions for a hunt," which thus appears to be the original reading.

4.b. Confusion in dictation has produced an inner Greek variant, BF reading ὤμων, "shoulders," whereas AMN read ὄνων, "donkeys." There is no reason to change MT.

5.a. The Greek tradition witnesses a double expression for footware, perhaps reflecting changing fashions in the ancient world.

5.b. For כול, "all," LXX lacks an equivalent, but appears to have two equivalents for נקדים, "crumbling" or "moldy" (appearing again only in 1 Kgs 14:3). LXX represents an attempt to parallel the reading with v 12, where MT duplicates v 5, but Greek does not (See Margolis, 153–54).

6.a. LXX reads "to Joshua and to Israel." Here textual history has sought to alleviate problems introduced into the text in its literary development. "Man of Israel" appears in vv 7–8, while "men" appear in v 14. The Massoretic tradition added "men of Israel" to v 6 to prepare for v 7. LXX then smoothed out tradition by eliminating the role of "man of Israel" altogether and explicitly underscoring the role of Joshua. Other Greek traditions underscored Israel by reading "all Israel."

7.a. Keᵗhib wrote a plur. verb form, interpreting "man of Israel" collectively, as is normally the case. Qᵉre suggests sing. reading to secure strict grammatical agreement. LXX changed the subject to "sons" of Israel and so read plur. Manuscript, Targum, and version support can be shown for both Hebrew interpretations.

9.a. LXX lacks "to him," an addition in MT making the obvious explicit.

9.b. LXX repeats "name" whereas Hebrew changes from שם, "name" to שמעו, "reputation." MT represents original tradition.

10.a. LXX lacks "two," perhaps because it was written as β and dropped out before the same letter beginning the following word (Margolis, 156) or the Hebrew tradition may have added it as a common phrase (Deut 3:8, 4:47; Josh 2:10; 24:12).

10.b. The LXX copyist has taken "Amorite" over from the preceding line instead of "Heshbon."

10.c. LXX adds the verb "who lived in" which is not necessary, but possible, in Hebrew. LXX also added "and in Edrei," a popular phrase taken over from Deut 1:4; Josh 12:4; 13:12, 31 (cf. Num 21:33; Deut 3:1, 10).

11.a. LXX added the interpretative note "Having heard. . . ."

12.a. "At our homes" does not appear in LXX and may be amplification in the Hebrew tradition.

14.a. A simple transposition has changed Heb. האנשים, "the men," to הנשאים, "the chiefs," in LXX tradition, but this is anticipatory to v 15. Cf. similar error in Judg 8:15.

14.b. The literal translation would be "took from their supplies." This may be interpreted either as eating, based on the evidence of closing a covenant agreement with a meal, or as testing the evidence of the supplies. The latter seems more fitting with the present narrative, since the point is that the supplies were old, the food inedible (cf. Schmitt, *Du sollst*, 34–35).

14.c. LXX avoids the anthropomorphic "mouth of Yahweh" (Margolis, 159–60).

17.a. LXX lacks the date formula, which may be added in the Hebrew in light of similar formulas in 1:11; 2:16; 3:2; 9:16.

18.a. LXX reads "all the chiefs," underlining the Israelite commitment. The LXX's reason for omitting "congregation" is not obvious. In v 19, MT has "all," lacking in LXX.

20.a. LXX has introduced a doublet "having let them live, we will preserve them for ourselves." This is an interpretation of the Heb. infinitive absolute construction (cf. GK§113z).

21.a. The opening words are unnecessary in light of v 19 and are omitted by LXX. MT tradition has introduced the verse as a summary, as is shown by the imperfect consecutive "and then they became," which the versions have changed to the future in order to incorporate the statement in the quotation.

21.b. Strong Greek evidence supports the reading, "and all the congregation did" before "just as." This was necessary when the previous sentence was read in the future rather than the past. Syr introduces the etiological formula "to this day," even while reading the entire quotation as future. This shows how the tradition could insert the etiological formula at a very late date to interpret the material.

22.a. LXX reads sing. pronouns "me" and "you," for the Heb. plurals, thus intensifying the role of Joshua as representative of the community.

23.a. LXX makes some radical modifications. "Servitude" is understood as a single servant, so that the description becomes "a hewer of wood," with no reference to drawers of water. The anachronistic reference to the temple is observed resulting in the change to "cutter for me and my God."

24.a. LXX dramatizes the scene, adding "us and" as object of destroy.

25.a. Reversing the pattern of v 22, LXX has plur. pronouns for MT sing. This continues in 26a, where LXX pluralizes the verb, before introducing Joshua as explicit subject of "rescued," to which the etiological formula is added.

27.a. LXX continues the pattern of vv 18, 19, 21 by referring to "all" the congregation.

27.b. LXX has "God" rather than the personal name Yahweh. LXX then introduces Yahweh at the end of the verse where MT has no divine name. Auld should be followed in arguing for LXX originality here (VTSup 30 [1979] 12–13).

27.c. LXX has an explicit etiological statement, "Through this the inhabitants of Gibeon became wood cutters and drawers of water of the altar of God until today." This may well have dropped from the MT through homoeoteleuton (C. D. Ginsburg, *Introduction to the Massoretico-Critical Edition of the Hebrew Bible* [London: Trinitarian Bible Society, 1897] 175–76).

Form/Structure/Setting

The first two verses of chap. 9 clearly form a transition from the previous section. The subject they introduce, however, does not appear in chap. 9 but only in chap. 10. The larger unit for the editor is thus chaps. 9 and 10. By itself, chap. 9 is a complete narrative with its own purpose, as shown by the concluding formula in v 27. Its character as an independent narrative unit is witnessed also by 10:1–2, which refers back to it. Thus the unit we study here is 9:1–27, recognizing that 1–2 represent an introduction to the larger narrative in chaps. 9 and 10.

Chapter 9 consists of two narratives which have been editorially tied together and then interpreted in the light of Joshua's role (cf. Halbe, *VT* 25 [1975] 629–30). The first unit comprises vv 3–15. The disjunctive clause (v 3) is a typical narrative introduction setting forth the point of view of the Gibeonites, who react to the startling victories of Israel over their neighbors. Imperfect consecutives in 4–6a build up the narrative tension around the deception of the Gibeonites. Dialogue then takes over to form the narrative climax. This climbs slowly to its height in v 14, where the tension is resolved. Israel has fallen for the deception, without inquiring of Yahweh. The denouement appears in typical imperfect consecutive, formulaic fashion in v 15. Gibeon has received life.

The narrative has no etiological formulas, yet functions etiologically (cf. Halbe, *VT* 25 [1975] 628). It explains the position of Gibeon among Israel, a position of treaty partner protected by the might of Israel's army. The interesting thing is that the story is not told from Israel's perspective. Rather it reflects Gibeon's (cf. Hertzberg, 68; Gray, 97). They laugh at Israel, the mighty military power which allows a foreign army into the midst of its camp (v 6). There the all-victorious commander receives them and gives them the customary military order for name, rank and serial number (v 8), yet never receives his answer in any explicit terms (9a). On the other hand, the commands of the Gibeonite elders (v 11) were followed to the letter (vv 6, 8). Gullible Israel immediately accepts their evidence and takes their provisions (v 14). Here a word play lets this be taken to mean not only accept the evidence, but also to eat of it (cf. above, *Notes* 14.b. and Hertzberg, 67). Such eating can symbolize acceptance of the strangers into the camp and provide a basis for temporary protection (cf. Halbe, *VT* 25 [1975] 620, note 50). This not being enough, Israel makes a permanent treaty with them, something always done in the name of the god(s), but Israel never turned to inquire of her own God (v 14b).

When and where would such a story be told? We gain hints from 2 Sam 21:1–4. In the days of Saul and David, Gibeonites exerted their own pressures and enjoyed their own privileges. This came to be too much for Saul, so that he tried to exterminate them, only later to have Gibeon gain revenge on his family. Gibeon then served as a major sanctuary for the nation until Solomon completed the Jerusalem temple (1 Kgs 3:4–5). Quite likely in the period of prosperity under David, the Gibeonites would have used this story to illustrate their superiority over their politically superior neighbors. Its origin may even be earlier.

History changed things fast. Solomon enslaved the foreigners in his kingdom (1 Kgs 9:20–21; cf. Ezra 2:43–58; Neh 7:46–60; Haran). Israel took over the story and used it to explain the new situation. To do so, they added their own ending, preserved in vv 16–21. Again, the narrative is opened by the common temporal clause (16) introducing the point of tension—a covenant with neighbors, not foreigners (16b). This theme was then inserted back into the earlier narrative (v 7, opposing the view of Otto, *Mazzotfest*, 89–92, and of Halbe, *Privilegrecht*, 341–42). The latter's chief interest is in the parallel law in Exod 34:12a, blinding him to the fact that the theme does not belong to 9:1–15 but only to the secondary narrative in 16ff). Imperfect consecutives then build up narrative tension (vv 17–18) and reverse the direction of march of the earlier narrative (cf. v 6). Dialog forms the climax (vv 18b–21a) and centers on the point of tension, the covenant with neighbors. The extended dialog places Israel in a real dilemma. She cannot follow the law and kill them (Deut 7:2; Exod 34:12a; cf. Deut 20:16–18), for she has made a covenant with them. She must preserve them alive, and yet they must know once and for all Israel's superiority. Finally the plan evolves (v 21). The practice of Solomon was justified from Israel's own tradition (cf. Halbe, *VT* 25 [1975] 633–34).

The Deuteronomistic historian has taken over the material and fit it into his own scheme centering on the role of Joshua. To do this, he has not employed a narrative pattern. Rather he has taken up a legal pattern, that of gaining revenge for a crime through cursing, a pattern found also in Gen 4:9–16 (cf. Halbe, *VT* 25 [1975] 623–24). Guilt is established through a question (v 22) which uses the language of both narratives. The verdict is given in form of a curse (v 23a) and sentence (v 23b). The convicted criminals do not appeal the verdict (cf. Gen 4:13–14) but submit to it (vv 24–25). The Deuteronomist can then show the greatness of Joshua (vv 26–27). This final paragraph is not the only contribution of the Deuteronomist. He has also expanded the confession of faith in the opening narrative with his own particular interests (9bβ–10).

The final composition in chap. 9 is thus composed of three units, each with its own setting and purpose, yet the three have been combined into a remarkable whole. The first section now reports the trickery of the Gibeonites, setting them in a bad light through the following context, while setting forth Joshua as a peacemaker (v 15a). The second unit (16–21) then concerns only Israel. The Gibeonites are referred to but never appear. Nor does Joshua. Israel decides their fate. Joshua then appears as mediator to announce the verdict to the Gibeonites, while protecting them from the Israelites (v 26).

Comment

The scene of action widens unexpectedly. No longer does Israel face simply one city-state and its army. She has become so important that coalitions are formed against her. The threat presented by Israel is pictured as being so great that it forced the racially diversified former enemies to join together against Israel.

The expression "beyond Jordan" refers here to the area west of the Jordan, as the following description shows. The more usual referent is the area east of the Jordan as in v 10. Of the nineteen lists of nations, only Deuteronomy 20:17 corresponds to this one (Blenkinsopp, *CBQ* 28 [1966] 207). The geographical description includes only the southern part of the country and the Mediterranean coast, preparing for the conquest summary in 10:40, where the list is expanded to include the southern Negeb but does not include the coastal plain up to the Lebanon.

² The editor makes two points in the second verse. The kings were unanimous, and they fought against Joshua as well as Israel. Again the role of Joshua is highlighted.

³ Not everyone joined the coalition. Joshua's reputation caused part of the population to attempt devious means to escape the Israelite threat. Gibeon is identified with el-Jib, five and a half miles (nine kilometers) north of Jerusalem in the territory of Benjamin (Josh 18:25). Pritchard's excavations (VTSup 7 [1960] 8–12) have revealed extensive occupation in Early Bronze I (ca. 3150–2850), Middle Bronze II (2000–1750), early Iron Age I (1200–1150), when the first city wall was built; with the peak of prosperity in Iron Age II (1000–586). The city was not occupied during the Late Bronze period, when the conquest is usually dated. Thus Bimson (*Redating*, 205–6) uses it as evidence for redating the conquest.

⁴ The Gibeonites thus acted with "cunning." The verbal root ערם occurs five times in the OT being applied by Saul to David in 1 Sam 23:22 in a two-sided meaning. From Saul's perspective it is a bad characteristic, while from the narrator's it is admirable. The term is cast in a bad light in Job 5:13 and Ps 83:4, while a good connotation appears in Prov 15:5 and 19:25. Outside our passage the adjective occurs four times, negatively in Exod 21:14, but positively in Prov 1:4; 8:5, 12. Double entendre is used in our passage as in 1 Sam. From the Gibeonite point of view, they were quite wise in what they did, whereas the Israelite version saw this as deceptive and wrong.

⁶ Israel is located again at Gilgal rather than Shechem as in 8:30–35, showing again the lateness of that section. The story is thus tied to the earlier narratives of the book, probably by the early collector. This does not show that the story itself originated or was used in the sanctuary at Gilgal, though this possibility cannot be totally excluded.

The "man of Israel" is introduced here (see *Notes* 6.a.). The term has been a major factor in the numerous attempts to find parallel sources (cf. the latest attempts by Schmitt, *Du sollst*, 30–37, and Otto, *Mazzotfest*, 89–92). Such attempts have failed to note the two distinct narrative structures, while being unable to find complete parallel accounts. The expression "man of Israel" is a collective noun, often referring to the Israelite army (Judg

7:23; 9:55; 20:11–48; 1 Sam 13:6; 14:22; 17:2, 19–25; 2 Sam 17:24; 23:9).
A military undertone may be present in all uses of the term, but a few passages
(Judg 8:22; 21:1; 2 Sam 16:18; 17:14; 19:42–44) may support Schmitt's contention (*Du sollst,* 38) that the expression represents more clearly than others
the democratic element in Israel's society. Schmitt is correct in saying that
the expression is used in the early years of the monarchy and then again in
Deuteronomistic literature. In Josh 9 the expression appears only in vv 6–7
and represents the work of tradition history in joining the narrative of 3–
15 with that of 16–21, shifting blame away from Joshua. In so doing the
tradition shows that Israel violated the ancient law of Exod 34:12. The Deuteronomistic historian read this in light of the Deuteronomic law of Deut 20:15–
18.

The Hivites are not documented in extra-biblical texts and may reflect
early linguistic confusion with the Horites or Hurrians (E. A. Speiser, "Hivite,"
IDB 2 [1962] 615). Originally at home in Armenia, they travelled far and
wide in the Ancient Near East between ca. 2200 and 1000 B.C. Quite early
they entered Syria-Palestine so that contingents were still found among the
"native" population when the Israelites entered the land. The Bible connects
them especially with Shechem (Gen 34:2), Gibeon (Josh 11:19); and the northern mountains (Judg 3:3; Josh 11:3). (See further, Speiser, "Hurrians," *IDB*
2 [1962] 664–66; H. A. Hoffner, "The Hittites and Hurrians," in D. J. Wiseman
(ed.) *Peoples of Old Testament Times* [Oxford: Oxford University Press, 1973]
221–28; F. W. Bush, "Hurrians," *IDBSup* [1976] 423–24).

The expression ל ברית כרת, "to make a covenant agreement with," refers
to an agreement between an overlord and his vassals (cf. M. Weinfeld, "ברית,"
TWAT 1 [1973] 784). Such an agreement would place obligations on the
vassals with promises being given by the overlord (cf. E. Kutsch, *Verheissung
und Gesetz* [BZAW 131; Berlin: Walter de Gruyter, 1973] 53). The treaty would
be sealed with an oath, equivalent to a self-curse and would seek to establish
peace between the two parties (cf. v 15). In the original context the reference
would be to the political treaty by which Gibeon obtained favored status
among Israel. It would presuppose a time when Israel had sufficient power
to be in a political position to be the overlord of a political treaty. From
the Deuteronomistic perspective the treaty would be a covenant with foreign
nations forbidden by the law (Deut 7:2) and in conflict with the covenant
tying Israel as vassal to Yahweh, her divine overlord (7:4).

[8] The Gibeonites use the polite language of Near Eastern diplomacy by
referring to themselves as Joshua's servants. The later tradition understood
the term literally as referring to the servile status of the Gibeonites over
against Israel.

[9] The divine promise is again seen at work, as the inhabitants of the land
tremble in fear before Yahweh and his great reputation (cf. 2:9; 5:1). God
continues to do his part. The Deuteronomist has taken the opportunity to
give content to the confession in 9b–10. For the original collector, the fame
of Yahweh rested on his victories over Jericho and Ai, but for the Deuteronomist the victories in Egypt and Transjordan formed the basis for Yahweh's
reputation.

[10] As often in Hebrew narrative, a historical flashback repeats or paraphrases

what has already been narrated (cf. vv 4–5). The Gibeonite travelers claim to be legitimate representatives of their people, commissioned by the ruling elders and all the citizens. Thus Israel makes covenant not with the political authorities but only with representatives whose only credentials are their own testimony and their dilapidated condition.

14 The climactic verse condemns Israel for not following the normal pattern of seeking the divine will before making such an agreement. From the Gibeonite point of view, this represented the superiority of Gibeonite cunning. For the biblical narrator it was Israel's sin.

15 Quite surprisingly, Joshua stands condemned by this verse. He made the covenant and established peace. The verse makes sense only on Gibeonite tongues, where the authority of Joshua is claimed for the Gibeonite privileges. The later editor has counterbalanced this through the addition of 22–27, where v 15 gives reason for Joshua's curse. Verse 15b is the literary link by which 16–21 was joined to the preceding narrative. Thus it introduces the chiefs of the community into the narrative. These terms are often used to cite priestly redaction, but this has been shown false by M. Noth (*Das System der zwölf Stämme Israels* [Stuttgart: W. Kohlhammer Verlag, 1930] 102–3, 151–62; cf. O. Calberini, "Il nāsi biblico nell' epoca patriarcale e arcaio," *BeO* 20 [1978] 64–74; Blenkinsopp, *CBQ* 28 [1966] 211; J. Milgrom, "Priestly Terminology and the Political and Social Structure of Pre-Monarchic Israel," *JQR* 69 [1978] 65–76).

17 The Gibeonites are shown to be more than a small group of isolationists. They controlled a whole group of cities. The three satellites of Gibeon are included in the list of Benjamite cities in Josh 18:25–28. Cephirah is mentioned in Ezra 2:25; Neh 7:29; 1 Esdr 5:19 and is usually located at Khirbet Kefireh about four miles (seven kilometers) southwest of Gibeon. This has been disputed by K. Vriezen, "Hirbet Kefire—Eine Oberflächeuntersuchung," *ZDPV* 91 [1975] 149–58). Beeroth means "wells." It is mentioned in 2 Sam 4:2; Ezra 2:25; and Neh 7:29. It has been variously located at el-Bireh, seven kilometers northeast of Gibeon; tell en-Nasbeh, twelve kilometers north of Jerusalem; Nebi Samwil, a mile south of Gibeon; Khirbet el-Burj, on the ridge above Nebi Samwil; Biddu, the modern city near Khirbet el-Burj; Khirbet Raddana in the outskirts of Bireh. In the midst of all of this A. Kuschke now claims, on the basis of reports from Z. Kallai-Kleinmann, that the location of Beeroth may be considered to be clarified on the basis of discoveries at Ras et-Tahūne on the northwest edge of el-Bireh "Gibeon," *Biblisches Reallexikon,* 2nd ed. [Tübingen: J. C. B. Mohr, 1977] 97; cf. Bimson, *Redating,* 219; S. Cohen, "Beeroth," *IDB* [1962] 375; A. F. Rainey, "Beeroth," *IDBSup* [1976] 93; Y. Aharoni, "Khirbet Raddana and Its Inscription," *IEJ* 21 [1971] 133–35; S. Yeivin, "The Benjamite Settlement in the Western Part of their Territory," *IEJ* 21 [1971] 141–54; J. A. Callaway and R. E. Cooley, "A Salvage Excavation at Raddana, in Bireh," *BASOR* 201 [1971] 9–19).

Kiriath-Jearim appears under slightly differing names in Josh 15:9, 11, 60; 18:14; Judg 18:12; 2 Sam 6:2; 1 Chr 13:6; Ezra 2:25; Neh 7:29. It is usually located at Deir el-Azar, slightly over ten kilometers west of Jerusalem.

18 The theme of leadership which has so dominated the entire book appears again. The entire community murmured just as they had done in the wilder-

ness. This was directed against the leaders who prevented them from carrying
out the divine command (cf v 7 which ties the two units together) and from
killing the Gibeonites (18a; cf. Coats, *Rebellion*, 40–43). The leadership question thus becomes acute. How do leaders who have allowed themselves to
be tricked into disobedience work their way out of the situation and justify
themselves before their own congregation? Here the wilderness motif has
been turned upside down, for in the wilderness the leaders were justified,
while the congregation was guilty. Here the congregation is justified, while
the leaders are at fault.

¹⁹ The immediate justification is that an oath cannot be broken. This was
understood in ancient treaties. The ironic note here is that the oath was
sworn in the name of Yahweh, and thus binding, though the action had been
carried through without consulting Yahweh. Breaking the treaty would not
only result in human wrath, but would bring down divine wrath (v 20).

²¹ The leaders are able to go one step further and develop a plan of action,
just as cunning as that of the Gibeonites. Unable to kill the foreigners in
their midst, they reduce them to insignificant service (cf. Deut 29:10). This
was certainly not the Gibeonite understanding. They sought military protection in exchange for military loyalty. Israel turns the tables by reducing them
to slaves doing menial tasks for the community. Thus the leaders regain
the confidence of the community, resulting in their word being carried out.
Here is a different understanding of leadership from that connected with
Moses in the Pentateuch. Here is a call for leaders to be responsive to the
complaints of the people and to justify their own actions. Such justified complaint, though, is based on the authority of the Mosaic law.

²² The theme changes drastically with the final section. No longer is the
guilt of the leaders in question. Now the Gibeonites are brought to trial
before Joshua. As is proper in treaty violations, the condemnation comes in
the form of a curse (cf. Deut 27) which condemns the descendants to servitude.
The precise definition of this servitude in 23b is anachronistic for the time
of Joshua—when Israel had yet to build a house for God—and is loosely
connected syntactically to the sentence. Thus it probably represents a later
addition in light of the Jerusalem temple.

²⁴ The Gibeonite defense shows their Yahwistic piety, as they paraphrase
the Deuteronomistic credo. They were no different from all other kings in
their reaction to Israel. Terribly frightened, they simply sought to save their
scalps with a clever plan. Having been found out, they submit to Joshua
and his judgment (v 25).

²⁶ The action of Joshua is thus justified by the accused. He does not have
to justify himself before the citizens. Having brought the Gibeonites to submission, he prevents Israel from killing them, in contrast to the crafty plan which
the chiefs of the community had to devise to regain community confidence.
He simply condemned the Gibeonites to menial service at the sanctuary in
conformance with Israelite legal practice. This explains the position of the
Gibeonites among Israel. They are foreigners permitted to live, but their
very presence is a living lesson for both Israel and for foreigners. Foreigners
learn that they cannot trick their way into the people of Yahweh, even with
pious confessions of faith. Israel learns the supreme danger which threatens

its life and leadership when decisions are made without consulting Yahweh and when the Mosaic law is not followed.

[27] The final phrase of the verse is syntactically awkward and represents Deuteronomistic phraseology (Weinfeld, *Deuteronomy,* 324, no. 1). The reference in Deuteronomy is to the Jerusalem temple (cf. 1 Kgs 8:14–21). The leadership of Joshua thus provided servants for the temple God planned in Jerusalem. Where such servants served prior to Solomon remains unclear. At least one stage of the tradition probably referred this to Gibeon. An even earlier stage could have been connected with Gilgal, though this is less certain.

Explanation

Chapter 9 looks backward and forward as it seeks to teach Israel her identity. It looks back to the story of Rahab, where foreigners were allowed to become part of the people of God, dwelling in their midst (6:25). It looks forward to chap. 10, where the existence of foreigners in her midst forces Israel into war, but thus enables her to carry out her program of conquest. Thus it raises in a very clever way the question of Israel and foreigners.

The problem was acute for Israel throughout her history. Her Exodus tradition admitted that Israel included a "mixed multitude" (Exod 12:38). Despite the conquest, Canaanite enclaves remained among her (Judg 1:21–36; Josh 13:1–7, 13). In the Exile, Israel then lived in the midst of foreign people, a situation that did not change upon the return (Ezra 9:1–10:44). The book of Joshua allows some pious foreigners who prove their loyalty to Israel to be accepted into the community (6:25), but warns that those who seek to deceive the people, those who entice them after other gods (Deut 7), those whose piety is out of self-interest, face the judgment of Yahweh and his people.

In setting up such a situation, the book also points out the problems of leadership in Israel. Leaders are not allowed to act on their own authority without consulting deity. They cannot assume the loyalty of the people when they act in such a godless manner. They cannot ignore divine law. Rather they find themselves trapped by their own actions. The leader is required to execute justice by proper legal channels. Only then can he expect the loyalty of the people. Such acts of loyalty then become part of Israel's sacred tradition and prepare the way for the service of God at the holy temple God chooses to dwell in among Israel.

The Southern Sweep (10:1–43)

Bibliography

Abel, F. M. "Les stratagèmes dans le Livre de Josué." *RB* 56 (1949) 332–35. **Alfrink, B.** "Het 'Still Staan' van Zon en Maan in Jos. 10:12–15," *Studia Catholica* 24 (1949) 238–68. **Alt, A.** "Josua." *Werden und Wesen des Alten Testaments,* ed. P. Volz, F. Stummer, and J. Hempel. BZAW 66. Berlin: Alfred Töpelmann, 1936, 13–29. (=*Kleine Schriften zur Geschichte des Volkes Israel.* Vol. 1. München. C. H. Beck'sche Verlagsbuchhandlung, 1953, 176–92.) **Balaban, M.** "Kosmische Dimension des Wunders von Gibeon." *Communio Viatorum* 12 (1969) 51–60. **Bimson, J. J.** *Redating the Exodus and Conquest.* JSOTSup 5. Sheffield: University of Sheffield, 1978, 210–15. **Blenkinsopp, J.** *Gibeon and Israel.* Cambridge: Cambridge University Press, 1972, 41–52. **van den Bussche, H.** Het zogenaamd zonnewonder in Jos. 10:12–15." *Collationes Gandavenses* 1 (1951) 48–53. **Christensen, D. L.** *Transformations of the War Oracle in Old Testament Prophecy.* HDR 3. Missoula, MT: Scholars Press, 1975, 41–43, 49–50. **Dus, J.** "Gibeon—eine Kultstätte des Šmš und die Stadt des benjaminitischen Schicksals." *VT* 10 (1960) 353–74. **Eisler, R.** "Joshua and the Sun." *AJSL* 42 (1926) 73–85. **Elliger, K.** "Josua in Judäa." *PJ* 30 (1934) 47–71. **de Fraine, J.** "De miraculo solari Josue, Jos. 10, 12–15." *VD* 28 (1950) 227–36. **Fuller, R. C.** "Sun, Stand Thou Still." *Scripture* 4 (1951) 305–13. **Gruenthaner, M. J.** "Two Sun Miracles of the Old Testament," *CBQ* 10 (1948) 271–90. **Halpern, B.** "Gibeon: Israelite Diplomacy in the Conquest Era." *CBQ* 37 (1975) 303–16. **Heller, J.** "Der Name Eva." *ArOr* 26 (1958) 636–56. ———. "Die schweigende Sonne." *Communio Viatorum* 9 (1966) 73–78. **Holladay, J. S.** "The Day(s) the Moon Stood Still." *JBL* 87 (1968) 166–78. **Hollenberg, J.** "Die deuteronomischen Bestandtheile des Buches Josua." *Theologische Studien und Kritiken* 1 (1874) 497–99. **von Hoonacker, A.** "Das Wunder Josuas." *TGI* 5 (1913) 454–61. **Jacobs, L.** *Jewish Biblical Exegesis.* New York: Behrman House, 1973. 92–99. **Jones, G. H.** " 'Holy war' or 'Yahweh war'?" *VT* 25 (1975) 653–55. **Kleber, A.** "Josue's Miracle." *AER* 56 (1917) 477–88. **Lambert, G.** "Josué è la bataille de Gabaon." *NRT* 76 (1954) 374–91. **Matthes, J. C.** "Das Solstitium Jos. 10:12–14." *ZAW* 29 (1909) 259–67. **Maunder E. W.** "A Misinterpreted Miracle." *Expositor* 36 (1910) 359–72. **van Mierlo, J.** "Das Wunder Josues." *ZKT* 37 (1913) 895–911. **Miller, P. D.** *The Divine Warrior in Early Israel.* HSM 5. Cambridge, MA: Harvard University Press, 1973, 123–28. **Möhlenbrink, K.** "Die Landnahmensagen des Buches Josua." *ZAW* 56 (1938) 264–65. **Mowinckel, S.** "Hat es ein israelitisches Nationalepos gegeben?" *ZAW* 53 (1935) 130–52. ———. *Tetrateuch-Pentateuch-Hexateuch.* BZAW 90. Berlin: Alfred Töpelmann, 1964, 39–40. **Noth, M.** "Die fünf Könige in der Höhle von Makkeda." *PJ* 33 (1937) 22–36. (=*Aufsätze zur biblischen Landes- und Altertumskunde.* Vol. 1. Neukirchen-Vluyn: Neukirchener Verlag, 1971, 281–93.) **Otto, E.** *Das Mazzotfest in Gilgal.* BWANT 107. Stuttgart: W. Kohlhammer Verlag, 1975, 92–93, 318–19. **Phythian-Adams, W. J.** "A Meteorite of the Fourteenth Century B.C." *PEQ* 78 (1946) 116–24. **Quell, G.** "Das Phänomen des Wunders in Alten Testament." *Verbannung und Heimkehr,* ed. A. Kuschke. Tübingen: J. C. B. Mohr, 1961, 259–61, 273–74. **Reid, J.** "Did the Sun and Moon Stand Still?" *ExpTim* 9 (1898) 151–54. **Richter, W.** *Traditionsgeschichtliche Untersuchungen zum Richterbuch.* BBB 18. Bonn: Peter Hanstein, 1963, 181–86. **Rösel, H.** "Wer kämpfte auf kanaanäischer Seite in der Schlacht bei Gibeon, Jos. X?" *VT* 26 (1976) 505–8. **Rudolph, W.** *Der "Elohist" von Exodus bis Josua.* BZAW. 68. Berlin: Alfred Töpelmann, 1938, 204–9. **Sawyer, J. F. A.** "Joshua 10:12–14 and the Solar Eclipse of 30 September 1131 B.C." *PEQ* 104 (1972) 139–46. **Schmid, H.** "Erwägungen zur Gestalt Josuas in Überlieferung und Geschichte." *Judaica* 24 (1968) 55. **Schunck, K. D.** *Benjamin.* BZAW 86. Berlin: Alfred Töpelmann, 1963, 18–39. **Stolz, F.** *Jahwes und Israels Kriege.* ATANT 60. Zürich: Theologischer Verlag, 1972, 85–87. **Thils, G.** "De solis institione secundum Iosue 10, 12–14." *Collectanea Mechliniensia* 30 (1945) 153–56. **Vèronnet, A.** "L'arrêt du soleil par Josué." *Revue du clergé francais* 41 (1905) 585–603. **de Vaux, R.** *Histoire ancienne d'Israël.* Vol. 1. Paris: J. Gabalda, 1971, 576–82. (=*The Early History of Israel.* Tr. D. Smith. London: Darton, Longman & Todd, 1978, 627–35.) **Weimar, P.** "Die Jahwehkriegserzählungen in Exodus 14, Josua 10, Richter 4, und I Samuel 7." *Bib* 57 (1976) 38–73. **Wellhausen J.** *Die Composition des Hexateuchs und der historischen Bücher des Alten Testa-*

ments. 2nd ed. Berlin: Georg Reimer, 1889, 128–29. **Wright, G. E.** "The Literary and Historical Problem of Joshua 10 and Judges 1." *JNES* 5 (1946) 105–14. **Yeivin, S.** *The Israelite Conquest of Canaan.* Istanbul: Nederlands Historisch-Archaeologisch Instituut in het Nabije Oosten, 1971, 80–83.

Translation

¹ *When Adoni-Zedek,* [a] *the king of Jerusalem, heard that Joshua had captured The Ruin and put it to the ban, that just as he had done to Jericho and to its king, so he had done to The Ruin and to its king and that the residents of Gibeon had made peace* [b] *with Israel* [c] *and were living among them,* [d] ² *then he feared exceedingly, because Gibeon was a great city, comparable to one of the city-state capitals, and because it was greater than The Ruin,* [a] *all its men being mighty warriors.* ³ *So Adoni-Zedek, king of Jerusalem, sent to Hoham,* [a] *king of Hebron, and to Piram, king of Jarmuth, and to Japhia, king of Lachish, and to Debir, king of Eglon, saying,* ⁴ *"Come up* [a] *to me and help me so that we may punish Gibeon, for she has concluded a peace treaty with Joshua and with the sons of Israel."* ⁵ *The five kings of the Amorites* [a] *— the king of Jerusalem, the king of Hebron, the king of Jarmuth, the king of Lachish, the king of Eglon—they and all their armies assembled* [b] *and encamped against Gibeon. They battled against her.*

⁶ *The men* [a] *of Gibeon sent to Joshua to the camp* [b] *at Gilgal, saying, "Do not abandon your vassals. Come up to us quickly. Save us! Help us! for all the kings of the Amorites, who live in the hill country, have gathered themselves against us.* ⁷ *So Joshua went up from Gilgal, he and all his combat troops with him and all the valiant warriors.*

⁸ *Then Yahweh said to Joshua, "Have no fear of them, for into your hand I have given them. Not one man of them shall stand before you."*

⁹ *Joshua came to them suddenly, traveling all night from Gilgal. Then Yahweh threw them into a panic before* [a] *Israel. He* [b] *inflicted a crushing defeat upon them in Gibeon, then pursued them on the road ascending to Beth Horon,* [c] *and defeated them clear to Azekah and Makkedah.* ¹¹ *While they were fleeing before Israel, being on the descent from Beth Horon, Yahweh hurled down upon them huge* [a] *stones from heaven unto Azekah, and they died. More died from the hailstones than the sons of Israel killed with the sword.* [b]

Then [a] *Joshua spoke to Yahweh before the sons of Israel in the day of Yahweh's* [b] *giving over the Amorites, and he said in the sight of Israel:* [s]

"O sun, in Gibeon stand still:
O moon, in the valley of Aijalon.

¹³ *Still stood the sun*

> *And the moon remained*
> *Till the nation* [a] *took vengeance on its enemies."*

Is it not written in the book of the Upright? [b] *The sun remained at the halfway point of the heavens and did not hurry to set for about a whole day.* ¹⁴ *There has never been a day like it before or since when Yahweh listened to the voice* [a] *of man, for Yahweh fought for Israel.*

^{15a} *Joshua and all Israel with him returned to the camp at Gilgal.* ¹⁶ *These five kings fled and hid in the cave at Makkedah.* ¹⁷ *It was reported to Joshua, "The five kings have been found hidden in the cave in Makkedah."*

¹⁸ *Joshua said, "Roll big* ^a *boulders into the mouth of the cave, and station men in front of it to guard it.* ¹⁹ *But you all should not stand around. Pursue after your enemies. Destroy* ^a *them. Do not give them a chance to enter into their cities, for Yahweh, your God,* ^b *has given them into your hand."*

²⁰ *As Joshua and the sons* ^a *of Israel completed inflicting the crushing defeat upon them, almost totally destroying them, a remnant did remain* ^b *from them, and they entered the fortified cities.* ²¹ *All the people returned to the camp* ^a *to Joshua at Makkedah unharmed. Not a single man threatened* ^b *the sons of Israel.* ²² *Joshua said, "Open the mouth of the cave and bring out to me* ^a *these five kings from the cave."* ²³ *They obeyed. They brought out to him these five kings from the cave—the king of Jerusalem, the king of Hebron, the king of Jarmuth, the king of Lachish, the king of Eglon.* ²⁴ *As a man was bringing them—these kings—* ^a *to Joshua, Joshua called out to all the men* ^b *of Israel and said to the commanders of the troops who had gone with him, "Come near. Place your feet on the necks of these kings."* ^c *They came near and placed their feet on their necks.*

²⁵ *Joshua said to them, "Be not afraid* ^a *nor terrified. Be strong and brave, for Yahweh will act accordingly against all your enemies whenever you all are fighting them."* ²⁶ *Afterward,* ^a *Joshua struck them and killed them and hung them on five trees. They were hanging on the trees until the evening.* ²⁷ *At sunset, Joshua issued the command, and they brought them down from the trees and threw them into the cave where they had hidden. They placed big boulders on the mouth of the cave until this very day.*

²⁸ *But as for Makkedah, Joshua* ^a *captured it that day and smote it with the sword and its king.* ^b *He put them to the ban, including everything alive in it. He did not let anything remain.* ^c *He did to the king of Makkedah just what he had done to the king of Jericho.* ²⁹ *Joshua and all Israel with him passed over from Makkedah to Libnah. He battled Libnah.* ³⁰ *Yahweh gave it, too, into the hand of Israel along with its king. He smote it with the sword and everything alive in it. He did not let anything in it remain. He did to its king just what he had done to the king of Jericho.* ³¹ *Joshua and all Israel with him crossed over from Libnah to Lachish. He encamped against it and battled against it.* ³² *Yahweh gave Lachish into the hand of Israel. She captured it on the second day and smote it with the sword and everything alive* ^a *in it according to all which he had done to Libnah.* ³³ *Then Horam, king of Gezer, went up to help Lachish. Joshua smote him* ^a *and his people until nothing at all remained for him.* ³⁴ *Joshua and all Israel with him crossed over from Lachish to Eglon. They encamped against it and battled against it.* ^{35a} *They captured it on that day and smote it with the sword and everything alive in it. In that day* ^b *he set out the ban according to all which he had done to Lachish.* ³⁶ *Joshua and all Israel with him went up from Eglon* ^a *to Hebron. They battled against it.* ³⁷ *They captured* ^a *it and smote it with the sword and its king and all its cities and everything alive in it. He did not let anything remain, according to all which he had done to Eglon. He put it to the ban and everything alive in it.* ³⁸ *Joshua and all Israel with him turned to Debir. He battled against it.*

³⁹ *He* ^a *captured it and its king and all its cities. They smote them with the sword and put everything alive in it to the ban. He did not let anything remain. Just as*

he had done to Hebron,[b] *so he did to Debir and its king and just as he had done to Libnah and to its king.* [40] *Joshua smote all the land, the hill country and the Negeb and the Shephelah and slopes and all* [a] *their kings. He did not let anything remain. Everything that breathed he put to the ban just as Yahweh, the God of Israel, commanded.* [41] *Joshua smote* [a] *them from Kadesh Barneah to Gaza, along with all the land of Goshen and unto Gibeon.* [42] *All these kings and their land Joshua captured at one time because Yahweh, the God of Israel, fought for Israel.* [43] *Joshua and all Israel with him returned to the camp at Gilgal.*

Notes

1.a. LXX renders the royal name Adoni-bezek, which appears in Judg 1:5–7. Noth, followed provisionally by Soggin (119), adopts LXX reading here. Hertzberg (72) is more probably correct in rejecting this. Adoni-bezek is original to Judg 1 and related to the locality of Bezek. Late textual tradition did not understand this and sought to identify him with the king of Jerusalem in Josh 10.

1.b. LXX interpreted the Hebrew root שלם to mean "deserted."

1.c. LXX adds Joshua along with Israel as object of the action, another element in the tradition's continued effort to glorify Joshua.

1.d. LXX lacks "and were living among them," a motif used in 9:7 to connect the two narrative elements and added here by even later tradition to make the connection with chap. 9 explicit.

2.a. LXX lacks "and because it was greater than the Ruin," an addition in the MT to enhance the ensuing achievement (Benjamin, *Variations*) and to make the tie to the larger tradition explicit.

3.a. The names are transmitted quite differently by LXX: Hoham becomes Ailam, a name reappearing in LXX for Horam in v 33. Pir'am becomes Phidon, through faulty Hebrew transmission. Japhia becomes Jephthah. Eglon becomes Odollam (cf. Margolis, 172).

4.a. LXX gives a dynamic equivalent, adding δεῦτε, "hurry up."

5.a. LXX reads "Jebusite" for MT "Amorite," connecting the tradition more closely to Jerusalem (cf. 15:8, 63; 18:28; Judg 1:21; 2 Sam 5:6).

5.b. LXX lacks "they assembled," an addition in the tradition showing that the appeal of v 4 was carried out.

6.a. LXX read "inhabitants" for "men," thus repeating the expression of v 1.

6.b. LXX adds the redundant "of Israel," whereby the tradition makes the identity explicit.

10.a. LXX adds "the sons" which may have fallen out after the similar לפני "before." This recurs in v 11.

10.b. LXX makes Yahweh the explicit subject, while Syriac and Targumic evidence shows a plural subject, a phenomenon witnessed by G, S, and Frg. Tg. for the following verbs. This seeks to avoid the picture of God pursuing and striking.

10.c. For Beth-Horon, LXX reads Ωρωνω, otherwise a Moabite city (Isa 15:5; Jer 48:3, 5, 34; Moabite stone). Dittography of the final ן may be the ultimate cause of confusion. LXX is more difficult reading but cannot be accepted.

11.a. LXX reads "hail," anticipating the following line.

11.b. LXX redundantly adds "in the battle," perhaps reflecting an early textual variant (Benjamin, *Variations*).

12.a. For the use of אז to unite a clearly recognizable unit to the context loosely, see Dus, *VT* 10 (1960) 358, n.1.

12.b. LXX reads God for Yahweh and continues "gave over the Amorites into the hands of Israel, when he smashed them in Gibeon and they were shattered before the sons of Israel, and Joshua said. . . ." C. D. Ginsburg (*Introduction to the Masoretico-Critical Edition of the Hebrew Bible;* [London: Trinitarian Bible Society, 1897] 176), Benjamin and Soggin (119) are right in seeing this as homoeoteleuton. Auld (VTSup 30 [1979] 13) is probably correct in seeing God here and in v 14 as the original reading, explaining the corruption of ἔθνος, "nation" to θεός, "god," within the Greek transmission of v 13.

12.c. LXX lacks "in the sight of Israel," which may have entered the tradition after the previous line was omitted in the Hebrew tradition.

13.a. The use of גוי, "nation," to refer to Israel is somewhat rare and is often changed to גויו, on the basis of haplography of the preceding מ (Delitzsch, Noth, Hertzberg, 74; Gray, 110; etc.). Israel is pictured as גוי in 5:6, and R. E. Clements ("גוי," *TWAT* 1 [1973] 970–73) shows that Israel was often referred to as גוי prior to the postexilic priestly writings. Emendation without textual support is not in order here.

13.b. The quotation formula is lacking in LXX. Alfrink, Sawyer, (*PEQ*104 [1972] 140) and Benjamin argue for priority of LXX, while most commentators ignore the fact. Auld (VTSup 30 [1979] 13) suggests that a later edition introduced the citation formula on the basis of 2 Sam 1:18. The citation interrupts the context. The later tradition would have had no reason to omit the reference.

14.a. LXX omits "voice" to tone down the anthropomorphism (Benjamin).

15.a. V 15 does not appear in LXX, nor does the corresponding v 43. These probably represent the work of the later tradition tying the entire tradition to Gilgal (cf. Auld, VTSup 30 [1979] 13; Benjamin; *Variations*).

18.a. "Big" does not appear in LXX in vv 18 and 27 and may represent later amplification of the narrative.

19.a. זנב derives from the noun "tail." It is used here and in Deut 25:18 to mean seize and destroy or attack the rear guard (cf. LXX).

19.b. LXX reads "our God" in both instances in this verse, following a regular pattern of differentiation from MT (Auld, VTSup30 [1979] 11–12). This may reflect liturgical usage of the tradition personalizing references to deity.

20.a. LXX reads "every son," an attempt of the later tradition to underline the total involvement of the community.

20.b. שריד, "remnant, survivor," is used in two formulaic expressions in Joshua: "until no remnant at all remained for him" (8:22; 10:33; 11:8; cf. Deut 3:3; 2 Kgs 10:11; Num 21:35); "he did not cause a remnant to remain" (10:28, 30, 37, 39, 40; cf. Deut 2:34). Only in 10:20 does a verbal form of the root appear: "but a remnant remained." LXX abbreviates the sentence but reflects the rare verbal usage. LXX represents free rendering.

21.a. LXX lacks "to the camp" a regular LXX feature by which the camp is never located outside Gilgal (cf. 8:13; 18:9).

21.b. The final element of the verse is an idiom elsewhere associated with a dog (Exod 11:7) and translated literally "to point the tongue at," meaning "to threaten." LXX translates "to grumble, murmur." The function of לאיש literally "to a man," is debated in the present text. The initial ל is usually deleted as dittography, making "man" the indefinite subject. It could be read adverbially, meaning totally, unanimously. The indefinite subject would then be expressed by the verb form. The older suggestion to supply "dog" as subject as in Exodus is no longer taken seriously.

22.a. "To me" is lacking in LXX and may have been added as the tradition underscored the authority of Joshua. Similarly, LXX lacks "to him" in v 23 as well as the introductory formula of obedience there.

24.a. "These kings" is superfluous and is omitted by LXX. Later tradition underlines the explicit obedience to Joshua.

24.b. LXX reads, "Joshua called together all Israel and the chief commanders of the battle who went out with him, saying to them . . ." "Man of Israel" in MT may have been inserted on the basis of chap. 9. A few Hebrew MSS do not witness it, nor does the Syriac. MT makes explicit that the address was only to the commanders and may reflect later tradition.

24.c. LXX lacks "these kings," having only the possessive pronoun "their." The text may have had the suffix הם which later copyists took for the initial letters of המלכם, "kings," or later tradition may have sought to formulate command and execution exactly alike.

25.a. LXX has not understood the general form of the oracle of salvation and has applied it to the specific case. "Do not fear *them.*"

26.a. LXX omits "afterward he struck them." The text is redundant and perhaps represents later tradition's attempts to unite the text with v 24 after the intrusive note in 25.

28.a. LXX has the indefinite "they" as subject. Later tradition again underscored the role and authority of Joshua.

28.b. "And its king" is out of place in the formulary style of the section and is omitted by LXX. Later tradition sought to make all the formulaic statements complete. The addition included "them" in the following clause.

28.c. LXX also witnesses tendency to complete the formulaic expressions by adding καὶ διαπε-φευγώς = ופליט (cf. 8:22; Jer 42:17; 44:14; Lam 2:22). A similar tendency appears in LXX in vv 30, 33.

33.a. "And everything alive in it" does not appear in LXX and represents tendency to full formula. LXX, on the other hand, has plural subjects (cf. v 28) avoiding any possibility of understanding Yahweh as subject of such human activities. The Hebrew subject is ambivalent, being capable of interpretation as Yahweh, Israel, or Joshua. Israel is most likely in the context. Greek completes the formula with "he utterly destroyed it."

34.b. LXX adds formulaically "with the edge of the sword."

35.a. LXX adds "and Yahweh gave it over into the hand of Israel," again inserting the full formulation (Benjamin suggests homoeoteleuton in MT).

35.b. LXX avoids repetition of "in that day," which may have been added by the tradition to underscore the miraculous.

36.a. LXX omits "from Eglon" which may again represent full formulation in the tradition.

37.a. LXX lacks "they captured it" and changes the subject to singular. No mention is made of the king, since his death was presupposed in v 26. This omission drew with it the following "and its cities."

39.a. Evidence from a few Hebrew manuscripts and a Targum support the plural subject.

39.b. Filling out the form, LXX adds "and its king," but then omits the final "just as . . ." clause, which is syntactically awkward but which rounds off the section 29–39 as a literary unit and which would not have been added by the later tradition.

40.a. LXX lacks "all," which has been added by tradition to underline the completeness of the conquest.

41.a. "Joshua smote" does not appear in LXX and may reflect later amplification.

43.a. Cf. note 15a.

Form/Structure/Setting

The temporal clause of v 1 marks the transition to the new section, tying the material both to the preceding narrative and to 9:1–2. The MT has a concluding formula in v 15a, but the LXX gives the more original reading (Notes, 15a). With its insertion of 15, the tradition has noted that a narrative unit is complete at that point. However, the following material was closely tied to 1–14 by the compiler and continues his theme. This is concluded by the summary formula of v 42. The tradition has again marked the end of the unit by adding v 43. A new transition is made in 11:1, paralleling in form that of 10:1. Thus the unit for study is 10:1–42 (43).

As has long been recognized, the unit has several traditional components. Verses 1–11 represent a typical miraculous holy war narrative, introduced by the temporal clause (1–2), leading to the imperfect consecutives building up narrative tension. These are skillfully augmented by parallel dialogue sections (vv 4, 6b) by which both sides expand the action to their allies. The climax occurs in the salvation oracle (v 8), the expected resolution then being described in 9–11. The formulaic conclusion comes in 11b.

Traditional poetry appears in 12bB, 13aA, with an introduction in 12a–bA and a summary conclusion in 13aB, b, 14.

A new narrative begins in midstream with v 16. It presents an unexpected variant ending to the previous narrative, having no narrative introduction of its own. It does have a distinctive setting. While vv 1–11 center on Gibeon (v 10) and the descent of Beth-Horon (v 11), vv 16–27 center on Makkedah (16). The two have been linked through the introduction of Makkedah into the first narrative (v 10).

The second narrative apparently reaches its climax quickly in the report to Joshua (v 17) and his response (18), but the continuation confuses the issue and complicates the plot. A new issue is at stake—the remnant. Joshua's orders are supplemented (v 19), and only these supplementary orders are carried out (v 20). The scene then shifts back to the starting point at the cave (21), where new orders (22) appear to contradict the original ones. These, however, are carried out (23), giving rise to yet another command (24) and then a general formula of encouragement (v 25). An apparent concluding formula appears then in 26, only to be continued unexpectedly with the etiological ending (27). Narrative form has disintegrated. Narrative tension quickly disappears. The narrative sidetrack in 19–20 prepares for the formulaic list of 29–39. The narrative continuation in 21–27 is an illustration of holy war technique and theology with the etiological formula being secondary interpretation (B. Childs, "A Study of the Formula, 'Until This Day,' " *JBL* 82 [1963] 288). V 28 provides a holy war summary for the preceding.

Verses 29–39 form a unit as shown by the summary formula concluding the section and pointing back to its beginning. That Libnah, Lachish, Eglon formed an original unity (Schunck, Benjamin, 31–33; Weimar, *Bib* 57 [1976] 52–53) is possible, but not proven. The unit represents a logical pattern of conquest in Judah, one quite possibly taken by Sennacherib and Nebuchadnezzar (cf. Wright, *JNES* 5 [1946] 109–12; Halpern, *CBQ* 37 [1975] 314–15; N. Na'aman, "Sennacherib's Campaign to Judah and the Date of the *lmlk* Stamps," *VT* 29 [1979] 61–86). It is thus a typical conquest summary.

The theological summary appears in 40–42.

Thus formally, the chapter contains a holy war narrative, a poetic fragment with prosaic introduction and conclusion, a narrative fragment transformed into a secondary etiology to illustrate holy war technique, a typical conquest itinerary, and a theological summary.

What lies behind these materials? How have they received their present form? The solutions to the tradition history behind the battle of Gibeon are myriad. Alt (*Kleine Schriften* 1, 187–89) saw it as the one battle in which Joshua was firmly anchored. Noth expressed doubts about Joshua's anchorage in the tradition, but held to the historical battle between Israel and Canaanite city states. Sawyer (*PEQ* 104 [1972] 139) dates the material exactly to an eclipse of the sun which lasted four minutes on 30 September 1131 B.C. beginning at 12:40 P.M. Rösel (*VT* 26 [1976] 506–7) limits the action to Jarmuth and Azekah against Gibeon. Weimar (*Bib* 57 [1976] 61–62) transposes the narrative to a battle pitting Gibeon against Israel. Schunck (*Benjamin,* 37–39) travels the other direction to see a coalition of Ephraimites, Benjaminites, and Judahites joining forces against the Amorites. For Dus (*VT* 10 [1960] 360–61) the story is an etiological invention of the compiler to explain a heroic song, whose true origin lay in a polemical curse against the cities of the Sun and Moon god. The list of theories is almost endless.

A few facts appear clear. The first narrative rests on old Jerusalem tradition of a king of Jerusalem whose name contained the divine component Zedek (cf. Gen 14:18). Its locus is confined to the area of Gibeon and Beth-Horon. At least the kings of Jarmuth and Azekah, whose cities play no role in the following traditions, were included (so Rösel, *VT* 26 [1976] 506–7). The tradition told how the coalition against Gibeon was defeated by a nighttime march of Joshua.

The original home of such a tradition may well have been the same as that of chap. 9: Gibeon. The Gibeonites used it to explain how Israel's great hero Joshua had shown himself true to the treaty which bound Israel and Gibeon together. They used it to protest against the treatment they received at the hands of Saul and Solomon.

The Israelite compiler transformed the tradition into an example of holy war narrative. To do so, he utilized yet another tradition of Israelite battle on the descent of Beth-Horon going toward Azekah (v 11). No other contours of the tradition are apparent. He inserted into the original Gibeon narrative the Israelite holy war narrative elements: great fear of the enemy (v 2); the salvation oracle (v 8), and the theological summary (v 11b).

The Compiler used the poetic fragment to make the miracle more prominent. The poem may well be related to pieces such as Exod 15:21; Judg 5; Num 21:14–15; 21:27–30 commemorating early military achievements. Its precise context is forever lost. It could well be related originally to the same context as the core of 1–10a. As such it would be a prayer for the sun not to rise and for the moon to remain in control (Gray, 110). The compiler has interpreted it in a different perspective. He has created a chapter of pursuit by introducing 10b. The miracle is one of extended daylight for him (13b). In 14 he reiterated the holy war theme, while also underlining the unique position of Joshua.

The Makkedah tradition concerned five kings buried in a cave there, quite possibly the five kings listed in v 23, whose joint actions near Makkedah are much more probable than in the vicinity of Beth-Horon. The Compiler has then inserted all these kings into the earlier narrative. He has also inserted his pursuit motif to transform the burial story into a lesson for holy war. Burial in the cave is only a temporary measure while Israel pursues the remnant. He also added the etiological formula to show the validity of his holy war lesson for the contemporary generation.

Finally the Compiler used a conquest itinerary to create the final leg of his pursuit. The tradition behind such a list can probably never be recovered. Certainly it stands in tension with the traditions of Josh 15:13–19; 16:10; Judg 1:10–15, 20; cf. 1 Kgs 9:16. For the compiler, the tradition illustrated his own theological conclusion (40–42).

The Compiler has thus given the chapter its basic form. Repeated Deuteronomistic redactional levels are not evident (*contra* Weimar, *Bib* 57 [1976] 51–62). Rather a few modest changes may have been introduced to underline the totality of the destruction (cf. v 20, the total destruction refrain in vv 28, 30, 33, 37, 39, 40, and perhaps v 25).

Comment

[1] The opening verse ties the conquest narratives together into a unit, referring back to Jericho (chap. 6), Ai. (chaps. 7–8), and Gibeon (chap. 9). [2] The following verse introduces the holy war ideology which dominates the chapter. In so doing it harks back to the theme of 2:9, the fear of the inhabitants of

the land before the mighty acts of Yahweh. This demonstrates that despite the covenant made with inhabitants of the land, Israel remains in proper relationship to Yahweh. Joshua's measures have been sufficient. The plural verb form has no antecedent in the present context. It may represent an earlier form of the narrative (Noth) or simply refer to the inhabitants of Jerusalem without specifically introducing them into the narrative. The comparison of Gibeon with Ai probably represents the Gibeonite city at the time of the Israelite monarchy (cf. J. B. Pritchard "Gibeon's History in the Light of Excavation," VTSup 7 [1960] 4–5, 11–12). The description serves to emphasize the even greater power of Israel and her God. It appears to imply that Gibeon had the power of one of the city-states but did not have a king. It is often surmised that a council of elders ruled the city (cf. 9:11).

Excavations in Jerusalem and references in Near Eastern documents show that Jerusalem occupied a prominent place in Palestine by the nineteenth century (execration tablets). Apparently the wall erected in that era lasted until the seventh century. The city's wide range of influence in the southern hill country is well documented in the Amarna Letters, seven of which come from its king, Abdi-Khepa. It became Israelite only with its capture by David (2 Sam 5:6–10).

Hebron has ancient patriarchal traditions preserved in Gen 23:1–7; 13:18; 18:1; Num 13:22. Its conquest is attributed to Caleb in Josh 15:13; Judg 1:20. It is located about nineteen miles (thirty kilometers) south of Jerusalem, controlling the road south to Beersheba and two passes to the coastal plain.

Jarmuth is generally identified with Tell Jarmuth (Khirbet Yarmouk), three miles (five kilometers) southwest of Beth Shemesh and (twenty-five kilometers) southwest of Jerusalem. A brief trial excavation has revealed only Early Bronze Age remains (ca. 2650–2350). Thus its location is not certain. An Amarna age letter found at Tell el-Hesi mentions Jarmuth, but no other biblical narratives do.

Lachish has a long history reaching into prehistorical times. It is notorious for its expansionist policies in the fourteenth century as evidenced in the Amarna Letters, eighteen of which have been discovered there. Three kings are named: Zimreda, Shipti-Balu, and Yabni-Ilu. The city is mentioned here for the first time in the Bible. It is located at Tell ed-Duweir, eighteen miles (thirty kilometers) southeast of Ashkelon and fifteen miles (twenty-five kilometers) west of Hebron. Late Chalcolithic and Early Bronze Age settlements are followed by signs of eighteenth century settlement, with an extensive Late Bronze Age settlement representing the city's prime, even without defensive walls (D. Ussishkin, "Excavations at Tel Lachish," Tel Aviv 5 [1978] 91). This thirteenth century city was destroyed by fire and abandoned for a considerable period. The most recent excavator attributes the burning to Joshua (D. Ussishkin, Tel Aviv 5 [1978] 92).

Eglon is such a center of archaeological debate that the recent Supplement to the Interpreter's Dictionary of the Bible gives two articles, one by A. Rainey (252), supporting Tell 'Aitun, seven miles (twelve kilometers) southeast of Lachish and ten miles (seventeen kilometers) southwest of Hebron, and one by D. G. Rose (252–53) supporting Tell el-Hesi, seven miles (eleven kilometers) west south west of Lachish. Tell el-Hesi was destroyed in the thirteenth century and reoccupied in the tenth. (For other suggested locations, cf. Gray, 108; Bimson, *Redating,* 212). Outside the present context, the Bible mentions Eglon only in Josh 12:12 and 15:39.

Debir appears here as the name of a king. In vv 38–39; 11:21; 12:13; 15:7, 15, 49; 21:15; Judg 1:11, and 1 Chr 6:43, it is a city. Its location is a matter of scholarly debate. Proposals include Tell Beit Mirsim, thirteen miles (twenty kilometers) southwest of Hebron; Khirbet Tarrameh, five miles (nine kilometers) southwest of Hebron; or Khirbet Rabud, seven and a half miles west of Hebron. M. Kochavi ("Debir," *IDBSup* [1976] 222) calls it the largest and most important Canaanite city south of Hebron.

⁴ Israel's inroads into the land threaten the stability of the establishment. The king of Jerusalem takes drastic measures, calling together the major city-state chieftains of the south. The Amarna letters illustrate such tactics well. There we see Shuwardata of Hebron protesting against the strong-arm policies of 'Abdu-Heba of Jerusalem (Letter 280, *ANET,* 487), but then we learn that the same two kings have joined together against Hapiru opposition (Letter RA, xix, *ANET,* 487). Other letters show the king of Jerusalem constantly appealing to the Pharaoh for help against his enemies.

⁶ Gibeon responds in kind, calling upon her ally for protection in face of invasion. Joshua is pictured as maintaining his headquarters at Gilgal (cf. v 10), so that Gilgal may be the eventual source of the Israelite tradition. The appeal employs the typical ploy of exaggeration. Now "all the kings of the Amorites," not just five, are involved.

⁷ Joshua proves himself true to his commitment, even when the commitment was made under false pretenses. He takes his entire fighting force with him.

⁸ But the victory does not rest with Joshua and his power. The victory depends upon the divine Word and divine action. A prophetic oracle of salvation insures victory for God's commander.

⁹ Divine assurance does not exclude human wit and action. Joshua stages a surprise dawn attack after an all-night march. From Gilgal to Gibeon would entail a march of about eighteen miles (thirty kilometers). Soggin (127) claims it could be carried out in eight to ten hours. The Hebrew text of 9:17 claims that it took three days for Joshua to reach Gibeon the first time. The notice there may intentionally point to the present verse to underline the remarkable achievement of Joshua and his men here.

¹⁰ Yahweh sent the enemy into a panic before the unexpected reinforcements. This panic, Heb. הּמם is a technical term in holy war narratives, binding Exod 14; Josh 10; Judg 4; and 1 Sam 7 together (cf. Richter, *Untersuchungen,* 52–53; Weimar, *Bib* 57 [1976] 38–39, 70–73). It is closely tied to storm phenomena (cf. Exodus 14:24; 1 Samuel 7:10; Josh 10:11; cf. further, H.-P. Müller, "המם," *TWAT* 2 [1977] 449–54).

The narrative may well have ended at one time with the great victory at Gibeon (10a), but the present context uses the narrative as an introduction to its real theme, the pursuit. This begins on the ascent of Beth Horon. The name probably represents an early Canaanite sanctuary for the god Horon, who is mentioned in the execration texts and in Ugaritic materials. The city is actually in two parts, an upper and a lower, dominating the northern pass to the Shephelah. Upper Beth-Horon is five miles (eight kilometers) northwest of Gibeon, while the Lower Beth Horon lies six and a half miles (eleven kilometers) northwest of Gibeon.

Azekah is usually located at Tell-ez-Zakariyel, fifteen miles (twenty-five kilometers) south of Beth Horon and fifteen miles (twenty-five kilometers) northwest of Hebron. It has always been a strategic military outpost as shown by its appearance in the Lachish letters (*ANET,* 322) and in a recently discovered inscription of Senacherib (N. Na'aman, "Sennacherib's campaign to Judah and the date of the *lmlk* stamps," *VT* 29 [1979] 61–86). Its capture opened the way through the Elah Valley to Lachish. Excavations carried out at the turn of the century have been subject to varying interpretations (cf. E. Stern, "Azekah," *EAEHL* 1 [1975] 141–43). It certainly had a long history prior to the Israelite occupation.

Makkedah is introduced into the text here in an awkward fashion to join the narrative to that which follows. The main tradition centers on the cave here (vv 16–27), while v 28 turns the attention to a city. Its location remains quite uncertain. V. Gold ("Makkedah," *IDB* 3 [1962] 228) suggests Tell es-Safi, which others would identify with Libnah or Gath (E. Stern, "Es-Safi, Tell," *EAEHL* 4 [1978] 1024–27; cf. Bimson, *Redating,* 212–13). In any case, the pursuit goes southward.

11 The center of interest for the Compiler is the act of God. It makes little difference to him that the greatest part of the miracle would be sending hail stones that killed only enemies. Israel's experience has shown that God provides victory for his people in battle. Israel does not have to depend upon her own power. She can rely on her God, when her God can rely upon her. The point made is that the victory was much more due to the power of God than to that of Joshua. This was a message of real comfort to the readers of the Deuteronomistic history, when in exile they found themselves in a much weaker position militarily than did Joshua. R. B. Y. Scott ("Meteorological Phenomena and Terminology in the Old Testament," *ZAW* 64 [1952] 19) has shown that such hail storms in the Palestinian spring can produce stones two inches in diameter.

12 The last half of 12a certainly is an editorial link with the present context. The original context for the first part of the verse stands open to debate. It could well have been linked to the poem in the original source. The nature of the poetic miracle is another subject of wide debate. The Hebrew verb דמם can mean "to be motionless" or "to be silent." It may have meant that the heavenly bodies did not shine (Noth) or that the sun stood still and did not move, as it is interpreted by the Compiler (v 13b). Such poetry may have been motivated by a cosmic eclipse (Sawyer, *PEQ* 104 [1972] 139–46), by a Palestinian hailstorm (Scott *ZAW* 64 [1952] 19–20) or by an understanding of heavenly signs and portents by which proper positions of the heavenly bodies are important for earthly events (Holladay, *JBL* 87 [1968] 176). The precise context of the original poem will probably never be discovered.

Other questions are more important for theological exegesis. If one does not emend the text, the poem is a direct address to the heavenly bodies. This is normal for Israel's neighbors, where the moon and sun would be seen as gods. It is astounding in Israel, where even the creation story refuses to name the sun and moon, being content to refer to the greater and lesser light (Gen 1:14–19). Such language could easily be interpreted as worship of and prayer to the heavenly deities. The biblical writer carefully avoids this. Joshua speaks to Yahweh through such language (12a). Thus the importance of Joshua is underscored. He is a man of prayer empowered to command the great "gods" of Israel's neighbors. But he can do so only because Yahweh listens to him (v 14).

The tradition has understood the poem to be an excerpt from an ancient collection (v 13; cf. *Notes*). This is called the book of Jashar (="Upright") here and in 1 Sam 1:18. The LXX in 1 Kgs 8:12–13 refers to a book of Song, which represents a transposition of two letters in the Hebrew from ישר to שיר. The name and contents of the book again are not the most important issue. What is noteworthy is that the Hebrew tradition understood its scripture as based on even more ancient sources. This implies the removal of the final authors of Scripture from eye witnesses to compilers of early traditions and sources, just as critical scholarship has shown on other grounds. The criteria for authority and canonicity in the OT is not that of having been an eyewitness of the events. Rather, it is that of having been inspired by God to use the traditions of the nation to interpret the identity of the nation for the future. The book of Joshua is based on old traditions and sources, but its final form was achieved only in the exilic period, and even then, as comparison with the LXX and other versions quickly shows, the text was not fixed. The material was authoritative, but open for new interpretation in light of new experiences with God. Only at a quite late date was the canon seen as unchangeable text. Even then the process of interpretation continued, giving rise to the oral traditions recanonized by the Jewish community into the Talmud.

The Compiler of the text sees the poetic fragment as giving further witness to his theme, that God fights for Israel. Here is the central motif of holy war theology. Addressed to the exilic community in its final form, the book does not encourage the people to retrace the steps of Joshua in totally demolishing all enemies so much as to trust Yahweh to fulfill his promises to his people and to do the necessary fighting for them, even against overwhelming odds. Israel is not to waste her time planning battle strategy and gathering armies. She is to spend her energies finding and doing the will of God, being Israel.

16–28 The Compiler continues his pursuit motif, though all opposition appeared to be destroyed. His reason appears in v 19. Israel must complete her assigned duties. God fights for Israel. He also fights with and through Israel. She cannot expect the victory, however, if she does not do her part. She did not carry out God's battle plan at Ai and was defeated (chap. 7). She risked her identity as people of God by letting the Gibeonites trick her (chap. 9). Now she again faces the challenge. Will she complete her work for God? God has given the enemy into her hands. But she must take the enemies. She cannot stand around and celebrate victory, when total victory and total obedience are not yet realities.

20 Israel had lost valuable time, however, and did not totally achieve her objective. A remnant remained. The pursuit must continue. But first, Israel

must learn another lesson. After the battle, the people return to camp in שלום (v 21). The people who follow God's orders and complete the battle for God are led back to the camp and find they have wholeness, safety, health. This state, not that of battle, is the goal for the people of God. This is the gift of God to the obedient people. It is the offer to be given enemies before entering into battle (Deut 2:26; 20:10). It is the reward for battle properly carried out. No one threatens the obedient Israel (v 21).

It is noteworthy that here (v 21) the camp is at Makkedah. The Compiler does not seem to have an ideal of the exclusiveness and importance of the camp at Gilgal as did the later tradition (see Notes to v 15, 21).

22-27 The attitude of obedience is further illustrated as Joshua issues commands and the people obey. At the same time the section illustrates the authority of Joshua, the leader of Israel. An important point is that the military commanders are shown to be obedient to the authority of Joshua. In the present context this paints a picture of the man of God's choosing, the man obedient to the Mosaic law (chap. 1) as having power over the military strongmen. Priorities in leadership are set up for Israel.

The picture of placing the foot on the neck of the enemy as a sign of triumph is also the background for Ps 18:41 (= 2 Sam 22:41; cf. G. Schmuttermayr, *Psalm 18 und 2 Samuel 22.* [SANT 25. München: Kösel-Verlag, 1971] 160; M. Dahood, *Psalms* I, [AB. Garden City, NY: Doubleday, 1966] 116; cf. Exod 23:27; Isa 51:23; *ANEP,* No. 393).

25 The present passage is not meant simply to report the events of the past. It has a message for the people of Israel, a message of courage and comfort. The words once delivered to Joshua as he took up his task (1:7, 9, 18) are now given by him to Israel. The people of God have no need to fear their enemies. God fights for his people, protects and guides them with his presence. The conquest was not a once-and-for-all event. It is typical of God's work for his people. Whenever an obstacle stands before people of God, they need not fear. God is there to conquer for his people.

27 Even as Joshua speaks words of encouragement and promise of future victory, he exemplifies the other half of the equation. He obeys the law which God gave Moses, in this instance Deut 21:22–23. The land God is giving his people must not be defiled by a body hanging overnight (Deut 21:23). Joshua obediently takes the bodies down and buries them fittingly in the hole they tried to use for refuge. Now they have eternal refuge from life's worries. This place of refuge is important for Israel. It is a reminder of what God has done for her and of the significance of that past act for the present day. The people who experience divine victory are all too prone to forget. Israel has reminders all over her countryside calling her to remember and to obey.

28-39 The conquest list completes the history of pursuit. As Joshua had obeyed, so Israel sets out again to follow God into battle. They are not satisfied with victory. They must obey the divine command to totally obliterate any opposition in the land which might tempt them to follow other gods (Deut 20:16–18). The present formulation of the list shows that Israel did precisely what her law commanded (cf. vv 30, 32, 33, 35, 37, 39, 40). Thus after the catastrophe at Ai and the foolhardy action with Gibeon, Israel once again assumes her place as totally obedient people of Yahweh, fulfilling the command of Yahweh to the letter. At the same time, Yahweh has shown himself to be a God who accepts a people who follow him despite their past mistakes.

Libnah occurs unexpectedly for the first time here. This shows that the list is independent from the original narrative. The location of Libnah is disputed. The meaning of the name is "white," which has often led to an identification with Tell es-Safi (see above to location of Makkedah). Elliger (*PJ* 30 [1934] 47–71) has suggested Tell Burnat, sixteen miles south of Lachish. A. Rainey ("Libnah," *IDBSup* [1976] 546) argues that Tell es-Safi can no longer be considered at all. Tell el-Judeideh has also been suggested (A. Negev [ed.], "Judeideh [Tell El-]" *Archaeological Encyclopedia of the Holy Land,* [London: Weldenfeld & Nicolson, 1972] 176), but this is more commonly identified with Moresheth-Gath, the home of the prophet Micah (M. Broshi, "Judeideh, Tell," *EAEHL* 3 [1977] 694). Wright suggests that Tell Burnat began in the late Bronze Age and would have been only a small fortified outpost ("A Problem of Ancient Topography: Lachish and Eglon," *HTR* 64 [1971] 444).

33 Gezer is located on the boundary of the Judean hills guarding the road leading from the way of the sea to the Valley of Ajalon and on to Jerusalem. It is referred to frequently in Egyptian sources and plays an important role in the Amarna correspondence. Here it is shown as responding to the distress of a neighboring city-state just as the king of Jerusalem called for help from his neighbors. The defeat does not include destruction of the city (cf. 16:10; Judg 1:20; 1 Kgs 9:15–17).

41 The Compiler has a different geographical span in view—that of the Davidic empire. Here is the land that belongs to Israel. Israel's persistent pursuit reaped rewards. The traditions at hand do not include all the land involved, but the editor draws from the available traditions the conclusion that God has fulfilled his promises and given all the southern territory to his people. In so doing, he does not note that his sources speak at best of a "victorious raid" (Soggin, 132) rather than a battle of conquest leaving settlers behind in each conquered city. This is unimportant for the writer. He looks back on a history of Israel with God, a history in which Israel occupies the land. He seeks to use the traditions available to him to show how Israel has gained this land. The traditions give him every right to talk about the great military victories of Joshua and Israel. This is precisely what he does not emphasize. He speaks of the great victories of God fulfilling his promises to his people. Yahweh has fought for his people and given them the land.

Explanation

A complex set of traditions serves the Compiler as he sets out the fulfillment of God's promises to Israel and the way in which God fulfills such promises. A basic tradition of Israel's faithfulness to her commitment to Gibeon is transformed into an introduction to a story of pursuit. The story of physical pursuit is interspersed with the teachings about Israel's pursuit of her spiritual identity as people of Yahweh. The pursuit is pictured on the physical plain as the conquest of the southern territory. Such a conquest is made possible through the use of a basic tradition of victory at Gibeon, punishment at Makkedah, and a list of cities on the conquest itinerary. These sources are brilliantly transposed into a spiritual pilgrimage to the goal of being people of God.

The identity given the people of God has several components. As throughout the early chapters of the book, particular emphasis is laid on the role of Israel's leader. Joshua is shown to be the leader without parallel in that God listened to his command. Such a definition of leadership is not left without modification. Joshua is immediately pictured as the leader who carries out the divine commands. He does not tarry to celebrate victory, but rather continues the pursuit until the battle is won. Fulfilling the role given him in the first chapter, he displays the fearless courage of leadership and admonishes his generals to do likewise. He can convert the near-tragedy of the covenant with foreigners living in the land into an example of the obedience and victory of God's people.

Obedience to the divine law is a second component. This is the law of holy war as spelled out in Deuteronomy. Such obedience laid particular emphasis on the total annihilation of the enemy. Such thoughts bring shivers to the modern conscience. The editor of Joshua knew that such a program had not been carried out consistently. Too many people remained in the land. Chapter 10 is careful to avoid any mention that Jerusalem was destroyed. The motif has aims far beyond pure historical description. The motif shows the great lengths to which Joshua and his people went to obey God. It underlines the total victory God gave *once*. It thus spelled hope that an exiled Israel might again win the land once more occupied by foreigners. An Israel punished because she trusted her covenants with foreign powers more than she did her covenant with Yahweh might receive yet another chance if she could find leadership like that of Joshua and obedience like that of the nation in the period of conquest. Would the exiled nation pursue God as steadfastly as Joshua pursued his opponents and God's law? Or would they continue their pursuit of the enemy's gods? Would Israel again allow Yahweh to fight for Israel? Would the day come again when Israel returned to her camp in safety with no man threatening her?

Northern Annihilation (11:1–23)

Bibliography

Abel, F. M. "Les stratagèmes dans le Livre de Josué." *RB* 56 (1949) 335–38. **Aharoni, Y.** "New Aspects of Israelite Occupation in the North." *Near Eastern Archaeology in the Twentieth Century,* ed. J. A. Sanders. Garden City, NY: Doubleday, 1970, 254–67. ———. "Problems of the Israelite Conquest in the Light of Archaeological Discoveries." *Antiquity and Survival* 2 (1957) 131–50. **Alt, A.** "Erwägungen über die Landnahme der Israeliten in Palästina." *PJ* 35 (1939) 17–19. (=*Kleine Schriften zur Geschichte des Volkes Israel.* Vol. 1. München: C. H. Beck'sche Verlagsbuchhandlung, 1953, 134–35.)

Bardtke, H. *Bibel, Spaten und Geschichte.* Göttingen: Vandenhoeck & Ruprecht, 1969, 200–209. **Bimson, J. J.** *Redating the Exodus and Conquest.* JSOTSup 5. Sheffield: University of Sheffield, 1978, 185–200. **Bright, J.** *The Authority of the Old Testament.* Nashville: Abingdon, 1967, 241–51. **DeVries, S. J.** "Temporal Terms as Structural Elements in the Holy-War Tradition." *VT* 25 (1975) 80–83. **Fritz, V.** "Das Ende der spätbronzezeitlichen Stadt Hazor Stratum XIII und die biblische Überlieferung in Jos. 11:1–15 und Ri. 4:1–3, 23, 24." *UF* 5 (1973) 123–39. **Gray, J.** "Hazor." *VT* 16 (1966) 26–52. **Maass, F.** "Hazor und das Problem der Landnahme." *Von Ugarit nach Qumran,* ed. J. Hempel and L. Rost. BZAW 77. Berlin: Alfred Töpelmann, 1958, 105–17. **Malamat, A.** "The Period of the Judges." *The World History of the Jewish People* 1:3, ed. B. Mazar. Tel-Aviv: Massada, 1971, 135–40. **Mazar, B.** "Beth She'arim, Gaba, and Harosheth of the Peoples." *HUCA* 24 (1952–53) 75–84. **Mowinckel, S.** *Tetrateuch-Pentateuch-Hexateuch.* BZAW 90. Berlin: Alfred Töpelmann, 1964, 40–41. **Noth, M.** "Der Beitrag der Archäologie zur Geschichte Israels." VTSup 7 (1960) 272–73. (*=Aufsätze zur biblischen Landes- und Altertumskunde.* Vol. 1. Neukirchen-Vluyn: Neukirchener Verlag, 1971, 43–44.) ———. "Hat die Bible doch recht?" *Festschrift für Günther Dehn,* ed. W. Schneemelcher. Neukirchen: Neukirchener Verlag, 1957, 14–15. (*=Aufsätze* 1, 25–26). **Otto, E.** *Das Mazzotfest in Gilgal.* BWANT 107. Stuttgart: W. Kohlhammer Verlag, 1975, 93–95. **Rudolph, W.** *Der "Elohist" von Exodus bis Josua.* BZAW 68. Berlin: Alfred Töpelmann, 1938, 209–11. **Schmid, H.** "Erwägungen zur Gestalt Josuas in Überlieferung und Geschichte." *Judaica* 24 (1968) 56. **Schunck, K. D.** *Benjamin.* BZAW 86. Berlin: Alfred Töpelmann, 1963, 26–28. **Stolz, F.** *Jahwes und Israels Kriege.* ATANT 60. Zürich: Theologischer Verlag, 1972, 88. **Weippert, M.** *Die Landnahme der israelitischen Stämme.* FRLANT 92. Göttingen: Vandenhoeck & Ruprecht, 1967, 40–43. (*=The Settlement of the Israelite Tribes in Palestine.* Tr. J. D. Martin. London: SCM, 1971, 33–37.) **de Vaux, R.** *Histoire ancienne d'Israël.* Vol. 1. Paris: J. Gabalda, 1971, 599–605. (*=The Early History of Israel.* Tr. D. Smith. London: Darton, Longman & Todd, 1978, 655–67.) **Yadin, Y.** *Hazor.* London: Oxford University Press, 1972, 9–11, 128–34, 198–99. **Yeivin, S.** *The Israelite Conquest of Canaan.* Istanbul: Nederlands Historisch-Archaeologisch Instituut in het Nabije Oosten, 1971, 83–85. ———. "The Israelite Settlement in Galilee and the Wars with Jabin of Hazor." *Mélanges bibliques rédigés en l'honneur de André Robert.* Paris: Bloud & Gay, 1957, 95–104.

Translation

[1] *When Jabin, king of Hazor, heard, he sent to Jobab, king of Madon,* [a] *and to the king of Shimron and to the king of Achshaph,* [2] *and to the kings who were in the northern* [a] *hill country and in the Arabah south* [b] *of Chineroth and in the Shephalah and in the hills* [c] *of Dor on the west* [d]. [3] *Now the Canaanites from east and west and the Amorites and the Hittites and the Perizzites and the Jebusites in the hill country,* [4] *and the Hivites under Hermon in the land of Mizpah came out—they and all their armies* [a] *with them, a multitude as numerous as the sands on the seashore—along with horses and chariots of immeasurable number.* [5] *All these kings assembled together according to their agreement and came and encamped together at the waters of Merom to do battle with Israel.*

[6] *Yahweh said to Joshua, "Do not fear them, for tomorrow at this time I am giving all of them* [a] *dead to Israel; while their horses you will hamstring, and their chariots you shall burn with fire."* [7] *Joshua came and all the warriors with him* [a] *against them beside the waters of Merom suddenly and attacked them.* [b] [8] *Yahweh gave them into the hand of Israel. They smote them and pursued them unto Great Sidon and unto Misrephoth-mayim and unto the valley of Mizpeh to the east. They*

smote them until nothing at all remained for them. ⁹ *Joshua did to them just what Yahweh said to him. Their horses he hamstrung, and their chariots he burned with fire.*

¹⁰ *Joshua turned at that time and captured Hazor, and its king he smote* ᵃ *with the sword because Hazor had previously been the head of all these kingdoms.* ¹¹ *They* ᵃ *smote every person in it with the edge of the sword, applying the ban.* ᵇ *Nothing remained of all that breathed. Hazor he burned with fire.* ¹² *All the cities of these kings and all their kings Joshua captured. He smote them with the edge of the sword, putting them to the ban, just as Moses, the servant of Yahweh, commanded.* ¹³ *The only exception was that all the cities standing on their tells, Israel did not burn, with the exception of Hazor alone, which Joshua* ᵃ *did burn.* ¹⁴ *At the same time, all the spoil of these cities* ᵃ *and the cattle, the sons of Israel appropriated for themselves. It was only all the people that they smote with the edge of the sword until they had utterly destroyed them. They did not leave anything breathing.* ¹⁵ *Just as Yahweh commanded Moses, his servant, thus Moses commanded Joshua, and thus Joshua did. He did not leave one thing undone from all that Yahweh* ᵃ *commanded Moses.*

¹⁶ *Joshua took all this land, the hill country and all the Negeb and all the land of Goshen and the Shephelah and the Arabah and the hill country of Israel and its Shephelah.* ¹⁷ *From Mount Halak going up to Seir clear unto Baal-Gad in the valley of the Lebanon under Mount Hermon, all their kings he captured. He smote them and killed them.*

¹⁸ *For many days Joshua did battle with all these kings.* ¹⁹ *There was not a city which made peace* ᵃ *with the sons of Israel except for the Hivites dwelling in Gibeon. They captured absolutely everything in battle.* ²⁰ *For it had been Yahweh's idea to harden their hearts to encounter Israel in battle in order that they could put them to the ban without their having opportunity to plead for mercy. Indeed this was so that they might annihilate them just as Yahweh commanded Moses.*

²¹ *Joshua came at that time and cut off the Anakim from the hill country, from Hebron, from Debir, from Anab, and from all the hill country of Judah and from all the hill country of Israel.* ᵃ *With their cities, Joshua put them to the ban.* ²² *None of the Anakim remained in the land* ᵃ *of the sons of Israel with the exception that in Gaza, Gath,* ᵇ *and Ashdod, they remained.* ²³ *Joshua took all the land according to all which Yahweh spoke to Moses. Joshua gave it out for a possession of Israel according to their lots by their tribes. Meanwhile, the land had rest from battle.*

Notes

1.a. LXX transliterates the geographical references in this chapter in unexpected ways. Madon becomes Marrōn. Shimron becomes Sumoōn (LXX ᴬ-Somerōn-Samaria). Achshaph becomes Azeiph.

2.a. LXX read צפון, "northern," as צידן, "Sidon," as in v 8 and then added "the great" as v 8.

2.b. LXX reflects a confusion of letters in the Hebrew copying tradition, reading נגד, "over against," for MT נגב, "south."

2.c. The Hebrew נפות, "hills," occurs only here and in 1 Kings 4:11, both times with Dor. Its meaning is uncertain, possibly referring to sand dunes near Dor (Soggin, 134).

2.d. "On the west" was taken by LXX with the next verse to achieve parallelism, translating the word "seacoast" first of the Canaanites and then of the Amorites.

4.a. Copying mistakes have transformed MT מחניהם, "armies" into LXX מלכים, "kings," parallel to v 5. This led to the dropping of "all" by LXX.

6.a. LXX read the sign of the direct object with a suffix rather than MT sign of direct object plus "all of them." The MT may result from dittography of the following חללים.

7.a. LXX lacks "with him against them," which may have entered the text as dittography of the following עלﬞ-מי.

7.b. LXX amplifies the narrative with specific geography: בהר "in the hill country," which may have arisen in confusion with the preceding בהם.

10.a. LXX lacks "he smote with the sword," perhaps through haplography (Holmes, Benjamin).

11.a. The textual tradition is confused in the uses of singular and plural subjects in this verse (cf. *BHS*).

11.b. LXX emphasizes the extent of the ban by adding πάντας, "all."

13.a. LXX reads "Israel" for Joshua, continuing the confusion of subjects (cf. 11k). MT may reflect continued tendency of tradition to emphasize the role of Joshua.

14.a. LXX lacks "of these cities and the cattle," possibly an addition by the later tradition to limit the case to this time and not let it be understood as a general practice. A similar tendency is at work in MT addition of אדם, "people," not attested by LXX.

15.a. LXX reads "Moses commanded him," which may reflect simple mistakes in copying (Benjamin, *Variations*), but more probably reflects the later tradition's refusal to leave the last command to Moses.

19.a. LXX abbreviates the verse: "there was not a city which Israel did not take. They took them all in battle." This makes Israel the controlling subject, rather than the enemy city and eliminates the concept of making peace. The omission of the reference to the Gibeonites may reflect the original tradition which later was augmented to make explicit connection to chap 9.

21.a. LXX reads "from all the family of Israel and from all the hill country of Judah." Here the tradition has intensified the meaning while missing the geographical distinction between the two kingdoms. That more than a copyist's error is involved (Benjamin, *Variations*) is seen in the transposition of Israel before Judah.

22.a. LXX lacks "in the land" and interprets Israel as the agent of the action.

22.b. LXX lacks "Gath," which later tradition may have added or which may have dropped out within the Greek tradition (Margolis, 225–26).

Form/Structure/Setting

An introductory formula parallel to that of 10:1 marks the opening of the new section. Its conclusion is problematical. Verse 9 is a formulaic conclusion, but 10 obviously seeks to continue the previous narrative. Verse 15 contains yet another concluding formula. Verse 16, however, introduces a summary parallel to 10:40. The summary can be taken as an independent unit, but the parallel in 10:40 shows that it is intended to be read with the preceding narrative. Verse 20 then gives the concluding formula. This leaves vv 21–23 isolated as a small unit by themselves consisting of a specific notation (21–22) and a general summary transitional statement (23). Though these might be treated in isolation, it is easier in the present format to handle them along with the preceding section to which they are loosely connected.

A holy war narrative describing the victory of Joshua and Israel over a Canaanite coalition near the waters of Merom forms the center of the chapter. This begins with the temporal clause in v 1, builds dramatic tension through the imperfect consecutive clauses of vv 4 and 5, reaches its climax in the dialogue of v 6, and then is resolved in the formulaic imperfect consecutive clauses of vv 7 through 9. Within the narrative, certain interpretative elements appear, particularly the long list in v 3. The obedience theme of v 9 may be attributed to the theological interpretation of the Compiler. The Compiler has shaped the narrative into the same pattern as that of chap. 10. Thus the introduction in v 1 has no real reference point. We are not told what was heard. The conclusion of the battle (v 8aB,b) is placed in the same pursuit thematic characteristic of chap. 10. Interestingly, the tradition is tied in no way to Gilgal or any other Israelite site. No direct clue is available for detecting the original home of the tradition. One would search for it among the peoples of whom the tradition had later meaning, namely the northern tribes, possibly the later Israelite inhabitants of Hazor.

Verse 10 opens a new section of the narrative, one even more closely patterned on chap. 10. No narrative tension is established. Rather, battle reports are summarized in theological terms. The basic question concerns what tradition lies behind such standardized reports. The only report with concrete details concerns Hazor, which had been "head of all these kingdoms." Recent archaeological reports have verified a massive destruction of Hazor in the thirteenth century following a celebrated history.

Hazor was known from the nineteenth century onward as a major city in Palestine. The Mari letters describe some of its extensive trade relationships. Egyptian correspondence from the sixteenth to the fourteenth century reveal Hazor to be a city of importance for the Egyptian empire. The Amarna correspondence shows its troubled relationships with its Palestinian neighbors, its declared loyalty to the Egyptian pharaoh, and friendly relations with the Hapiru. Here the ruler is given the title of "king," an unusual occurrence among Palestinian city-state heads.

Excavations headed by Yadin (*Hazor*, 23–26) have excavated the city's history back to the twenty-seventh century. In the fourteenth and thirteenth centuries the city covered one hundred seventy-five acres, ten times the area of Jerusalem, Megiddo or any other Palestinian city excavated. The population may have numbered 40,000. This city met violent destruction to be replaced in the twelfth and eleventh centuries by an unfortified, temporary settlement resembling others of the period in Galilee often identified as Israelite settlements. Joshua 11 can thus be related to the destruction of the massive Late Bronze Age Hazor, the largest city of Canaan (cf. Yadin, *Hazor*, 129–34; Maass, "Hazor," 113–17; Gray, 117, 120–21; Schunck, Benjamin, *Variations*, 27–28 etc.). Bimson (*Redating*, 185–200), on the other hand, rewrites current archaeological theory and dates the destruction of Hazor by Joshua to the last decades of the fifteenth century.

Having posited the connection between Joshua 11 and the destruction of Hazor revealed by excavation, the commentator must be careful not to say too much. The biblical account itself reports the long fight Israel had to wage to conquer the area (v 18) and the fact that only Hazor of all the major cities was burned (v 13). The loose literary connection between 1–9 and 10–15 (cf. "at that time" v 10) cautions against making firm chronological statements. At best we have an old Israelite tradition preserved by the settlers of Iron Age Hazor describing the destruction of the city. The important point for the tradition was not when and why. The question was how. The answer reverberates even today: God gave it into our hands.

On the other hand, the commentator must not be satisfied with saying too little, while attributing too much to the invention of tradition. This appears to be the tendency of Fritz when he posits a destruction of Hazor by the Sea Peoples and reduces Josh 10–11 and Judg 4 to the free creation of tradition based on the existence of the ruins of Hazor. His tradition-history studies appear to assume a unilinear growth of tradition in which conflicting traditions cannot circulate at the same time. It is precisely the creative genius of the Compiler of the conquest narratives that he has collected the wide range of traditions and used them to create the picture of how God gave Israel the land. A list of cities as in Josh 12 and the ruins of Hazor do not create the narrative traditions behind Josh 10–11. Fritz (*UF* 5 [1973] 123–39) must be heard when he warns against assuming that other city-states or other groups could not have taken such a large city and that only a tribal confederation under Joshua could have taken it. The veracity of the tradition is not founded on the size of Hazor. It is founded on the nature and growth of traditional narrative itself. The correlation between tradition and excavation is not proved but has more probability than a reconstruction without literary support.

Verses 16 through 20 are formulated by the Compiler to provide a parallel summary to that of 10:40–41.

Verses 21 through 23 take up the special tradition of the Anakim, also mentioned in Num 13:22, 28, 33; Deut 1:28; 2:10–11, 21; 9:2; Josh 14:12, 15; 15:13, 14; 21:11; Judg 1:20. These were the "giants" possessing the land desired by Israel. They centered in Hebron from which they were driven out by Caleb (Josh 14:12–15; 15:13–14; Judg 1:20). Our passage, again given in theological report style, attributes their destruction to Joshua. The sudden geographical switch from north to south, the loose literary connection ("at that time," v 21), and the report in Deut 9:2 lead to the assumption that these verses are a literary construction of the Deuteronomist filling out his picture of Joshua.

The final verse is a literary summary and transition pointing backward through chaps. 1 through 11 and pointing forward to chaps. 13 through 21.

Comment

[1] The conquest of the north, as that of the south (chap. 10), is pictured as Israel's response to enemy attack. Israel's victories over Jericho and Ai led Gibeon to seek a peace agreement, but led the two dominant kings—those of Hazor and Jerusalem—to form military alliances with their erstwhile enemies to resist the new military power emerging on the scene. Jabin appears as king of Hazor in Judg 4:2, 7, 17, 23, 24, which is then taken up in Ps 83:10. Since Jabin is not involved in the action of Judg 4, does not appear at all in the parallel account in Judg 5, and is said to have been killed in our section, the tradition of his activity has aroused great scholarly interest. W. Richter (*Traditionsgeschichtliche Untersuchungen zum Richterbuch.* [BBB 18, Bonn: Peter Hanstein, 1963] 56–63) has demonstrated the secondary role of Jabin in the Judg narrative. The attempt by Fritz (*UF* 5 [1973] 123–39) to prove that Jabin is secondary to Judg 4 but still tradition historically prior to the appearance in Josh 11 must be rejected as assuming a unilinear develop-

ment of tradition. Bimson (*Redating*, 195), on the other hand, argues on the basis of Mari evidence, that Jabin was a dynastic name of several kings (cf. Yadin, *Hazor*, 5–6).

The town of Madon appears only here and in the list of 12:19. It is usually located at modern Khirbet Madin due to the similarity of names. This would place it five miles west of Tiberias on the mountain called Qarn Hattin. Y. Aharoni (*Land*, 106) argues for the LXX reading, locating the city by the waters of Merom.

Shimron appears here, in 12:20, and in the list of cities of Zebulon in 19:15. The original name may have been Shimʿon (Aharoni, *Land*, 106). It is usually identified with Khirbet Sammuniyeh five miles (eight kilometers) west of Nazareth in the Esdraelon Valley, but Gray (118) suggests Marun er-Ras, ten miles (seventeen kilometers) northwest of modern Safed, north of the Sea of Chinneroth.

Achshaph appears here, in 12:20, and in the list of Asher cities in 19:25. It is generally identified with Tell Kisan, six miles (ten kilometers) south east of Acco, but Gray (118) suggests Tell Iksif, five and a half miles (nine kilometers) east of Marun er-Ras.

If the traditional identifications are correct, then the Canaanite coalition is pictured as covering the area between the Jordan River and the Mediterranean Sea north of Megiddo. Gray's suggestions would narrow the area to the immediate vicinity of Hazor and the Sea of Chinneroth. In either case, the great northern stronghold trembles and plots before the fame of Israel and her God.

² Verse 2 uses general geographical description to extend the coalition. The kings are neither named nor given specific location. The northern hill country is the mountainous area northwest of the Sea of Chinneroth. The Arabah south of Chinneroth is not a precise description. Arabah usually refers to the Jordan River Valley between the Sea of Chinneroth and the Dead Sea. Occasionally, it refers to the continuation of the depression south of the Dead Sea to the Gulf of Aqabah. In v 2 the expression may refer either to the area immediately south of the Sea of Chinneroth or to the area near the Sea immediately south of the city of Chinneroth on the northwestern shore of the Sea. If the latter is meant, it is unique in OT usage.

Unique language certainly appears in "the Shephalah." The term occurs twenty times and always refers to the area between the Philistine plain and the southern hill country (e.g. Josh 9:1; 10:40; cf. D. Baly, *The Geography of the Bible* [New York: Harper & Row, 1957] 142). The reference here may be to the northern continuation between Mount Carmel and Shechem even though this area is more hilly than the southern Shephalah (cf. G. A. Smith, *The Historical Geography of the Holy Land* [London: Hodder and Stoughton, 1894] 203; Baly, *Geography*, 144).

Dor is identified with Khirbet el-Burj, twelve miles (twenty kilometers) south of Mount Carmel. An inscription of Ramses II from the thirteenth century is the first mention of Dor. The Bible mentions it only here, 12:23; 17:11; Judg 1:27; 1 Kgs 4:11; and 1 Chr 7:29. Located in the territory of Asher, it was assigned to Manasseh but was not captured (17:11–12; Judg 1:27). The account of Wen-Amon (*ANET*, 26) lists its ruler as Beder (ca.

1100) and identifies him as a member of the Sea Peoples, who are closely related to the Philistines. Limited excavations in 1923–24 revealed the city's founding in the Late Bronze Age with a thirteenth century destruction, possibly by the Sea People (cf. G. Foerster, "Dor," *EAEHL* 1 [1975] 334–37). The biblical writer thus describes the forces opposing Joshua as in control of the land from the Esdraelon plain north at least to Dan and stretching from the Jordan Valley to the Mediterranean Sea. Their defeat means Israelite control of the North.

3 Not only all the territory, but also all the peoples are involved. The Canaanites are located by the Mediterranean Sea and the Jordan River as in Num 13:29, which also lists the Hittites, Jebusites, and Amorites as dwelling in the hill country. Elsewhere the Jebusites are closely identified with Jerusalem (15:8, 63; 18:28; Judg 1:21; 19:10–11; 2 Sam 5:6, 8; 24:16, 18; cf. Josh 18:16). The Hivites are located in the northern extremities of the land in Judg 3:3 and 2 Sam 24:7.

The use of the extended list of nations rests on an old tradition and serves a specific theological function. The territory occupied by these nations is promised to Abraham (Gen 15:18–21), and again to the nation suffering in Egypt (Exod 3:8, 17). The promise becomes the basis of divine demand in Exod 13:5; 23:23; 34:11, and can be used to exemplify the seriousness of divine anger (Exod 33:2). Deuteronomic literature then takes the motif to demonstrate the necessity that the nations in the land be totally exterminated (Deut 7:1; 20:17). Victory over the peoples becomes the sign that God fulfills his promises (Josh 3:10). This is brought to reality in 9:1; 11:3; 12:8 and serves again as the basis for divine command (24:11). The reality is that Israel has not fulfilled the divine command (e.g. Josh 15:63; Judg 1:21, 27:36; 3:1–5). Solomon achieved a solution by enslaving these peoples (1 Kgs 9:20–21). (For study of the lists and literature see J. Halbe, *Das Privilegrecht Jahwes* [FRLANT 114; Göttingen: Vandenhoeck & Ruprecht, 1975] 140–47.)

4 The holy war narrative emphasizes the impossible task facing the people of God. Israel had to face an innumerable army that had the best modern equipment. The odds were insurmountable. Yet for Israel God by himself was a majority against which no army was large enough.

5 As in the case of the Jerusalemite coalition, so the northern kings overcame a history of fighting one another to join forces against the supreme threat of Israel. Their camp is located at the waters of Merom, mentioned only here in the biblical literature. Egyptian texts from about 1500 also include Merom in a list of Palestinian cities (*ANET*, 243, 256; Aharoni, *Land* 150). Ramses II (ca. 1300) also mentions it (*ANET*, 243). It is generally identified with Meirūn, four miles west of Safed, but Aharoni (*Land*, 206) argues that a suitable tell is lacking there. He prefers to see the name preserved in Jebel Marun and Marun er-Ras, so that the site of the town would be the nearby Tell el-Khirbeh. The battle site is thus quite close to Hazor.

6 The central feature of the holy war narrative is the intervention of Yahweh by means of an oracle of salvation promising victory and telling his people not to fear. The oracle here also gives battle directions. Israel is to cut the hamstrings of the horses, thus taking away the advanced weaponry of the enemy. Such action is cruelty to animals (Gen 49:6) but is good battle strategy

for a people who do not know how to utilize chariots themselves(2 Sam 8:4).

⁷ As in the attack on the southern coalition, surprise is Joshua's best weapon (cf. 10:9). Throughout the book, the biblical writer sees no discrepancy between attributing the victory to Yahweh and describing clever human military tactics. Israel tells her military history as a history directed by God. Human tactics may be described, but the ultimate glory and praise is given only to Yahweh.

⁸ As in chap 10, the battle narrative is transformed suddenly into a pursuit narrative. The pursuit leads to Great Sidon. This is the ultimate limit of the tribe of Asher (19:29), twenty-five miles (forty-two kilometers) north of Tyre on the Mediterranean coast. Asher could not conquer it (Judg 1:31). Only 2 Sam 24:6 appears to assume that Israel ever controlled the region. Joshua 13:1–6 assumes that the land of the Sidonians, including Misrephoth-maim, was not conquered by Joshua. The latter is the traditional frontier city between Lebanon and Palestine (Soggin, 135) to be identified with Khirbet el Musrife at the northern end of the Plain of Acco, but Aharoni (*Land,* 216) says excavations there do not reveal remains from the Late Bronze or Early Iron Age. Aharoni notes the possibility of identifying it with the river Litani.

Mizpah is a common Palestinian place name, since the word means watch-tower. The precise place meant here cannot be determined. It represents the eastern extreme, just as Sidon and Misrephoth-maim represent the western boundaries. Joshua is said to have covered the entire northern territory promised to Abraham and finally conquered by David. The understanding here is that Joshua did not gain permanent control, but he did show that God had fulfilled his promises by giving victory throughout the territory. This parallels the conception of 10:41. Not only was God faithful in fulfilling his promises, but Joshua was faithful in carrying out the divine commands. He destroyed the various peoples of Palestine (cf. 10:40).

⁹ Joshua's obedience even extended to the manner in which he dealt with the horses and chariots (cf. v 6). The interest here in underlining the obedience of Joshua makes the chronological order unclear. The command in v 6 appeared to indicate the battle strategy. Israel was to hamstring the chariot horses so that the chariots could not be used against Israel. Here the fulfillment of the command is placed at the end, so that it could appear to represent the final act in the victory celebration (cf. 2 Sam 8:4). The tradition probably understood the act here as the surprise strategy which enabled Israel to win the battle.

¹⁰ Biblical tradition accurately remembers the greatness that was Hazor as shown by archaeological excavation and inscriptional evidence. The largest tell in Palestine, Hazor had controlled the northern country for centuries. Her proud history and strong army did not save her when Yahweh decided to give the land to his people. ¹¹ Thus Hazor fell to the fate commanded by God for all cities in the land (Deut 7:2; 20:17). ¹² A similar fate met all the kings who had conspired with Hazor against Israel. Joshua thus completed the task set out for him in chap. 1. He stood tall as the example of leadership for the people of God. That example was not to be seen simply in his military prowess. Rather, that example was epitomized in his fulfillment of the Mosaic

law. God's perfect leader chose to follow God's perfect command and thus reap God's perfect victory.

¹³ Israel tried to be honest and face facts in her use of tradition to create a self-understanding for the people of God. Israel did not claim to be perfect. Israel had failed. She had not burned all the cities. In fact, of the major cities of the north, only Hazor was burned. Much remained left to do (Josh 13:1–6). Joshua had fulfilled the task given him. Israel had not. Israel could set Joshua up as the example for all later leaders to follow. She could never set up any period of her history as the time of pristine obedience. Even in the conquest, Israel had not gone far enough. When Israel recited her history, she confessed the greatness of God, who fulfilled his promises to Israel. She also confessed her own sins in not living up to the demands made upon her by God.

¹⁴ As in Ai (8:2, 27), so here Israel is allowed to take booty to enrich herself. This is a rather loose interpretation of the rules in Deut 20. It shows that already the legal material was interpreted in differing ways rather than being seen as a strict legalism with no exception. The continuing word of God was the dominant factor (8:27; 11:15).

¹⁵ The major emphasis of the section is seen in the repetition in 15 of what was already made clear in v 12. The conquest narratives from the story of the spies sent to Jericho to the destruction of Hazor and the north stands as a monument to the great faithfulness of Joshua to the Mosaic law. It thus stands as a goal for all future leaders of Israel. Rather than being lawmakers, the kings of Israel are law takers and law keepers.

¹⁶ Verse 16 is formed as a linguistic parallel to 10:40, but it functions in a different way. Whereas 10:40 summarizes the conquest of the immediately preceding narrative unit, 11:16 summarizes the entire conquest both north and south. The hill country, Negeb, land of Goshen, Shephelah, and Arabah are all southern features. The only question is the precise territory designated by Goshen. This designates the Egyptian delta where the family of Joseph settled in Gen 45–50; Exod 8:18 (Eng.=8:22); 9:26. In Josh 10:41 and 11:16 it appears to refer to a part of the southern territory conquered by Israel, while in 15:51 it is a city in the hill country assigned to the tribe of Judah. Aharoni (*Land,* 38) describes the Judean land of Goshen as "the broad intermediate zone designated as a border region between the hill country and the Negeb." The description of the northern territory is interestingly brief in light of the preceding narrative. Only the hill country and its Shephelah is mentioned. The latter appears to have the same referrent as in v 2.

Verse 17 makes the geographical description more precise. Mount Halak is identified with Jebel Halaq, about forty miles (sixty-seven kilometers) southwest of the Dead Sea. Seir normally refers to the major mountain range of Edom, though Josh 15:10 and Deut 1:44 point to a Seir in Judah. The reference here is to Edom. This represents the southern limit of the Israelite victory march, corresponding to the reference to Kadesh Barnea in 10:40. The northern limit is described as Baal Gad. Aharoni is most honest when he admits (*Land,* 217), "the exact identification of Baal-gad is not known." Eissfeldt ("Die ältesten Bezeugungen von Baalbek als Kultstatte," *Forschungen und Fortschritte* 12 [1936] 51–53) equates it with modern Baalbek. Joshua's victory march is pictured as reaching the limits of the Davidic kingdom. Whereas 10:40 gave the east-west boundary, 11:16 gives the north-south boundary of Joshua's triumphs.

Verse 18 reveals quite clearly the nature of the biblical tradition. Joshua fought a long time with these kings. Only exemplary narratives have been preserved by the biblical tradition. The conquest and occupation of the land was a long and complicated affair. The narratives preserved are sufficient to serve the biblical purpose. They show that God fulfilled his promises and gave the land to his people, defeating the occupants against overwhelming odds.

[19] At one place the tradition claims to give the complete picture. Israel learned its lesson after one mistake. She did not sign peace agreements with any of the other inhabitants of the land. She responded to God's faithfulness at this point by fulfilling the divine command.

[20] Israelite obedience was made easier by God, who caused the inhabitants of the land to resist any temptation to plead for peace. The theme of hardening the heart is shared with the plague narratives in Exod 4:21–14:18. In the plague narratives the motif served to "describe the resistance which prevented the signs from achieving their assigned tasks" (B. S. Childs, *The Book of Exodus* [Philadelphia: Westminster, 1974] 174; cf. his discussion and literature, 170–75). Here the motif serves to force Israel to obey, rather than to be merciful (cf. Hertzberg, 83). Here is a biblical lesson which has always been difficult for the people of God to learn. Deuteronomy commanded Israel to obey God, destroy the inhabitants, have no mercy, make no covenant, make no marriages (7:1–3). Such a command had a divine purpose. It removed the temptations to follow other gods. From the days of the Judges and especially from the period of Solomon onward, the great temptation was to make political alliances through covenants and political marriages between royal families (1 Kgs 11:1–8; 16:31; 20:30–43). To protect Israel against the major sin of idolatry, God commanded her not to show mercy to the enemy. To enable her to keep his commandment, God caused her enemies to fight her rather than seek mercy and peace.

[21-22] The Anakim were the villains of the spy narratives (Num 13:28, 33; Deut 1:28). God promised specifically to destroy them (Deut 9:1–3). The conquest narrative thus concludes with the specific fulfillment of the promise. Interestingly, an exception clause is appended to the report. The Anakim remained in the territory of the Philistines. This prepared for the future narratives of combat with the Philistines which dominate the book of Samuel and appear in the Samson narratives, particularly the giant Goliath (1 Sam 17:4; cf. 2 Sam 21:18–22).

[23] The final verse of the chapter summarizes the conquest and the work of Joshua. Chapter 1 has been realized. With strength and courage, Joshua has conquered the whole land, the land promised to Abraham and eventually ruled by David and Solomon. Every promise and every command given by Yahweh to Moses has been fulfilled. Joshua gave out the land to the people, who had rest from fighting. With this verse the identity of Israel is realized. Israel is the obedient people of God dwelling in the land given by God, having to fight no longer because she has totally subdued the enemies of

God. But Israel did not maintain the ideal, as the historian knows only too well (24:31; Judg 2:6–15). The example of Joshua thus loomed ever larger in the history of Israel. He was the obedient leader serving as the example for all his successors.

Explanation

Using the tradition of a victory over a coalition led by the king of Hazor, the biblical writer describes how God gave the northern territory to Israel. In so doing he carefully retains the traditions which show that only Hazor was burned of all the cities and that the battle for the Promised Land lasted a long time. Thus he reveals much about his historical procedures and sources. He has not attempted to preserve all the details. On the basis of his faith and the word of God which has been entrusted to him, he has testified to the greatness of God in providing the entire land for Israel. God has devised a strategy for Israel's entire life, a strategy revealed in the book of Deuteronomy. This strategy for life has then been entrusted to the human agent Joshua. Divine encouragement and instruction has combined with human faithfulness to accomplish the total victory. Even though much remains to be done (13:1–6), the victory can be described as total because the work of Joshua has been carried out in total faithfulness. The task for the historian has not been to describe every detail of what had been done, nor every detail of what remained. The major emphasis of the historian has been to demonstrate how Israel obtains her land. This can then be held up as the example for all future generations. Throughout the years of monarchy, of exile, and even through the years of the postexilic period, the example could be read as a call to similar obedience awaiting the act of God again fulfilling his promises to his people.

Victory's Victims (12:1–24)

Bibliography

Fritz, V. "Die sogenannte Liste der besiegten Könige in Josua 12." *ZDPV* 85 (1969) 136–61. **Hollenberg, J.** "Die deuteronomischen Bestandtheile des Buches Josua." *Theologische Studien und Kritiken* 1 (1874) 499–500. **Ottosson, M.** *Gilead.* Lund: C. W. K. Gleerup, 1969, 117–19. **Schmitt, G.** *Du sollst keinen Frieden schliessen mit den Bewohnern des Landes.* BWANT 91. Stuttgart: W. Kohlhammer Verlag, 1970, 116–20. **Wüst, M.** *Untersuchungen zu den siedlungsgeographischen Texten des Alten Testaments.* Wiesbaden: Dr. Ludwig Reichert Verlag, 1975, 12–24, 28–57.

Translation

[1] *Now these are the kings of the land whom the sons of Israel smote and then possessed their land beyond the Jordan toward the sunrise, from the valley of the Arnon unto Mount Hermon and all the* [a] *Arabah eastward:*

² *Sihon, the king of the Amorites whose residence was in Heshbon. He was ruling from Aroer,*[a] *which is upon the bank of the River Arnon, and the middle of the river and half of the Gilead on unto the River*[b] *Jabbok, the border of the sons of Ammon.* ³ *And the Arabah unto the Sea of Chinneroth eastward and unto the Sea of the Arabah, the Salt Sea eastward, the way of Beth*[a]*-jeshimoth and southward*[b] *under the slopes of Pisgah.*

⁴ *The boundary*[a] *of Og, the king of Bashan, one of the remnant of the Rephaim,*[b] *who resided in Ashtaroth and in Edrei.* ⁵ *He ruled over Mount Hermon and Salecah and all Bashan unto the border of the Geshurites*[a] *and the Maacathites and half of Gilead, unto*[b] *the border of Sihon, king of Heshbon.*

⁶ *Moses, the servant of Yahweh, and the sons of Israel smote them. Moses, the servant of Yahweh*[a]*, gave it for an inherited possession to the Reubenites and to the Gaddites and to half the tribe of Manasseh.*

⁷ *Now these are the kings of the land*[a] *whom Joshua and the sons of Israel smote beyond the Jordan westward from Baal-gad in the Valley of Lebanon unto Mount Halak going up to Seir, the land which Joshua gave to the tribes of Israel for a possession according to their lots, in the hill country, and in the Shephelah, and in the Arabah, and in the slopes and in the wilderness and in the Negeb, the Hittites, the Amorites, the Canaanites, the Perizzites, the Hivites, and the Jebusites:*

⁹ *The king of Jericho, one:*   *the king of Ai, which is beside Bethel, one;*
¹⁰ *The king of Jerusalem, one;*   *the king of Hebron, one;*
¹¹ *The king of Jarmuth, one;*   *the king of Lachish, one;*
¹² *The king of Eglon, one;*   *the king of Gezer, one;*
¹³ *The king of Debir, one;*   *the king of Geder,*[a] *one;*
¹⁴ *The king of Hormah, one;*   *the king of Arad,*[a] *one;*
¹⁵ *The king of Libnah, one;*   *the king of Adulam, one;*
¹⁶ *The king of Makkedah,*[a] *one;*   *the king of Bethel,*[b] *one;*
¹⁷ *The king of Tappuah, one;*   *the king of Hepher, one;*
¹⁸ *The king of Aphek, one;*   *the king of Lashsharon,*[a] *one;*
¹⁹ *The king of Madon,*[a] *one;*   *the king of Hazor, one;*
²⁰ *The king of Shimron-meron,*[a] *one;*   *the king of Achshaph, one;*
²¹ *The king of Taanach, one;*   *the king of Megiddo, one;*
²² *The king of Kedesh,*[a] *one;*   *the king of Jokneam by Carmel, one;*
²³ *The king of Dor in Haphath-Dor, one;*   *the king of Goiim in Gilgal,*[a] *one;*
²⁴ *The king of Tirzah, one;*   *all the kings were thirty-one.*[a]

Notes

1.a. LXX transliterated Arabah, but added "land of" before it. This may represent a confused dittography from the preceding τήν in the Greek, since in vv 3 and 8, the transliteration is made properly. LXX does have trouble understanding Arabah (Benjamin, *Variations*) as seen in 4:13; 5:10; 8:14; 11:16; 13:32; 18:18.

2.a. Aroer has been confused in part of the Greek tradition with Arnon.

2.b. LXX lacks "River" though the word occurs in the parallel passage Deut 3:16.

3.a. LXX lacks בית, literally "house of," a component of many geographical names reflecting the presence of sanctuaries. In 13:20 LXX renders the בית.

3.b. The Hebrew תימן can mean "south," as in Job 39:26; Zech 9:14; Isa 43:6. It can also refer to Edom or the southern part of Edom (cf. R. de Vaux, "Téman, ville ou région d'Édom?" *RB* 76 [1969] 379–85). LXX interprets it in the latter sense for our passage, being followed by NEB. The term is missing from the parallel passage in 3:17 and is probably a directional addition by the editors here in parallel to the earlier reference to the "east."

4.a. LXX lacks "boundary," being followed by most modern commentators. In this instance LXX may have been as good a form critic as modern commentators who notice that a territorial list is not called for by the introduction in vv 1–2. MT is the more difficult reading and must be accounted for.

4.b. LXX interprets Rephaim as "giants."

5.a. LXX ᴮ has confused Geshurites with more common Girgashites.

5.b. "Unto" is lacking in MT but present in LXX. It has fallen out due to haplography with the previous word.

6.a. LXX and V lack the second "servant of the Lord," possibly an addition of traditional terminology within the Massoretic tradition.

7.a. LXX read "Amorites" for "land." The words evidence some similarity in Hebrew, leading to confusion of the two traditional phrases in the Hebrew textual transmission.

9.a. LXX simply lists the kings without using the schematic "one" throughout the list.

13.a. LXX ᴮ reads Asei for Geder, but the original Greek tradition reflected MT (cf. Margolis, 237).

14.a. LXX ᴮ has given two variant forms of Arad (cf. Fritz, *ZDPV* 85 [1969] 142, n. 27).

16.a. LXX has transmitted Makkedah in several corrupt forms (cf. Brooke, McLean; Margolis, 238).

16.b. LXX makes no reference to Bethel, perhaps because of previous mention in v. 9 (Margolis, 238–39), but it is more probable that the reference to Bethel entered the textual tradition at a quite late stage.

18.a. The MT לשרון is evidently to be understood as the preposition ל plus the noun Sharon (cf. Isa 33:9; 35:2; 65:10; 1 Chr 5:16; 27:29; Cant 2:1). The MT uses the prepositional construction only here. G apparently read "the king of Aphek of Sharon" (Margolis, 239–40), though LXX ᵇ reads "the king of Ephek tēs 'Arōk," while LXX ᴬ omits 18b entirely. The first modification of the simple king of a city-state form in the list led the later tradition to modify the text. MT divided the double name into two, while LXX ᴬ tradition omitted the unusual form.

19.a. LXX omits "the king of Madon," probably understanding it as a doublet of "the king of Maron," which it lists in the following verse (Fritz, *ZDPV* 85 [1969] 142).

20.a. Shimron-meron occurs only here in the OT. LXX read them as two separate cities, though the spellings of both have suffered within the LXX transmission. Elsewhere the two distinct cities appear in the MT and are to be presupposed as original here, though MT does represent the more difficult reading.

22.a. LXX transposed Kedesh before Taanach in v 21.

23.a. MT translates literally, "the king of the nations of Gilgal." LXX reads "the king of goiim of Galilee," which is most often taken as the correct reading, since the list deals with kings in the region of Galilee. Fritz (*ZDPV* 85 [1969] 143) says MT cannot be understood. The MT tradition represents an attempt to bring Gilgal, the central point of the early tradition into the list.

24.a. Corresponding to its transmission of the tradition, LXX reads the number as twenty-nine.

Form/Structure/Setting

The introductory formula of v 1 clearly marks a new beginning, while the concluding formula in 24b brings the unit, indeed the entire first major division of the book in chaps. 1 through 12 to a close.

The unit itself has two clear subdivisions marked by the similar introductory formulas in v 1 and v 7. The subdivisions are formulated in close parallelism to one another. The striking differences thus call all the more for explanation. Verse 1 explicitly states that they "possessed their land," whereas v 7 places the parallel statement at the end of the sentence and modifies it to read, "the land which Joshua gave to the tribes of Israel for a possession according to their lots." The latter prepares the way for the following chapters which

detail the giving of the land to the tribes and which note areas which were
not yet conquered, but of which the tribes had to take possession for themselves.

Verses 1 through 6 list the territories of each of the two kings conquered
separately, while vv 7 through 24 first list the entire territory (v 8) and then
the various kings. Why is this so? The most likely explanation is that the
editor had two types of material available to make the descriptions. The first
came from Deut 1–3 and summarized the eastern conquest. (That the geographical descriptions developed in the highly complex literary reflections
described by Wüst [*Untersuchungen,* 12–24], must be doubtful.) The other
was a list of towns in the western sector. Since vv 1–6 (as well as 7–8) represent
the Deuteronomistic editor's summary of the material in Deut 1–3 and in
Josh 11, the form critical interest here is on vv 9–24. Fritz (*ZDPV* 85 [1969]
136–61) has recently attempted to show that vv 10–24 represent a list of
cities fortified by Solomon, v 9 simply being a resume of chaps. 6 through
8. Schmitt (*Du sollst,* 116–20), on the other hand, assumes that all of the
names come from conquest reports either preserved in Numbers and Joshua
or available to the editor but not preserved for us. Soggin (143), from still
another perspective, argues that the list must be "very ancient" because it
disagrees with the "official version" of chaps. 1–11 and because "the picture
of Palestine which it presents gives the best description, though it is not
always complete, of the city states of the region as they appear a century
and a half earlier in the el-Amarna archives."

Certainly v 9 summarizes chaps. 6 through 8. Verses 10–12a follow precisely
10:3 (=5, 23). Despite the arguments of Noth and Fritz, it is doubtful that
the names were introduced into chap. 10 on the basis of chap. 12. Rather,
the procedure in 1–9 shows us the literary dependence of the editor of chap.
12 on earlier literature.

Eglon is followed in v 12 by Gezer. This, too, shows dependence on 10:33
where Gezer is closely related to the defeat of Lachish and then Eglon. Debir
follows (12:13) just as in 10:38, omitting Hebron (10:36), which has already
been listed here (12:10). It would appear then that the information in 12:14–
24 is that which is dependent upon a source outside Joshua. It is quite possible
that the results of Fritz apply to this list.

Comment

[1] For the writer of Joshua, possession of the land beyond Jordan is an
established fact. He summarizes it here to demonstrate the continuity in God's
leadership of Israel into the land and to prepare for the distribution of the
land in the following chapters. In so doing he uses a form of superscription
familiar from the Deuteronomistic superscriptions of Deuteronomy (1:1; 4:44;
28:69; cf. G. Seitz, *Redactionsgeschichtliche Studien zum Deuteronomium.* [BWANT
93; Stuttgart: W. Kohlhammer Verlag, 1971] 31). The territory is described
as extending from the River Arnon in the south to Mount Hermon in the
north (cf. Deut 3:8). The Arnon separated Moab from the kingdom of Sihon
(Num 21:13, 26). Snow-covered Mount Hermon rises 9,100 feet above sea
level and supplies the headwaters for the Jordan River. "All the Arabah" is

a summarizing term related to Deut 4:49 intending to show that Israel controlled all the eastern Jordan Valley.

[2] Sihon's capture is taken from the tradition of Num 21:21–30, as repeated in Deut 1:4; 2:24–37; 29:6–7 (Eng. 7–8). Rumors of the defeat paved the way for Israelite victories west of the Jordan (Josh 2:10; 9:10). His capital was Heshbon. Tell Hesban across the Jordan River from Jericho retains the name but has no remains earlier than the seventh century B.C. (S. H. Horn, "Heshbon," *EAEHL* 2 [1976] 510). Horn suggests nearby Jalul as a good candidate ("Heshbon," *IDBSup* [1976] 410). The Moabites later controlled the city (Isa 15:2, 4; 16:8–9). Sihon's kingdom is described as reaching from Aroer on the Arnon to the Jabbok. Aroer was not a town, but a fortress guarding an important highway (E. Olávarri, "Aroer," *EAEHL* 1 [1975] 98). Evidence of Late Bronze Age settlement has been excavated.

"And the middle of the River" is a difficult phrase related to 13:16 and Deut 2:36 where a city is mentioned. Gray (124) suggests that the present text has lost an original reference to the city or "watchpost." Wüst notes, however, (*Untersuchungen,* 12) that chap. 12 gives geographical boundaries while chap. 13 traces border cities. Our text thus places the boundary in the middle of the river valley. The territory is understood to include half of Gilead. Gilead is used as a geographical term to denote a vague area east of the Jordan, north and south of the Jabbok (cf. Ottosson, *Gilead,* 9). Our text sees the Jabbok as dividing Gilead into two halves. Wüst's (*Untersuchungen,* 12–24) detailed syntatical and literary arguments for a complicated literary development constantly reinterpreting the boundaries are at their weakest here. The stereotyped Deuteronomistic phraseology shows a conception of the land of the Ammonites extending east of the Jordan between the Arnon and the Jabbok (cf. Judg 11:12). The victory over Sihon, king of the Amorites, gives Israel control of the land of the Ammonites.

[3] Verse 3 describes the land of Sihon from another perspective which is not quite clear. Whereas v 2 described the northern and southern boundaries, here the east and west limits appear to be in view. Only the western boundary is located. This is the Jordan Valley between the Sea of Chinnereth, later called the Sea of Galilee, and the Sea of the Arabah or the Salt Sea, later called the Dead Sea. This is more closely defined with the addition of "the way of Beth-jeshimoth," a city whose exact location is unknown but has been sought in the area at the north end of the Dead Sea at least since the time of Eusebius of Caesarea (ca. A.D. 324). "Southward under the slopes of Pisgah" makes the identification still more exact. The mountain of Moses' death lies opposite Jericho (Deut 34:1; cf. 3:27) and was also the scene of a confrontation between Balaam and Balak (Num 23:14). Otherwise the name occurs only in geographical lists (Num 21:20; Deut 3:17; 4:49; Josh 13:20). The twice repeated "eastward" is the only indication of the eastern boundary (cf. v 1). It is interesting that in giving the imprecise east-west boundary, the description extends the north-south boundary above the River Jabbok. The intention is to underline the completeness of Israel's conquest of the Trans-jordan territory.

[4] Having ended the reference to Sihon with a long territorial description, the Massoretic text then introduces the "boundary of Og" rather than the

expected introduction simply of the person of Og. He ruled Bashan, the
northern portion of Transjordan renowned for its fertility (Amos 4:1), forests
(Isa 2:13), and mountains (Isa 33:9). Only at the height of her power could
Israel maintain control of Bashan. Og was among the remnant of the Rephaim,
ancient inhabitants of the land (Gen 14:5; 15:20), who gave their name to
the land of Bashan (Deut 3:13; cf. Josh 17:15), as well as to a valley separating
Judah and Benjamin west of the Jordan (Josh 15:8; 18:6). Tradition identified
several different groups renowned for their stature as Rephaim (Deut 2:11,
20), but Og came to be recognized as the last survivor (Deut 3:11; Josh
13:12). Ashtaroth, the first of Og's royal cities, is usually identified with tell
Ash'-ari, twenty-four miles (forty kilometers) south of modern Keneitra and
twenty miles (thirty-nine kilometers) east of the Sea of Chinneroth (cf. S.
Cohen, "Ashteroth-Karnaim," *IDB* 1 [1962] 255). It is also mentioned in
Gen 14:5; Deut 1:4; Josh 9:10; 13:12, 31; 1 Chr 6:56, in the Amarna Letters
(cf. Ottosson, *Gilead,* 12), and other Egyptian texts (*ANET,* 242, 329, 486).
Edrei is the battle scene in Num 21:33. Otherwise it is mentioned in connection
with Og (Deut 1:4; 3:1, 10; Josh 13:12, 31). The Egyptians also refer to it
(*ANET,* 242). It is identified with modern Dera halfway between Damascus
and Amman.

⁵ The meager traditional evidence available is used to describe the borders
of Og. The northern border is Mount Hermon (cf. v 1). Salecah is the extreme
eastern border of Bashan, possibly identified with modern Salkhad, the defensive center of the Jebel el-Druze. The Geshurites and Maacathites represented
peoples Israel could not drive out of the land (Josh 13:2, 13) until the time
of David (1 Sam 27:8; 2 Sam 10:6–14). Their territory furnished a border
point for Israel to the east (Deut 3:14; Josh 13:11). Later David entered
into a marriage alliance with the king of Geshur (2 Sam 3:3), and Absalom
fled there for refuge (2 Sam 13:37–15:8). The southern boundary is simply
taken from v 2.

⁶ The summary statement underlines the work of Moses. Transjordan has
been given the two and a half tribes (Deut 3:12–13; cf. Josh 13: 8–32). Here
again, Moses set the example which Joshua followed.

⁷ That Joshua followed the example is made abundantly clear in v 7, which
combines the language of vv 1 and 6 with the information of 11:17, given
in reverse order. One notable modification is made. Joshua distributed the
territory according to the lots. This harmonizes with the presentation in 18:10
to which the present verse points (cf. 14:2).

⁸ Verse 8 takes pains to show that Joshua distributed all the land he had
conquered. Here again the picture becomes clear that Joshua first conquered
the major part of the land in battle, but then later gave it out to the tribes
to possess, even though much work remained to be done in conquering the
land (13:2–6), the task being completed only by David.

⁹ Chaps. 1–12 cannot tell the story of the conquest of Bethel, yet the city
is so important that it comes in for specific mention in the text in a manner
unlike any other city (7:2; 8:9, 12, 17). The original list here may not have
included the king of Bethel (v 16; cf. *notes,* 16.b.).

In a dramatic fashion the extent of the conquest is forced upon the reader
via the long list of kings. Most of the cities have been discussed previously.

[13] Geder is graphically close to Gezer and could be an early scribal error. (cf. Gray). Aharoni suggests the error is for Gerar, "the most important Canaanite city in the western Negeb" (*Land,* 210; "The Land of Gerar," *IEJ* 6 [1956] 27). At any rate, it cannot be located nor can its occupational history be described.

[14] Hormah was the scene of Israelite defeat (Num 14:45 cf. Deut 1:44) and victory (Num 21:3). The territory lay in the southern end of Judah (Josh 15:30) and was allotted to Simeon (19:4). Judah and Simeon joined to conquer it (Judg 1:17). There David later gained early support (1 Sam 30:30). Earlier Egyptian texts also refer to Hormah (Aharoni, *Land* 133). The exact location is a matter of scholarly debate. Aharoni suggests Tell Masos ("Nothing Early and Nothing Late: Rewriting Israel's Conquest," *BA* 39 [1976] 71–72), seven miles (twelve kilometers) east of Beersheba. Excavation evidences shows occupation from the end of the thirteenth century until a major destruction ca. 1000. Defensive walls appear never to have been built. Fritz ("Arad in der biblischen Überlieferung (Num 21:1–3) und in der Liste Schoschenks I," *ZDPV* 82 [1966] 340–41) suggests it must be north of Beersheba. Bimson (*Redating,* 203–4) uses the Middle Bronze evidence from Tell Masos to date the Israelite destruction to the fifteenth century.

Arad is tied closely to Hormah in Num 21:1–3 and is settled by the Kenites in Judg 1:16. The excavator Aharoni has suggested that Israelite Arad is to be identified with Tell Arad, eighteen miles (thirty kilometers) east-northeast of Beersheba. The site was settled, however, only in the Early Bronze Age and then again about the eleventh or twelfth century. Aharoni thus suggests that the Arad mentioned in Numbers is to be located at Tell Malhata, where Middle Bronze (ca. 1550) fortifications were found followed by an Israelite fortress of the tenth century (*BA* 39 [1976] 56–57). Bimson takes this as further support for his dating (*Redating,* 204–5). The lack of Late Bronze and Early Iron evidence for Tell Arad is a key in Fritz's dating of the present list to the period of Solomon.

[15] Adullam is a city in southern Judah (15:35; Neh 11:30) mentioned in an oracle of doom by Micah (1:15). A nearby cave served as a hiding place for David (1 Sam 22:1; 2 Sam 23:13). Its traditions go back to Jacob (Gen 38). On the basis of Eusebius and a nearby locality which has preserved the name, Adullam is identified with esh-Sheikh Madhkur, nine and a half miles (sixteen kilometers) east-northeast of Beit Jibrin. Surface explorations have revealed Iron Age remains.

[17] Tappuah is the name of two cities, the one in Judah (15:34) and the other on the boundary of Ephraim and Manasseh (17:7–8; 16:8). Our context shows the latter is meant here. It is located at Tell Sheikh Abu Zarad nine miles (fifteen kilometers) southeast of Nablus. Surface explorations indicate settlement in the Late Bronze Age and in the Iron Age.

Hepher is the personal name of one of the clans of Manasseh (Num 26:33; 27:1; Josh 17:2–3). The only other geographical reference is 1 Kgs 4:10. It has been identified with et-Tayibeh, three and a half miles south of Tulkarm by Alt ("Das Institut im Jahre 1925," *PJ* 22, [1926] 68–69) but with Tell el-Muhaffar by Wright ("The Provinces of Solomon," *Eretz Israel* 8 [1967] 63*), with Tell Ibshar eight miles (thirteen kilometers) northwest of Tul Kerm by B. Maisler ("Die westliche Linie des Meerwegs," *ZDPV* 58 [1935] 82–83). Uncertainty of location makes a description of the occupational history impossible.

[18] Aphek is identified with Ras el-Ain at the mouth of the Yarmuk River just east of Tel-Aviv. Egyptian sources make several references to it (*ANET*, 242, 246, 329). Recent excavations have revealed a long history of occupation. Substantial settlement and building are witnessed in both the Middle and Late Bronze Ages with a destruction level ending the Late Bronze Age ca. 1200. The excavators attribute this to the Sea Peoples (M. Kochavi, "Tel Aphek, 1976" *IEJ* 27 [1977] 54). It was later a scene of vital battles for Israel (1 Sam 4:1; 29:1; 31:1–7).

Lashsharon probably is to be connected with Aphek and referred to the Plain of Sharon (cf. *notes*, 18.a.).

[21] Taanach was a Levitical city in western Manasseh (Josh 21:25 cf. 17:11) but was not immediately conquered (Judg 1:27). It served as the site of the famous battle by the waters of Megiddo (Judg 5:19) and is mentioned in the list of Solomon's taxation districts (1 Kgs 4:12). It is well known in Egyptian sources (*ANET*, 235–36, 243, 490). It is located at Tell Taannek five miles (eight kilometers) southwest of Megiddo. Excavation has revealed occupation reaching back into the Early Bronze Age, ca. 2700. A long gap is followed by Middle Bronze settlement beginning about 1700. Some destruction evidence closes the Middle Bronze settlement. Late Bronze settlement was interrupted by Thutmose III about 1468. Significant occupation resumed in the late thirteenth century only to be destroyed about 1125 (A. Glock, "Taanach," *EAEHL* 4 [1978] 1138–47).

Megiddo is a vital defense station controlling the entrance of the international highway Via Maris into the Jezreel Valley. Thus it appears repeatedly in Egyptian texts (*ANET*, 228, 234–38, 242–43, 477, 485, cf. 263–64). The territory was given to Manasseh (Josh 17:11), but not conquered (Judg 1:27). By its waters, Deborah and Barak battled Sisera and the kings of Canaan (Judg 5:19). Solomon strengthened its defenses (1 Kgs 9:15) and levied taxes on it (1 Kgs 4:12). There Ahaziah of Judah died from battle wounds (2 Kgs 9:27), and Josiah was slain by Pharaoh Neco (2 Kgs 23:29–30). Excavations have revealed its defenses reaching back into the Early and Middle Bronze Ages and its settlement into the Chalcolithic (before 3300). The pottery evidence for dating the Middle Bronze Age Strata of Megiddo forms one of the central links in Bimson's arguments for dating the conquest in the fifteenth century (*Redating*, 151–65). A destruction level at the end of the Late Bronze Age is evident.

[22] Kedesh is a common geographical name and may have been used by several different towns. The specific one meant here is the subject of debate (cf. Fritz, *ZDPV* 85 [1969] 152–53).

Jokneam lies near the border of Zebulon (Josh 19:11) and was a Levitical city (21:34). Thutmose III mentions it (cf. A. Ben-Tor, R. Rosenthal, "The First Season of Excavations at Tel Yoqne'am, 1977," *IEJ* 28 [1978] 60). Recent excavation has shown Late Bronze Age and Iron Age settlement, though the evidence for the earliest Iron Age settlement does not appear to be extensive (*IEJ* 28 [1978] 57–82).

²³ The meaning of גוים לגלגל is uncertain (see *notes,* 23.a.). Gilgal is the central location of the first Joshua narratives. Goyim is part of the name Harosheth-hagoyim in Judg 4, which does not appear in the poetic parallel in Judg 5 nor anywhere else in the Bible. Goyim is not evidenced as an independent name. The locality meant here is thus unknown.

²⁴ Tirzah is located at Tel el-Farah, seven miles (eleven kilometers) northeast of Nablus, on a major highway. It belongs to the group of cities in the central highlands (16b–17) and is somewhat out of place here. The name is used for a woman in the genealogy of Manasseh (Num 26:33; 27:1; 36:11; Josh 17:3). Later it served briefly as the royal residence of the northern kingdom (1 Kgs 14:17–16:23; cf. 2 Kgs 15:14–16). As such it was renowned for its beauty (Cant 6:4). Excavations have shown settlement reaching back to the Neolithic and Chalcolithic periods, as well as in the Early Bronze Age. Middle Bronze Age II occupancy follows six hundred years of desolation. A strong city wall was built about 1700. Late Bronze Age evidence is poorly preserved but is shown by pottery to have continued until 1400 and possibly into the thirteenth century. Signs of destruction are attributed by the excavator to the Israelites. The Iron Age period saw continued use of the sanctuary first used in the Middle Bronze Age (cf. R. de Vaux, "El-Far 'a, Tell, North." *EAEHL* 2 [1976] 395–404).

The Iron Age pottery dates from the tenth and ninth centuries, but de Vaux does not want to exclude earlier Israelite occupation ("Tirzah," *Archaeology and Old Testament Study,* ed. D. W. Thomas, [London: Oxford University Press, 1967] p. 376; cf. Fritz, *ZDPV* 85 [1969] 155).

Explanation

Using all the sources available to him, the final editor of Joshua described the total victory of Joshua over the kings of Canaan. The description was not complete. Shechem is not mentioned, and the hills of Ephraim are sparsely represented, as is the territory north of Hazor. Completeness is not the object. The writer seeks to compile a list that will impress the readers with the greatness of the feat of God in working for Israel and of the greatness of the leadership of Joshua in following the example of Moses and completing the task first given to Moses. Still, the writer is aware that much remains to be done. Israel is not given an identity of rest and accomplishment. Even as she basks in the glory of victory and obedience, she faces a new task ahead. She has won the territory, now she must drive out the remaining inhabitants and settle it. She has not been called to a life of constant warfare and celebration of victory. She has been called to a life in the land which God has given her, a life to be lived in accordance with the life style prescribed by God. The first step in fulfillment of that calling is the division of the land. That follows immediately. When that is complete, Israel will have her identity set before her, an identity of life in the land obeying Yahweh, the giver of the land and the law.

I. God's Geographical Guidance (Joshua 13–19)

These chapters promise nil theologically, at least at first glance. Who has even bothered to read through the long lists of towns and borders, much less attempted to discover geographical grounds for Christian faith? The commentary seeks to show that such seeking and sorting is worth the effort. God's inspired writer has taken up the geographical traditions of his people and preserved them in his own pattern to demonstrate precisely those points his exiled readers needed to hear. He turns boundary lists into a part of the story of God's actions for his people and of the promises of God for a people who still do not live on the land. The secret lies in the leadership of a faithful servant of God, who will allocate the land and wait for God to drive out the remaining enemies (see 13:6–7).

For a while, Israel must be willing to occupy that portion of the land available to them, keeping faith that God will dispossess the present occupants of the land that remains at the proper time. Israel, even Israel in exile, can occupy the land, if they follow the leadership examples of Joshua and Caleb, showing complete loyalty to Yahweh, dividing the land for the good of all the people, not one special office or class, and faithfully claiming and fulfilling the promises God has given. In all of this Israel must accept God's authority over all her political authorities. God had provided even the political boundaries and divisions for Israel. Could Israel see the priority of Torah, of God's teaching, as being more important for her life than the challenge of establishing political power? Joshua 13–19 placed that challenge squarely before an Israel seeking again to dispossess the enemy and possess the land.

II. Lots for the Land (13:1–19:51)

Bibliography

Aharoni, Y. "The Province List of Judah." *VT* 9 (1959) 225–46. **Alt, A.** "Eine galiläische Ortsliste in Jos. 19." *ZAW* 45 (1927) 59–81. ———. "Judas Gaue unter Josia." *PJ* 21 (1925) 100–116. (=*Kleine Schriften zur Geschichten des Volkes Israel*. Vol. 2. München: C. H. Beck'sche Verlagsbuchhandlung, 1953, 276–88.) ———. "Das System der Stammesgrenzen im Buche Josua." *Beiträge zur Religionsgeschichte und Archaeologie Palästinas*. Leipzig: A. Deichert, 1927, 13–24. (=*KS* 1, 193–202.) **Bächli, O.** "Von der Liste zur Beschreibung, Beobachtungen und Erwägungen zu Jos. 13–19." *ZDPV* 89 (1973) 1–14. **Cross, F. M.** and **Wright, G. E.** "The Boundary and Province Lists of the Kingdom of Judah." *JBL* 75 (1956) 202–26. **Elliger, K.** "Die Grenze zwischen Ephraim und Manasse." *ZDPV* 53 (1930) 265–309. ———. "Tribes, Territories of." *IDB* 4 (1962) 701–10. **de Geus, C. H. J.** *The Tribes of Israel*. Studia Semitica Neerlandica 18. Assen: Koninklijke Van Gorcum, 1976, 70–83. **Gottwald, N. K.** *The Tribes of Yahweh*. Maryknoll, NY: Orbis, 1979, 155–63, 173–74, 179–84, 197–98, 365–66, 375, 728–

31. **Hölscher, G.** *Geschichtsschreibung in Israel.* Lund: C. W. K. Gleerup, 1952, 345–49. **Kallai-Kleinmann, Z.** "Note on the Town Lists of Judah, Simeon, Benjamin and Dan." *VT* 11 (1961) 223–27. ———. "The Town Lists of Judah, Simeon, Benjamin and Dan." *VT* 8 (1958) 134–60. ———. *The Tribes of Israel. A Study in the Historical Geography of the Bible* (Hebrew). Jerusalem: 1967. ———. "Tribes, Territories of." *IDBSup* (1976) 920–23. **Kuschke, A.** "Historisch-topographische Beiträge zum Buche Josua." *Gottes Wort und Gottes Land,* ed. H. G. Reventlow. Göttingen: Vandenhoeck & Ruprecht, 1965, 90–109. **Mayes, A. D. H.** *Israel in the Period of the Judges.* London: SCM, 1974, 67–73, 128–30. **Mittmann, S.** *Beiträge zur Siedlungs-und Territorialgeschichte des nördlichen Ostjordanlandes.* Wiesbaden: Otto Harrassowitz, 1970, 208–46. **Mowinckel, S.** *Tetrateuch-Pentateuch-Hexateuch.* BZAW 90. Berlin: Alfred Töpelmann, 1964, 51–76. ———. *Zur Frage nach dokumentarischen Quellen in Josua 13–19.* Oslo: Dybwad, 1946. **North, R.** "Israel's Tribes and Today's Frontier." *CBQ* 16 (1954) 146–53. **Noth, M.** "Studien zu den historisch-geographischen Dokumenten des Josuabuches." *ZDPV* 58 (1935) 185–255. (=*Aufsätze zur biblischen Landes- und Altertumskunde.* Vol. 1. Neukirchen-Vluyn: Neukirchener Verlag, 1971, 229–80.) ———. *Überlieferungsgeschichtliche Studien.* Tübingen: Max Niemeyer Verlag, 1943, 45–47. ———. "Überlieferungsgeschichtliches zur zweiten Hälfte des Josuabuches. *Alttestamentliche Studien Fr. Nötscher zum 60. Geburt-Stag,* ed. H. Junker and J. Botterweck. BBB 1. Bonn: Peter Hanstein, 1950, 152–67. **Rudolph, W.** *Der "Elohist" von Exodus bis Josua.* BZAW 68. Berlin: Alfred Töpelmann, 1938, 237–38. **Schmitt, G.** *Du sollst keinen Frieden schliessen mit den Bewohnern des Landes.* BWANT 91. Stuttgart: W. Kohlhammer Verlag, 1970, 81–120. **Schunck, K. D.** *Benjamin.* BZAW 86. Berlin: Alfred Töpelmann, 1963, 142–67. **Simons, J.** *The Geographical and Topographical Texts of the Old Testament.* Leiden: E. J. Brill, 1959, 109–207. ———. "The Structure and Interpretation of Joshua XVI–XVII." *Orientalia Neerlandica.* Leiden: E. J. Brill, 1948, 190–215. **Täubler, E.** *Biblische Studien: Die Epoche der Richter.* Tübingen: J. C. B. Mohr (Paul Siebeck), 1958. **Tengström, S.** *Die Hexateucherzählung.* Lund: C. W. K. Gleerup, 1976, 73–78. **de Vaux, R.** *Histoire ancienne d'Israël.* vol. 2. Paris: J. Gabalda, 1973, 46–48. (=*The Early History of Israel.* Tr. D. Smith. London: Darton, Longman & Todd, 1978, 727–30.) **Wellhausen, J.** *Die Composition des Hexateuchs und der historischen Bücher des Alten Testaments.* 2nd ed. Berlin: Georg Reimer, 1889, 130–35. **Wüst, M.** *Untersuchungen zu den siedlungsgeographischen Texten des Alten Testaments.* Wiesbaden: Dr. Ludwig Reichert Verlag, 1975. **Yadin, Y.** "The Fourfold Division of Judah." *BASOR* 163 (1961) 6–12. **Yeivin, S.** *The Israelite Conquest of Canaan.* Istanbul: Nederlands Historisch-Archaeologisch Instituut in het Nabije Oosten, 1971, 247–66.

Introduction to History of Research

The book of Joshua follows its description of the conquest of the land with a parallel description of the distribution of the land by lots among the various tribes. The territory of the tribes is given in long lists of cities and territories. Close observation of the lists has revealed that the treatment of the various tribes is quite unequal. This has provoked a number of scholarly theories concerning the origin and development of Josh 13–19.

The traditional theory utilizes the literary critical methods developed for the Pentateuch and finds parallel sources. Thus Wellhausen separated the basic Priestly materials from older JE ones and noted that originally 18:1 must have stood prior to chap. 14. Steurnagel divided most of the material between P and a secondary Deuteronomic writer. Eissfeldt found materials belonging to J, E, and P.

The work of Albrecht Alt and Martin Noth changed the course of research.

Alt separated three types of materials form-critically, namely (1) isolated notes connected with Judg 1; (2) town lists; and (3) border descriptions. He then introduced the method of territorial history to date the various materials, since the town lists and border descriptions did not seem to cover the same territory. He dated the southern town lists to the time of Josiah, with the northern town lists reflecting Assyrian practice taken over by Josiah. The border descriptions, in which Simeon, Dan, and Issachar are apparently ignored, reflected the tribal territories immediately before the rise of the monarchy. Such lists were originally used to settle tribal border disputes.

Noth compared Josh 15 and Num 34 to show that border points remained the same but the connecting descriptions did not. He thus theorized that the original lists contained only border points without connecting descriptive text. The editor's lack of familiarity with the north resulted in a task only partially and inconsistently completed. Noth doubted that town lists had ever existed for Galilee, but did seek to show that both early border descriptions and Josianic town lists for territory east of the Jordan had been used.

Noth also developed a revolutionary literary critical theory, saying that the Priestly editor had no part in Josh 13–19, this being the work of a redactor closely akin to the Deuteronomic school.

Continuing research has disputed both the literary and territorial decisions of Noth. Sigmund Mowinckel argued that the lists could not arise prior to the monarchy, since no political center existed to establish and maintain such boundaries. For him the knowledge displayed in Josh 13–19 is simply that of an educated postexilic Jew familiar with the ethnic and political traditions and realities of his time. He would not have had written documents, since these could not have survived the tragedy of 587.

Gustav Hölscher (*Geschichtsschreibung*, 345–49) also attributed the border descriptions to P, while reserving the town lists for an even later hand, at least those of Judah and Benjamin being genuine documents from the Persian period.

Frank Cross and George Ernest Wright (*JBL* 75[1956] 202–26) modified Noth to the extent that a Simeonite boundary list could be reconstructed, the Danite list in chap. 19 had to be considered separately from the other town lists, and the town list was to be dated in the reign of Jehoshaphat (873–849).

Z. Kallai-Kleinmann refuses to cut out later additions to the lists but sees each as prepared from the perspective of the tribe involved. The boundary system thus derives from David's census as completed with Solomon's acquisition of Gezer, not from the premonarchical period. The town lists must each be dated separately. The list of Judah, for example, comes from the period of Jehoshaphat, but only after being edited in the time of Hezekiah. The Dan list is Solomonic, while that of Benjamin is from the time of Abijah. The earliest is that of Simeon, which is connected with David's census.

Yohanan Aharoni also excluded Dan from the town list but then sought to explain the exclusion of Jerusalem from Judah. This led him to seek a date for the combined Judah-Benjamin list. He excludes 15:45–47 on the basis of form and content and finally dates the resulting list in the time of Uzziah.

Klaus-Dietrich Schunck accepts Kallai-Kleinmann's methodology, separating the town lists, and then reconstructs a complicated growth of the material. Davidic origin is argued for 15:2–12a, which was then supplemented in the time of Rehoboam by 16:1–3. This in turn was one source for 18:12–20, a late literary combination. Old tribal borders are found in 15:5b–11 and 16:5–7. Turning to the town list, Schunck followed Aharoni except in a few details. He saw 18:21–24 and 19:41–46 as provinces being added by Josiah.

Siegfried Mittmann worked with Josh 13 to argue that it came from Solomon's administration and described territories around regional centers rather than fixed border points.

Sh. Yeivin also saw the town lists as including administrative centers. He agrees with Aharoni that the Judah-Benjamin list comes from the period of Jehoshaphat, but sees the territory of Joseph being that of the period of the judges as are those of Zebulon, Naphtali, and probably Asher. The Danite list is Davidic as are those of the east Jordan tribes. The Simeonite list comes from the time of Hezekiah.

A. D. H. Mayes showed that the distinction is between border descriptions and city lists, not fixed border points. He argued that the southern border descriptions can be understood only in the time of the United Monarchy. The lists of east Jordan are secondary literary productions based on Num 32.

This last point is taken to the ultimate extreme by Manfred Wüst, who works out a complex literary interaction to show the development of all the texts dealing with east Jordan. The only traditional sources are a brief town list in 13:16, 26a and a traffic route in 13:17, 19, 20, 27a.

Sven Tengström uses chaps. 19 and 21 to show that nothing forbids the assumption that the description of the tribal borders and the settlement of the tribes was formed from the beginning in light of the twelve tribe system. Thus he sees the substance of Josh 13–21 as being early. The fact that only the borders of the central tribes are exhaustively described and that Jerusalem, called by its ancient name Jebus, belongs to Benjamin, leads Tengström to locate the origin of the document in central Palestine prior to the monarchy.

Using Aharoni's observation that the basic descriptions give only the internal borders of Benjamin, Manasseh, Ephraim, Zebulon, Asher, and Naphtali, thus differing little from the Israel of Ishbosheth in 2 Sam 2:9, C. H. J. de Geus dates the original boundary system in the period of the judges, allowing for the addition of Judah and the Josephites after the division of the monarchy.

Most recently, Norman Gottwald has worked sociologically to show that the boundary lists would have had no social setting prior to the census of David, in connection with which they would be used to assess the human and material resources available to the king. He describes a repeated use of the materials by each of the major Pentateuchal sources, resulting in substantial losses in all of the lists.

The literary problems of the section are thus complicated and demand new questions and new solutions. The study that follows will be aware of such problems, but will, as proper in the present commentary format, concentrate upon the theological issues involved.

Divide What You Have! (13:1–7)

Bibliography

Auld, A. G. "Textual and Literary Studies in the Book of Joshua." *ZAW* 90 (1978) 412–17. **Japhet, S.** "Conquest and Settlement in Chronicles." *JBL* 98 (1979) 205–18. **Maisler, B.** *Untersuchungen zur alten Geschichte und Ethnographie Syriens und Palästinas.* Giessen: A. Töpelmann, 1930, 59–63. **Rudolph, W.** *Der "Elohist" von Exodus bis Josua.* BZAW 68. Berlin: Alfred Töpelmann, 1938, 211–14. **Smend, R.** "Das Gesetz und die Völker." *Probleme biblischer Theologie*, ed. H. W. Wolff. München: Chr. Kaiser Verlag, 1971, 497–500. **Wüst, M.** *Untersuchungen zu den siedlungsgeographischen Texten des Alten Testaments.* Wiesbaden: Dr. Ludwig Reichert Verlag, 1975, 222–27.

Translation

[1] Now when Joshua was old, advanced in years, Yahweh said to him,[a] "You have become old,[b] you have advanced in years, but there remains a great amount of land to possess. [2] This is the land which remains: all the regions [a] of the Philistines and all of the Geshurites,[b] [3] from the river [a] which is opposite Egypt unto the border of Ekron northward (it is reckoned to the Canaanites), the five chiefdoms [b] of the Philistines—those of Gaza, and Ashdod, Askelon,[c] Gath and Ekron—along with the Avvim.[4] Southward [a] all the land of the Canaanites from Arah [b] which belongs to the Sidonians unto Aphek unto the border of the Amorites; [5] also the land of Byblos [a] and all Lebanon eastward from Baal Gad [b] under Mount Hermon unto Lebo Hamath. [6] All the inhabitants of the hill country from Lebanon unto Misraphoth Mayim, all the Sidonians, I will dispossess them before the sons [a] of Israel, only cause it to fall to Israel for an inheritance just as I commanded you. [7] Now divide this land into an inheritance of the nine tribes and the half tribe of Manasseh." [a]

Notes

1.a. LXX makes the text more explicit, reading "Joshua" for the MT pronoun "him."

1.b. LXX omits "you have become old" which may represent a later filling of the text to achieve exact correspondence.

2.a. LXX does not witness "all," which is likely a later amplification. גלילית, traditionally translated "regions," still remains a mystery, for the term cannot mean "regions" in Josh 22:10–11. Nor does this seem appropriate for Ezek 47:8. Connection to the Philistines is also made in Joel 4:4 (Eng.=3:4).

2.b. Again "all" may be later amplification, not appearing in LXX. הגשורי is read by LXX here and in 1 Sam 27:8 as Τεσειρει, a reading attested by the Massoretic Qere in the Samuel passage. LXX adds here "and the Canaanites," a scholarly gloss on the basis of 13:13, 15:63, 16:10, 17:12, Judg 1:19–35.

3.a. שיחור refers to the Nile or one of its branches in Isa 23:3; Jer 2:18. Here and in 1 Chr 13:5 it refers to a traditional boundary point between Israel and Egypt, more often called the נהל, e. g. Num 34:5; Josh 15:4, 47. (For the more limited meaning in Egyptian sources, see Wüst, *Untersuchungen*, 33–34). The meaning was already a mystery to early translators, so that LXX used the vague "uninhabited land." This is complicated by the description מצרים על־פני "opposite, in the vicinity of Egypt," (cf. J. Drinkard, " 'AL Pene as 'East of' " *JBL* 98 [1979]

285–86). This appears to locate Shihor outside of Egypt and may show dependence on 1 Sam 15:7 (cf. M. Wüst, *Untersuchungen*, 37).

3.b. סרן is a technical term borrowed from the Philistines and applied exclusively in the twenty-one OT occurrences to the five city-state rulers of the Philistines.

3.c. LXX unifies the grammatical structure, adding the conjunction before Ashkelon and Gath.

4.a. Definition and grammatical construction become quite unclear beginning with v 4. מתימן may be either a geographical location "Teman" preceded by the preposition "from" (LXX, BDB, Ezek 25:13) or a direction "southward" (KB, cf. Isa 43:6). If the latter meaning is adopted, then the phrase is usually connected to the preceding verse (Soggin, Noth, most modern translations and commentators). The text may be read with "southward" referring to the following description of the land of the Canaanites going southward from Sidon to Aphek.

4.b. ומערה has puzzled translators since the LXX which read "facing Gaza, and the Sidonians . . ." The Heb. term as it stands can be a proper name "Mearah" or refer to a cave. Buhl, followed by Steurnagel and Hertzberg, inserts a prepositional *mem* to read "from Me'ara." Noth, Soggin (provisionally) and the *Hebrew Text Project* repoint the text to read "from Arah." Our geographical uncertainty makes restoration or explanation of the text impossible. The reference is apparently to an unknown Sidonian town.

5.a. LXX reads the opening of v 5: "and all the land of Galilath of the Philistines," which appears to be a transliteration of the Hebrew expression in v 2. The MT refers to the land of the Giblites, a term used in 1 Kgs 5:32 (=Eng. 5:18), Ps 83:8 and Ezek 27:9 for Byblos, as rightly interpreted by the LXX in Ezekiel. LXX here appears to be based on a defective Hebrew text.

5.b. The Greek tradition has corrupted Baalgad, perhaps reflecting the tendency of the tradition to excise names containing Baal.

6.a. LXX omits "sons," a common phenomenon in the transmission of the text (cf. Auld, VTSup 30 [1979] 10–11).

7.a. The transition between v 7 and v 8 in MT is syntactically difficult. LXX adds at the end of v 7: "from the Jordan unto the Mediterranean Sea toward the setting of the sun, you shall give it. The Mediterranean Sea will serve as boundary." (See v 8 for the continuation). Abel, Soggin, the *Hebrew Text Project*, and Auld argue correctly that the LXX text is original here. LXX's verb translates a Heb. nominal construction in 13:27; 15:12; and Num 34:6 (cf. Josh 15:47; 23:4) and a verbal construction in 18:20. LXX's verbal interpretation is probably correct in all instances.

Form/Structure/Setting

The transitional nature of 13:1 is clear from the nominal beginning and from its relationship to similar transitions in 23:1 and 1:1 (cf. Smend, "Das Gesetz"). The imperative of v 7 concludes the section prior to the transition to historical review in v 8. This is shown by the change from first to third person reference to God, thus concluding the divine quotation after v 7. The precise structure of the section offers particular difficulties, as Hollenberg noted in the last century. This has led Noth to speak of a piling up of secondary additions of the first, second, and third order (p 76). Bright separates vv 2–6 as having belonged originally to chaps. 1–12. Wüst (*Untersuchungen*, 30–40, 221–39) describes an even more detailed literary growth of the section than does Noth (pp 73–75). Confusion results from three points: 1) the relationship of 13:1–7 with 10:40–43 and 11:16–23, 2) the precise description of the land that remains, and 3) the double imperative in vv 6–7 and its connection with chap. 18, on the one hand, and with 13:8–33 on the other.

The structural solution can come only with the realization of the two distinct types of tradition which appear in Josh 1–12 and 13–19. The first half of the book is built on ancient oral traditions which have gained literary form quite early. Our text represents a reinterpretation of those early traditions by a Deuteronomistic editor, who has framed the early tradition with his compositions in chaps. 1 and 12, as well as with brief statements in chaps. 8, 10, 11. In chaps. 13–19 literary activity dominates. Oral narrative form is conspicuous only by its absence. Such literary activity presupposes the entire literary plan of the Deuteronomist in Deut 1 through 2 Kgs 25.

Chapter 13 is a major dividing point in this plan. Here the major shift in Israel's identity is made. She moves from a people fighting for the land to a people living in the land. This shift is accomplished literarily in total awareness of the promises of Josh 1, the conquest of Josh 2–12, and the later conquests in Judg 1 and in the reign of David (e.g. 1 Sam 30; 2 Sam 5; 8; 10). The literary form chosen at this point is complex and significant. It is based on the tradition witnessed by Gen 27; 49; and Deut 33, that of the elder spokesman giving his final blessing to his family/nation, a blessing which is determinative for the future of the audience. With a narrative statement (1a) and divine address (1bA), the way is prepared for Joshua's final address. Ten chapters intervene before that address appears (chap. 23). Why? The common answer is literary redaction, a claim which can be neither proved nor disproved. A more important fact is theological. Joshua's task is no longer to point forward to future blessing. Joshua's task is to teach proper life style for those who possess the blessing (chap. 23). Before that can be done, the land itself must be not only conquered, but also settled. Joshua's final act is thus divided into two parts. He not only gives his farewell advice; he also gives out the land (chaps. 14–21). The speaking and the action are joined into one complex event by the parallel introductory formulas (13:1; 23:1b). The action is placed first because it is the presupposition on which the speaking is based.

The action itself is based on a complex of traditions, each of which must be incorporated into the final formulation. The traditions include:

1) The settlement of the territory east of the Jordan by the tribes of Gad, Reuben, and half of Manasseh (cf. Num 32; Deut 3:12–22).
2) The promised borders of the land (Num 34; Josh 1; cf. 1 Kgs 8:65).
3) The land that remained for later conquest (Judg 1).

The divine speech thus contains four major parts:

a) A description of the present situation (v 1).
b) A description of the land that remains (vv 2–5).
c) A promise to complete the conquest eventually (6a).
d) A description of Joshua's present task and a command to begin immediately (6b–7).

Comment

[1] This verse introduces the theological tension central to the book of Judges and to the remainder of the Deuteronomistic history, namely life in the Land of Promise *shared* with the inhabitants of the land. At this point no reason is given for the inhabitants remaining. It is simply stated as a fact. The emphasis here is on the role of Joshua, as was so often the case in chaps. 1–12.

Joshua cannot complete the task of conquering the land. He is too old. He has fought a long time (11:18); he has been entirely faithful (11:15). All that remains is to detail the achievement already summarized in 11:23 (cf. 12:7), the partitioning of the land. Such a detailed description is first interrupted by a description of the work that remains after Joshua, a work already hinted at in 11:13.

² The land that remains has three sections:

1) The land of the Philistines and their southern "allies," vv 2–3.
2) The Phoenician coast, v 4.
3) The northern mountain country of Lebanon, v 5.

Such a division reflects the task facing David and the kingdom attributed to Solomon. The Philistines are understood to have been conquered by David (1 Sam 27; 2 Sam 8:1; 21:15–22; 23:8–17), while the only reference to control of Phoenicia comes in 1 Sam 24:6–7. Solomon apparently exercised domination of Lebanon (1 Kgs 9:19; 8:65), based on the Syrian wars of David (2 Sam 8:3–12; 10:1–19).

The territory of the Philistines heads the list of land that remains. This is appropriate in view of the role ascribed to the Philistines in the period of the judges and the early monarchy (Judg 3:31; 10:6–7; 13–16; 1 Sam 4–7; 13–14; 17–19; 23:1–6, 27–28; 27–29; 31; 2 Sam 5:17–25). A hint that the Philistines were not conquered has already appeared in 11:22.

The Philistines appear to have entered Palestine with a group usually called Sea Peoples coming down from eastern Asia Minor and Crete. They established their settlements in their five major cities (v 3) during the twelfth century. Philistine existence continued in Palestine until their deportation by Nebuchadrezzar II in 604 B.C. (K. A. Kitchen, in *Peoples of OT Times*, ed. D. J. Wiseman [1973] 53–78; contrast A. Nibbi, *The Sea Peoples and Egypt* [New Jersey: Noyes Press, 1975]).

The Geshurites are normally located in Syria north of the territory conquered by the Trans-Jordan tribes (Deut 3:14; Josh 12:5; 13:11–13). David eventually gained influence there through a marriage alliance (2 Sam 3:3=1 Chr 3:2), but this produced the rebel Absalom, who retreated to his maternal home (2 Sam 13:37–38). Interestingly, the area was not explicitly listed in David's fights with the Syrians (2 Sam 8, 10).

In the present context, northern Geshurites cannot be intended. A more fitting group is mentioned in 1 Sam 27:8, where David apparently attacks a group south of the Philistine cities. Textual problems in both texts, along with the lack of further information, makes identification difficult.

³ The territory of the Philistines and Geshurites is described in geographical detail. It reaches from Shihor to Ekron, the northernmost Philistine city. This appears to attribute to the Geshurites the wilderness between Gaza, the southernmost Philistine city, and the Egyptian border.

The mention of Shihor indicates that the editor is using a tradition distinct from others within the Deuteronomistic history and related only to that of 1 Chr 13:5. Shihor is usually located inside Egypt (cf. *Note* e), whereas the writer understands it as a border point of Egypt. Either he extends the Israelite claim well within the normal boundaries of Egypt (cf. Japhet, 209), or he uses the grammatical construction of 1 Sam 15:7 to distinguish the Shihor as the eastern boundary of Egypt (cf. M. Wüst, *Untersuchungen*, 37–38). In either case, he points to the time of its conquest under Saul and David (cf. 1 Sam 27:9). For the location of the borders of Canaan and Egypt, see now N. Naʾaman, "The Brook of Egypt and Assyrian Policy on the Border of Egypt" *Tel Aviv* 6 [1979] 68–90).

The reference to the Canaanites is not clear in the context. It may refer to a special tradition in which the coastland belonged to the Canaanites as opposed to the other members of the lists of the inhabitants of the land (Num 13:29; Deut 1:7; Josh 5:1; 11:3; cf. B. Maisler, *Untersuchungen*, 54–74). Otherwise, in the relatively few references in Deuteronomy-Joshua, the term applies to the entire land west of the Jordan (cf. Josh 22:9–11, 32). Here this would include the Philistine and Geshurite territories under the more comprehensive term used in Deut 11:30; 32:49; and Josh 5:12; 14:1; (cf. Gen 10:19) and would separate the land into two categories, that belonging to Israel and that belonging to the Canaanites, preparing for the future conflicts between the religion of Israel and that of Canaan.

The Philistines centered in five city-state complexes. Gaza, the southernmost of the five, was apparently the home of the temple of Dagon destroyed by Samson (Judg 16:23–30). The city had been a major Egyptian center in the Amarna period (*ANET*, 235, 258, 489). The summary statement of Josh 10:41 includes Gaza in the area defeated by Joshua, but 11:22 shows that Anakim remained there as opposed to the conditions in the land of Israel. Judg 1:18 (note negative added by LXX) assigns its conquest to Judah, to which it was allotted in Josh 15:47. Finally, 1 Kgs 5:4 (Eng.=4:24) gives Gaza as the western border of Solomon's empire, but the mention is missing in LXX and stands in some tension with 5:1 (cf. J. Gray, *I & II Kings* [2nd ed; OTL. Philadelphia: Westminster, 1970] 140–41). Traditionally, Gaza formed the southern border of Canaan (cf. Na'aman, *Tel Aviv* 6 [1979] 75–76).

Ashdod is identified with the modern village of Isdud, located nine miles (fourteen and a half kilometers) northeast of ancient Ashkelon and three and a half miles (six kilometers) southeast of modern Ashdod. Ugaritic texts refer to the textile industry at Ashdod. Its temple of Dagon was later disturbed by the Ark (1 Sam 5:1–9). Archaeology has uncovered defense walls dating to the last half of the seventeenth century B.C. Late Bronze Age finds indicate settlement from 1450–1230 with a large, but not total, destruction layer marking the end. M. Dothan, the excavator, attributes this to a first wave of Sea Peoples, preceding the settlement by the Philistines in the twelfth century (*EAEHL* 1, 108). The earliest Philistine stratum revealed an image of an enthroned mother goddess. The early Philistine city was one of the largest cities of its time in Palestine, covering almost eighty acres.

Ashkelon stands between Gaza and Ashdod and is the only Philistine city which was located on the seacoast itself. It appears among the cities cursed by the Egyptians in the nineteenth century execration texts (*ANET*, 329) and was later the object of the wrath of Ramses II (1304–1234; *ANET*, 256) and of Merneptah about 1230 (*ANET*, 378a). A cult of the Egyptian god Ptah may have been established there (*ANET*, 263b). During the Amarna period, the king of Ashkelon claims total obedience to the pharaoh (*ANET*, 490), but the king of Jerusalem apparently charges the Ashkelon king with treason (*ANET*, 488a).

Gath remains a topic of debate for biblical geographers and archaeologists. G. E. Wright has repeatedly argued for the identification with Tell esh-Sheri°ah, fifteen kilometers south of Tell el-Hesi ("Fresh Evidence for the Philistine Story." *BA* 29 [1966] 78–86; "A Problem of Ancient Topography: Lachish and Eglon." *HTR* 64 [1971] 446=*BA* 34 [1971] 84). Israeli archaeologists have contended that this is too far south and suggested identifying Gath with Tell es-Safi, half way between Gezer and Lachish (A. Rainey, "Gath," *IDBSup* [1976] 353, with literature; E. Stern, *EAEHL* 4 [1978] 1024–27; N. Na'aman, "Sennacherib's 'Letter to God' on his Campaign to Judah," *BASOR* 214 [1974] 35; "Sennacherib's Campaign to Judah and the Date of the *lmlk* Stamps" *VT* 29 [1979] 67; A. Negev [ed.], AEHL [1972] 121–22). Neither suggestion is entirely satisfactory (H. Weippert, *Biblisches Reallexikon* [2 ed.; 1977] 86).

Excavation reports from Tell esh-Sheri°ah show an important Canaanite settlement with strong Egyptian influence during the seventeenth to the thirteenth centuries, ending in a large destruction during the middle of the twelfth century, followed by Philistine occupation in the eleventh century. In the eighth-seventh century stratum, two Hebrew ostraca appeared. (Cf. E. D. Oren and E. Netzer, "Tel Sera° (Tell esh-Shari°a)" *IEJ* 24 [1974] 264–66; E. D. Oren, *EAEHL* 4 [1978] 1059–68). The excavators identify it with Ziklag, against Wright.

Tell es-Safi was escavated in 1899 with results less than satisfying by today's standards. The city was apparently settled in the Early Bronze Age. Philistine pottery was found as were Hebrew stamps (cf. Stern). Thus both sites suggested for Gath seem to indicate periods of Philistine and of Israelite settlement. This would agree with the report in 2 Chr 11:8 that Rehoboam controlled Gath.

The Hebrew ark caused problems for Gath (1 Sam 5:8–9). According to 1 Sam 7:14, Samuel restored Gath and Ekron to Israel. Victory over Goliath of Gath allowed Israel to chase the Philistines back to their homes in Ekron and Gath (1 Sam 17, especially v 52). David lived with the king of Gath until he secured Ziklag as a present from the Philistines (1 Sam 27:1–7). David finally defeated Gath (2 Sam 21:20–22), but there remained a Philistine king in Gath under Solomon (1 Kgs 2:39).

The site of Ekron remains shaded in archaeological dispute. W. F. Albright finally identified it with Aqir ("Syria, The Philistines, and Phoenicia," *CAH* II, Ch. XXXIII, 26, n. 3; cf. H. J. Sroebe, *Das Erste Buch Samuelis* 141). Israeli archaeologists follow J. Naveh, ("Khirbat al-Muquanna°-Ekron: An Archaeological Survey," *IEJ* 8 [1958] 166–70) in locating Ekron at Khirbet el-Muqanna° (Tel Miqne) (cf. A. Rainey, "Ekron," *IDBSup* [1976] 255; T. C. Mitchell, *Archaeology and Old Testament Study*, ed. D. W. Thomas [1967] 405–6). Judah received the city (15:45–46; cf. 11), but so did Dan (19:43). Judah captured it according to Judg 13: 1:18 MT, but LXX has the negative here. Her god later tempted Israel (1 Kgs 1:2–16).

Having listed the five Philistine cities, the text then adds "and the Avvim."

This is related to Deut 2:23, where the Avvim are said to have been conquered by the Caphtorim, probably Sea Peoples related to the Philistines.

⁴ The structure and meaning of this verse are not clear (see *Notes*). Apparently the more confined meaning of Canaan is used here (cf. *Comment* to v 3), being defined as the northern coastal region of the Phoenicians reaching down to Aphek. This is distinguished from the land of the Amorites, who are elsewhere said to inhabit the hill country (Num 13:29; Josh 5:1). The site of Arah, or whatever the original name of the textually obscure Sidonian city may be, is obscure. The tribe of Asher was unable to conquer Sidon (Judg 1:31). Only 2 Sam 24:6–7 implies that David controlled Phoenicia. Otherwise Tyre and Sidon are free kingdoms allied with David and Solomon (2 Sam 5:11; 1 Kgs 5:15–24 [=Eng. 5:1–10]; 9:11–14).

The Bible knows several sites named Aphek:

1. A city given to Asher but not conquered (19:30; Judg 1:31), possibly near Acco.

2. A city east of the Jordan on the road to Damascus (1 Kgs 20:26–30; 2 Kgs 13:14–19, 25).

3. A site sometimes identified with the present text is the modern Afqa, fifteen miles east of ancient Byblos in Lebanon.

4. The most famous of the cities called Aphek is a city-state in the plain of Sharon located at modern Tel Rosh haʾAyin close to the source of the Yarkon River, just east of modern Tel Aviv. The city appears in the nineteenth century execration texts from Egypt (*ANET*, 329). Settlement in the fourth millennium with a walled city in the early third millennium has been demonstrated by excavations (M. Kochavi, "Tel Aphek (Ras el-ʿAin)" *IEJ* 22 [1972] 238–39). A Middle Bronze Age palace (M. Kochavi, "Tel Aphek," *IEJ* 23, [1973] 245–46) and Late Bronze Age occupation concluded with a massive destruction layer around 1200, with Iron Age settlement also destroyed by fire (M. Kochavi, "Tel Aphek," *IEJ* 24 [1974] 261–62; cf. R. Giveon, "Two Unique Egyptian Inscriptions from Tel Aphek," *Tel Aviv* 5 [1978] 188, n. 1).

The excavator suggests that the thirteenth century destruction be attributed to the Sea Peoples and reports now that in the Israelite layer a cult site has been discovered which was destroyed in the eighth century (M. Kochavi, "Tel Aphek," *IEJ* 26, [1976] 51–52). Its king is listed among those defeated by Joshua (12:18). During the days of Samuel and Saul it served as a mustering point for Philistine troops (1 Sam 4:1; 29:1). Thus it is conceived here as among the land that remains to be conquered by David when he conquered the Philistines.

Verse 5 describes a third region which remained unconquered, that of the far north. This begins above Sidon at Gebal or Byblos and stretches eastwards. Lebanon refers to the western mountain range rising from the Phoenician coast to a height of 8300 feet and the country dominated by the mountain range. It is a component part of the land promised to Moses and Joshua (Deut 1:7; 3:25; Josh 1:4), but it was not conquered by Joshua (Josh 11:17; 12:7). In our passage it appears to represent the western border of the section of territory, whose eastern border is represented by the line from Baal Gad to Lebo-Hamath. Lebanon appears to be under Solomonic domination in 1 Kgs 9:19, while the Solomonic borders reached to Lebo-hamath (1 Kgs 8:65).

Verse 6 serves as a summary statement of all that has gone before, but actually includes at best only vv 4 and 5. Sidonians is given as a term for all the inhabitants of the Phoenician coast and of the mountains of Lebanon. Misraphoth Mayim represented the northern border of Joshua's conquests (cf. 11:8).

The theological point of the whole section comes in v 6aβ, the divine promise. God will do that which Joshua is too old to do. Israel may lose its perfectly obedient leader, but she will not lose the leadership of God. He has made his promise (Exod 34:24; Num 32:21; 33:52-53; Deut 9:3-5; 11:23; 18:12; Josh 3:10). The term יָרַשׁ (hiph'il) "dispossess" becomes almost a re-frain in the following chapters of Joshua, most often to describe Israel's in-ability to dispossess the inhabitants (13:13; 15:63; 16:10; 17:12, 13; contrast 13:12; 14:12; 15:14; 17:18). This all points forward to the repeated promise in 23:5 with the associated warning in 23:13, reaching the climax in Judg 2:20-23.

6b-7 The emphasis in our chapter is on the task which Joshua must yet fulfill despite his old age. He has yet another command of Yahweh to obey. He must distribute the land to those tribes who will live west of the Jordan. The tribes of Reuben, Gad and half of Manasseh have already received their portion east of the Jordan from Moses (Num 32). Joshua must now finish the task first given Moses in Num 26:52-56. The importance of this task for Joshua is demonstrated by the repetition of the command. It is first given as Joshua's sign of obedience which insures that Yahweh will dispossess the nations (cf. Deut 11:22-23). It is repeated as something to be done at this precise moment. Joshua is given not only a general command for the future, but also a specific task to be begun immediately. Completion of the task is interrupted by vv 10-33, a historical resumé of what Moses did. This gives a complete picture of the tribal possessions in one section.

Explanation

Joshua 13:1-7 turns the corner from conquest to settlement. It should represent the end of the story. The long journey from Egypt to the Promised Land is finally over. The people have won the land. They need only divide it among themselves and live on it according to the laws God has been so good to give them. Historical reality was not that simple. Israel still faced a major task. The western coast, the southern wilderness and the northern mountain land remained under foreign control. And the hero, who had brought victory to Israel through his obedience to Yahweh, was too old to carry on his victorious ways. Now what?

The reader expects a repetition of Deut 31 and 34. The only question remaining is, who will be the new leader? Our writer surprises us. New leader-ship is not the issue. Leadership rests in the hands of God. He will carry out his promise (v 6). The central issue remains one of obedience to divine command. Will the conquering hero now distribute the land to the people? Here we see the true audience to whom the book is written. It is written to an Israel which has experienced false leadership, leadership which would not divide the conquered land among the people. The issue is expressed in its sharpest terms by Ezek 45. Israel's history with kingship had been a history of oppression in which rulers claimed too much land for themselves, evicting the rightful owners, and refusing to distribute the land (vv 8–9). The story of Naboth's vineyard in 1 Kgs 21 gives a perfect example of what many kings must have done in Israel. Our writer uses the example of Joshua to remind all future generations of Israel how a leader of God's people must act. He must act just as Yahweh commanded (v 6b). Land which he conquers, he must distribute. Thus the writer has shown that Joshua distributed the land as soon as he conquered it (11:23; 12:7). Only such obedient action could bring cessation of war (cf. 11:23). Israel must not wait until she conquers all the land to distribute it. The whole history of Israel showed that there was constantly land remaining to be conquered. The writer explained this fact in Judg 2. Here his emphasis is on proper action for a people in possession of less than all the land. His message is particularly for Israel ready to return from Babylonian exile. Thus Israel has suffered punishment because of the action of her kings. Now she is called to reflect upon her history and learn from the past. When God gives her the land once more, she is to distribute it equally as God has commanded. No one ruler nor any ruling class may slice up the land for itself. The land belongs to Yahweh. He gave it to his people, just as he conquered it for his people.

Reviewing Moses' Allotments (13:8–33)

Bibliography

Bartlett, J. R. "Sihon and Og, Kings of the Amorites." *VT* 20 (1970) 257–77. **Bergman, A.** "The Israelite Occupation of Eastern Palestine in the Light of Territorial History." *JAOS* 54 (1934) 169–77. ———. "The Israelite Tribe of Half-Manasseh." *JPOS* 16 (1936) 224–54. **Glueck, N.** "Explorations in Eastern Palestine, 1–4." AASOR 14 (1933–34) 1–114; AASOR 15 (1934–35); AASOR 18–19 (1937–39); AASOR 25–28 (1945–49). **Kaufmann, Y.** *The Religion of Israel from its beginnings to the Babylonian exile.* Tr. M. Greenberg, Chicago: University of Chicago Press, 1960, 200–202. **Kuschke, A.** "Historisch-topographische Beiträge zum Buche Josua." *Gottes Wort und Gottes Land*, ed. H. G. Reventlow. Göttingen: Vandenhoeck & Ruprecht, 1965, 90–102. **Mayes, A. D. H.** *Israel in the Period of the Judges.* London: SCM, 1974, 69–70. **Mittmann, S.** *Beiträge zur Siedlungs- und Territorialgeschichte des nördlichen Ostjordanlandes.* Wiesbaden: Otto Harrassowitz, 1970, 231–46. **Noth, M.** "Gilead und Gad." *ZDPV* 75 (1959) 14–73. (= *Aufsätze zur biblischen Landes- und Altertumskunde.* Vol. 1. Neukirchen-Vluyn: Neukirchener Verlag, 1971, 489–543.) ———. "Israelitische Stämme zwischen Ammon und Moab." *ZAW* 60 (1944) 11–57. (= *Aufsätze* 1, 391–433.) ———. "Die israelitischen Siedlungsgebiete im Ostjordanland." *ZDPV* 58 (1935) 231–55. (= *Aufsätze* 1, 262–80.) ———. "Jabesh-Gilead. Ein Beitrag zur Methode alttestamentlicher Topographie." *ZDPV* 69 (1953) 28–41. (= *Aufsätze* 1, 476–88.) ———. "Das Land Gilead als Siedlungsgebiet israelitischer Sippen." *PJ* 37 (1941) 50–101. (= *Ausätze* 1, 347–90.) ———. "Die Nachbarn der israelitischen Stämme im Ostjordanlande." *ZDPV* 68 (1946–

51) 1–50. (= *Aufsätze* 1, 434–75.) **Ottosson, M.** *Gilead, Tradition and History.* Lund: C. W. K. Gleerup: 1969, 118–35. **Simons, J.** "Two Connected Problems Relating to the Israelite Settlement in Transjordan." *PEQ* 79 (1947) 27–39, 87–101. **de Vaux, R.** *Histoire ancienne d'Israël.* Vol. 1. Paris: J. Gabalda, 1971, 511–45. (= *The Early History of Israel.* Tr. D. Smith. London: Darton, Longman & Todd, 1978, 551–92.) ———. "Notes d'histoire et de topographie transjordaniennes." *RB* 50 (1941) 16–47. (= *Bible et Orient.* Paris: Éditions du Cerf, 1967, 115–49.) **Wüst, M.** *Untersuchungen zu den siedlungsgeographischen Texten des Alten Testaments, 1 Ostjordanland.* Wiesbaden: Dr. Ludwig Reichert Verlag, 1975.

Translation

[8] *With it* [a] *the Reubenites and the Gaddites took their inheritance which Moses had given to them beyond the Jordan eastward just as Moses the servant of Yahweh had given to them:* [9] *from Aroer which is beside the river Arnon along with the city in the midst of the river valley and all the plain* [a] *of Medeba unto Dibon;* [b] [10] *also* [a] *all the cities of Sihon, king of the Amorites who ruled in Heshbon, unto the border of the sons of Ammon;* [11] *and Gilead and the territory of the Geshurites and the Maacathites, along with* [a] *all of Mount Hermon and all Bashan unto Salecah;* [12] *all the kingdom of Og in Bashan which he ruled in Ashtaroth and in Edrei (he remained from the remnant of the Rephaim; Moses had smitten them* [a] *and dispossessed them).* [13] *However, the sons of Israel did not dispossess the Geshurites and the Maacathites.* [a] *Geshur* [b] *and Maacath have lived in the midst of Israel until this day.* [14] *Only to the tribe of Levi, did he not give an inheritance; the gifts devoted to* [a] *Yahweh, the God of Israel, that is his* [b] *inheritance, just as he said to him.* [c]

[15] *Moses gave to the tribe of the sons* [a] *of Reuben for their clans.* [16] [a] *This is the territory that belonged to them: from Aroer which is beside the River Arnon along with the city in the midst of the river valley and all the plain by* [b] *Medeba;* [17] *Heshbon and all its* [a] *cities which are in the plain; Dibon* [b] *and Bamoth-Baal and Beth-Baal-meon* [c] *and* [18] *Jahazah and Qedemoth and Mephaath* [19] *and Kiriathaim and Sibmah and Zereth Shahar in the hill of the valley* [20] *and Beth Peor and the slopes of Pisgah and Beth Jeshimoth;* [21] *along with all the cities of the plain and all the kingdom of Sihon, king of the Amorites who* [a] *ruled in Heshbon, whom Moses smote along with the princes of Midian: Evi and Reqem and Zur and Hur and Reba,* [b] *the vassal princes under Sihon, dwelling in the land.* [22] *Also Balaam, son of Beor, the one who practiced divination, the sons of Israel killed with the sword together with their battle casualties.* [a] [23] *So this was the border of the sons* [a] *of Reuben: the Jordan and its* [b] *territory. This is the inheritance of the sons of Reuben for their clans: the cities and their villages.* [c]

[24] *Moses gave to the tribe of Gad,* [a] *to the sons of Gad for their clans.* [25] *This is the territory which belonged to them: Jazer and* [a] *all the cities of Gilead with half the land of the sons of Ammon unto Aroer, which is over against Rabbah;* [b] [26] *also from Heshbon unto Ramath-mizpeh and Betonim; also from Mahanaim unto the territory of Debir;* [a] [27] *also in the valley of Beth Haram and Beth Nimrah* [a] *and Succoth and Zaphon, the remainder of the kingdom of Sihon, king of Heshbon; the Jordan and territory unto the end of the Sea of Chinnereth beyond the Jordan to the east.* [28] *This is the inheritance of the sons of Gad for their clans,* [a] *the cities and their villages.*

[29] *Moses gave to half the tribe of Manasseh. This is* [a] *what belonged to half the*

tribe of the sons of Manasseh for their clans: [30] *their territory was from Mahanaim,
all Bashan, all the kingdom of Og, the king of Bashan, and all Havvoth-Jair, which
are in Bashan, namely sixty cities,* [31] *and half of Gilead, and Ashtaroth and Edrei,
cities of the kingdom of Og in Bashan. This belonged to the sons of Machir, the
son* [a] *of Manasseh, for half of the sons of Machir for their clans.* [32] *These are what
Moses caused to be inherited in the plains of Moab, beyond the Jordan east of Jericho.*
[33] *But* [a] *to the tribe of the Levites, Moses did not give an inheritance; Yahweh, the
God of Israel, he is their inheritance, just as he spoke to them.*

Notes

8.a. As at the end of v 7, so the beginning of v 8 represents a difficult Hebrew text. The
pronominal suffix has no apparent antecedent. From the context, it must refer to the half of
the tribe of Manasseh not included in v 7. The LXX text reads "to the (two) tribes and to the
half tribe of Manasseh, to Reuben and to Gad, Moses gave what was beyond the Jordan eastward.
Moses, the servant of the Lord, gave to him (!) [9] from. . . ." Codex Vaticanus does not even
contain the number two. The text has apparently been disturbed quite early, so that various
textual traditions have tried to restore its meaning. Holmes, Auld, Soggin, Gray, and the Text
Project all adopt some modified form of LXX reading. The text thus has a long history of
corruptions, so that hopes of restoring a "pristine" text are faint, but a clumsy redactor cannot
be blamed for all the problems either (as Wüst, *Untersuchungen,* 85–87, does).

9.a. LXX consistently transliterates Hebrew מישׁר "plain" throughout this passage rather
than translating it.

9.b. The Greek omits "unto Dibon" and reads the first term "from Daidadan," which is
probably a corruption of both place names. A prepositional *mem* has probably dropped out of
the Hebrew text, which reads "all the plain from Medeba to Dibon."

10–11.a. LXX omits the introductory conjunction, probably correctly. The preceding may
be summarized as the cities formerly ruled by Sihon. Similarly in v 11, LXX omits the conjunction
prior to "all Mount Hermon," summarizing the territory of the Geshurites and Maacathites as
comprising Mount Hermon and Bashan.

12.a. The LXX sing. suffix refers explicitly to the "kingdom" of Og, while the Heb. plur.
suffix is ambiguous, the nearest antecedent being the "Rephaim." LXX may represent early
exegesis, since the earlier traditions (Deut 2:11, 20; 3:11, 13; Josh 12:4; cf. Num 21:33–35)
nowhere refer to an Israelite victory over the Rephaim.

13.a. LXX adds "and the Canaanites," just as was done in v 2. This, too, represents early
exegesis for which the Canaanites are the archenemy.

13.b. Continuing its exegetical glosses, LXX adds "the king of" before Geshur, implying
that a captive king dwelled among the Israelites. Geshur here is in Transjordan as opposed to
the Geshur in the southwestern Negeb in v 2.

14.a. LXX does not render אשׁי. The term is dependent upon Deut 18:1 and may represent
a later exegetical gloss (see Auld). Its meaning is usually related to אש, "fire," but Hoftijzer
("Das sogenannte Feueropfer" VTSup 16 [1967] 127–34), may be correct in defining it as gifts
given to deity on the basis of a vow.

14.b. Having omitted אשׁי the LXX referred the pronoun "that (or) he" to Yahweh and
interpreted "tribe" as collective, thus using plur. pronouns, as does MT in v 33. The singular
of MT conforms to Deut 18:2; 10:9 and may represent glosses from there. A LXX gloss makes
Yahweh the explicit subject of "he spoke."

14.c. At the end of the verse LXX adds, "And this is the allotment which Moses allotted
to the sons of Israel in the plains of Moab beyond the Jordan over against Jericho." This is
apparently a summary statement closing the section, parallel to that of v 32. As such, it reinterprets
the function of 8–14, reading it as parallel to the other tribal allotments. Instead, the verses
seek to summarize the territory occupied by Israel beyond the Jordan. Despite Margolis and
Holmes, Auld agrees that the LXX addition is secondary, but on grounds of a complicated
literary theory.

15.a. As often, LXX does not witness "sons." For the combination סטה בני "tribe of the
sons of . . . ," see Auld, VTSup 30 (1979) 10–11.

16.a. The MT duplicates v 9 but here LXX reads ἥ ἐστιν κατὰ προσωπον φαραγγος Αρνων, καὶ ἥ πόλις ἥ ἐν τῇ φάραγγι Αρνων rather than ἥ ἐστιν ἐπι τοῦ χειλους λειμαρρου Αρνων καὶ τὴν πόλιν τὴν ἐν μέσῳ τῆς φαραγγος . . . Here LXX thus does not make it clear that the edge or shore of the river is specified, but then adds a second "Arnon" while not specifying "the midst of." Either LXX is inconsistent here in its translation techniques or had a slightly different text before it.

16.b. MT reads עַל "upon, over," while a large number of Heb. mss and the Tg witness עַד, "unto." LXX also apparently read עַד, but did not read "Medeba." V 16 is closely related to v 9, where similar textual problems occur. Textual evidence would tend to support the reading עַד חשבון, "unto Heshbon," but textual emendation here is not based so much on textual evidence as on geographical, structural, and literary presuppositions.

17.a. LXX does not translate the pronominal suffix. The antecedent for the suffix is apparently Heshbon. The Heb. syntax would be more easily understood if the suffix were not present. Again, the text may be emended only after the literary problems have been analyzed (see Wüst, *Untersuchungen,* 126–128).

17.b. Greek adds the conjunction before Dibon, separating it clearly from the preceding construction.

17.c. LXX transmission of the city names is quite inconsistent in vv 17–19 (cf. Margolis, Brooke-McLean).

21.a. LXX lacks "who ruled in Heshbon," a traditional phrase which may have entered the text here from v 10.

21.b. LXX, Vg, and Tg transliterate רבע "Reba" as a fifth vassal king and are followed by most modern translations. Soggin (p. 150) suggests translating the term as "four," which would involve repointing the text at least. The term is related to that of Num 31:8 and most likely is to be considered as a proper name.

The Greek tradition shows confusion in the final words of the verse. Vaticanus reads: τὸν Ῥοβε ὁρχοντα ἐναρα Σειων καὶ τοὺς κατοικοῦντας Σειων, ". . . Robe, the chief, the war spoils of Seion, and the inhabitants of Seion." Margolis restores: ἁρχοντας παρὰ Σηων καὶ τοὺς κατοικοῦντας τὴν γῆν, "the rulers on behalf of Seon. And the inhabitants of the land . . . ," but Margolis admits that the orthography of the royal name is difficult and appears to interpret Seion as a geographical entity. MT is to be preferred, but the Greek tradition reminds us of the exegetical difficulties faced by the first translators of the text.

22.a. LXX does not witness "the sons of Israel" or "with the sword" and translates the difficult Heb. phrase אל חלליהם as ἐν τῇ ῥοπῇ "in the decisive moment" (Vaticanus) or ἐν τῇ τροπῇ, "in the battle route" (Margolis based on Coptic). Neither reading is preferable to the MT, but both show the difficulty the early tradition had in understanding the text.

As is often the case, there appears to be confusion between the Heb. prepositions אל "to" and עַל "upon, on account of" (cf. BHS).

23.a. LXX, as often, omits "sons."

23.b. The Heb. text reads literally, "the Jordan and territory (or border)." The meaning is clearer than the syntax.

23.c. The Heb. pronominal suffix is feminine and refers to cities. LXX apparently duplicated the pronoun and referred it back to the Reubenites, "their cities and their villages." MT is the most difficult reading and should be retained.

24.a. MT preserves a double reading of which the LXX preserves "to the sons of Gad," while Syr witnesses "to the tribe of Gad." The original text, parallel to vv 15 and 29b, may have read "to the tribe of the sons of Gad."

25.a. LXX omits the conjunction before "all," which could be interpreted as defining Jazer as including all the cities of Gilead.

25.b. The important Vaticanus Greek witness is apparently corrupt here (cf. Margolis), but gives an interesting interpretation, reading: "unto Araba, which is over against Arad," extending the territory quite far south.

26.a. Again Greek, though probably corrupt (Margolis), preserves variant geographical readings: "and from Heshbon unto Araboth over against Massepha, and Botanei and Baan unto the territory of Daibon." The final city is read by MT as Lidebor. LXX understood the initial *lamedh* as a preposition. What is probably the same city is variously pointed in the MT לוֹ דְבָר 2 Sam 9:4–5; לֹא דְבָר, 2 Sam 17:27; לֹא דָבָר, Amos 6:13; and לִדְבָר, here.

27.a. LXX again has distinct readings for the opening two geographical locations. Vaticanus reads, καὶ Ἑνα δῶμ καὶ ὁ θαργαει και βαιναθαναβρα. Margolis may be correct in restoring the middle term to Beth Haran, as in Num 32:36.

28.a. Using the language of 7:12, LXX inserts, "The necks they turned in face of their enemies because it was according to their clans." Why or how this was introduced into the text at this point is not clear.

29.a. LXX does not witness, "This is what belonged to half the tribe of the sons of Manasseh." The form used here is distinct from that of vv 15–16 and 24–25. This may be explained either on literary grounds or as a textual corruption, in which case the beginning of v 30 would have been falsely copied in the middle of v 29, with v 30 then being modified. The original text may have read: Moses gave to half the tribe of Manasseh for their clans. This is the territory which belonged to half the tribe of the sons of Manasseh: from Mahanaim and all Bashan and all the kingdom of Og (adding conjunctions with LXX).

29.a.–31.a. LXX interprets the text reading, "sons of Machir, the sons of Manasseh, and to half of the sons of Machir, the sons of Manasseh, . . ."

33.a. LXX omits v 33, which repeats with slight changes v 14 (cf. Auld, "Textual and Literary Studies in the Book of Joshua" *ZAW* 90 [1978] 412).

Form/Structure/Setting

The structure of the section is distinct in the Massoretic and Greek traditions. The Hebrew text does not have a formulaic beginning. Rather it is tied very loosely to the preceding by a sentence (v 8), whose syntax is difficult to decipher (see *Notes*). Verses 8–12 describe in a long list the territory which the tribes east of the Jordan took after Moses gave it to them. The territory is listed from south to north and covers all the land between the river Arnon and Mount Hermon. This is divided into several sections:

1) The city of Aroer along with the city in the midst of the Arnon Valley (9a);

2) The northern Moabite tableland described in a north-south direction of Medeba to Dibon (9b);

3) The territory captured from Sihon, the Amorite king in Heshbon, described in a west-east direction, ending at the border of the Ammonites (10);

4) Gilead, apparently assumed to be the territory between Heshbon and the Yarmuk River (11);

5) The land of the Geshurites and the Maacathites, assumed to be north of the Yarmuk below Mount Hermon (11);

6) Mount Hermon, the northern border in the Anti-Lebanon range (11);

7) Bashan, apparently understood as the land east of the territory of the Geshurites and Maacathites, reaching in a west-east direction to Salecah. Bashan is further identified as the kingdom of Og, centering around two cities, Ashtaroth in the north and Edrei in the south (11–12a).

Having listed the territory included in Israel's inheritance east of the Jordan, the writer then notes two exceptional cases (13–14). Israel failed to capture the extreme northern territory of Geshur and Maacath, resulting in a situation in the editor's day in which the two enemy kingdoms exist within Israel. The other exception is unexpected in the context. It notes that the Priestly Levites did not receive territory from Moses. The notice has no relationship to the eastern tribes. Rather it is a summarizing notice, insuring reference to all tribes of Israel within vv 1–14.

Verses 15–33 in the Hebrew tradition contain three subsections, denoting the territory of Reuben (15–23); Gad (24–28); and the half tribe of Manasseh (29–31). Verse 32 forms a concluding summary. Almost choruslike, the MT then repeats the notice about Levi (v 33).

Each territorial description is introduced by the notice that Moses gave the territory to the tribe for its clans. The territory is described. A final notice indicates that this is the inheritance of the tribe for its clans, the cities and their villages. This formal structure is quite disturbed in the final section on Manasseh.

Within each section the territory is divided into certain units. Reuben's territory begins at the southern limit of Aroer and the Arnon Valley and includes all the plain to (cf. *Notes*) Medeba (16). This is more closely defined as Heshbon and all its cities in the plain (17a). These cities are then listed, though the order followed is difficult to determine (17b–20). The cities are again characterized as the cities of the plain and as the kingdom of Og (21), to which a historical note is attached (21b–22).

Gad's territory is described in a variety of ways. First, it is defined generally as Jazer and all the cities of Gilead (25aA). This is more closely defined in each direction. To the east it includes half of the territory of the Ammonites reaching to Aroer by the Ammonite capital of Rabbah (25aB,b). The southern territory begins at Heshbon, reaching unto Ramath-mizpeh and Betonim (26a). The northern territory begins at Mahanaim, extending to Debir (or Lo-Dabar, cf. *Notes*) (26b). The western section represents the remainder of the kingdom of Sihon not allotted to Reuben. This is more closely identified as the Jordan Valley reaching northward to the Sea of Chinnereth (27).

The territory of eastern Manasseh is described in two sections. The general description extends from Mahanaim northward, a territory which can be designated as all Bashan, as all the kingdom of Og, with the notation that this included all Havvoth-Jair (30). V 31 appears to be a very brief historical note, somewhat parallel to 21b–22, attributing the eastern territory to Machir, a territory including half of Gilead and the capital cities of Og in Edrei and Ashtaroth. One would expect here a note similar to Num 32:40 that Moses gave these to Machir. One also expects the closing formula זאת נחלה לחצי בני מנשה למשפחותם, "this is the inheritance of half of the sons of Manasseh for their clans." LXX may point to early textual corruption at this point (cf. *Notes*).

The source for this information has been a matter of intense scholarly debate. The standard explanation is that of Martin Noth, working on the analogy of the discoveries of Albrecht Alt with regard to the tribal lists in chaps. 15–19. Noth isolated at least fragments of an eastern list of towns and of fixed border points in vv 15–33. The town list (17b–19 [20?], 27aA) he connected to Alt's western town list, dated to the time of Josiah. Likewise, he saw the border points (16, 17a?, 20?, 25b?, 26, 27aBb) as connected to the western document compiled by one of the judges of Israel to settle or prevent border disputes.

Rudolph (*Der Elohist,* pp. 214–216) agreed that town lists lay behind Josh 13, but was not sure these could be seen as towns conquered by Josiah. He denied the presence of border lists, seeing rather geographical reference points to describe certain regions. The Priestly writer divided the territory into two parts of Reuben and Gad, thus creating pure fiction, according to Rudolph. Similarly Glueck (*AASOR* 18–19 [1937–39] 249–51) argues that Noth's boundary lines fit neither the kingdom of Sihon nor the territory of the Israelite tribes. What is more, they follow no natural boundaries and accord with no archaeological findings. They are no more the eastern boundary of the tribes than Dan to Beersheba is the eastern border of western Palestine.

Mittmann accepts the division between a town list and boundary description, but notes the literary differences between chaps. 13 and 15, thus denying a common source to the two. Moreover, the border points lay too far apart and do not form a meaningful boundary line. For Mittmann, it was the redactor who transformed an original list into a border description parallel to that of Josh 15. The original list was an administrative document from the time of Solomon outlining the areas of authority of each of the regional centers.

Wüst also works with the assumption of originally distinct territorial description and town lists, but for him the original territorial description was limited to "from Aroer unto Medeba" (v 16) and "from Heshbon unto Ramath-mispeh (and Betonim?)" (v 26a). "And all the plain" was added to v 16 from v 17, where it headed the city list, thus uniting the two lists. Description of Aroer and the city in the middle of the valley were added to equate precisely the Israelite boundary with that of Sihon (Num 21:13, 26). The addition of the material concerning half-Manasseh in vv 29–30 brought the expansion of the Gaddite territory "from Mahanaim unto the territory of Lodebar" (26b) so as to claim all the territory east of the Jordan for Israel (see his summary on p 144). Such a border separation represents, for Wüst, the border between Israel and Moab described by the Moabite Stele and in Jer 48:2; 49:3 rather than actual tribal history.

Wüst separates the city list in Josh 13:17–20, 27 from that in Num 32:34–38. The list in Numbers, he finds originally limited to Dibon, Ataroth, Aroer, and Atroth-shophan in Gad. The original Reubenite list included Heshbon, Elealeh, Kiriathaim, Baal-meon and Sibma. The two lists were built around the regional centers of Dibon and Heshbon and must come from a time prior to ninth century Moabite expansion, and thus from the time of Solomon at the latest (cf. *Untersuchungen*, 152–53; 182).

The Joshua city list, unlike that of Numbers, was not originally separated by tribes, but rather represented ancient, undatable highway routes in Trans-Jordan, since it is hard to imagine the route as a border line. One of the routes ran from Dibon to Bamoth-Baal and then diverted from the major northern route to Medeba to follow the northwestern route to Beth-baal-meon, Kiriathaim, and Beth-jeshimoth, joining a road to Beth-haram, Beth-nimrah, Succoth, and Zaphon. A second route ran from Sibma over Zereth-sharar to Beth-peor. This was inserted by an editor into the original route to extend the territory northward. A later editor added the slopes of Pisgah to join the road to the Jordan Valley again. Later editorial work divided the route into three parts: the plain, (v 17), the hill of the valley (v 19b), and in the valley (v 27). Only at this stage was the material taken up by the editor of Josh 13 and split into two parts for Reuben and Gad. The editor then extended the towns of Gad through use of information gathered from Num 32:1 and Judg 11:33, creating Josh. 13:25.

Wüst has thus reduced the boundary list to such an extent that it loses function and meaning, while creating a system of roads running in all directions but without a *Sitz im Leben* for preservation. The pre-history of the lists remains in darkness, only the literary intentions being capable of illumination.

Levitical Cities

City	Joshua		Numbers			Josh 21	Chr 6		Deuteronomistic	Prophetic
	13	Other	21	32	Other		Heb.	Eng.		
Aroer	9, 16	12:2	—	34	—	—	—	—	Deut 2:36; 3:12; 4:48; 2 Kgs 10:33; 2 Sam 24:5; Judg 11:26	Jer 48:19
Medeba	9, 16	—	27–30	—	—	—	—	—	—	Isa 15:2
Dibon	9, 17	—	30	3, 34	33:45f.	—	—	—	—	Isa 15:2, 9; Jer 48:22
Heshbon	10, 17, 21, 26, 27	9:10; 12:2, 5	25–34	3, 37	—	39	66	81	Deut 1:4; 2:24, 26, 30; 3:2, 6; 4:46; 29:6(7); Judg 11:11, 26	Isa 15:4; 16; 8–9; Jer 48; 2, 34, 45
Salecah	11	12:5	—	—	—	—	—	—	Deut 3:10	—
Ashtaroth	12, 31	12:4 9:10	—	—	—	—	56	71	Deut 1:4	—
Edrei	12, 31	12:4	33	—	—	—	—	—	Deut 1:4; 3:1, 10	—
Bamothbaal	17	—	19–20	—	22:41	—	—	—	—	—
Bethbaalmeon	17	—	—	3, 38	—	—	—	—	—	Jer 48:23; Ezek 25:9
Jahaz	18	—	23	—	—	36	63	78	Deut 2:32; Judg 11:20	Isa 15:4; Jer 48:21, 34
Kedemoth	18	—	—	—	—	37	64	79	Deut. 2:26	—
Mephaath	18	—	—	—	—	37	64	79	—	Jer 48:21
Kiriathaim	19	—	—	37	—	—	61 (?)	76 (?)	—	Jer 48:1, 23 Ezek 25:9
Sibmah	19	—	—	3, 38	—	—	—	—	—	Isa 16:8, 9; Jer 48:32
Zereth-shahar	19	—	—	—	—	—	—	—	—	—
Beth Peor	20	—	—	—	—	—	—	—	Deut 3:29; 4:46; 34:6	—
Baal Peor Peor		22:17	—	—	23:28; 25:3, 5, 18; 31:16	—	—	—	(Ps 106:28)	Hos 9:10
Slopes of Pisgah Top of Pisgah	20	12:3 —	— 20	—	— 23:14	—	—	—	Deut 3:17; 4:49 Deut 3:27; 34:1	—
Beth-jeshimoth	20	12:3	—	—	33:49	—	—	—	—	Ezek 25:9
Princes of Midian	21	—	—	—	31:8; cf. 25:18	—	—	—	—	—
Jazer	25	—	32	1, 3, 35	—	39	66	81	2 Sam 24:5; (1 Chr 26:31)	Isa 16:8–9; Jer 48:32
Aroer by Rabbah	25	—	—	—	—	—	—	—	cf. Judg 11:33	—
Rabbah	25	—	—	—	—	—	—	—	2 Sam 11:1; 12:26–29; 17:27	Amos 1:14
Ramath-mizpeh	26	—	—	—	—	—	—	—	—	—
Betonim	26	—	—	—	—	—	—	—	—	—
Mahanaim	26, 30	—	cf. Gen 32:3 (=Eng. 2)	—	—	38	65	80	2 Sam 2:8, 12, 29; 17:24, 27; 19:33; 1 Kgs 2:8; 4:14	—
לדבר (see Notes)	26	—	—	—	—	—	—	—	(2 Sam 9:4, 5; 17:27)	Amos 6:13
Beth-haram	27	—	—	36(=Beth Haran)	—	—	—	—	—	—
Beth-nimrah	27	—	—	3, 36	—	—	—	—	—	—
Succoth	27	—	cf. Gen 33:17; Ps 60:8= 108:8	—	—	—	—	—	1 Kgs 7:46; Judg 8	—
Zaphon	27	—	—	—	cf. 26:15	—	—	—	—	—
60 Cities of Jair	30	—	—	41	—	—	—	—	Deut 3:14; 1 Kg. 4:13; Deut 3:14; 1 Kg. 4:13; Judg 10:4	cf. 1 Chr 2:23

The literary editor attempts to incorporate all the information at his disposal into an allocation of the territory east of the Jordan parallel to that west of the Jordan. His starting point is the specific geographical understanding of the Deuteronomic tradition, which says:

1) Aroer is the southern boundary of the land occupied by Israel (Deut 2:36; 3:12; 4:48; Josh 12:2; 13:9, 16; 2 Kgs 10:33; cf. 2 Sam 24:5). The Mesha stele (1. 26; *ANET*, 320) and Jer 48:19 presuppose Moabite occupation of Aroer, whereas Num 32:34 and Judg 11:26 witness Israelite occupation.

2) The border could be more precisely defined as the city in the midst of the river valley (3:9, 16; cf. Deut 2:36; 3:16; Josh 12:2; 2 Sam 24:5). This makes clear that the border is precisely that of the kingdom of Sihon over against Moab (cf. Num 21:24; 22:36; Wüst, *Untersuchungen*, 133–43).

3) All the high plain north of the Arnon reaching up to Medeba and Heshbon belonged to Israel (Deut 3:10; Josh 13:9, 16, 17, 21; cf. the city of refuge in the plain, Deut 4:43; Josh 20:8). By the time of Jeremiah, the cities of the plain are Moabite (Jer 48:8, 21; cf. *ANET*, 320).

4) The expression "who ruled in Heshbon" (vv 10, 21) is confined to this chapter. The related expression "king of Heshbon" (v 27) is a Deuteronomistic emphasis (Deut 2:24, 26, 30; 3:6; 29:6 (Eng. =7); Josh 9:10; 12:5; Judg 11:19; cf. Neh 9:22). Outside Deuteronomistic literature the regular expression is "who lived in Heshbon" (Num 21:34; taken up by Deuteronomy in Deut 1:4; 3:2; 4:46; Josh 12:2) or "city of Sihon" (Num 21:26–27). Later Heshbon belonged to Moab (Isa 15:4; 16:8–9; Jer 48:2, 34, 45).

5) Salecah (v 11) is introduced as the extreme limit of Bashan, territory of Og, by the Deuteronomist (Deut 3:10; Josh 12:5; cf. 1 Chr 5:11).

6) That Ashtaroth is (a) the residence of Og by itself (Josh 9:10) or (b) along with Edrei is a city of Og (13:31) or the residence of Og (Deut 1:4; Josh 12:4) or the city where Og ruled (13:12) appears only in Deuteronomistic literature. Numbers 21:33 knows only of a battle at Edrei (cf. Deut 3:1), whereas in Deut 3:10 the cities of Og are Edrei and Salecah.

7) The identification of Og as part of the ancient giant Rephaim appears only in Deuteronomistic literature (Deut 3:11; Josh 12:4; 13:12). In fact, connection of the ancient Rephaim with the conquest of east Jordan occurs only in Deuteronomistic materials (Deut 2:11, 20; 3:13; cf. Josh 17:15). Otherwise, the Rephaim appear only in Genesis 14:5; 15:20; 1 Chr 20:4.

8) Kedemoth is known only here, as a wilderness station from which messengers were sent to Sihon (Deut 2:26), and as a Levitical city (Josh 21:37; cf. 1 Chr 6:64 [Eng. = 6:79]).

9) Mephaath is mentioned only here and as a Levitical city in 21:37 (cf. 1 Chr 6:64 [Eng. = 6:79]). Jeremiah pronounced judgment upon the city as Moabite (48:21).

10) Beth-Peor (v 20) is a geographical site where Israel stopped in the wilderness and received Mosaic commands (Deut 3:29; 4:46) and near which Moses was buried (Deut 34:6). In Numbers the place name is Peor (23:28) and represents the great place of sinning with the Baal of Peor (25:3, 5, 18; 31:16; cf. Josh 22:17; Ps 106:28; Hos 9:10).

11) The "slopes" of Pisgah (v 20) appears only in Deuteronomistic literature (Deut 3:17; 4:49; Josh 12:3). Otherwise, the reference is to the top of

Pisgah (Num 21:20; 23:14; Deut 3:27; 34:1). אשׁד, "slope," appears in the singular only in the poetry of Num 21:15. The plural "slopes" appears only in Josh 10:40; 12:8.

12) Beth-jeshimoth is part of Og's kingdom only in Josh 12:3 and here (v 20). Otherwise, it appears in the itinerary of Num 33:49 and as a Moabite city (Ezek 25:9).

13) Aroer, which is over against Rabbah (v 25), is mentioned explicitly only here and is perhaps to be seen as a misinterpretation of Judg 11:33 (Mittmann, "Aroer, Minnith und Abel Keramim." *ZDPV* 85 [1969] 63–75; Wüst, *Untersuchungen,* 169–175). In the narrative literature, only the Deuteronomist mentions Rabbah, the Ammonite capital (Deut 3:11; 2 Sam 11:1; 12:26–29; 17:27; cf. Amos 1:14; Jer 49:2–3; Ezek 21:25; 25:5). Rabbah's location west of the Jabbok has led the Deuteronomist to speak of half of Gilead (12:2, 5; 13:31) and half of the land of the Ammonites (13:25; cf. Num 21:24; Deut 2:19, 37; 3:16). A hint at the wider claims of the Ammonites is given in Judg 11:13, a claim somewhat supported by their ability to attack across the Jordan in the period of the Judges (Judg 3:10–11). Only with Saul (1 Sam 11:11; 14:47) and David (2 Sam 8:12; 10–12) were they finally defeated.

14) Aside from the etiology in Gen 32:3 (=Eng. 2), Mahanaim (vv 26, 30) appears only in Deuteronomistic traditions (Josh 21:38; 2 Sam 2:8, 12, 29; 17:24, 27; 19:33; 1 Kgs 2:8; 4:14).

15) Amos 6:13 is the only non-Deuteronomistic tradition concerning לדבר (13:26—see Notes; cf. 2 Sam 9:4–5; 17:27).

16) Succoth appears first in the etiology of Gen 33:17 and then only in the Deuteronomistic tradition of Judg 8, except for the psalmic allusion (Ps 60:8 = 108:8).

17) Only Deuteronomistic literature knows of the sixty cities of Jair (v 30; cf. Deut 3:4; I Kgs 4:13).

Despite the abundance of traditions and expressions which belong solely to Deuteronomistic literature, Josh 13 is not a new creation by the Deuteronomist, for it builds also upon traditions witnessed in Numbers:

1) Num 21:21–35 speaks of the capture of cities of Sihon and Og, specifically Heshbon, Jahaz, Edrei, Dibon, and Medeba.

2) Num 21:26–28 established the Arnon as the border between Sihon and Moab, after Sihon had defeated Moab.

3) Num 32 establishes the claim of Reuben and Gad to the land of Jazer and of Gilead (v 1). Verses 33–41 add "half of Manasseh" to the story. The tradition shares with Josh 13 the cities of Dibon (v 3, 34; cf. Num 21:30); Beth Baal Meon (vv 3, 38); Kiriathaim (v 37); Sibmah (v 38, cf. Sebam in v 3); Jazer (vv 3, 35; cf. 21:32); Beth Haram (v 36 = Beth Haran); Beth Nimrah (vv. 3, 36); and the villages of Jair (v 41).

4) Num 31:8 witnesses a close literary relationship with 13:21–22.

5) Bamoth Baal is anchored in the Balaam tradition (Num 22:41) and the wilderness itinerary (21:19–20).

Several of the cities are also rooted in the tradition of Levitical cities (Josh 21; 1 Chr 6): Heshbon, Ashtaroth, Jahaz, Kedemoth, Mephaath, Jazer, and Mahanaim.

We have then a Deuteronomistic author taking up parts of the Numbers traditions and parts of the Levitical city traditions. In his own distinctive linguistic tradition, he incorporates them into a description of the tribal allotments in the territory east of the Jordan. The result is not a map nor a description of the goodness of the land (Bächli). The result is a description of the work of Moses based on available traditions, a description which lays Israel's claim to the land east of the Jordan.

Comment

[8] The function of the entire narrative is shown in the opening verse. The eastern tribes have taken (לקחו) their inheritance and thus have followed explicitly the command of Moses. This is the pattern set out for the tribes west of the Jordan who have not taken their land, that is, have not yet settled down upon it. Much more, it is the pattern for all of the life of the people of God. They are to take the inheritance given them by God and follow the commandments given by Moses.

[9] For Aroer, cf. 12:2 and Wüst, *Untersuchungen,* 133.

Medeba is about fifteen miles southeast of the point where the Jordan enters the Dead Sea, present-day Madeba. Excavations have produced only a single tomb from pre-Roman times, and it is dated ca. 1200 B.C. (M. Avi-Yonah, *EAEHL* 3, 820).

Dibon became the capital of Moab and was the home of King Mesha (*ANET,* 320). It is two and a half miles (four kilometers) north of the Arnon river, across the valley from modern Dhiban. Num 32:34 attributes its Israelite fortification to Gad, but Josh 13:17 assigns it to Reuben. Occupation goes back to the Early Bronze Age, but this is followed only by Iron Age occupation. (A. D. Tushingham, *EAEHL* 1, 330–33).

[10] For Heshbon, cf. 12:2 and Wüst, *Untersuchungen,* 149, n. 493.

[11] For Salecah, see 12:5.

[12] For Ashtaroth and Edrei, see 12:4.

[13] This introduces a series of statements in Joshua and in Judg 1:19–36 describing territories not conquered by Israel, thus reflecting a task still before the people (cf. v 6) and providing a basis for the theological judgments of Judg 2–3. Theological judgment is only implied in the present context. Historically, the territories in the extreme north were controlled by Israel only under David (2 Sam 3:3; 10:6–14).

[14] The reference to the Levites insures that all the tribes of Israel are mentioned in the present context and shows that the instructions of Num 18:20–24; Deut 10:6–9; 18:1–5 (cf. Lev 25:29–34; Num 18:6; 26:62; Deut 12:12; 14:27, 29) were faithfully carried out. This prepares for the setting out of Levitical cities in chap 21.

The specific formulation of the text (see *Notes*) refers to Deut 18:1. The Levites are God's priests and receive their livelihood from his altar, not from the land (cf. J. Hoftijzer, "Das sogenannte Feueropfer," VTS up 16 [1967] 114–34, especially 124–25). Thus the Levites do not need the land, nor do they have time to work the land. They are dedicated to God's work (cf. G. Minette de Tillesse, "Sections 'tu' et sections 'vous' dans le Deuteronome,"

VT 12 [1962] 70–72; J. A. Emerton, "Priests and Levites in Deuteronomy," *VT* 12 [1962] 134–35).

[17] Bamoth-baal means "high places of Baal" and is to be identified with Mesha's Beth-bamoth (*ANET*, 320), but its location is uncertain. This passage joins Num 22:41 in locating it near the Arnon (cf. Wüst, *Untersuchungen*, 153–54, n. 505). It may be *gebel `aṭarus*, situated at el-ḳuwezije (M. Ottosson, *Gilead*, 123).

Beth-baal-meon is identified with Ma'in, four miles (eight kilometers) southwest of Medeba, despite the lack of archaeological remains predating the Roman period (cf. R. de Vaux, *Bible et Orieht*, 123; E. D. Grohman, "Baal-Peor"*IDB* 1 [1962] *IDB* 332; M. Ottosson, *Gilead*, 87).

[18] Jahaz is variously located: H. Libb, ten kilometers north of Dibon, (de Vaux, *Bible et Orient*, 119–20); `Aleiyan (J. Liver, "The Wars of Mesha, King of Moab," *PEQ* 99 [1967] 15–16, n. 5); Khirbet el-Medeiyineh (Y. Aharoni, *The Land of the Bible*, 379); Khirbet Iskander (A. Kuschke, "Beiträge," 92), to name only a few suggestions.

Kedemoth is notoriously difficult to locate, being variously placed at ḳaṣr ez-za'feran, es-salije, Khirbet er Remeil (cf. M. Ottosson, *Gilead*, 123; S. Cohen, "Kedemoth,"*IDB* 3 [1962] 4) or `Aleiyan (Y. Aharoni, *The Land of the Bible*, 380).

Mephaath was located by Alt at Khirbet nef'a, eight to nine kilometers south of Amman ("Das Institut im Jahre 1932," *PJ* 29 [1933] 28–29), but Aharoni (*The Land of The Bible*, 381) suggests Tel Jawah, about ten kilometers south of Amman with A. H. van Zyl (*The Moabites* [Leiden: E. J. Brill, 1960] 94, n. 7).

[19] Kiriathaim is generally located with Kuschke ("Beiträge," 93; cf. *ZDPV* 77 [1961] 24–31) at Khirbet el-qureye, ten Roman miles west of Medeba; but Aharoni maintains a location at Quaryat el-Makhaiyet (*The Land of the Bible*, 380).

Sibmah is situated by Kuschke ("Beiträge," 92) "possibly" at Khirbet qurn el-kibš (cf. M. Ottosson, *Gilead*, 87–88), but this is denied by Wüst, who needs the tell for Zereth-shahar (*Untersuchungen*, 160–161 and n. 539), but has no counterproposal.

Zereth-shahar is placed at Khirbet el-libb by Kuschke ("Beiträge," 92), at ez-Zarat by Aharoni (*The Land of The Bible*, 385; cf. Ottosson, *Gilead*, 124), but at Khirbet qurn el-kibš by Wüst (*Untersuchungen*, 160–161).

[20] Beth Peor seems now to be located at Khirbet 'Uyun Musa (O. Henke, "Zur Lage von Beth Peor," *ZDPV* 75 [1959] 155–63; cf. Kuschke, "Beiträge," 93–94; Wüst, *Untersuchungen*, 154, n. 508), but Soggin (157) continues to identify it with Khirbet eš-šaikh jayil.

Pisgah is a mountain in the Abarim range across from Jericho and is usually identified with Ras Siyagha (Kuschke, "Beiträge," 93–94; *AEHL*, 747). Ottosson (*Gilead*, 124) identifies it as rugm el-heri. At any rate, Wüst (*Untersuchungen*, 163, n. 541) is correct in emphatically denying that it is a town name.

Beth-jeshimoth is "certainly located" at Tell el-'azeme (Kuschke, "Beiträge," 92; cf. Wüst, *Untersuchungen*, 154, n. 510; Ottosson, *Gilead*, 124).

[21] Our chapter shares the tradition of the defeat of the Midianite kings with Num 31. Our author identifies the "princes of Midian" as vassal princes

of Sihon, thus joining the Sihon tradition and the Balaam tradition, which appears alone in Num 31.

²⁵ Jazer remains a point of discussion, though the German school appears to be settling with some discomfort on Tell el-ᶜareme (Kuschke, "Beiträge," 99–102; R. Rendtorff, "Zur Lage von Jaser," *ZDPV* 76 [1960] 124–35; W. Schmidt, "Zwei Untersuchungen im wadi nāᶜūr," *ZDPV* 77 [1961] 46–55; Wüst, *Untersuchungen*, 117, n. 386, and 147, n. 489), while the Israelis lean more toward Khirbet es-Sar, about eight miles west of Amman (*AEHL*, 161; Aharoni, *The Land of The Bible*, 379).

The tension between v 25 and v 10 in the description of the Ammonite-Israelite border cannot be solved by the radical text critical work of B. Obed ("A Note on Josh. XIII 25," *VT* 21 [1971] 239–41; cf. Wüst, *Untersuchungen*, 167, n. 555). Rather the verse seeks to explain the fact that Ammon controlled the city of Rabbah, west of the Jabbok, when the latter was actually the boundary line between Ammon and Israel (cf. 12:2) and that Israel fought for this territory under Jephthah (Judg 11) and finally captured Rabbah only under David (2 Sam 12:26; cf. Wüst, *Untersuchungen*, 164–75). Thus, at the time of Joshua, Israel controlled only that territory reaching to an Aroer which lay west of the Ammonite capital Rabbah, modern Amman.

²⁶ Ramath-mispeh has been variously located (cf. the summary of Ottosson, *Gilead*, 127) with the German school now tending to accept Khirbet el-qarᶜa (R. Hentschke, "Ammonitische Grenzfestungen südwestlich von Amman," *ZDPV* 76 [1960] 115–19; Kuschke, "Beiträge," 97 with nn. 38–41), although Wüst is certainly correct in noting that all locations are finally based on literary and form critical hypothesis (*Untersuchungen*, 143, n. 475; cf. the uncertainty of Ottosson, *Gilead*, 127, and Aharoni's suggestion of Khirbet Jelᶜad with a question mark, *The Land of The Bible*, 383).

Betonim is located without doubt at Khirbet el-batne, six kilometers southwest of es salt by Kuschke ("Beiträge," 96) in agreement with most modern scholars (e. g. Mittmann, *Beiträge*, 236, n. 84; Ottosson, *Gilead*, 127; Aharoni, *The Land of The Bible*, 375), but Wüst (*Untersuchungen*, 120) does not appear to be totally convinced.

Mahanaim is also located without doubt by Kuschke ("Beiträge," 96) at Tell heggag, three kilometers south of Penuel (cf. Mittmann, *Beiträge*, 222, n. 34), but this, too, has to be set over against Aharoni's identification with Tell edh-Dhahab el Gharbi (*The Land of The Bible*, 381; cf. *AEHL*, 191–92).

Insofar as לדבר can be identified as Lodebar (see *Notes*), it is located in comparison with Amos 6:13, but all locations are based on questionable literary and historical hypotheses (cf. Wüst, *Untersuchungen*, 127–29). The location remains totally unknown.

²⁷ Beth Haram appears to be Tell er-Rameh or a nearby Tell (see the discussion by Wüst, *Untersuchungen*, 148–49, n. 492).

Beth-nimrah is either Tell Nimrin (Wüst, *Untersuchungen*, 148, n. 491) or Tell el-Bleibil (Aharoni, *The Land of The Bible*, 374; Ottosson, *Gilead*, 128).

Succoth is generally identified with Tell Der ᶜAlla (Wüst, *Untersuchungen*, 131, n. 435), though H. J. Franken, who excavated the site, denies the identification and seeks to locate Succoth at Tell el-Aḥṣaṣ (*EAEHL* 1, 321).

Zaphon is usually located at Tell es-Saᶜidiye (Wüst, *Untersuchungen*, 131–

32, n. 436), though other suggestions have been made (cf. Ottosson, *Gilead*, 128, n. 60; Mittmann, *Beiträge*, 219–20, n. 31).

Explanation

This section surprises the reader. He expects to hear of Joshua's immediate obedience to the command of Yahweh (v 7). Instead, he finds a lengthy list of territory east of the Jordan for which Joshua has no responsibility. Why? The only explanation is that the theology of leadership continues to play the dominating role in the book. Joshua is the leader who did just what Moses said and just what Moses did, thus experiencing the divine presence just as Moses did (cf. chap. 1). It was particularly the east Jordan tribes who had had questions about Joshua, wanting to make sure that the divine presence was with Joshua as it had been with Moses (1:17). Now we see Joshua bringing about for them that which Moses promised. The tribes east of Jordan can now take and possess the land which Moses gave them. Thus God has proven to be with Joshua. Joshua has proven to be the leader with conviction and courage (1:18). This serves as an example to all generations of the rewards of obedience to God and his chosen leader. It also presents an example for all future leaders who seek to give Israel rest in her land. They must be leaders of conviction and courage following the example and commandments of Moses by following the example of Joshua. Then they, like Moses and Joshua, can lay claim to the hotly disputed land east of Jordan.

But in the midst of the chapter lies a hint of warning. Some enemies remain. The task is not finished. After the aged Joshua passes from the scene, new leadership will be needed to rid Israel of the menace of the Geshurites and Maacathites (v 13). Thus the chapter becomes a call to leadership as well as an example of leadership. This call will be constantly repeated through the next chapters, finding its climax in Judg 1–3. A similar hint appears elsewhere in the chapter. Israel is given only half the land of the Ammonites (v 25). A strong enemy lurks on their border, an enemy who will soon test Israel's will and faith (Judg 3; 10–11; 1 Sam 11:11; 14:47; 2 Sam 10–12), an enemy who will threaten Israel until the final days of her existence (2 Kgs 24:2; Jer 40:14; 41:10, 15). Will Israel be faithful so that her God and his leader can drive them out? Or will Israel succumb to the religious temptations of the Ammonite god (1 Kgs 11:1–8, 33; cf. 2 Kgs 23:13)? From the first, Israel is reminded that faithfulness to the example of Moses and Joshua leads to defeat of enemies, but temptation and further tasks continually lie before Israel. One final note of warning lurks in v 22. God has defeated one man who tried to practice divination. Such activity is outlawed in Israel (Deut 18:14). But can Israel remember the lesson?

Thus our surprise at these verses turns to respect, as we see an author seeking to set up a theological example for the people of Israel, calling forth obedient, courageous leadership for the task ahead, while giving encouragement on the basis of the past faithfulness of God.

Beginning with Caleb   (14:1–15)

Bibliography

Auld, A. G. "Textual and Literary Studies in the Book of Joshua." *ZAW* 90 (1978) 412–17. **Beltz, W.** *Die Kaleb-Traditionen im Alten Testament.* BWANT 98. Stuttgart: W. Kohlhammer Verlag, 1974, 30–37, 64–70. **Noth, M.** *Überlieferugsgeschichte des Pentateuch.* Stuttgart: W. Kohlhammer Verlag, 1948, 143–50. ————. *Überlieferungsgeschichtliche Studien.* Tübingen: Max Niemeyer Verlag, 1943, 44–47. **Rudolph, W.** *Der "Elohist" von Exodus bis Josua.* BZAW 68. Berlin: Alfred Töpelmann, 1938, 217–18. **Wüst, M.** *Untersuchungen zu den siedlungsgeographischen Texten des Alten Testaments, I Ostjordanland.* Wiesbaden: Dr. Ludwig Reichert Verlag, 1975, 202–12.

Translation

¹ *These are what the sons of Israel inherited* [a] *in the land of Canaan, which Eleazar, the priest, and Joshua, the son of Nun, and the heads of the fathers of the tribes distributed as* ² *the inheritance to the sons of Israel by the lot* [a] *of their inheritance, just as Yahweh commanded by the hand of Moses* [b] *for the nine* [c] *and a half tribes.* ³ *For Moses had given the inheritance of the two and a half tribes* [a] *beyond the Jordan, but to the Levites he did not give an inheritance in their midst.* ⁴ *Because* [a] *the sons of Joseph comprised two tribes—Manasseh and Ephraim—they did not give a share to the Levites in the land, except cities to live in with their pasture lands for their cattle and goods.* [b] ⁵ *Just as Yahweh commanded Moses, so the sons of Israel did: they apportioned the land.*

⁶ *The sons of Judah approached Joshua in Gilgal, and Caleb, the son of Jephuneh the Kenizzite, said to him, "You know the thing which Yahweh spoke to Moses, the man* [a] *of God, on my account and on your account in Kadesh Barnea.* ⁷ *I was forty years old when Moses, the servant of Yahweh,* [a] *sent me from Kadesh Barnea to spy out the land. I returned the word to him just as it was on my heart.* [b] ⁸ *My brothers who went up with me caused the heart of the people to melt,* [a] *but I remained totally loyal to Yahweh, my God.* ⁹ *Moses swore in that day, 'Surely the land on which your foot made its way will become an inheritance for you and for your sons forever, because you remained totally loyal to Yahweh, my God.'* [a] ¹⁰ *Now it is a fact that Yahweh has given me life, just as he spoke, for these forty-five years since that time when Yahweh spoke this word to Moses when Israel walked in the wilderness, so that right here today I am eighty-five years old.* ¹¹ *Still today I am just as strong as the day when Moses sent me; my strength now is just the same as it was then for war or for daily activities.* [a] ¹² *So now give me this mountain which Yahweh spoke about in that day, for you heard on that day that the Anakim are there and large fortified cities. If, however, Yahweh be with me,* [a] *then I will dispossess them, just as Yahweh spoke.* ¹³ *Then Joshua blessed him and gave Hebron to Caleb, the son of Jephuneh,* [a] *for an inheritance.* ¹⁴ *Therefore, Hebron has belonged to Caleb, the son of Jephuneh, the Kennizite, until this day because of the fact that he was totally loyal to Yahweh the God of Israel.* ¹⁵ *Now the name of Hebron had previously been*

Kiriath-Arba; he had been a great man among the Anakim. ^a *Then the land had peace from war.*

Notes

1.a. The Hebrew uses two forms, first the Qal, then the Pi'el, of the verbal root נחל in this verse. LXX has interpreted the sentence as parallel to its interpretation of 13:32, while the MT finds a closer parallel in 13:14b (LXX, omitted in MT). LXX (and Syr) has even changed the second verb into the singular, while retaining the compound subject. Auld uses the textual and syntactical difficulties as a reason to suspect editorial layers.

2.a. MT uses a construct relationship at the beginning of v 2, thus continuing the sentence of v 1. Most modern commentators and translators separate the construct relationship by repointing בְּגוֹרָל on the basis of LXX and Tg. readings. This would introduce a new sentence: "Their inheritance was by lot. . . ." The final fulfillment formula appears to refer back to Num 34:13, where Joshua, Eleazar, and the heads of the fathers of the tribes of the sons of Israel do not appear. Thus the original text most likely separated vv 1 and 2 into two sentences. The later tradition understood the fulfillment in a broader sense to incorporate passages such as Num 26:1, 52–56; 32:2, 28; 34:16–29, thus joining vv 1 and 2 into one sentence (but cf. Wüst, *Untersuchungen,* 202–203).

2.b. LXX read Joshua instead of Moses, connecting the statement to the act of distribution rather than that of commanding.

2.c. Several Hebrew manuscripts, Syr, and Frg.Tg. insert "to give" before "to the nine and a half tribes." This interprets v 2 as a separate sentence and supplies a verb which would be implied by the context.

3.a. LXX represents a tradition corrupted by homoeoteleuton, "for Moses had given the inheritance of the two and a half tribes" falling out after the preceding "and a half tribes."

4.a. The Hebrew syntax of 4 is parallel to that of v 3, both beginning with כִּי clauses and a perfect verb. The second part of each verse explains why the Levites did not gain a share in the inheritance. In each verse the verb of the second part continues the subject of the first part, so that 4b appears to state that the sons of Joseph did not give a portion to the Levites. This has led to early attempts to clarify the syntax, as seen in the passive reading of the LXX, followed by most modern translations with the notable exceptions of Noth and Hertzberg. In any reading, the subject remains indefinite, at best.

4.b. The Greek tradition is either corrupt or did not understand the Heb. ולקנינם, which it translates lamely with a repeated "and their cattle" (cf. Margolis, 269). The Heb. term apparently means "purchased goods," unless Noth is correct in seeing a stereotyped paronomastic construction meaning "all my earthly goods."

6.a. Tg adds a prophetic dimension to the text by translating "man of God" as "prophet of God" (Sperber, *The Bible in Aramaic* IV B, 49).

7.a. As often, LXX has "God" instead of Yahweh (see Auld, "Joshua" VTSup 30 [1979] 12–13).

7.b. "Just as it was on my heart" reads literally: "just as with my heart." LXX has changed this to "according to his mind," thus saying Caleb spoke what Moses wanted to hear. On the basis of 1 Kgs 8:17–18; 10:2, Noth translates, "just as I made up my mind to do." F. Stolz (*THAT* 1, 863) speaks of the capacity for critical judgment. Deut 15:9 uses the same expression דבר עם לבב to express the idea of "thought, idea, matter about which one is thinking." In our passage the meaning seems to be that the report of the things was precisely that which Caleb remembered from his experiences (cf. Hertzberg).

8.a. MT has a purely Aramaic form המסי for the Heb. המס, which appears in Deut 1:28, a verse to which our text is related (cf. GKC§ 75ii).

9.a. The Greek tradition read the suffix as second person, with evidence for both the sing. and plur. readings.

11.a. The final idiom may refer to military maneuvers (cf. 1 Sam 29:6) or to daily activities (cf. 2 Kgs 11:8; 19:27 = Isa 37:28; Ps 121:8). It apparently represents a sign of adult strength not usual for a child (1 Kgs 3:7) or an old man (Deut 31:2 and here). LXX interprets the idiom in a military sense here by transposing "for war" to the end of the sentence.

12.a. MT has the pronoun attached to the sign of the accusative, though there is no preceding verb. Thus the text must necessarily be read with strong manuscript and versional support as the preposition אִתִּי, "with me."

13.a. LXX fills out the phrase with "the son of Kenaz," with a slightly different construction than it has used in vv 6, 14.

15.a. LXX reads the city as Kiriath Argob. This may result from textual corruption (Margolis), but could also reflect confusion with the Argob of Bashan (Deut 3:4, 13, 14; 1 Kgs 4:13). Similarly, instead of reading great man (אָדָם), LXX read (μητρόπολις) "metropolis," possibly reflecting a Heb. אֵם (cf. Margolis).

Form/Structure/Setting

Verses 1 and 15 mark off the section with clear introductory and concluding formulas. Each of the formulas is related to similar formulas elsewhere in the book. In 11:23aB a variation of the introductory formula occurs, followed immediately by the precise closing formula which we find in 14:15. For the present structure of the book, this signals that the thought of chap. 11 is being taken up and expanded after the excurses-like summaries of chaps. 12 and 13. In these chapters two distinctive forms appear. The first begins with the demonstrative pronoun—"this, these," parallel to 13:1:

1) 12:1: kings defeated east of the Jordan;
2) 12:7: kings defeated west of the Jordan;
3) 13:2: land remaining to be possessed;
4) 13:23b: inheritance of Reuben;
5) 13:28: inheritance of Gad;
6) 13:32: inheritance distributed by Moses.

The second uses the verb נתן to describe the gift of some land for the people to possess, parallel to 11:23aB:

1) 12:6a: Moses gave east Jordan to the two and a half tribes;
2) 12:7b: Joshua gave west Jordan to the tribes of Israel;
3) 13:8b: Moses gave the land to the two and a half tribes, who now possess it (cf. 12:1aB; 13:12bB);
4) 13:15: Moses gave to the sons of Reuben;
5) 13:24: Moses gave to Gad;
6) 13:29: Moses gave to half of Manasseh.

With 14:1 we thus reach a turning point. After having briefly summarized the victories east and west, the giving of the land east and west, along with the possessing and distribution for inheritance of the land in the east, we now turn to the distribution and possession of the land in the west. Chapter 14 does not, however, immediately describe the act of distribution and possession for the nine and a half tribes. This must await the following chapters. Instead, we have in chap. 14 what appear to be two excurses. Closer examination reveals that even these two themes are closely related to the structure of the book. Verses 2–5 take up the Levitical theme of 13:14, 33 and carry it a step further, preparing in turn for the Levitical distribution and possession in chap. 21. Verses 6–15 reach back to Num 13:14; Deut 1:21–36 (cf. Num 26:65; 32:12) to bring up the promise to Caleb, the faithful spy. Here, too, the narrative structure of giving is carried forward (v 13), and the theme of possession is introduced (v 14a). The Caleb theme is not yet complete (see 15:13–19; Judg 1:11–15), yet the reason for its presence here is perfectly clear as the *Comment* and *Explanation* will seek to show.

The question of form and setting must also be addressed. For the first section, it is quite clear that we have a literary composition seeking to reflect upon the themes of obedience to divine command, possession of the land, and the plight of the Levites. As such, the verses reflect a long history of theological work in Israel.

The Caleb narrative leads in a different direction. Its present form is that of an etiological narrative, with the concluding "unto this day" formula (14). Childs has shown, however, that the etiological element here "no longer reflects an ethnic etiology, but a theological doctrine of the deuteronomist. The presupposition for such a theological appropriation is an existing tradition" ("A Study of the Formula 'Until this Day,'" *JBL* 82 [1963] 287). The narrative structure lets the form-critical problem appear in yet another light. The narrative begins abruptly (v 6) without the normal temporal or nominal opening. Still, the opening sentence gives a geographical setting and introduces the characters: Joshua and the men of Judah. This gives way to confrontation between Caleb and Joshua in the form of a long monologue by the former. Repetition within the monologue reveals the major points being made:

1) The age and continued strength of Caleb reflect divine blessing upon him (7a, 10, 11);

2) Caleb has been obedient to Moses and to Yahweh (7b, 8b, 9b, 14);

3) The land has been promised to Caleb (9, 10aB, 12aB, 12bB).

It is this last point where significant nuances are made. Moses swore to give the land over which Caleb had walked to him (v 9; cf. v 7). Caleb then asked only for a mountain (12a), which still represented a large amount of territory encompassing several cities (12b). Joshua gave Caleb only the city of Hebron (13a). This gains special significance in light of the early tradition in Num 13–14. This narrative centers around two poles, the faithfulness of Caleb, who "remained totally loyal to Yahweh" (14:24; cf. 32:11, 12), and the rebellion of the other spies (13:28, 31; 14:4). The story then relates the punishment of the rebels (14:39–45), but mentions only the promise to Caleb (14:24). The story of Num 13–14 is thus incomplete. It lacks one element: the heroic acts of Caleb bringing the heroic saga to its promised fulfillment. Joshua 14:6–15 is precisely the missing element but with a surprising twist. Caleb is not given the land, nor even the mountain, but only the city. Who would have told the story in this way? The clue may well lie in 6a. The story has its roots in Gilgal, even though "this mountain" (12) is far from Gilgal. As in earlier Gilgal narratives, especially chaps. 7–8, a polemical element lies behind the narrative. The conquest hero Joshua is shown to win out over the demands of the Judean hero Caleb. This takes on added significance in light of 1 Sam 30:14, where a portion of the southern Negeb is claimed by the Calebites in the time of the intense struggle between the Judean David and the Benjaminite Saul. David's part in the Hebron polemic is seen in 1 Sam 25, when the Calebite Nabal does not recognize David. This results finally in the death of the Calebite and the marriage of his widow to David, who thus gains claim to Calebite property. Ultimately, it was at Hebron that David consolidated his strength and was crowned for the first time (2 Sam 2:1–4), but it was also at Hebron that Absalom was crowned in revolt against his father David (2 Sam 15). Thus control of Hebron was an important element in political strategy in early Israelite history. Our narrative appears to be an early chapter in that history when Benjamin claimed control of Hebron but graciously blessed the Calebites by granting control of Hebron to them.

The Deuteronomistic history has taken up the old narrative and given it a new interpretation. Caleb becomes the example of the faithful leader, who is totally loyal to Yahweh. As such, he is rewarded with the first inheritance in the Promised Land, an inheritance continuing until this day (v 14). It is precisely such an inheritance which the exiled readers of Joshua sought in vain.

Comment

¹ The verbal root נחל is paired with the similar use with Moses as subject in 13:32, pointing back to the only previous use of the verb in the book, at 1:6 (see *Comment* there). The cognate noun is the key term which holds the final half of the book of Joshua together (11:23; 13:6, 7, 8, 14, 23, 28, 33; 14:2, 3, 9, 13, 14; 15:20; 16:5, 8, 9; 17:4, 6, 14; 18:2, 4, 7, 20, 28; 19:1, 2, 8, 9, 10, 16, 23, 31, 39, 41, 48, 49, 51; 21:2; 23:4; 24:28, 30, 32). The proliferation of the term in this section and, particularly, the verbal use at the key points of structure (11:23; 13:32; 14:1; 16:4; 19:49, 51) show that the Deuteronomist has invested the term with great theological significance, even if the earlier tradition used it simply as "settlement, homestead" (*contra* G. Gerlemann, "Nutzrecht und Wohnrecht. Zur Bedeutung von אחזה und נחלה," *ZAW* 89 [1977] 312–25). God has given a homestead for his people to be theirs through the generations. It is precisely chap. 14 which cautions against taking the inheritance language too far. The land is an inheritance for a people totally loyal to Yahweh, as Caleb was. It is God's gift to his people. It is not a basis for the people's claim on God.

The land of Canaan here refers to all the territory west of the Jordan (cf. 5:12; 22:9–11, 32), as compared to the more limited meaning in 13:3–4 (see *Comment* there).

Eleazar, the son of Aaron (Exod 6:23, cf. Lev 10; Num 3:1–4, 32; 20:22–28) appears for the second time in the Deuteronomistic history (cf. Deut 10:6). He fulfills the task set out in Num 34:17 for himself, Joshua, and the leaders of the tribes named in the following verses. Here these leaders are called "heads of the fathers of the tribes" in agreement with the language of Num 32:28. They thus join Joshua in fulfilling the command of Josh 13:7.

² The language of lots also comes from Numbers (26:55–56; 33:54; 34:13) and appears here for the first time in the Deuteronomistic history. The lots appear to be stone objects used to gain impartial decisions. These were often (Prov 16:33), if not always, interpreted as decisions given by God. The precise nature and use of the lots remains unclear (cf. J. Lindblom, "Lot-Casting in the Old Testament," *VT* 12 [1962] 164–78; E. Renner, *A Study of the Word*

goral in the OT, Heidelberg dissertation, 1958; W. Dommershausen, *TDOT* 2, 450–56; H. H. Schmid, *THAT* 1 [1971] 412–15). They are understood here to be capable of impartially revealing the divine decision concerning the distribution of the land, so that no tribe can claim to have been cheated in the process.

"Just as Yahweh (Moses) commanded," the *Ausführungsformel* (literally, "the formula of carrying out," thus the obedience formula; cf. G. Liedke, *THAT* 2 [1976] 530–36) has played a leading role in the structure of Joshua to this point (1:7, 13; 4:10; 7:11; 8:27, 31, 33, 35; 10:40; 11:12, 15, 20; 13:6; cf. 1:16, 18; 4:8; 9:24). It repeatedly demonstrates that God determines the actions and fortunes of Israel. The people of God are not called to act on their own initiative and desire, nor to set their own goals. God has set the goals and issues the commands which lead to their achievement. The introduction to the distribution of the land of Canaan is thus introduced (v 2) and concluded (v 5) by the obedience formula.

³ Verse 3 summarizes briefly the statement of chap. 13 as an explanation why the division in "the land of Canaan" is only to nine and a half tribes.

⁴ Verse 4 seeks to solve the mathematical problem: nine and a half plus two and a half plus one equals twelve. The answer is simple, divide one tribe into two, thus adding still one more tribe to the equation. The entire problem centers around the existence of two systems for naming the tribes of Israel, one including Joseph and Levi (Gen 49:1–27; 29:31–30:24; Deut 27:12–13; Gen 35:23–26; Exod 1:2–4; Gen 46:8–25; I Chr 2:1–2; Ezek 48:31–35) and the other omitting Levi and dividing Joseph into Ephraim and Manasseh (Gen 48; Num 26:5–51; 1:5–15; 2:3–31; 10:14–28; 7:12–83; 1:20–43; 34:16–28; Ezek 48:1–29). The early poetic passage in Deut 33 combines both systems, while the even earlier poetry of Judg 5 does not even name twelve tribes. Two lists in 1 Chr 12:25–38 and 27:16–22 bring further complexities. The problem has been most recently discussed by H. Seebass, "Erwägungen zum altisraelitischen System der zwölf Stämme," *ZAW* 90 [1978] 196–219; M. Metzger, "Probleme der Frühgeschichte Israels," *VF* 22 [1977] 30–43; C. H. J. de Geuss, *The Tribes of Israel;* N. Gottwald, *The Tribes of Yahweh,* 345–75, 887–89; B. Lindars, "The Israelite Tribes in Judges," VTSup 30 [1979] 95–112.

Our text solves the problem by saying that Joseph was divided into two tribes, thus taking away the tribal portion of Levi. This rested on the tradition that Jacob adopted the sons of Joseph as his own (Gen 48:5–6) and on the appointment of the Levites as priests (cf. Num 18; Deut 10:9; 12:12; 14:27, 29; 18:1; Josh 13:14, 33).

The Levites are not left unprovided for. They are promised cities and pasture lands, thus preparing the way for chap. 21.

⁵ Verse 5 underlines Israelite obedience. It joins 11:23 in giving a summary statement of what is yet to be described in detail. Thus the writer underlines at each step that Israel's actions correspond to the divine will.

⁶ The actual distribution begins with the tribe of Judah (cf. 15:1). This is a distinctive emphasis over against chaps. 1–12, where the central tribes of Benjamin and Ephraim-Manasseh appear in the spotlight. As seen in the section on *Form/Structure/Setting*, the material used here appears to have origi-

nated in Benjamin. In the final biblical account, tribal polemic and enmity have been overcome. The emphasis now is on each tribe getting its assigned portion. Judah comes first, because its representative Caleb plays a special function for the editor.

Gilgal, the center of activity in chaps. 1–12 (e.g. 4:19; 5:9; 10:6), is mentioned only here in the second half of the book. Whether this gives a setting for the following chapters or only for this particular incident can be debated. Its origin in the material probably rests on the history of tradition of the narrative itself (see *Form/Structure/Setting*).

The Kenizzites are related to the Edomites through the genealogy of Esau in Gen 36:11, 15, 42, but both Caleb and Kenaz are connected to the tribe of Judah in 1 Chr 4:11 (LXX 13, 15). The importance of the Calebite-Kenizzite tradition appears also in the fact that the first judge comes from this line (Judg 3:9–11).

אִישׁ הָאֱלֹהִים, "man of God" is a title of honor which appears to have roots in the Northern prophetic tradition (see particularly 1 Kgs 13; 1 Sam 9:6–8; 1 Kgs 17:17–24; 2 Kgs 1:9–16; 4–8), even though literarily, it appears almost exclusively in the Deuteronomistic history or sources dependent upon it (cf. W. E. Lemke, "The Way of Obedience," *Magnalia Dei, The Mighty Acts of God* [ed. F. M. Cross, W. E. Lemke, and P. D. Miller; Garden City, NY: Doubleday, 1976] 312–14; 323, n. 77). The term is applied to Moses in relatively late literature (Deut 33:1; Ps 90:1; Ezra 3:2; 1 Chr 23:14; 2 Chr 30:16), except for our passage, which may well be the source of the designation for Moses. This ties Moses into the prophetic circles, but also accords him honor above the ordinary prophets (J. A. Holstein, "The Case of *'ish ha' elohim'* Reconsidered: Philological Analysis versus Historical Reconstruction," *HUCA* 48 [1978] 69–81, with bibliography; cf. J. Kühlwein, *THAT* 1, 136–37; N. P. Bratsiotis, *TWAT* 1 [1971] 250–52). The usage here may reflect the use of the tradition by the early prophetic circles in the north. The title is used by Caleb to underline the authority by which he makes his request of Joshua.

"On your account," apparently includes Joshua within the faithful spy tradition as is done in Num 13:16; 14:6, 30, 38; 26:65; 32:12. The remainder of the story here with the possible exception of 12b ignores Joshua's participation, (note especially v 8) as also Num 13:30–33; 14:24.

[7] Kadesh-Barnea was the significant staging point for Israelite activities in the wilderness (Num 13:26; 20:1, 14, 16, 22; cf. 32:8; 33:36–37; 34:4; Deut 1:2, 19, 46; 2:14; 9:23). Josh 10:41 lists it as the southern limit of Joshua's activities. It is generally located at Tell el-Qudeirat, but finds here indicate occupation only from the tenth century (M. Dothan, *EAEHL* 3 [1977] 697–98).

[8] "I remained totally loyal to Yahweh" is a rare expression in the Hebrew text, appearing to have its basic source in the Caleb tradition (Num 14:24; 32:12; Deut 1:36). It gives the thematic expression to the present text (vv 9, 14; cf. M. Rose, *Deuteronomist und Jahwist.* [Zürich: Theologischer Verlag, 1980]). It is taken up only one time outside the Caleb tradition, that being in the Deuteronomistic judgment against Solomon (1 Kgs 11:6), marking the beginning of Israel's downfall. The Deuteronomist thus appears to take

the Caleb tradition as the prime example of how Israel should act. The writer thus restricts the language to reference to Caleb's perfect example and to the moment when Israel began its irreversible trend in the opposite direction.

¹⁰ The forty-five years over against v 7 appears to give five years for the conquest between the forty years in the wilderness and the present day.

¹² The Anakim are connected to the primeval wicked giants, the Nephilim (Num 13:33; cf. Gen 6:4), also known by various other names (Deut 2:10–11, 20–21). They are particularly tied to Hebron (Num 13:22, 28). Here is another step on the way to fulfillment of the divine promise to destroy these enemies (Deut 9:2; cf. *Comment* on 11:21). For Caleb that destruction depends only on the divine presence (cf. 1:5, 9, 17).

¹³ Joshua blessed Caleb in the same manner as the patriarchal fathers blessed their sons (e.g. Gen 27; 24:60; 32:1 = Eng. 31:55; 48:9, and so on). This showed his position of authority over against Caleb (cf. Exod 39:43; 2 Sam 19:40 = Eng. 19:39). For Caleb this signified the promise of success, fertility, military achievement (cf. J. Scharbert, *TDOT* 2, 279–308; G. Wehmeier, *Der Segen im Alten Testament* [Basel: Friedrich Reinhardt, 1970] 143–46). The blessing represents a promise for steady continued success over a long period of time, not just in one particular moment or event (C. Westermann, *Theologie des Alten Testaments*, 88–101). In this case, the blessing is for the work of Caleb and his descendants in Hebron.

¹³ For Hebron, see *Comment* on Josh 10:3. It is the first inheritance ¹⁴ given to be a home for Israelites west of the Jordan. The writer uses an etiological formulation to lay claim to Hebron even in his own day (cf. *Form/Structure/Setting*).

¹⁵ The etiological note called for explanation, based on the patriarchal traditions (Gen 23:2; 35:27). The name "Kiriath Arba" means literally "the town of the four." Scholars have interpreted this variously: highways, parts of the city, cities, four clans, etc. (See E. Lipiński, "'Anaq-Kiryat ʾArbaʿ-Hébron et ses Sanctuaires Tribaux," *VT* 24 [1974] 41–55.) Our text understands Arba not in the meaning four, but as the name of a man, a hero of the primeval Anakim. This seeks to show the power of God in granting Israel control over a city with such a proud and powerful history.

Looking back to 11:23, the editor emphasizes that he is taking up the story which had ended at that point and carrying it a step further. He does this by underlining the conditions which make the next step possible. After all the battles of conquest, God has brought peace to the land so that Joshua and his cohorts can distribute the land to the various tribes of Israel. God is the giver of victory in battle. He is also the provider of peace for normal existence.

Explanation

The editor of Joshua has placed two quite distinctive pieces of literature together to prepare for the actual distribution of the Promised Land. First, he has taken up the written traditions of the book of Numbers and shown that the entire process of land distribution followed the precise pattern that God had set out in his earlier instructions to Moses. The right persons distributed the land. The proper persons received the land. The excluded persons were sent to their own land. The privileged priests were given no land responsibility, though their interests and needs were taken care of. Even the problem of the number of tribes created by the exclusion of the Priestly tribe was explained as within the purpose of God. The division of the land was not the work of a king arbitrarily giving out gifts to those who served him or bribing those whose power and influence he needed. The division of the land was for the good of the people, according to the plan of God.

Secondly, the editor took up oral tradition with a long history behind it and used it to show that the tribe of Judah, that tribe which endured longest in the history of God's people, had received the first inheritance. Actually, it was not all the tribe of Judah, but only the man Caleb. This, too, fulfilled the promises of the book of Numbers. Thus it stood in God's plan. But it did more. It showed that God could give territory among his people to people with foreign connections, for Caleb was a Kennizite and thus related to the Edomites, the people so cursed by Israel at the time of her exile (cf. Obadiah; Ps 137:7; Jer 49:7–22; Isa 63). It was not his family connections which brought forth blessing upon Caleb. Blessing came forth because Caleb totally followed Yahweh. This complete loyalty to Yahweh established Caleb as the perfect example of those who received the land from Yahweh. It reminded later generations who had lost the land that they had done so because they had followed the example of Solomon, who refused to follow Yahweh, but instead went to foreign lands and followed the desires of the worshipers of foreign gods (1 Kgs 11). This began the path which led to Israel's destruction.

Thus the editor shows that Deut 27 and 28 proved true in Israel's history. Caleb the loyal man received the promised blessings, while the writer's audience knows that ultimately Israel was not loyal and received the threatened curses.

Joshua 14 thus sets forth two major points, which continue to have value for the people of God. Life in all its dimensions is to be lived according to the plans set forth by God, not by the greedy, selfish plans designed by man. Blessing comes ultimately to the man who totally follows God.

Judah and Joseph (15:1–17:18)

Bibliography

See introduction to 13:1–19:51 above.

Aharoni, Y. "The Northern Boundary of Judah." *PEQ* 90 (1958) 27–31. **Albright, W. F.** "The Northern Boundary of Benjamin." AASOR 4 (1922–23) 150–55. ———. "The Site of Tirzah and the Topography of Western Manesseh." *JPOS* 2 (1931) 241–51. **Alt, A.** "Megiddo im Übergang vom kanaanäischen zum israelitischen Zeitalter." *ZAW* 60 (1944) 67–85. (= *Kleine Schriften zur Geschichten des Volkes Israel.* Vol. 1. München: C. H. Beck'sche Verlagsbuchhandlung, 1953, 256–73.) ———. "Zur Geschichte von Beth-Sean. 1500–1000 v. Chr." *PJ* 22 (1926) 108–20. (= *KS* 1, 246–55.)

Beltz, W. *Die Kaleb-Traditionen im Alten Testament.* BWANT 98. Stuttgart: W. Kohlhammer Verlag, 1974, 30–37. **Dahl, G.** "The 'Three Heights' of Joshua 17:11." *JBL* 53 (1934) 381–83. **Danielus, E.** "The Boundary of Ephraim and Manasseh in the Western Plain." *PEQ* 90 (1958) 122–44. **Dever, W. G.** "Gezer." *EAEHL* 2 (1976) 428–43. **Elliger, A.** *Die Frühgeschichte der Stämme Ephraim und Manasse.* Dissertation, Rostock, 1972. **Elliger, K.** "Michmethath." *Archaeologie und Altes Testament,* ed. A. Kuschke and E. Kutsch. Tübingen: J. C. B. Mohr (Paul Siebeck), 1970, 91–100. ———. "Neues über die Grenze zwischen Ephraim und Manasseh." *JPOS* 18 (1938) 7–16. ———. "Thappuah." *PJ* 33 (1937] 7–22. **Fernandez, A.** "Los Límites de Efraim y Manasés." *Bib* 14 (1933) 22–40. **Garsiel, M.** and **Finkelstein, I.** "The Westward Expansion of the House of Joseph in the Light of the ʿIzbet Ṣarṭah Excavations." *Tel Aviv* 5 (1978) 192–98. **Glock, A. E.** "Taanach." *EAEHL* 4 (1978) 1138–47. **James, F.** "Beth-Shean." *EAEHL* 1 (1975) 207–12. **Jenni, E.** "Historisch-topographische Untersuchungen zur Grenze zwischen Ephraim und Manasse." *ZDPV* 74 (1958) 35–40. **Kaiser, O.** "Stammesgeschichtliche Hintergründe der Josephgeschichte. Erwägungen zur Vor- und Frühgeschichte Israels." *VT* 10 (1960) 1–15. **Kallai-Kleinmann, Z.** *Judea, Samaria, and the Golan.* Jerusalem: Publications of the Archaeological Survey of Israel I, 1972. **Kellermann, D.** "Überlieferungsprobleme alttestamentlicher Ortsnamen." *VT* 28 (1978) 423–32. **Kingsbury, E. E.** "He Set Ephraim before Manasseh." *HUCA* 38 (1967) 129–36. **Kuschke, A.** "Das Deutsche Evangelische Institut für Altertumswissenschaft des Heiligen Landes. Lehrkursus 1959." *ZDPV* 76 (1960) 38–39. **Lance, H. D.** "Gezer in the Land and in History." *BA* 30 (1967) 34–47. **Mazar, A.** and **Kelm, G.** "Canaanites, Philistines, and Israelites at Timna/Tel Batash." (Hebrew) *Qadmoniot* 13 (1980) 89–97. **Namiki, K.** "Reconsideration of the Twelve-Tribe System of Israel." *AJBI* 2 (1976) 29–59. **North, R.** "Israel's Tribes and Today's Frontier." *CBQ* 16 (1954) 146–53. ———. "Three Judean Hills in Josue 15,9f." *Bib* 37 (1956) 209–16. **Noth, M.** "Der Beitrag der samarischen Ostraka zur Lösung topographischer Fragen." *PJ* 28 (1932) 54–57. **Otto, E.** *Jakob in Sichem.* BWANT 110. Stuttgart: W. Kohlhammer Verlag, 1979, 227–60. **Ottoson, M.** *Gilead, Tradition and History.* Lund: C. W. K. Gleerup, 1969, 136–43. **Phythian-Adams, W. J.** "The Boundary of Ephraim and Manasseh." *PEFQS* (1929) 228–41. **Sauer, J. A.** "A Review of Gezer II (HUC)." *Basor* 233 (1979) 70–74. **Simons, J.** "The Structure and Interpretation of Joshua XVI–XVII." *Orientalia Neerlandica.* Leiden: E. J. Brill, 1948, 190–215. **Talmon, S.** "The List of Cities of Simeon." (Hebrew) *Eretz Israel* 8 (1967) 265–68. **Wächter, L.** "Zur Lage von Michmethath." *ZDPV* 84 (1968) 52–62. **Wallis, G.** "Thaanath-Silo." *ZDPV* 77 (1961) 38–45. **Yadin, Y.** "Megiddo." *EAEHL* 3 (1977) 830–56. **Zobel, H. J.** *Stammesspruch und Geschichte.* BZAW 95. Berlin: Alfred Töpelmann, 1965, 112–26.

Translation

15:1 *The lot* [a] *belonged to the tribe of the sons* [b] *of Judah for their clans: beginning at* [c] *the border of Edom, the wilderness of Zen to the Negeb, the southern end.* [d] *² Their southern border was the end of the Salt Sea from the tongue facing the Negeb. ³ It goes out south* [a] *of the ascent of the Scorpions, to Zin, goes up south of Kadesh Barnea, passes over to Hezron, goes up to Adar, turns to Qarqaʿ.* [c] *⁴ It passes over to* ʿAzmon, *goes out to the Brook of Egypt. The limits of the boundary are* [a] *at the sea. This will be for you all* [b] *the southern boundary.*

⁵ The boundary to the east is the Sea of Salt unto the end of the Jordan.

The border on the north side is from the tongue of the Sea at the end of the Jordan. ⁶ The border goes up to Beth Hagal and passes north of Beth Arabah. The border goes up to the stone of Bohan, the son of Reuben. ⁷ The border goes up to

Debir ^a *from the Valley of Achor, then to the north is turning to Gilgal,* ^b *which is in front of the ascent of Adummim, which is south of the valley. Then the border* ^c *passes to the waters of* ^c*En Shemesh. Its limits are at* ^c*En Rogel.* ⁸ *The boundary goes up the valley of the son of* ^a *Hinnom to the shoulder of the Jebusites on the south (that is Jerusalem). The boundary goes up to the top of the mountain which is in front of the Valley of Hinnom to the west, which is at the end of the Valley of the Rephaim to the north.* ⁹ *The boundary then bends from the top of the mountain to the spring of the waters of Nephtoah* ^a *and goes out to the cities of Mount* ^c*Ephron.* ^b ¹⁰ *The border bends to Baalah (that is Kiriath-Jearim). The border turns from Baalah westward to Mount Seir,* ^a *passes to the shoulder of Mount* ^b *Jearim to the north (that is Chesalon). It goes down to Beth Shemesh and passes to Timnah.* ^c ¹¹ *The border goes out to the shoulder of Ekron to the north. The border bends to Shikkeron, passes over Mount Baalah and goes out to Jabneal. These are the limits of the border to the west.*

¹² *The border on the west* ^a *is the Mediterranean Sea and territory. This is the border of the sons of Judah all around for their clans.*

¹³ *But to Caleb, the son of Jephuneh, he gave a portion in the midst of the sons of Judah according to the speech of Yahweh* ^a *to Joshua, namely, Kiriath Arba, the father of Anak (It is Hebron).* ¹⁴ *Caleb* ^a *dispossessed from there the three sons of Anak: Sheshai, Ahiman, and Talmai, the descendants of Anak.* ¹⁵ *He* ^a *went up from there to the inhabitants of Debir. (The name of Debir previously was Kiriath Sepher.)* ¹⁶ *Caleb said, "Whoever strikes against Kiriath Sepher and captures it, I will give to him Achsah, my daughter, for a wife."* ¹⁷ *Othniel, son of Kenaz, brother of Caleb, captured it. Then he gave to him Achsah, his daughter, for a wife.* ¹⁸ *When she came, she allured* ^a *him into asking from her father a field. She alighted* ^b *from the donkey. Then Caleb said to her, "What is wrong with you?"* ^c ¹⁹ *She said, "Give me a blessing, because the land of the Negeb you have given me. Also give me pools of water." Then he gave to her the upper pools and the lower pools.*

²⁰ *This is the inheritance of the tribe of the sons of Judah for their clans.* ^a ²¹ *The cities in their entirety* ^a *belonged to the tribe of the sons of Judah to the boundary of Edom in the south:* ²² *Kabzeel, Eder, Jagur;* ²³ *Kinah, Dimonah, Adadah; Kedesh, Hazor, Yithnan;* ^a ²⁴ *Ziph, Telem, Baaloth;* ²⁵ *Hazor-Hadattah,* ^a *Kiriath-Hezron (that is Hazor);* ²⁶ *Amam, Shemah, Moladah;* ²⁷ *Hazar-Gaddah, Heshmon, Beth Pelet;* ²⁸ *Hazar-Shual, Beersheba, Bizyothyah;* ^a ²⁹ *Baalah, Iyim, Ezem;* ³⁰ *Eltolad, Chesil, Hormah;* ³¹ *Ziklag, Madmannah, Sansannah;* ³² *Lebaoth, Shilhim, Ayin, and Rimon,* ^a *in all twenty-nine cities* ^b *and their villages.*

³³ *In the Shephelah: Eshtaol, Zorah, Ashnah;* ³⁴ *Zanoah, En Gannim, Tappuah, Enam;* ³⁵ *Yarmuth, Adullam, Socoh, Azekah;* ³⁶ *Shaarim, Adithayim, Gederah, and Gederothayim,* ^a *fourteen cities and their villages.*

³⁷ *Zenan, Hadashah, Migdal-Gad;* ³⁸ *Dilean, Mizpeh, Yokteal;* ³⁹ *Lachish, Bozkath, Eglon;* ⁴⁰ *Cabbon, Lahmas, Chitlish;* ⁴¹ *Gederoth, Beth-Dagon, Naamah, and Makkedah, sixteen cities and their villages.*

⁴² *Libnah, Ether, Ashan;* ⁴³ *Yiphtah, Ashnah, Nezib;* ⁴⁴ *Keilah, Achzib, and Mareshah, nine cities and their villages.*

⁴⁵ *Ekron and her suburbs and her villages;* ⁴⁶ *from Ekron and to the sea, everything which is beside Ashdod and her villages.* ⁴⁷ *Ashdod, her suburbs and her villages, Gaza, her suburbs and her villages unto the brook of Egypt, and the (Mediterranean)* ^a *Sea and territory.* ⁴⁸ *And in the hill country: Shamir, Yattir, and Socoh;* ⁴⁹ *Dannah,*

Kiriath Sannah (it is Debir); ⁵⁰ *Anab, Eshtemoh, Anim;* ⁵¹ *Goshen, Holon, and Giloh, eleven cities and their villages.*

⁵² *Arab, Dumah, and Eshan;* ⁵³ *Yanim, Beth Tappuah, Aphekah;* ⁵⁴ *Humtah, Kiriath Arba (it is Hebron), and Zior, nine cities and their villages.*

⁵⁵ *Maon, Carmel, Ziph, Yuttah;* ⁵⁶ *Jezreel, Yokdeam, Zanoah;* ⁵⁷ *Kayin, Gibeah, and Timnah, ten cities and their villages.*

⁵⁸ *Halhul, Beth-zur, Gedur;* ⁵⁹ *Maarath, Beth-Anoth, and Eltekon, six cities and their villages.* ª

⁶⁰ *Kiriath Baal (that is Kiriath Jearim) and Rabbah, two cities and their villages.*

⁶¹ *In the wilderness: Beth-Arabah, Middin, Secacah;* ⁶² *Nibshan, the City of Salt, and En Gedi, six cities and their villages.*

⁶³ *But as for the Jebusites, the inhabitants of Jerusalem, the sons of Judah were not able to dispossess them. The Jebusites have lived with the sons of Judah* ª *in Jerusalem until this day.*

¹⁶:¹ *The lot* ª *went out to the sons of Joseph from the Jordan by Jericho to the waters* ᵇ *of Jericho eastward, the wilderness going up from Jericho into the hill country of Bethel.* ² *It goes out from Bethel to Luz,* ª *passes over to the territory of the Archites, Ataroth.* ³ *It goes down westward to the territory of the Japhletites unto the territory of lower Beth-Horon and unto Gezer.* ª *Its limits are at the sea.*

⁴ *The sons of Joseph, Manasseh and Ephraim, received their inheritance.* ⁵ *The territory of the sons of Ephraim belonged to their clans: The border of their inheritance to the east was Ataroth-Adar unto Upper Beth Horon.* ⁶ *The border goes out to the Sea. Michmethath is on the north. The border turns eastward to Taanath-Shiloh, passes over it* ª *eastward to Janoah.* ⁷ *It goes down from Janoah, Atarroth, and to Naarath, touches Jericho and goes out to the Jordan.* ⁸ *From Tappuah the border goes westward to the river Kanah. Its limits are the sea. This is the inheritance of the tribe of the sons* ª *of Ephraim for their clans.* ⁹ *Cities are also set apart for the sons of Ephraim in the midst of the inheritance of the sons of Manasseh, all the cities and their villages.* ¹⁰ *But they* ª *did not dispossess the Canaanites who live in Gezer, and the Canaanites lived in the midst of Ephraim until this day, and they became slaves doing forced labor.*

¹⁷:¹ *The lot* ª *belonged to the tribe of Manasseh, for he was the firstborn of Joseph, to Machir, the first-born of Manasseh, the father of Gilead, for he was a man of war. Gilead and Bashan belonged to him.* ² *It belonged to the remaining sons of Manasseh for their clans, to the sons of Abiezer, to the sons of Helek, to the sons of Asriel, to the sons of Shechem, to the sons of Hepher, and to the sons of Shemida. These were the sons of Manasseh, the son of Joseph,* ª *the males, by their clans.* ³ *But Zelophehad, the son of Hepher, the son of Gilead, the son of Machir, the son of Manasseh, had no sons, only daughters. These are the names of his daughters: Nahlah, Noah, Hoglah, Milcah, and Tirzah.* ⁴ *They approached Eleazer, the priest, Joshua, the son of Nun, and the chiefs, saying, "Yahweh commanded Moses* ª *to give us an inheritance in the midst of our brothers." He gave to them, in accord with the commandment of Yahweh, an inheritance in the midst of the brothers of their father.* ⁵ *The sections of Manasseh fell out ten,* ª *disregarding the land of Gilead and Bashan which is beyond the Jordan,* ⁶ *because the daughters of Manasseh* ª *inherited an inheritance in the midst of his sons, while the land of Gilead belonged to the remaining sons of Manasseh.*

⁷ *The boundary of Manasseh was from Asher, that is Michmethath, which is across from Shechem, and the boundary goes southward to the inhabitants* ᵃ *of En Tappuah.* ⁸ *The land of Tappuah belonged to Manasseh, but Tappuah on the border of Manasseh belonged to the sons of Ephraim.* ⁹ *The border went down to the river Kanah. These cities* ᵃ *south of the river belonged to Ephraim in the midst of the cities of Manasseh, but the boundary of Manasseh was north of the river. Its limits were the sea.* ¹⁰ *To the south belonged to Ephraim and to the north to Manasseh. Its boundary was the sea. They touched Asher to the north and Isaachar to the east.* ¹¹ *There belonged to Manasseh in Isaachar and in Asher: Beth-shean and its suburbs, Yibleam and its suburbs, with the inhabitants of Dor and its suburbs, and the inhabitants of En Dor and its suburbs, and the inhabitants of Taanach and its suburbs, and the inhabitants of Megiddo and its suburbs, the three of Napheth.* ᵃ ¹² *The sons of Manasseh were not able to dispossess these cities. The Canaanites were determined to live in this land.* ¹³ *When the sons of Israel became strong, they set the Canaanites to forced labor, but they did not completely dispossess them.*

¹⁴ *The sons of Joseph spoke with Joshua, "Why have you given to me* ᵃ *for an inheritance one lot and one section, though I am a great people, (since) up to this point, Yahweh has blessed me?"* ¹⁵ *Joshua said to them, "If you are a great people, go up for yourself into the forest and create for yourself there in the land of the Perizzites and the Rephaim,* ᵃ *since the hill country of Ephraim is too restrictive* ᵇ *for you."* ¹⁶ *Then the sons of Joseph* ᵃ *said, "The hill country is not enough for us, but iron chariots are among all the Canaanites who live in the land in the valley, to those in Beth-Shean and her suburbs and to those in the Valley of Jezreel."* ¹⁷ *Joshua said to the house of Joseph, to Ephraim and to Manasseh,* ᵃ *"You are a great people with great power.* ¹⁸ *To you will belong not one lot, for the hill country* ᵃ *will belong to you, though it is forest. Creating it, you shall possess its farthest limits, because you will dispossess the Canaanites, though they have iron chariots, even though they are strong.*

Notes

A quick glance at a critical edition of the Hebrew or Greek text reveals immediately the complexity of the textual situation in these chapters. The problems of transliterating and transmitting the many proper names makes it impossible to comment on textual variants of almost every name in the text. We must confine ourselves to the most important variants, quite a task in itself.

15:1.a. The Hebrew text uses הגורל, "lot," in 15:1; 16:1; 17:1, whereas the LXX seems to presuppose הגבול, "border, territory," in each instance. Auld ("Textual and Literary Studies in the Book of Joshua," *ZAW* 90 [1978]) argues on the basis of 21:20, 40 and 1 Chr 6:51 that the LXX has preserved the earlier text form. He concludes that "chs. 13–17 of Joshua were without mention of *gwrl* or 'lot' until a very late stage in their development" (416–17). Steuernagel and Holzinger argue, on the other hand, that LXX has corrected the texts in light of 18:5ff. Both conclusions depend upon larger literary presuppositions. Whichever is correct, it shows that the copyists continued to interpret as well as transmit the text for a long period until its final stabilization in the first Christian century.

15:1.b. LXX does not translate "sons"; cf. Auld, Joshua, VTSup 30 (1979) 10–11.

15:1.c. MT has only one preposition, אל, "towards, at," in the verse. LXX has translated this with ἀπό, "from," and has also introduced the same preposition before "the wilderness." This could represent a loss by haplography (Soggin).

15:1.d. MT has two expressions for "southwards," forming somewhat of a tautology (Soggin). LXX has clarified this with language from Num 20:16 (Margolis; *Text Project*). The attempt in MT appears to be to describe the boundary beginning at Edom and reaching to the extreme end of the Wilderness of Zin (cf. Num 34:3–4).

15:3.a. LXX reflects מנגד "in front of, opposite," rather than MT מנגב "south of."

15:4.a. The written text (Kethib) has a sing. verb following the pattern of the context, while the Massoretes chose to read (Qere) a plur. verb in grammatical agreement with the subject.

15:4.b. MT suddenly returns to direct address with a second pers. plur. suffix, which the LXX changes in line with the context to third pers. plur. (cf. Vg). Noth explains it as an addition from Num 34:6–7, while Soggin follows the LXX; but MT can be retained (with Text Project).

15:5.a. LXX interprets the text, adding "all" before the Sea of Salt.

15:7.a. Steuernagel describes the text as corrupt to the foundations. LXX reads, "and the boundary continues on to the fourth part of the Valley of Achor." Margolis bases this on a corruption in the old Hebrew script between דברה מעמק (MT) and רבעה מעמק. Noth admits his own uncertainty in interpreting MT דבר as a preposition meaning "behind." The MT, despite its difficulties, is preferable.

15:7.b. Instead of "then northward turning to Gilgal," LXX reads "and then goes down toward the districts" (Text Project). Steuernagel and Noth follow LXX, explaining צפנה פנה as dittography. Noth reads גלילות on the basis of 18:17, while Steuernagel translates Gilgal as "circle of stones" (cf. Hertzberg), saying it does not fit geographically here. The Text Project turns Noth's argument around and sees LXX as a correction based on 18:17 (cf. Bright). Gray and Bright seek to avoid geographical difficulties by seeing a second Gilgal coming in view. No easy or even probable solution is apparent.

15:7.c. LXX lacks "border."

15:8.a. LXX lacks "son of."

15:9.a. The consonants can be read "the spring of Merneptah," after the Egyptian Pharaoh (cf. Noth).

15:9.b. LXX reads "to mount Ephron," followed by Noth (cf. Soggin with reference to Baldi). Margolis and Text Project suggest an original reading of עִיֵי "ruins."

15:10.a. LXX transposes the verb in front of "to Mount Seir," instead of behind it.

15:10.b. LXX confuses letters in reading הר "mount" as עיר "city." Similarly Beth Shemesh, "house of the sun," becomes "city of the sun."

15:10.c. Some Mss and LXX read the city Timnah as the common word תימן (cf. v 1), "south."

15:12.a. LXX reads "their border." MT witnesses slight confusion caused by dittography, which has appeared in another form in LXX.

15:13.a. LXX reads, "speech of God, and Joshua gave to him the city Arbok, the metropolis of Enak." On the use of God for Yahweh, see Auld, "Joshua," VTSup 30 (1979) 12–13. For the last part, cf. 14:15. The grammatical restructuring is for clarity, since the Heb. does not specify a subject for "he gave." LXX loses, however, the theological emphases of God's word directed to Joshua. Steuernagel says this is done because such a word has not been previously reported.

15:14.a. LXX adds the unnecessary "son of Jephunneh," transposes two of the names, and omits the final "descendants of Anak." The phrase is also lacking in Judg 1:10 and is dependent upon Num 13:22. Interestingly, LXX adds the phrase in Judges. Auld notes ("Judges I and History: A Reconsideration," VT 25 [1975] 270) that MT of Judg 1:11–15 agrees with LXX tradition in Josh 15:15–19.

15:15.a. LXX inserts the explicit subject, "Caleb."

15:18.a. Translation is complicated by the use of vocabulary of whose meaning we are uncertain and by complex textual variants. ותסיתהו is a Hiphil from סות, meaning "lead away, seduce, incite, provoke" (Holladay). It "always has a pejorative sense" (Soggin; cf. Noth, Ehrlich). Steuernagel and R. C. Boling (Judges [AB 6a; Garden City, N.Y.: Doubleday, 1975] 56–57) follow some evidence from LXX and Vg in making the subject masculine, Boling translating, "he nagged her." The argument of Noth and Soggin that only Caleb and his daughter are involved is not true to the text. Certainly, here the conversation is between the newly-weds, even though Othniel is not mentioned by name. The implication is that the bride used her feminine charms to gain a request from her new husband. One cannot defend the emendation on grounds of protecting the image of the first judge (against Boling; cf. Text Project). The problem that in the following scene the wife confronts her father is to be explained in the sense that she gained her husband's agreement before carrying out her plan. Auld may be correct in following LXX in restoring: לאמר אשאל מאת אבי (VT 25 [1975] 271).

15:18.b. The verb ותצנח has caused all sorts of scholarly consternation and conjecture. G. R. Driver went so far as to suggest "she broke wind" (NEB; "The Problems of Interpretation in the Heptateuch." *Mélanges biblíque rediges en l'honneur de André Robert* [Paris: Blood & Gay, 1966] 75–76), but this "has not found wide acceptance" (Boling, *Judges*, 57). E. W. Nicholson must be followed when he concludes ("The Problem of צנח," *ZAW* 89 [1977] 259–66), "the problem of the meaning of צנח still remains" (265). Thus we join him in following tradition and translating "she alighted" (cf. Boling).

15:18.c. The Heb. reads literally, "What to you?" The implication is often "What is it to you?" "What ails you?" "What do you want?" (BDB, 552).

15:20.a. LXX omits "for their clans."

15:21.a. LXX reads Ἐγενήθησαν δὲ πόλεις αὐτῶν πόλεις πρὸς τῇ φυλῇ υἱῶν Ἰουδα . . . , "There were their cities, cities belonging to the tribe of the sons of Judah." Margolis interpreted this as forming two headings, a general one for 21b–62 and a special heading for the cities of the Negeb in 21b–32. He sees MT merging these into one. The meaning of מקצה is weakened into a pronoun by LXX. Modern translators usually render "furthermost" (JB) or "in the extreme south" (RSV). It may also mean the whole, all of the cities (cf. BDB, 892; cf. NEB).

15:23.a. LXX joins the last two names into Hazor-Yithnan, probably correctly (cf. *Text Project*, Soggin, Margolis).

15:25.a. LXX read Hazor-Hadattah as חצרתה "and her villages," thus relating it to the previous verse, possibly correctly. Noth sees it as a later addition.

15:28.a. Bizyothyah is given by LXX with "and her villages" (בנותיה), which is supported by Neh 11:27 and is probably correct, needing only a slight change in the Heb. text (cf. *Text Project; BHS;* Soggin).

15:32.a. LXX seems to have read ʿ En Rimmon as one word (Margolis), probably correctly (cf. Soggin, *Text Project; BHS;* Neh 11:29).

15:32.b. MT lists thirty-six cities before this note, showing the continuing change in the transmitted text. LXX says twenty-nine cities also, but it lists thirty.

15:36.a. LXX presupposes וגדרתיה, "her villages" probably correctly (Soggin, *BHS,* but denied by *Text Project*). The change brings exactly fourteen cities into the list, whereas MT lists fifteen.

15:47.a. MT reads the "Territory Sea," a confusion with the following word caused by the change of one letter. LXX preserves the correct reading, "The Great Sea," i.e. the Mediterranean.

15:59.a. LXX adds a verse omitted by homoeoteleuton from MT: "Tekoa, Ephrathah (that is Bethlehem), Peor, Etam, Culon, Tatam, Shoresh, Cerem, Gallim, Bether, and Manocho, eleven cities and their villages" (following the *Text Project* reconstruction, though recognizing with Margolis that "the corruptions defy emendation.").

15:63.a. LXX does not transmit "with the sons of Judah," which may well represent a later dogmatic reflection (cf. Auld, *VT* 25 [1975] 274–75).

16:1.a. See 15:1a.

16:1.b. LXX does not read "to the water of Jericho," an awkward expression, but the resulting Greek "would be senseless here" (Margolis). The expression insures that the border is understood to have been outside Jericho, so that Jericho is not included in Joseph's territory.

16:2.a. LXX has skillfully rearranged the text to read: "and will go up from Jericho into the hill country, the wilderness into Bethel-Luz, and they will go out to Bethel and run along the borders of Achatarothi . . ." In so doing, it has provided no evidence for a more original text.

16:3.a. LXX places "and unto Gezer" at the end of v 5.

16:6.a. LXX does not repeat "border" as the subject and omits the accusative pronoun "it," smoothing out the construction somewhat. This continues with the omission of the opening verb of v 7. Soggin refers to MT as incomplete here.

16:8.a. LXX does not reflect "sons" (cf. Auld, "Joshua," VTSup 30 [1979] 10–11).

16:10.a. LXX adds "Ephraim" as explicit subjects and then inserts at the end an explicit reference to 1 Kgs 9:16 "until Pharaoh, king of Egypt, came up and took it and burned it with fire. He killed the Canaanites and the Perizzites, and all the inhabitants of Gezer. Pharaoh gave it in the dowry of his daughter." This results in the omission of the final clause of MT (cf. Judg 1:29), which may itself be a later insertion of a traditional phrase (cf. Auld, "Judges I and History," *VT* 25 [1975] 275, n. 52).

17:1.a. See 15:1a. LXX also adds "sons" before Manasseh.

17:2.a. LXX omits "sons of Manasseh, the son of Joseph," which may be a later specification by the tradition. Similarly, in the next verse, the genealogical expansion after "son of Hepher," is not represented by LXX. Also in v 4, "son of Nun" does not appear in LXX.

17:4.a. LXX reads the idiomatic "by the hand of Moses."

17:5.a. LXX reads somewhat more smoothly: "Their portion fell: from Anassa and the plain of Labek, which is part of the land of Gilead, which is beyond the Jordan." This omits all reference to Bashan, which may have been added because of its traditional ties with Gilead.

17:6.a. LXX reads "daughters of the sons of Manasseh," making the genealogy of v 3 explicit. The LXX omission in v 3 necessitated this. LXX also then changes "his sons" to "their brothers."

17:7.a. Margolis speaks of deep-seated corruption here and does not even attempt to restore part of the verse in LXX. LXX may be translated: "and the borders of the sons of Manasseh were Delanath, which is before the sons of Anath, and it goes up to the borders, to Jamin and Jassib to the fountain of Thaphthoth. ⁸ It shall be Manasseh . . ." Noth, Soggin, Gray, Hertzberg see the LXX as correct in reading ישבי, "inhabitants," as the name of a town, Yashib. The *Text Project* takes the construction as a compound name of a town: Yashib-en-tappuah. Restoration on the basis of such corruptions is extremely difficult.

17:9.a. Steuernagel describes the beginning and end of the verse as incapable of being understood, explaining the problem through a series of editorial glosses. LXX reads: "And the borders shall go down to the valley of Karana on the south over against the valley of Jariel. Tereminthos (=Terebinth or Turpentine tree) belongs to Ephraim in the midst of a city of Manasseh. The borders of Manasseh on the north are unto the brook. And its limit is the Sea." Our translation inserts an article before "these cities," which is the minimum required to make sense of the text. LXX shows that the tradition may have worked on the text to eliminate the name אלה, "cultic tree."

17:11.a. The text here gives us great difficulties, as Steuernagel pointed out. Auld (*VT* 25 [1975] 280) says it is "grammatical nonsense . . . in all its versions." LXX omits Yibleam and its suburbs, the inhabitants of En Dor and its suburbs, the inhabitants of Taanach and its suburbs, then translates the final phrase, "the third part of Mapheta and its suburbs." LXX adds Taanach. George Dahl ("The 'Three Heights' of Joshua 17:11," *JBL* 53 [1934] 381–83) suggested that the final phrase was a marginal note later incorporated into the text. The note sought to show that Dor, the third town in the list, should be read as Naphath Dor, distinguishing it from En-Dor. He noted that all other occurrences of Naphath are with Dor (Josh 11:2; 12:23; 1 Kgs 4:11). He argued that En-Dor was an even earlier attempt to identify precisely Dor, since it does not appear in the parallel texts in Judg 1:27 and 1 Chr 7:29. The major modern commentaries and the *Text Project* agree with Dahl. Noth accepts this but sees En Dor as the original and Dor the first gloss. Auld (*VT* 25 [1975] 281) sees with Holmes the possibility of the LXX preserving the more original text with only three names and then suggests that a verse or two is missing from the text so that "two originally separate notes had become telescoped."

17:14.a. LXX made the suffix plur. in accord with the context. LXX also gives no translation of the difficult Heb. עד אשר עד כה "up to this point" or possibly "to such an extent" (cf. Noth). Perles (*Analekten zur Textkritik des Alten Testaments* [1922] 6) suggested reading עד as an abbreviation of עד דבר, "because of the fact that" (cf. Noth, Soggin, Hertzberg, *BHS*).

17:15.a. LXX omits "in the land of the Perizzites and the Rephaim," which could be later introduction of traditional terminology. Budde, Rudolph, Schmitt (*Du sollst*, 93) see Rephaim as dittography from Mount Ephraim. The Heb. term "to create" is the *Piel* form rather than the normal *Qal* and seems to indicate a technical meaning, "clearing ground."

17:15.b. The verb אצל occurs eight times in the *Qal* and twice in the Hiphil. Only here is the meaning "to be too narrow, restricted" suggested for it. Otherwise, it means "to urge, be urgent, be in a hurry." Certainly, the *Text Project* is correct in rejecting NEB's conjecture uniting the verb and the prepositional phrase into a single form, אצלך, "beside you."

17:16.a. LXX offers a text with somewhat different emphases: "They said, 'The Mount Ephraim does not satisfy us. Choice horses and iron belong to the Canaanites, to the ones dwelling in it in Beth Shean and in its villages, and in the Valley of Jezreel.'" The explicit subject "sons of Joseph" is not repeated. The hill country becomes Mount Ephraim. "Among all" disappears, as does "in the land in the valley."

17:17.a. LXX is addressed "to the sons of Joseph," rather than to "the house of Joseph, to Ephraim and to Manasseh," the latter possibly reflecting later specification by the tradition. LXX also makes the statement a conditional one by inserting "if" at the beginning.

17:18.a. LXX harmonizes the text a little by reading "forest" for "hill country," then omitting "its farthest limits." LXX then concludes: "You will be stronger than he in strength." Steuernagel sees a corrupt text to be explained by later insertions from vv 15–16. Hertzberg simply accepts the final Greek sentence as correct. Noth follows R. Smend (*Die Erzählung des Hexateuch*, 333) in inserting a negative into the text, "You cannot drive out the Canaanites." Soggin correctly denies this. The *Text Project* also rejects such interpretive modifications. But Auld, working on Judg 1:19 which has the negative, is uncertain as to how to read our passage (*VT* 25 [1975] 273).

Form/Structure/Setting

The introductory formula of 15:1 clearly opens this section and takes up the theme of 13:6–7; 14:2. One may look for the conclusion of the section at several points. We choose 17:18 for two reasons:
1) 18:1 makes a definite break through geographical change;
2) Conflict with the Canaanites concludes each of the sub-sections in 15–17, ending at 17:18, but does not appear in 18–19.
The major structures within 15–17 are clear. The major sections begin with "The lot belonged to . . ." (15:1; 16:1; 17:1). They end with a reference to the previous inhabitants and their relationship to Israel, using the key word "dispossess."
Each sub-section has its own structures:

I. THE LOT OF JUDAH (CHAP. 15)
   A. The borders of Judah (1–12)
      1. The southern border (1b–4)
      2. The eastern border (5a)
      3. The northern border (5b–11)
      4. The western border (12)
   B. The exception: Calebites in Hebron, Debir, and the Negeb (13–19)
   C. Summary (20)
   D. The list of Judah's cities (21–62)
   (Note: Two types of structural markers are used in this section, a larger geographical one, which we mark with letters, and a smaller one noting the total number of cities, which we mark with numbers.)
      a. On the southern border of Edom (21b–32)
         1. Twenty-nine cities (21b–32)
      b. In the Shephelah (33–47)
         2. Fourteen cities (33–36)
         3. Sixteen cities (37–41)
         4. Nine cities (42–44)
         5. (No summary) Philistine territory (45–47)
      c. In the Hill Country (48–60)
         6. Eleven cities (48–51)
         7. Nine cities (52–54)
         8. Ten cities (LXX nine) (55–57)
         9. Six cities (58–59)
         10. Eleven cities (59a LXX only)
         11. Two cities (60)
      d. In the wilderness (61–62)
         12. Six cities (61–62)
   E. Jebusites remain with Judah in Jerusalem (63)

II. THE LOT OF THE SONS OF JOSEPH (CHAP. 16)
   A. The southern boundary (1b–3)
   B. The inheritance of Manasseh and Ephraim (4–9)
      1. The Borders of Ephraim (5–9)
         a. Southern border (5b–6aα)
         b. Eastern (?) border (6aβ–7)
         c. Northern border (8)
         d. Summary conclusion (8b)
         e. The Exception: Ephraimite cities in Manasseh (9)
      2. Canaanites remain with Ephraim in Gezer (10)
III. THE LOT OF THE TRIBE OF MANASSEH (17:1–13)
   A. The Exception: Machir, the first-born, has Gilead and Bashan, east
      of the Jordan (1b)
   B. That which belongs to the remaining sons of Manasseh (2–11)
      1. The remaining sons of Manasseh (2)
      2. Fulfilling the promise to the daughters of Zelophehad (3–4)
      3. Summary (5–6)
      4. The Borders of Manasseh (7–11)
         a. Southern border (7; cf. 16:6–8)
         b. The Exception: Ephraimite city in Manasseh (8)
         c. Southern border continued (9aα)
         d. The Exception: Ephraimite cities in Manasseh (9aβbα)
         e. The Western Border (9bβ)
         f. Summary distinction (10a)
         g. Northern border (10bα)
         h. Eastern border (10bβ)
         i. The Exceptions: Manassite cities in Issachar and in Asher (11)
   C. The Canaanites remain in Manasseh (12–13)
IV. NARRATIVE EPILOGUE AS THEOLOGICAL CONCLUSION (17:14–18)

This clear structure has been achieved through the use of several types
of traditional materials:

   1) Border descriptions (15:1–12; 16:1b–3, 5–8; 17:7–10)
   2) List of Judean cities (15:21–62)
   3) Caleb tradition (15:13–19)
   4) Canaanites who remain tradition (15:63; 16:10; 17:12–13, 15–16, 18)
   5) The Zelophehad tradition (17:3–4)
   6) The Josephite expansion tradition (17:14–18)

Each of these must be examined briefly to understand the type of materials
at our writer's disposal and how he was led by God to interpret them for
his own and succeeding generations.
   1) The border descriptions are apparently the oldest materials used. The
same tradition is used to prepare the southern border in 15:1–4 as in Num
34:3–5, where it serves for all Israel. The function of a southern border is
not clear from a political standpoint, since it is not clear over against whom
such borders would be established nor what function they would serve. Such

a border may be fashioned simply to parallel the important northern border (Cf. Y. Aharoni, *The Land of the Bible,* 233; C. H. J. de Geuss, *The Tribes of Israel,* 80). Again, the eastern Judean border is simply a natural lake, the crucial point being the northern dividing line. It is the northern border which occupies the majority of the space and is the most detailed. What is remarkable here is the fact that Jerusalem is denied to Judah. This may be explained (1) as arising from the continued Jebusite occupation prior to David's conquest of the city; (2) as reflecting the Judean administrative procedure whereby Jerusalem is mentioned separately from Judah and is the "city of David," that is under the king's personal control; (3) or as representing a Benjaminite claim to the city, perhaps based on the tradition of the war with the king of Jerusalem (cf. chap. 10; Judg 1:21). The third alternative would join it to the other elements of tradition within the book of Joshua which reflect an early polemic between the tribes of Judah and Benjamin.

The next list is the southern border of the sons of Joseph (16:1–3), again a vital tradition for Benjamin, for which it serves as the northern border (cf. 18:12–13). E. Otto (*Jakob in Sichem,* 233) takes up again the arguments of Schunck and Täubler that 16:1–3 represents tradition after the division of the monarchy. The other extensive list is the eastern border of Ephraim and the Jordan, which is usually claimed for Manasseh. It is not impossible that Benjamin also laid claim to this territory. The setting of the boundary lists may well be tribal disputes centering in Benjamin, Ephraim, and Manasseh, the very centers of the narratives of chaps. 1–12, and the center of the kingdom of Saul, the Benjaminite, and his son (cf. 1 Sam 7:15–17; 2 Sam 2:8–9). The setting may have been within larger groups, such as the six northern tribes of Ephraim, Manasseh, Benjamin, Zebulon, Asher, Naphtali (Aharoni, *The Land of the Bible,* 233). Such material could well have been preserved in the Benjaminite sanctuary of Gilgal, along with the other materials of Josh 1–11. As such it was gradually removed from its political usage and became part of the religious tradition of the people, showing how Yahweh, not the political process, had given the land to the tribes of Israel (cf. S. Tengstrom, *Die Hexateucherzählung,* 77–78). E. Otto, (*Jakob in Sichem,* 227–45) has tried to show recently that the disputes centered in Ephraim and Manasseh.

2) The city lists show by their combination of two structural systems that they have been used in varied situations within their history. The division into twelve units reflects the administrative system of the monarchy (Alt), while the divisions into four areas may well have military functions (Yadin). Such political subdivisions were naturally altered through the generations to fit new historical circumstances. But the biblical writer saw them in an entirely new light. God showed him that such political systems reflected the divine work in bringing all of the cities of Judah under the control of Israel. God gave not only the land, not only the tribal areas, but each of the cities to his people. Political leaders may administer the land under their political systems, but the ultimate destiny of the land and its cities remained in the hands of Yahweh, the God who gave the land to his people.

3) It is difficult to describe the narrative structure of the Caleb narrative, because the introduction (15:13) is only a link, resuming the narrative from 14:15. V 14 may be the original opening of the narrative, since it is at this

point that we find the same story repeated, with a few insignificant variations, in Judg 1:11–15. Beltz (*Kaleb-Traditionen,* 36) is correct in seeing v 14 as a good continuation of 14:13, the original conclusion of that segment of the Caleb narrative. Whatever the original introduction and context, 15–19 provides a well-formed narrative based on oral foundations. The setting is given in the somewhat foolhardy challenge of Caleb (v 16) promising his daughter to whatever brave soul would conquer the city. The challenge is taken up and carried out by Othniel, leading to the climatic dialogue (18–19). Here, surprisingly, Othniel is a silent onlooker. The new bride does all the talking. She uses her feminine charms to gain his acceptance to her proposition. Then she goes back to her father with the proposition. The father knew his daughter. At first sight, he could tell something was up and so immediately asked what was troubling her. She did not try to turn on the feminine charm with her father. Rather, she returned to the child's role: "Give me, daddy, give me. I've been cheated, daddy. It's not fair." Immediately, her father gave in, complying with the request of his daughter.

This has usually been understood as an etiological narrative (Noth) even though the traditional etiological formula, "unto this day," does not appear. Certainly it functions so in the present context. But its original context is not etiological. Beltz comes to a somewhat representative conclusion that the story is Calebite tribal tradition seeking to represent Caleb as a sovereign nomadic prince, who conquers his own territory of Hebron and then cleverly strengthens his own position by concluding a marriage agreement with economic advantages. This is precisely not the tone of the story. Caleb does not go out and find the best possible marriage contract. Rather, he invites any rascal off the street to have his daughter if he can win one battle. Then his own daughter continues her spoiled ways to gain economic advantages for herself over against her father. Certainly the tribe of Caleb could have found a better way to make a hero out of their nomadic prince. Rather, the tone of the narrative in chap. 14 is continued, wherein Caleb gets the bad end of the deal. Again, tribal polemic is probably involved, though in this case the precise background of such polemic is not clear. Certainly the tradition has been taken up into Scripture and used to show how God was working to provide land for his faithful servant, bringing blessing to his people.

4) The tradition of the Canaanites who remain has usually been assumed to have its original place in Judg 1, from which it has been borrowed for use in Joshua. Auld ("Judges I and History," *VT* 25 [1975] 261–85) argues for the priority of the Joshua narratives (cf. C. H. J. de Geuss, *The Tribes of Israel,* 82–83, 85–86). The notices are carefully placed in our section at the end of units to give theological interpretation to the units. Thus they are not in an original *Sitz im Leben* but in a carefully constructed literary context.

Judges 1:1–21 is a Judean tradition showing the powerful occupation of the tribe of Judah, even against Jerusalem. It does note that Judah could (LXX) not drive out the Canaanites, who were too strongly armed. The final verse then deals with the reality that Jerusalem was not occupied until the time of David. It does so by blaming not the Judeans, but the Benjaminites. The connection of Benjamin with Jerusalem can belong only to the early pre-monarchical tradition. Joshua 15:63 then reflects the later tradition or a different perspective to blame Judah for not occupying Jerusalem (cf. S. Teng-ström, *Die Hexateucherzählung,* 77–78).

In the second half of Judges one turns to the northern tribes and begins on the positive note that Yahweh was with them and gave them victory (22–26) (cf. the attempt to date the list under Solomon by T. N. D. Mettinger, *Solomonic State Officials,* 116, n. 24a). This positive possibility is used, however, only as a contrast for the response of the northern tribes. All that can be said about the rest of the north is that they failed to do what God told them to do. Such a list may well represent ancient (liturgical?) tradition. Certainly the several examples together reflect more of an original setting than the isolated appearance in Joshua. Joshua also shows some interpretations of the material. The strict form of the Ephraim notice (1:29) has been adapted to the Joshua context (16:10), and the etiological formula added, to underline the point of the Joshua text that the action had relevance for the later day. The significance of the addition of the forced labor formula, uniquely absent from Ephraim in Judg 1, is not clear.

The Manasseh reference is modified at one small but significant point. Joshua 17:12 notes that Manasseh was not able to drive out the inhabitants, whereas Judg 1:27 says simply they did not. Here we appear to have a northern interpretation of the tradition, just as in Judg 1:19, we saw a southern interpretation. For Joshua, the inhabitants in Manasseh are simply part of the remaining peoples whom God is promising to drive out (13:6). For Judges, the Canaanites there represent the sin of Manasseh. This is shown conclusively in the final notice in Josh 17:18. The concluding narrative in 17:14–18 shows that the theme of the remaining Canaanites has definitely been the central point for the inspired writer of this section. Only here does he take up the problem of the strength of the Canaanites, a theme introduced in Judg 1 only for the Judeans (1:19). Joshua 17:18, however, includes no mention of Israel not conquering. Rather, the narrative is told to promise that Israel will conquer the Canaanites (18). The theme of the Canaanites who remain is thus taken by the writer of Josh 15–17 from its original literary setting in Judg 1 in order to give a theological promise to the people of God. Both Judg 1 and Josh 15–17 may represent earlier collections of material, the one from Judah, the other from the circle of Joseph—Ephraim—Benjamin, using common tradition in polemic against each other. The biblical author has taken up the old materials and used them in two places to demonstrate the truth which God had revealed to him within the old traditions.

5) The Zelophehad tradition (17:3–4) has its roots in Num 27:1–7. Joshua has not preserved a true narrative structure. Rather, it represents a literary creation, taking the information from Num 27 and using it to demonstrate the faithful obedience of Joshua to the commandments of Moses, the theme which we have seen to be dominant in the book.

6) Finally, the Josephite expansion tradition must rest on ancient tradition. It deals with precisely the part of the land which proved most troublesome for Israel to conquer, namely the city of Beth Shean and the Valley of Jezreel. It represents the problem of tribes conquering individual territory, a problem which the writer of Joshua would not have invented. The narrative is told in the dialogue style so common to ancient Israelite narrative. Still, it must

be conceded that much of the present narrative reflects the vocabulary and
purpose of the literary context: "inheritance, lot, blessing, Rephaim, Perizzites
(?), the chariots and iron of the Canaanites (taken from Judg 1:19, cf. above),
limits, dispossess." G. Schmitt, *Du sollst*, 89–97, has correctly disputed the
common assumption that two parallel narratives appear in 14–15, 16–18 (cf.
e.g. Soggin). The biblical writer appears to have taken an old tradition, perhaps
one in which Joshua arbitrated land disputes between tribes (Alt, Hertzberg),
and used it to show how God had provided for the needs of all his people
and had promised success over the Canaanites.

In this section, then, as throughout the book, we find the biblical author
taking up old traditions which have been meaningful in the life of his people
for generations and using them to teach the word of God to his readers for
his day.

Comment

1-12 The first lot is given the tribe of Judah. This represents not the order
of birth of the sons of Jacob but the order of political priority for the editor
of the biblical narrative. His major concern is with Judah, the only representative of Israel left in his day. For him Judah is the first to receive its inheritance,
the last to fall, and the only remaining hope for restoring the lot of the
people of God.

15:3 The Ascent of the Scorpions (עקרבים) has recently been recognized
in other ancient near eastern literature (M. Görg, "Zum 'Skorpionenpass'
[Num XXXIV 4; Jos. XV 3], *VT* 24 [1974] 508–9). For a description of the
boundary as a whole, see Y. Aharoni, *The Land of the Bible*, 63–65; Noth,
77, 86–87).

6 That Reuben should have descendants west of the Jordan has given rise
to the theory that one time Reuben lived west of the Jordan (for discussion
and rejection of the theory, cf. R. de Vaux, *Histoire Ancienne*, = *Early History*,
576–81).

8 The border here is carefully defined to go just south of Jerusalem itself,
while the corresponding description for Benjamin places it just inside Benjaminite territory (18:16). This is a major point used by scholars in trying to
date the list (cf. Soggin, 173–74).

9 On 15:9f, see Robert North, *Bib* 37 (1956) 209–16. On Ephron, see
K.-D. Schunck, "Ophra, Ephron und Ephraim," *VT* 11 [1961] 188–200.

13 The basic reason for incorporating the Caleb tradition at this point is
to demonstrate again that everything was done according to the divine word,
even when no specific reference can be made to where such a command
was given. The command to Joshua is simply the command given to Moses
and fulfilled through Joshua (cf. Judg 1:20), or it is based on a tradition
which was not incorporated into the completed Scriptures.

14 The three sons of Anak are taken up from Num 13:22. The tribe of
Judah is said to have killed them in Judg 1:11.

15 For Debir, see 10:3, *Comment.*

17 Othniel is also named as the first of the Israelite judges, the only one
to represent the southern clans (Judg 3:9–11).

[19] For "blessing," see 14:13. Here the word has the simple meaning of "wedding present," but the deeper meaning illustrated in Deut 28:1–14 is also implied.

[20] The narrative summary shows that the Caleb-Othniel tradition has been incorporated as part of the tradition of the tribe of Judah. Territory occupied by Caleb and Othniel is seen to be territory given by God to the tribe of Judah. Here, again, we see the Israelite understanding which does not separate primary and secondary causes. What from a human perspective may be deemed the work of man is judged ultimately to be the lot given by God.

[21-62] The list of cities according to their political and military subdivisions is incorporated to show from still another perspective the greatness of God's gift to Judah. Judah controlled not only the borders, but life inside the borders. Not all cities of Judah are named, certainly, but the implication is that Judah received title to all the cities and land within her borders. Again, what might appear to be simply political bases of power are interpreted by the biblical writer as parts of the divine domain given by God to his people. The biblical author's audacity in incorporating a political document into his theological literature represents a highly significant theological understanding of human priorities and responsibilities. Political documents and administration are not the ultimate authority. Political literature is not the final law. Above, beyond, and behind all political activity and authority stands the ultimate authority of God.

[21] For cities in the Negeb during the Iron Age, cf. V. Fritz, "Erwägungen zur Siedlungsgeschichte des Negev in der Eisen I-Zeit (1200–1000 v. Chr.) im Lichte der Ausgrabungen auf der Ḫirbet el-Mšāš," *ZDPV* 91 (1975) 30–45.

[37-41] For cities around Lachish, see now D. Kellermann, *VT* 28 (1978) 429–32.

[45-47] This district does not have the normal concluding formula. It includes three of the five Philistine cities and a territory which Israel did not control prior to the monarchy and seldom during the monarchy. Thus Wright and Cross ("The Boundary and Province Lists of the Kingdom of Judah," *JBL* 75 [1956] 218) concluded, "The territory makes no sense as a political district, not only because of its size, but because neither Israel nor Judah ever controlled it all." Thus, for Cross and Wright, it is "an editor's addition to the province list in order to fit it for his purpose of describing the total claim of the tribe of Judah" (cf. Alt, "Judas Gaue unter Josia," *PJ* 21 [1925] 106n. = *KS* II, 278, n. 3).

[60] Kiriath-jearim may also appear in 18:28, though the text there is not clear. This has led to long discussions over the relationship between the extremely short town list of 15:60 and the Benjaminite list (cf. Y. Aharoni, "The Province-List of Judah," *VT* 9 [1959] 226–30; K.-D. Schunck, *Benjamin*, 153–67). Aharoni appears correct in his assertion that "there seems no reason to maintain that Kirjath-jearim and Rabbah cannot have been a separate province. . . . It is therefore obvious that other factors than size or the number of towns were decisive in determining the area of the provinces" (*VT* 9 [1959] 229–30).

[63] The biblical writer's emphasis is seen in his concluding remarks on Judah.

They were not able to dispossess the Jebusites and thus had to endure their presence in Jerusalem up to the writer's day. This casts a spell over the entire future history of Jerusalem for the writer, despite David's victory over the Jebusites (2 Sam 5:6–10). When we consider that the major part of the Deuteronomistic history centers on the activities of the kings of Judah in Jerusalem, this note becomes even more important. The government in Jerusalem was a government impaired by the fact that it had not accomplished the first command of God. It had not driven the Jebusites out of the capital city. Judah thus lived its life in the shadow of temptation from Jebusite gods and Jebusite practices. All of this stood in opposition to the command of Deut 7:1–26; 20:16–18. Solomon might make the remaining nations slaves (1 Kgs 9:20–21), but this still was not what Yahweh had commanded (cf. Josh 9). For the problem of Jerusalem prior to David, see N. Gottwald, *The Tribes of Yahweh*, 568–71.

16:1-3 The next allotment does not go to a tribe, as such. Rather it goes to the sons of Joseph. This is a very careful formulation, seeking to maintain both the tradition that Joseph was the original son of Jacob and that the tribe of Joseph had been divided into two parts, named after his two sons (cf. the detailed review of research and evidence by C. H. J. de Geuss, *The Tribes of Israel*, 70–96; E. Otto, *Jakob in Sichem*, 253–54). The boundary marked here is that between Ephraim and Benjamin and has parallels in 16:5; 18:11–13 (Aharoni, *The Land of the Bible*, 235–36). That the list is a replacement for the Judean list in 15:5b–11 from the time of Rehoboam is quite doubtful (against K.-D. Schunck, *Benjamin*, 147).

2 Luz is identified as the original name of Bethel in Gen 28:19; 35:6 (cf. 48:3); Judg 1:23; Josh 18:13.

An Archite was David's friend and counselor, who proved instrumental in defeating the revolt of Absalom (2 Sam 15:21–37; 16:15–17:23). The Archites may have been a clan of Benjamin (S. Cohen, "Archite," *IDB* 1 [1962] 209) or, more likely, remnants of ancient inhabitants of the land (Soggin, Hertzberg).

3 The Japhletites are mentioned only here and in the genealogical list of 1 Chr 7:30–40, where they are included as descendants of Asher.

Gezer was not conquered by Ephraim (16:10 = Judg 1:29), but only came into Israel's possession when the Egyptian Pharaoh gave it to Solomon as a wedding present (1 Kgs 9:15–17; cf. 2 Sam 5:25).

4 The note that the Josephites received (נחל) their inheritance parallels the statement in 14:1 concerning the people of Israel as well as that in 13:8 (לקח) concerning the tribes east of the Jordan. Interestingly, no such summary is given for Judah (cf. 15:20), nor for the tribes listed in chaps. 18 and 19.

6-8 For topographical problems here, see A. Kuschke, "Beiträge," 102–6; E. Otto, *Jakob in Sichem*, 238–42. For Michmethath, see K. Elliger, "Michmethath," 91–100. For Janoah, see E. Otto, "Survey-archäologische Ergebnisse zur Geschichte der früheisenzeitlichen Siedlung Janoah (Jos 16, 6, 7)," *ZDPV* 94 (1978) 108.

8 Elliger ("Die Grenze zwischen Ephraim und Manasse," *ZDPV* 53 [1930] 267) has made much of the observation that Tappuah is only fully discussed at 17:7–8 (cf. C. H. J. de Geuss, *The Tribes of Israel*, 78–81; E. Otto, *Jakob in Sichem*, 231–32).

[9] The border irregularities, placing cities of one tribe within the boundaries of another, point to the early date and historical soundness of the border descriptions. For the translation and topographical discussion of the text, cf. C. H. J. de Geuss, *The Tribes of Israel,* 76–77.

[10] This verse points to the time of Solomon, when Israel gained control of Gezer and put the foreign population to work on building projects of the monarchy (1 Kgs 9:15–22; cf. 5:27; 2 Sam 20:24; T. N. D. Mettinger, *Solomonic State Officials,* 128–39). This points to progress beyond the point of 15:63, where the Jebusites simply dwell in the land. Here we begin to see the structure of the present section, pointing toward 17:18.

17:1 The present text underlines the unusual order of the allotment. Manasseh, the first-born, received his allotment after his younger brother Ephraim (cf. Deut 21:15–17). This follows the pattern set in Gen 48. It also represents the leadership exercised by Ephraim during the period of the Judges as seen in the book of Judges.

Machir appears as an independent tribe in Judg 5:14, where Manasseh is not mentioned. This has given rise to a long history of scholarly debate over the relationship of Manasseh and Machir, which has been surveyed recently by R. de Vaux, *Histoire ancienne,* 538–41, 589–98 (=*Early History,* 584–87, 642–53; cf. S. Mittmann, *Beiträge,* 213–14, n. 15). In our context, Machir is mentioned as the representative of Manasseh east of the Jordan (cf. Num 32:39–40; Deut 3:15; Josh 13:31).

2-3 The genealogical relationships given here are complicated. Hepher appears to be a son of Manasseh in v 2, but a son of Gilead, the son of Machir, the son of Manasseh, in v 3. Such genealogical information is related to that of Num 26:29–33; 27:1, 36:1, 10 (cf. Hertzberg; J. Liver, "The Israelite Tribes," *The World History of the Jewish People* III: *Judges,* 207–8). Several of the names also appear as geographical locations: Shechem (e.g. Josh 24:1); Hepher (1 Kgs 4:10; Josh 12:17); Gilead (e.g. Josh 13:11, 25); Tirzah (Josh 12:24; 1 Kgs 14:17; 2 Kgs 15:14). The Samarian Ostraca have places named Abiezer, Helek, Shechem, Shemida, Noah, Hoglah (*DOTT,* 205).

The section is included here to stress again that Joshua carried out all the commands of Moses and Yahweh (Num 27:1–11; cf. 36:1–13).

[5] Manasseh received ten shares, one each for the clans of Manasseh except for Hepher, and one each for the five daughters of Zelophehad, the son of Hepher, who appear to have inherited just as much as each of the sons of Manasseh. It is interesting that the ten parts are set over against Gilead and Bashan, making a total of twelve. Gray goes so far as to suggest, "the debate seems to concern not so much land as status in a sacral confederacy of the clans of Manasseh, perhaps the reorganization of an originally smaller confederacy at Shechem." Whatever the historical background, for the present editor the point remains the obedience of Joshua and the allotment to Manasseh.

For 7–8, see A. Kuschke, "Beiträge," 102–107; E. Otto, *Jakob in Sichem,* 234–38.

8-11 Cf. *Comment* on 16:9.

[12] The cities of Dor, Megiddo, Taanach, Ibleam, and Beth-Shean represent a string of Canaanite strongholds in the Valley which Israel did not control until the period of the monarchy, when under David and Solomon they became Israelite centers whose inhabitants were forced to work for the king (cf. *Com-*

ment on 16:10). Here the writer seeks to show that Israel gained control, but they never did do what God told them to do and what he promised to do with them, namely drive out all the inhabitants. Here is a sign of Israel's disobedience which accounts for the problems described in Judges, climaxing in the withdrawal of the divine promise in Judg 2:21–23.

¹⁴ The term blessing continues to play an important role in the section (cf. 14:13; 15:19). The tribe of Joseph is connected to the patriarchal blessings promising that the people of God would increase in numbers. The problem of the narrative is set up in that the blessing of land is not equal to the blessing in numbers.

¹⁵ Joshua sets a test before the Josephites—if they are so great, and thus so blessed by God, let them show that God is with them. Let them create for themselves a place to live in the midst of the powerful inhabitants of the land. This is especially true since they are in such a hurry to get outside the confines of Mount Ephraim (for the restricted geographical sense of the term, see G. Schmitt, *Du sollst,* 91–92).

¹⁶ The Josephites plead their case further. They face a losing struggle. The hill country is too small, here seemingly to refer again to the restricted sense of Mount Ephraim. The valley is not available, because the Canaanites with their iron weapons protect it. Again the old narrative points out with 17:11 that the Israelites could not control the string of cities near the Jezreel Valley. The Josephites have not, however, answered Joshua's challenge. Rather, they have avoided the issue.

¹⁷ Joshua replies with an answer that at the same time is conciliatory and challenging. He accepts the fact that they are a great and thus blessed people. He emphasizes their great power, thus their great potentiality. He concedes the necessity to grant their request, that is that they have more than one lot. This, in turn, explains how the house of Joseph came to be viewed as comprising two tribes—Manasseh and Ephraim.

¹⁸ The gaining of the second lot is set forth in a challenge and a promise. The challenge is the one put forward in v 15. They must create the second lot—a place in the wooded hill country. Thus they will extend beyond the hill country of Ephraim to control the entire hill country (cf. Schmitt). The challenge is now modified with renewed promise. Joseph, unlike Judah, and unlike Ephraim and Manasseh, will defeat the Canaanites despite the great power of the enemy. Thus even the promise of victory is a challenge to fight.

Explanation

Long lists of boundaries and cities invite us to skip on to the next section. We do so at the cost of missing a central part of the message of the book. Here we find finally the fulfillment of the command to Joshua in 13:6–7. The land west of the Jordan was given out to the tribes. Such distribution of the land was not a simple process, however. It involved the responsibility to carry out the promises of Moses (15:13–19; 17:3–6). It involved the necessity to accept the land given out (16:4). It also involved the necessity to solve tribal dissatisfaction (15:19; 17:14–18). It involved the challenge to create a living space for some of the tribes (17:14–18). It also involved the challenge to fight for territory possessed by other peoples (15:16; 17:18), a challenge which Israel did not always meet successfully (15:63; 16:10; 17:12; cf. Judg 1–3). Israel thus knew that she had experienced the blessing of God, but she also knew that her failure to meet the challenge threatened to cost her the blessing (Judg 2).

Our section provides the basis for the remainder of the Deuteronomistic history and its problem. It sets up the problem which confronted Israel for the rest of her history. Could she again become the obedient children of God, as she had been under Joshua (cf. Judg 2:6–10)? Or would Israel always be the people facing the challenge of God but seeking ways to avoid that challenge? Would Israel always be the people who wanted another lot from God without fulfilling the conditions set out by God? God had set out her boundaries. He had shown each tribe what territory they could expect to control under God's leadership. But he also showed each tribe that the allotment was not a guaranteed gift. With the allotment of the land went the allotment of the Torah, directing life in the land and among the tribes. The remainder of the Deuteronomistic history through 2 Kings demonstrates to Israel this close connection between Torah and gift of the land.

Israel finally went her own way instead of God's way. She chose to live in Yahweh's land while serving the gods of other peoples and other lands. When this happened, God raised up prophets and historians to warn Israel. She would not learn from her preachers or her historians. Thus God took back the land, gave it to foreign rulers, and led Israel back across the wilderness into exile. Ultimately, the land had to be taken away from the people of God. They had to lose the gift to appreciate it.

A deeper study into the text has revealed yet another level of meaning. The seemingly endless lists of hard-to-pronounce cities and topographical features began life as political documents. As such, they served as the basis for arbitration between tribes and as the basis for administering political districts. God in his wisdom led Israel's historians to take up the political documents to teach Israel religious truth. This religious truth, in turn, had great relevance for everyday life in the political arena. Here we see the close connection in Israel between political reality and divine Word. God can use the political reality to prepare the foundations for his word to his people. He can then use his word to seek to change the political reality.

The Shiloh Selections *(18:1–19:51)*

Bibliography

Aharoni, Y. "Anaharath." *JNES* 26 (1967) 212–15. ———. *The Land of the Bible.* Tr. A. F. Rainey. London: Burns & Oates, 1967, 235–39. ———. "The Province List of Judah." *VT* 9 (1959) 225–46. **Albright, W. F.** "Egypt and the Early History of the Negeb." *JPOS* 4 (1924) 149–61. ———. "The Topography of the Tribe of Issachar."

ZAW 44 (1926) 225–36. **Alt, A.** "Bemerkungen zur Ortsliste von Benjamin (Jos 18, 21–28); *ZDPV* 78 (1962) 143–58. ———. "Eine galiläische Ortsliste in Jos. 19." *ZAW* 45 (1927) 59–81. ———. "Judas Gaue unter Josia." *PJ* 21 (1925) 100–116. (=*Kleine Schriften zur Geschichten des Volkes Israel.* Vol. 2. München: C. H. Beck'sche Verlagsbuchhandlung, 1953, 276–88.) ———. "Saruhen, Ziklag, Horma, Gerar." *JPOS* 15 (1935) 294–324. (=*KS* 3, 409–35.) ———. "Das System der Stammesgrenzen im Buche Josua." *Beiträge zur Religionsgeschichte und Archaeologie Palästinas.* Leipzig: A. Deichert, 1927, 13–24. (=*KS* 1, 193–202.) **Bächli, O.** "Von der Liste zur Beschreibung, Beobachtungen und Erwägungen zu Jos. 13–19." *ZDPV* 89 (1973) 1–14. **Cross, F. M.** and **Wright, G. E.** "The Boundary and Province Lists of the Kingdom of Judah." *JBL* 75 (1956) 202–26. **Kallai-Kleinmann, Z.** "Note on the Town Lists of Judah, Simeon, Benjamin and Dan." *VT* 11 (1961) 223–27. ———. "The Town Lists of Judah, Simeon, Benjamin and Dan." *VT* 8 (1958) 134–60. **Kuschke, A.** "Historisch-topographische Beiträge zum Buche Josue." *Gottes Wort und Gottes Land*, ed. H. G. Reventlow. Göttingen: Vandenhoeck & Ruprecht, 1965, 106–9. ———. "Kleine Beiträge zur Siedlungsgeschichte der Stämme Asser und Juda." *HTR* 64 (1971) 291–313. **Mazar, B.** "The Cities of the Territory of Dan." *IEJ* 10 (1960) 65–77. **Mettinger, T. N. D.** *Solomonic State Officials.* K. D. Lund: C. W. K. Gleerup, 1971, 124–26. **Miller, J. M.** "Geba/Gibeah of Benjamin." *VT* 25 (1975) 145–66. **Noth, M.** "Der alttestamentliche Name der Siedlung von Chirbet Kumran." *ZDPV* 71 (1955) 111–23. (=*Aufsätze zur biblischen Landes- und Altertumskunde.* Vol. 1. Neukirchen-Vluyn: Neukirchener Verlag, 1971, 332–43.) ———. "Studien zu den historisch-geographischen Dokumenten des Josuabuches." *ZDPV* 58 (1935) 185–255. (=*Aufsätze* 1, 229–54.) **Schmitt, G.** *Du sollst keinen Frieden schliessen mit den Bewohnern des Landes.* BWANT 91. Stuttgart: W. Kohlhammer Verlag, 1970, 106–9. **Schunck, K. D.** *Benjamin.* BZAW 86. Berlin: Alfred Töpelmann, 1963, 149–69. **Strange, J.** "The Inheritance of Dan." *ST* 20 (1966) 120–39. **Talmon, S.** "The Town Lists of Simeon." *IEJ* 15 (1965) 235–41. **Vink, J. G.** "The Date and Origin of the Priestly Code in the Old Testament." *OTS* 15 (1969) 63–73.

Translation

18:1 *All the congregation of the sons of Israel assembled together at Shiloh. They pitched the tent of meeting, the land lying under control before them.* 2 *There remained among* [a] *the sons of Israel seven tribes who had not obtained their inheritance.* 3 *Joshua said to the sons of Israel, "How long will you all prove yourselves to be lazy cowards* [a] *in regard to entering* [b] *to possess the land which Yahweh the God of your fathers has given you all?* 4 *Provide for yourselves three men of each tribe so that I may send* [a] *them, so they may get about the business of exploring the land in order to write it up in view of their inheritances and so they may come to me.* 5 *They will apportion it into seven portions. Judah will remain on its territory to the south, while the house* [a] *of Joseph remains on their territory to the north.* 6 *But you will write up seven portions for the land and bring them to me here, so that I may cast for you all the lot here* [a] *before Yahweh our God.*

7 *"But there will be no portion for the Levites* [a] *in your midst, because the priesthood of Yahweh is his inheritance. Gad, Reuben, and half the tribe of Manasseh have taken their inheritance beyond the Jordan to the east, which Moses, the servant of Yahweh, gave to them."*

8 *The men rose and went. Joshua commanded the ones going to write up* [a] *the land, saying, "Go, explore in the land, and write it up. Then return to me. Here* [b] *I will throw the lot for you all before Yahweh in Shiloh.* 9 *Then the men* [a] *went*

and passed over the land. [b] *They wrote it up according to cities for seven portions in a book. Then they came* [c] *to Joshua to the camp of Shiloh.* [d] [10] *Joshua threw the lot for them in Shiloh before Yahweh,* [a] *and Joshua apportioned there the land to the sons of Israel in accordance with their portions.*

[11] *The lot came up for the tribe of the sons* [a] *of Benjamin according to their clans. The territory of their lot was between the sons of Judah and the sons of Joseph.*

[12] *The territory belonged to them on the north side from the Jordan. The border goes up to the shoulder north of Jericho. It goes up into the hill country to the west. Its limits are toward the wilderness of Beth-Aven.* [13] *The border goes up from there to Luz, to the shoulder of Luz to the south (that is Bethel). The border goes down Ataroth Adar* [a] *over the hill country which is south of lower Beth Horon.* [14] *The border bends and turns round on the west side southward from the mountain which is opposite of Beth Horon to the south. Its limits are at Kiriath Baal (that is Kiriath Jearim, the city of the sons of Judah). This is the western side.* [15] *The south side begins at the edge of Kiriath Jearim.* [a] *The border goes out westward* [b] *and goes out to the spring of the waters of Nephtoah.* [16] *The border goes down to the edge of the mountain which is opposite the vale of Ben Hinnom which is in the Valley* [a] *of the Rephaim to the north. It goes down the vale of Hinnom to the shoulder of the Jebusites to the south. It goes down ʿEn Rogel.* [17] *It turns northward* [a] *and goes out ʿEn Shemesh and goes out to Geliloth, which is opposite the ascent of Adummim. It goes down the stone of Bohan, the son of Reuben.* [18] *It crosses over to the shoulder of Mul* [a]-*haʿarabah to the north. It goes down to the ʿArabah.* [19] *The border passes over to the shoulder of Beth Hoglah to the north. Its limits are the border at the tongue of the Salt Sea northward to the southern end of the Jordan. This is the southern border.* [20] *The Jordan bounds it on the eastern side. This is the inheritance of the sons of Benjamin to its borders all around for their* [a] *clans.*

[21] *Cities belonged to the tribe* [a] *of the sons of Benjamin for their clans: Jericho, Beth Hoglah, ʿEmek Keziz;* [22] *Beth Haʿarabah, Zemarayim, Bethel;* [23] *Avvim, Parah, ʿOphrah;* [24] *Chephar-ha-ʿammonai, ʿOphni,* [a] *Gebaʿ, twelve cities and their villages.*

[25] *Gibʿon, Ramah, Beʾeroth;* [26] *Mizpeh,* [a] *Chephirah, Mozah;* [27] *Rekem, Yirpeʾel, Tarʾalah;* [28] *Zelaʿ-ha-ʾeleph,* [a] *and the Jebusite (that is Jerusalem), Gibeʿath-Kiriath, fourteen cities and their suburbs. This is the inheritance of the sons of Benjamin for their clans.*

[19:1] *The second lot came out for Simeon, for the tribe* [a] *of the sons of Simeon for their clans. Their inheritance was in the midst of the inheritance of the sons of Judah.* [2] *There belonged to them in their inheritance: Beersheba, Shebaʿ,* [a] *Moladah;* [3] *Hazar-Shuʿal, Balah, ʿAzem;* [4] *ʾEltolad, Bethul,* [a] *Hormah;* [5] *Ziklag, Beth-ham-markaboth, Hazar-Susah;* [a] [6] *Beth-Lebaʾoth, and Sharuhen,* [a] *thirteen cities and their suburbs.* [7] *ʿAyin Rimmon,* [a] *ʿEther, and ʿAshan, four cities and their suburbs,* [8] *and all the suburbs which* [a] *surrounded these cities unto Baʿalath-Beʾer, Raʾmath of the Negeb.* [9] *This is the inheritance of the tribe of the sons of Simeon for their clans. Out of the district of the sons* [a] *of Judah was the inheritance of the sons of Simeon. Because the allotment of the sons of Judah was too large for them, the sons of Simeon received an inheritance in the midst of their inheritance.*

[10] *The third lot came up for the sons of Zebulon for their clans. The border of their inheritance reached unto Sarid.* [a] [11] *Their border goes up to the west and Marʿalah. It reaches Dabbasheth* [a] *and reaches to the river valley which is opposite Yokneʿam.*

¹² It turns from Sarid eastward to the sunrise ᵃ upon the border of Kisloth-tabor. It goes out to Dabrath and goes up to Japhiaᶜ. ¹³ From there it passes over eastward to the sunrise to Gath-Hepher, ᶜEth-Kazin.ᵃ It goes out to Rimmon, being bent to Neᶜah.ᵇ ¹⁴ The border turns itselfᵃ about northward to Hannathon. Its limits are the Vale of YiphtahᵓEl. ¹⁵ And Kattath, Nahalal, Shimron, Yid'alah, and Bethlehem, twelve cities and their suburbs.ᵃ ¹⁶ This is the inheritance of the sons of Zebulon for their clans, these ᵃ cities and their suburbs.

¹⁷ For Issachar the fourth lot came out for the sons of Issachar and their clans.ᵃ ¹⁸ Their territory was: Jezreel, Chesuloth, Shunem; ²⁰ Hapharayim, Shiᵓon,ᵃ ᵓAnaharath; Rabbith, Kishyon, ᵓEbez; ²¹ Remeth,ᵃ ᶜEn-Gannim, ᶜEn-Haddah, Beth Pazzez. ²² The border reached Tabor, Shahazumah,ᵃ and Beth Shemesh. The limits of their territory were the Jordan, sixteen cities and their suburbs. ²³ This is the inheritance of the tribe of the sons of Issachar for their clans, the cities and their suburbs.

²⁴ The fifth lot went out to the tribe of the sons of ᵃ Asher for their clans. ²⁵ Their territory was: Helkath,ᵃ Hali, Beten, ᵓAchshaph; ²⁶ Alammelech, ᶜAmᶜad, and Mishᵓal. It reached Carmel to the west and Shihor-Libnath. ²⁷ It turned eastward to Beth Dagon and reaches Zebulon and the Vale of Yiphtah-ᵓEl to the north,ᵃ Beth ᶜEmek and Neᶜiel. It goes out to Cacul-Missemo'l; ²⁸ Ebron,ᵃ Rehob, Hammon, Kanah unto Sidon the Great. ²⁹ The border turns to Ramah and unto the city ᵃ of the Fortress of Tyre. The border turns to Hosah. Its limits are the sea, from the district of ᵓAchzib, ³⁰ ᶜUmah,ᵃ ᵓAphek, and Rehob, twenty-two cities and their suburbs. ³¹ This is the inheritance of the tribe of the sons of Asher for their clans, these ᵃ cities and their suburbs.

³² For the sons ᵃ of Naphtali, the sixth lot went out to the sons of Naphtali for their clans. ³³ Their territory was from Heleph, from ᵓElon (=the oak) in Zaᶜanannim, ᵓAdami-han-nekeb, and Yabneᵓel unto Lakkum. Its limit was the Jordan. ³⁴ The border turned westward to ᵓAznoth-Tabor. It went out from there to Hukok. It reaches Zebulon on the south and Asher on the west and Judah of the Jordan ᵃ on the east. ³⁵ The fortified cities are: Ziddim, Zer, Hammath, Rakkath, Chinnereth; ³⁶ ᵓAdamah,ᵃ Ramah, Hazor; ³⁷ Kedesh, ᵓEdreᶜi, ᶜEn-Hazor; ³⁸ Yirᵓon, Midgal-ᵓEl, Horem, Beth-ᶜAnath, and Beth Shemesh, nineteen cities and their suburbs.ᵃ ³⁹ This is the inheritance of the tribe of the sons of Naphtali for their clans, the cities and their villages.ᵃ

⁴⁰ For the tribe of the sons of ᵃ Dan for their clans came out the seventh lot. ⁴¹ The territory of their inheritance ᵃ was Zorᶜah, ᵓEshtaᵓol, the city of Shemesh; ⁴² Shaᶜalabbin,ᵃ ᵓAyyalon, Yithlah; ⁴³ Elon, Timnatha, ᶜEkron; ⁴⁴ ᵓEltekeh, Gibbethon, Baᶜalath; ⁴⁵ Yehud,ᵃ Bene-Berak, Gath-Rimmon; ⁴⁶ the waters of Yarkon, and Rakkon,ᵃ with the territory opposite Joppa. ⁴⁷ The territory of the sons of Dan ᵃ went away from them. The sons of Dan moved up and did battle with Leshem. They captured it and smote it with the sword. They dispossessed it and settled down in it. They called Leshem, "Dan," after the name of Dan, their father. ⁴⁸ This is the inheritance of the tribe of the sons of Dan for their clans, these cities and their suburbs.

⁴⁹ They finished distributing as an inheritance the land according to its boundaries. Then the sons of Israel gave an inheritance to Joshua, the son of Nun, in their midst. ⁵⁰ According to the word of Yahweh,ᵃ they gave him the city which he requested: Timnath-Serah in the hill country of Ephraim. He built up the city and settled down in it.

⁵¹ These are the inheritances which Eleazar, the priest, and Joshua, the son of

Nun, and the heads of the fathers of the tribes of Israel distributed as an inheritance by lot in Shiloh before Yahweh at the entrance of the tent of meeting. They finished apportioning the land.

Notes

18:2.a. The preposition appears to be missing in the Targumic and Greek traditions, but is necessary in the Heb. construction.

18:3.a. The Heb. Hithpael participle occurs only here and in Prov 18:9. The perfect appears in Prov 24:10. The basic meaning of the root רפה is "to become slack, quit working." It can also refer to the loss of courage (2 Sam 4:1; Isa. 13:7).

18:3.b. LXX does not reflect the idiomatic "to enter" of the Heb., but also omits "to you all" and simplifies "God of your fathers" to "our God." The latter appears in the Heb. of v 6 and may reflect the fluidity of tradition in using various traditional divine epithets (cf. Auld, VTSup 30 [1979] 12–13) (cf. *Comment*).

18:4.a. The Heb. text has an opening imperative followed by a series of imperfects joined by simple *waws*. This expresses purpose or result (cf. e.g. T. O. Lambdin, *Biblical Hebrew,* 119). LXX has gone its own way in reproducing this verse, omitting any reference to "I may send them," reading לפי "in view of, according to," as לפני "before, in the presence of *me,*" interpreting נחלתם, "their inheritances," as "just as it ought to be divided," and writing the final phrase of v 4 and the opening one of v 5 as if they were imperfect consecutives, describing past actions: "They came to him and he divided to them seven portions." This strengthens the role of Joshua, but stands in contradiction to v 6 in both MT and LXX.

18:5.a. LXX reads "sons," rather than "house," repeating its reading in 17:17.

18:6.a. LXX and Syr omit the second "here," which is redundant.

18:7.a. LXX adds "sons-of" before Levites. The sing. suffix on inheritance referring back to the plur. Levites has caused scribes in Hebrew, Greek, Aramaic, and Syriac traditions to use the plur. suffix.

18:8.a. LXX ignores כתב, "to write up," in this verse, interpreting it as "to explore, pass through the land," in both instances. Still, the LXX in the following verse and v 4 expresses the theme of writing.

18:8.b. LXX^A and Syr place "here" with the preceding sentence, followed by the JB, but rejected correctly by the *Text Project*.

18:9.a. LXX does not reflect specific subject for the sentence.

18:9.b. LXX adds "and they saw it," taking up the idiom of 2:1.

18:9.c. LXX reflects the Hiphil of בוא, "they brought," but has no object. The confusion arose because the MT reflects the command "to come to me" in v 4 as well as "to bring them to me" in v 6.

18:9.d. LXX omits reference to the camp at Shiloh here. Scribes could have added this to the textual tradition in light of v 1.

18:10.a. LXX omits the second half of v 10, beginning with "and Joshua . . ." This may represent a later scribal insertion underlining obedience to the command of 13:6–7.

18:11.a. LXX omits "sons" before Benjamin and Judah, while using it before Joseph. LXX also adds "the first" to "lot" in analogy to the remainder of chaps 18–19.

18:13.a. Ataroth Adar appears also in 16:5. The *Text Project*, later editions of the JB, and Soggin prefer to read "Ataroth-Orech" here, based on 16:2, seeing MT as assimilation to 16:5. LXX gives support for the change. Our verse certainly parallels 16:2 rather than 16:5, so that "Ataroth-Orech" may be original here.

18:15.a. LXX reads the older name Kiriath Baal here (cf. 15:60; 18:14) and may preserve the older reading.

18:15.b. LXX reads, "goes across to Gasin, to the spring. . . ." The opinion of the scholars is quite divided here, as a comparison of modern translations quickly reveals. Noth, Hertzberg, and NIV follow MT, the first two with questions. Holzinger and Steuernagel are content to point out that the text is corrupt. NEB simply omits the section. RSV follows 15:9 (MT) in reading here "from there to Ephron, to. . . ." Soggin and JB follow LXX in reading "Gazin." The *Text Project* interprets LXX in another manner (cf. Margolis) and reads "towards Iyyim/ the ruins and goes. . . ." Gray says the MT is absurd and goes his own way in reconstructing from the LXX, "and the border went out west of Moza to the spring. . . ," or "and the border went out to Moza and went out to the spring. . . ." Here we are dealing with a text which has been misunderstood at a very early stage and probably can never be properly restored.

18:16.a. LXX^B apparently reads, "The border goes down to the end; this is in front of the Vale of Sonnam, which is at the end of the Valley of Rephaim to the north." Margolis explains this as an inner-Greek corruption, but Hertzberg uses it to reconstruct "at the end of the Valley . . ." here. Syriac and Targumic evidence is often used (cf. Hertzberg, Noth) to restore "Ben" before the second Hinnom. Haplography with the preceding גי, "vale," is possible here, but total consistency is not necessary.

18:17.a. The opening "it turns northward" does not appear in LXX. We "remain in the dark" concerning its meaning (Noth), so that it may not be original. LXX also reads the more frequent "Beth Shemesh" for "ʿEn Shemesh."

18:18.a. LXX reads Beth-ha-ʿarabah with 15:6, 61; 18:22 over against MT which can be understood either as a proper name, "Mul-ha-ʿarabah," or as a preposition, "opposite, facing the ʿArabah." The *Text Project* is probably correct in retaining MT over against Soggin, RSV, JB, NIV, Noth, Hertzberg.

18:18.b. LXX^B reads, "They shall go down to the borders on the shoulder of the sea to the north. This is the limit of the border on the tongue of the sea of Salt on the north unto the end of the Jordan to the south." This omits the reference to the Arabah (18b) and to Beth Hoglah, for which is substituted a second reference to the sea. Margolis explains LXX^B as homoioteleuton and corruption, whereas *BHS* suggests that MT represents dittography, thus explaining the omission of "to the Arabah and it passes over." Both traditions thus represent corruption, the original text probably reading: "the border went down to the shoulder of Beth-Hoglah" (cf. Steuernagel).

18:20.a. LXX omits the pronominal suffix.

18:21.a. LXX omits "tribe."

18:24.a. LXX lacks an equivalent for ʿOphni, which may be explained as dittography for the preceding name.

18:26.a. The LXX has different order in 26–28.

18:28.a. Zelaʿ-ha-ʾeleph appears to represent one town in MT, since there is no conjunction separating them. The same can be said for Gibeʿath-Kiriath. The final note lists fourteen cities, understanding each of the compounds as two cities. LXX appears to have read the final two as Gibeath and Kiriath-Jearim (cf. Margolis, vv 14–15). LXX's summary (28) reads: "thirteen cities," apparently understanding Zelaʿ-ha-ʾeleph as one name. Jearim may have fallen from the text due to haplography.

19:1.a. LXX simplifies the text, omitting "for Simeon, for the tribe of," and "for their clans." This is a pattern followed by LXX in each of these formulaic introductions (cf. 18:11; 19:10, 17, 24, 32, 40), but the only point of consistency which even LXX has achieved is the use of the same verb and the use of the number of the lot in every case. Here again is evidence that the copying tradition was somewhat free in reproducing formulaic materials. MT is actually more consistent in including "sons of" and "for their clans" in every instance. Such consistency could be the work of the later copying tradition.

19:2.a. LXX is to be followed in reading "Shemaʿ," MT reflecting dittography of the preceding word (cf. 15:26). The word may not have appeared in the original list at all, since vv 1–6 include fourteen names, while the summary in 6b has only thirteen cities (cf. Steuernagel).

19:4.a. 15:30 witnesses Chesil here, whereas 1 Chr 4:30 has Bethuʾel.

19:5.a. The final two names are quite differently witnessed in 15:31 (cf. 1 Chr 4:31; Neh 11:28).

19:6.a. Again, 15:32 shows different readings, but our chapter preserves the preferred readings.

19:7.a. Written as one term in MT, ʿAyyin Rimmon appears to be considered two cities in the concluding summary, making four cities listed. LXX adds Talcha (LXX^B) or Tachan (Margolis, cf. 1 Chr 4:32), which may have fallen from MT tradition in confusion with עתר, which follows. The proper spelling of the latter may be עתך (cf. 1 Sam 30:30; Josh 15:42 LXX).

19:8.a. The syntax of v 8 is difficult in MT, but the omission of the opening "all the suburbs which" by LXX only makes it even more difficult. LXX also apparently understands בעל as a verb form (see Margolis).

19:9.a. In moves typical of the copying tradition, LXX omits "sons" before Judah, then adds "tribe of" before the first "sons of Simeon." The term חבל "district," appears only here and 17:5, 14 within the boundary lists. This verse also contains the primary terms נחלה and חלק for the inheritance or allotment.

19:10.a. LXX omits "sons" (cf. 19:1.a.). It reads the final place as Shadud. This is usually accepted following Alt ("Das Institute in Jahre 1925," *PJ* 22 [1926] 59–60), but *Text Project* retains MT. The same problem appears in v 12.

19:11.a. LXX understood the first verb form as a noun, Gola. Margolis sees the middle part of the verse as too corrupt for translation in the LXX, but the LXX[B] reads ἐπὶ βαιθαραβα, "to Beth'Araba," for MT "Dabbasheth and reaches." The final part of Dabbasheth represents the consonants for the Heb. word "shame," used sometimes to replace "unholy elements" (e.g. Ish-bosheth, 2 Sam 2:8 for Esh-baal, 1 Chr 8:33; 9:39). LXX appears to have a text which omits the "shameful element" entirely and combines the first part of the word with the following verb form.

Despite great scholarly comment, there is no reason to emend "to the west" (cf. Soggin).

19:12.a. The effect of familiar language is witnessed by LXX, which inserts Beth before Shemesh, forming the familiar Beth Shemesh (cf. 18:17) rather than the directional "rising of the sun."

19:13.a. LXX reads "'Irah-Kazin," thus "to the city of Kazin," which may be correct. Neither of the terms appears elsewhere in the OT (Cf. A. van Selms, "The Origin of the Name Tyropoean in Jerusalem," *ZAW* 91 [1979] 173).

19:13.b. Soggin calls MT here incomprehensible. Scholarship is almost unanimous in seeing the article on המתאר, "being bent" as belonging to the preceding Rimmon as a directive ה and then reading ותיר, the frequently used "it turns." This may well be correct, though it remains a conjecture without solid textual basis.

19:14.a. LXX does not witness the accusative pronoun which most commentators delete as incomprehensible (Soggin).

19:15.a. Judg 1:30 gives variants of Kattath and Nahalal, while LXX gives its consistent variant Sumoon for Shimron (cf. 11:1; 12:20). LXX[B] reads "Jericho" instead of Yid'alah, other Greek, Heb., Syr, and Vg texts reading Yir'elah. The summary statement is omitted here, 22b, 30b, 38b, perhaps because of the difficulty of finding the precise number of cities in each section (but cf. Steuernagel).

19:16.a. There is strong Heb., Greek, Aramaic, and Latin support for the addition of tribe before "sons of," while LXX omits "these," as redundant after v 15.

19:17.a. LXX omits the repetitive "for the sons of Issachar for their clans," but this is the normal formula, whereas the surprising feature here is the opening "for Issachar" (cf. 19:1.a.).

19:19.a. LXX adds a city, possibly to be restored as Be'eroth (*BHS*) or Deberoth (Margolis), since this makes the arithmetic of v 22 easier, but the LXX may simply have repeated הרבית from v 20 (Margolis), which appears in 21:28 and 1 Chr 6:57 as Dabrith.

19:21.a. Remeth appears in 21:29 as Yarmuth and in 1 Chr 6:58 as Ra'moth.

19:22.a. The various traditions have transmitted Shahazumah in different ways. LXX read the last part as a separate word, ימה, "westwards." LXX did not transmit 22b (cf. 19:15.a.).

19:24.a. LXX omits "to the tribe of the sons of" and "for their clans." (Cf. 19:1.a.).

19:25.a. LXX added "from" to turn the list of cities into the expected border description (but see Soggin).

19:27.a. LXX again makes the border description explicit, adding "and the border went to."

19:28.a. For 'Ebron, 21:30, 1 Chr 6:39, and many mss. here read 'Abdon, which may be original.

19:29.a. For עיר, city, LXX reads עין, spring. The final two words of the verse are usually corrected following Judg 1:31, LXX, and the annals of Sennacherib (*ANET*, 287) to "Mahlab and 'Achzib," or a similar vocalization (cf. *Text Project*).

19:30.a. LXX may have read 'akko, Acco, for Omah (cf. Judg 1:31). Again, LXX omits the final section (cf. 19:15.a.).

19:31.a. LXX omits "these" (cf. 19:16.a.).

19:32.a. LXX omits "the sons of" and "to the sons of Naphtali for their clans" (cf. 19:1.a.).

19:34.a. "Judah of the Jordan" is a strange and inexplicable name for an unknown locality (Soggin). LXX does not reflect "Judah." NEB takes it to mean lowlands, while the *Text Project* considers it "the corrupt form of a place name which at present cannot be reconstructed," suggesting the translation "Jehuda at/on the Jordan." Soggin may be more nearly correct when he suggests that Judah arose through dittography from Jordan (cf. Bright).

19:36.a. LXX apparently read the cities as Hazzorim, Hamath, Deketh, Chinereth, and 'Armay. Alt (*ZAW* 45 [1927] 72, n. 2) explained the opening words of the verse as dependent upon similar phrases in 28, 29, which he considered to be later additions there. He is followed by Noth, Hertzberg, Kaufmann, and *BHS*. There is little evidence for such a radical solution.

19:38.a. LXX omits the final summary (cf. 19:15.a.).

19:39.a. LXX omits the final "for their clans. . . ." This is the only instance where LXX does not attest this stereotyped formulaic ending.

19:40.a. LXX omits "the tribe of the sons of" and "for their clans" (cf. 19:7.a.).

19:41.a. LXX does not witness "inheritance," while the textual tradition also witnesses confusion between עִיר, עִין, and Beth Shemesh (*BHS*) as often.

19:42.a. Judg 1:35; 1 Kgs 4:39 and some Heb. mss provide the basis for reading Shaᶜalebim.

19:45.a. For Yehud, LXXᴮ offers Hazor, "a real variant" (Soggin), which leads the *Text Project* to include both names in the text (cf. O. Eissfeldt, "רָקוֹן Jos 19, 45 und ἡ Ἰουδαια I Makk 4, 15 = *el-jehudije*," *ZDPV* 54, [1931] 271–278 = *Kleine Schriften*, vol. 1 [Tübingen: J. C. B. Mohr, 1962] 274–79).

19:46.a. LXX reads "and on the west of Yarkon, the border opposite Joppa," thus reading יָמָה for מִי and not witnessing Rakkon, which appears nowhere else in the OT. This has led to a wide variety of translations (cf. *Text Project*, which ultimately retained MT). Rakkon may well represent dittography from Yarkon, the LXX representing the original text here.

19:47–48.a. The textual tradition in these verses is quite complex. LXX has introduced much of the language of Judg 1:34–36 but in a distinctive interpretation: "The sons of Dan did not drive out the Amorites who pressed upon them in the hill country. The Amorites did not allow them to come down into the valley. They forced them out of the territory of their allotment. And the sons of Judah (!) came and warred against Lachish (!), and captured it and smote it with the mouth of the sword. They settled down in it and called the name of it Lasenndan. The Amorites continued to live in Elom and in Salamin. And the hand of Ephraim (!) weighed down upon them, and they become tributaries to them." If nothing else, this shows clearly how the text continued to be open to interpretation and addition among the copyists. Auld ("Judges I and History," *VT* 25 [1975] 277–78) buttresses the argument of Holmes that LXX represents the original text here.

19:50.a. LXX has God for Yahweh (cf. Auld, VTSup 30 [1979] 12–13). LXX records Joshua's lands as Timnath-heres (cf. 24:30, Note).

Form/Structure/Setting

The two chapters clearly form a separate unit with the change of location (18:1) and the concern for the seven remaining tribes (v 2). The section actually concludes with 19:48, the final verses representing a conclusion to chaps. 13–19 as a whole, though 19:51 does point back to 18:1.

The introductory section gives the general setting (v 1), the task that remains (v 2), exhortation and plans for fulfilling the task (vv 3–7), recapitulation of the instructions (v 8), obedient carrying out of the instructions (vv 9–10). This is followed by the listing of the allotments to each of the remaining seven tribes:

1) Benjamin (11–28)
   a. Northern border (12–13) (cf. 16:1–3)
   b. Western border (14)
   c. Southern border (15–19) (cf. 15:6–11)
   d. Eastern border and summary (20)
   e. Lists of cities (21–28)

2) Simeon (19:1–9)
   a. City list (2–7) (cf. 1 Chr 4:28–33; Josh 15:26–32, 42)
   b. Border extension and summary (8)
   c. Explanation (9)
3) Zebulon (10–16)
   a. Southern border to the west (10b–11)
   b. Southern border to the east (12)
   c. Eastern border (13)
   d. Northern border (14)
   e. City list (15) (cf. Judg 1:30)
   f. Summary (16)
4) Issachar (17–23)
   a. City list (18–21) (cf. 21:28–29)
   b. Northern border (22a)
   c. City list summary (22b)
   d. Summary (23)
5) Asher (24–31)
   a. City list (25–26a)
   b. Western border (26b)
   c. Southern border (27a)
   d. Eastern border (27b)
   e. City list (28a) (cf. 21:30–31)
   f. Northern border (28b)
   g. Western border in the north (29)
   h. City list (30) (cf. Judg 1:31)
   i. Summary (31)
6) Naphtali (32–39)
   a. Southern border to the east (33)
   b. Southern border to the west (34abA)
   c. City list (35–38) (cf. 21:32; Judg 1:33)
   d. Summary (39)
7) Dan (40–48)
   a. City list (41–45) (cf. 15:10–11, 33, 45–46, 57; 21:23–25; Judg 1:35)
   b. Historical reflection (46–47) (cf. Judg 1:34–36).
   c. Summary (48).

The conclusion shows that Joshua, the faithful leader, was not neglected in accordance with divine command (49–50). The final verse then ties the introductions in 14:1 and 18:1 into a summary conclusion.

The section has generally been analyzed as the work of a redactor using the latest materials of the Pentateuch, as well as some older traditions.

Vink (*OTS* 15 [1969] 63–73) has tried to show that the tradition here is to be understood as sophisticated etiology developed by the Priestly writers in the later Persian period seeking to arbitrate between groups at Samaria and in Jerusalem by developing a program of resettlement for the rich Disaspora Jews. Shiloh is chosen because of its location halfway between Samaria and Jerusalem.

Schmitt (*Du sollst*, 106–9) has shown that the section does not fit the

"Priestly" understanding of the lot given out by Eleazer and the heads of the tribes along with Joshua. The appointment of a commission to divide the land represents the origin, not the conclusion or middle point of a tradition. Thus Schmitt concludes that a second land distribution tradition lies behind the present narrative. Gray, though holding to the theory of Priestly influence, also sees original tradition behind the section, namely in the role of Joshua as land arbitrator and in the role of a boundary commission to settle boundary disputes on the basis of written records. He has also noted the distinction that in 14–17, Judah and Joseph were shown taking the initiative to gain their allotment, while here "the formality of the transaction is surprising." Bächli (*ZDPV* 89 [1973] 1–14), too, has underlined the age of the commission tradition.

Certainly it is difficult to imagine the later editors totally rewriting the land distribution narratives in the distinct form and setting of 15–17 and 18–19 without a basis in the tradition itself. It is equally difficult to imagine that the *Ortsgebundenheit* of tradition history would be so totally contradicted by this one tradition, where the name Shiloh appears not once, but four times within ten verses. The most important argument against the originality of Shiloh here is the geographical one. How can the tradition speak of Shiloh originally and describe Judah as being south and Joseph being north (v 5)? This may be answered in either of two ways. First, it is precisely 5b which finds its context outside the present narrative and can be suspected of being an editorial link to 15–17. Second, Shiloh stands quite near the northern boundary point of Ephraim and perhaps even near the northeastern corner of her territory. Such a standpoint could represent a time in the tradition when the house of Joseph was limited to the territory of Manasseh. This would explain to some degree the extensive interest in Benjamin evident in both chaps 15–17 and in 18–19, Benjamin being precisely the point of contention between the house of Joseph and the house of Judah, with the basically unsettled Ephraimite hill country between.

Whatever the setting which produced the land distribution tradition here, the interesting thing is the nature of the tradition itself. First it deals with seven tribes, which seem to have little relationship at first glance. This is particularly true of Simeon, settled so far to the south. It is precisely Simeon which has no border descriptions and whose city list is most heavily dependent upon lists witnessed independently elsewhere. If anywhere, it is with Simeon that an original list has given place to later historical situation. But the earliest Simeonite tradition places Simeon precisely in the area of Manasseh, near Shechem, in the days when Levi remained a secular tribe (Gen 34:25–31). Here, again, may be a clue to the antiquity of the tradition. A further clue may rest in the territory allotted Dan, for here his allotment is in the far western edge of the country, which the tradition itself has then had to explain by the note that Dan lost this territory (19:47). Judg 1:35 notes that the house of Joseph eventually controlled this territory.

The other interesting element here is the use of the verb כתב, "to write," five times (4, 6, 8, 8, 9), climaxing with reference to the book (9). The story is not simply an editorial introduction to the following land allotment. It is a traditionally unique account centering not so much on the allotment as on the book to be written. Here is an ancient tradition, which appears to have its home in Shiloh and which accounts for the preservation of a book containing tribal allotments. It is precisely this tradition which can account for the preservation of premonarchical border lists for the tribes. Such tradition is tied to the person of Joshua, the one who ultimately uses the book not only to give out land allotments, but also to justify a second allotment for the house of Joseph (cf. 17:14–18) and settle other such tribal disputes.

Despite the present common framework, the lists themselves reveal different forms. Simeon and Dan have no borders at all, only city lists. Issachar is also reduced basically to a city list, except for the border fragment in 19:22a. Naphtali has only the extensive southern border followed by the city list. Zebulon, on the other hand, has extensive border descriptions with only a fragmentary city list (v 15). Only Benjamin and Asher have extensive border and city lists, both having more than one of the latter.

The mixture of form, and the repetition of form and content, show the historical nature of the material before us. The great debate about dating each of the components may never be solved. The point is clear: each of the components has its own history within the political life of Israel prior to being incorporated into the present text. The present text then has its own history of interpretation prior to reaching its final form, as the *Notes* have clearly demonstrated. This indicates that the material served Israel as a living political and religious instrument for many generations before it was finally put into its present form.

The final section (49–51) rests upon the tradition that Joshua lived in the city of Timnathserah in the hill country of Ephraim. Such a tradition would be preserved by his descendants through the generations before it entered into the written record.

Comment

18:1 The עדה "congregation," is almost unanimously taken as a linguistic clue to late Priestly editing (the most extensive study is that of L. Rost, *Die Vorstufen von Kirche und Synagogue im Alten Testament* [BWANT 76; Stuttgart: W. Kohlhammer, 1938]). Recent studies have rejected this consensus. J. Milgrom ("Priestly Terminology and Social Structure of Pre-monarchic Israel," JQR 69 [1978] 66–76) has shown that עדה "can only be conceived as an *ad hoc* emergency body called together by the tribal chieftains whenever a national trans-tribal issue arose. . . . Once the monarchy was firmly established, there was no further use for the עדה, and it disappears." The congregation may be composed of the entire nation with women and children, of adult males or of national representatives. It must be noted that Milgrom does not try to show that עדה was never used by later editors, only that its basic setting was the ancient Israelite institution.

The tent of meeting occurs only in this section (19:51) in the book of Joshua. Deut 31:14 is the only appearance in that book. Koch (*TDOT* 1, 118–30) represents the scholarly consensus in saying that the term cannot be demonstrated in use prior to the Priestly writer (124). There is, however, no sound evidence to deny the motif to the early tradition. The tent is established outside the camp by Moses and guarded by Joshua (Exod 33:7–11; cf. Num 11:16–29). The tent was the place where Moses brought Joshua to be commissioned by God (Deut 31:14). What is interesting is the close tie in each of the ancient narratives between Joshua and the tent, as well as the close tie between Shiloh and the tent (1 Sam 2:22; Ps 78:60).

The tent was "originally related to the prophetic aspect of Yahwism. . . . It constituted a spatial vehicle for oracular communication. The tent was an empty shelter which at times could be filled with the presence, but only the presence of a God in dialogue with man. . . . It sought to answer the human quest for the disclosure of the divine will on specific occasions" (S. Terrien, *The Elusive Presence* [San Francisco: Harper & Row, 1978] 175–76; cf. his fuller discussion pp. 175–86; M. Haran, *Temples* 260–75; B. Childs, *Exodus,* 590–93; W. H. Schmidt, *Glaube* 107–9; J. Lewis, "The Ark and the Tent," *Rev Exp* 74 [1977] 537–41.)

In our passage the use of the tent of meeting is explicitly theological. The tradition itself may have been used to explain how the tent came to be in Shiloh. In the present literary context of the Bible, the tent shows that Israel completely obeyed the will of God and that the division of the land to the seven tribes took place in the divine presence. It is also striking that the setting up of the symbol of access to Yahweh is done only when the land had rest from war. Here is the picture which the inspired writers want Israel to remember. They receive their land when they provide a place for Yahweh to speak to them. Such is done in an atmosphere of peace, not of war. Obedience to God does not bring renewed fighting and conquest. Obedience to God brings peace and life in the land he has given (cf. Judges, where the saviors bring peace to Israel until she rebels).

Verse 2 connects explicitly with the previous theme of the land given already to the tribes beyond Jordan and to Ephraim, Manasseh, and Judah, leaving seven tribes still landless. In context with v 1, this says that even though land had been given to many of the tribes, all Israel continued to gather together until the task was completed.

Verse 3 continues this thought by addressing all Israel, not just the seven tribes. The first words of the address are totally unexpected. They lament the laziness and lack of courage displayed by Israel. The position at the beginning of the context and the unexpected content show that this is central to the message of the section. Israel is told that possession of land depends on her activity and courage (cf. chap. 1). No one can blame Yahweh, if Israel does not have her land. Yahweh has given it to her. Here the traditional language must refer back to the conquest narratives of chaps. 1–12. Israel simply has not shown the necessary faith and courage to take the gift given by God. It is noteworthy that only here in the book of Joshua is reference made to the God of your fathers. This refers to the patriarchal tradition of Genesis and the appearance of God to each of the patriarchs (cf. A. Alt, "Der Gott der Väter," *KS* 1, 1–78, *Essays on Old Testament History and Religion* [Tr. R. A. Wilson; Oxford: Basil Blackwell, 1966] 1–77; F. M. Cross, Canaanite Myth and Hebrew Epic, 1–75; C. Westermann, *Genesis 12–50* [Darmstadt: Wissenschaftliche Buchgesellschaft, 1975] 94–123). Here it almost separates the current generation from claim to the title people of Yahweh. Yahweh is the God of their fathers, not the God of a disobedient people unwilling to take what he has offered them.

4 Lamentation and rebuke is not the final word. Even to a disobedient, reluctant people, God gives new marching orders. A commission is chosen to survey the land, write their findings in a book, and divide the land into seven parts. It is the work of this commission and its followers, who continually brought the lists up to date according to contemporary political conditions, which insured the preservation of the material. It is the commission who showed that Israel could not be condemned totally. These representatives of all the tribes of Israel listened to Joshua's instructions from God and set out immediately to accomplish their task.

Verse 5 ties back clearly to v 2 and through it to chaps. 15–17 to show why only seven portions need to be made despite the tradition of twelve tribes of Israel.

6 The task of Joshua is reduced to throwing the lot. This placed subsequent responsibility for the division of the land itself upon the tribal representatives. Joshua had only to give out what had already been divided. In turn, this showed that the distribution of the land had been agreed upon by the tribal representatives as being fair and equitable. God could not be criticized for making an unfair division of the land. God's part was simply to show which tribe received the parts already divided and designated by the commission. Now that the tribes have indicated their readiness to obey, the reference to God changes. He is no longer the "god of your fathers" (v 3). He is "our God."

7 The role of the Levites is again underlined (cf. 13:14, 33; 14:3–4). This continues to prepare the way for chap. 21, but also adds a piece of information. In 13:14 we saw that the sacrificial fires were the inheritance of Levi. In 13:33, it was God himself. Now it is the Priestly office. Within the canonical context, this ties back to Exod 29:9; 40:15; Num 25:13; and particularly Num 18:1–7. Joshua again shows himself obedient to the Mosaic tradition in setting apart the Levites for their role as priests.

Similarly, the writer is careful to include the tradition of the tribes east of the Jordan (chap. 13). Every care is taken to show that all the people of Yahweh, all twelve tribes, are cared for and involved.

9 The commission obeys their instructions. The interesting note is made that the land is written up by cities, thus connecting the tradition to the lists of cities which follow as well as the pure border descriptions. The ספר is a written document which did not necessarily take "book" form (Bächli, *ZDPV* 89 [1973] 11).

The camp appears for the first time in chaps. 13–19, though even here it does not appear in LXX. In chaps. 5–10, the Israelite camp is normally at Gilgal, so that many scholars wish to connect this passage with Gilgal also. However, the book of Joshua knows several other places where Israel's camp stood (1:11; 3:2; 8:13; 10:21), as had the Pentateuchal narrative with its wandering in the wilderness. Shiloh is here made the final camp for Israel, again an indication of the concern to legitimize the worship of Shiloh.

10 As the theme of the tent of meeting has already indicated, all the action took place before Yahweh. Here Joshua and Israel showed their obedience to God. They divided the land according to his plans and will, not human pride and selfishness.

11 In accord with the plan of chaps. 15–17, Benjamin is placed between Judah and Joseph. This and the placing of Benjamin first in the list shows the important role played by Benjamin in the tradition. On genealogical grounds (e.g. Gen 35:16–20, 49:1–27), Benjamin would be last.

18:12–19:48 The extended lists of different form, extent, and probably date are included here to lay claim to all of Palestine for the people of Yahweh. We will not try to settle the extended debate over the original setting, extent, and date of each of the component parts. The significant point to make in a commentary is this: Israel recognized that her God had provided all the land she needed for each of her tribes. This is significant in view of later stories of tribal dispute and warfare (Josh 22; Judg 17–21). God created the conditions for peace in Israel. Her own leaders had outlined the conditions and judged them to be fair. God through the lot had shown his approval. Still, parts of Israel were never satisfied.

18:11–28 It is noteworthy that both Bethel and Jerusalem, the major cult sites of Israel and Judah, respectively, are attributed to Benjamin (cf. vv 13, 16, 22, 28).

19:1 The tribe of Simeon apparently had disaster early in its history (Gen 49:7; the notable absence in Deut 33; Judg 5). Its territory thus is simply part of that of Judah. This is explained by the extraordinary statement that Judah's territory was too large for her (v 9). Such a statement stands in stark contrast to the narrative of Joseph in 17:14–18.

10 Judg 1:30–33 notes cities which Zebulon, Asher, and Naphtali could not conquer. These notices are not referred to here. Here we see how the biblical writer used his information for his own purposes. The task here is to underline the obedience of the tribes in carrying out God's directions and to emphasize the greatness of God's gift to his people. Judges then steps back to show how Israel failed to obey totally and thus had to suffer repeatedly through her history.

47–48 This style of working is shown clearly in vv 47–48. Here information is taken up from Judg 1, but the accent is moved. In Judges the accent is on the power of the Amorites to press Dan back, thus punishing Dan. Here the emphasis is on the subsequent victory of Dan (cf. Judg 18), given a setting with the simple note that their territory went away from them. Our passage thus seeks to show that even under the conditions of lost property, God was able to give his people an inheritance in the land. Even when a tribe lost its original lot, God replaced it. This was of particular importance to the readers of the Deuteronomistic history in exile. They had lost all their inheritance. They had no more lot.

49 The gift of land ends on a special note. The people of Israel take the initiative away from Joshua. They give him land. This is written, however, neither to glorify the unselfishness of Israel, nor the greatness of Joshua. Rather, it is another example that Israel did what God commanded (v 50). It does imply that God blessed the individual leader as well as the nation for faithful obedience. Here Joshua's relationship to a tribe is not even stated. This occurs only in 1 Chr 7:20–29.

⁵¹ The concluding summary ties back to 14:1 (cf. 17:4) to show that the total task of distributing the land west of the Jordan was done precisely as Moses had outlined it. This verse pictures the whole process from 14:1 on as occurring in Shiloh (cf. 14:6). The important note, introduced in v 49 and taken up again here, is that Israel completed her task.

Explanation

Again long lists of names may well bar us from digging into the theological understanding which this section seeks to give us. Scholarship has virtually exhausted itself seeking to recover the historical setting of the various lists. It has tended to ignore the theological structure and understanding which the biblical writer has created.

First, he has set seven lazy tribes who lack courage over against the two most powerful tribes, whose representatives demanded their territory and more—immediately. In so doing he has seemed to promise success to the powerful ones in their fight against the strong Canaanites (17:18). Over against this he has set the example of the tribe of Dan, who lost their territory to the Canaanites, yet were able to fight and gain another territory. Neither group is ultimately cursed. Rather, both groups represent the needs of the people of God. Over against a strong enemy, the powerless people of God are promised victory. Even after defeat and loss of land, the way is laid out for new hope, new land, new victory. We see Israel on its land and wanting more just as Israel is pushed off its land and needing desperately a new foothold—in either case Israel can look to past example and find that God is able to provide the needs of the people.

The chapters make one thing perfectly clear. Success is conditioned on obedience, on faithfulness to the word of God. The Israel who is not willing to march forward at God's command finds talk of the God of your fathers. Only the Israel which shows it is ready for immediate obedience can hear of "our God."

Certain perspectives on such obedience are given. First, such obedience involves action at the place where God has shown himself ready to meet his people. Israel must come to the tent of meeting and find the divine will. There she must find the lots which God has given her.

But the first divine word is not that of the lot for the tribes. Rather, the first divine word is one of warning and direction. Israel cannot simply receive the gifts directly from the hand of God. She must do her part. Having done her part and received the gift, she can blame neither her leader nor her God, for Israel's representatives have marked off the equal parts. Israel's representatives have accepted as fair the division of the land. The division has been recorded as a guide to all future generations. No more can tribes fight over territory. They simply come to the divine representative and seek the answer in the book. Contemporary wishes and egotistical demands do not decide the case. God has already provided for guidelines to be set out. He has placed his decision in a book. On the basis of the book, the people can know what the divine will is.

Having received the land, Israel is called to a life in the land. The opening verse characterizes the life. It is a life of peace in a land under control. This is God's desire and God's provision. When Israel loses control of her land, she cannot blame God. She must look back to the tradition which tells her how she received the land. There she will see that the land was given to an obedient people. Then she must measure her own life against the standard set up in the beginning.

The gift of the land brought blessings not only to the nation as a whole and to the individual tribes. It also brought blessing to the faithful leader. God commanded Israel to reward the individual for his faithfulness. Thus the Deuteronomic understanding of blessing and curse is expressed not only on the corporate, but also on the individual level. This, too, stands as a source of encouragement to Israel through the years as many of her people become dispersed from the main body of the people of God.

III. Life in the Land   (*Joshua 20–24*)

Chapters 1–12 and 13–19 lend themselves naturally to history of research study. Each section deals basically with one type of material and can be handled easily under one theme. Chapters 1–12 concern the conquest. Chapters 13–19 deal with land allotment and tribal territories. When we turn to Joshua 20–24, we encounter a new phenomenon. Chapter 19 has given a definite closing formula to the section begun in chapter 13. The allotment of the land has been finished. Chapter 20, however, does not begin with a theological introduction, such as we found in chapter 1 and again in chapter 13. Nor is the theme of chapter 20 the same as that of the following chapters, if we define theme strictly by contents. Each of the five chapters has its own type of contents and its own history of tradition. Thus any history of research must deal with each chapter individually rather than trying to work with the section as a whole.

At this point, we do need to justify separating the book at this place rather than at chapter 21, where the division is often made. The division at chapter 21 rests on the concluding summary in vv 43–45. This is defensible as being true to the contents of the book. Such a separation, however, must deal with chapters 20 and 21 as appendices to the major section of land distribution. Closer examination appears to reveal a different criteria for separation. The first 19 chapters have constantly laid out before Israel the promise of the land and the demand of Torah for life in the land. The final five chapters describe the beginnings of life in the land and show Israel's first steps of obedience as well as their first conflicts. These chapters become examples of life in the land for Israel forever and aye. This way of life separates Israel from her neighbors and marks the path of Israel for the future. Such a life makes provisions for the underprivileged of the community, those suspected of murder, the gravest suspicion under which a person could live, and the landless Levites, open to the mercy of the community if special provisions are not made. Only when Israel begins to establish such life in the land can she hear the word that the promise has been fulfilled.

The Israel of the fulfilled promise has not heard the final word. She must realize that she is the Israel of internal disputes and find ways to settle those disputes. Such pointers to dispute settlement are given in the final three chapters. Here Israel finds her practical everyday identity. Israel is the people of the central sanctuary, settling disputes through priestly mediation, recognizing the unity of east and west, and pledging themselves to live under the covenant which God has given them through his faithful leader. Israel is thus ready for life in the land without their leader. They have God's covenant.

Setting Up Sanctuaries   (20:1–9)

Bibliography

Auld, A. G. "Cities of Refuge in Israelite Tradition." *JSOT* 10 (1978) 26–40. **David, M.** "Die Bestimmungen über die Asylstädte in Josua XX. Ein Beitrag zur Geschichte des biblischen Asylrechts." *OTS* 9 (1951) 30–48. **Delekat, L.** *Asylie und Schutzorakel am Zionheiligtum.* Leiden: E. J. Brill, 1967, 290–320. **Dinur, B.** "The Religious Character of the Cities of Refuge and the Ceremonies of Admission into Them." (Hebrew) *Eretz Israel* 3 (1954) 135–46. **Greenberg, M.** "The Biblical Conception of Asylum." *JBL* 78 (1959) 125–32. ———. "City of Refuge." *IDB* 1 (1962) 638–39. **Löhr, M.** *Das Asylwesen im Alten Testament.* Halle: Max Niemeyer Verlag, 1930. **Loewenstamm, S. E.** "Law." *The World History of the Jewish People.* First Series, Vol. 3: Judges, ed. B. Mazar. Jerusalem: Masada Press, 1971, 258–62. **Nicolsky, N. M.** "Das Asylrecht in Israel." *ZAW* 48 (1930) 146–75. **van Oyen, H.** *Ethik des Alten Testaments.* Gütersloh: Gütersloher Verlagshaus Gerd Mohn, 1967, 121. **Phillips, A.** *Ancient Israel's Criminal Law.* Oxford: Basil Blackwell, 1970, 99–109. **Seitz, G.** *Redaktionsgeschichtliche Studien zum Deuteronomium.* BWANT 93. Stuttgart: W. Kohlhammer Verlag, 1971, 111–13. **Weinfeld, M.** *Deuteronomy and the Deuteronomic School.* Oxford: Clarendon Press, 1972, 236–39.

Translation

[1,2] *Yahweh spoke to Joshua, "Speak to the sons of Israel, 'Set up for yourselves the cities of refuge which I spoke about to you all by the hand of Moses,* [3] *to which the killer may flee, who has struck down a person inadvertently without knowing.[a] They[b] will become for you all for refuge[c] from the avenger of blood.*

[4] *" 'He may flee to one of these cities. He shall stand at the entrance of the gate of the city and shall speak in the ears of the elders of that city about his case. They shall take him into the city unto themselves and give him a place. He shall live there with them.* [5] *But if the avenger of blood should pursue after him, they shall not deliver the killer into his hand, since without knowledge he smote his neighbor, not having hated him in the past.* [6] *He shall dwell in that city until he can stand before the assembly for judgment, until the death of the one who will be high priest in those days. Then the killer will return and enter his own city and his own house, to the city from which he fled.' "*

[7] *Then they sanctified[a] Kadesh in Galilee in the hill country of Naphtali, and Shechem in the hill country of Ephraim, and Kiriath ʾArbaʿ (that is Hebron) in the hill country of Judah.* [8] *Beyond the Jordan, east of Jericho,[a] they set up Bezer in the wilderness in the plain of the tribe of Reuben, and Ramoth in Gilead of the tribe of Gad and Tolan in Bashan from the tribe of Manasseh.* [9] *These were the cities appointed for all[a] the sons of Israel and for the sojourner who sojourns in their midst to flee there—anyone smiting a person inadvertently—so that he may not die by the hand of the avenger of blood until he has stood before the assembly.[b]*

Notes

3.a. LXX has no equivalent for "without knowing," a phase apparently taken from Deut 19:4, where it is translated in LXX by the same term used here and normally for שְׁגָגָה, "inadvertently." The parallel section in Num 35:11 does not contain "without knowing."

3.b. LXX gives an explicit subject "the cities," as in Num 35:12.

3.c. LXX has inserted Num 35:12b at this point: "and the killer shall not die (from the avenger of blood-Josh 20:3, not Num 35:12) until he should stand before the assembly in judgment." The "until" clause appears in MT in 20:6.

All the remainder of vv 4–6 is not transmitted by LXX^B. LXX^A corresponds to MT with minor variants. Holmes (71) can simply note that it is generally admitted that LXX gives the more original text." Soggin sees the addition as an "interpretative interpolation." Parts of vv 4–6 can be explained as language taken up from the parallel passages in Num 35; Deut 4:41–43; 19:1–13:

4a = Deut 4:42b; 19:11b; cf. 19:5b.
5aA//19:6aα
5aB//19:12 (?)
5b//19:4b
6//Num 35:28.

Even so, 4aβ,b, the unique language of 5aB and 6 are not adequately explained. The most extensive attempt appears to be that of Holzinger.

7.a. LXX διέστειλεν, "he separated," appears only here for Heb קדשׁ, "sanctify." It translates קרה, Hiphil, "cause to happen, direct, select," in Num 35:11. Hollenberg ("Die deuteronomischen Bestandtheile des Buches Josua," *Theologische Studien und Kritiken* 1 [1874] 462–506) suggested that בקרה was the proper reading here. Even Holmes rejected this, but Auld has taken it up again. LXX is again here assimilating the text to Num 35.

8.a. Jericho is difficult syntactically here and is omitted by the LXX. It may reflect scribal use of 13:32.

9.a. LXX does not translate "all," which may be the emphasis of later tradition.

9.b. LXX adds "in judgment" in conformity with v 6 (= LXX v 3) and Num 35:12.

Form/Structure/Setting

The opening divine speech in v 1 marks the beginning of a new section. The formulaic summary of v 9 and the switch of characters and subject matter in 21:1 show that 20:9 ends the section.

The unit is divided into two parts: divine command (1–6) and human obedience (7–8) with the closing summary (v 9).

The divine command has a very complex structure:

v 1–2a: Divine citation formula;
2b: Apodictic command tied to previous command;
3: Purpose for command;
4: Procedure explained;
5: Casuistic explanation from different perspective;
6: Procedure completed.

Human obedience is set forth in two parallel parts: setting up cities west (7) and east (8) of the Jordan.

The summary of v 9 then introduces new vocabulary and carries the procedure only to the court of judgment, not to the return from the city of refuge (contrast v 6).

The tradition behind the city of refuge can be studied only through comparison of the parallel accounts in Exod 21:12–14; Num 35; Deut 4 and 19, along with similar practices in Israel's environment.

The Book of the Covenant (Exod 20:22–23:33) opens a section on cases concerning injury to persons (21:12–36) with the general regulation: "Whoever smites a man resulting in death shall die." This is immediately modified for the case when one did not lie in wait but God was the one who let the victim fall into his hand. Then God will set up a place where he can flee. This in turn is modified to say that if the man was boiling mad (or arrogant) with his neighbor so as to murder him with scheming and cunning, he is to be taken away from God's altar to die. Exodus thus presupposes either only one or an indefinite number of places where the man who only did what God permitted to happen, not being himself involved emotionally or intellectually, can flee. This place appears to be connected with the sanctuary and its altar by the further modification.

Numbers 35 is concerned to set up both cities for the Levites (cf. Josh 21) and places of refuge, the latter being part of the former (v 6). The actual command to set aside cities of refuge begins only in v 9. Here the number six (cf. v 6) appears only in v 13, whereas vv 9–11 may be interpreted as seeing an indefinite number of cities set up west of the Jordan. The cities are called "cities of refuge" (מקלט). The killer who smites a person inadvertently (בשגגה) can flee there from before the avenger (גאל) and is not to die before he stands before the assembly (עדה) for judgment. The note is then made that three of the cities shall be beyond the Jordan and three in the land of Canaan (v 14). The cities are not confined to Israelites but also apply to the sojourner (גר) and alien (תושב). A long list of cases is given for which the city of refuge is not open, so that the avenger of blood can kill the murderer (vv 16–21). Included here are mention of hatred and lying in wait (v 20). A list of applicable cases follows (vv 22–23) including not lying in wait and not having been an enemy or having sought his evil (22–23). The court procedure is then spelled out (24–28). The assembly (עדת) shall judge *between* the killer and the avenger of blood, rescuing the killer from the avenger of blood and returning him to the city of refuge to which he fled. This seems to imply that the jurisdiction lies not with the assembly in the city of refuge but with the assembly in the killer's home town or in the town where the crime was committed. This assembly returns the killer to the city of refuge. There the killer remains "until the death of the high priest who anointed him with holy oil" (v 25). The killer is not permitted to leave the territory of the city of refuge. Should he do so, the avenger of blood may kill him without guilt. When the priest dies, the killer may return to his *land* and his *possessions*. The following legislation then notes that ransom may not be paid to allow the killer to return to the land until the death of the priest. The entire law is related to the belief that blood pollutes the land, which can only be redeemed by the blood of one who shed blood.

Deuteronomy 4:41–4 then notes that Moses divided out three cities beyond the Jordan for the killer who killed his neighbor without knowledge (בבלי דעת), not hating him in the past. The three cities are then named: Bezer in the wilderness of the plain of the Reubenites, Ramoth in Gilead of the Gaddites, and Golan in Bashan of the Manassehites.

Deuteronomy 19 commands Israel to divide out three cities in the land (that is, west of Jordan) and establish the way. The territory is to be divided into thirds for *every* killer to flee there. The killer is defined as the one "who smote his neighbor without knowledge (בבלי דעת) not hating him in the past" (v 4). A specific example is given of one who may "flee to one of these cities and live, lest the avenger of blood should pursue after the killer" (vv 5–6). A possibility is then mentioned in case Yahweh should multiply their land. Then they may add three more cities, presumably within the land of Canaan. This is connected with the commandment not to shed innocent blood in the midst of the land so that blood (guilt) will not be upon the people. Attention turns to the case of the man not eligible for refuge because he hates his neighbor and sets up ambush against him, smiting him so that he dies. If this man flees to one of these cities, the elders of his city shall take him and give him to the avenger of blood, and he shall die. This burns out the innocent blood from Israel and is good for Israel.

A comparison of the passages can be charted in the following manner:

	Exod 21	Num 35	Deut 4	Deut 19	Josh 20
1. No. of cities	1 or indefinite	v. 6—6	3 in east	v. 2—3 west	2—indef
		9—indef.		7—3 west	7—3 west
					8—3 east
		13—6		8,9—3 + 3 (all west?)	9—indef
2. Verb used	Set up	Give—6,13,14	divide	divide—2,7 add—9	Give—2,8 Sanctify —7
		Select—11			
3. Group eligible	Israel	Israel—10 Sojourner—15 Alien 15	East Jordan	West (?)	Israel—1 Sojourner—9
4. Conditions of eligibility					
a. Not lie in wait	13	22	—	—	—
b. Inadvertent	—	12,15	—		3,9
c. Did not know	—	—	42	4	3,5
d. Not hate			42	4,6	5
5. Name of cities	—	—	Eastern		Six
6. Process	—	12, 24–28, 32–33	—	12 (guilty)	4—6,9
a. Entrance		Escape avenger		Escape Avenger	Escape avenger
b. Trial		Killer & Avenger before עדה of home town		—	1) Killer before elders at gate 2) before עדה
c. Verdict					
Guilty		Avenger kill		Elders give to avenger	—
Innocent		עדה return to city of refuge		—	Elders accept into city of refuge
d. Length of sentence		Till death of priest		—	Till death of priest
e. Condition of sentence		Not leave city of refuge or be killed by avenger. Cannot be ransomed		—	
f. Release		To his own land		—	To his town
7. Nature of Refuge	Altar	Levitical City	—	City	City gate
8. Presupposition	—	Blood guilt on land—32	—	Blood guilt on land—10, 13	—

Interestingly, all accounts share the expression "to flee there," and all but the brief Exodus account share the same terms for Avenger of Blood, killer, and neighbor. The major verbal distinction is the technical term "City of refuge" shared only by Num 35 and Josh 20. Josh 20:9 also introduces a unique term, "cities of appointment" (?).

In light of the similarities and differences in the accounts, scholars have suggested various theories concerning the age and growth of the tradition of the cities of refuge.

Nicolsky (*ZAW* 48 [1930] 146–75) sees Josh 20 as a literary composition totally dependent upon Num 35 and Deut 19. He sees the original nomadic regulations as a burden for the cult, since it had to bear the cost of providing for the refugee. Acceptance of the refugee was understood as bringing premature, atoning death to the high priest of the sanctuary. Thus, originally, lots would have been cast periodically to determine which sanctuary would have had to serve as place of refuge. The original custom would have been available to others than simply killers, but the particular law was preserved because it served the later lawgivers' purpose of combating the anarchical elements of tribal law. The Deuteronomists sought to centralize worship and secularize the law, so that the altar is replaced with the city and the priestly responsibility with that of the elders. The priestly writer's compilation is a postexilic projection of a custom no longer practiced but retaining a number of earlier customs. He sees as uniquely Israelite the limitation to unintentional murder and the fact that the deity in no way protects, even for a limited time, a recognized lawbreaker, punishing even the inadvertent murderer.

Löhr (*Asylwesen*) shows numerous examples in international treaties dealing with political asylum, while claiming that the distinction between intentional and unintentional murder goes back into primitive tribes. He, too, sees Josh 20 as a compilation, basically dependent upon Num 35. Only 1–3, 7–8, even then, belong to the original passage. He claims that blood revenge is not presupposed in Exod 21, because the "dying you shall surely die" formula presupposes official procedures of justice, not blood revenge. He emphasized that the stay in the city of refuge is a type of atonement for the refugee and suggests that the custom rests ultimately on Canaanite customs taken over by Israel.

Moshe Greenberg (*JBL* 78 [1959] 125–32; *IDB* 1, 638–39) emphasizes the theological, religious nature of the materials, which cannot be accounted for on humanitarian or political grounds. He underlines the fact that every killer is guilty to some degree (cf. Gen 9:6; Exod 21:28ff). The development in the law is an advance over prior customs of regarding homicide as a purely private matter which the families settle. The law develops from a temporary asylum at the altar to an indefinite asylum in the city. Here expiation takes place through the death of the priest. He sees the six cities named as being under Israelite control only during the united monarchy, so that this is the time when the program of regulating blood revenge was conceived, though the conception of asylum apart from the particular cities is doubtless older, functioning with a multiplicity of priesthood and going back to the earliest age of Israel. Deuteronomy turns it into a purely humanitarian institution.

M. David (*OTS* 9 [1951] 30–48) sees Josh 20 as a post-exilic compilation using Num 35 which has later been changed in light of Deut 19. This would use language that had no relevance for the contemporary situation, since free cities no longer existed. The same goes for the use of the term עדת, which is made to decide on matters which are too narrow for the time and interests of the national assembly. This raises for David the question of the entire idea of cities of refuge as opposed to asylum in the temple is not an idea which never had any practical significance.

Delekat (*Zionheiligtum*, 290–320) goes to another extreme. He assumes that the editing inserting Josh 20:4–6 must have been practiced sometime in the postexilic period. The only time he can find is that of John Hyrcanus when Hebron was regained. Thus he sees in Joshua a correspondence to the practice of the Hellenistic cities. The practice of cities of refuge is, of course, much older, he supposes, reaching back to a time when the cities were autonomous. This would be the time of the judges. He sees elders as the leading officers of the עדת, so that real differences do not exist between Deuteronomy and Numbers. Delekat argues strongly that atonement is not the point at issue, since the natural death of a man cannot be seen as atonement. Only the long separation from home could be seen as atoning.

Starting from the mention of anointing in Num 35:25, Delekat argues that this is involved with legal practices of adoption rites in the Ancient Near East, whereby one is anointed and thus freed from his adoption. The refugee then has been adopted by the high priest. This is parallel to the near eastern *Paromone* relationship in which a slave is joined to a master for the lifetime of the master. At the death of the master, i.e., the high priest, the refugee is free to go home. This is practically and politically advantageous for the new high priest.

Delekat also argues that the city of refuge was limited to a certain area, at first the temple region, within a city. The secularization of Deuteronomy could seek to make this another special section of the city. Delekat cannot imagine that it would be easy to find a section where people would welcome the refugees.

Loewenstamm ("Law," 258–62), sees the law of refuge as belonging to the first beginnings of Israel, though its functioning was improved during the United Kingdom. He seeks to combine elements of all the passages to reconstruct the legal institution as a whole.

Recently, Auld (*JSOT* 10 [1978] 26–40) has argued that the lists of cities of refuge are developed from Josh 21. Joshua 20 takes over a phrase of uncertain meaning, ערי מקלט from 1 Chr 6:40–45, takes city names from the top of the lists of Levitical cities in Josh 21, and interprets them in light of Deut 19.

From all of this, we can conclude that the institution of refuge is extremely old and shared by Israel with many peoples in all parts of the world. It is a necessity for a community in which murder was not regulated by political courts but by local families. The institution of asylum or refuge placed a needed limitation on the zeal of enraged families seeking to carry out blood revenge. Such institutions originate in the tribe and thus find their center in a local place, a sacred place. The biblical laws show long reflection and frequent adjustment to new political and sociological situations. The case easiest to note is the law of release. Numbers 35 sends the man back to his own *land*. This apparently stems from a society in which farming and agriculture were still predominant. Joshua 20 has changed this to his own *town*, where now an urban society is presupposed. Again the change from the interest in the altar (Exod 21) to the city gate (Josh 20) reflects a similar situation.

The institution of city of refuge thus has served Israel for many centuries, gradually being adjusted to new conditions. Each of the passages dealing with the institution has also been influenced by the context into which it has been placed. For Josh 20, this is clear. The context is that of fulfillment of the earlier Mosaic commands. This has brought the language of both Num 35 and Deut 19 into the passage in order to show that every element of the command has been fulfilled. Still, Josh 20 appears to maintain some tradition which other laws do not reflect, namely the tradition of the conditions of entrance once the place of refuge has become an established city and the place of the trial the city gate. Joshua 20 thus adapts the ancient institution to the urban setting controlled by the elders of the city. It also introduces the names of the three western towns. It is interesting here, that the extra towns presupposed possible by Deut 19:9 are not mentioned. The names of the towns reflect holy places long sacred to Israel. This shows that even with the turning over of many of the duties to the town elders, the towns themselves remained those with ancient sacral associations. It is difficult to accept here the literary sleight of hand of Auld in transforming the city list traditions into derivations from the literature of Josh 21. Rather, the whole development of the tradition shows the growth of the city of refuge institution from that of local holy places among the tribal elements to ancient sanctuaries in the land, to established cities of refuge now under the control of the elders of the land. What is not clarified is the relationships of the elders to the עדת. Delekat may be correct here in seeing the elders as leading officers of the עדת.

Comment

[1-2] The important element for the book of Joshua is the fulfillment of the command to Moses. Here we see that the dominant theological hand of the book is still at work.

[3] Unintentional sin is the subject matter of Lev 4 (cf. Num 15:27–29), where it is clear that such sin is still regarded as bringing guilt upon the person committing it. Such sin has to be dealt with ritually. This sets the background for understanding the city of refuge. It is not only a place of safety but also a place where the sinner must pay the consequences of his sin. It is at the same time refuge and prison.

The avenger of blood is related to the larger question of the גאל in Israel. This is tied to the responsibility of the family for their own. The list of persons who may function as גאל is given in Lev 25:48–49. He has the legal responsibility to protect the rights of his endangered relative. The most familiar examples of the גאל in operation appear in Ruth 3–4 and in Jer 32:6–7. Blood revenge is illustrated well by the story of 2 Sam 14:1–11. All of this rests in ancient family law in a society which has not developed public prosecution and legislation. Such ancient customs, however, were prolonged for a long time in altered form within the urbanized society.

Phillips (Criminal Law, 99–109) argues that the "go'el of blood" was not connected with ancient tribal customs of vengeance, but was a representative appointed by the elders. His theory is a bit contrived and appears to ignore the sociological history behind the city of refuge.

⁴ The elders of the city represent an important political and legal institution in the Ancient Near East. The functionings of such a body are illustrated in Ruth 4:1–12; 1 Sam 11:3; 16:4. The roots of such an institution are not in city life, but in nomadic tribal life, so that even after Israel settles into the land, her tribes retain elders (Judg 11:4–11). They also play a role in some of Israel's early narratives (Exod 17:5–6; Num 11:14–17; 16:25). They play a particular role in the Deuteronomic law (5:23; 19:12; 21:1–9, 18–21; 22:13–21; 25:5–10; 27:1; 29:9 [=Eng. 10]; 31:9, 28). In Joshua they play only a minor role, appearing in our passage; 7:6; 8:10, 33; 23:2; 24:1, 31.

⁵ One of the first refinements in the law of blood revenge is the attempt to define criteria for determining whether the murder is inadvertent or not. One such criteria is previous relationships between the parties. Has one hated the other or not?

⁶ Here the עדה appears to reflect the ancient usage (cf. 18:1). The assembly of the local town sat in judgment on the one who applied for refuge. Certainly, when the עדה became "all Israel," such an institution could not function in regard to every murder case.

The death of the high priest was taken by early rabbinic authorities to refer to atonement. This is taken to its logical end in the discussion of Nicolsky, but the opinion of Delekat, deriving this from adoption and slave regulations, is probably closer to the original development. The refugee became attached to the temple cult as a worker for the high priest and gained freedom upon the death of the priest, allowing the new priest to assemble his own staff, while providing support for the priesthood among the newly freed men as they returned home.

⁷ The use of the cultic term "to sanctify" has usually caused comment and reason for textual change. Perhaps this too reflects the ancient usage, when the cities were regarded as part of the cult.

⁹ The conclusion is in the form of the conclusions of 13–19 and shows that the same literary hand is still at work. For him the cities of refuge represent an "all Israel" institution, taking in even the גרים, the strangers who live outside their own kinship circles and thus do not have the status or privileges of a normal citizen (cf. 8:33, *Comment*).

Explanation

The book of Joshua seeks in all its parts to demonstrate the faithful obedience of Joshua to the instructions God gave Moses. In so doing, the book reaches back into the Pentateuch and into Deuteronomy for traditions in which Moses received a command from Yahweh for later action.

The present text of Joshua goes further than simply emphasizing the obedience of Joshua. It shows the nature of the law which Joshua has carried out. The law is an attempt to adapt tribal, nomadic practices to new sociological realities of urban life. The old practices still hang on. Blood revenge cannot be ignored. It stands as a threat to the life of the community. On the other hand, killing cannot be dismissed or handled lightly. The newly urbanized society must find a way to deal with both sides of the problem. The city of refuge seeks to find the middle ground for dealing with that problem. In it God sets up for Israel an institution to protect the man who has been guilty of a crime which he did not plan, and for which he had no motivation.

The institution involves two legal steps, according to Josh 20. First, the elders of the city must be satisfied and allow the man into the city. Next the general assembly of the city must hear the case. The interesting note is that the man does not simply go free even though he has proven that he acted without malice aforethought. Proven innocent, the man remains a virtual prisoner in the city of refuge, most probably in the service of the priest and/or temple of the city. Restoration to normal, free life comes only at the death of the priest. From the earliest rabbinic times onward, this has been interpreted in the sense of Priestly atonement. Such exegesis is historically improbable. Yet it shows how even after the practice of using the city of refuge had died out, the community continued to work with the text in new sociological conditions to try to gain insights into the will and workings of God with sinful man.

The Christian community, likewise, is called upon to delve into the old text and seek new insights for new sociological conditions. Such insights must begin where the text does, with the call to obedience to God's life style. Beyond that, the community is called to reflect upon its whole understanding of crime and punishment. We cannot ignore the centuries of traditions which have resulted in our present penal codes and practices. We cannot, however, simply take for granted that such practices have somehow been given us by divine revelation and need never to be altered. The Christian community must take seriously its responsibility to examine penal institutions and practices and seek to find the ways God would lead us to reform such practices. The innocent man should not suffer unduly and the guilty man should be given sufficient protection and hope for new opportunities as well as sufficient punishment.

The Levitical Cities   (21:1–42)

Bibliography

Aharoni, Y. *The Land of the Bible.* Tr. A. F. Rainey. London: Burns & Oates, 1967, 268–73. **Albright, W. F.** *Archaeology and the Religion of Israel.* 2nd ed. Baltimore: The Johns Hopkins Press, 1946, 121–25. ———. "The List of Levitical Cities." *Louis Ginzberg Jubilee Volume I.* New York: The American Academy for Jewish Research, 1945, 49–73. **Alt, A.** "Bemerkungen zu einigen judäischen Ortslisten des Alten Testaments." *ZDPV* 68 (1951) 193–210. (= *Kleine Schriften zur Geschichten des Volkes Israel.* Vol. 2. München: C. H. Beck'sche Verlagsbuchhandlung, 1953, 289–305.) ———. "Festungen und Levitenorte im Lande Juda." *KS* 2, 306–15. **Auld, A. G.** "The Levitical Cities': Texts and History." *ZAW* 91 (1979) 194–206. ———. *Studies in Joshua: Text and Literary*

Relationships. Dissertation, Edinburgh, 1976, 235–80. **Cazelles, H.** "David's Monarchy and the Gibeonite Claim (II Sam XXI, 1–14)." *PEQ* 87 (1955) 171, 174. **Cody, A.** *A History of Old Testament Priesthood.* AnBib 35. Rome: Pontifical Biblical Institute, 1969, 159–65. **Gunneweg, A. H.** *Leviten und Priester.* FRLANT 89. Göttingen: Vandenhoeck & Ruprecht, 1965, 64–65, 123–24. **Halpern, B.** "Sectionalism and the Schism." *JBL* 93 (1974) 519–32. **Haran, M.** "Studies in the Account of the Levitical Cities." *JBL* 80 (1961) 45–54, 156–65. ——. *Temples and Temple-Service in Ancient Israel.* Oxford: Clarendon Press, 1978, 84–87, 112–31, 148. **Japhet, S.** "Conquest and Settlement in Chronicles." *JBL* 98 (1979) 205–18. **Klein, S.** "Die Priester-, Leviten-, und Asyl-städte." *Qobes of the Jewish Palestine Exploration Society* (1935) 81–94. **Löhr, M.** *Das Asyl-wesen im Alten Testament.* Halle: Max Niemeyer Verlag, 1930, 28–30, 33–34. **Mazar, B.** "The Cities of the Priests and the Levites." VTSup 7 (1960) 193–205. **Mettinger, T. N. D.** *Solomonic State Officials.* Lund: C. W. K. Gleerup, 1971, 98–101. **Möhlenbrink, K.** "Die levitischen Überlieferungen des Alten Testaments." *ZAW* 52 (1934) 184–231. **Nielsen, E.** "Politiske forhold og kulturelle strømninge i Israel og Juda under Manasse." *DTT* 29 (1966) 1–10. **Noth, M.** "Überlieferungsgeschichtliches zur zweiten Hälfte des Josuabuches." *Alttestamentliche Studien Fr. Nötscher zum 60. Geburtstag,* ed. H. Junker and J. Botterweck. BBB 1. Bonn: Peter Hanstein, 1950, 164–67. **Ross, J. P.** *The "Cities of the Levites" in Joshua XXI and I Chronicles VI.* Dissertation, Edinburgh, 1973. **Spencer, J. R.** *The Levitical Cities, A Study of the Role and Function of the Levites in the History of Israel.* Dissertation, Chicago, 1980. **Strauss, H.** *Untersuchungen zu den Über-lieferungen der vorexilischen Leviten.* Dissertation, Bonn, 1960, 132–39. **Tengstrøm, S.** *Die Hexateucherzählung.* Lund: C. W. K. Gleerup, 1976. 75–78. **Tsafrir, Y.** "The Levitic City of Beth-Shemesh in Judah or in Naphtali?" (Hebrew) *Eretz Israel* 12 (1975) 44–45, 119*. **de Vaux, R.** *Ancient Israel: Its Life and Institutions.* Tr. J. McHugh. New York: McGraw-Hill, 1961, 366–67. ——. *Histoire ancienne d'Israël.* Vol. 1. Paris: J. Gabalda, 1971, 493. (= *The Early History of Israel.* Tr. D. Smith. London: Darton, Longman & Todd, 1978, 530.) **Wellhausen, J.** *Prolegomena zur Geschichte Israels.* 5th ed. Berlin: Georg Reimer, 1899, 156–65. (= *Prolegomena to the History of Israel.* Tr. J. S. Black and A. Menzies. Edinburgh: A. & C. Black, 1885, 159–67.) **Yeivin, S.** *The Israelite Conquest of Canaan.* Istanbul: Nederlands Historisch-Archaeologisch Instituut in het Nabije Oosten, 1971, 262–64.

Translation

[1] *The heads of the fathers of the Levites* [a] *approached Eleazer, the priest, and Joshua, the son of Nun, and the heads of the fathers of the tribes of the sons of Israel.* [2] *They spoke to them in Shiloh in the land of Canaan, "Yahweh commanded by the hand of Moses to give to us cities of residence along with their pastures* [a] *for our cattle."* [3] *The sons of Israel gave to the Levites from their inheritance according to the word of Yahweh these cities and their pastures:*

[4] *The lot came out for the clans of the Kohathites. There belonged to the sons of Aaron, the priest, from the Levites, from the tribe of Judah and from the tribe of the Simeonites and from the tribe of Benjamin by lot thirteen cities.* [5] *To the sons of Kohath who remained from the clans* [a] *of the tribe of Ephraim and from the tribe of Dan and from half of the tribe of Manasseh by lot ten cities.*

[6] *To the sons of Gershom from the clans of the tribe of Issachar and from the tribe of Asher and from the tribe of Naphtali and from half the tribe of Manasseh in Bashan by lot* [a] *thirteen cities.*

[7] *To the sons of the Merarites for their clans from the tribe of Reuben and from the tribe of Gad and from the tribe of Zebulon twelve cities.* [8] *The sons of Israel*

gave to the Levites these cities and their pastures just as Yahweh commanded by the hand of Moses by lot.

⁹ They ª gave from the tribe of the sons of Judah and from the tribe of the sons of Simeon these cities which he called ᵇ them by name: ¹⁰ It belonged to the sons of Aaron from the clans of the Kohathites from the sons of Levi,ª since the first ᵇ lot belonged to them, ¹¹ and they ª gave to them Kiriath-arba, the father of Anak (it is Hebron), in the hill country of Judah and ᵇ its pasture surrounding it. ¹² But the field of the city and its suburbs, they ª gave to Caleb, the son of Jephunneh, into his possession.ᵇ

¹³ To the sons of Aaron, the priest,ª they gave the city of refuge of the killer, namely Hebron and its pasture, along with Libnah and its pasture; ¹⁴ Jattir and its pasture, Eshtemoa and its pasture; ¹⁵ Holon ª and its pasture, Debir and its pasture; ¹⁶ ꜥAyin ª and its pasture, Juttah and its pasture, Beth Shemesh and its pasture—nine cities from these two tribes.

¹⁷ From the tribe of Benjamin: Gibeon and its pasture, Geba ᶜ and its pasture; ¹⁸ Anathoth and its pasture, Almon ª and its pasture—four cities. ¹⁹ All the cities of the sons of Aaron, the priest, were thirteen cities and their pastures.ª

²⁰ To the clans of the sons of Kohath, the Levites, who were remaining from the sons of Kohath, belonged cities of their lot ª from the tribe of Ephraim. ²¹ They gave to them the city of refuge of the killer, namely Shechem and its pasture in the hill country of Ephraim,ª and Gezer and its pasture; ²² Kibzaim ª and its pasture, Beth Horon and its pasture—four cities.

²³ And from the tribe of Dan: Elteke⁾ and its pasture, Gibbethon and its pasture; ²⁴ Aijalon and its pasture, Gath-Rimmon and its pasture—four cities.

²⁵ From half of the tribe of Manasseh: Tanaach and its pasture, Gath Rimmon ª and its pasture—two cities.

²⁶ All the cities were ten and their pastures for the clans of the sons of Kohath who remained. ²⁷ To the sons of Gershon from the clans of the Levites from half the tribe of Manasseh: the city of refuge of the killer, namely, Golan in Bashan and its pasture, Beeshterah ª and its pasture—two cities.

²⁸ From the tribe of Issachar: Kishyon and its pasture, Deberath and its pasture; ²⁹ Jarmuth ª and its pasture, En-Gannim and its pasture—four cities.

³⁰ From the tribe of Asher: Mishal and its pasture, ꜥAbdon and its pasture; ³¹ Helkath ª and its pasture, Rehob and its pasture—four cities.

³² From the tribe of Naphtali: the city of refuge of the killer, namely Kedesh in Galilee and its pasture, Hammoth-Dor ª and its pasture, Karthan and its pasture—three cities. ³³ All the cities of the Gershonites for their clans were thirteen cities and their pastures.

³⁴ For the clans of the sons of the Merarites, the Levites who were remaining: from the tribe of Zebulon: Jokneam and its pasture, Kartah and its pasture; ³⁵ Dimnah and its pasture, Nahalal and its pasture—four cities.ª

³⁶ And ª from the tribe of Reuben: Bezer and its pasture, Jahaz and its pasture; ³⁷ Kedemoth and its pasture, Mephaath and its pasture—four cities.

³⁸ And from the tribe of Gad: the city of refuge of the killer, namely Ramoth in Gilead and its pasture, Mahanaim and its pasture; ³⁹ Heshbon and its pasture, Jazer and its pasture—in all four cities.

⁴⁰ All the cities were for the sons of the Merarites for their clans who remained from the clans of the Levites. Their lot ª was twelve cities.

⁴¹ *All the cities of the Levites in the midst of the possession of the sons of Israel were forty-eight cities and their pastures.* ⁴² *There is* ᵃ *for each of these cities a city with its pasture surrounding it; thus it was for all of these cities.*

Notes

Textual study is complicated by the appearance of virtually the same material in 1 Chr 6:39–66 (=LXX and Eng. 6:54–80). City names often differ quite radically in MT, LXX, and Chronicles. We can note only the most significant of these.

1.a. LXX has "sons" preceding Levites rather than Israel. The expression, taken up from 14:1 and 19:51, is "heads of the fathers of the tribes of the sons of Israel," from which our passage creates a related formula for the Levites, so that "sons" may belong originally in both formulas.

2.a. LXX uses two different terms to translate מִגְרָשׁ, "pasture," a form of περισπόρια occurring in vv 2–11, 34–42, while a form of ἀφωρισμένα occurs in thirty-five other places in the chapter (cf. Holmes, 72). L. Delekat ("Zum hebräischen Wörterbuch," *VT* 14 [1964] 22) says 21:2–11, 34–42 must not have appeared originally in the Greek. Delekat does show that the original reading should be מִגְרָשֶׁהָ, thus singular, throughout the chapter, the meaning of the word being the territory outside the city walls legally claimed by a city.

5.a. LXX does not reproduce "clans" in vv 5–6 but does so in v 7, where MT uses "for" or "according to" their clans instead of the "from" or "out of" their clans used in vv 5–6. *BHS* and *BHK*, Noth, Soggin and many others make vv 5–6 conform to 7, while Holmes appears to favor LXX. The *Text Project* retains MT. The form "from, out of" the clans appears in Joshua only in 21:5, 6, 10, 27, 40. Except for vv 5 and 6 the expression separates one clan from related clans. The expression may well be a later insertion into 5–6 (cf. LXX) or a dittography there of the *mem* for an original *lamedh*. The corresponding 1 Chr verses compound the confusion, 6:46 reading "from" while v 47 reads "for, according to."

6.a. 1 Chr 6:47 does not reflect "by lot" or "half." LXX joins Chronicles in inserting "lot" in the following verse rather than here. Vv 4–7 are developed formulaicly with "by lot" an essential part. The "by lot" of v 8 does not fit the pattern there and may reflect a later marginal correction which should have been inserted into v 7 rather than 8.

9.a. LXX has a sing. verb with a compound subject: "the tribe of the sons of Judah and the tribe of the sons of Simeon gave (sing.) and from the tribe of the sons of Benjamin these cities. They were assigned (or named) ¹⁰ to the sons of Aaron. . . ." 1 Chr 6:50 also mentions the tribe of the sons of Benjamin. This follows the pattern of Josh 21:4, 9–19 and may reflect an original text, though it is also possible that a later copyist may have sought to make the pattern complete by inserting reference to Benjamin here.

9.b. Translations have paraphrased the Heb. idiom here, while 1 Chr 6:50 has harmonized the grammar to the context by pluralizing the verb and "names." Holmes' suggestion of an original וַיְקַדְּשׁוּ "they sanctified," on the basis of 20:7 is quite fanciful. We can remain with MT (Soggin).

10.a. 1 Chr 6:39 does not reflect "from the sons of Levi," a formulation which is not duplicated elsewhere in the chapter and may be secondary in the current context, making the Levitic relationship of the Aaronic priests explicit.

10.b. "The first" does not appear in LXX or Chronicles and may be secondary amplification.

11.a. LXX continues the sing. verb (cf. 9.a.) but without definite subject and reflects אֵם, "mother," rather than אָב, "father," as in 15:13. 1 Chr reads "land of Judah" rather than "hill country of Judah." All of this reflects peculiarities of transmission and translation rather than actual textual variants. The omission of any reference to Kiriath Arba in Chronicles could reflect an original text. The reference may well be a later insertion based on 15:13 (*BHS*).

11.b. LXX introduces the contrasting note here rather than at the beginning of the next verse as in MT.

12.a. LXX makes Joshua the subject, a harmonizing interpretation based on 14:13 and 15:13. In the same vein, LXX makes the gift "to the sons of Caleb," avoiding further repetition.

12.b. The final word "into his possession" is superfluous in the context and omitted by the Chronicler.

13.a. Both LXX and 1 Chr 6:42 omit "the priest," which may represent the later addition of a traditional title (cf. Holmes). LXX continues its sing. verb here.

15.a. The pointing of חֹלֹן is not certain in light of חִילֵן in 1 Chr 6:43, often seen to reflect an original חִילֵן.

16.a. עַיִן is the Heb. word for "eye" or "fountain" and is often interpreted as unsuitable as a place name (Noth). ʿAshan of LXX and 1 Chr 6:44 is often seen as original. Juttah is one of eight cities not listed in Chronicles (cf. Aharoni, *The Land of the Bible*, 270–271).

18.a. עַלְמוֹן becomes Gamala in LXX[B] and ʿAlemeth in 1 Chr 6:45, where the order of the cities is transposed.

19.a. "And their pastures" is not represented in LXX, while in 1 Chr 6:45, the summary reads: "all their cities were thirteen cities with their clans." The latter represents a Hebrew copyist's substitution of one familiar term in the context for another, while LXX represents either the earliest version of the text or accidental haplography.

20.a. 1 Chr 6:51 reads גְּבוּלָם, "their territory" instead of "their lot." LXX reflects an inner Greek error seemingly based on Heb. "their territory." The combination "cities of their lot" occurs only here in the MT. "Cities of their territory" is no more frequent. A unique linguistic formulation has led to early textual corruption with Chronicles perhaps reflecting the "original" text (cf. Auld, "Textual and Literary Studies in the Book of Joshua," *ZAW* 90 [1978] 41; "Cities of Refuge in Israelite Tradition," *JSOT* 10 [1978] 32).

21.a. LXX does not witness "in the hill country of Ephraim" which may be a later geographical specification on analogy of v 11 (cf. Auld, *JSOT* 10 [1978] 32).

22.a. LXX witnesses textual confusion with a double reference to suburbs, a total of four cities, but the omission of Kibzaim, so that only three cities are named. 1 Chr 6:53 reads Jokmeam. Albright and Aharoni want to retain both names. This could only represent an early form of the list prior to the present numerical totals. A copyists' error is more likely. Noth derives Jokmeam from the Priestly name of 1 Chr 23:19; 24:23.

25.a. Gath-Rimmon is certainly dittography from v 24. LXX[B] gives ʾIebatha; 1 Chr 6:55 Bileam. Some Greek mss reflect Beth Shean, which Hollenberg adopts (*Theologische Studien und Kritiken* 1 [1874] 462–506). Usually today, Ibleam is read (Soggin, *Text Project*, Aharoni, etc.).

27.a. Beʿeshterah apparently reflects an initial preposition, which is faithfully reflected in the Greek tradition. 1 Chr 6:56 reads ʿAshtaroth, which is usually adopted today. Hertzberg makes the interesting suggestion "Beth Ashteroth."

29.a. Jarmuth is rendered Remmath by LXX (cf. 19:21) and Raʾmoth by 1 Chr 6:58. The original reading is uncertain. ʿEn-Gannim becomes "Pegen of the scribes" in LXX and ʿAnem in 1 Chr 6:58. MT is usually retained.

31.a. Helkath becomes Hukok in 1 Chr 6:60, but this is probably secondary (Noth).

32.a. Hammoth-Dor is rendered Nemmath by LXX[B] with many other variants in the Greek tradition. 1 Chr 6:61 reads Hammon. Hammath is generally read here on the basis of 19:35. Soggin carries this further and reads the following Karthan as Rakkath with 19:35. LXX reads the latter as Themmon, while 1 Chr 6:61 reads Kiriathaim. Aharoni holds the latter for a possible reading and includes Dor as a separate city.

35.a. 1 Chr 6:62 abbreviates in a radically altered form, reading Rimmono and Tabor as the only cities. LXX reads Maan, Kadesh, Gella, and correspondingly totals only three cities. Kartah of MT appears suspiciously like dittography from Karthan of v 32 (Aharoni). Rimmon may represent the original reading corrupted into Dimnah, though the latter is the more difficult reading. Aharoni suggests reading Kartah as (Chisloth?)-Tabor. Noth correctly notes the tendency of the tradition to replace unknown names with town names known from the tradition.

Soggin notes that the participle "who are remaining" is meaningless in the context. One can better say that it differs in function from the original formulaic usage in vv 5, 20, and 26, where it distinguishes the rest of the clan of Kohath from the Aaronites, who also belong to the clan. In vv 34, 40, the expression marks off the Mararite clans as the remaining Levites after cities have been allotted to the Kohathites and the Gershonites.

36.a. The major Hebrew tradition does not include vv 36–37, though some later Heb. mss. do witness them. Such omission, however, makes the arithmetic of v 41 in error. This is probably a case of early haplography. Reconstruction of the verses is done on the basis of LXX and 1 Chr 6:63–64. The LXX appears to give the earliest reading (*Text Project*).

40.a. As in v 20, the early tradition confused "lot" and "territory," the latter being witnessed in LXX. 1 Chr 6 concludes with Josh 21:39a.

42.a. MT changes unexpectedly to an imperfect verb expressing either present, future, or imperative meanings. LXX witnesses a difficult construction with a prepositional element rather than a verb. *BHS* is typical of modern scholarship in suggesting the insertion of a conjunction before the verb, thus reflecting a past meaning. This has, however, no textual basis. At best, the construction is difficult.

At the end of v 42, LXX adds a long section paralleling 19:49b–50: "Joshua finished dividing the land into their territories. The sons of Israel gave Joshua a portion, acccording to the word of Yahweh. They gave him the city which he requested. Timnath-serah they gave him in the territory of Ephraim. Joshua built the city and resided in it." LXX then adds: "Joshua took the knives of stone with which he had circumcised the sons of Israel, those born in the way in the wilderness. He deposited them in Timnath-Serah." The repetition of the first part makes it suspect, though Holmes argues that a Hebrew reviser deleted it. Hertzberg describes the final section as a legend spun from 5:2ff. It is highly unlikely that the LXX translators would invent such a story and place it here. Rather they appear to be working with older tradition, about which we know nothing further (cf. Soggin).

Form/Structure/Setting

The section is clearly marked off by the concluding formula in 20:9, the new narrative introduction in 21:1, and the concluding summaries in 21:41–42. The content and summarizing character of 21:43–45 then mark them off as a separate theological summary.

The structure of the section is clear and becomes even more clear when compared to that of the related material in 1 Chr 6:39–66 (Eng. 6: 54–81):

Josh 21:1–42	1 Chr 6:39–66
Larger context: division of land to tribes by lot, chaps. 13–21.	Larger context: list of genealogy of Israel, chaps. 4–8, specifically the genealogy of Levi, 5:27–6:66.
1–3 Narrative setting based on Num 35:1–8.	39a List introduction.
4a Lot falls for Kohathites (connecting to chaps. 14–19).	
4b Thirteen cities from Judah, Simeon and Benjamin for Aaron by lot.	39b For Aaron of the Kohathites by lot.
5 To rest of Kohathites from Ephram, Dan, ½ Manasseh, ten cities.	
6 To Gershon from Issachar, Asher, Naphtali, ½ Manasseh, thirteen cities.	
7 To Merari from Reuben, Gad, Zebulon twelve cities.	
8a List introduction (=v 3);	
b Obedience formula.	
9 List introduction from Judah and Simeon.	
10–12 First lot gives Aaron of the Kohathites Hebron, but field and suburbs are Caleb's (10a=4b; joins to 14:6–15; 15:13–14).	40–41 Hebron in land of Judah given to Aaron, but field and suburbs to Caleb.
13–16a Nine cities listed for Aaron (form parallels 4–7; content parallels 10–12).	42–44 Eight cities listed for Aaron (42a=39b–40).
16b Summary: nine cities from two tribes (related to v 9).	
17–18a Four cities listed from Benjamin.	45a Three cities listed from Benjamin.
18b Summary: four cities.	

Josh 21:1–42	1 Chr 6:39–66
19 Summary (vv 13–18): Thirteen cities for Aaron	45b Summary: Thirteen cities for Aaron.
20a For the rest of the Kohathites (cf. 5).	46a For the rest of the Kohathites,
	46b Summary: Ten cities from ½ Manasseh (text? cf. 21:5).
	47 To Gersham from Issachar, Asher, Naphtali, Manasseh in Bashan, thirteen cities (=21:6).
	48 To Merari from Reuben, Gad, Zebulon, twelve cities (=21:7).
	49 Introduction: Given to Levites (cf. 21:8a)
	50 List introduction from Judah, Simeon, Benjamin (cf. 21:9).
20b Their lot from Ephraim.	51 For Kohath from Ephraim (cf. 21:20; 6:46a).
21–22a Four cities listed.	52–54 Six cities listed.
22b Summary: four cities.	
23–24 Four cities listed with summary from Dan.	
25 Two cities listed from ½ Manasseh with summary.	55 Two cities listed from ½ Manasseh for rest of Kohathites.
26 Summary: Ten cities for the rest of the Kohathites.	
27a For Gershon:	56a For Gershom:
27b Two cities listed from ½ Manasseh with summary.	56b Two cities listed from ½ Manasseh.
28–29 Four cities listed from Issachar with summary.	57–58 Four cities listed from Issachar.
30–31 Four cities listed from Asher with summary.	59–60 Four cities listed from Asher.
32 Three cities listed from Naphtali with summary.	61 Three cities listed from Naphtali.
33 Summary: Thirteen cities for the Gershonites.	
34a For Merarites:	62a For Merarites:
34b–35 Four cities listed from Zebulon with summary.	62b Two cities listed from Zebulon.
36–37 Four cities listed from Reuben with summary.	63–64 Four cities listed from Reuben.
38–39 Four cities listed from Gad with summary.	65–66 Four cities listed from Gad.
40 Summary: Twelve cities for the Merarites.	
41 Summary: Forty-eight cities for the Levites.	
42 Summary definition of the cities.	

The two sections contain basically the same material. The order differs in regard to 21:5–9 and 6:46–50. Joshua introduces a narrative setting based on Num 35:1–8 and tying back to its own narrative in chaps. 14–19 with particular reference to the motif of the lot (14:2; 15:1; 16:1; 17:1, 14, 17; 18:6, 8, 10, 11; 19:1, 10, 17, 24, 32, 40, 51), to the plight of the Levite (13:14, 33; 14:3–4; 18:7), and to the narrative of Caleb (14:6–15; 15:13–14). Joshua also gives comprehensive numerical summaries. The Chronicler never mentions the tribe of Dan, and does not include the tribe of Simeon in the Aaronic cities.

The only summary in 1 Chr (v 45b) does not square with the preceding lists numerically.

Scholars have generally agreed that Chronicles uses Joshua, but Ross (*Cities*) and Auld have recently argued for the Chronicler's originality here. Such would go against the pattern of the Chronicler, who elsewhere is heavily dependent upon earlier biblical sources. Auld (ZAW 91 [1979] 200) must admit that 6:39–41 is an insertion into Chronicles from an "earlier edition" of Josh 21. One must go further. The isolated summary in 6:45b belongs to the larger group of summaries which mark Josh 21 but play no significant role for 1 Chr 6. The same can be said for the summary statistics in 46–48, which are correlated to the larger lists of cities and their summaries. The references to lot (6:39, 46, 48, 50) reflect an original element of Joshua, not Chronicles. The double repetition of Hebron has its sense within the larger Joshua context, but represents only a precise copying of material in the Chronicler. What is more important, the change of order can best be explained from the Chronicler's perspective. In the context of Joshua, the important element was to give the total picture of all the cities of the Levites prior to giving the individual details. Thus the summaries are placed at the first (vv 5–7 with the introduction in 4). For the Chronicler, the important point is to keep the distinction between what belongs to Aaron and what belongs to the Levites. Thus everything to do with Aaron is shifted to the first part of the text, to be followed by the summaries. The Chronicler often uses this procedure. Everything points to the originality of Josh 21. It is this form of the text which we must study to discover an original form and setting.

Several points become obvious within Josh 21. Repetition occurs in 3, 8, 9 and in 4b, 10, 13. The natural function of such verses is to introduce a following list. Two such lists occur: 5–7 and 13–40. The question of priority goes to the latter, which is summarized by the former. Vv 3 and 8 form a framework for the section 1–8 and witness the same vocabulary and intention. This leaves v 9 as the original introduction to 13–40. V 4 introduces the theme of lot, thus connecting the material back to chaps. 14–19, and introduces the form of the list in vv 5–7. V 10 continues the lot theme and serves to introduce 11–12, which duplicate 13a in order to tie the narrative to chaps. 14–15. This means that the original introduction to the list in 13–40 appears in 9 and 13.

It is thus 9 and 13–40 which stands open to further investigation seeking to determine its form and setting. Such investigation has led to various results. Kaufmann saw it as a utopian ideal developed in the earliest stages of Israel's existence. Tengström (*Die Hexateucherzählung*, 75–78) seeks to join it to his pre-monarchical Shechemite Hexateuch. Klein and Albright have used archaeological information to place it in the time of David, which de Vaux wants to shift to a time after the division of the kingdom. Haran (*JBL* 80 [1961] 45–54, 156–65) connects it to his priestly school in the time of Ahaz and Hezekiah. Alt followed by Noth seeks to join the list to his other Josianic lists. The classical view is that of Graf and Wellhausen seeing the list as a postexilic utopian ideal of the priestly school.

Recent scholarship has begun to reach almost a consensus. This is based

on the work of Mazar (VTSup 7 [1960] 193–205), who noted the function
of the Levites as devoted supporters of the Davidic-Solomonic monarchy
used to administer both the cultic and political affairs of the frontiers of
the empire (cf. 1 Chr 26:29–32). This explains the point made repeatedly
by Noth and Alt that the territory covered by the cities has unexpected gaps
in the very stronghold of the kingdom itself, namely in central Judah between
Jerusalem and Hebron and in the center of the northern kingdom in the
territory of Ephraim and Manasseh. Mazar noted that the Levites were settled
only in those cities recently conquered by David and retaining strong Canaanite traditions and probably strong Canaanite population elements. This explains two other factors. Albright had pointed out the inclusion of cities which
remained to be conquered under Joshua, namely Tanaach, Ibleam, Gezer,
Nahalol, Aijalon, Dor, Bethshean (cf. Judg 1). Judg 17–18, 19 and laws such
as Deut 14:29; 16:11, 14; 26:11–12 appear to represent Levites as homeless
wanderers dwelling where they can find Priestly employment. It is not improbable that, prior to David, Levites had begun to live in certain cities, particularly
cities which were themselves sanctuaries and places of refuge or which were
near such cities. The monarchy simply brought the institutionalizing of such
practices, likely based on an Egyptian model (Mazar). In later times, the measures against the Levites and the local sanctuaries, particularly by Jeroboam
(2 Chr 11:13–15) and Josiah (2 Kgs 23:8) intensified the need to find places
of residence and service for the Levites. Our list thus has its setting in the
time of the United Monarchy, but mirrors an institution which may have
functioned, particularly in Judah, for many generations, indeed for the life
of the kingdom itself. The Chronicler's use of the material may reflect continued life of the institution in a new form in the postexilic community. The
institution itself can be seen from two perspectives. From that of the monarchy,
it was designed to strengthen government control and influence through
the employment of men of high reputation and long-standing tradition. From
the perspective of the Levites, it provided security and meaningful employment for a group which lived its life on the economic borderline, while permitting them to continue their tradition of priestly employment at the same
time.

Comment

[1] The opening verse connects back to 14:1; 17:4; 19:51. The Levitical motif
is taken up from 13:14, 33; 14:3–4; 18:7. To this point no provision has
been made for levitical residence. Rather the point has been that Levites
cannot have material possessions and responsibilities as do the other tribes,
since they are devoted to Yahweh and his service. The gift of cities of residence
was foreshadowed in 14:4.

[2] The fulfillment of Mosaic commands, a theme so vital to the entire book,
relates back to Num 35:1–8. The intriguing element here is that the recipients
of the promise, the Levites, take the initiative rather than Joshua or the other
Israelite leaders (cf. Num 27:1; 36:1). It is emphasized here and particularly
in Numbers 35:3 that the pasture land is for the cattle to graze, not for

farm land to be worked and exploited economically by the Levites. The cattle would, presumably, be for the immediate food and clothing needs of the family and for personal sacrifices.

³ The cities are pictured almost as a sacrifice given by the various tribes to the Levitical priests.

⁴ The choice of the cities and their distribution among the various Levitical clans is incorporated into the lot system employed previously for the distribution of the land among the tribes. The first lot does not fall upon the first born (cf. Gen 46:11; Exod 6:16; Möhlenbrink). Rather the lot falls on the ancestor of Aaron. This is made clear by the abrupt change of subjects in 4a and 4b from clans of Kohath to sons of Aaron.

The thirteen cities have caused much comment (cf. especially Albright). The total of forty-eight cities would suggest a pattern of four cities from each tribe. The pattern is broken only here and with the tribe of Naphtali. Tsafrir has suggested that Beth Shemesh (v 16) originally referred to the city of that name in Naphtali (cf. Judg 1:33) and was secondarily transferred to Judah. This is not impossible, but far from proven. The irregularity of the numerical system could argue for its authenticity. It may be that the tradition of thirteen Aaronic cities was originally separate from that of forty-eight Levitical cities. This is particularly interesting in the light of two facts. The Chronicler does not include Simeon, thus possibly leaving nine cities from Judah. Numbers 35:8 calls for a distinction in number of cities according to the size of the tribe. The unevenness of distribution may be the original tradition, while later systematizers have developed a theory of four cities per tribe.

⁵ Dan is pictured in its original western position rather than the later move northward (Judg 18). Its connection is with northern Ephraim and Manasseh rather than the southern Judah (cf. Judg 15:9–13) or the more proximate Benjamin.

⁶ The other half of Manasseh is located geographically east of the Jordan in Bashan as usual, but is connected uniquely with the western tribes of Issachar, Asher, and Naphtali. Such connection points to ancient tradition in which related Levitical clans lived in these regions.

⁷ Zebulon is joined to the eastern tribes of Reuben and Gad, again pointing to ancient tradition in which Levitical distribution did not coincide with the normal tribal listing.

V 8 summarizes the section by calling renewed attention to the obedience to divine command.

⁹ The actual list of cities is introduced here, following the theological introduction. The significance of 9b is not clear. Is it an attempt to say Israel renamed the cities? Or does it try to say that long ago the forty-eight cities were explicitly listed, so that no contemporary king has a right to tamper with the list, taking one city off and adding another on?

¹⁰ The preeminent role of Aaron is again emphasized in that his "sons" receive the first lot. This serves to introduce the following verses.

¹¹⁻¹² These verses become necessary in light of the Caleb traditions (14:6–15; 15:13–14) and the Levitic city tradition of v 13. They clarify that the city itself and its immediate pastures were set apart for the Levites, while

the surrounding villages controlled by the city-state of Hebron along with all the agricultural fields belonged to the Calebites. Here the Levites are excluded from exercising direct political power and from developing an economic power base. אחזה, "possession," appears here for the first time in Joshua. It is used most often in Lev 25 and 27; Num 32 and 35; and Ezek 44–48. It appears again in Josh 21:41; 22:4, 9, 19. Gerleman has recently argued ("Nutzrecht und Wohnrecht. Zur Bedeutung von אחזה und נחלה," *ZAW* 89 [1977] 313–18) that it refers specifically to the use of land for cultivation rather than to possession of the land. He would translate the present passage "with the right of cultivation." In the context of Joshua, such an interpretation overlooks the theological overtones of the context. The emphasis is not so much upon agricultural rights as upon permanent possession and control of the territory. Such control is still understood in terms of the land as belonging to God and given to the tribe for its use.

¹³ Each of the cities of refuge is included within the Levitical cities as indicated in Num 35:6. Noth has argued that such inclusion is secondary. His theory rests on his previous literary theory that 13:18 and 19:35bB quote from a form of Josh 21 which does not include the cities of refuge. Such literary analysis is very tentative and without much textual support. Numbers 35:6 might point to a tradition of forty-two Levitical cities, but this, too, is quite speculative. Since cities of refuge were probably tied to ancient altars, it would be quite appropriate for such cities to become cities of the Levitical priests. This must not, however, mean that every Levitical city was an ancient sanctuary.

For Hebron, see *Comment* on 10:3.

For Libnah, see *Comment* on 10:29.

¹⁴ Jattir is modern Khirbet ʿAttir, thirteen miles south-southwest of Hebron and fourteen miles northeast of Beersheba. See 15:48; 1 Sam 30:27.

Eshtemoa is modern es-Samuʿ eight and a half miles (fourteen kilometers) southwest of Hebron. An Iron Age deposit of silver jewelry and ingots was found there. See 15:50; 1 Sam 30:28.

¹⁵ Holon has not been located. See 15:51. For Debir, see *Comment* on 10:3.

¹⁶ ʿAyin appears as a place name here, 15:32; 19:7; and Num 34:11. The latter is geographically distinct, while the other two passages may refer to ʿEin-Rimmon. ʿAshan, usually read here with LXX (cf. *Notes*), is located at Khirbet ʿAsan, a mile and a half northwest of Beersheba.

Juttah is identified with Yatta, five and a half miles southwest of Hebron. See 15:55. With Beth-Shemesh, the list moves radically northwestward onto the Philistine border. It is located near modern Beth-Shemesh, twelve and a half miles (twenty kilometers) west of Jerusalem. Though unmentioned in ancient literature outside the Bible, it apparently has deep roots in history, an eighteenth-century city having been excavated. It is named House of the Sun, apparently in reference to a temple for the sun god, and is apparently identical with ʿIr Shemesh, the city of the sun, assigned to Dan in 19:41. See 15:10; 1 Sam 6; 1 Kgs 4:9; 2 Kgs 14:11, 13; 2 Chr 28:18 (Cf. *EAEHL* 1, 248–53).

¹⁷ The Benjaminite Levites may have served in the Jerusalem sanctuary. This may explain the absence of Jerusalem from the list. It is possible that

the list reflects the Davidic time before Jerusalem became the major sanctuary, the high place being at Gibeon (1 Kgs 3). For Gibeon, see above on Josh 9–10, Cf. 18:25.

Geba is the Benjaminite city (18:24) on the northern border of Judah (2 Kgs 23:8; Zech 14:10), identified with modern Jeba six miles north-northeast of Jerusalem. See 1 Sam 13–14; 2 Sam 5:25; 1 Kgs 15:22; Isa 10:29; Ezra 2:26; Neh 7:30; 11:31; 12:29.

¹⁸ Anathoth is famous for its connections with Jeremiah and his Priestly ancestors (Jer 1:1; 11:21–23; 29:27; 32:7–9; cf. 1 Kgs 2:26). It is located at Ras el-Kharrubeh, three miles north of Jerusalem. Its name may have been associated with a temple to the Canaanite goddess Anath. See Isa 10:30; Ezra 2:23; Neh 7:27; 11:32.

Almon is mentioned only here (cf. *Notes*). It is located at Khirbet Almit, a mile northeast of Anathoth.

²⁰⁻²⁶ The remainder of the clan of Kohath is allotted former Canaanite strongholds on the borders of Ephraim, Dan, and half of Manasseh. Only Shechem, the city of refuge, represents the heartland of Ephraim and Manasseh.

²¹ Shechem is the key city in the history of the Hexateuch, according to Tengström. Judg 8–9 show that it was a strong Canaanite center of Baal worship even during Israel's early history with mention of Baal-berith, the Baal of the covenant in 8:33. It has significant patriarchal connections in Gen 12:6; 33:18–35:4; 37:12–14, but has no conquest narrative in Joshua, only the cultic references in 8:30–35 and 24:1–28. It is placed within the borders of Manasseh in 17:7 but does not appear in the city lists. Excavations have uncovered occupation levels dating back to ca. 3600 B.C. with major occupation between 1900 and 1540 and between 1450 and 1125. Excavations have amply illustrated the cultic importance of Shechem (cf. E. F. Campbell, *IDBSup* [1976] 821–22; E. F. Campbell "Amarna Notes," 39–54; G. E. Wright, *EAEHL* 4 [1978] 1083–94; K. Jaros, *Sichem*; K. Jaros, B. Deckert, *Studien*; E. Otto, *BN* 6 [1978] 19–26; *idem, Jakob in Sichem* 108–58). See also 1 Kgs 12:1, 25; Hos 6:9; Jer 41:5; Ps 60:8 (=Eng. v 6)=108:8 (=Eng. v 7).

Gezer is far southwest of Shechem, a reason used to theorize that the cities of refuge are a secondary addition to this list. It is located at Tell Jezer five miles (eight kilometers) south-southeast of Ramleh and evidences settlement at least as early as 3300 B.C. It was deserted from 2500 until 1900, and its fortifications were built only about 1650. Here a massive sanctuary with ten sacred pillars has been revealed. Destruction came about 1470, possibly from Thutmose III of Egypt, the city being rebuilt only after 1400. In the fourteenth century, ten of the Amarna letters come from kings of Gezer. Merneptah of Egypt claims to have destroyed Gezer about 1232, but the archaeological evidence is ambiguous at this point. Gezer was allotted to Ephraim but not conquered (16:3, 10). Philistines took over the city in the twelfth century and controlled it up to the time of the Israelite monarchy (cf. 1 Kgs 9:15–17). Solomon apparently built new fortifications, but destruction came soon, probably at the hand of Pharaoh Shishak, ca. 924. Israel regained the city but lost it to Assyria in 733. Hezekiah may have regained control (N. Na'aman, "Sennacherib's Campaign to Judah and the date of the *lmlk* Stamps," *VT* 29 [1979] 76). It was destroyed again by Babylon in 586. (Cf. W. G. Dever, *EAEHL* 2 [1976] 429–43). See *Comment* on 10:33.

²² Kibzaim occurs only here. No location is known. Possibly it is a textual corruption of Jokneam (or Jokmeam; see *Notes*), which would have to be distinguished from the northern city mentioned in 12:22; 19:11; and 21:34, and from Jokmean of 1 Kgs 4:12.

Beth Horon is usually divided into a lower part, on the boundary of Benjamin and Ephraim (16:3; 18:13), and an upper part, also on the southern boundary of Ephraim (16:5). See 1 Kgs 9:17; 2 Chr 25:13; *Comment* on 10:10.

²³ Elteke' in Dan (19:44) was the site of a battle between Sennacherib of Assyria and Egypt in 701 (*ANET*, 287b). Elliger locates it at Tell el-Melat northwest of Gezer (*BHH* 1, 385, 567). There is also an Altaku mentioned in the conquest lists of Hor-en-heb, Seti I, Ramses II, and Ramses III (*ANET*, 242).

Gibbethon in Dan (19:44) came into Philistine possession early in the divided monarchy (1 Kgs 15:27; 16:15–17). Elliger identifies it with ʿAgir, four kilometers west of Tell el-Melat (*BHH* 1, 385, 567), but others identify it with Tell el-Melat (*AEHL* [1972] 127).

²⁴ Aijalon of Dan (19:42) remained under Amorite control (Judg 1:35), despite the victory of Josh 10:12. It is identified with Yalo near Emmaus, twelve miles (twenty kilometers) northwest of Jerusalem. See 1 Sam 14:31; 2 Chr 11:10, 28:18.

Gath-Rimmon of Dan (19:45) may be Tell Jerishe in modern Ramat Gan near the Yarkon River. Excavations there have traced settlement back to about 2300. Only after 2000 was the settlement fortified, but it was destroyed in the middle of the sixteenth century. Rebuilding followed quickly. Destruction came again in 1200, followed by Philistine occupation. This was destroyed, possibly by David. The Israelite city did not last long, however, probably being destroyed by Pharaoh Shishak about 920 B.C. (Cf. N. Avigad, *EAEHL* 2 [1976] 575–78).

²⁵ Tanaach belonged to Manasseh though located in Issachar (17:11), and continued in Canaanite hands (Judg 1:27). See *Comment* on 12:21.

Ibleam (see *Notes*) also belonged to Manasseh though located in Issachar (17:11) and remained in Canaanite hands (Judg 1:27). It is located at modern Bel ameh, two kilometers south of Jenin. See 2 Kgs 9:27; 15:10 (? LXX).

²⁷⁻³³ The clan of Gershon gains cities on both sides of the Sea of Galilee, in a rare union of groups east and west of the Jordan. This may reflect royal policy-seeking to create forces to unify the territory.

²⁷ Golan is known only in the city of refuge tradition. It may be Sahm el-Jalan on the eastern bank of the River el-ʿAllan.

If Ashteroth is the correct reading (see *Notes*), it may reflect the ancient capital city of Og (see *Comment* on 12:4).

²⁸ Kishyon in Issachar (19:20) may be related to the Kishon of Judg 4:7, 13; 5:21; 1 Kgs 18:40. Its location remains uncertain with Tell el-Muqarqash and Tell el-ʿAjjul having been suggested (G. W. van Beek, "Kishon," *IDB* 3 [1962] 38).

Daberath on the border of Zebulon (19:12) is located at Daburiyeh west of Mount Tabor. (See, however, G. Biton, "Haddabrat—A Defined Place Name," *Beth Mikra* 24 [1978] 73–74.)

²⁹ Jarmuth is the name of a Judean city (15:35; cf. 10:3, 5, 23; 12:11; Neh 11:29). Our verse is the only reference to Jarmuth in Issachar (cf. *Notes*). It has been tentatively identified with Kaukab el-Hawa (*AEHL* [1972] 162).

ᶜEn-Gannim refers not to the Judean city (15:34), but to the one in Issachar (19:21). A tentative identification has been made with Khirbet Beit Jann, modern Jenin (but see G. W. van Beek, "En-Gannim," *IDB* 2 [1962] 101).

³⁰ Mishʾal of Asher (19:26) appears in early Egyptian texts and has been variously identified with Tell Kisan, Tell en-Nahl, and Tell Abu Hawan, all in the Plain of Acco, the exact location being unknown.

ᶜAbdon of Asher (cf. ᶜEbron, 19:28 with *Notes*) may be located at Khirbet ᶜAbdeh, four miles East of Achzib (G. W. van Beek, "Abdon," *IDB* 1 [1962] 4).

³¹ Helkath (cf. *Notes*) of Asher (19:25) is tentatively placed at Tell el-Harbaj in the southeastern corner of the plain of Acco (A. Alt, "Das Institute im Jahre 1928," *PJ* 25 [1929] 38–39), but this is quite uncertain (Noth).

Rehob of Asher (19:28, 30) was not actually conquered (Judg 1:31). Suggested locations include Tell el-Gharbi, also called Berweh, seven miles east-southeast of Acco (G. W. van Beek, "Rehob," *IDB*, 4 [1962] 29) or even less likely Tell el-Balat (*AEHL* [1972] 269).

³² Kedesh in Naphtali (19:37) was the gathering point for Israel's troops in Judg 4–5. (V. Fritz, "Die sogenannte Liste der besiegten Könige in Josua 12," *ZDPV* 85 [1969] 152, would separate the two places; cf. *EAEHL* 2 [1976] 406; 3 [1977] 702–3). It is located at Tell Qedes, six miles (ten kilometers) north of Hazor. Excavation has shown occupation reaching back into Early Bronze I (ca. 3000) with only sporadic evidence for Late Bronze and Iron Age settlement (Y. Aharoni, *EAEHL* 2 [1976] 406). See 2 Kgs 15:29.

Hammoth-Dor (see *Notes*) is probably the Hammath of Naphtali (19:35). Its name indicates that it was a spa with hot baths. It is identified with Hamman Tabariyeh, south of Tiberias on the western shore of the Sea of Galilee. Dor is a city south of Mount Carmel on the Mediterranean sea coast (cf. *Comment* on 11:2).

Karthan or Rakkath (see *Notes* and 19:35) has been tentatively located at Khirbet el-Qureiyeh (*IDB* 3 [1962] 3) and Tell Eklatiyeh (or Knetriyeh) northwest of Tiberias (Noth).

³⁴⁻⁴⁰ The clan of Merari receives cities in two widely separated geographical areas: Zebulon in the northwestern part of Palestine and the wide-ranging areas of Reuben and Gad east of the Jordan and below the Sea of Galilee. This unlikely "invention" may well rest on the historical tradition of widely separated elements of the Levitical clan, reaching back into the period when the clan was wandering sojourners within Israel (contrast Noth).

³⁴ Jokneam is near the border of Zebulon (19:11). See *Comment* on 12:22.

Kartah appears only here in the Bible. It is located at ᶜAtlit (C. N. Johns, *EAEHL* 1, [1975] 130), where Middle/Late Bronze Age and eighth-seventh century occupation has been uncovered (134) or at el Artiqeh (*AEHL* [1972] 177). Others admit that the location is completely unknown (Noth; *IDB* 3 [1962] 3).

[35] Dimnah appears only here and is to be equated with Rimmon (see *Notes*), on the border of Zebulon (19:13). This may be located at modern Rummaneh, six miles north-northeast of Nazareth (V. R. Gold, "Rimmon," *IDB* 4 [1962] 99; cf. *AEHL* [1972] 269).

Nahalal of Zebulon (19:15) was not conquered (Judg 1:30). Attempts have been made to identify it with the contemporary village of Malul in the Jezreel Valley and with Tell en-Nahl at the southern end of the Plain of Acco (*AEHL* [1972] 227; *IDB* 3 [1962] 496). See *Notes*.

[36] Bezer is mentioned only as a city of refuge. A tentative location is suggested by E. D. Grohman (*IDB* 1 [1962] 407), at modern Umm el-ʿAmad, eight miles northeast of Medeba.

Jahaz of Reuben (13:18; see *Comment* there). See Judg 11:20; Isa 15:4; Jer 48:21, 34.

[37] For Kedemoth and Mephaʿath of Reuben, see *Comment* on 13:18.

[38] Ramoth-Gilead, missing from the lists of chap. 13, was capital of Solomon's sixth province (1 Kgs 4:13). Only recently has scholarly consensus begun to locate it at Tell er-Ramith, seventy miles south of Damascus. The only problem lies in the lack of evidence for pre-Solomonic settlement, perhaps another indication of the date of the list (H. M. Jamieson, "Ramoth-Gilead," *IDBSup*, [1976] 726; M. Ottosson, *Gilead*, 32–34). The excavator, Paul W. Lapp, could write, "The question of the identification . . . has not been conclusively proved by the excavations, but the case is as strong or stronger than for many biblical sites." He notes that the site is smaller than one would expect from the literary evidence (*The Tale of the Tell* [Pittsburgh: The Pickwick Press, [1975] 119). Noth (*Könige I* BKAT IX; Neukirchen: Neukirchener Verlag, [1968] 413) and Mittman (*Beiträge*, 225) accept the identification. See 1 Kgs 22; 2 Kgs 8:28–29; 9:1–14.

For Mahanaim in Gad, see 13:26, *Notes;* Gen 32:3; 2 Sam 2; 17:24–27; 19:33; 1 Kgs 2:8; 4:14.

[39] For Heshbon, see 12:2, *Notes;* 9:10; 13:10, 17, 21, 26, 27; Num 21; 32:3, 37; Deut 1:4; 2:24–35; 3:2, 6; 4:46; 29:6; Judg 11:19, 26; Isa 15:4; 16:9; Jer 48:2, 34, 45; 49:3; Cant 7:5; Neh 9:22.

Jazer of Gad was discussed in the *Comment* on 13:25. See Num 21:32; 32:1, 3, 35; 2 Sam 24:5; Isa 16:8–9; Jer 48:32; 1 Chr 26:31.

[41-42] The final summary ties back to Num 35 to show that the exact requirements set out there have been met. God's word has been followed explicitly.

The LXX (see *Notes*) conclusion carries the obedience motif further and reiterates the obedience of Israel in giving Joshua a place to live as well as the obedience of Joshua in occupying the city and in preserving the sacred relics, which would now, presumably, be at the disposal of the priests of Timnath-Serah. If LXX represents later interpretation, it shows that the tradition continued to develop the theme central to the story itself.

Explanation

Take special care of the poor clergy! This is the theme of the complex formed by Num 35 and Josh 21, along with the relevant Deuteronomic laws. Tradition has pictured the Levitical priests in a precarious economic situation.

This narrative complex gives the reason and the remedy for the situation. The reason is simple. The Levites belong to God and must serve him, not their own financial interests. They must depend upon him for their livelihood. God, not land and agricultural riches, are the inheritance of the Levites (cf. 13:14, 33). The priesthood, not farm work, occupies their time (18:7). The remedy is equally simple. The tribes of Israel are responsible to support their priests. Part of this support involves a "parsonage." Each tribe gives of its own cities for the priests. It gives offerings of which the priests gain a part for their own food (13:14; cf. Lev 2:3, 10; 5:13; 6:9, 11, 19, 22=Eng. 6:16, 18, 26, 29; 7:6–10, 14, 31–36; 8:31). Such provision for the priests was, however, open to abuse (1 Sam 2:12–17). Ultimately, the possibility of such abuse vanished with the destruction of the temple. Still, the precedent and principle had been established. The Christian church found that it needed only the priesthood of Jesus the Christ (cf. Hebrews), but the problem opened itself in a new form. The church had gifted men who served as evangelists and teachers and pastors. Paul, though seeking to provide for his own living, reminded his followers that the ones "who proclaim the gospel should get their living by the gospel" (1 Cor 9:14; cf. Matt 10:10). Joshua 21 thus represents the first step in a long road, the road to the rights of the minister. Paul notes the other side of the picture in his own example. Such rights cannot be asserted by the minister on his own behalf when this puts obstacles in the way of others (1 Cor 9:12).

A new set of problems is opened up by the original setting of the material. If the archaeological and historical evidence can be interpreted to place the list in the early period of the monarchy, then the problem of the relationship of the priesthood to the government is opened. Apparently, the original intention of the material was to provide not only the necessities of life for the priest, but also to provide loyal supporters for the government in areas of political unrest and insecurity. It is interesting to note at this point that the biblical record has ignored this original setting and understood the materials only from a later context. The major OT image is that of the prophet who stands to advise and even rebuke the king.

Gifts from God's Goodness   (21:43–45)

Bibliography

Smend, R. "Das Gesetz," 501–503.

Translation

⁴³ *Yahweh gave to Israel all the land which he had sworn to give to their fathers, and they possessed it and lived in it.* ⁴⁴ *Yahweh gave them rest all around, according to everything which he had sworn to their fathers. Not a single man stood before them from all their enemies; rather all their enemies, Yahweh gave into their hand.*

[45] *Not a single word fell from every good word which Yahweh spoke to the house* [a]
of Israel. Everything came to pass.

Notes

[a] LXX has "sons" rather than "house" of Israel, another instance of the use of different familiar formulas within the textual tradition.

Form/Structure/Setting

The passage is a theological conclusion to the entire book up to this point. Though written with the narrative imperfect consecutives, the section stands apart from what precedes and follows in content. The previous section has a concluding summary in 41–42, while the transitional אָז, "then," introduces a new subject in 22:1.

The section is easily seen as a literary summary composed by the editor of the book in his favorite Deuteronomistic vocabulary. The explicit theological themes of Deuteronomy and Joshua are taken up and brought to a conclusion. Deuteronomy 1:8 says that Yahweh has set (נתן) before them the land. Israel is to go and possess (ירשׁ) the land which Yahweh swore to their fathers to give (נתן) to them and to their seed after them. Deuteronomy 1:34 presents another divine oath, this time explaining why the generation in the wilderness would not see "the good land which I swore to give to your fathers." In 4:21–22 God swore that Moses would not enter the good land, but "you all will pass over and will possess this good land." The oath sworn to the fathers is a motivating force in the homiletical portions of Deuteronomy (6:10, 18, 23; 7:8, 13; 8:1, 18; 9:5; 10:11; 11:9, 21; 19:8; 26:3, 15; 28:9, 11; 30:20; 31:7, 20, 21, 23; 34:4). Joshua picks up this theme immediately in 1:6, where Joshua is promised that he will cause the people to inherit the land "which I have sworn to their fathers to give them." Joshua 2–11 is summarized in 11:23, Joshua conquering the land and providing rest from war. The distribution of the land in 13–21 concludes with a parallel summary in our section. The history of promise has become reality.

The theme that Yahweh will give rest from war is introduced in Deut 3:20 in the speech to the Trans-Jordan tribes, whose armies are to pass over armed until Yahweh gives rest to their brothers as he already has to them. This is the goal of Israel's march across the Jordan. This is taken a step further in 12:9–10 where obtaining rest is the sign for beginning worship (cf. Josh 22–24). In Deut 25:19 achieved rest is the sign to send all the Amalekites to their eternal rest. Joshua continues this theme in 1:13–15 with explicit reference back to Deut 3:20. The Trans-Jordan tribes are to remain until "Yahweh gives rest for your brothers as for you all and they possess, also they, the land which Yahweh your God is giving to them." Rest from war is achieved in 11:23. Our v 44 brings this to a climax. The promised rest has arrived. This is then completed in 22:4 with the dismissal of the eastern soldiers, the condition of rest serving then as the introduction to 23:1. (Note also 2 Sam 7:1, 11; 1 Kgs 5:18 [= Eng. 5:4]; 8:56.)

Verses 44b–45 interpret more precisely the significance of the preceding fulfillment. Taking up the language of holy war oracles (10:8), the biblical writer explains that not just in one battle, but in the whole land every single enemy soldier has fallen. This is emphasized by the contrast sentence stated first with the enemy as subject and the verb negated, then without conjunction but with the normal sentence order reversed, with the enemy as object and God as subject of a positive verb. This is the material situation. The enemy is defeated. But that is not the main point to be made. The conclusion (v 45) is the theological point. This is expressed in sentence structure parallel to 44b. A negative sentence precedes a positive one. The final clause is made shorter here, ending the section with stylistic impact.

Form and style combine, then, to give force to the theological climax of the book. Having told the stories of conquest and of distribution with particular reference to the obedience of Israel and its leader, the editor now draws his theological conclusion.

Comment

43 The editor emphasizes here the completeness of God's action. In so doing, he ignores the tradition concerning the incompleteness of Israel's action (13:1–6, 13; 15:63; 16:10; 17:12–13; cf. Judg 1:19, 21, 27–35). Here we see the manner in which biblical writers interpreted their source material. They emphasized the point of view they needed to make in the context, underlining one perspective. In a different context, a different element of the tradition could be taken up and underlined. This is seen by a comparison of the present text with that of Josh 13:1–7 or Judg 1. The theme here is the faithfulness of God in fulfilling his promises. God did his part. No matter what the political situation of Israel in a later generation, be it the division of the kingdom, the fall of the northern kingdom, or the destruction of Jerusalem and the Exile, Israel could not blame God. God had faithfully done for Israel what he promised. Blame belonged on Israel's shoulders, not God's. The same theme is placed on a universal perspective in Gen 1–3, where the world God created is good. Man is responsible for bringing divine punishment and thus "evil" into the world. Evil is explained both on the national and on the universal level as God's disciplining action in response to man's guilt, man's false exercise of his freedom.

For the theme "Promise to the fathers," see C. Westermann, *Die Verheissungen an die Väter* (= *The Promises to the Fathers*).

44 The meaning of the Deuteronomist's rest theology is clearly seen here. Rest is peace, absence of enemies and war. See Josh 1:12–18. The verse is a counterpart to chap. 12, which concluded the first section of the book. It is the fulfillment of God's promise in Exod 33:14. Both major sections of the book thus end with a statement about God's faithfulness in totally defeating the enemy. As in v 43, the editor underlines one side of the whole. Israel won all her battles and gained control of the land. The one-time slave-people now become masters of their destiny and fate. This did not erase the other factor of life. Enemies still abounded. War was still a threat. The book of Joshua stands as an example of how to act in that future threat in order to obtain the same result. War, as peace, is to be conducted in accordance to divine command. The obedient people defeat their enemies and find God's gift of peace. This is the message of Joshua. This must not be misread as a call to universal war. It is a call to face all aspects of life in faith in the faithful God.

[45] Here is the major emphasis of the section. God's word can be trusted. God fulfills his promises. The faithful community of God reads history as the story of God's directing promises.

Explanation

The small section summarizes the theological point of the book of Joshua. The entire book is to be read in light of these three verses, particularly the last. God directs history for his disobedient people through his warning and judging word. The prophets then exemplify particularly this latter statement. Still again, the word of promise takes precedence in the production of the prophetic books (note the discussion of R. E. Clements, *Old Testament Theology*, 131–54).

Such theology sounds good to the modern ears, but it seldom takes root in the modern assembly of the people of God. It raises many more questions than it calls forth answers. Who in the community can claim to hear the promising and/or judging word of God for the present? Who can point to fulfillment of God's word in present historical events? Who can read from history the word of command to God's people for the present situation? Our secular age has basically dismissed any thought of God's continuing control of history. It has definitely dismissed any thought of God directing the events of history through his word to his prophetic spokesmen. Was this something confined to the nation of Israel when it had a political face? How does the people of God interact with political reality today? That is the question posed by Josh 21:43–45. Whatever method the present generation may find to hear, interpret, and live out the word of God in present political reality, Josh 21:43–45 tells that community, on the basis of long experience with God, that both God's promising and his judging word will become historical reality. God is faithful. The question is the stance of the people of God: obedient or disobedient!

Authority and Aim of an Altar   (22:1–34)

Bibliography

Boecker, H. J. *Redeformen des Rechtslebens im Alten Testament.* WMANT 14. Neukirchen: Neukirchener Verlag, 1964, 35–41, 118. **Cholewinski, A.** *Heiligkeitsgesetz und Deuteronomium.* Rome: Pontifical Biblical Institute, 1976, 24–26. **Coats, G. W.** "Conquest Traditions in the Wilderness Theme." *JBL* 95 (1976) 177–90. ———. *Rebellion in the Wilderness.* Nashville: Abingdon, 1968, 32–37. **Diebner, B.** and **Schult, H.** "Die Stellung der Jerusalemer Orthodoxie zu den Yhwh-Altären in der Diaspora. Eine historische-kritische Spekulation zu Jos. 22:9–34." *DBlatt* 7 (1976) 33–37. **Dus, J.** "Der Brauch der Ladewanderung im alten Israel." *TZ* 17 (1961) 15–16. ———. "Die Lösung des Rätsels von Jos. 22." *ArOr* 32 (1964) 529–46. **Eissfeldt, O.** "Monopol-Ansprüche des Heiligtums von Shilo." *OLZ* 68 (1973) 327–33. (= *Kleine Schriften*, Vol. 6. Tübingen: J. C. B. Mohr (Paul Siebeck), 1979, 8–14.) **de Fraine, J.** "De altari Reubenitarum." *VD* 25 (1947) 301–13. **Hermisson, H. J.** *Sprache und Ritus im altisraelitischen Kult.* WMANT 19. Neukirchen: Neukirchener Verlag, 1965, 99–101. **Kloppenborg, J. S.** "Joshua 22: The Priestly Editing of an Ancient Tradition." *Bib* 62 (1981) 347–71. **Menes, A.** "Tempel und Synagoge." *ZAW* 50 (1932) 270–71. **Möhlenbrink, K.** "Die Landnahmensagen des Buches Josua." *ZAW* 56 (1938) 246–50. **Otto, E.** *Das Mazzotfest in Gilgal.* BWANT 107. Stuttgart: W. Kohlhammer Verlag, 1975, 170–71, 362. **Rudolph, W.** *Der "Elohist" von Exodus bis Josua.* BZAW 68. Berlin: Alfred Töpelmann, 1938, 238–40. **Schmid, R.** *Das Bundesopfer in Israel.* SANT 9. München: Kösel-Verlag, 1964, 87–90, 116. **Snaith, N. H.** "The Altar at Gilgal." *VT* 28 (1978) 330–35. **de Vaux, R.** *Histoire ancienne d'Israel.* Vol. 1. Paris: J. Gabalda, 1971, 536–38. (= *The Early History of Israel.* Tr. D. Smith. London: Darton, Longman & Todd, 1978, 581–84.) **Vink, J. G.** "The Date and Origin of the Priestly Code in the Old Testament." *OTS* 15 (1969) 73–77.

Translation

¹ *Then Joshua called to the Reubenites,*[a] *the Gaddites, and to the half tribe of Manasseh* ² *and said to them, "You all have obeyed all that Moses, the servant of Yahweh, commanded you, and you have obeyed my voice according to all that I have commanded you.* ³ *You all have not abandoned your brothers these many days up until this day, so that you have fulfilled* [a] *the obligation* [b] *of the commandment of Yahweh, your God.* ⁴ *Now, Yahweh, your* [a] *God, has given rest to your* [a] *brothers just as he spoke to them. Therefore, turn and go for yourselves to your tents, to the land of your possession, which Moses, the servant of Yahweh,* [b] *gave to you beyond the Jordan.* ⁵ *Only, be exceedingly careful to obey the commandments and the Torah, which Moses, the servant of Yahweh, commanded you,* [a] *to love Yahweh, your* [a] *God, and to walk in all his ways* [b] *and to obey his commandments and to cleave to him and to serve him with all your heart and with all your being."* ⁶ *Joshua blessed them and sent them away, and they went to their tents.*

⁷ *Now half of the tribe of Manasseh, Moses had set up in Bashan, while half of it Joshua had set up with their brothers beyond* [a] *the Jordan to the west. It was also the case* [b] *that when Joshua sent them to their tents, he blessed them and said to them,* ⁸ *"With great wealth,* [a] *return to your tents and with exceedingly large herds of cattle, with silver and gold, with bronze and iron, and with a large quantity of clothing. Divide the booty from your enemies with your brothers."*

⁹ *The sons of Reuben and the sons of Gad and half the tribe* [a] *of Manasseh turned and went away from being with the sons of Israel, away from Shilo which was in the land of Canaan, to go to the land of Gilead, to the land of their possession which they themselves had seized to possess it, according to the word of Yahweh by the hand of Moses.* ¹⁰ *They came to Geliloth of the Jordan, which was in the land of Canaan, and the sons of Reuben* [a] *and the sons of Gad and half the tribe of Manasseh built there an altar by the Jordan, an altar visible for miles.*

¹¹ *The sons of Israel heard, "The sons of Reuben and the sons of Gad and half the tribe of Manasseh have just built an altar at the edge of the land of Canaan, at the region of the Jordan on the side of the sons of Israel."* ¹² *The sons of Israel*

listened,[a] *and all the congregation* [b] *of Israel assembled themselves at Shiloh to march up against them for war.*

[13] *The sons of Israel sent Phinehas, the son of Eleazar* [a] *the priest, to the sons of Reuben and to the sons of Gad and to* [b] *half the tribe of Manasseh to the land of Gilead,* [14] *and along with him ten chiefs, one each of the house of the father* [a] *for all the tribes of Israel, each the head of the house of their fathers (they belonged to the clans of Israel).* [15] *They came to the sons of Reuben* [a] *and to the sons of Gad and to half the tribe of Manasseh to the land of Gilead. They spoke with them,* [16] *"Thus says all the assembly of Yahweh,*[a] *'What is this disobedience with which you all have disobeyed the God of Israel to turn today from following after Yahweh, in that you have built for yourselves an altar of your rebellion today* [b] *against Yahweh?* [17] *Was the sin of Peor too little for us, the sin which we have not cleansed from among us until this day? It brought a plague against the congregation of Yahweh.*

[18] *"But you all are turning today from following after Yahweh. It will be so that you will rebel today against Yahweh, then tomorrow he will become angry with all the assembly* [a] *of Israel.* [19] *Now, indeed, (if) the land of your possession is impure,* [a] *pass over for yourselves to the land of the possession of Yahweh, where the tabernacle of Yahweh is dwelling, and seize for yourselves a possession in our midst. But against Yahweh, do not rebel, and against us, do (not) rebel* [b] *by building for yourselves an altar aside from the altar of Yahweh our God.* [20] *Did not Achan, the son of Zerah, disobey with a disobedience of the ban so that upon all the assembly of Israel came the anger, despite the fact that he was but one man? Did he not die on account of his sin?'"*

[21] *The sons of Reuben and the sons of Gad and half the tribe of Manasseh answered and spoke with the heads of the clans of Israel,* [22] *"El, God, Yahweh! El, God, Yahweh! He knows. May Israel know! If in rebellion or if in disobedience against Yahweh, then you (sing.)* [a] *do not save us this day* [23] *for* [a] *building for ourselves an altar to turn from following after Yahweh. And if (it was) to send up upon it a burnt offering and a sacrifice, or if to make upon it a peace offering, may Yahweh himself seek (us) out!* [24] *In truth, was it not because of anxiety from the state of affairs that we did this thing, in that we said, 'Tomorrow your sons will say to our sons, "What is there between you and Yahweh, the God of Israel?* [25] *But a boundary Yahweh has set up between us and you all, the sons of Reuben and the sons of Gad,* [a] *namely the Jordan. There is no portion for you all in Yahweh." Your sons would cause our sons to cease fearing Yahweh.'* [26] *We said, 'Let us act for ourselves,* [a] *building the altar.'*

[27] *"It is not for burnt offerings and not for sacrifices. Indeed, it is a witness between us and between you all, and between our generations after us to perform the service of Yahweh before him with our burnt offerings and with our sacrifices and with our peace offerings. But your sons will not say tomorrow to our sons, 'There is no portion for you all in Yahweh.'* [28] *We said, 'When they talk to us and to our generations in the future, then we will say, "See the model of the altar of Yahweh which our fathers made. It is not for burnt offering nor for sacrifice, but it is a witness between us and between you all." '* [a] [29] *Far be it from us that we should rebel against Yahweh to turn today from following after Yahweh to build an altar for burnt offering and for sacrifice and for offering except for the altar of Yahweh our God* [a] *which is before his tabernacle."*

[30] *Phinehas, the priest, and the* [a] *chiefs of the assembly and the heads of the clans*

of Israel who were with him heard the words which the sons of Reuben and the sons of Gad and the sons ᵇ of Manasseh spoke. It was good in their eyes. ³¹ Phinehas, son of Eleazar ᵃ the priest, said to the sons of Reuben and to the sons of Gad and to the sons of Manasseh, "Today we know that Yahweh is in our midst, because you all have not disobeyed Yahweh in this disobedience. In that way, you have delivered the sons of Israel from the hand of Yahweh."

³² Phinehas, the son of Eleazar ᵃ the priest, and the chiefs returned from being with the sons of Reuben and the sons of Gad,ᵇ from the land of Gilead, to the land of Canaan to the sons of Israel and reported unto them the matter. ³³ The matter was good in the eyes of the sons of Israel, and the sons of Israel ᵃ blessed God. But they did not command to go up against them for war to utterly destroy the land where the sons of Reuben and the sons of Gad ᵇ were living. ³⁴ The sons of Reuben and the sons of Gad ᵃ named the altar, because it was a witness between us that Yahweh is the God.

Notes

1.a. LXX reads "sons of Reuben and sons of Gad" rather than Reubenites and Gadites, another of many examples of variant expressions interchanged within the tradition. Similar variation is evidenced in the manuscript variation between the two Heb. words מטה and שבט for "tribe."

3.a. The verbal construction with *waw* and perfect demands discussion. Within the narrative context, the simple perfect or imperfect consecutive is expected. LXX thus has aorist. Holmes says the MT must be a "modified imperative." He follows Steuernagel, Holzinger, and Driver in omitting the conjunction and connecting the "up until this day" with "you have obeyed." GKC § 112ss lists seven examples of a "longer or constant continuance in a past state" represented by perfect with conjunction. GKC § 112ff discusses the perfect consecutive used to introduce the apodosis. This may be the meaning here, 3a expressing the fulfilled condition and 3b giving the result.

3.b. LXX omits משמרת, "obligation," perhaps because it did not understand the nuance of the construction discussed in the previous note.

4.a. LXX uses "our" perhaps to prevent any restriction of Yahweh to the Transjordan tribes. Cf. v 5.

4.b. LXX does not witness "the servant of Yahweh," which may be a later addition of a frequent title.

5.a. LXX reads "us." Cf. 4d. Similarly LXX reads "our God."

5.b. "To walk in all his ways" does not appear in Syriac and could be a later insertion on the basis of Deut 10:12; 13:4.

7.a. The Massoretic tradition has preserved different readings of the preposition: *Kethib*= מ, *Qere*= ב.

7.b. The two Heb. particles appear to serve separate functions here. גם functions at sentence level (KB³, 188, no. 8) to emphasize the following action. כי introduces a temporal clause, the main clause then being introduced by the imperfect consecutive.

8.a. LXX does not witness "and he said to them saying" and thus changes the following construction to read: "And with great wealth they returned to their homes, and exceedingly large herds of cattle and silver and gold and iron and a large quantity of clothing. They divided the booty of the enemies with their brothers," omitting the opening verb of v 9. Following the lead of Dillmann, Holmes changes the Qal imperative חלקק to a Pi'el indicative introducing, in a somewhat unusual fashion, a circumstantial clause to be translated, "Having divided . . . ." He says later tradition misunderstood the verbs as imperatives and then inserted the opening line of v 8 and the opening word of v 9. Holzinger is correct, however, in preferring MT as more difficult reading. LXX understood the division of spoil as resulting in the wealth and thus transformed the sentence which originally spoke of a wish (command) for division of spoil in future victories (cf. Steuernagel).

9.a. LXX brings parallelism by adding "sons" to Manasseh also.

10.a. Here and in vv 11 and 15 LXX transposes Gad before Reuben. LXX understood גלילות as Gilgal, but it means "districts, regions" in 13:2. The term is a proper name in 18:17 and may be so understood here (so Soggin, Noth). LXX translates the same term "Gilead" in v 11 (cf., however, Snaith, *VT* 28 [1978] 330–35).

12.a. "The sons of Israel listened" repeats the phrase of 11a and does not appear in LXX, Syr or Vg. It may represent dittography. Holmes' suggestion of homoeoteuleuton in LXX is less likely.

12.b. LXX does not reproduce "congregation," perhaps an addition in line with vv 16, 17, 18, 20, 30 in which "sons" does not appear, but contrast 18:1.

13.a. LXX completes the genealogy with "sons of Aaron."

13.b. Cf. 9.a.

14.a. Syriac does not witness "of the house of the father," which could represent partial dittography from 14b (Noth, Soggin). MT is the more difficult reading and is supported by LXX, whereas Syr deletes the phrase in both parts of the verse (cf. *Text Project*). Holzinger calls 14b "untranslatable."

15.a. Cf. 10.a.

16.a. The tendency of the tradition to interchange familiar phrases is witnessed by Heb. and Tg. manuscripts reading "Israel," while other Heb., Gk. and Arabic evidence points to "sons of Israel" (cf. *BHS*).

16.b. LXX does not witness the second "today," which may be dittography in MT or simplification by LXX.

18.a. LXX omits "assembly." Cf. 12.b.

19.a. LXX reads "too little" for impure. Holmes follows Masius in suggesting an inner-Greek error: μιαρα>μικρα. Holzinger may be correct in saying LXX did not understand the text.

19.b. For "against us, do not rebel," LXX reads, "do not rebel against the Lord," after having read the preceding, "do not become rebellious against God." This may point to variant readings incorporated into the text (Steuernagel). MT reads first מרד "rebel," followed by the preposition ב then followed by the sign of the accusative. The latter occurs nowhere else in the OT. Ehrlich, followed by Noth and Soggin, suggests reading the Hiph'il, thus creating a usage nowhere witnessed in MT. Holmes suggests that the MT rests on the LXX repetition with ביהוה later being changed to ואותנו. Either the writer used a rare grammatical form for variety, or the text has become so disturbed that the original reading cannot be restored. If one reads the MT, then the pointing of Leningrad must be changed with many Heb. witnesses from אֶל, "to," to אַל, "not" (*Text Project*).

20.a. The syntax of this verse is extremely difficult. LXX introduces an extra "Behold," at the beginning, and follows its regular pattern of transcribing the name Achar (cf. 7:1). Thus it reads, "Behold, did not Achar the one of Zara transgress a transgression in regard to the bann, and upon all the assembly of Israel wrath came. This one alone himself died on account of his own sin." Rahlfs (*Septuaginta*) regards LXX B as having suffered haplography and, based on LXX A, restores: "And this one was alone. Not only this one died on account of his own sin." LXX does not appear to witness the negative, while Hebrew does not have an equivalent for "alone." Nor does Hebrew represent an express interrogative unless one carries it over as understood from the sentence initial interrogative. Holmes explained the text as a result of two interpolations, first "one" from Deut 24:16, then after the LXX, "not" on the basis of 7:24ff., where Achan's family also died. Soggin translates, "And if only he had perished alone for his iniquity!" following the Vulgate in reading לֹא for לֹא. With all this, the interpretation of Steuernagel remains the most likely. He accepts the interrogative context, suggesting perhaps emendation to add the interrogative particle. He then ties "and he was one man" to the preceding clause as a conditional clause. The final clause then shows the gravity of the divine anger.

22.a. The second person address to deity is surprising in context of the immediately preceding third person reference. Most commentators thus read the third person here with LXX, Syr, and Vg. Such change of persons is not uncommon in Hebrew and should not so readily be ignored (Hertzberg, Gray). Holmes' change to "the God of Israel" on the basis of v 16 is too speculative.

23.a. The Heb. infinitive construction ties back to the preceding verse. LXX, followed by many modern commentators, simplifies the construction by introducing "and if" at the beginning. This results in ignoring the "and if" which does occur in the Heb. in the middle of the verse. LXX also expands the divine title to "following after Yahweh our God."

25.a. LXX does not reproduce "the sons of Reuben and the sons of Gad," probably a later insertion to give explicit identification.

26.a. An attempt is often made to provide an object for the verb "to make," (cf. Soggin, Noth), but עשה can have an absolute sense "to act."

28.a. LXX transposes "between us and between you all" and adds from the context "and between our sons."

29.a. LXX does not witness "our God," while Syr adds "of Israel," again witnessing the tendency of the tradition to interchange familiar expressions. LXX may be original here.

30.a. LXX adds "all" and omits "the heads of the clans," which may be an insertion of the tradition on the basis of 13b.

30.b. MT's "sons of Manasseh" here and in 31 incorporates the addition by LXX in vv 9 and 13 but omits the normal reference to the half tribe. LXX here reads "half tribe" without "sons," showing the fluctuation in the transmission of the text.

31–32.a. LXX does not witness "the son of Eleazer," which may be an amplification of the tradition. Cf. 13.a.

32.b. The absence in MT of reference to Manasseh is surprising and is corrected by LXX. Cf. vv 33, 34.

33.a. The tradition could not accept a blessing in the mouth of the people. Thus LXX represents a theological correction in its reading, "They blessed the God of the sons of Israel." This resulted in the addition in LXX of a preceding, "and they spoke to the sons of Israel."

33.b. See 32.a.

34.a. LXX inserts Joshua as the subject, relegating the tribes to the possessors of the altar. Again LXX includes the half tribe of Manasseh (cf. 32b., 31a.). This also resulted in the final clause reading "and he said that it is between *them* that the Lord is *their* God." Many scholars seek on the basis of Syr. to find an explicit name for the altar, namely "Witness" (Steuernagel, Holmes), or "Gilead" (Dillmann, Holzinger) or something scandalous (Noth, Soggin). The MT can be interpreted in at least three ways, the last line being causal, a name, or a quotation (*Text Project*).

Form/Structure/Setting

Chapter 22 can be subdivided in several distinct ways, as a glance at different commentaries quickly reveals. This lies in the nature of vv 1–8. They clearly form a theological summary, building a bridge back to the message of 1:12–18. As such, they tie to the theme of 21:43–45. At the same time, they have a message of their own and can be considered independently. But in the context of the book as a whole, they now function as a transition to the narrative concerning the East Jordan tribes in vv 9–34. This is seen by the structural markers of the chapter. אז, "then," (v 1) clearly marks a new beginning, separating the chapter from the previous one. The reversed sentence order of v 7 might be taken as the sign of a new section, but its content clearly shows that it is being set off as a contrast to what precedes, not as a new section within the larger structure. Similarly, v 9 introduces a new phase in the narrative, but the imperfect consecutive ties it closely to the preceding structure, while the subject matter gives both a conclusion to what preceded and an introduction to what follows. Syntax and content thus join the entire chapter into a single unit. This is concluded with the formulaic conclusion of v 34, a temporal clause marking a new opening at 23:1.

This structural description of the chapter shows that it contains two basic subsections: an opening theological summary (1–8) and the narrative (9–34). A formal analysis of each of these reveals the original setting and purpose of each. Verses 1–8 form the editor's conclusion to the East Jordan tribes' participation in the conquest. As so often in such editorial summaries, it is given in monologue form (1–6, 8), interrupted only by a brief historical review (7). It can be outlined:

I. Dismissal of East Jordan Tribes (1–6)
  A. Introduction—v 1
  B. Commendation—v 2
  C. Reason for commendation detailed—v 3
  D. Results of obedience—v 4
  E. Command for the future—v 5
  F. Blessing, dismissal, and departure—v 6
II. Dismissal of Eastern Manasseh (7–8)
  A. Historical setting—v 7
  B. Blessing in imperative form—v 8

The narrative section has two major parts. The first (9–12) is a narrative introduction to the second (13–14), which follows the pattern of official consultations seeking to avoid formal judicial action (cf. Boecker, *Redeformen*):

I. Narrative introduction (9–12)
  A. Departure from Israel to Gilead—v 9
  B. Arrival at Jordan and construction of altar—v 10
  C. Angry reaction of Israel: preparation for Holy War—vv 11–12
II. Consultation to avoid judicial and military involvement (13–34)
  A. Delegation sent—vv 13–15
  B. Messenger speech—vv 16–20
    1. Formula of accusation—vv 16a
    2. Detailed testimony describing guilt—v 16b
    3. Precedent case used to predict consequences—vv 17–18
    4. Alternative proposal to settle dispute—v 19a
    5. Warning against present policies—v 19b
    6. Precedence case to support warning—v 20
  C. Defense testimony—vv 21–29
    1. Introduction—v 21
    2. Oath of purgation—v 22
    3. Sworn denial of accusation—v 23
    4. Formula of appeasement under oath—vv 24–28
      a. Appeasement formula with oath—v 24a
      b. Conditions motivating action—vv 24b–25
      c. Purpose of action—vv 26–28
      d. Oath of innocence—v 29
  D. Resolution—vv 30–34
    1. Defense testimony accepted—v 30
    2. Verdict announced—v 31
    3. Announcement to accusers—v 32
    4. Acceptance and response by accusers—v 33
    5. Response of Accused—v 34.

Formal analysis raises two questions. Where was such legal language employed to tell such a narrative? In what context was the narrative preserved?

Neither question can be answered with certainty. The cultic nature of the material suggests its origin within priestly circles of Israel. This is reinforced by the strange fact that Phinehas, the priest, not Joshua, is the major character of the narrative. Two sanctuaries appear in the narrative: Shiloh and the one of the East Jordan tribes on the Jordan. The LXX may be correct in identifying the latter with Gilgal (cf. 10 l, Notes; Soggin, Snaith (*VT* 28 [1978] 330–35), Otto (*Mazzotfest*), Möhlenbrink (*ZAW* 56 [1938] 246–50). The present narrative is certainly a victory for the Shiloh tradition. Sacrificial worship is restricted to Shiloh, being forbidden at Gilgal. This stands over against the history of Gilgal, which was carefully legitimated and used as an official sanctuary (Josh 4:19–5:15), served as the center for festive treaty-making (Josh 9:6–15), and had a tradition of sacrificial offerings (1 Sam 10:8; 11:15; 13:8–14; 15:12–15, 21; Amos 4:4–5; cf. H. J. Stoebe, *Das erste Buch Samuelis*, 210–11). As the Samual passages show, Gilgal was closely tied to King Saul. Samuel himself, however, had roots in Shiloh (1 Sam 1–4). These roots were torn away by the Philistine conquest in which Shiloh lost its priesthood, its ark, and probably its existence or at least its cultic significance (1 Sam 4; Jer 7:12, 14; 26:6, 9; Ps 78:60; cf. A. Kempinski, *EAEHL* 4 [1978] 1098–1100). (But see now M. Rose, *Deuteronomist und Jahwist*.) The Name Phinehas was part of the Shilonite priestly tradition (1 Sam 1:3; 2:34; 4:4, 11, 17, 19; 14:3).

If the tradition has ancient roots, then, it would have to be located in the period prior to Samuel, when the Shiloh sanctuary occupied a strong position in Israel's cultic life (cf. Judg 21:12, 19), a time when the Ephraimites were asserting themselves over against the tribe of Benjamin and the East Jordan tribes (Judg 12:1; 19–20; cf. 8:1). The tradition would then mark an agreement between the Israelites centered at Shiloh with the tribes from East Jordan and whomever else, e. g. Benjamin, who maintained the sanctuary at Gilgal (cf. Möhlenbrink, *ZAW* 56 [1938] 246–50; Otto, *Mazzotfest*). Such an agreement would have recognized the central place of Shiloh to the detriment of the Gilgal sanctuary. The actual power of the agreement would have been short-lived, since Shiloh soon lost its cultic significance. The Shiloh tradition lived on, however, in the exiled priesthood in Anathoth (1 Kgs 2:27).

This Shiloh tradition may have exercised an important influence on the book of Joshua as a whole. The major section of the book is dominated by Gilgal narratives, but the closing section reflects the importance of Shiloh (18:1–22: 34). Did the tradition as a whole gain its contours at the time of Shiloh's dominance?

It is this old story, rooted in the feuding of Israelite tribes and cults, which has been taken up by the biblical writer to proclaim the word of God in a quite different setting. The exile has produced further divisions within the people of God. The worship place is no longer Shiloh, but Jerusalem, where the temple lies in ruins. Worship may well again center around a holy tent within the sacred ruins. The men of power and influence, however, are no longer there. They live in Babylon in exile. They face the question of worship far beyond the Jordan. The old narrative finds a resolution for the new crisis in worship. Worship beyond the Jordan, in exile, away from God's land of possession, can be carried out. Such worship, however, cannot be the normal sacrificial worship of Jerusalem (cf. Menes, *ZAW* 50 [1932] 270–71). Such tension lived on, however. Joshua 22 stood as an ever real need for the people of Israel during the exile and during the years of the second temple. Its function became even more acute with the rise of yet another schism within the people of God. Ezra and Nehemiah reflect the growing tension between the people of the north around Samaria and the people of Jerusalem. Joshua 22 provided a possible solution for even this tension (Vink, *OTS* 15 [1969] 73–77), but the solution was never accepted and realized. Thus an old tradition spoke to ever new historical realities within the people of God. It is probable that each of these new situations has left its mark on the tradition itself, as God used his word to work out the tensions among his people.

Comment

¹ מטה, "tribe," occurs only here and v 14 in this chapter, in which שבט, its synonym, appears seven times. This follows a pattern of the book. In chaps. 1–12, מטה appears only with Achan in 7:1, 18; שבט thirteen times. In chaps. 13–21, מטה is used fifty-three times, while שבט appears only with notices about the Levites (13:14, 33), and in Deuteronomistic introductions (13:7; 18:2, 4, 7), aside from what are probably editorial notes in 13:33 and 21:16. This makes it probable that the notation here in 22:1 is also a later editorial note, adding half of Manasseh to a section in which it was not originally included, since the specific note about half of Manasseh comes in vv 7–8.

The concern with the East Jordan tribes here is significant. The entire Joshua narrative is framed by concern for those parts of the people of God living outside the actual "Promised Land." This may reflect the setting of the major editorial work of the book.

² The command of 1:13–15 and the pledge of 1:16–18 have been realized. No reasons can be given to condemn those tribes dwelling outside the Promised Land. They have been faithful to the two great commanders of Israel, Moses and Joshua.

³ The specific praise of faithfulness to the brothers in the land has specific relevance for the period of the exile. Babylonian Jews cannot be condemned for unfaithfulness. No one geographical group of God's people has a monopoly on faithfulness and obedience.

The term משמרת, "obligation to God" or "charge given by God" appears in several highly significant summary contexts (Gen 26:5; Lev 8:35; 18:30; 22:9; Num 9:19, 23; Deut 11:1; 1 Kgs 2:3; 2 Chr 13:11; otherwise only 2 Chr 23:6; Mal 3:14).

⁴ The result of faithfulness is rest, the precise reward promised in 1:15 (cf. 21:43–44). The reward, however, is for the brothers, since the East Jordan tribes already have their rest (1:13). They now simply receive the command to return and enjoy that rest. This has particular significance in light of the following narrative in which the brothers bring accusation of unfaithfulness against the East Jordan tribes. The accusing West Jordan tribes can enjoy their "rest" only because of the faithfulness of their East Jordan brothers.

⁵ Return to rest does not mean return to forget or neglect obligation.

God demands faithfulness in peace and prosperity as well as in war and danger. The command echoes that given to Joshua in 1:7. It is a summary of the charge of Deuteronomy (cf. Deut 10:12–13, 20; 11:1; 6:4–15; 13:4–5 [Eng. 3–4]; 30:15–20). It is the definition of people of God. The man-God relationship is not a legalism done in fear, nor a business transaction done with pride of achievement. It is a love and devotion relationship, obeying and worshiping out of free choice.

⁶ Blessing is not necessarily connected with the cult for ancient Israel. Here it is simply part of the formula of taking leave and saying goodbye. Included is the wish for luck and prosperity (v 8; cf. G. Wehmeier, *Der Segen*, 154; Gen 32:1 [Eng. 31:55]; 47:7, 10; 2 Sam 19:40 [Eng. 19:39]; 13:25).

⁷ A historical review takes up the notes of Num 32:33; 34:14–15; Deut 3:13; Josh 1:12–15; 17:1–13. The isolated notice about half the tribe of Manasseh is unexpected in this context. It may be related to the similar phenomenon in Num 32 and have ultimate historical roots. The second part of the verse must refer to the dismissal of only the eastern half of the tribe.

⁸ Here the formal blessing receives content. Again, it is striking that such blessing is given only to the one group. It may relate to a reputation as a "man of war" (Josh 17:1). The concluding imperative note may be understood in several ways. It may be an admonition to share your current wealth with the families who stayed beyond the River; but it may also be a programmatic note for the future, calling for the East Jordan tribes to remember their western brothers after future military successes. This would fit the emphasis on unity in the following narrative.

⁹ Repeating the departure note of 6b, now including Manasseh, the narrative proper begins by distinguishing between the East Jordan tribes and the sons of Israel as well as between the land of Canaan and the land of Gilead. This may well reflect ancient designations in a period before the unity of the twelve tribes was self-evident. The important point for the editor here is that the East Jordan tribes were obeying Yahweh and the Mosaic commandments.

¹⁰ The altar is located in the land of Canaan, which, according to the previous verse, means west of the Jordan. The location may reflect an ancient understanding of the land west of the Jordan as that controlled by Yahweh and thus suitable for an altar to Yahweh (cf. v 19). Historically, it may reflect an ancient tie between the East Jordan tribes and the Benjaminites with their sanctuary at Gilgal.

¹¹ Scholarly controversy over the location of the altar centers on the meaning of the phrases אֶל־מוּל and אֶל עֵבֶר. The first means "the front side of" (Exod 26:9; 28:25, 27, 37; Josh 8:33). Perhaps Josh 9:1 is the best parallel here, speaking of the territory in front of, that is, this side of, the Lebanon. The other is more difficult. It can mean "on the other side of, beyond" as in Deut 30:13. It can, however, refer to the side, the edge of something: Exod 28:26 (=39:19); Ezek 1:9, 12 (=10:22). It is apparently this latter meaning which is intended in our passage. The altar is a border shrine within the land of Canaan but on its very edge and serving for those tribes who are not precisely part of the sons of Israel, but rather live in the land of Gilead. This explains their fear of separation and exclusion.

¹² For the assembly or congregation of Israel, עֵדָה, see *Comment* on 18:1.

The original purpose was to engage in immediate battle, a practice not un-known among Israelite tribes (cf. Judg 19–21; the Judah-Benjamin conflict represented by David and Saul; the ultimate dissolution into two kingdoms).

¹³ Abruptly and unexpectedly, the strategy changes. An investigation com-mission is appointed. This is in the best Israelite tradition of seeking to avoid court and military conflict when possible (see Boecker, *Redeformen*), a tradition that was certainly not realized in all instances.

Phinehas plays a unique role here, being the only leader besides Joshua to take the initiative in any action within the book. He is the son of Eleazer, who is on the inheritance commission with Joshua (14:1; 19:51; 21:1), but who never acts independently. Here Phinehas takes center stage away from Joshua. The later tradition modified this by inserting Joshua into v 34 (LXX; see *Notes*). Outside his birth (Exod 6:25), Phinehas appears only in the Baal of Peor incident (Num 25; cf. Ps 106:30), the resulting war against Midian (Num 31:6) and the note inserted into Judg 20:28. It is interesting to note that the tradition connects him here with Shiloh, in Judg 20 apparently with Bethel, and in Josh 24:33 with Gibeah.

¹⁴ The commission includes a representative of the nine full tribes and the western half of Manasseh. For the term נשיא, "chief," see Comment on 9:15 (cf. 13:21; 17:4). The house of the father, בת אב, is generally the third division within Israelite society under the tribe (שבט or מטה) and the clan (משפחות or אלפים), but here the meaning is not so clear. The term may be given an extended meaning to serve as a synonym for "tribe," or it may seek to describe each of the "chiefs" as being the head of his extended family as well as chief of his tribe. For a full discussion of the term, see N. Gottwald, *The Tribes of Yahweh*, 258–67, 285–92, and J. Flanagan, "Chiefs in Israel," JSOT 20, 1981, 47–73).

¹⁶ The speech is opened with the official "messenger formula" so well known from the prophets (see the summary of recent study by W. E. March, "Prophecy," *Old Testament Form Criticism*, ed. J. H. Hayes. [San Antonio: Trinity University Press, 1974] 146–57). The accusation is that Israel has "disobeyed, transgressed," מעל (See *Comment* on 7:1). This late linguistic expression may reflect the use of the material in the exilic community. Otherwise, it is the only use of the term which has been preserved from the early tradition.

The accusation is not without its irony. An act of religious devotion, build-ing an altar, is defined as rebellion against God. This presupposes that God has ordained only one legitimate altar (Deut 12; cf. the recent discussion by A. D. H. Mayes, *Deuteronomy*, 61–63, 220–29). An earlier stage of the tradi-tion may have interpreted this to mean that God had specifically legitimated certain sanctuaries, setting them apart from the Canaanite shrines (see 5:13–15). The accusation would then be that the new altar was constructed at man's initiative, not God's. The emphatic "for yourselves" may point in this direction.

¹⁷ The prosecution uses a precedence case to strengthen their accusation. This is based on the tradition of Num 25, which is also used by the Deutero-nomist in Deut 4 as the extreme example of Israel following other gods. This sets up the prosecution understanding. The altar will lead the East Jordan tribes to worship other gods, the primary sin. The sin of Israel at Beth Peor

has lasting effects. טהר, "cleanse oneself, purify from among us," is at home in priestly circles, particularly the legislation in Lev 14–16. Our text appears to mean more than cultic ritual. It refers to excluding all worship of foreign gods (cf. Gen 35:2; H. Ringgren, *TWAT* 3 [1978] 314).

נגף, "plague," appears to be a specifically priestly term referring to numinous divine punishment, which can be averted only by following divine instructions (Exod 12:13; 30:12; Num 8:19: 17:11–12 [Eng. 16:46–47]).

18 The prosecution predicts the results of the crime, divine anger on the entire community (cf. 9:20; Deut 29:27 [Eng. 29:28]). קצף, "wrath, anger," is used only twice for human anger. The verb is used for divine anger in a majority of the cases, particularly in Deuteronomistic and Priestly circles (G. Sauer, *THAT* 2 [1976] 665). Human sin and rebellion rouse the divine wrath. Here we see the responsibility of the community for its members and the sense of unity within the community, so that the sin of a part brings punishment on the whole.

19 The prosecution seeks to avoid the punishment. They offer an alternative solution, marked grammatically by an exclusive sentence (Andersen, *Sentence* 170–74) separating the proposed solution from the threatened punishment. The presupposition is that East Jordan's land is impure. טמא is a Priestly term dominating Lev 11–15, Num 19, Deut 14. This impurity is not caused by disobeying purity codes, however. East Jordan is impure because it is not Yahweh's possession. Rather it is simply "your possession." That means it is land where Yahweh does not live, land which his presence has not sanctified and purified (cf. Amos 7:7). Again, the charge of the prosecution is that the accused have taken their own initiative, chosen their own land and their own altar, and thus have forsaken God. The alternative solution is to forsake their land and their altar and come into Yahweh's possession. This is a self-sacrificial proposal, for it means that the ten tribes will have to share their land with the East Jordan tribes (Cf. Gen 13:8–9).

The משכן, "tabernacle" of Yahweh shows his presence in the land of the sons of Israel. The expression is a part of priestly language (Exod 26–27, 36–40; Num 1–10; for literature see A. R. Hulst, *THAT*, 2 [1976] 908). It is based, however, on an old Shiloh tradition (M. Haran, *Temples*, 194–204).

Even though the altar is built, the warning is given, "Do not rebel." This underlines the contrast of choices available. Worship at an altar is viewed as a necessity by both parties. The point is, which altar has been properly legitimated by God and which is contaminated by worship by foreign gods?

20 Another precedence case is used to illustrate the drastic nature of the punishment. The example of Achan (Josh 7) shows that individual sin brought disaster for the whole community. It also shows that the guilty party had to die for his sin. This should stand as warning enough for anyone who would disobey God. On this solemn note, the prosecution rests its case.

21 "The heads of the clans of Israel" picks up the last phrase of the somewhat overloaded v 14 and may reflect an ancient military division in ancient Israel (cf. N. Gottwald, *The Tribes of Yahweh*, 270–78). The use of such a term in the original tradition would correspond to the military overtones given the tradition by v 12.

22 The defense opens its testimony with a solemn proclamation of three different names for God. The first, *El*, is the name of the Canaanite high god taken over into the names of the gods of the fathers (e.g. El Shaddai, Gen 17:1; 28:3; 35:11; 43:14; 48:3; 49:25; Exod 6:2–3; El 'Olam, Gen 21:33; El 'Elyon, Gen 14:18–22; El Ro'i, Gen 16:13; El Berith, Judg 9:46; El the God of Israel, Gen 33:19–20; cf. B. W. Anderson, "Names of God," *IDB* 2 [1962] 407–17). *Elohim* is the generic name for God, which is grammatically plural, having the Hebrew plural ending ים. Most often, as here, it refers to the one God. Yahweh is the personal name of Israel's God revealed to Moses (Exod 3; 6). The defense case begins with a solemn vow that God knows the truth and the plea that Israel may soon learn. This is strengthened by an oath formula, directed in the Hebrew text directly to God, and asking that he not bring them victory if they are guilty. The assumption here is that the final word in the dispute belongs neither to the accuser nor to the accused but to God. The term again gives military overtones to the scene.

²³ A second oath formula (23b) adds a new perspective to the argument. The defense understands the accusation to deal with the problem of sacrifice, terms never introduced by the accusers. This may well reflect the Priestly use of the tradition in a time when the Jerusalem temple began to claim sole authority for sacrifice. Three types of sacrifice are named. The עולה is the whole burnt offering (Exod 29:18; Lev 1). מנחה is a vegetable offering which normally accompanies the whole burnt offering, though in special circumstances the term assumes more specific meanings (cf. R. Rendtorff, *Geschichte des Opfers*, 168–98). זבחי שלמים is a compound term apparently joining two originally separate types of sacrifices (Rendtorff, 151). The זבח began as a private family sacrifice (e.g. 1 Sam 1–2) in which the animal is eaten by the worshipers. The שלמים is the offering given at the conclusion of the ceremony of the whole burnt offering. The joining of the terms appears to be the result of cult centralization as demanded by Deut 12, so that family sacrifices were limited to the temple area with the priest carrying out certain blood rituals originally associated with the שלמים alone (Rendtorff, *Geschichte des Opfers*, 162–68; cf. B. Lang, *TDOT* 2 [1980] 17–29).

Again the oath leaves punishment to Yahweh.

²⁴ The accused state their case in a form that seeks to appease their accusers by justifying their actions and the motives behind them. They were motivated by דאגה "anxiety, concern" (see Jer 49:23; Ezek 4:16; 12:18f.; Prov 12:25) over the current state of affairs. This is stated in terms of the younger generation and future possibilities. It reflects present anxiety. The relationship between the different groups in Israel was not one of trust. Rather the East Jordan group felt threatened with expulsion from the communal worship of Yahweh and from the community which worshiped him.

²⁵ The anxiety had roots in a theological issue, the definition of the Promised Land. The geographical feature of the Jordan River could easily take on theological significance as a boundary of God's people (cf. Ezek 48). This would relegate everyone east of the Jordan to other lands with other gods (cf. Deut 32:8; 4:19). This is the other side of the argument of the accusers, who supposed that the East Jordan group had fallen away to other gods. The countercharge from the East Jordan tribes is, "You all are arbitrarily cutting us off from worshiping Yahweh."

²⁷ The East Jordan tribes interpret their altar as a perpetual witness that they do belong to Yahweh, a witness, which, if accepted, would avoid future confrontations on the subject. The Jordan is a symbol of separation. The altar is a symbol of unity. The sacrifices differ significantly here, the private זבח and the final שלמים being separated. Also this verse, read in isolation, could be interpreted as presupposing that the altar of witness would also be an altar of sacrifice. This may be the oldest level of tradition in the narrative.

²⁸ The altar is patterned on the one used by the sons of Israel, namely the one in Shiloh, since that altar has been patterned after God's model (cf. Exod 25:9–40). Here the East Jordan altar is explicitly limited to the witness function, sacrifice being excluded.

²⁹ The defense testimony closes with an oath of innocence based on pure motives. This actually takes judgment from the hand of men and gives it to God, as did the opening oath (vv 22–23).

³⁰ The commission is satisfied with the defense testimony. "It was good in the eyes of" is a formula accepting proposals or testimonies (Gen 41:37; Lev 10:20; Deut 1:23; 1 Sam 18:5; 2 Sam 3:36; 18:4; 1 Kgs 3:10; Esth 1:21; 2:4; cf. Gen 45:16; Lev 10:19; Esth 2:9).

³¹ The agreement shows that God has made the judgment (cf. vv 22–23, 29) and thus that God is present among them. This is precisely the theme dominating Josh 1 (vv 5, 9, 17). Amidst the arguments of men, the promised presence of God reveals itself and brings peace. By proving their innocence, the East Jordan tribes have delivered all Israel from the threatened punishment (cf. vv 18, 20).

³² The commission did not have the final word. They had to make their report to the sons of Israel as a whole. The report was accepted with thanksgiving to God. Notice that when men bless God, it simply means to give thanks for his blessings (Gen 24:27, 48; G. Wehmeier, *Der Segen*, 160–62). A situation which threatened war and total destruction resulted in worship and a new relationship of trust.

³⁴ The altar functions as a witness to both groups, not just of national unity. The function is much greater. It shows that the unifying factor is Yahweh. Even more, the altar witnesses to the divinity of Yahweh himself, a divinity proved by his presence in transforming a situation which threatened war and total destruction into a new relationship of unity and trust.

Explanation

The passage opens up new light on the struggles through which God had to lead his people before they could join one another in worship and proclamation of his deity. The problem was not simply the enemy who possessed the land (Josh 1–12). It was not simply jealousy among tribes and desire for more land (Josh 17:14–18). The problem was threatened warfare among the tribes themselves because they could not trust one another and because they accused one another of apostasy. Such accusation was not based on credal statements. Rather it was based on different modes and places of worship. Behind it all lay not only religious, but also political and professional motivations. Here the basic nature of the Israelite legal system prevailed, as it called for the parties to seek to arbitrate their disputes and avoid fights in the courts or on the battle fields. Both parties, each from its own perspective, offered compromise solutions. The accusers listened to the reasoning of the defendants, even when this meant admitting implicitly their own possible guilt, namely that they could well have denied the other group the right to worship God. A compromise was reached which reunited the people of God and led them to bless his holy name.

Soon after the agreement was reached, the parties involved disappeared from historical importance. The altar of Shiloh was destroyed. The Transjordan tribes lost more and more of their independence to conquering enemies. The tradition, however, lived on. New generations found God speaking to them in new ways through the old tradition. Each could emphasize a different aspect—the mode of worship, the place of worship, the tribal connections, the geographical boundaries, the definition of people of God and place of God, the charges of apostasy. Each generation interpreted the tradition in light of its new circumstances, from the division of the monarchy to the ever developing schism between Jerusalem and the Samaritans.

The major interpretation came when the material was placed in its present literary context. Here it closed out the action of the conquest and served as a bridge to the ups and downs of the Judges. As such, it became the example of how Israel should settle its tribal, religious, political, and legal conflicts. It gave a final definition of the unity of Israel as the twelve-tribe people of God on both sides of the Jordan River. Most of all it identified Yahweh as *the God,* a claim proved by his presence in unifying the disputing people of Israel, giving a separated people his blessing instead of his wrath. As such, the chapter became the illustration of how the blessings and curses of God (Deut 27–28) worked out in the history of God's people. It showed that the determining factor was neither the place of the cult nor the geographical location of the peoples. Cult and geography could separate. Proclamation of Yahweh as the present God unified.

The Commander's Concluding Charge
(23:1–16)

Bibliography

Baltzer, K. *Das Bundesformular.* WMANT 4. Neukirchen: Neukirchener Verlag, 1960, 71–73. **Bright, J.** *The Authority of the Old Testament.* Nashville: Abingdon, 1967, 241–51. **Floss, J. P.** *Jahwe dienen—Göttern dienen.* BBB 45. Bonn: Peter Hanstein, 1975, 331–34. **Halbe, J.** *Das Privilegrecht Jahwes Ex. 34, 10–26.* FRLANT 114. Göttingen: Vandenhoeck & Ruprecht, 1975, 347–49. **Lubsczyk, H.** *Der Auszug Israels aus Ägypten.* Erfurter Theologische Studien 11. Leipzig: St. Benno-Verlag, 1963, 138–45. **McCarthy, D. J.** *Treaty and Covenant.* 2nd ed. AnBib 21A. Rome: Pontifical Biblical Institute, 1978, 203. **Perlitt, L.** *Bundestheologie im Alten Testament.* WMANT 36. Neukirchen: Neukirchener Verlag, 1969, 19–22. **Rudolph, W.** *Der "Elohist" von Exodus bis Josua.* BZAW 68. Berlin: Alfred Töpelmann, 1938, 240–44. **Schmitt, G.** *Du sollst keinen Frieden schliessen mit den Bewohnern des Landes.* BWANT 91. Stuttgart: W. Kohlhammer Verlag, 1970, 148–50. **Smend, R.** "Das Gesetz und die Völker." *Probleme Biblischer Theologie,* ed. H. W. Wolff. München: Chr. Kaiser Verlag, 1971, 501–4. **Wilms, F. E.** *Das Jahwistische Bundesbuch in Exodus 34.* SANT 32. München: Kösel-Verlag, 1973, 194–96.

Translation

[1] *Many days after Yahweh had given rest to Israel from all their enemies all around, when Joshua became old in years,* [2] *Joshua called to all* [a] *Israel, to their elders, and to their heads, and to their judges and to their officials. He said to them, "I have become old; I have increased in years.* [3] *But you all have seen all that Yahweh, your* [a] *God, has done to all these nations on your behalf, because Yahweh, your God, it is indeed, who has fought for you all.* [4] *See, I have allotted to you all these remaining nations as an inheritance for your tribes, from the Jordan and all the nations which I have cut off* [a] *and the great sea at the going down of the sun.* [5] *But Yahweh, your God, is the one who will push them out on your behalf.* [a] *He will dispossess them from before you all in order that you all may possess their land just as Yahweh, your God, spoke to you all.* [6] *And you all must have great courage to obey carefully all that is written in the book of the Torah of Moses, so as not to turn from it to the right nor to the left,* [7] *and so as not to mix with these nations, these* [a] *remaining with you all. The name of their gods you all shall not call to memory nor shall you all swear* [b] *(by them), nor shall you all serve them, nor shall you all bow down in worship to them.* [8] *But you all stick to Yahweh, your God, just as you all have done until this day.* [9] *Yahweh has dispossessed from before you all great and mighty nations, but as for you all, no man has stood before you all until this day.* [10] *One man from you all pursues a thousand, for Yahweh, your God, it is he indeed who has fought for you all, just as he spoke to you all.* [11] *You all must guard yourselves* [a] *carefully to love Yahweh, your God,* [12] *for if you all ever turn away and stick with the rest* [h] *of these nations who remain with you all so that you all would relate yourself in marriage with them and would mix with them and they with you all,* [13] *be fully aware that Yahweh, your God,* [a] *will no longer continue to disposses these nations from before you all. They will become for you all a trap and a snare* [b] *and a whip in your sides and thorns in your eyes until you all wander away lost off of this good land which Yahweh, your God, has given to you all.* [14] *But as for me, right now today I am going the way of all the earth. You all know with all your hearts and with all your being that not one word has fallen from all the good* [a] *words which Yahweh, your God, spoke concerning you all. They all* [b] *have come to pass for you all.* [15] *Not one word has fallen from among them. And it will be the case that just as every good word which Yahweh, your God,* [a] *spoke to you all, has come upon you all, just so Yahweh will bring upon you all every evil word until he has destroyed you all from upon this good land which Yahweh, your God, has given to you all.* [16] *When you all transgress the covenant of Yahweh, your God, that he commanded you all, and you all go off and serve other gods and bow down in worship to them, then the anger of Yahweh will burn against you all, and you will quickly wander away lost from upon this good land which he has given to you all."*

Notes

2.a. LXX adds traditional "sons of."

3.a. LXX quite consistently reads first person plural for second person plural of MT in this chapter.

4.a. The text of 4b is problematic, changing from reference to the future allottment of remaining nations to a boundary description to a reference to past destruction of nations, and back to a boundary description. LXX witnesses the same text. Working from the Vulgate, Grätz, followed by Steuernagel, has suggested that "all the nations which I have cut off" be transposed before "from the Jordan" and that "and unto the" be added before "great sea." Holmes notes that Jerome's text appears to have been more confused than ours. Holmes thus suggests seeing "all the nations . . . cut off" as a pre-LXX gloss. He may be correct, but we must be clear that this is a literary judgment, not one based on textual evidence. The phrase has its apparent origin in Deut 12:29; 19:1, where it stands in close connection to ירש, "dispossess." Perhaps it represents an early gloss to v 5, which has been accidentally copied from the margin into v 4. This may be supported by the textual disturbances which have affected v 5.

5.a. LXX reads: "But the Lord (y)our God will push them out from before us (you), until that they should perish. He will send against them the wild beasts until they utterly destroy them and their kings from before you. You will, possess their land, just as the Lord, our God, said to you." Hollenberg (*Theologische Studien und Kritiken* 1 [1874] 462–506) suggests that LXX has the proper text, which has fallen from MT through homoeoteuleuton. Holmes counters that it is a deliberate work of a Hebrew scribe who summarized the omitted words with והוריש אתם מלפניכם, "he will dispossess them from before you." Steuernagel points to Deut 7:20 as the source, to which Soggin adds Exod 23:28. A much more likely candidate is Lev 26:22, in which הכריתה also occurs (cf. previous *Note*). The reference to the kings might be corruption from the Leviticus passage or Midrashic joining to Josh 10:40; 11:12, 17; Deut 7:24. Only one thing is clear. The tradition has interpreted the passage to the extent that the original reading cannot be recovered.

7.a. The expression בגוים האלה הנשארים האלה אתכם, "with these nations, these remaining with you," is awkward and probably the result of conflation (R. Boling, "Some Conflate Readings in Joshua-Judges," *VT* 16 [1966] 296–97).

7.b. Conflation may also explain the presence of the two *Hiphil* forms, "not call to memory," and "not swear by." The latter must be read as Niphal (cf. Syr, Vg, Tg). LXX omits the latter form altogether.

11.a. MT reads literally, "and you should guard yourselves exceedingly for your souls." LXX has no equivalent for the idiomatic usage of "for your souls."

12.a. MT again represents a conflated text. Cf. 7.a. There is considerable Hebrew evidence for reading "all" in place of "the rest." LXX omits the word. The tradition found various ways of emphasizing this important point.

13.a. LXX does not witness "Your God," which may be a later usage of a familiar refrain.

13.b. שטט, "snare," occurs nowhere else in the Hebrew Bible and is evidently a copying error for the similar שטים.

14.a. "Good" does not appear in LXX. It is the addition of a familiar phrase on the basis of v 15, where it is necessary in light of the explicit opposition to the "evil word."

14.b. LXX and Vg. reflect textual variations in the last half of the verse, in which expansion and/or dittography have occurred.

15.a. LXX omits "your God" the two times it appears in this verse, but adds it the one time it does not occur, showing again the flexibility of the copying tradition in using divine titles.

16.a. LXX omits the final half of the verse, which is an abbreviated version of Deut 11:17. Holmes argues that the verse must be a late insertion which did not understand that 16 was the protasis of 15 without which 15 becomes an unconditional threat. Such exegetical decisions cannot serve as the basis of textual ones. It is possible that the original writer intended an unconditional threat. The form of v 15 is not that of a conditional sentence. Rather, it is a complete sentence in itself. Verse 16a is then a temporal clause for which 16b forms a proper main clause. The evidence appears to favor the MT as original, though it is not impossible to understand 16a as an interpretation of 15b, which then, itself, was interpreted through 16b.

Form/Structure/Setting

The temporal clause of v 1 clearly marks the beginning of a new narrative. The threat of 15–16 closes the narrative content. For this reason, we divide our exegesis at this point. The grammar, however, of 24:1 connects this closely to the preceding, so that one might well argue that the two chapters form a unit.

Every verse of the chapter displays Deuteronomistic theology and vocabulary (cf. the lists of M. Weinfeld, *Deuteronomy*, 320–59). The only remaining literary question reduces to the number of Deuteronomists or the stage of Deuteronomistic activity at which the chapter was written (cf. Smend, *Das Gesetz;* Halbe, *Privilegrecht*). The form of the chapter may be approached from two perspectives. The opening verse connects it with the deathbed blessings of the patriarchs (Jacob, Gen 48–49; Joseph, Gen 50:22–26; Moses, Deut 33 and the book of Deuteronomy; David, 2 Sam 23:1–7; 1 Kgs 2:1–9; cf. Weinfeld, *Deuteronomy*, 11–14). The content and form, however, are distinctive, having many connections with the "Covenant Formulary" (Baltzer, *Das Bundesformular;* McCarthy, *Treaty and Covenant*):

1) Antecedent History, vv 3–5
2) Statement of substance (or basic principle), vv 6–8
3) (Transformed) blessing, vv 9–10
4) Restatement of basic principle, v 11
5) Curse, vv 12–13, 15–16.

The content thus relates to that of a covenant renewal ceremony, but again in a distinctive manner. The liturgy of covenant renewal has become the sermon of a dying leader. Baltzer relates this to the Hittite vassal treaties, where the aged king appoints his successor and secures the allegiance to him from the next generation. He fails to note that Josh 23 knows of no successor. Here the burden is placed strictly on the congregation. He does note that blessing and curse have become successive events in history. The content of covenant renewal has become the sermonic blessing of the patriarch in a unique way, for the final and dominating word is a curse, not a blessing. This reveals the setting for which the message is intended, namely that of the Israelite community of the Exile who have experienced both blessing and curse. Joshua 23 explains why God had brought the curse upon Israel. As Perlitt (*Bundestheologie*) has shown, the arc of tension runs from Josh 23 to 2 Kgs 17, where the curse is realized. The arc of tension runs even further. It connects also to 2 Kgs 21:1–16; 23:26–27, where the curse of Josh 23 is realized even more fully. But Josh 23 has also a narrower arc of tension, which runs simply to Judg 2, particularly vv 6–23 and 3:1–6, where the transgression of the covenant begins and the curse is initiated (cf. especially vv 20–23). Joshua 23 thus plays a key role in the biblical story. It foreshadows the remainder of the history of Israel, placing that history under the dark shadow of curse from its very inception.

The chapter not only points forward. It also has backward connections. As in Exod 19:4–6 Israel looked back to the Exodus, so in 23:3–4 Israel looks back at the conquest. As in Exod 23:23–33 God promised Israel to drive out their enemies and commanded Israel not to worship other Gods, so in Josh 23:5–13. As Exod 33:1–3 illustrated the curse of divine wrath, so 23:13, 15–16 threatened such a curse upon Israel. As Exod 34 depicts the covenant with Israel based on God defeating the enemies and Israel refraining from any contact with the gods of the enemies, so Josh 23 presupposes such a covenant and the dire consequences of disobedience. This is the theology which is preached in the entire book of Deuteronomy, finding its climax in the blessings and curses of chaps. 27–29. It is the theology which introduces the book of Joshua (especially 1:1–9). Finally, the setting of Josh 23 repeats that of chap. 13, an aged Joshua facing Israel with much land yet to be divided.

Joshua 23 is thus a centerpiece, taking up the themes stretching from Sinai onward and casting their light into the period of the judges, into the divided monarchy and finally into the Babylonian Exile. As such, Josh 23 is the theological explanation of the history of Israel herself.

Comment

[1] Unlike other narrative texts, this one has no specific setting in time or space. It simply connects to 13:1, when Joshua was old, and 21:44, when God had given rest. The setting thus marks Israel at the moment she had dreamed of from the Exodus onward (Exod 33:14). But it also marks the crisis of leadership transition. The message which follows is at the same time one for prosperity, and also for crisis.

[2] The list of leaders joins those of the first half of the book: *elders* (6:21; 7:6; 8:10, 33; cf. 20:4) *judges* (8:33; cf. K. W. Whitelam, *The Just King* [JSOTS 12; Sheffield: JSOT Press, 1979] 198); and *officials* (1:10; 3:2; 8:33), with those of the second half: *heads* (14:1; 19:51; 21:1; 22:14, 21, 30). Interestingly, there is no mention of chiefs nor priests. The setting is a meeting of the "secular" leaders of the community.

[3] Joshua begins by defining Israel through looking at her history. Israel is the people for whom Yahweh fights against all the nations (Exod 14:14, 25; Deut 1:30; 3:22; 20:4; Josh 10:14, 25, 29, 42), thus fulfilling his promise to be with them (contrast Exod 33:1–3 and Josh 1:5, 9, 17). Without divine presence and assistance in battle, Israel has no identity. This summarizes chaps. 1–12.

[4] Despite Israel's triumphs, she had a nagging problem. Enemies remained in the land God had given her (13:1–7), precisely in the land between the Jordan and the Mediterranean (cf. the problem of chap. 22). Just as God had portioned out the land to the tribes (14–19), so he now has apportioned out the nations (cf. 13:6, the only other appearance of the *Hiph'il* of the verb נפל in Joshua). This represents the other side of the picture from that emphasized in 21:43–45. Israel has the land. She must no longer fight for it. But she still has nagging enemies. Judges 1:1–3:6 takes up the same problem from various perspectives (cf. Exod 23:27–31).

[5] God's promise to push out the remaining nations takes up the promises of Deut 6:19 and 9:3–4. To "dispossess them" reaches back to Exod 34:24; Num 32:21; Deut 4:38; 9:4–5; 11:23; 18:12; Josh 3:10; 13:6 (cf. Judg 11:23). The promise to "possess them" takes up the language of the promise to

Abraham in Gen 15:7 (cf. 22:17; 24:60; 28:4). This is underlined in Lev 20:24. The promise begins to be fulfilled in Num 21:24, 35, but remains the overarching promise repeated in Num 33:53 and the task of Israel throughout Deuteronomy (1:8, 21, 39, and over sixty times). Thus it is not surprising that Joshua's marching orders are to go and possess the land (1:11, 15). At the end of the conquest, he still faced more land to possess (13:1) and implored the tribes to possess the land (18:3). The concluding summary is likewise in terms of possession (21:43), but even then the task remains (23:5). Thus Israel saw God fulfilling his promises, but constantly placing a new task before his people.

⁶ The task is not, however, stated in military terms. Rather it is in terms of obedience to God's will (1:7–8; Exod 24:7; Deut 28:58, 61; 29:19–20, 26 [Eng. 29:20–21, 27]; 30:10; 31:24, 26; Josh 8:31, 34; cf. Exod 34:27–28).

⁷ The major concern of the Deuteronomistic law is now summarized. Israel's identity hangs on her uniqueness. Whereas the nations serve many gods, she serves only one. She must avoid all contact with the nations in order to avoid all temptation from their gods. Specifically, she is not to call to remembrance the names of their gods (Exod 23:13; Isa 26:13), that is to praise them and to acknowledge their divine power. If the MT is correct (cf. *Notes*), she is not to take oaths in the name of other gods (cf. Deut 6:13; 10:20), that is to call upon other gods to guarantee the fulfillment of promises, for this is at the same time a recognition of the power of the god (C. A. Keller, *THAT*, 2 [1976] 860–61; cf. Jer 5:7; 12:16; Zeph 1:5). She is not to serve other gods, but only Yahweh (Exod 3:12; 20:5; 23:24–25, 33; Deut 4:19, 28; 6:13; 7:4, 16; 8:19; 10:12, 20; 11:13, 16; 12:2, 30; 13:5, 7, 14; 17:3; 28:14, 36, 47, 64; 29:17, 25; 30:17; 31:20; Josh 22:5, 27). Such service includes cultic worship (cf. especially Num 4; 8; 18), but extends to the total binding of oneself as a servant to God (cf. Deut 28:47–48; Floss, *Jahwe dienen*). Finally, Israel must not bow down in worship to other gods (Exod 20:5; 23:24; 32:8; 34:14; Lev 26:1; Num 25:2; Deut 4:19; 5:9; 8:19; 11:16; 17:3; 29:25; 30:17). Here is Yahweh's claim to the absolute allegiance of his people, a claim totally unique in Israel's environment, where everyone worshiped many gods, even though the national god was seen as the chief god or the king of the gods. For Israel, Yahweh claimed to fulfill all the functions for which other nations needed a multitude of gods. The problem was that Israel could never really come to believe the claim totally. She constantly sought the favors of the gods who had claimed to give fertility to the land long before Israel entered it or the gods who seemed at the moment to have military power. In all circumstances, Yahweh demanded absolute allegiance of his "slave people," if they did not want to return to the slavery in Egypt.

⁸ The writer uses an oath formula to call upon Israel to cling to Yahweh (cf. Deut 10:20; 11:22; 13:5; 30:20; Josh 22:5). The other choice is for the sicknesses of Egypt to cling to Israel (Deut 28:60). The writer encourages Israel by noting that she has succeeded in such total loyalty up to this point. Such language is applicable only to the conquest generation, being just the opposite of the wilderness generation and all succeeding ones.

⁹ A historical review similar to verse three is inserted as a reason for maintaining total loyalty. Yahweh's actions have proved his claims. The promise of Josh 1:5 has been fulfilled.

¹⁰ The blessings of Deut 28:7 and 32:30 have been realized. God has fought for Israel (cf. v 3). The repeated refrain is that God has kept his word.

¹¹ The point of the entire oration comes somewhat unexpectedly. In a context of fighting and demands, the expected response is loyal love (cf. 22:5).

¹² The reverse response is to cling to other gods (cf. v 9). The result would be a new people, a mixture of the remaining nations and Israel. But this people would not be the people of Yahweh. Israel must do everything in her power to avoid losing her unique identity. The only way to retain the identity is through absolute loyalty to Yahweh. Solomon found the truth of this claim, to his despair (cf. 1 Kgs 11).

¹³ The mood changes dramatically. The imperative call to obedience moves to threatened punishment for disobedience. As with the entire chapter, the remaining nations take center stage. They represent the threat. God has promised to take care of that threat (vv 4–5). He has asked Israel to ignore the threat and the temptation which comes with it (vv 7, 11–12). If Israel does not do her part, then God will not do his. Here is the danger of freedom. God seeks man's free response of love. God does his part to deserve and receive such love. God does not force his attentions upon man. But the man who ignores God's claims finds God's punishment. Here the punishment fits the crime. Mixing with the nations brings further opportunities for such mixing. God refuses to drive them out (contrast v 5). When they remain, they are troublesome temptations for further mixing, further loss of Israel's unique identity, and thus for further punishment. The ultimate result is that Israel loses her land and wanders away lost, the same condition as her original ancestor (Deut 26:5; אבד, "to wander aimlessly, lost"; "to perish," as here; cf. Lev 26:38; Deut 4:26; 7:20; 8:19, 20; 11:17; 28:20, 22; 30:18). The sad thing is that Joshua gives nothing new to Israel. They have known it all along. God has constantly warned his people. They are at fault. They do not listen. Thus they lose the gift of God.

¹⁴ Amid the threat, Joshua adds a poignant plea. Will they not listen to the voice of an old, dying man? Can they not accept his personal testimony? If not, can they not look deep within themselves and accept the reality of what they know? God has failed in nothing. Everything he said, he has done. God has been, is, and will be faithful. What is Israel's response?

¹⁵ Joshua must quickly note the reverse side of the picture. Not only God's good, pleasing promises come true. He also has the power and the will to bring his "evil words" to pass. Here all the threats of Deuteronomy and particularly the curses of 28:15–68 stand at the center of attention. Yahweh's major gift to Israel has been her land. It is precisely this gift (v 13) which he will take away.

¹⁶ Verse 16 summarizes the threat in terms of God's wrath aroused by a broken covenant, ending the theological summary precisely where chapter 7 began (cf. 7:1). Again, the cause of divine wrath centers on broken loyalties, serving other gods, worshiping them (cf. v 7). The warning of Deut 6:15; 7:4; 11:17; 29:24–27 [Eng. 29:25–28] is pictured as historical reality in terms similar to Deut 31:16–18. Warning has become almost certainty. The gods of the nations appear as an almost irresistable temptation for Israel.

Explanation

The last sermon of the dying hero and leader is the favorite form used by the Deuteronomistic historian to preach to his audience, as seen by its use for the entire book of Deuteronomy and by its concluding place here in Joshua. Covenant theology is the central theme of the Deuteronomist. Our chapter combines the favorite form and theme to summarize the major message in sixteen verses packed with the favorite language of the Deuteronomist. Here is theological dynamite.

In the context of Joshua's day, the message is a doomladen warning. Rest is not the final word for life in the land. Temptation lurks in the presence of the gods of the peoples remaining in the land. Blessing can last only as long as total faithfulness to Yahweh lasts. When Israel begins to experiment with other gods, trying to be like the nations and worship every god possible, doom is imminent. Doom means loss of the promised and given land. Doom means aimless wandering, searching for a home like the ancient patriarchal father. Doom means destruction, death, disintegration of the people of God.

For Israel in the monarchical period, the message was even more grave. Marriage and mixing with the remaining nations began with Solomon, resulting in mixing with foreign gods, just as our passage predicts. Doom also began with the division of the kingdom. Could total destruction be far behind? Then when the north has fallen, can Judah have hope to escape? No! Manasseh sealed her doom.

The Deuteronomistic message is aimed particularly at exiled Israel. Doom has come. The people of God have wandered into a foreign land. Does this mean their God has fought and lost? Must Israel search for another god, one who can fight and win with modern weaponry and in modern political reality? You are asking the wrong questions says the Deuteronomist. The answer is not in political power in the short term. The answer is the longer historical perspective. God proved his power to conquer long ago. The exile only proves God's power to be self-consistent, fulfilling his evil word as well as his good word. God has found another way to show his right to claim total allegiance. The question must now be directed to Israel. Has she learned the lesson of history? Is she ready to face her own disloyalty, her own faithlessness with the gods of the nations? Chapter 23 shows exiled Israel why she is in the position she is in. But that is not the end. One chapter remains to give hints on how to regain her lost position.

Commitment to the Covenant (24:1–28)

Bibliography

(Note: The bibliography on Joshua 24 is too vast to list. The following list attempts to give the most important materials on the major problems of the chapter and to note sources for more extensive bibliographic aids.)

A. *Exegesis*

Baltzer, K. *Das Bundesformular.* WMANT 4. Neukirchen: Neukirchener Verlag, 1960, 29–37. (= *The Covenant Formulary in the Old Testament.* Tr. D. E. Green. Oxford: Basil Blackwell, 1971, 19–27.) **Becker, J.** *Gottesfurcht im Alten Testament.* Rome: Pontifical Biblical Institute, 1965, 114–15. **Buber, M.** *The Prophetic Faith.* New York: MacMillan, 1949, 13–18. **Floss, J. P.** *Jahwe dienen—Göttern dienen.* BBB 45. Bonn: Peter Hanstein, 1975, 334–71. **Giblin, C. H.** "Structural Pattens in Jos 24, 1–25." *CBQ* 26 (1964) 50–69. **Hollenberg, J.** "Die deuteronomischen Bestandtheile des Buches Josua." *Theologische Studien und Kritiken* 1 (1874) 485–89. **L'Hour, J.** "L'Alliance de Sichem." *RB* 69 (1962) 5–36, 161–84, 350–68. **Jaroš, K.** *Sichem.* Orbis Biblicus et Orientalis 11. Freiburg: Universitätsverlag, 1976, 129–53 (bibliography). **Kraus, H. J.** *Gottesdienst in Israel.* 2nd ed. München: Chr. Kaiser Verlag, 1962, 160–66. (= *Worship in Israel.* Tr. G. Buswell. Richmond: John Knox Press, 1966, 134–41.) **Liedke, G.** *Gestalt und Bezeichnung alttestamentlicher Rechtssätze.* WMANT 39. Neukirchen: Neukirchener Verlag, 1971, 180–86. **Lubsczyk, H.** *Der Auszug Israels aus Ägypten.* Leipzig: St. Benno-Verlag, 1963, 136–43. **Mayes, A. D. H.** *Israel in the Period of the Judges.* London: SCM, 1974, 34–41. **McCarthy, D. J.** *Treaty and Covenant.* 2nd ed. AnBib 21A. Rome: Pontifical Biblical Institute, 1978, 221–42, 279–84, 290–98 (bibliography). **Mendenhall, G. E.** *Law and Covenant in Israel and the Ancient Near East.* Pittsburgh: Bible Colloquium, 1955, 41–44. **Möhlenbrink, K.** "Die Landnahmensagen des Buches Josua." *ZAW* 56 (1938) 250–54. **Muilenburg, J.** "The Form and Structure of the Covenantal Formulations." *VT* 9 (1959) 357–60, 364–65. **Noth, M.** *Das System der zwölf Stämme Israels.* Stuttgart: W. Kohlhammer Verlag, 1930, 133–40. **Perlitt, L.** *Bundestheologie im Alten Testament.* WMANT 36. Neukirchen: Neukirchener Verlag, 1969, 239–84. **Rudolph, W.** *Der "Elohist" von Exodus bis Josua.* BZAW 68. Berlin: Alfred Töpelmann, 1938, 244–53. **Schmidt, W. H.** *Alttestamentlicher Glaube in seiner Geschichte.* 2nd ed. Neukirchen: Neukirchener Verlag, 1975, 18, 102–4. **Schmitt, G.** *Der Landtag von Sichem.* Arbeiten zur Theologie 15. Stuttgart: Calwer Verlag, 1964. (bibliography). **Seebass, H.** *Der Erzvater Israel.* BZAW 98. Berlin: Alfred Töpelmann, 1966, 5–8, 87–102. **Sellin, E.** *Gilgal.* Leipzig: A. Deicherische Verlagsbuchhandlung Werner Scholl, 1917, 50–56. **Smend, R.** "Das Gesetz und die Völker." *Probleme Biblischer Theologie,* ed. H. W. Wolff. München: Chr. Kaiser Verlag, 1971, 503–4. **de Vaux, R.** *Histoire ancienne d'Israël.* Vol. 1. Paris: J. Gabalda, 1971, 610–14. (= *The Early History of Israel.* Tr. D. Smith. London: Darton, Longman & Todd, 1978, 667–72.) **Vriezen, T. C.** "Exodusstudien Exodus I." *VT* 17 (1967) 336–38. **Weinfeld, M.** *Deuteronomy and the Deuteronomic School.* Oxford: Clarendon Press, 1972, 59–66. **Wellhausen, J.** *Die Composition des Hexateuchs und der historischen Bücher des Alten Testaments.* 2nd ed. Berlin: Georg Reimer, 1889, 135–36.

B. *Shechem*

1. ARCHAEOLOGY

Boling, R. G. "Bronze Age Buildings at the Shechem High Place: ASOR Excavations at Tananir." *BA* 32 (1969) 82–103. **Buhl, R. J.** "The Excavation of Tell er-Ras on Mt. Gerazim." *BA* 31 (1968) 58–72. **Campbell, E. F.** "Shechem (City)." *IDBSup* (1976) 821–22 (bibliography). ———. "Two Amarna Notes: The Shechem City-State and Amarna Administrative Terminology." *Magnalia Dei: The Mighty Acts of God,* ed. F. M. Cross, W. E. Lemke and P. D. Miller. Garden City, NY: Doubleday, 1976, 38–54. **Campbell, E. F., Ross, J. F.,** and **Toombs, L. E.** "The Eighth Campaign at Balâṭah (Shechem)." *BASOR* 204 (1971) 2–17. **Campbell, E. F.** and **Wright, G. E.** "Tribal League Shrines im Amman and Shechem." *BA* 32 (1969) 104–16. **Elliger, K.** "Sichem." *BHH* 3 (1966) 1781–83. **Horn, S. H.** *Jaarbericht van het Voorziatisch-Egyptisch gezelschap* (*genootschap*) 20 (1968) 71–90. **Jaroš, K.** *Sichem.* Freiburg: Universitätsverlag, 1976, 11–66 (bibliography). **Jaroš, K.** and **Deckert, B.** *Studien zur Sichem-Area.* Freiburg: Universitätsverlag, 1977. **Otto, E.** *Jakob in Sichem.* BWANT 110. Stuttgart: W. Kohlhammer Verlag, 1979, 108–58, 212–18. ———. "Überlieferungen von Sichem und die Ausgrabungen auf tell balaṭa. Rezensionsartikel zu: Jaroš, K., *Sichem* (OrBibl 11, 1976)." *Biblische Notizen* 6 (1978) 19–26. **Seger, J. D.** "Shechem Field XIII, 1969." *BASOR* 205 (1972) 20–35. **Toombs, L. E.** and **Wright, G. E.** "The Fourth Campaign at Balaṭah (Shechem)." *BASOR* 169 (1963) 1–26, 32–60. **Vogel, E. K.** "Bibliography of Holy Land Sites Compiled in Honor of Dr. Nelson Glueck." *HUCA* 42 (1971) 76–77 (bibliography). **Weippert, H.** "Sichem." *Biblisches Reallexikon,* ed. K. Galling. 2nd ed. Tübingen: J. C. B. Mohr (Paul Siebeck), 1977, 293–96 (bibliography). **Wilhelm, G.** "Ausgrabungen in Tell Balaṭa und Tell er-Ras." *AfO* 23 (1969–70) 183–86. ———. "Ausgrabungen in Tell Balaṭa." *AfO* 24 (1973) 213–15. **Wright, G. E.** *Shechem: The Biography of a City.* New York: McGraw-Hill, 1965. ———. "Shechem." *Archaeology and Old Testament Study,* ed. D. W. Thomas. Oxford: Clarendon, 1967, 355–70. ———. "Shechem." *EAEHL* 4 (1978) 1083–94 (bibliography). **Wright, G. R. H.** "Co-ordinating the Survey of Shechem over Sixty Years." *ZDPV* 89 (1973) 188–96. ———. "Shechem and League Shrines." *VT* 21 (1971) 572–603. ———. "Temples at Shechem." *ZAW* 80 (1968) 1–35. ———. "Temples at Shechem—a Detail." *ZAW* 87 (1975) 56–64.

2. TRADITION

Alt, A. "Josua." *Werden und Wesen des Alten Testaments,* ed. P. Volz, F. Stummer, and J. Hempel. BZAW 66. Berlin: Alfred Töpelmann, 1936, 27–29. (= *Kleine Schriften zur Geschichten des Volkes Israel.* Vol. 1. München: C. H. Beck'sche Verlagsbuchhandlung, 1953, 191–92.) ———. "Die Wallfahrt von Sichem nach Bethel." *Alexander von Bulmerincq Festschrift.* 1938, 218–30. (= *KS,* 1, 79–88.) **Auerbach, E.** "Die grosse Überarbeitung der biblischen Bücher." VTSup 1 (1953) 1–10. **Bächli, O.** *Amphiktyonie im Alten Testament.* TZ Sonderband 6. Basel: Friedrich Reinhardt Verlag, 1977, 103–6, 110–14. **Clements, R. E.** "Baal-Berith of Shechem." *JSS* 13 (1968) 21–32. **Craigie, P. C.** "El Brt. ELDN. (RS 24. 278, 14–15)." *UF* 5 (1973) 278–79. **Dus, J.** "Mose oder Josua?" *ArOr* 39 (1971) 16–45. **Gottwald, N. K.** *The Tribes of Yahweh.* Maryknoll, NY: Orbis Books, 1979, 550–52, 563–67. **Herrmann, S.** *Die prophetischen Heilserwartungen im Alten Testament.* BWANT 85. Stuttgart: W. Kohlhammer Verlag, 1965, 78–92. **Irwin, W. H.** "Le sanctuaire central Israélite avant l'établishment de la monarchie." *RB* 72 (1965) 165–71, 182–84. **Jaroš, K.** *Sichem.* Freiburg: Universitätsverlag, 1976, 67–127. ———. *Die Stellung des Elohisten zur Kanaanäischen Religion.* Göttingen: Vandenhoeck & Ruprecht, 1974, 147–73, 213–31, 256–57. **Keller, C. A.** "Über einige alttestamentliche Heiligtumslegenden." *ZAW* 67 (1955) 143–54. **Lipinski, E.** "El-Berith." *Syria* 50 (1973) 50–51. **Maag, V.** "Sichembund und Vätergötter." VTSup 16 (1967) 205–18. **Nielsen, E.** "The Burial of the Foreign Gods." *ST* 8 (1954) 103–22. ———. "Historical Perspectives and Geographical Horizons. On the Question of North-Israelite Elements in Deuteronomy." *ASTI* 11 (1977–78) 77–89. ———. *Shechem, A Traditio-Historical Investigation.* Copenhagen: Gad, 1955. **Otto, E.** *Jakob in Sichem.* BWANT 110. Stuttgart: W. Kohlhammer Verlag, 1979, 227–60. **von Rad, G.** *The Problem of the Hexateuch and Other Essays.* Tr. E. W. T. Dicken. Edinburgh: Oliver & Boyd, 1965, 1–78. **Reviv, H.** "The Government of Shechem in the El-Amarna-Period and in the Days of Abimelech." *IEJ* 16 (1966) 252–57. ———. "The Pattern of the Pan-tribal Assembly in the Old Testament." *Journal of Northwest Semitic Languages* 8 (1980) 85–94. **Rowley, H. H.** *From Joseph to Joshua: Biblical Traditions in the Light of Archaeology.* London: Oxford University Press, 1950, 124–29. **Sellin, E.** *Gilgal.* Leipzig: A. Deicherische Verlagsbuchhandlung Werner Scholl, 1917, 80–94. **Tengström, S.** *Die Hexateucherzählung.* Lund: C. W. K. Gleerup, 1976. **Toombs, L. E.** and **Wright, G. E.** "The Fourth Campaign at Balaṭah (Shechem)." *BASOR* 169 (1963) 27–32. **Wijngaards, J. N. M.** *The Dramatization of Salvific History in the Deuteronomic Schools. OTS* 16 (1969). **Wright, G. R. H.** "The Mythology of Pre-Israelite Shechem." *VT* 20 (1970) 75–82.

C. *Short Historical Creed*

Brekelmans, C. H. "Het 'historische Credo' van Israeel." *Tijdschrift voor Theologie* 3 (1963) 1–10. **Carmichael, C.** "A New View of the Origin of the Deuteronomic Credo." *VT* 19 (1969) 273–89. **Childs, B. S.** "Deuteronomic Formulae of the Exodus Traditions." VTSup 16 (1967) 30–39. **Craigie, P. C.** *Deuteronomy.* NICOT. Grand Rapids: Eerdmans, 1976, 321. **Cross, F. M.** *Canaanite Myth and Hebrew Epic.* Cambridge, MA: Harvard University Press, 1973, 79–144. **Durham, J. I.** "Ancient Israelite Credo." *IDBSup* (1976) 197–99 (bibliography). **Harrelson, W.** "Life, Faith, and the Emergence of Tradition." *Tradition and Theology in the Old Testament,* ed. D. Knight. Philadelphia: Fortress Press, 1977, 11–30. **Huffmon, H. B.** "The Exodus, Sinai and the Credo." *CBQ* 27 (1965) 101–13. **Hyatt, J. P.** "Were There an Ancient Historical Credo in Israel and an Independent Sinai Tradition?" *Translating and Understanding the Old Testament,* ed. H. T. Frank and W. L. Reed. Nashville: Abingdon, 1970, 152–70. **Jenks, A. W.** *The Elohist and North Israelite Traditions.* SBLMS 22. Missoula, MT: Scholars Press, 1977, 12–16. **Lang, B.** "Glaubensbekenntnisse im Alten und Neuen Testament." *Concilium* 14 (1978) 499–503. **Lohfink, N.** "Zum 'kleinen geschichtlichen Credo' Dtn. 26, 5–9." *TP* 46 (1971) 19–39. **McCarthy, D. J.** "What Was Israel's Historical Creed?" *Lexington Theological Quarterly* 4 (1969) 46–53. **Mayes, A. D. H.** *Deuteronomy.* NCB. London: Oliphants, 1979, 332–33. **Merendino, R. P.** *Das deuteronomische Gesetz: eine literarkritische, gattungs- und überlieferungsgeschichtliche Untersuchung zu Dt. 12–26.* BBB 31. Bonn: Peter Hanstein, 1969, 346–71. **Miller, P. D.** *The Divine Warrior in Early Israel.* HSM 5. Cambridge, MA: Harvard University Press, 1973, 166–75. **Nebeling, G.** *Die Schichten des deuteronomischen Gesetzeskorpus; Eine traditions- und redaktionsgeschichtliche Analyse von Dt. 12–26.* Dissertation, Münster, 1970, 238–45. **Nicholson, E. W.** *Exodus and Sinai in History and Tradition.* Oxford: Basil Blackwell, 1973. **von Rad, G.** *The Problem of the Hexateuch and Other Essays.* Tr. E. W. T. Dicken. Edinburgh: Oliver & Boyd, 1965, 1–78. **Richter, W.** "Beobachtungen zur theologischen Systembildung in der alttestamentlichen Literatur anhand des 'Kleinen geschichtlichen Credo.'" *Wahrheit und Verkündigung,* ed. L. Scheffczyk *et al.* München: Ferdinand Schöningh, 1967. **Rost, L.** *Das kleine Credo und andere Studien zum Alten Testament.* Heidelberg: Quelle & Meyer, 1965, 11–25. **van Seters, J.** *Abraham in History and Tradition.* New Haven, CT: Yale University Press, 1975, 142–43. **Thompson, T. L.** "The Joseph and Moses Narratives." *Israelite and Judean History,* ed. J. H. Hayes and J. M. Miller. Philadelphia: Westminster, 1977, 162–66. **Vriezen, T. C.** "The Credo in the Old Testament." *Studies on the Psalms: Ou Testamentiese Werkgemeenschap in Suid-Afrika.* Potchefstroom: Pro Rege—Pers Beperk, 1963, 5–17, **Wallis, G.** "Die geschichtliche Erfahrung und das Bekenntnis zu Jahwe im Alten Testament." *TLZ* 101 (1976) 801–16 (history of research). **Wassermann, G.** "Das kleine geschichtliche Credo (Dtn. 26,5ff) und seine deuteronomische Übermalung." *Theologische Versuche II,* ed. J. Rogge and G. Schille. Berlin: Evangelische Verlagsanstalt, 1970, 27–46.

D. *Covenant*

Barr, J. "Some Semantic Notes on Covenant." *Beiträge zur Alttestamentlichen Theologie,* ed. H. Donner, R. Hanhart, and R. Smend. Göttingen: Vandenhoeck & Ruprecht, 1977, 23–38. **Buis, P.** "Les formulaires d'alliance." *VT* 16 (1966) 396–411. **Campbell, E. F.** "Moses and the Foundations of Israel." *Int* 29 (1975) 146–51. **Clements, R. E.**

Old Testament Theology. Atlanta: John Knox Press, 1978, 96–103. **Eichrodt, W.** "Darf man heute noch von einem Gottesbund mit Israel reden?" *TZ* 30 (1974) 193–206. **Fohrer, G.** "Altes Testament—'Amphiktyonie' und 'Bund'?" *TLZ* 91 (1966) 801–16, 893–904. **Halbe, J.** *Das Privilegrecht Jahwes Ex. 34, 10–26.* FRLANT 114. Göttingen: Vandenhoeck & Ruprecht, 1975, 506–26. **Hillers, D. R.** *Covenant: The History of a Biblical Idea.* Baltimore: Johns Hopkins Press, 1969. **Jepsen, A.** "Berith. Ein Beitrag zur Theologie der Exilszeit." *Verbannung und Heimkehr,* ed. A. Kuschke. Tübingen: J. C. B. Mohr (Paul Siebeck), 1961, 161–79. **Kutsch, E.** *"berît,* Verpflichtung." *THAT* 1 (1971) 339–52. ————. *Verheissung und Gesetz; Untersuchungen zum sogenannten "Bund" im Alten Testament.* BZAW 131. Berlin: Walter de Gruyter, 1973. **Loersch, S.** *Das Deuteronomium und seine Deutungen.* Stuttgart: Verlag Katholisches Bibelwerk, 1967, 95–103 (history of research). **McCarthy, D. J.** *"Berith* and Covenant in the Deuteronomistic History." VTSup 23 (1972) 65–85. ————. *"Berith* in OT History and Theology." *Bib* 53 (1972) 110–21. ————. "Ebla, *horkia temnein, ṭb šlm.* Addenda to *Treaty and Covenant."* *Bib* 60 (1979) 247–53. ————. *Old Testament Covenant: A Survey of Current Opinions.* Oxford: Basil Blackwell, 1972. (history of research, bibliography). ————. *Treaty and Covenant.* 2nd ed. AnBib 21A. Rome: Pontifical Biblical Institute, 1978 (bibliography). **Martin-Achard, R.** "Trois ouvrages sur l'alliance dans l'Ancien Testament." *RTP* 110 (1978) 299–306. **Mayes, A. D. H.** *Deuteronomy.* NCB. London: Oliphants, 1979, 64–71. ————. "King and Covenant: A Study of 2 Kings 22–23." *Hermathena* 125 (1978) 34–47. **Nötscher, F.** "Bundesformular und 'Amtsschimmel.'" *BZ* 9 (1965) 181–214. **Schmidt, W. H.** *Alttestamentlicher Glaube in seiner Geschichte.* 2nd ed. Neukirchen: Neukirchener Verlag, 1975, 104–7. **Wächter, L.** "Die Übertragung der Beritvorstellung auf Jahwe." *TLZ* 99 (1974) 801–16. **Weinfeld, M.** *"Berith*—Covenant vs. Obligation." *Bib* 56 (1975) 120–28. ————. *"berîth."* TDOT 2 (1975) 253–79. **Westermann, C.** "Genesis 17 und die Bedeutung von *berit."* *TLZ* 101 (1976) 161–70. ————. *Theologie des Alten Testaments in Grundzügen.* ATD Ergänzungsreihe 6. Göttingen: Vandenhoeck & Ruprecht, 1978, 34–37. **Wilms, F. E.** *Das Jahwistische Bundesbuch in Exodus 34.* SANT 32. München: Kösel-Verlag, 1973, 213–33. **Zimmerli, W.** "Erwägungen zum 'Bund.' Die Aussagen über die Jahwe *berit* in Ex. 19–34." *Wort-Gebot-Glaube,* ed. H. J. Stoebe. ATANT 59. Zürich: Zwingli Verlag, 1970, 171–90. ————. *Old Testament Theology in Outline.* Tr. D. E. Green. Atlanta: John Knox Press, 1978, 48–58 (bibliography).

Translation

¹ *Joshua gathered all the tribes of Israel to Shechem.* [a] *He called the elders of Israel* [b] *and her heads* [c] *and her judges and her officials, and they appeared before God.* ² *Joshua said to all the people, "Thus said Yahweh, the God of Israel, 'Beyond the river your fathers have lived since time immemorial* [a]*—Terah, the father of Abraham and the father of Nahor—and they served other gods.*

³ *'I took your father Abraham from beyond the river and caused him to go through all the land of Canaan.* [a] *I multiplied his seed and gave him Isaac.* ⁴ *I gave* [a] *to Isaac Jacob and Esau. I gave to Esau Mount Seir to possess it as an inheritance, but Jacob and his sons went down to Egypt.* [b] ⁵ *I sent Moses and Aaron,* [a] *and I struck Egypt, just as I did in its midst.* [b] *Afterward, I brought* [c] *you all out.* ⁶ *I brought your fathers* [a] *from Egypt, and you all came to the sea.* [b] *The Egyptians pursued after your fathers* [c] *with chariots and with horsemen to the Reed Sea.* ⁷ *They cried out* [a] *to Yahweh, and he set darkness* [b] *between you all and between the Egyptians. He brought upon it the sea. It covered them. Your eyes saw what I did in Egypt.* [c]

You all lived in the wilderness many/days. ⁸ *I brought you all* ᵃ *to the land of the Amorites, the ones who dwell beyond/the Jordan. They fought you all,* ᵇ *and I gave them into your hand.* ᶜ *You all possessed their land, and I destroyed* ᵈ *them before you all.* ⁹ *Balak, the son of Zippor, king of Moab, rose and fought against Israel. He sent and called Balaam, the son of Beor,* ᵃ *to curse you all.* ¹⁰ *But I did not consent to listen to Balaam, and he actually blessed you all.* ᵃ *I delivered you all from his hand.* ¹¹ *You all passed over the Jordan and came to Jericho. The lords* ᵃ *of Jericho—the Amorites, the Perizzites, the Canaanites, the Hittites, the Girgashites, and Hivites, and the Jebusites—fought against you all. I gave them into your hand.* ¹² *I sent the hornet (?)* ᵃ *before you all, and it drove them out from before you all, namely the two kings of the Amorites. But it was not by your sword nor by your bow.* ᵇ ¹³ *I gave* ᵃ *to you all a land in which you* ᵇ *did not exert yourself and cities which you all did not build, and you all lived in them. (I also gave) vineyards and olive orchards, which though you all did not plant, you all are eating.'*

¹⁴ *"This being the case, fear Yahweh. Serve him totally and faithfully. Turn away from the gods* ᵃ *which your fathers served beyond the rivers and in Egypt. Serve Yahweh.* ¹⁵ *But if it is wrong* ᵃ *in your view to serve Yahweh, then choose for yourselves today whom you all will serve, either the gods whom your fathers* ᵇ *served, who were beyond the river, or the gods of the Amorites, in whose land you all are living. But in any case, I and my house, we will serve Yahweh."* ᶜ

¹⁶ *The people answered and said, "Far be it from us, the forsaking of Yahweh to serve other gods, for Yahweh is our God.* ᵃ ¹⁷ *He is the one who brought us up and our fathers from the land of Egypt, from the house of service, and who did before our eyes these great signs. He protected us in all the way in which we went and among all the peoples through whose midst we passed.* ¹⁸ *Yahweh drove out all the peoples, indeed the Amorite living in the land, from before us.* ᵃ *Yes, we also will serve Yahweh, because he is our God."*

¹⁹ *Joshua said to the people, "You all are not able to serve Yahweh, because a holy God is he, a jealous deity* ᵃ *is he, one who will not forgive your sins and transgressions.* ²⁰*If you should forsake Yahweh and serve strange, foreign* ᵃ *gods, he will turn and do evil to you all. He will finish you all off after* ᵇ *having been so good to you all."*

²¹ *The people said to Joshua, "No, but it is Yahweh whom we will serve!"*

²² *Joshua said to the people, "You all are witnesses against yourselves, that you have chosen for yourselves Yahweh to serve him."*

They said, "Witnesses." ᵃ

²³ *"This being the case, turn away from the strange foreign gods which are among you all, and stretch out your hearts to Yahweh, the God of Israel."*

²⁴ *The people said to Joshua, "Yahweh, our God,* ᵃ *we will serve. His voice we will obey."*

²⁵ *Joshua cut a covenant for the people that day. He set up for them statutes and judgments in Shechem.* ᵃ ²⁶ *Joshua* ᵃ *wrote these words in the book of the Torah of God. He took a huge stone and set it up there under the oak which was in the sanctuary of Yahweh.* ᵇ ²⁷ *Joshua said to all the people, "This stone right here will be among us* ᵃ *for a witness, since it has heard all the words of Yahweh, which he spoke with us.* ᵇ *It shall be among you all for a witness,* ᶜ *lest you should deny your* ᵈ God."*

²⁸ *Joshua sent the people away, each to his inheritance.*

Notes

Soggin's translation, incorporating several textual variants, displays graphically the complicated textual history of the chapter. We expect no less from such a theologically central chapter.

1.a. The LXX tradition obtains consistency here and in v 25 reading Shiloh for Shechem in line with 18:1, 8, 10; 19:37; 21:2; 22:9, 12. This represents a quite early textual tradition (cf. Wright-Orlinsky, *BASOR* 169 [1963] 28, n. 31) and shows the early tradition's concern for consistency. It may also represent early anti-Samaritan feelings. No attempt to support the LXX as original has gained acceptance (cf. Auld, VTSup 30 [1979] 14; Holmes, 8; Schmitt, *Landtag*, 9).

1.b. LXX avoids repetition by substituting "their" for "Israel."

1.c. LXX omits "their heads" and translates "elders" with a different term than used in 23:2, though the two lists are the same in Hebrew.

2.a. Here is an example of Heb. עולם, often translated "forever," used in a context referring to the past. The term in itself thus does not cover all time from the beginning to the end.

3.a. LXX does not witness "Canaan," which is probably a later interpretation using familiar idiomatic language (cf. Holmes, 5).

4.a. LXX omits "I gave" as stylistically superfluous.

4.b. LXX adds, "And they became there a nation great and numerous and powerful. And the Egyptians afflicted them." The note is taken over from MT of Deut 26:5b–6, adding a note of blessing over against the darkness of the content and the note of blessing on Esau, the ancestor of the proverbial enemy, Edom. Just because the words can be easily retroverted into Hebrew is no reason to argue for their originality (against Hollenberg, Holmes).

5.a. LXX does not have "I sent Moses and Aaron," a phrase representing a later phase of the tradition when all authority was derived from Moses and Aaron. The language may in fact be derived from Mic 6:4 (cf. L'Hour, *RB* 69 [1962]; Soggin).

5.b. "Just as I did in its midst" is variously interpreted and transmitted by the versions (cf. Soggin), who did not understand the "global reference to all the acts which God performed in Egypt" (*Text Project*, cf. Soggin). Thus the versions introduced the traditional language of signs and wonders. The conjunction כאשר here may either be interpreted causally, "in accordance with the facts" (or things) or temporally "when" (cf. Williams, *Syntax*, 50, § 260, 262).

5.c. Here LXX changes to third person reference to deity, a pattern maintained with consistency through v 13, possibly for "motives of reverence" (Holmes) or due to the use of "sermonic language" (Schmitt). More likely, the LXX tradition was coping with the evident change of speakers which occurs unexpectedly in v 14 (MT). LXX transfers the change to v 5.

6.a. The repetitiousness of 5b and 6a do not appear in the versions (cf. Soggin) and probably represent two variants which have both been incorporated into the text tradition (Schmitt). This forms a part of the larger problem in that LXX repeatedly has first person plural rather than second person plural in the following section. Since this occurs with pronouns rather than verbs (Rudolph), Schmitt thinks it reflects a wrong understanding of a dictated text by a Greek copyist. It may involve an attempt to identify Joshua more closely with Israel and hang together with the change of speaker effected by LXX in v 5 (see 5.c. above). Holmes could say that Dillmann and all later scholars take all mention of "the fathers" as a later redaction.

6.b. LXX amplifies with traditional "Red Sea."

6.c. LXX "our fathers." See 6.a. above.

7.a. LXX reads "We cried." Cf. 6.a. and 6.c.

7.b. Greek uses two terms "clouds and darkness" to interpret the Hebrew מאפל, a word occurring only here in MT and probably meaning "darkness" (See Köhler, "Archaeologische Nr. 20, 21," *ZAW* 44 [1926] 62). LXX is based on the tradition of Exod 14:20. LXX continues "between us." See 6.a. and 6.c.

7.c. LXX reads "and your eyes saw that which the Lord did in the land of Egypt," uncharacteristically retaining the second person plural pronoun, but speaking of God in the third person (cf. 5.c.) and adding "land."

8.a. LXX: "He brought us" (cf. 5.c., 6.a.).

8.b. LXX B omits "They fought you all," which appears to be based on Num 21:23. The phrase may represent later interpretation underlining the wickedness of the enemy (cf. 4.b.).

8.c. LXX reads: "The Lord gave them into our hands" (cf. 5.c., 6.a.).

8.d. LXX: "You all destroyed." (Cf., 6.a.).

9.a. LXX omits "son of Beor" (Holmes notes the similar omission in 22:31, 32.) MT may represent expansion with traditional language. LXX also reads "to curse us" (cf. 6.a.).

10.a. LXX: "The Lord your (sing.) God (cf. 5.c.) was not willing to utterly destroy you (sing.). He greatly blessed us (cf. 6.a.). "He delivered us out of their hands and he gave them over." Despite Hollenberg's and Holmes' textual error interpretation, we must see that a theological issue was raised by the later tradition. The verse is based on Deut 23:6 (Eng. 5), which in turn is based on the tradition of Num 22–24, especially 23:11, 27; 24:10. Behind the Greek tradition is apparently an unwillingness even to use the term שמע, "to hear, to obey" with God as subject and man as object. Similarly, the most natural reading of the Greek is that God is the subject of the blessing, not Balaam. (Vg and Syr explicitly use first person.) The addition of the final phrase represents the use of traditional language, perhaps even an alternative reading in the Greek tradition to the preceding phrase, or a dittography out of v 8 or 11.

11.a. LXX avoids the connotations of the Heb. Baals, "lords," of Jericho and uses the more neutral "residents of." Again, second pers. pronouns become first, while the Lord becomes the third pers. subject (cf. 5.c., 6.a.). The different versions give different orders in the list of nations.

12.a. LXX and the early versions render הצרעה as wasps or hornets. Most modern commentators follow Köhler, ("Hebräische Vokabeln I," ZAW 54 [1936] 291) in understanding the word to mean "scourge, terror, discouragement." However, Mayes, Deuteronomy, 188, on 7:20, and Childs, Exodus, 446, 451, on 23:28 retain the traditional "hornet." The verse retains the subject and pronoun changes (5.c. and 6.a.). What is remarkable is the reading "twelve kings" instead of two, which is usually followed in modern scholarship. The "Two" tradition comes from Sihon and Og east of Jordan, while the present context refers to the kings mentioned in chaps. 1–11 conquered west of the Jordan.

12.b. MT followed faithfully by LXX has second pers. sing. with the weapons. Most commentators take this as an early gloss, perhaps using language from Gen 48:22; Hos 1:7; 2 Kgs 6:22, none of which exactly duplicate the language. Otherwise, one must use the Syr as the basis for emendation to plur. suffixes, but certainly the Syr represents only later accommodation to the context. As it stands, the text can be taken only as a divine aside to Joshua personally, or an attempt to make the emphatic statement more personal.

13.a. Greek retains third pers. subject but now speaks to "you all." This removes Joshua from the reception of the land (cf. 19:50; 21:42 LXX).

13.b. MT again mysteriously reads second pers. sing. LXX and other versions read plur. Perhaps the sing. is an accommodation to the preceding second pers. sing. within the copying tradition. Perhaps the singular context of Deut 6:10, which is paraphrased here, was influential at this point.

14.a. LXX adds "strange" on the basis of v 23, as well as MT, not LXX, v 20. LXX continues to speak of "our fathers" (cf. 5.c.).

15.a. LXX softens the expression from "if it is evil in your eyes," to "if it does not please you all."

15.b. The Greek renders unexpectedly "the gods of your fathers," using the second person and the "technical term" for the patriarchal gods. Holmes suggests the possibility that LXX is original here, MT being revised to parallel the preceding verse and avoid the sacred idiom. LXX may simply represent a sermonic idiom to make the call to decision more personal in all its components, thus the return unexpectedly to the more personal second person and the use of the shocking idiom. Schmitt may be correct in suggesting a Greek syntactical simplification.

15.c. LXX adds "because he is holy," giving away the punch line of v 19 too quickly.

17.a. LXX apparently did not understand the Heb. syntax and translated "The Lord our God, he is God" (cf. Holmes).

Syr omits "and our fathers," which is often taken as a later gloss (Holzinger, Holmes), but Schmitt is certainly correct in questioning whether Syr represents better textual tradition. Cf. 5.c. The LXX omission of "land" has better claim to originality, the longer expression representing a later use of traditional idiom. Similarly, the LXX omission "from the house of bondage, and who did before our eyes these great signs" may represent later insertion of traditional language (cf. Deut 6:22; 7:19).

18.a. The Heb. syntax is difficult here, so that the Greek reverses the order to read, "the Amorite and all the nations dwelling in the land before us." Holmes suggests that "all the nations" is a gloss later added to LXX. Cf. BHS.

19.a. LXX omits the second reference to God, in which the Hebrew switches from Elohim to El. LXX simplifies the syntax (Holmes).

20.a. The Hebrew term נכר means both strange and foreign. LXX chooses here the term "other" rather than "foreign."

20.b. LXX does not read the temporal conjunction but rather the causal ἀνθ᾽ ὧν, perhaps reflecting confusion with the Heb. תחת אשר, which Holmes takes to be original, being the more difficult text. The exact nuance of the Greek conjunction is not clear, and it probably represents a misreading of the Hebrew.

22.a. LXX omits, "And they said, 'Witnesses.' " The phrase does not fit the following syntax, where Joshua is not mentioned as subject again, so that the phrase may be a later insertion seeking to make clear the conscious confession and thus basis for guilt of the people. But see Schmitt, *Landtag.*

24.a. Two mss and LXX omit "our God," which may be a later addition of conventional language, used again to magnify the guilt of the people.

25.a. LXX: Shiloh, see 1.a. Here LXX adds, "before the tent of the God of Israel," clearly an addition based on the tradition of the tabernacle at Shiloh (cf. 18:1).

26.a. LXX omits "Joshua" here, possibly a later addition to magnify explicitly the work of Joshua, but more likely a Greek simplification avoiding repetition of v 25.

26.b. "In the sanctuary of Yahweh" becomes "before the Lord" in LXX, avoiding setting the tree within the sanctuary.

27.a. LXX again removes Joshua from responsibility, reading "among you all." LXX also does not have "all" the people, possibly a later attempt to underline the responsibility of the entire community.

27.b. LXX adds "today," a later emphasis perhaps on the basis of liturgical usage. The attempts of Holmes and Driver to argue for the originality of this reading and those of the following notes is ill-founded at best.

27.c. LXX uses prophetic language to make the passage relevant to its own time rather than simply a report of past history, adding "in the last days."

27.d. LXX applies the lesson to its own day sermonically by the simple maneuver of rendering the conjunction "lest" in a more general sense "whenever." It also underlines the authoritative and faithful role of Joshua by reading, "Yahweh, my God."

Form/Structure/Setting

The opening imperfect joins chap. 24 closely to the preceding narrative syntactically. The relationship is underlined by repeating the same audience (23:2a=24:1b). The two narratives have many similarities:

1) Opening survey of history (23:3–5; 24:2–13) leading to conclusions for present behavior (23:6–13; 24:14–15).

2) Description of the consequences of disobedience (23:13, 15–16; 24:19–20).

3) Call for total allegiance to Yahweh, forbidding the worship of other gods (23:7, 12, 16; 24:2, 14–24, 27). Syntax and content thus tie chaps. 23 and 24 tightly together.

Radical distinctions separate the chapters:

1) The setting is temporal, the old age of Joshua, in 23; but geographical, Shechem, in 24.

2) Past history centers on the allotment of the land in 23, but on the victories of Yahweh in 24.

3) Allegiance to Yahweh is expressed by obedience to the book of the law in 23, but by "serving" Yahweh in 24.

4) Disobedience is expressed by marriage entanglements with the peoples left in the land in 23, but by continued worship of the gods of the ancestors in 24.

5) The major distinction is in form, 23 being the farewell speech of a dying leader, while 24 is a ceremonial dialogue between the leader and the representatives of the people.

A key to analyzing the chapter lies in understanding this ceremonial form. Such analysis should give clues to the original setting of the material and to the preservation and transmission of the materials. The present Massoretic text may be outlined as follows:

1) Cultic assembly at Shechem before God, v 1.
2) Prophetic proclamation in divine first person of God's choice and direction of Israel, vv 2–13.
3) Prophetic call to obedience in prophetic first person, vv 14–16.
4) Oath of allegiance by people responding to the divine history of salvation, vv 17–18.
5) Warning of consequences of decision, vv 19–20.
6) Reaffirmation of allegiance, v 21.
7) Formal ceremony binding Israel to her decision, vv 22–24.
8) Establishment of documents to implement and preserve the agreement, vv 25–27.
9) Dismissal of assembly, v 28.

The text is thus a "report of covenant making" (McCarthy, *Treaty and Covenant*, 241). From where has such a report come? Does it represent an original union of a Yahwistic group led by Joshua with a non-Yahwistic group with patriarchal connections living in the land to form Israel, a theory held in various forms by Sellin, Noth, de Vaux, Jaroš, Maag, Seebass, and Nielsen among others? Or are we dealing with a form used repeatedly within Israel to renew the covenant, as held by Muilenburg, Baltzer, and so on? Or do we have a small historical creed used in the Festival of Weeks at Gilgal and a covenant renewal form used at the Feast of Booths in Shechem (von Rad)? Or do we basically have a literary production reflecting the theological reflections of the early Deuteronomistic movement (Perlitt)? Or is it only a postexilic scribe using both Deuteronomistic and Priestly traditions who has composed the present composition (L'Hour)? Or is the present text so complicated that seven layers of tradition can be isolated (Floss)? Or is the text so artistically put together with the repetition of key ideas seven and twelve times that we must argue for literary unity (Giblin)? Joshua 24 raises complex questions whose answers would lead us far in understanding the political, sociological, and religious history of Israel. At present we can take only first steps into this morass of questions.

Certain things seem reasonably sure. Despite Perlitt's profound attempts, no one can explain the presence of Shechem in the present text apart from historical memory and/or cultic connections. This becomes even clearer in light of Gen 12:6; 33:18–20; 34:1–35:5; 37:12–17; Deut 11:26–32; 27:1–26;

Josh 8:30–35; Judg 8:31–9:57. Shechem is not necessarily the place where the Hexateuchal narratives originated (Tengström, *Die Hexateucherzählung*), but it is a place with ancient Israelite connections. The connections include many things which reappear in Josh 24, i.e. the divine leadership of Abraham through the land (Gen 12:6); the putting away of the gods of the fathers (Gen 35:4); the divine epithet El (Yahweh) the God of Israel (Gen 33:20); the connection of deity and covenant (berith) as seen in the Shechemite divine name Baal-(El-)Berith (Judg 8:33; 9:4, 46); a sanctuary with sacred stones and tree (Gen 33:20; 35:4; Deut 27:2, 4–8; Judg 9:4, 6, 18, 46). The chapter can in no way be called a literary invention. It preserves too many phenomena which can be explained only as originating in the ancient worship at Shechem. Again, the present language of the chapter is neither Deuteronomistic or post-Deuteronomistic. Even Perlitt must concede that it represents an early stage of Deuteronomic development (cf. McCarthy). On the other hand, any connection with a Pentateuchal E source has not and cannot be proved (cf. Jenks, *The Elohist*, 60–63). The question boils down to the history and antecedents of the Deuteronomistic movement. The best proposal remains that northern traditions have fed the Deuteronomistic movement, particularly traditions with origins in Shechem. The problem which scholarship faces is the determination of the form and age of such traditions. Shechem as a cult center apparently died out quite early, being destroyed in the period of the judges (Judg 9) and not being given new cultic authority even when it gained political power (1 Kgs 12:25–29). Thus the traditions themselves must be quite early. This is supported by the ready acceptance of trees and stones in the sanctuary. The tradition is early. What about the form?

Recent study has centered on von Rad's theory that vv 2–13 form an early credal statement used in Israel and connected with Deut 6:21–23 and 26:5–9. The radical distinction in content, form, language, and context among these passages had led to a rejection of von Rad's contention that the early creed represented the original cultic form from which the Hexateuch developed (Cf. Hyatt, Rost, Richter, Wallis). Joshua 24 is particularly important here, since the creed is in divine first person rather than in the third person of creedal confession, and since it is so much more detailed than the others. In fact, the "creed" in Josh 24 cannot be seen as a standard form taken over from another context. The content of vv 2–13 fits specifically the specific intent of the following call for allegiance. Those elements are chosen which show God's superiority over other gods. The first person divine speech and the context-determined content show that a brief historical creed does not form the basis for Josh 24:2–13. At best, we can speak only of a general topic known and used in a variety of forms and content within Israelite life (cf. McCarthy, *Lexington Theological Quarterly* 4 [1969] 46–53). This may point back to a practice within Israel of telling the great deeds of God in various contexts—children's catechism, festival celebrations, private offerings and confessions, and so on. Use of such a "topic" may be very ancient and widespread in Israel. Its very flexibility in usage and in context prohibits closer definition of the history of its development and usage. The details of Josh 24 over against the Deuteronomy passages probably points to the more advanced form of Josh 24. To establish an advance in the age of the material does not, however, establish a precise date, particularly not a monarchical date for the materials.

The other element which has been used to determine the age of the form is the use of forms and language from the near eastern, particularly the Hittite, treaties (cf. Mendenhall, Baltzer, Hillers). These follow the pattern?

1. Preamble introducing the king (cf. v.2);
2. Antecedent history describing previous relationships between the two parties (cf. vv 2–13);
3. A basic stipulation governing future relationships (cf. vv 14, 16, 18b, 21, 23, 24);
4. Specific stipulations;
5. The invocation of the gods as witnesses (cf. vv 22, 27);
6. Blessings and curses (cf. vv 19–20).

Such a structure cannot be found in its entirety. We do not have a treaty between Yahweh and his people. Rather we have a report of the making of an agreement. Such a report is based on political models which would be available in Israel's environment throughout her history, but which would most likely be known to Israel after she has become a political entity involved in the processes of such treaty-making. It is precisely at Shechem where we find Israel having her first and fiercest contacts with political entities (cf. Gen 34; Judg 9). It is precisely here where covenant traditions appear to be most ancient (cf. Mayes, *Deuteronomy*, 68). It is precisely here that the tradition of disposing of foreign gods is at home (Gen 35:4). This is important in view of the fact that Josh 24 centers only on this commandment rather than on a law code. It is likely that this concentration on one commandment marks an early stage of Israel's covenant tradition, later supplemented by the extensive list of commandments.

Thus the most likely hypothesis concerning the age and form of the tradition behind Josh 24 is that it represents an ancient Shechemite cultic ceremony in which Israel affirmed her allegiance to Yahweh as the God of Israel rather than to the other gods of her environment. This marks the major turning point in the identity of Israel over against her neighbors. The ceremony itself may indeed reach back to the very beginnings of Israel's life in the Promised Land. This cannot be proved, for such a ceremony was not a sterile rite which remained unchanged. Rather, the tradition remained alive and dynamic, giving identity to Israel through many generations. An original ceremony may have centered on disposing of foreign gods. Such a ceremony, however, would not have remained at the center. The center gradually shifted to the call to allegiance to Yahweh in light of past failures and current temptations, focusing on the pledge to serve Yahweh rather than on putting away the gods. Such a shift would not be total. Worship of other gods remained a reality within Israel's existence until far into the postexilic period. Thus the call to put away the foreign gods came repeatedly to Israel, not only from her prophets but also from her cultic ceremonies.

The preservation of the cultic tradition is problematic. The Shechemite sanctuary may have vanished from existence in the period of the judges. Its traditions were preserved, perhaps in the national sanctuary at Bethel (cf. Otto, *Jakob in Sichem*). With the fall of the northern kingdom, the traditions became the property of the developing Deuteronomistic traditions, whose origins and carriers remain shrouded in darkness. As such, they gained new significance in the battle against the gods of the enemies beyond the river, first the Assyrians and then the Babylonians. Finally, they became part of the literary deposit of the book of Joshua. Indeed, they became the climax of the book. This climactic element becomes clear in light of other cultic elements in the book. The opening section of the book, given in cultic language, climaxes in the ceremony of circumcision, rolling away the "reproach of Egypt" (5:9), and in the Passover, preparing the way for the presence of the Holy in Israel's midst (5:13–15). Disobedience of the law (7:1) leads to a ceremony of judicial cleansing but also causes Israel to set up a cultic institution to remind her of the consequences, i.e. blessings and cursings, of her relationship to the Torah (8:30–35). The division of the land at the cultic centers (14:6; 18:1; 19:51; cf. 21:2) is threatened by intertribal jealousy, settled through an "altar of witness" (22:28, 34). It is thus fitting that the climax of the book is not human warning (chap. 23), but cultic affirmation (chap. 24). Within the context of the Deuteronomistic history, the book of Joshua does not seek to teach a new law or issue a new warning to the people. The book of Joshua seeks to illustrate from history the identity of Israel. It is only with Joshua that we have a leader who does not go wrong. It is only with Joshua that we have a people who have been perfectly obedient (22:2–3). It is only with Joshua that Israel commits herself totally to Yahweh alone as God (chap. 24). After Joshua, the history of Israel goes downhill. Joshua 24 thus marks the high point of Israel's history, the full realization of her identity as people of God.

Comment

[1] The text begins in midstream. The use of אסף "to gather," to begin a narrative is unique in the biblical literature. It belongs in midstream after a setting and purpose for the gathering has been established (e.g. Gen 29:22; Exod 3:16; 4:29; Num 11:16, 24). The narrative appears to be purposely atemporal, setting itself up as an example for repeated use.

Shechem surprises us again with its appearance, just as it did in 8:30–35. Though never mentioned in Chaps. 1–11 nor in the city lists of 13–19, it is set apart as a city of refuge (20:7) and as a Levitical city (21:21). The Amarna letters and other Near Eastern materials witness to relationships between the city of Shechem and less settled elements of the population during the Middle and Late Bronze ages (see especially, E. Otto, *Jakob in Sichem*, 159–69). Our passage does not make it clear if the cult site involved is actually in the city of Shechem or is a sanctuary outside the city associated with Mount Ebal and Gerizim (cf. Deut 27; Josh 8:30–35). The relationship between the narrative and the discovery of a sanctuary of Tananir on Gerizim is also unclear (cf. Otto, *Jakob in Sichem*, 158), though Otto is probably correct in disavowing any connection. Tananir does show that holy places could exist outside the town, perhaps in connection with more unsettled elements of the population. See further 21:21, Comment.

The reference to the tribal leaders connects the cultic assembly closely to the farewell speech of Joshua (23:2) and involves the leaders of Israel's "secular" life in the religious responsibility and commitment of the people.

"They appeared (or took their stand) before God" is an expression rarely used in the OT and seems to be connected with the popular assembly of Israel (1 Sam 10:19), perhaps having its ultimate derivation in the language of the court (Job 33:5; 41:2; Prov 22:29; cf. Exod 8:16; 9:13).

² Joshua addresses all the people, not just the leaders. "Thus says the Lord" represents the introduction to the prophetic messenger speech (cf. a summary of recent literature in J. Hayes, *Old Testament Form Criticism*, [San Antonio: Trinity University Press, 1974] 149–55). McCarthy (*Treaty and Covenant*, 224) wants to find the form originating in the royal decrees and treaties. In our context, the form is definitely used in a prophetic sense rather than in the literary form of a treaty.

"The God of Israel" is apparently closely connected to the tradition of Shechem (cf. the summary by E. Otto, *Jakob in Sichem*, 78–81) reaching back probably to the earliest period of the existence of a group called Israel (cf. Gen 33:20). Our passage specifically identifies Yahweh, not El, as the God of Israel.

The saving history begins with the patriarchs beyond the River, taking the historical summary a step beyond Deut 26:5 and two steps beyond Deut 6:21. This is based on the genealogical tradition preserved in Gen 11:24–32. The "fathers" are narrowed down specifically to Terah to show that the dividing line of service of other gods can be drawn with the decision of Abraham (cf. Gen 12: 1–6). The understanding that the fathers had other gods may be related to Gen 35:1–4.

The service of other gods is the theme of the entire chapter. The expression "other gods" picks up the opening motif of the Decalog (Exod 20:3; Deut 5:7; cf. Exod 23:13) and sounds the theme of the entire Deuteronomistic history (Deut 6:14; 7:4; 8:19; 11:16, 28; 13:3, 7, 14; 17:3; 18:20; 28:14, 36, 64; 29:25; 30:17; 31:18, 20; Josh 23:16; Judg 2:12, 17, 19; 10:13; 1 Sam 8:8; 26:19; 1 Kgs 9:6, 9; 11:4, 10; 14:9; 2 Kgs 5:17; 17:7, 35, 37, 38; 22:17). Only the northern prophet Hosea (3:1) and Jeremiah with his close relations to the Deuteronomic school and its editors (Jer 1:16; 7:6, 9, 18; 11:10; 13:10; 16:11, 13; 19:4, 13; 22:9; 25:6; 32:29; 35:15; 44:3, 5, 8, 15) utilize the expression "other gods."

"To serve" includes worship but cannot be limited to the cultic sphere. Perlitt is correct in saying that the theme is the object of worship, not the type of worship (*Bundestheologie*, 257). Service here describes "the recognition of a relationship of dependence upon Yahweh, based on the liberation from Egypt" (Floss, *Jahwe dienen*, 371). Here is the theme of the whole chapter, indeed of the biblical narrative from Deut 1 through 2 Kgs 25: will Israel accept the unconditional claim of God to be her only God?

³ Two central promises of the patriarchal narratives, the presence of God directing the patriarchs and the gift of a large family are proclaimed as having been fulfilled. The journey through the land of Canaan is based on Gen

12:5–9. The history is a selective history, ignoring Ishmael (Gen 16:16) [4] but citing Esau (Gen 25:25) in order to make a theological point: God had established Esau much earlier than Jacob, not because Esau was more blessed, but because God chose to use Jacob for his further purposes (cf. Hertzberg). Thus a moment of historical darkness did not mean that God had forgotten or forsaken his people for some other. This was extremely important for the exilic audience of the Deuteronomist.

[5] Moses and Aaron are introduced (see *Notes*) as representatives of the two sources of authority for the late Israelite community, the priesthood and the Torah of Moses. The emphasis of the historical review is not on human authority but upon divine action. Any authority derived from Moses and Aaron is secondary. God himself is the sole source of primary authority. He sent out the humans from whom authority is secondarily derived.

The tradition that Yahweh "struck Egypt" is apparently tied to the early Passover tradition (Exod 12:23; cf. 12:27; 7:27) and appears outside of it only in our passage.

"I brought you out" is an expression particularly loved by the Deuteronomistic literature (see P. Humbert, "Dieu fait sortir," *TZ* 18 [1962] 357–61; " 'Dieu fait sortir.' complementaire," Note *TZ* 18 [1962] 433–36; B. Childs, VTSup 16 [1967] 30–39), but based on old, probably northern traditions (Richter, *Beobachtungen,* 178–86). Our passage may reflect one of the earliest liturgical uses of the formula, a practice which has led to the variation between "you all" and "your fathers" (cf. *Notes*). The Exodus out of Egypt occurs prior to the deliverance at the Sea and is viewed as the beginning of the wilderness traditions (cf. G. W. Coats, "The Traditio-Historical Character of the Reed Sea Motif," *VT* 17 [1967] 253–65). The Egyptian pursuit mirrors Exod 14:9, 23; while Israel's cry is picked up from Exod 14:10 to emphasize the initiative and grace of God over against the ineffectiveness of Israel. [7] The "cry" motif was especially meaningful for the exilic audience of the Deuteronomist.

Rather than the regular term for darkness (cf. Exod 14:20), the writer uses a term akin to the plague narrative (Exod 10:22) to intensify the aura of divine action and power.

Liturgy covers the generation gap, so that "your eyes saw" can be used, ignoring the death of a generation in the wilderness. The witness formula "your eyes have seen" is a favorite device of the Deuteronomic school to convict its audience (Deut 4:3; 11:7; in singular in 3:21; 4:9; 7:19; 10:21; 29:2).

The Pentateuch pictures the wilderness as the period of Israel's murmuring and God's punishment, even while depicting miraculous acts of God which preserve Israel's life. Our writer suffices with a brief mention, letting the audience fill in the details and interpretation. His focus is on God's guidance and victories.

[8] In line with its theme of divine victory, the text pictures the encounter with the nations east of the Jordan as military victories (cf. Num 21:23–25, 32, 33–35; 31:1–12), ignoring the circuit around Edom tradition (Num 20:14–21; Deut 2:2–8). Amorites here refers to the inhabitants of the territory east of the Jordan (cf. Josh 2:10 with 3:10).

⁹ The East Jordan summary is followed by a specific example which fits the purpose of the text, that of Balaam (cf. Num 22–24; Josh 13:22). The present Numbers context shows God defeating the intention of a foreign king and a prophet to preserve his people, but also shows his people responding with service of other gods (Num 25:2–3). Our text preaches loudly against such a response.

¹⁰ Here is a picture of the prophetic relationship to God. God does not listen to or obey the prophet. God directs the prophetic action and word. Not even the prophet has a claim upon Yahweh. God remains totally free to act as he chooses. Thus here the intention to curse is changed to blessing. Israel understood her relationship to the prophet to be a dangerous one. She stood in his hand. But God demonstrated that he delivered Israel even from the hands of prophets who would curse her. As long as Israel remained people of Yahweh, she had no cause to fear even revered divine spokesmen. God's victory over a prophet thus becomes part of divine saving history.

¹¹ Continuing its emphasis, the text describes even the event at Jericho as a battle, over against the miraculous emphasis of Josh 6. This is not sufficient reason to look for distinct literary sources. Rather it shows how the same tradition is viewed and used from different perspectives in different contexts. The introduction of the list of nations here seeks to use the Jericho example to subsume the entire conquest of the land. A similar summarizing technique appears in v 12, using the ancient language of the "hornet" or "panic" (see Notes) to describe the conquest of the two (twelve?; see Notes) kings of the Amorites (now in West Jordan; cf. v 8).

¹²ᵇ⁻¹³ Two brief notes, the first becoming quite personal with the singular "you" (cf. Notes), make the point of the entire historical survey. God, not man, has acted. Israel's blessings, Israel's entire identity, is a result of divine choice and action, not human power. The point is made in the language of Deut 6:10–11, another context centering on the service of other gods. Our text apparently presupposes that the people are already living in the cities and using the fields.

¹⁴ The text abruptly changes speakers and mood. The prophetic Joshua now assumes the role of an attorney pleading for the proper verdict for his client (cf. Isa 5:3; Exod 10:17; 19:5; H. Wildberger *Jesaja 1–12* [BKAT X; Neukirchen: Neukirchener Verlag, 1972] 169–70). He demands two actions be taken. First, the people are to enter into the proper relationship to Yahweh. Second, they are to rid themselves of all other claimants to lordship over them. The proper relationship includes the proper attitude of reverence and awe in response to the majestic acts of God and the proper action of service in its widest sense (see *Comment* on v 2). Such service is qualified by a pair of terms. תמים, "totally," can refer to the completeness of a day or year (Josh 10:13; Lev 23:15; 25:30; cf. 3:9), but most often refers to the perfection of an animal to be sacrificed (Exod 12:5; 29:1; Lev 1:3, 10; sixteen other times in Leviticus; eighteen times in Num 6; 19; 28–29; ten times in Ezek 43–46). In reference to men, it is used only with Noah (Gen 6:9); as a command to Abraham (17:1); and for the original inhabitant of Eden (Ezek 28:15). It is the action expected of the people with their rulers (Judg 9:16, 19). Its basic home is in cultic literature, where it describes the actions of God (Deut

32:4; 2 Sam 22:31=Ps 18:31; Ps 19:8). It is the demand made on the person who would enter the cultic worship (Ps 15:2) and the confession of innocence by the worshiper (2 Sam 22:24=Ps 18:24; cf. 37:18; 84:12; 101:2, 6). The wisdom wirters use the term sparingly to refer to the righteous man who is blessed before God (Job 12:4; 36:4; Prov 2:21; 11:20; 28:10). Here then is a norm set up for men (Deut 18:13), but seldom ascribed to a man. The man who achieves it is often the victim of ridicule (Job 12:4; Amos 5:10).

The other element describing service of God is אמת, "faithfully." This, too, is seldom attributed to a person (cf. Neh 7:2; Jepsen, *TWAT* 1 [1971] 335) and finds its basic usage in the Psalms. It designates a quality within men that cannot be presupposed, that of trustworthiness and faithfulness in speech and deed in relationship to other people and to God (cf. Jepsen, *TWAT* 1 [1971] 337). Joshua thus demands an attitude and actions which are beyond the normal, expected attitudes and actions of men. He demands the same type of response to God that God has already shown to men, that of total loyalty and dedication.

Floss (*Jahwe dienen*, 351–52) contends that the command to put away the gods comes too late, being expected prior to the positive command (Gen 35:2–3; Judg 10:15–16; 2 Chr 33:15–16). He neglects to note that in each case the attitude and decision for Yahweh precedes the actions of putting away the gods and building the altars. Only if he would go against his own contention that "to serve" has wider connotations than "to worship, sacrifice," could his case be maintained. Joshua calls for proper allegiance, on which basis he can then call for a change of practice.

The interesting point is that Israel is charged with false worship not only in the time of their ancestors, but also in the time of their stay in Egypt. The presupposition appears to be that Israel has never yet served Yahweh correctly. They have merely cried to him in time of need (cf. v 7). Israel is in the new land. The new land presents them with a new life style. The land has known a life style worshiping Baal and El and the other gods and goddesses for many centuries. On the other hand, Israel has a history of worship, worship connected with the gods of the patriarchs and the gods of Egypt. Over against this history, stands the quite brief history of God's actions for Israel.

[15] Joshua concludes his case by spelling out the alternatives facing Israel, with the language "in your eyes" connecting back to v 7. The call for Israel to choose is unique in several respects. 1) God is normally the subject, having chosen Israel (Deut 4:37; 7:6, 7; 10:15; 14:2; 1 Kgs 3:8; Isa 41:8–9; 43:10; 44:1–2; 49:7; Ezek 20:5; Ps 33:12; 47:5 [=Eng 47:4]; 135:4; Neh 9:7). Yet his very choice forces a decision on Israel, for it is made in the midst of many attractive "religions." The doctrine of election may well have been formulated precisely in the battle against the Canaanite religion (cf. Seebass, TDOT 2 [1975] 83–84. 2) The only choice for Israel's neighbors was which god to serve at the moment, in the present crisis. Polytheism, the worship of many gods, was the natural presupposition in Israel's environment. Ultimate choice was unnecessary, heretical, basically stupid. 3) Cultic activities presupposed that the god of the cult was known and chosen before cultic worship began. The task of the cult was celebration, not choice.

Joshua thus forced Israel to make a choice which never confronted her neighbors, a choice which would determine the nature of her cult from that moment on, a choice which spotlighted as no other the unique quality and demand of Yahweh. In the hour of choice, Israel's freedom remains totally protected. No prophetic threats thunder down upon her (cf. Schmitt, *Landtag*, 37). She is simply asked to view God's history and determine if it proves his superiority over other claims to deity. The decision is not one to be made in isolation, for Joshua leads the way, proclaiming that his family has already chosen Yahweh. When Israel chooses Yahweh, she has a leader to show her the way.

16 In an oath, the people follow Joshua's leadership.

17-18 Their answer is totally proper employing a long string of cultic clichés describing the salvation history. Each of the statements differs from those of Joshua. Whereas Joshua emphasized the victories of Yahweh against nations who fought Israel, the people emphasize the signs and wonders which provided for the needs of a people escaping from the house of bondage and protected them in the unknown, dangerous way across the wilderness, finally providing them a place to live.

19-20 Joshua's answer is perhaps the most shocking statement in the OT. He denies that the people can do that which he has spent the entire chapter trying to get them to do. Having won their statement of faith and allegiance, he rejects it. Why? The classic answer is that vv 19–20 represent a later insertion in light of the exile (Rudolph, Noth, Möhlenbrink, Floss). Schmitt (*Landtag*, 12) argues, however, that only difficult experiences such as the fall of the northern kingdom are presupposed, the verses warning Israel that she cannot serve Yahweh in the manner she imagined. McCarthy, in light of the treaty tradition, speaks (*Treaty and Covenant*, 236) of a historicizing of the curses and blessings with the understanding that the evil must come about. "The curse and the blessing are no longer alternatives, but one follows the other as a fact." He explains this (p 240) as being impossible in the covenant context, being derived rather from the prophetic tradition of Amos 3:1–2 and Isa 6:9–10 (cf. Hertzberg). None of these solutions takes the present context seriously enough. The issue at stake in the entire chapter is the service of other gods, presented as a present reality for Israel. Her experience is that of the service of gods who make less demands than does Yahweh. She has been able to serve such gods. She could build images for them, dress them, perfume them, build a house for them, bring sacrifices to feed them, carry them in processions, even bury them in appropriate moments (Gen 35:4; cf. 31:34). The scholarly theology of the priesthood of these gods might have denied the possibility; but for the common worshipers, it was certainly within their possibilities to serve the gods they knew, indeed, to serve several of them simultaneously. Joshua has detected this in the response of the people. They see God as the one who is bound to protect them along their way, so they can protect him by serving him. Joshua demands a service with deeper motivation. He wants service based on the nature of God himself. Joshua has described this nature in the acts of gracious election, creating a people through salvation history. Now he defines this nature with two theologically loaded terms, terms which explain why Israel cannot serve Yahweh.

First, God is holy. This is, aptly enough, language taken over from the Canaanite tradition itself (H. P. Müller, *THAT* 2, 593, 598, 602). It is in a category all by itself in describing an attribute belonging to deity, namely the numinous, mysterious element which separates him from all creation and creatures. In its earliest tradition Israel understand this holiness both as a saving and as a destructive power (T. Vriezen, *An Outline of Old Testament Theology* [2nd ed.; Oxford: Basil Blackwell, 1970] 299; cf. 1 Sam 6:20). The demonstration of the destructive power of holiness is not simply an impersonal, automatic entity in itself, however. It must be understood as the power of a God who feels himself personally insulted by the unimpressed (Müeller, *THAT* 2, 597). The holiness of God impresses the worshiper to imitate the purity of God, acting in accordance with the demands of God (Exod 22:30 [=Eng. 22:31]; Lev 19:2). The true worshiper of Yahweh is impressed by the numinous holiness of God, so impressed that he knows he cannot meet the demands of such a god. He cannot serve such a god.

Similarly, God is jealous and zealous. Here again, terminology is taken from Israel's environment, where the gods are jealous among themselves. Yahweh's uniqueness lies precisely in his jealousy over against his worshipers. He loves them so much that he wants their undivided love in return. He will not share them with any other god. God turns his jealous indignation against the unfaithful worshiper, not against the rival lover. He punishes the people who try to serve him along with some other god. God's jealousy cannot tolerate this. He has given undivided love and wants the same from them (cf. Exod 20:5; 34:14–16). Thus Eichrodt can call the jealousy of God "the basic element in the whole Old Testament idea of God" (*Theologie des Alten Testaments,* I [3rd ed; Berlin: Evangelische Verbugsanstalt, 1933] 133, n. 15=*Theology of the Old Testament,* I [Tr. J. A. Baker; Philadelphia: Westminster, 1961] 210, n. 1).

The nature of God himself prevents Israel from serving him. His holy purity and jealous love both tie him in total devotion to his people and tie them off from fulfilling his demands. This has drastic consequences. God will not forgive Israel's sins (cf. Exod 23:21). His expectations of them are too high. His love for them is too great. He cannot easily ignore their wrongdoings, their casual flirtations with other gods. The gods of the neighbors would simply wait for the worshiper to come back. Yahweh goes out to discipline the errant lover until she returns.

20 The consequences receive explicit definition. Israel's temptation is not just to serve other gods. It is to serve "strange, foreign" gods, gods to whom Israel does not belong, gods who have done nothing for Israel. Such service is the easy way out for Israel. She can fulfill the wishes of the strange gods. But such service is foreign to Israel, for it denies her very origins and identity. Still, it remains a tempting option throughout her existence. When Israel exercises this option, Yahweh's course of action is clear. He will reverse salvation history. Israel will be totally destroyed. This is the basic definition of Israel's relationship with God, a definition the prophets played on in various ways for centuries. God has created the relationship and takes it with utmost seriousness. He expects Israel to do the same and will give them reason to do so when they do not.

²¹ In light of the nature of Yahweh and his demands, the people again respond, more somberly and succinctly, but still positively. Israel has obligated herself to Yahweh.

²² Joshua assumes the role of judge and swears Israel in as witnesses against herself. Normally, other gods would serve as witnesses in the Ancient Near East. Israel's pledge of allegiance to Yahweh has excluded them from consideration (see v 27). Israel must observe her own behavior and attest their fidelity or infidelity to their oath. Her free choice is to reject the gods of her tradition and turn to the God who has given her identity and hope.

²³ Having gained Israel's commitment, Joshua places the demand on her once more (cf. 14). The demand is now quite personal. The gods are no longer those of the fathers beyond the river and in Egypt. The gods are the ones in the midst of the people today. The present generation is not exempt from the sin of the fathers. The ceremony of putting away the gods, however it may have been carried out, (cf. Nielsen, *ST* 8 [1954] 103–22), was not enough in itself. The important ingredient was one of personal dedication. Israel did not have only to stretch out her hands in ritual worship. She had to stretch out her innermost being, her heart, in total devotion.

²⁴ Finally, Israel gives an extended answer demonstrating she has understood Yahweh's demands. They accept Yahweh as their God (cf. v 17). They promise to serve him (18b). They pledge to listen obediently to his voice, something they had not mentioned previously. Here is the central statement of the chapter. The identity of Israel stands not in her confession of faith nor in her cultic loyalty. The basic identity of Israel resides in the conversation she carries on with God, listening to his word and obeying it. This, and only this, is true service of Yahweh.

²⁵ On this basis, Joshua establishes the agreement between Israel and Yahweh. The term *berith*, "covenant," has been the subject of great dispute recently. Kutsch and Perlitt have argued that it entered Israel's theology with the Deuteronomistic school. Weinfeld and particularly McCarthy (e.g. *Bib* 53 [1972] 110–21) object that Exod 19, 24, and 34; 2 Sam 23:5 and Hos 8:3 point to pre-Deuteronomic levels using *berith* theology. More recently, Barr has tended in this direction also. Again, the problem hangs together with the pre-history of the Deuteronomistic literary activity. In this case, the connections of Shechem with El- or Baal-Berith appear to provide the connecting link (cf. McCarthy, *Treaty and Covenant*, 222–23 with note 20). The Deuteronomists may well have brought ancient northern covenant traditions into Jerusalem. The basis of the covenant agreement is חק ומשפט, literally "statute and judgment." The singular is unusual, appearing also in the early tradition in Exod 15:25. The content of the "law" mediated by Joshua is not given. Certainly later tradition would understand it as the Mosaic law of Sinai. That this was the original intention of the tradition has been deeply questioned by Schmitt (e.g. *Landtag*, 14–15, 23–25). The present context does not emphasize the stipulations of the agreement between Yahweh and Israel. Rather, it focuses on the central stipulation, that of complete loyalty and service of the Lord of the covenant. All other stipulations are simply presupposed as common knowledge of the people.

It may be that the geographical designation (in Shechem) at one time directed the audience to the site where the other stipulations could be found if desired. In the literary context of Josh 24, the geographical designation simply ties the report to old tradition and concludes the dialogue by taking up the geographical motif set out in v 1.

26 Verse 26a actually duplicates the document clause of 25b and makes it more explicit. It uses the language of the Deuteronomist and may well reflect an updating of the tradition, identifying the statute and judgment of Joshua with the book of the Torah of God (cf. 1:7–8; 8:31–34; 22:5; 23:6). If so, then it may reflect the practice of revising the Torah itself, since here Joshua apparently adds the agreement he has made to the Torah. This might, indeed, point to a conscious addition of the book of Joshua itself to the Torah of Moses.

An ancient practice underlies 26b. A great stone is set up under a tree within the sanctuary. G. E. Wright has tried to show that the excavations of Shechem have uncovered cultic areas featuring cultic stones or Masseboth. E. Otto (*Jakob in Sichem*, 108–58) has recently called this explanation into question, again showing the necessity and difficulty of interpreting the "hard facts" of archaeology in relationship to literary witnesses. Whatever the final archaeological interpretation proves to be, Josh 24 attests to a period when stones were used with cultic significance by Israel (cf. Gen 28:18–22; 31:13, 44–52; 35:14, 20; Exod 24:4; Josh 4; 2 Sam 18:18, cf. Isa 19:19). The legal literature of Israel roundly condemns such pillars (Exod 23:24; 34:13; Lev 26:1; Deut 7:5; 12:3; 16:22), but this did not stop the practice (Hos 3:4; 10:1–2; Mic 5:12 [Eng. 5:13]; Ezek 26:11; 1 Kgs 14:23; 2 Kgs 3:2; 10:26–27; 17:10; 18:4; 23:14). Throughout Israel's history, the sacred stone remained ambiguous, interpreted by many as a continuation of the ancient tradition commemorating God's acts for Israel and Israel's commitment to Yahweh, but seen by many others as a continuation of Canaanite practices forbidden by Yahweh. The biblical writers came down hard on the side of the latter party. Still, some traditions of "acceptable use" of cultic stones were preserved, one of them being the present passage. (See G. A. Barrois, "Pillar," *IDB* 3 [1962] 815–17; C. Graesser, Jr., "Pillar," *IDBSup* [1976] 668–69; K. Jaroŝ, *Die Stellung* 147–79, 208–11).

Along with the cultic stone appears the sacred tree, though the tradition has changed the Hebrew pointing of the word (cf. *BHS*). A similar tree is associated with Shechem in Gen 12:6; 35:4; Deut 11:30; Judg 9:6, 37. Other such trees appear in Judg 6:11, 19; Gen 13:8; 14:13; 18:1; Judg 4:11; 1 Sam 10:3. Another type of holy tree appears in Gen 21:33 (cf. 1 Sam 22:6; 31:13). Use of trees within the sanctuaries also came under condemnation (Deut 12:2; 2 Kgs 16:4; Isa 1:29; 57:5; Hos 4:13; Jer 2:27; 3:6; Hab 2:19; Ezek 6:13; 20:28; see Jaroŝ, *Die Stellung*, 213–57; J. A. Soggin, *TWAT* 2 [1976] 357). Here then, our text shows a very early period in the history of Israelite religion when stones and trees were used unthinkingly and innocently in the cult and became such a fixed part of the tradition that later writers did not remove them.

The sanctuary is interpreted as belonging to Yahweh. This may indicate a division between an Israelite sanctuary near Shechem and the Shechemite sanctuary of Baal-Berith inside the city itself (cf. Judg 9). The Israelite sanctuary was the site of a ceremony sealing the agreement. Details of the ceremony are not given. Perhaps sacrifices or meals were a part of such ritual (cf. Exod 24). For our context, this is unimportant. The intention is not to preserve the ritual but to impress upon the audience the importance of the basic stipulation.

27 Having completed the ceremony, Joshua explains the significance to the people. The subjective witness of the people (v 22) is complemented by the objective witness of the stone (cf. Gen 31:51–52). Here is an ancient understanding which attributes "life" to the cultic stone (cf. McCarthy, *Treaty and Covenant*, 223).

"The words of Yahweh" are difficult to define. The natural expectation would be that the stone was witness to divine statutes written upon it (cf. Deut 27; Josh 8:30–35). The only words of Yahweh recorded in our passage, however, are the historical summary in vv 2–13. Here again, ancient ritual is summarized but remains secondary to the context. The words must be the stipulations of the agreement (v 25b), but these have been minimized in interest of the call to obedience to the one basic stipulation. Israel's temptation is not to violate some secondary stipulation. Israel's punishment would not come from a legalistic god who finds that she has not carried out a ritual properly. Israel's temptation and the danger of punishment came under the basic commandment: thou shalt have no other gods. כחש, "to deny" appears with deity as the object only here, Jer 5:12, Isa 59:13; Job 31:28; and Prov 30:9. This does not prove that it is late language (Schmitt, *Landtag*, 22 against L'Hour, *RB* 69 [1962]).

28 The agreement is concluded. The people may return to the inheritances which God has given to them. The identity of Israel is complete. She is a people sworn to serve only Yahweh living in her land given her by Yahweh.

Explanation

Joshua 24 completes the book by giving the theological definition of the people of God. Here we suddenly find highly loaded theological language, defining God and the God-man relationship. This makes the chapter one of the most important chapters in the OT for biblical theologians. But the chapter is not simply theological reflection, as contended by some recent writers. Its foundations were in the very roots of Israel herself, when ancient cultic symbols continued to be used and the religion of the fathers could be seen as a temptation to other gods. Thus the chapter has played a very important role for historians of Israel and her religion. In all of the effort to incorporate the message of the chapter into a theological, historical, or religious system, the intent of the chapter in its canonical context can easily be overlooked.

Joshua 24 is atemporal. It sets itself up as an occasion which has validity for all Israel through all time. It does not belong to the period immediately after the conquest, nor to the period immediately after the distribution of the land. It does not belong to the ceremony celebrating Joshua's final speech to Israel before he dies (chap. 23). It belongs to no specific time and thus to all times. It is ever a call to the people of God to examine their identity over against the true identity of people of God as set out in the chapter.

That identity as God's people hinges on two things. The first is the action of God in the history of his people. Such action is set out as having occurred prior to any service of Yahweh by the people. Salvation history can in no way be connected to God's reward for the behavior of his people. God chose to act in his own freedom in the hope that the people he delivered from slavery would respond in the same freedom and choose to serve him. The chapter implies that such a free choice was not immediately forthcoming. In this, it stands with the wilderness narratives of the Pentateuch. A people having experienced the saving acts of God can easily turn to murmuring or to serving other gods. God sends his leader to assemble the people and remind them of the greatness of God's actions for them. Only under such leadership does Israel respond. Thus Josh 24 is a fit ending for the activity of Joshua. Joshua here becomes more than a pious, obedient hero of faith, more than a conquering hero of war, more than a just arbiter in legal disputes. Here Joshua becomes the courageous religious leader ready to set the example himself with his house and calls his people to follow. Such a call is not a summons seeking recognition and popularity for himself. It is a call issued with stern warning of the responsibility and consequences.

The call of Joshua to Israel is more than simply a narration of past history. It is a demand for discipleship, a call to hear and obey in faithfulness and loyalty the commands of God. Joshua forces Israel to understand the difference between their concept of god(s) and the true nature of Yahweh. He is the holy, jealous God, who expects his people to be satisfied with nothing less than perfection. He is not a God whom men can bribe. He is not a God who waits around patiently while Israel flirts with other gods. He is not a God who governs one small part of the world, while others take care of their shares. He is the only God, the one who has all power and all responsibility. More than anything else, he is the God who loves so much that he seeks the same whole-hearted love and devotion in return. Man is incapable of such total devotion, but this is no excuse. Man is called to demand such devotion from himself, to be satisfied with nothing less.

The sad story of Israel is that she refused even to try. Immediately following the generation of Joshua, she slipped into the easy way, the way of her neighbors. She chose the other gods (e.g. Judg 10). The remainder of the history of Israel is the story of God raising leaders—judges, kings, prophets—to call Israel back to himself, as Joshua had done. None had the success of Joshua. Never again did the entire people of God unite in commitment as in the time of Joshua. When a second Joshua arose (2 Kgs 23:24–25), it was too late. God had already begun the evil which he had threatened to bring upon a disobedient people. Finally, God called forth his own Son, bearing the same name, to seek to entice his people back to him. Even then the people refused, choosing to use the courts of the nations to bring condemnation and death upon Jesus. The words of Joshua now join the words of Jesus in calling forth in all nations for people who will come to the court of God, hear the new agreement which God seeks to make with his people, and take upon themselves the commitment to serve the God and Father of Jesus Christ in all circumstances. All too often, people have answered this agreement as did Israel of old. They have pledged their whole heart to God, but the first temptation has led them to halt between two opinions, serving the gods of the fathers, the gods of the lands, the gods of materialistic atheism, along with the Father. The timeless ceremony continues to beckon men to choose whom they will serve. He continues to warn them that such choice has serious consequences. He continues to remind them that the God offering the choice has already done more for his people than they can ever repay. He continues to be a jealous lover calling his people back to his holy courts for service.

Faithful to the Finish (24:29-33)

Bibliography

Auld, A. G. "Judges 1 and History: a Reconsideration." *VT* 25 (1975) 261–65. **Budde, K.** "Richter und Josua." *ZAW* 7 (1887) 93–166. **Hertzberg, H. W.** "Die Tradition in Palästina." *PJ* 22 (1926) 84–104. (=*Beiträge zur Traditionsgeschichte und Theologie des Alten Testaments.* Göttingen: Vandenhoeck & Ruprecht, 1962, 11–27.) **Kaiser, O.** "Stammesgeschichtliche Hintergründe der Josephgeschichte. Erwägungen zur Vor- und Frühgeschichte Israels." *VT* 10 (1960) 10. **Mowinckel, S.** " 'Rahelstämme' und 'Leastämme.' " *Von Ugarit nach Qumran,* ed. J. Hempel and L. Rost. BZAW 77. Berlin: Alfred Töpelmann, 1958, 143–44. **Noth, M.** *Überlieferungsgeschichtliche Studien.* Tübingen: Max Niemeyer Verlag, 1943, 6–10. **O'Doherty, E.** "The Literary Problem of Judges 1:1–3, 6." *CBQ* 18 (1956) 1–7. **Rendtorff, R.** *Das Überlieferungsgeschichtliche Problem des Pentateuch.* BZAW 147. Berlin: Walter de Gruyter, 1977, 165–67. **Richter, W.** *Die Bearbeitungen des 'Retterbuches' in der deuteronomischen Epoche.* BBB 21. Bonn: Peter Hanstein, 1964, 44–49 (history of research). **Rösel, H.** "Die Überlieferung vom Josua ins Richterbuch." *VT* 30 (1980) 342–50. **Rofe, A.** "The Composition of the Introduction of the Book of Judges (Judges II,6–III,6)." (Hebrew) *Tarbiz* 35 (1966) 201–13. ———. "The End of the Book of Joshua According to the Septuagint." (Hebrew) *Shnaton* 2 (1977) 217–27. **Schenke, H. M.** "Jacobsbrunnen—Josephsgrab—Sychar." *ZDPV* 84 (1968) 159–84. **Schmitt, H. C.** *Die nichtpriesterliche Josephsgeschichte: Ein Beitrag zur neuesten Pentateuchkritik.* BZAW 154. Berlin: Walter de Gruyter, 1980, 124–27. **Seebass, H.** *Geschichtliche Zeit und theonome Tradition in der Joseph-Erzählung.* 1978, 103–13. **Smend, R.** "Das Gesetz und die Völker." *Probleme biblischer Theologie,* ed. H. W. Wolff. München: Chr. Kaiser Verlag, 1971, 506–9. **Tengström, S.** *Die Hexateucherzählung.* Lund: C. W. K. Gleerup, 1976, 40–47. **Vriezen, T. C.** "Exodusstudien Exodus I." *VT* 17 (1967) 334–44. **Weimar, P.** *Untersuchungen zur Redaktionsgeschichte des Pentateuch.* BZAW 146. Berlin: Walter de Gruyter, 1977, 169. **Wright, G. R. H.** "Joseph's Grave under the Tree by the Omphalos at Shechem." *VT* 22 (1972) 476–86.

Translation

[29.a.] *After these things, Joshua, the son of Nun, the servant of Yahweh, died at the age of one hundred ten years.* [30] *They buried him in the territory of his inheritance, in Timnath-Serah,*[a] *which*[b] *is in the hill country of Ephraim, north of the mountain of Gaʿash.*[c] [31] *Israel*[a] *served Yahweh all the days of Joshua and all the days of the elders whose days extended beyond Joshua's and who knew*[b] *all the work*[c] *of Yahweh which he did for Israel.*

³² *At the same time, the bones of Joseph, which the sons of Israel had brought up from Egypt, they buried in Shechem, in the section of the field which Jacob had bought from the sons of Hamor,* ᵃ *the father of Shechem, with a hundred Qesitah.* ᵇ *They belonged* ᶜ *to the sons of Joseph as part of the inherited estate.*

³³ *Meanwhile, Eleazer, the son of Aaron,* ᵃ *died. They buried him in Gibeah of Phinehas, his son, which was given* ᵇ *to him in the hill country of Ephraim.* ᶜ

Notes

29.a. V 28–31 are repeated in Judg 2:6–9 with significant variations in wording and order, several of which are witnessed by LXX in our passage. Between 28 and 29, LXX inserts v 31 in agreement with Judg 2:7. The distinction in order is caused by the different functions of the two units, Joshua emphasizing the faithfulness of Joshua and its consequences, while Judges emphasizes the contrast between the obedience of Joshua's generation and the disobedience of the following ones. The originality of the Joshua section can be seen in that while Judges sought to modify the transitional temporal clause of v 29, which no longer served as an introduction (2:8), LXX retained the introductory clause even though it no longer fit the literary scheme. LXX represents the attempt to harmonize the two sections.

30.a. The name of Joshua's home is variously transcribed. This passage agrees with 19:50. LXX ᴮ in 19:50 reads ϑαμαρχαρης and the Old Latin, "Chamahares." In our passage LXX ᴮ reads ϑαμναϑασαχαρα with many variant readings. MT of Judg 2:9 reads Timnah-heres, reversing the order of the consonants, agreeing with LXX of Josh 19:50, but giving rise to still further complexity among Greek manuscripts. The original name may well have been Timnah-heres, "portion of the sun," which was later transposed to avoid any associations with sun worship.

30.b. Neither LXX nor Judg 2:9 witnesses the relative. They are supported by strong Heb. ms and Tg evidence.

30.c. LXX ᴮ reads Gilead here, but Gaas in Judg 2:9. After v 30, LXX reads, "There they laid with him in the tomb into which they buried him there the stone knives with which he had circumcized the sons of Israel in Gilgal, when he led them out of Egypt, just as the Lord had commanded them. There they are unto this day." This is a continuation of the LXX addition in 21:42, completing the etiological statement which would naturally surround a grave tradition. Such a tradition suits the function of the present section, illustrating the obedience of the people at the death of Joshua. The very "heresy" of attributing the leadership from Egypt to Joshua could also speak for the age of the tradition. Rofé has argued for the originality of the entire LXX conclusion, an argument which certainly cannot hold for the opening portion. Rösel's attempt (*VT* 30 [1980] 342–50) to refute the originality of the additions in v 30 are not convincing. Judges may have taken up the LXX rather than the MT text tradition. If the LXX formulation here is "illogical," this does not prove it is not original. The question certainly deserves more comment than it normally receives.

31.a. Judg 2:7 reads "the people," instead of "Israel." This is a modification to the context of Judges. The reference to Israel is necessary in the Joshua context, where Israel has not been mentioned. Judges mentions "Israel" in its addition in 6b. (cf. Richter, *Bearbeitungen,* 47).

31.b. LXX and Judg 2:7 read "saw" instead of "knew." The MT represents a more expansive content, including knowledge of the tradition, while the alternative limits it to being eyewitnesses. Such a change may have been made under the influence of 23:3 (Rösel, *VT* 30 [1980] 344), where the eyewitness function is limited to the conquest. Judg 2:10 represents a taking up of the language of the original context, not a cause for the change from "see" to "know" (against Richter, *Bearbeitungen,* 47).

31.c. The early versions read plural, "works," again in line with the tendency noted in 31.b. of emphasizing the deeds which could be seen with the eye rather than the comprehensive work of Yahweh. Judg 2:7 follows the same tendency in reading "great work of Yahweh."

32.a. LXX reads "Amorites" instead of "Sons of Hamor," adjusting to the more common designation of the inhabitants of the land rather than to the specific context picked up from Gen 33:19. LXX thus also adjusts "father of Shechem" to "inhabitants of Shechem."

32.b. The *Qesitah* is a unit of exchange taken over from Gen 33:19 and appearing elsewhere only in Job 42:11. Its exact meaning and value is unknown. LXX translated "lambs."

32.c. LXX reads "and he gave." The reason for the plural verb in Heb. is not apparent. The reference is certainly back to "the section of the field." The omission of "sons of" by LXX may be original, the Massoretic tradition adding it to underline the theme of inheritance in light of the report of Joseph's death and the context of the book.

33.a. LXX introduces an introductory formula parallel to that of v 29, disregarding the structure which sets both the story of Joseph (v 32) and that of Eleazer (v 33) in disjunctive clauses. LXX and other translations, along with two Heb. mss. add the traditional title "the priest."

33.b. LXX changes "buried" to passive and "was given" to active voice, while reading the locality as "Gabaar." The locality may either be interpreted as a proper name or as the "hill of Phinehas."

33.c. LXX introduces an extensive conclusion, "In that day the sons of Israel, taking up the ark of God, carried it around among themselves. Phinehas officiated in the place of Eleazer, his father, until he died. He was buried in Gabaar, which belonged to him. But the sons of Israel went away each into his place and into his own city. The sons of Israel worshipped the Astarte and the Astaroth and the gods of the nations around them, and the Lord gave them over into the hands of Eglon, the king of Moab. He ruled them eighteen years."

This ties directly into the beginning of Judges, omitting some of the literarily difficult passages of that book. Rofé has thus argued for its originality (cf. Rösel, *VT* 30 [1980] 349). The new literary formulation shown at the beginning of v 33 and the repetition of the material in Judg 3:14 point against the originality. The content and theme is that of Judges, not that of Joshua. Thus it appears that the later tradition has tried to make the tie between the two books explicit not only in Judg 2:6–10, but already in Josh 24.

Form/Structure/Setting

The very general temporal clause clearly marks the introduction to a new section in v 29. Verses 32–33 then introduce new subject matter, but do so with disjunctive clauses, which express a contrast to the preceding clauses. The section is thus structured as a unit. Judges 1:1 marks the next section by taking up the heading of this unit, namely the death of Joshua, as the point of temporal reference. This gives further indication that 24:29–32 is seen in the context as a literary unit.

The opening verses reflect the literary death report form found also in Gen 23:2, 19; 25:7–8; 35:28–29; Deut 34:5 (cf. Gen 35:19; 48:7; 49:33–50:13). Joshua 24:29 is unusual in placing the description of the life span after the death notice rather than prior to it. Verse 31 gives an interpretation of the death report. Verse 32 then takes up the narrative of Gen 33:18–19 combined with that of 50:22–26 (cf. Exod 13:19). Finally, verse 33 represents yet another death report, but with reversed order of subject and predicate in order to set it clearly into the literary framework of the preceding.

Behind such literary reports lies a long tradition of honoring the memory of the founding fathers at their grave sites. It is possible that the joining of the traditions represents a stage in the cultic history of Shechem, since all three grave sites are in the hill country of Ephraim.

Comment

[29] Joshua has completed his task. The people are safely in their inherited territories. They have been warned of the dangers that lie ahead and have joined in covenant to avoid these dangers. Joshua can exit the scene with honor. The honor is shown by giving Joshua a new title. In life he was the minister of Moses (cf. 1:1). In death he assumes the title reserved for Moses,

that of servant of Yahweh (cf. 1:1, 2, 7, 13, 15; 8:31, 33; 9:24; 11:12, 15; 12:6; 13:8; 14:7; 18:7; 22:2, 4, 5). Before he had assumed the title only as a formula of self-humiliation before the deity in prayer (5:14). The point being made is that the title, "servant of Yahweh," belongs supremely to Moses. The title is thereafter transferred only at death to the faithful follower of Moses. No man can claim the title for himself and use it to rule others. Others must confer it in respectful memory. Even in death, Joshua fell just short of Moses, having reached only one hundred ten years (cf. Deut 34:7).

³⁰ For Joshua's inheritance, see 19:50. The location north of Mount Gaʿash occurs only here and in the parallel in Judg 2:9. The name serves to locate one of David's thirty heroes (2 Sam 23:30=1 Chr 11:32), but is otherwise unknown.

³¹ Joshua's epitaph was not written on a marble gravestone. It was written in the lives of the leaders he influenced and the people he led. They served Yahweh. Here is the theological climax to the theme introduced in 22:5 and repeated like a chorus in 23:7, 16; 24:14, 15, 16, 18, 19, 20, 21, 22, 24. Ironically, the minister of Moses brought the people to obey Yahweh, while Moses saw only the perpetual murmuring and rebellion of the people (cf. Deut 31:27). Even Moses had to die outside the Land of Promise.

The obedience is traced to faithful knowledge of the tradition. As long as men remained alive who could keep the tradition in force, Israel obeyed. When the men who knew the tradition of Joshua died, then the people rebelled. It is precisely at this point that the book of Judges takes up our verses and transforms them from a conclusion to the faithful life of Joshua to an introduction to the failure of the generations after Joshua (see Judg 2:6–10).

³² The obedience finds concrete expression in the case of Joseph's remains. Israel remembers and carries out the oath given by the fathers to Joseph in Gen 50:25, when he died at precisely the age of Joshua. The burial ground is connected to the place where Jacob established an altar (Gen 33:19), presumably the same place where Abraham had also built an altar (12:7), the foundation for the sanctuary where Joshua mediated the covenant to Israel (Josh 24:1–28). But here the emphasis lay on the purchase of the land. Israel claimed Shechem not by conquest, but by legal purchase.

³³ Despite the role of Phinehas in chap. 22, the final death report is that of his father Eleazer, who played the central role in the division of the land (14:1; 17:4; 19:51). The land is named, however, for Phinehas. The location is unknown, though the association with Shiloh in chap. 22 might point in that direction.

Explanation

The patriarchs had wandered through the land, making claim to small portions through the building of altars and through purchase of burial plots. The final act of Joshua's generation is to cement their claim to the land by burying their heroes in the land, a land which a father could now give to his son (v 33).

Joshua left behind something more than simply a burial place. He left behind an epitaph carved in the lives of men. Unlike leaders before or after himself, he led men to serve Yahweh. Thus he became the prime example of Israelite leadership. His was the golden age when Israel won all her battles, occupied her land, and made her covenant with Yahweh. This could be explained only in one way. Joshua had fulfilled the command of God to have conviction and courage (cf. chap. 1), to obey all the Torah of Moses (1:7–8), and to expect the divine presence to guide him. For the faithful Joshua, God proved faithful. Joshua could bow out graciously in his own inheritance, knowing he had fulfilled his task. Behind him remained a few protectors of the tradition of the great acts of God, who could remind the people of Joshua's example. But they, too, soon passed away, leaving behind a generation who forgot Joshua and Moses. They initiated the beginning of the end, as shown quickly in the book of Judges, where our section is taken up again for an entirely new purpose. The same facts which have shown the faithfulness of Joshua can also function to introduce the unfaithfulness of a generation who forgot Joshua and his God (Judg 2:6–10). Such a generation finally forced Israel to look ahead to a new day, when a new Joshua appeared on the scene as the servant of God totally fulfilling the task of God and bringing the promise of a new kingdom of God unlimited by physical boundaries or human death.

Index of Authors Cited

Abba, R. 45
Abel, F. M. xxvii, 24, 36, 53, 63, 73, 80, 97, 105, 120
Aharoni, Y. xxxvii, xxxviii, 11, 17, 103, 120, 126, 127, 128, 129, 137, 141, 143, 144, 164, 165, 185, 188, 189, 190, 193, 218, 222, 231
Albright, W. F. xxxvii, xl, 73, 77, 78, 83, 150, 193, 218, 222, 225, 226, 227
Alfrink, B. 105, 110
Alt, A. xxx, xl, 105, 112, 120, 137, 141, 142, 158, 164, 185, 188, 189, 194, 199, 200, 204, 218, 225, 226, 231, 259
Andersen, F. I. 3, 19, 39, 65, 247
Anderson, G. W. xxxiv, 77, 248
Astour, M. 24
Auerbach, E. 259
Auld, A. G. xvii, 3, 15, 55, 78, 109, 110, 145, 146, 155, 157, 167, 168, 179, 180, 181, 182, 183, 186, 197, 200, 210, 211, 215, 216, 218, 222, 225, 263, 280
Auzou, G. 36
Avigad, N. 230
Avi-Yonah, M. xxxviii, 163

Baars, W. 63
Bächli, O. xxxv, 24, 95, 141, 163, 194, 205, 259
Balaban, M. 106
Baltzer, K. 7, 9, 73, 250, 253, 258, 266, 268
Baly, D. xxxviii, 17, 126
Bardtke, H. 121
Barr, J. 85, 260
Barrois, G. A. 277
Bartlett, J. R. 153
Barth, C. 18, 19–20, 59
Becker, J. 258
Beltz, W. 167, 176, 186
Benjamin, C. D. 25, 26, 27, 65, 77, 78, 109, 110, 111, 123, 124, 132
Ben-Tor, A. 138
Bergman, A. 153
Bimson, J. xxxvi, xxxviii, xli, 32, 63, 70, 73, 83, 101, 103, 106, 115, 116, 120, 124, 126, 137, 138
Biton, G. 231
Bleek, F. xxviii
Blenkinsopp, J. 95, 101, 103, 106
Boecker, H. J. 73, 80, 236, 242, 246
Boling, R. C. 180, 181, 252, 258
Bratsiotis, N. P. 173
Brekelmans, C. H. W. 63, 260
Briend, J. 73
Bright, J. xxx, xxxvi, xxxvii, xxxix, 58, 121, 146, 180, 200, 250
Brockelmann, C. 26, 90
Brook, A. E. xvii, 133
Broshi, M. 119
Buber, M. 258
Budde, K. 182, 280
Buis, P. 260
Buhl, R. J. 146, 258

Burgmann, H. 63
Bush, F. W. 102

Calberini, O. 103
Callaway, J. A. xxxvii, 73, 79, 83, 103
Calvin, J. xxviii
Campbell, E. F. 229, 258, 260
Campbell, K. M. 24
Carmichael, C. 260
Cazelles, H. 219
Childs, B. S. xxxi, 28, 56, 67, 81, 82, 112, 130, 170, 204, 260, 264, 271
Cholewinski, A. 236
Christensen, D. L. 106
Clements, R. E. 48, 110, 236, 259, 260
Clines, D. J. A. 50
Coats, G. W. 95, 104, 236, 271
Cody, A. 219
Cohen, S. 17, 103, 136, 164, 190
Conrad, J. 84
Cooley, R. E. 103
Cornfeld, G. 70
Craigie, P. C. 259, 260
Cross, F. M. 36, 73, 81, 141, 143, 189, 194, 204, 260
Culley, R. C. 95

Dahl, G. 176, 182
Dahood, M. 118
Dalman, G. 60
Danielus, E. 176
David, M. 210, 214
Davidson, A. B. 19
Deckert, B. 229
De Fraine, J. 106, 237
De Geuss, C. H. J. xxxiv, xli, 141, 144, 172, 185, 186, 190, 191
Delcor, M. 63
Delekat, L. 210, 215, 216, 217, 221
Delitzsch, F. xxvii, 26, 110
De Tillesse, G. M. 163
Deurloo, K. A. 53
De Vaux, R. xxxviii, xxxix, 36, 53, 63, 74, 83, 89, 96, 106, 121, 132, 139, 142, 154, 164, 188, 191, 219, 225, 237, 258, 266
Dever, W. G. 176, 230
De Vries, S. J. 36, 46, 60, 73, 120
Diebner, B. 236
Diepold, P. 12, 17
Dietrich, W. xx, xxix
Dillmann, A. 239, 241
Dinur, B. 210
Dommershausen, W. 29, 172
Dothan, M. 173
Drinkard, J. 145
Driver, G. R. 180, 239, 265
Durham, J. I. 260
Dus, J. 36, 43, 63, 67, 95, 106, 112, 236, 259
Dussaud, R. 73

Edwards, I. E. S. xxxix
Ehrlich, E. 180, 240
Eichrodt, W. 261, 275
Eisler, R. 106

Eissfeldt, O. 7, 67, 89, 93, 129, 142, 200, 237
Elder, W. H. 53
Elliger, K. xvii, 106, 119, 141, 176, 190, 230, 258
Emerton, J. A. 164

Fensham, F. C. 95
Fernández, A. 36, 176
Fichtner, J. xxxi
Field, F. xvii
Finkel, J. 53
Finkelstein, I. 176
Flanagan, J. 246
Floss, J. P. 250, 255, 258, 266, 270, 273, 274
Foerster, G. 127
Fohrer, G. xxxiv, 36, 261
Franken, H. J. 63, 165
Fritz, V. 121, 124, 125, 131, 133, 134, 137, 138, 189, 231
Füglister, N. 53
Fuller, R. C. 106

Gadd, C. J. xxxix
Garsiel, M. 176
Garstang, J. xxxix
George, A. 36, 53
Gerleman, G. 11, 92, 171, 228
Gevirtz, S. 63
Gfroerer, A. xxviii
Giblin, C. H. 258, 266
Ginsberg, C. D. 99, 109
Giveon, R. 157
Glock, A. 138, 176
Glueck, N. 17, 33, 153, 158
Gold, V. 116, 232
Golka, F. xxxii, 30
Görg, M. 7, 188
Gottwald, N. xxxiv–xxxv, xli, 141, 144, 190, 245, 257, 259
Gradwohl, R. 53, 58
Graesser, C. 277
Graf, K. 225
Gray, J. xxvii, 4, 7, 47, 59, 110, 115, 121, 124, 126, 135, 149, 155, 180, 182, 191, 197, 198, 202, 240
Greenberg, M. 210, 214
Greenspoon, L. xvii
Gressmann, H. xxvii, xxx, 36, 42, 53
Grintz, J. M. 73, 83, 95
Grohman, E. D. 164, 232
Gruenthaner, M. J. 106
Gunkel, H. xxx, 28
Gunneweg, A. H. J. xxxix, 219

Haag, H. 53
Halbe, J. 53, 56, 95, 99, 100, 127, 250, 253, 261
Halpern, B. 95, 106, 112, 219
Hammond, M. G. L. xxxix
Haran, M. 7, 95, 204, 219, 225, 247
Harrelson, W. 260
Hauff, 91
Hayes, J. H. xxxix, 270
Heller, J. 24, 106
Henke, O. 164

Hentschke, R. 165
Herrmann, S. xxxiv, xxxix, 259
Hermisson, H. J. 53, 73, 237
Hertzberg, H. W. xxvii, 44, 59, 65, 99, 109, 110, 130, 146, 168, 180, 182, 188, 190, 191, 197, 198, 200, 222, 223, 240, 271, 274, 280
Hillers, D. R. 261, 268
Hoffner, H. A. 102
Hoftijzer, J. 155, 163
Holladay, J. S. 106, 116, 180
Hollenberg, J. 15, 89, 91, 106, 131, 146, 211, 222, 252, 258, 263, 264
Holmes, S. 78, 123, 155, 182, 200, 211, 221, 223, 239, 240, 241, 252, 263, 264, 265
Hölscher, G. 2, 24, 28, 53, 73, 141, 143
Holstein, J. A. 173
Holzinger, H. xxviii, 7, 19, 179, 197, 211, 239, 240, 241, 264
Horn, S. H. 135, 258
Horst, F. 80
Huffmon, H. B. 260
Hulst, A. R. 36, 51, 247
Humbert, P. 271
Hyatt, J. P. 260, 267

Irwin, W. H. 269

Jacobs, L. 106
James, F. 176
Jamieson, H. M. 232
Japhet, S. 145, 219
Jaroš, K. 229, 258, 259, 266, 277
Jenks, A. W. 260, 267
Jenni, E. 176
Jepsen, A. 34, 261, 273
Johns, C. N. 231
Jones, G. H. 42, 106
Joüon, P. 3, 19, 39, 90

Kaiser, O. 36, 176, 280
Kallai-Kleinmann, Z. 103, 142, 143, 144, 176, 194
Kaufmann, Y. 153, 200, 225
Kearney, P. J. 96
Keel, O. 53, 61, 73, 78, 87
Keil, C. F. xxvii
Keller, C. A. 36, 43, 53, 89, 255, 259
Kellerman, D. 86, 93, 176, 189
Kelm, G. 176
Kempinski, A. 243
Kenyon, K. 32, 63
Kingsbury, E. E. 176
Kitchen, K. A. 148
Kittel, R. xvii
Kleber, A. 106
Klein, S. 219, 225
Kloppenborg, J. S. 237
Knierim, R. 16, 73, 80, 83
Knoebel, A. 91
Koch, K. 203
Kochavi, M. 115, 138, 151
Köhler, L. 76, 92, 263, 264
Kraeling, E. G. 17
Kraus, H. J. xxi, 36, 47, 53, 63, 67, 258
Kroeze, J. H. xxvii
Kühlwein, J. 173
Kuschke, A. 73, 83, 103, 142, 153, 164, 165, 176, 190, 191, 194
Kutsch, E. 53, 80, 85, 102, 261, 276

Laaf, P. 53, 60
Lambdin, T. O. 3, 39, 65, 77, 197
Lambert, G. 106

Lance, H. D. 176
Lang, B. 248, 260
Langlamet, F. 24, 28, 30, 31, 32, 36, 39, 40, 41, 43, 45, 47, 50
Lemke, W. E. 173
Lewis, A. L. 70
Lewis, J. 204
L'Hour, J. 89, 258, 263, 266, 278
Liedke, G. 172, 258
Lindars, B. 172
Lindblom, J. 171
Lipinski, E. 47, 174, 259
Liver, J. 96, 164, 191
Livingston, D. 73, 83
Lods, A. 73
Loersch, S. 261
Loewenstamm, S. E. 210, 215
Lohfink, N. 2, 5, 8, 13, 33, 71, 260
Löhr, M. 210, 214, 219
Long, B. O. xxi, 28, 36, 53, 73, 81
Lubsczyk, H. 53, 250, 258

Maag, V. 11, 259, 266
Maass, F. 121, 124
McCarthy, D. J. 24, 28, 29, 50, 67, 85, 89, 250, 253, 258, 260, 261, 266, 267, 270, 274, 276, 278
MacDonald, J. xvii
Macholz, G. 16, 73, 80
McKenzie, J. L. 63, 73
McLean, N. xvii, 133
Maier, J. 36, 43, 47, 53, 63
Maisler, B. 138, 145, 149
Malamat, A. 121
Mann, T. W. 36, 41
March, W. E. 246
Margolis, M. L. xvii, 19, 55, 66, 78, 98, 109, 123, 133, 155, 156, 168, 169, 179, 180, 181, 182, 197, 198, 199
Marquet-Krause, J. 73, 83
Martin-Achard, R. 261
Masius, A. xxviii
Matthes, J. C. 106
Maunder, E. W. 106
Mayes, A. D. H. xx, xxiv, 36, 142, 144, 153, 246, 258, 260, 261, 264, 268
Mazar, B. xxxix, 121, 176, 194, 219, 226
Mendenhall, G. E. xxiv–xxxv, xli, 258, 268
Menes, A. 237, 244
Merendino, R. P. 260
Mettinger, T. N. D. 187, 191, 194, 219
Metzger, M. 172
Meyer, R. xviii
Michel, D. 19
Milgrom, J. 103, 203
Miller, J. M. xxxvi, xxxviii, xxxix, 33, 194
Miller, P. D. 53, 106, 260
Mitchell, T. C. 150
Mittmann, S. 18, 142, 144, 159, 162, 165, 166, 191, 232
Möhlenbrink, K. xxviii, 36, 53, 63, 73, 89, 96, 106, 219, 227, 237, 243, 258, 274
Moran, W. L. 24, 30, 32
Mowinckel, S. 24, 36, 53, 73, 89, 96, 106, 121, 142, 143, 280
Muilenburg, J. 258, 266
Müller, H.-P. 115, 275

Na'aman, N. 112, 116, 149, 150, 229
Namiki, K. 176
Naveh, J. 150
Nebeling, G. 260
Negev, A. xxxviii, 119, 150

Netanyahu, B. xxxix
Netzer, E. 150
Nibbi, A. 148
Nicholsky, N. M. 210, 214, 217
Nicholson, E. W. 45, 181, 260
Nielsen, E. 89, 219, 259, 266, 276
North, R. 142, 176, 188
Noth, M. xx, xxvii, xxix, xxx, xxxiii, xxxiv, xxv, xxxvi, xxxviii, xxxix, xl, 2, 4, 7, 8, 9, 15, 26, 40, 56, 57, 61, 63, 65, 67, 73, 78, 81, 83, 89, 103, 106, 107, 110, 112, 114, 116, 121, 134, 142, 143, 146, 153, 158, 167, 168, 176, 180, 182, 186, 188, 194, 197, 198, 200, 219, 221, 222, 225, 226, 228, 231, 232, 240, 241, 258, 266, 274, 280
Notscher, F. 261

Obed, B. 165
O'Doherty, E. 280
Olávarri, E. 135
Oren, E. D. 150
Otto, E. xxi, xxix, xxiv, 2, 7, 15, 16, 24, 30, 36, 41, 43, 45, 47, 49, 53, 55, 60, 63, 67, 73, 96, 100, 101, 106, 121, 176, 185, 190, 191, 229, 237, 243, 259, 269, 270, 277
Ottosson, M. 131, 135, 136, 154, 164, 165, 166, 176, 232

Perles, F. 182
Perlitt, L. 12, 85, 250, 253, 258, 266, 267, 270, 276
Phillips, A. 210, 216
Phythian-Adams, W. J. 106, 176
Plöger, J. G. 17
Polzin, R. xxxii
Porter, J. R. 2, 36, 53, 86
Pritchard, J. B. xxxix, 48, 96, 101, 114
Preuss, H. D. 8, 12

Quell, G. 106

Rahlfs, A. xvii, xviii, 240
Rainey, A. F. 73, 83, 103, 114, 119, 150
Ramsey, G. W. xxxii, xxxv, xxxvi, xxxviii
Reid, J. 106
Rendtorff, R. 9, 11, 92, 165, 248, 380
Renner, E. 171
Reventlow, H. G. 5–6
Reviv, H. 259
Richter, W. 106, 115, 125, 260, 267, 271, 280, 281
Riesener, I. 9
Ringgren, H. 47, 247
Robinson, H. 86
Rofé, A. xvii, 280, 281, 282
Rose, D. G. 114
Rose, M. xxiv, xxx, xxxiii, 173, 243
Rösel, H. 96, 106, 112, 280, 281, 282
Rosenthal, R. 138
Ross, J. P. 219, 225, 258
Rost, L. 60, 92, 203, 260, 267
Roth, W. 73, 80
Rowley, H. H. 259
Rudolph, W. xvii, xxviii, 2, 24, 28, 36, 53, 63, 73, 89, 96, 106, 121, 142, 145, 158, 167, 182, 237, 250, 258, 263, 274

Sauer, G. 247
Sauer, J. A. 176
Sawyer, J. 106, 110, 112, 116
Saydon, P. P. 36

Scharbert, J. 73, 174
Schenke, H. M. 280
Schmid, H. H. 9, 17, 106, 121, 172
Schmid, R. 36, 57, 237
Schmidt, W. H. 165, 182, 204, 258, 261
Schmitt, G. 2, 74, 96, 98, 101, 102, 131, 134, 142, 188, 192, 194, 200, 202, 250, 258, 263, 265, 274, 276, 278
Schmitt, H. C. 280
Schmitt, R. 9, 36, 53
Schmuttermayr, G. 118
Schneider, W. 3, 77, 90
Schottroff, W. 63, 96
Schult, H. 236
Schulz, W. 16, 59
Schunck, K. D. 36, 82, 96, 106, 112, 121, 124, 142, 144, 188, 189, 190, 194
Scott, R. B. Y. 116
Seebass, H. 172, 258, 266, 273, 280
Segal, J. B. 53, 60
Seger, J. D. 259
Seitz, G. 134, 210
Sellers, O. R. 86
Sellin, E. 89, 258, 259, 266
Shea, W. H. xxxvi
Simons, J. 142, 154, 176
Simpson, C. A. 2, 15, 24, 36, 41, 53, 74
Smend, R. xx, xxix, xxxi, xxxv, 2, 7, 8, 82, 145, 146, 182, 233, 250, 253, 258, 280
Smith, G. A. xxxviii, 126
Snaith, N. H. 237, 240, 243
Snijders, L. A. 17
Soggin, J. A. xxvii, xxxi, xxxvi, 3, 19, 24, 26, 27, 36, 39, 40, 41, 49, 53, 56, 58, 59, 63, 66, 77, 78, 83, 89, 91, 97, 109, 115, 119, 122, 128, 134, 146, 155, 164, 179, 180, 181, 182, 183, 188, 190, 197, 198, 199, 200, 211, 221, 222, 223, 240, 241, 243, 252, 263, 277
Sollberger, E. xxxix
Speiser, E. A. 102
Spencer, J. R. 219
Sperber, A. xvii, 168
Stern, E. xxxviii, 116, 150
Steuernagel, C. xxvii, 40, 65, 142, 146, 179, 180, 182, 197, 198, 199, 239, 240, 241, 252

Spinoza, B. xxviii
Stoebe, H. J. 77, 150, 243
Stolz, F. 24, 36, 63, 74, 96, 106, 121, 168
Strange, J. 194
Strauss, H. 219

Talmon, S. 176, 194
Täubler, E. 142
Tengström, S. xxix, xxxiv, 2, 7, 36, 89, 142, 144, 185, 187, 219, 225, 229, 260, 267, 280
Terrien, S. 204
Thils, G. 106
Thomas, D. W. xxxix
Thompson, T. L. 260
Toombs, L. E. xxxvii–xxxviii, 258, 259, 260
Tricot, A. 74
Tsafrir, Y. 219, 227
Tuch, F. xxviii
Tucker, G. M. 24, 28, 29
Tushingham, A. D. 163

Ussishkin, D. 114

Van Beek, G. W. 230, 231
Van Den Bussche, H. 106
Van Der Woude, A. S. 85
Van Mierlo, J. 106
Van Oyen, H. 210
Van Selms, A. 199
Van Seters, J. 260
Van Zyl, A. H. 164
Veijola, T. xx, xxix, 2, 7, 8
Véronnet, A. 106
Vetter, D. 12
Vincent, A. 24, 64, 83
Vincent, L. H. 73
Vink, J. G. 89, 194, 200, 237, 244
Vogel, E. K. 259
Vogt, E. 36, 43
Von Hoonacker, A. 106
Von Rad, G. 7, 11, 12, 22, 28, 42, 45, 80, 85, 89, 259, 260, 266, 267
Vriezen, K. 103, 258, 260, 275, 280

Wächter, L. 176, 261
Wagner, S. 24, 28, 29, 74, 79

Wallis, G. 176, 260, 267
Wambacq, B. N. 53
Wassermann, G. 260
Weber, R. xvii
Wehmeier, G. 174, 245, 249
Weimar, P. 9, 106, 112, 113, 115, 280
Weinfeld, M. 5, 6, 8, 12, 15, 41, 84, 85, 93, 102, 105, 210, 253, 258, 261, 276
Weippert, M. xxxvii, 24, 70, 73, 121, 150, 259
Weiss, M. 32
Wellhausen, J. xxviii, 2, 15, 24, 36, 53, 64, 67, 74, 106, 142, 219, 225, 258
Wendel, A. 64
Werner, E. 70
Westermann, C. xxxii, 9, 11, 12, 28, 29, 53, 80, 174, 204, 235, 261
Whitelam, K. W. 254
Wiesmann, H. 36
Wijngaards, J. N. M. 36, 54, 260
Wilcoxen, J. A. 24, 28, 37, 54, 64, 67
Wildberger, H. 37, 54, 60, 272
Wilhelm, G. 259
Williams, R. J. 27, 263
Wilms, F. E. 250, 261
Windisch, D. H. 24
Wiseman, D. J. xxxix, 148
Wolff, H. W. 17
Woudstra, M. H. xxvii, xxix, xxxiii, xli, 37
Wright, G. E. 64, 107, 112, 119, 141, 143, 150, 189, 194, 229, 258, 259, 260, 263, 277
Wright, G. R. H. 260, 280
Wüst, M. 18, 131, 134, 135, 142, 144, 145, 146, 149, 154, 155, 156, 159, 161, 162, 163, 164, 165, 167, 168

Yadin, Y. xxxvii, 68, 69, 121, 124, 126, 142, 176, 185
Yeivin, S. 96, 103, 107, 121, 142, 144, 219

Zenger, E. 54
Zimmerli, W. 261
Zobel, H.-J. 34, 68, 176

Index of Principal Subjects

Abdon, 266
Achshaph, 156
Adullam, 168
Ai, 112
Aijalon, 265
Almon, 264
Altar, 120
Amphictyony, 18
Anakim, 155, 160, 208
Anathoth, 264
Anger of God, 112
Aphek, 168, 182
Arabah, 156
Arad, 168
Archaeology, 20–23
Archite, 224
Ark, 72–73, 122–123, 181
Aroer, 165
Ashdod, 180, 194
Ashkelon, 180
Ashtaroth, 166
Avvim, 181–182
Ayin, 263
Azekah, 146

Bamoth-baal, 197
Ban, 61, 100, 115
Beeroth, 133
Benjamin (tribe), 6–7
Beth-baal-meon, 197
Beth Haram, 199
Beth Horon, 146, 265
Beth-jeshimoth, 198
Beth-nimrah, 199
Beth Peor, 198
Beth Shemesh, 263
Betonim, 198
Bezer, 267
Blessing, 208, 226, 243

Canaanites, 180, 182, 205
Circumcision, 86
City of Refuge, 246–252
Compiler, 6–8
Corporate Personality, 115
Covenant, 11, 114, 131–132, 289, 293, 313–314

Daberath, 266
Debir, 145
Deuteronomistic Historian(s), 5–6
Dibon, 196
Dimnah, 267
Dor, 157

Ebal, 120–121
Edrei, 166
Ekron, 181
Eglon, 145
Elders, 113, 252
Eleazar, 205
Election, 310–311
Eltekeh, 265
En Gannim, 266

Eshtemoa, 263
Etiology, 8, 15–16

Faithful, 310

Gath, 181
Gath-Rimmon, 265
Gaza, 180
Geba, 264
Geshurites, 167, 179
Gezer, 149, 167, 225, 264
Gibbethon, 265
Gibeon, 130
Gilead, 166
Gilgal, 6, 204, 207
God, 10
God of your fathers, 2, 240
Gods, 291, 307
Golan, 265
Goshen, 159

Hammoth-Dor, 266
Hardening, 160
Hazor, 154, 159
Hebron, 144, 208
Helkath, 266
Heshbon, 165
History, 24–26
Hittites, 30
Hivites, 131, 157
Holy, 312
Holy War, 70, 144, 145–148, 157–158
Hormah, 167

Ibleam, 265
Inheritance, 38, 205

Jabin, 155–156
Jahaz, 197, 267
Jarmuth, 144, 266
Jattir, 263
Jazer, 198
Jealousy of God, 312
Jebusites, 157
Jericho, 60
Jerusalem, 157
Jokneam, 169
Jordan, 44
Joshua, role of, 32–33, 36, 116, 121–122, 147, 148, 150, 161, 167, 178, 183
Juttah, 263

Kadesh-Barnea, 207
Kartah, 267
Karthan, 266
Kedemoth, 197
Kedesh, 169
Kedesh in Naphtali, 266
Kenizzites, 207
Kibzaim, 265
Kiriath-Arba, 208
Kiriathaim, 197

Kiriath-Jearim, 133
Kishzon, 266

Lachish, 144–145
Land, 10, 37, 50, 123, 183–184, 240, 293
Law, 10, 35, 39, 50, 148, 150, 159
Leadership, 10, 39–40, 133, 148, 150, 159, 183, 199
Lebanon, 30, 182
Levites, 73, 197, 240, 261–262
Libnah, 149
Living God, 74–75
Lord of all the earth, 75
Lots, 205

Maacathites, 167
Madon, 156
Mahamaim, 199
Makkedah, 146
Man of God, 207
Man of Israel, 131
Masseboth, 314
Medeba, 196
Megiddo, 169
Mephaath, 197
Merom, 158
Messenger of Yahweh, 89
Minister of Moses, 33–34, 36
Mishal, 266
Mizpah, 158
Monotheism, 61
Moses, 33, 36, 38, 167

Nahalal, 267
Name of God, 113–114
Narrative Structure, 16–17

Og, 166

Panic, 145–146
Passover, 88–89
Philistines, 179
Phoenicia, 182
Pisgah, 166, 198
Possession of Land, 44, 183, 291
Presence of God, 38–39, 114, 148
Priests, 77
Prophets, 309

Ramoth-Gilead, 267
Ramath-Mispeh, 198
Rehob, 266
Remnant, 140
Rephaim, 166
Rest, 11, 49–50, 270

Sacrifice, 121
Salecah, 167
Septuagint, 2–5
Servant of Yahweh, 2, 33–34, 36, 320
Seir, 160
Shechem, 264, 304
Shephalah, 156
Shihor, 179
Shimron, 156

Shittim, 61
Sibmah, 198
Sidon, 158, 182, 183
Sihon, 165–166
Succoth, 199

Taanach, 168, 265
Tappuah, 168
Tent of Meeting, 239
Tirzah, 169
Transferrence Formula, 8

Trees, 314
Tyre, 182

Zaphon, 199
Zereth-shahar, 198

Index of Biblical Texts

A. The Old Testament

Genesis

1–3	235
1:14–19	117
2:2–4	21
4:9–16	100
4:13–14	100
6:4	174
6:9	272
9	85
9:6	214
10:16	97
10:19	149
11:24–32	270
11:31	11
12:1–6	270
12:2	48
12:5	11
12:5–9	271
12:6	229, 266, 267, 277
12:7	283
12:10	93
13:8	277
13:8–9	247
13:18	114
14:5	136, 161
14:13	277
14:18	112
14:18–22	248
15	85
15:3–4	17
15:7	17, 255
15:16	11
15:18	11
15:18–21	127
15:20	136, 161
16:13	248
16:16	271
17	55, 58, 85
17:1	248, 272
17:13–14	58
17:22–27	57
17:24	58
18:1	114, 277
19:9	93
20:1	93
21:4	58
21:10	17
21:23	93
21:33	248, 277
21:34	93
22:13	70
22:17	17, 255
23:1–7	114
23:2	174, 282
23:19	282
24:27	249
24:48	249
24:60	17, 174
25:7–8	282
25:25	271
26:3	93
26:5	12, 244
26:60	255
27	147, 174

28:3	248
28:4	17, 255
28:15	12
28:18–22	277
28:19	190
29:22	269
29:31–30:24	172
31:3	12
31:13	277
31:34	274
31:44–52	277
31:51–52	278
32:1	174, 245
32:3	162, 232
32:5	93
33:17	162
33:18–19	282
33:18–20	266
33:18–35:4	229
33:19	281, 283
33:19–20	248
33:20	267, 270
34	59, 268
34:1–35:5	266
34:2	102
34:14	57, 59
34:25	55
34:25–31	202
35:1–4	270
35:2	247
35:2–3	273
35:4	267, 268, 274, 277
35:6	190
35:11	248
35:14	277
35:16–20	206
35:19	282
35:20	277
35:23–26	172
35:27	174
35:28–29	282
36:11	173
36:15	173
36:42	173
37:3	77
37:12–14	229
37:12–17	266
38	137
41:37	249
42:15	39
42:25	16
43:14	248
45–50	129
45:16	249
45:21	16
46:8–25	172
46:11	227
47:4	93
47:7	245
47:9	93
47:10	245
48	172, 191
48–49	253
48:3	190, 248
48:5–6	172

48:7	282
48:9	174
49	147
49:1–27	172, 206
49:6	127
49:7	206
49:25	248
49:33–50:12	13
50:22–26	253, 282
50:24	11
50:25	283

Exodus

1–14	9
1:2–4	172
3	248
3:2	61
3:3	57
3:5	57
3:6	57
3:8	11, 127
3:11–12	26
3:12	8, 12, 255
3:16	269
3:17	11, 127
3:20	42
4	10
4:10	9
4:17	61
4:21–14:18	130
4:23–24	xxiii
4:25	58
4:29	269
5	16
6	248
6:4	11
6:16	227
6:23	171
6:25	246
7:17	39
7:27	271
8:16	270
8:18	129
9:13	270
9:26	129
10:17	272
10:22	271
12	50
12–13	69
12:3	50
12:4	60
12:5	72
12:12	70
12:13	247
12:14–20	56
12:21–27	61
12:23	70, 271
12:26–27	49
12:27	271
12:38	33, 71, 105
12:39	16
12:43–49	55, 58, 60
12:47	60
12:49	90
13:3–9	61

13:5	11, 127	28:26	245	22:9	244
13:9	13	28:27	245	23:5	60
13:11	11	28:37	245	23:5–8	61
13:14–15	49	29:1	272	23:6	56
13:19	282	29:9	205	23:14	60
14	10, 35, 115	29:18	92, 248	23:15	272
14–15	41, 50	30:6	44, 45	23:42	93
14:9	271	30:12	247	24:22	90
14:10	271	30:26	45	25	65, 228
14:14	254	31:7	45	25:29–34	163
14:19	61	32:8	255	25:30	272
14:20	263, 271	32:13	11	25:48–49	216
14:23	271	32:17	61	26:1	255, 277
14:24	115	32:17–18	10	26:22	252
14:25	254	33:1	11	26:38	256
14:31	9, 50	33:1–3	254	26:41	58
15:21	113	33:2	127	27	65, 228
15:25	276	33:7–11	204		
16:4	13	33:11	10	*Numbers*	
16:13–35	61	33:14	21, 235, 254	1–10	247
16:28	13	33:17–23	46	1:5–15	172
17	13	34	85, 254, 276	1:20–43	172
17:5–6	217	34:10	127	2:3–31	172
17:8–13	87	34:11	100, 102	3:1–4	171
17:9	61	34:12	277	3:31	45
18:16–20	13	34:13	255	3:32	171
18:24–25	16	34:14	275	4	255
19	85, 276	34:14–16	61	4:5	45
19:4–6	253	34:18	152, 254	4:5–15	45
19:5	272	34:24	255	6	272
19:6	48	34:27–28	44	7:12–83	172
19:7–8	19	35–40	247	7:89	44, 45
19:13	65	36–40	45	8	255
19:22	46	39:35	174	8:19	247
20:3	270	39:43	45	9:2	60
20:5	255, 275	40:3	45	9:3	60
20:11	21	40:5	45	9:5	60
20:22–23:33	211	40:15	205	9:11	60
20:25	58, 90, 92	40:21	45	9:12	60
21	214, 215			9:14	90
21:12–14	211	*Leviticus*		9:19	244
21:13	213	1	248	9:23	244
21:14	101	1:3	272	10:11–12	55
21:28	214	1:10	272	10:14–28	172
22:30	275	2:3	233	10:33	21, 45
23:3–4	253	2:10	233	10:33–35	45
23:12	21	2:14	60	10:35	68
23:13	255, 270	3:9	272	10:36	21
23:15	61	4	216	11	10
23:21	11, 275	5:13	233	11:4–9	61
23:23	127	6:9	233	11:11	10
23:23–33	254	6:11	233	11:12	11
23:24	255, 277	6:16	233	11:14–17	217
23:24–25	255	6:18	233	11:16	16, 269
23:27	118	6:19	233	11:16–29	204
23:27–31	254	6:22	233	11:23	10
23:28	252, 264	6:26	233	11:24	269
23:33	255	6:29	233	11:25–26	21
24	85, 276, 278	7:6–10	233	11:26–30	10
24:1–7	19	7:14	233	11:28	61
24:4	277	7:31–36	233	12:6–8	10
24:7	255	8:31	233	12:7–8	9
24:12	13	8:35	244	12:16	55
24:13	10	10	171	13–14	28, 36, 79, 170
25:16	45	10:19	249	13:2	79
25:21	45	10:20	249	13:3	55
25:22	44, 45	11–15	247	13:14	169
25–31	44	12:3	58	13:16	173
26–27	247	14–16	247	13:21	11
26:9	245	16	44	13:22	114, 125, 174, 180, 188
26:33	45	17:15	93	13:26	173
26:34	45	18:30	244	13:28	125, 130, 174
27	13	19:2	275	13:29	126, 149, 151
28	13	19:34	90	13:30	17, 79
28:25	245	20:24	255	13:30–33	173

13:33	125, 130	25:18	161	35:4	46
14:6	173	25:31	31	35:6	213, 228
14:6–9	79	26:1	168	35:8	227
14:8	79	26:5–51	172	35:9	213
14:16	11	26:29–33	191	35:10	213
14:23–24	11	26:33	137, 139	35:11	210, 211, 213
14:24	173	26:52–56	152, 168	35:12	211, 213
14:30	173	26:55–56	171	35:13	213
14:33–34	55	26:62	163	35:14	213
14:38	173	26:65	169, 173	35:15	213
14:43	12	27	7, 187	35:22	213
14:44	45, 68, 45	27:1	137, 139, 191, 226	35:24–28	213
14:45	137	27:1–7	187	35:25	215
15:27–29	216	27:1–11	191	35:32	213
15:29	90	27:12–23	6	35:32–33	213
16:14	12	27:17, 18	7	35:42	213
16:25	217	27:20–21	7	36:1	191, 226
16:28	39	28–29	272	36:1–13	191
17:11–12	247	28:16	56	36:4	65
18	172, 255	28:17	56	36:10	191
18:1–7	205	31	164, 165	36:11	139
18:6	163	31:1–12	271		
18:20–24	163	31:2–3	248	*Deuteronomy*	
19	247, 272	31:6	70, 246	1	147
20	16	31:8	156, 162	1–3	134
20:1	173	31:16	161	1:1	xx, 134
20:14	173	32	20, 21, 144, 147,	1:1–5	13
20:14–21	271		152, 162, 228, 245	1:2	173
20:16	173, 179	32:1	159, 162, 232	1:4	35, 98, 135, 136, 161, 232
20:22	173	32:2	168	1:5	8, 13
20:22–28	171	32:3	162, 232	1:7	4, 10, 11, 149, 151
21	232	32:8	173	1:8	11, 17, 234, 255
21:1–3	137	32:11–12	11	1:15	17
21:2	86	32:12	169, 173	1:16	93
21:3	137	32:20–23	20	1:19	173
21:13	134, 159	32:21	152, 254	1:19–25	79
21:14–15	113	32:27	50	1:19–46	28
21:15	162	32:28	168, 171	1:21	17, 25
21:19–20	162	32:28–32	19	1:21–36	169
21:20	135, 162	32:33	245	1:23	79, 249
21:21–30	135	32:33–41	162	1:25	79
21:21–35	35, 162	32:34	161, 162, 163	1:28	79, 125, 130, 168
21:23	263	32:34–38	159	1:30	254
21:23–25	271	32:35	232	1:34	234
21:24	17, 161, 255	32:36	156, 162	1:35	5
21:26	134, 159	32:37	162, 232	1:36	173
21:26–27	161	32:38	162	1:37–38	5
21:26–28	162	32:39–40	191	1:38	5, 6, 12
21:27–30	113	32:40	158	1:39	17, 255
21:30	162	32:41	162	1:44	129, 137
21:32	17, 28, 162, 232, 271	33:36–37	173	1:46	173
21:32–35	79	33:48–49	33, 44	2:2–8	271
21:33	98, 136, 161	33:49	30, 162	2:7	12
21:33–35	28, 155, 271	33:52–53	152	2:10–11	125, 174
21:34	79, 161	33:53	17, 255	2:11	136, 155, 161
21:35	17, 110, 255	33:54	171	2:12	17
22–24	264, 272	34	143, 147	2:14	55, 173
22:1	44	34:1–12	11	2:19	162
22:23	61	34:3–4	179	2:20	136, 155, 161
22:36	161	34:3–5	184	2:20–21	174
22:41	162, 164	34:4	173	2:21	17, 125
23:11	264	34:5	145	2:22	17
23:14	135, 162	34:6	146	2:23	151
23:21	70	34:6–7	180	2:24	17, 161
23:27	264	34:11	228	2:24–35	232
23:28	161	34:13	168, 171	2:24–37	135
24:10	264	34:14–15	245	2:26	118, 161
25	31, 246	34:16–28	172	2:26–3:11	35
25:1	30, 31, 44	34:16–29	168	2:30	161
25:2	255	34:17	171	2:31	17
25:2–3	272	34:28	211	2:34	71, 110
25:3	161	35	211, 212, 213, 214,	2:35	86
25:5	161		215, 216, 228, 232	2:36	135, 161
25:13	205	35:1–8	223, 224, 226	2:37	162
25:16–18	31	35:3	213, 226	3	20

Ref	Pages	Ref	Pages	Ref	Pages
3:1	53, 98, 136, 161	6:23	234	12:27	90
3:2	161, 232	7	20, 105	12:29	252
3:3	110	7:1	97, 127	12:30	255
3:4	162, 169	7:1-26	190	12:32	90
3:6	71, 161, 232	7:2	100, 102, 128	13:3	270
3:7	86	7:4	83, 102, 255, 256, 270	13:4	239
3:8	35, 98	7:5	277	13:4-5	245
3:10	98, 136, 161	7:6	273	13:5	255
3:11	136, 155, 161, 162	7:7	277	13:7	255, 270
3:12	17, 161	7:8	234	13:14	255, 270
3:12-13	136	7:9	85	14	247
3:12-22	147	7:10-11	85	14:2	273
3:13	136, 155, 161, 169, 245	7:13	93, 234	14:21	93
3:14	136, 148, 169	7:16	255	14:22-27	93
3:15	191	7:19	264, 271	14:27	163, 172
3:16	132, 161, 162	7:20	71, 252, 256, 264	14:29	93, 163, 172, 226
3:17	135, 161	7:24	252	15:4-18	93
3:18	17, 19	8:1	234	15:5	4
3:18-20	20, 21	8:1-20	61	15:9	168
3:19	19	8:18	234	16	57
3:20	17, 20, 21, 234	8:19	255, 256, 270	16:1	60
3:21	12, 271	8:19-20	85	16:1-8	61
3:21-22	5	8:20	256	16:9-17	93
3:21-28	6	9:1-3	130	16:11	93, 226
3:22	254	9:2	125, 174	16:14	93, 226
3:25	3, 151	9:3-4	254	16:18	16
3:27	135, 162	9:3-5	152	16:22	277
3:28	5, 6, 12	9:4-5	11, 254	17	93
3:29	161	9:5	234	17:2	85
4	17, 211	9:11	85	17:3	255, 270
4:2	90	9:23	173	17:14-20	13, 59
4:3	271	10	68	17:16	14
4:6	59	10:1-5	44	17:18	90, 93
4:8	13	10:2	90	17:18-19	8
4:9	271	10:4	90	17:18-20	23, 90, 94
4:12	84	10:6	171	17:19	90
4:13	85, 90, 94	10:6-9	163	17:20	14
4:19	248, 255	10:8	44, 45	18:1	172
4:23	85	10:9	155, 172	18:1-5	163
4:26	256	10:11	xxxii, 234	18:1-8	39
4:28	255	10:12	239, 255	18:2	155
4:31	85	10:12-13	245	18:12	152, 254
4:37	273	10:14	47	18:14	166
4:38	11, 254	10:15	273	18:20	270
4:39	33	10:16	58	19	211, 212, 214, 215, 216
4:41-43	211	10:18-19	93	19:1	213, 252
4:41-44	212	10:20	245, 255	19:1-13	211
4:42	211	10:21	271	19:2	213
4:43	161	11:1	244, 245	19:4	210, 211, 213
4:44	8, 13, 134	11:7	271	19:5	211
4:46	161, 232	11:9	234	19:5-6	213
4:47	17, 35, 98	11:13	255	19:6	211
4:48	161	11:16	16, 255, 270	19:7	213
4:49	135, 161	11:17	83, 252, 256	19:8	213, 234
5:2	85	11:21	234	19:9	213, 216
5:7	270	11:22	255	19:10	213
5:9	255	11:22-23	152	19:11	211
5:14	21, 93	11:23	152, 254	19:12	211, 213, 217
5:22	90, 94	11:24	3, 11	19:13	213
5:23	46, 217	11:24-25	8	20	67, 71, 86
5:31	17	11:26-29	90	20:1-4	12
6:1	17	11:26-32	266	20:4	254
6:3	11	11:28	270	20:5-9	16
6:4-15	245	11:29	90, 91, 95	20:10	118
6:10	11, 234	11:29-32	94	20:15-18	33, 102
6:10-11	272	11:30	149, 277	20:16-18	100, 118, 190
6:13	255	11:31	16	20:17	101, 127, 128
6:14	270	12	246, 248	21:1-9	217
6:15	83, 256	12:2	255, 277	21:5	39
6:18	17, 234	12:3	277	21:15-17	191
6:19	254	12:5-28	84	21:18-21	217
6:20-21	49	12:7	93	21:22-23	87, 118
6:21	270	12:9-10	21	21:23	118
6:21-23	35, 267	12:12	163, 172	22:13-21	217
6:22	264	12:13-14	90	23:6	264

23:15	46
24:8	4
24:14	93
24:16	240
24:17	93
24:19	93
24:19–21	93
25:5–10	217
25:18	110
25:19	21
26:3	234
26:5	256, 276
26:5–6	263
26:5–9	35, 267
26:11–12	226
26:12–13	93
26:15	84, 93, 234
26:16–19	90
27	94, 104, 175, 269, 278
27–28	59, 250, 254
27:1	90, 217
27:1–8	92
27:1–26	94, 266
27:2	267
27:2–4	92
27:4	91, 92
27:4–5	90
27:4–8	267
27:5	58, 90
27:5–7	92
27:6–7	90
27:8	90, 92
27:10	90
27:11–13	94
27:11–16	19
27:12–13	90, 93, 172
27:13	90, 91
27:16–26	93
27:19	93
28	175
28:1	4
28:1–14	93, 189
28:2	90
28:7	256
28:9	234
28:11	234
28:13	4
28:13–14	90
28:14	255, 270
28:15	4, 90
28:15–68	256
28:20	256
28:21	17
28:22	256
28:36	255, 270
28:42	17
28:43–44	93
28:45	90
28:47	255
28:47–48	255
28:58	90, 255
28:60	255
28:61	90, 255
28:63	17
28:64	255, 270
28:65	22
28:69	8, 134
29:2	271
29:6	161, 232
29:6–7	137
29:9	17, 217
29:9–10	93
29:9–14	93
29:10	104
29:15–28	85

29:17	255
29:19–20	90, 255
29:20	13
30:1	90
30:5	17
30:6	58
30:8	90
30:10	13, 90, 255
30:13	245
30:15–20	245
30:16	17, 93
30:17	255, 270
30:18	17, 256
31	9, 57, 68, 152
31:1–8	6
31:2	7, 168
31:3	5, 17
31:3–8	12
31:4	35
31:6	6, 12
31:7	5, 6, 234
31:7–8	5
31:8	8, 12
31:9	8, 44, 45, 90, 217
31:9–12	13
31:9–13	19, 90
31:11	90
31:12	93
31:13	17
31:14	7, 10, 203, 204
31:14–15	5, 6, 7
31:16–18	256
31:17	83
31:18	270
31:20	234, 255, 270
31:21	234
31:23	5, 6, 7, 8, 12, 234
31:24	90, 254, 255
31:24–26	13, 94
31:25	44, 45
31:26	44, 45, 90, 255
31:27	283
31:28	17, 217
32:4	273
32:8	248
32:8–9	48
32:17	xxiii
32:30	256
32:46	4, 13, 90
32:47	17
32:49	149
33	147, 206, 253
33:1	173
33:4	13
33:10	13
34	152
34:1	135, 162
34:1–3	11
34:4	234
34:5	7, 10, 282
34:6	161
34:7	283
34:9	6
34:10–12	7

Joshua

1	xxv, 5, 6, 10, 12, 13, 31, 44, 46, 51, 57, 58, 61, 70, 72, 91, 92, 94, 118, 128, 130, 147, 166, 204, 209, 284
1–6	28
1–9	33, 134
1–11	125, 134, 185, 264, 269
1–12	1, 5, 13, 133, 136, 146, 147, 172, 185, 204, 209, 244, 244, 249, 254

1:1	xviii, xxv, 7, 9, 10, 146, 282, 283
1:1–2	15
1:1–3	9
1:1–8	7
1:1–9	2–3, 2–14, 5, 6, 7, 8, 13, 15, 20, 21, 35, 254
1:1–18	xxi, xxv
1:2	xxv, 5, 7, 8, 9, 10, 16, 46, 283
1:2–5	5
1:2–9	5
1:3	xxv, 9, 12, 14
1:3–5	5
1:3–9	9
1:4	4, 9, 19, 151
1:5	xxv, xxvi, 9, 12, 14, 46, 85, 174, 249, 254, 255
1:5–9	7
1:6	xxv, xxvi, 56, 8, 9, 14, 128, 171, 234
1:7	6, 7, 8, 9, 10, 16, 90, 118, 172, 245, 249, 283
1:7–8	xxv, 46, 255, 277, 284
1:7–9	7
1:8	8, 9, 90, 128
1:9	xxvi, 6, 9, 12, 16, 85, 118, 174, 254
1:10	xxvi, 16, 44, 254
1:10–11	15
1:11	xviii, xxv, 16, 17, 27, 30, 41, 44, 98, 205, 255
1:12	20
1:12–15	19, 20, 22, 245
1:12–18	xxv, 15, 18, 18–23, 20, 50, 235, 241
1:13	xxv, xxvi, 10, 20, 21, 50, 172, 244, 283
1:13–16	xxv
1:13–15	234, 244
1:14	20, 21, 65
1:15	xxv, xxvi, 10, 20, 21, 244, 255, 283
1:16	172
1:16–17	21
1:16–18	xxvi, 35, 50, 244
1:16–19	19, 22
1:17	12, 21, 85, 166, 174, 249, 254
1:17–18	19
1:18	xxvi, 6, 21, 118, 172
2	xxiii, xxxiii, 18, 19, 27, 28, 30, 31, 33, 41, 44, 67, 68, 70, 79
2–6	xxxiii
2–11	234
2–12	147
2:1	xxi, 27, 30, 31, 32, 197
2:1–2	29
2:1–9	xxii
2:1–24	24–25, 24–35
2:2	32
2:3–5	29
2:4	30, 32
2:4–5	32
2:6	30, 31, 32
2:6–8	29
2:8	30, 31
2:8–11	31
2:9	xxiv, xxv, 102, 113, 281
2:9–11	xxi, 29, 31, 44, 51, 71, 79
2:10	xxvi, 98, 135, 271
2:11	xxv, xxvi, 79, 84
2:12	28, 29, 31, 32, 34
2:12–16	xxii, 31
2:12–21	30
2:13	32
2:14	29
2:15	30

2:15-21	30, 31	
2:16	30, 98	
2:17	30	
2:17-21	xxi, 31	
2:18	30, 34	
2:18-20	32	
2:18-21	30	
2:19	30	
2:19-20	30	
2:20	34	
2:21	30, 34	
2:22	30, 41	
2:22-23	xxii	
2:23	29	
2:23-24	27	
2:24	xxi, xxiv, 28, 29, 24, 34, 70, 79	
3	xxiii, 18, 19, 31, 45	
3-4	45, 60, 70, 82, 85	
3-5	84	
3-6	96	
3:1	xxi, 30, 31, 41, 42, 44	
3:1-7	44	
3:1-5:1	36, 36-37, 36-52, 37-38, 42	
3:2	41, 42, 44, 98, 205	
3:2-4	xxii, 18, 42	
3:2-17	15	
3:3	44, 45	
3:4	45	
3:5	xxi, 41, 42, 46	
3:6	xxii, 41, 42, 46	
3:7	xxi, xxv, xxvi, 42, 44, 50, 85	
3:8	xxi, 43, 46, 49	
3:8-10	42	
3:8-17	44	
3:9	42, 46, 48, 161	
3:9-11	42	
3:10	xxi, xxvi, 42, 46, 47, 85, 97, 127, 152, 254, 271	
3:10-11	39	
3:11	47	
3:11-14	xxii, 42	
3:12	41, 48	
3:13	45	
3:13-15	48	
3:13-17	48	
3:14-16	39	
3:15	39, 43, 48	
3:15-16	xxi, 42	
3:16	xxii, 41, 42, 48, 161	
3:17	39, 40, 42, 43, 133	
3:17-4:1	49	
4	277	
4:1-3	xxi, 42, 48, 49, 50	
4:1-14	44	
4:2	41	
4:2-3	48	
4:4-5	42, 49	
4:4-7	xxii, 42, 50	
4:6-7	41, 49, 50	
4:7	82	
4:8	xxi, 41, 42, 48, 49, 172	
4:9	xxi, xxiii, 41, 48, 49, 50	
4:10	xxi, xxv, 41, 44, 49, 50, 171	
4:11	xxii, 41, 42, 50	
4:12	xxi, 50	
4:12-13	44	
4:13	xxii, 50, 84, 132	
4:14	xxi, xxv, 44, 50	
4:15	49, 50	
4:15-18	50	
4:15-22	42	
4:15-23	xxi	
4:15-5:1	44	
4:16	45	
4:16-18	43	
4:17	49	
4:18	41, 50	
4:19	48, 55, 173	
4:19-20	41, 43, 50, 56	
4:19-5:15	243	
4:20	41	
4:21-22	234	
4:21-23	41, 43, 49, 51	
4:21-24	41	
4:22	51	
4:23	xxvi, 51	
4:24	xxi, xxvi, 51	
4:24-5:1	41, 44, 51	
5	xxiii, 50, 55, 63	
5-10	205	
5:1	xxi, xxv, 35, 55, 79, 84, 102, 149, 151	
5:2	55, 56, 58, 223	
5:2-3	xxii	
5:2-4	56	
5:2-9	xxii	
5:2-15	53-63, 54	
5:3	55, 58	
5:4	xxi, 56, 59	
5:4-5	55	
5:4-6	54	
5:5	56, 58, 59	
5:5-6	xxi, xxv	
5:6	56, 59, 110	
5:7	xxi, xxiii, 56	
5:7-8	56	
5:8	xxii, 55, 56, 58, 59	
5:9	xxi, xxiii, 56, 58, 59, 60, 61, 173, 269	
5:9-10	xxi	
5:10	60, 61, 69, 83, 132	
5:10-12	xxi, 56, 60	
5:11	55, 56, 60	
5:11-12	60	
5:12	xxiii, 61, 149, 171	
5:13	57, 61	
5:13-15	xxii, 57, 246, 269	
5:14	57, 84, 283	
5:15	57, 61	
6	xxiii, xxxii, 30, 31, 65, 67, 72, 82, 86, 113, 272	
6-8	134	
6:1	55, 65, 68, 70, 149	
6:1-3	xxii	
6:1-5	70	
6:1-27	63-72, 64-65	
6:2	xxiv, 65, 67, 70, 71	
6:3	xxi, 65, 66, 67, 68, 70	
6:3-5	65	
6:4	xxi, 65, 66, 69, 70	
6:4-5	66	
6:5	65, 68, 69, 70	
6:5-7	70	
6:6	xxi, 45, 66, 67, 69, 70	
6:6-7	67	
6:7	xxii, 66, 68, 70	
6:8	xxi, xxii, 45, 66, 69, 70	
6:8-9	70	
6:9	xxi, xxii, 66, 68, 70	
6:10	66, 67, 69, 70	
6:10-12	xxii	
6:11	66, 67, 70-71	
6:11-16	70	
6:12	66, 68, 69, 71	
6:13	xxi, xxii, 66, 68, 69, 70	
6:14	66, 68, 69, 71	
6:14-16	xxi	
6:15	66	
6:16	xxii, xxiv, 67, 69, 70, 71	
6:17	28, 30, 67, 70, 71	
6:17-19	xxi, 67, 69, 70	
6:18	71, 77	
6:19	71, 86	
6:20	xxi, xxii, 30, 65, 66, 67, 68, 69, 70	
6:21	xxi, 66, 67, 71, 254	
6:21-25	70	
6:22-23	28, 30, 67, 69	
6:22-25	xxi	
6:23	71	
6:24	xxiv, 67, 68, 69	
6:25	xxiii, xxxii, 28, 30, 66, 67, 70, 71, 105	
6:26	xxi, xxvi, 70, 71	
6:27	xxi, xxiii, 67, 70, 79	
7	xxiii, xxv, xxxii, 82, 85, 95, 117, 247	
7-8	73-88, 74-76, 88, 113, 170	
7:1	xxi, xxiii, 76, 79, 81, 83, 86, 240, 244, 256, 269	
7:1-3	130	
7:2	xxiv, 76, 77, 78, 79, 81, 83, 136	
7:2-5	xxxii, 79	
7:2-6	xxii	
7:3	79, 81, 84	
7:4	79, 84	
7:4-5	79	
7:4-9	81	
7:5	77, 78, 79, 82, 84	
7:5-26	xxxii	
7:6	77, 84, 217, 254	
7:6-9	81	
7:6-12	79	
7:7	22, 77, 82, 84, 85	
7:7-9	xxi, xxv	
7:8	77	
7:9	xxvi, 82, 84	
7:10	80	
7:10-12	xxi	
7:11	xxi, 77, 80, 85, 172	
7:12	80, 85	
7:13	77, 80, 81, 86	
7:13-14	xxii	
7:13-26	xxiii, 79	
7:14	77, 85	
7:15	xxi, 77, 78, 80, 81, 86	
7:16	77	
7:16-18	77, 80	
7:16-25	xxii	
7:17	77	
7:18	77, 244	
7:19	77, 85	
7:20	85	
7:21	77, 86	
7:22	77	
7:22-23	80	
7:23	77	
7:24	77, 86, 240	
7:25	77	
7:26	xxi, xxiii, xxxi, 76, 78, 79, 81, 83, 86, 80, 82, 95, 147	
8	xxii, xxiv, 78	
8:1	xxiii, xxiv, 78	
8:1-2	79, 81	
8:1-29	xxxii	
8:2	xxi, 78, 86, 129	
8:3	78, 84	
8:3-7	xxii	
8:3-9	80	
8:3-23	79	
8:5	78	
8:6	78	
8:7	xxiv, 78, 87	
8:8	xxi, 78, 87	
8:9	xxi, xxii, xxiv, 78, 87, 136	

8:10	84, 217, 254	
8:10–11	xxii, 77, 78	
8:10–12	81	
8:10–17	81	
8:11	78	
8:11–13	78	
8:12	xxiv, 78, 84, 136	
8:12–13	xxi	
8:13	78, 110, 205	
8:14	78, 32	
8:15	78	
8:15–16	78	
8:16	78, 136	
8:17	xxiv, 78, 87, 136	
8:18	xxi, xxv, 61, 78, 81, 87	
8:19	78, 81, 87	
8:20	78	
8:20–21	81	
8:20–22	xxii	
8:21	78	
8:21–23	81	
8:22	110, 111	
8:22–27	82	
8:23–25	xxi	
8:24	78	
8:24–29	79	
8:25	84	
8:26	xxi, xxv, 61, 78, 87	
8:27	86, 129, 172	
8:27–28	xxi	
8:28	xxi, 78, 79	
8:28–29	81	
8:29	xxi, 79, 81, 87	
8:30	89, 90, 91	
8:30–34	90	
8:30–35	xxi, xxii, xxv, xxvi, 79, 89–95, 91, 94, 101, 229, 267, 269, 278	
8:31	3, 10, 58, 90, 92, 172, 255, 283	
8:31–34	277	
8:31–35	13	
8:32	90, 92, 93	
8:33	10, 17, 45, 90, 93, 172, 217, 229, 245, 254, 283	
8:34	90, 93, 94, 255	
8:35	90, 91, 94, 172	
9	xxiii, xxiv, xxv, xxvi, 99, 100, 102, 105, 109, 110, 113, 117	
9–10	229	
9:1	4, 97, 126, 127, 245	
9:1–2	111	
9:1–3	xxi	
9:1–15	100	
9:1–27	xxxii, 95–105, 96–97, 99	
9:2	89, 98, 101	
9:3	xxiii, 99, 101	
9:3–15	99, 102	
9:4	97, 101	
9:4–5	xxii, 103	
9:4–6	99	
9:5	97, 98	
9:6	xxi, 98, 99, 100, 101	
9:6–7	xxi, 102	
9:6–15	243	
9:7	98, 100, 104, 109	
9:7–8	98	
9:8	99, 102	
9:8–9	xxii	
9:9	xxvi, 98, 102	
9:9–10	xxi, xxv, xxvi, 100, 102	
9:10	35, 98, 101, 102, 135, 136, 161, 232	
9:11	16, 98, 99, 114	
9:11–15	xxii	
9:12	98	
9:14	98, 99, 103	
9:15	xxi, 98, 99, 100, 102, 103, 246	
9:15–21	xxii	
9:16	98, 100	
9:16–21	xxiii, 100, 102, 103	
9:17	98, 103, 115	
9:17–18	100	
9:18	98, 99, 103	
9:18–21	100	
9:19	98, 99, 104	
9:20	98, 104, 247	
9:21	98, 99, 100, 104	
9:22	98, 100, 104	
9:22–23	xxi	
9:22–27	xxiii, 103	
9:23	xxiv, 98, 100, 104	
9:24	xxi, xxv, 98, 104, 172, 283	
9:24–25	100	
9:25	98, 104	
9:25–27	xxi	
9:26	99, 100, 104	
9:26–27	100	
9:27	xxi, xxiii, xxiv, 99, 105	
10	xxiii, 99, 105, 109, 115, 120, 124, 125, 134, 147, 185	
10–11	125	
10:1	xxiii, 109, 111, 113, 123	
10:1–2	xxi, 99, 111	
10:1–10	113	
10:1–11	111	
10:1–14	111	
10:1–43	105–120, 107–109, 111	
10:2	109, 113	
10:3	109, 134, 174, 188, 228, 231	
10:3–6	xxii	
10:4	109, 111, 115	
10:5	109, 231	
10:5–6	35	
10:6	xxi, 109, 111, 115, 173	
10:7	xxi, xxiii, 65, 115	
10:8	xxii, xxiv, 111, 113, 115, 235	
10:9	xxi, xxii, xxiii, 115, 128	
10:9–11	111	
10:10	xxii, 109, 111, 113, 115–116, 230	
10:10–11	xxi	
10:11	xxii, 109, 111, 113, 115, 116	
10:12	xxi, 109, 111, 116–117, 230	
10:12–13	xxii	
10:13	109, 110, 111, 116, 117, 272	
10:13–15	xxi	
10:14	xxiii, 109, 110, 111, 113, 117, 254	
10:15	xxi, xxiii, 110, 111	
10:16	111	
10:16–18	xxii, 111	
10:16–27	111, 116	
10:16–28	117	
10:17	112	
10:18	110, 112	
10:19	xxiv, 110, 112, 117	
10:19–20	xxi, 112	
10:20	110, 112, 113, 117	
10:21	110, 112, 117, 118, 205	
10:21–22	xxii	
10:22	110, 112, 245	
10:22–27	118	
10:23	xxi, 110, 112, 113, 231	
10:24	xxii, 110, 112	
10:25	xxi, xxvi, 6, 110, 112, 113, 118, 254	
10:26	xxii, xxiii, 110, 111	
10:26–28	xxi, 112	
10:26–39	xxi	
10:28	110, 111, 113, 116	
10:28–39	118	
10:29	228, 254	
10:29–29	111, 112	
10:30	xxiv, 110, 111, 113, 118	
10:31–39	xxii	
10:32	xxiv, 118	
10:33	109, 110, 111, 113, 118, 119, 134, 230	
10:34	111	
10:35	111, 118	
10:36	111, 134	
10:36–39	xl	
10:37	110, 113, 118	
10:38	134	
10:38–39	115	
10:39	110, 111, 113, 118	
10:40	xxi, xxvi, 101, 110, 111, 113, 118, 123, 126, 128, 129, 130, 162, 172, 252	
10:40–41	125	
10:40–42	112, 113	
10:40–43	146	
10:41	11, 111, 129, 128, 129, 149, 173	
10:41–42	xxiii	
10:41–43	xxi	
10:42	111, 254	
10:43	xxi, xxiii, 110, 111	
11	xxiii, 124, 125, 134, 147, 169	
11:1	122, 123, 124, 125, 199	
11:1–2	xxi	
11:1–9	124	
11:1–23	120–122, 121–122	
11:2	120, 126, 182, 231	
11:3	xxi, 102, 123, 127, 149	
11:4	123, 127	
11:4–9	xxii	
11:5	122, 123, 127	
11:6	xxiv, 123, 127	
11:7	123, 128	
11:7–9	123	
11:8	xxiv, 110, 122, 124, 152	
11:9	xxiii, 123, 128	
11:10	xxi, 123, 124, 128	
11:10–15	124	
11:11	123, 128	
11:11–12	xxi, xxv	
11:12	10, 128, 129, 172, 252, 283	
11:13	123, 124, 129, 148	
11:13–14	xxi	
11:14	71, 123, 129	
11:14–15	xxi	
11:15	xxv, 10, 123, 129, 148, 172, 283	
11:16	xxiii, 123, 129, 130, 132	
11:16–20	xxi, 125	
11:16–23	146	
11:17	4, 11, 129, 136, 151, 252	
11:18	124, 130, 148	
11:19	102, 123, 130	
11:20	xxv, 71, 123, 130, 172	
11:20–23	xxi	
11:21	115, 123, 125, 174	
11:21–22	123, 130	
11:21–23	123, 125	
11:22	11, 123, 148, 149	
11:23	xxv, xxvi, xl, 123, 130, 148, 153, 169, 171, 172, 174, 234	
12	125, 134, 135, 147, 169, 235	
12:1	132, 133, 134, 135, 147, 169, 235	
12:1–2	133	
12:1–6	xxv, 134	
12:1–13	xxi	
12:1–24	131–132, 131–139	

12:2	132, 135, 136, 161, 162, 163, 165, 232	13:12	xxxii, 98, 136, 152, 155, 161, 163
12:3	132, 135, 161, 162	13:13	xxii, 105, 136, 145, 152, 155, 163, 166, 235
12:4	98, 133, 135, 155, 161, 164, 230	13:13–14	157
12:5	133, 134, 136, 148, 161, 162, 163	13:14	155, 157, 163, 168, 169, 171, 172, 205, 224, 226, 233, 244
12:6	10, 133, 136, 169, 283	13:15	155, 156, 169
12:7	4, 133, 136, 148, 151, 153, 169	13:15–31	xxii
12:7–8	134	13:15–16	157
12:7–24	134	13:15–23	157
12:8	127, 132, 134, 136, 162	13:15–33	157, 158
12:9	78, 133, 134	13:16	135, 144, 155, 156, 158, 159, 161
12:9–10	234		
12:9–24	134	13:17	144, 156, 157, 158, 159, 161, 163, 164, 232
12:10	134		
12:10–12	134	13:17–19	156, 158
12:10–24	134	13:17–20	158, 159
12:11	231	13:18	164, 228, 232
12:12	115, 134	13:19	159, 164
12:13	115, 133, 134, 137	13:20	132, 135, 144, 158, 161, 162, 164
12:14	133, 137		
12:14–24	xxii	13:21	156, 158, 161, 164, 232, 246
12:15	137	13:21–22	158, 161
12:16	78, 133	13:22	156, 166, 272
12:16–17	139	13:23	156, 168, 171
12:17	137, 191	13:24	156, 169
12:18	133, 138	13:24–25	157
12:19	126, 133	13:24–28	157
12:20	126, 133, 199	13:25	136, 158, 159, 162, 165, 166, 191, 232
12:21	133, 138, 230		
12:22	133, 138, 230, 231	13:26	144, 156, 158, 159, 162, 165, 232
12:23	126, 133, 134, 139, 182		
12:24	133, 139, 191	13:27	144, 146, 156, 158, 159, 161, 165, 232
13	xxv, 4, 135, 144, 147, 158, 159, 162, 169, 172, 205, 209, 254		
		13:28	157, 169, 171
13–17	179	13:29	156, 157, 169
13–19	141–144, 142, 143, 146, 147, 200, 205, 209, 217, 269	13:29–30	159
		13:29–31	157
13–21	xxix, xxxii, xxxiii, 5, 13, 125, 144, 223, 234, 244	13:30	157, 158, 162
		13:31	98, 136, 158, 161, 162, 191
13:1	145, 146, 147, 169, 254, 255	13:32	132, 155, 155, 157, 168, 169, 171
13:1–6	xxv, 128, 129, 131, 235		
13:1–7	xxv, xl, 105, 145, 145–153, 146, 152, 235, 254	13:32–33	xxi
		13:33	155, 157, 169, 171, 172, 205, 224, 226, 233, 244
13:1–14	xxi, 157		
13:2	136, 145, 146, 148, 155, 169, 240	14	141, 169, 171, 171, 175, 186
		14–19	223, 225
13:2–3	148	14–20	224
13:2–5	147	14–21	147
13:2–6	136, 146	14–19	254
13:2–7	11	14:1	149, 168, 169, 171, 190, 201, 207, 221, 226, 246, 283
13:3	148, 150		
13:3–4	171	14:1–5	xxi
13:4	146, 148, 150, 152	14:1–15	167–168, 167–175
13:5	4, 145, 148, 151, 152	14:2	136, 168, 171, 172, 183, 224
13:6	xxv, 146, 147, 152, 153, 163, 171, 172, 187, 254	14:2–5	169
		14:3	168, 171, 172
13:6–7	xxv, 141, 146, 147, 152, 183, 192	14:3–4	205, 224, 226
		14:4	168, 172, 226
13:7	146, 155, 166, 171, 244	14:5	xxv, 172
13:8	10, 146, 155, 157, 163, 169, 190, 283	14:6	xxi, xxiii, xxiv, 168, 169, 170, 207, 269
		14:6–13	xxii
13:8–9	153	14:6–15	169, 170, 223, 224, 227
13:8–12	157	14:7	10, 168, 170, 173, 174, 283
13:8–14	155	14:7–8	28
13:8–32	136	14:8	168, 170, 173
13:8–33	xxv, 146, 153–166, 154–155	14:9	168, 170, 171, 173
13:9	155, 156, 157, 161, 163	14:10	170, 174
13:10	163, 165, 232	14:11	168, 170
13:10–11	155, 156, 157, 161	14:12	125, 152, 168, 170, 174
13:10–33	152	14:12–15	125
13:11	136, 157, 161, 163, 191	14:13	169, 170, 171, 174, 189, 192, 221
13:11–12	157		
13:11–13	148		
		14:13–15	xl
		14:14	169, 170, 171, 173
		14:14–15	xxi
		14:15	xxvi, 18, 125, 169, 174, 185
		15	143, 159, 183
		15–17	183, 187, 205, 206
		15–19	158
		15:1	172, 179, 180, 183, 224
		15:1–4	183, 184
		15:1–12	xxii, 183, 184, 188
		15:1–63	176–178
		15:1–17:18	176–193, 176–179
		15:2–12	144
		15:3	180, 188
		15:4	145, 180
		15:5	180, 183
		15:5–11	144, 183, 190
		15:6	188, 198
		15:6–11	200
		15:7	115, 180
		15:8	109, 127, 136, 180, 188
		15:9	103, 180, 188, 197
		15:10	129, 180, 228
		15:10–11	201
		15:11	103
		15:12	146, 180, 183
		15:13	18, 114, 125, 185, 186, 188, 221
		15:13–14	125, 223, 224, 227
		15:13–15	xxi
		15:13–19	xl, 113, 170, 183, 184, 192
		15:14	125, 152, 180, 185, 186, 188
		15:15	xviii, 115, 188
		15:16	180, 186
		15:16–19	xxii
		15:17	188
		15:18	180, 181
		15:18–19	186
		15:19	189, 192
		15:20	171, 180, 183, 189, 190
		15:20–62	xxii
		15:21	181, 189
		15:21–32	181, 183
		15:21–62	181, 183, 184, 189
		15:23	181
		15:25	181
		15:26	198
		15:26–32	201
		15:28	181
		15:30	137, 198
		15:31	198
		15:32	181, 198, 228
		15:33	201
		15:33–47	183
		15:34	137, 231
		15:35	137, 231
		15:36	181
		15:37–41	183, 189
		15:39	115
		15:42	198, 201
		15:42–44	183
		15:45–46	201
		15:45–47	143, 183, 189
		15:47	145, 147, 149, 181
		15:48	228
		15:48–51	183
		15:48–60	183
		15:49	115
		15:50	228
		15:51	129, 228
		15:52–54	183
		15:55	228
		15:55–57	183
		15:57	201
		15:58–59	83

15:59 181, 183
15:60 103, 183, 189, 197
15:61 198
15:61–62 183
15:63 xxii, xxv, xxxiii, xl, 109, 127, 145, 152, 181, 183, 184, 186, 189, 191, 193, 235
16 184
16:1 179, 181, 183, 200, 224
16:1–3 144, 183, 184, 185, 190
16:1–9 xxii
16:1–10 178
16:2 181, 190, 197
16:3 181, 190, 229, 230
16:4 171, 192
16:4–9 184
16:5 181, 190, 197, 230
16:5–6 184
16:5–7 144, 171
16:5–8 184
16:5–9 184
16:6 181
16:6–7 184
16:6–8 184, 190
16:7 181
16:8 137, 171, 181, 184, 190
16:9 171, 184, 191
16:10 xxii, xxiii, xl, 113, 119, 145, 152, 181, 184, 187, 190, 191, 192, 193, 229, 235
17 91
17:1 179, 181, 183, 184, 191, 224, 245
17:1–2 xxii
17:1–13 184, 245
17:1–18 178–179
17:2 181, 184, 191
17:2–3 191
17:2–11 184
17:3 139, 182, 191
17:3–4 184, 187
17:3–6 xxi, xxv, 192
17:4 171, 181, 182, 207, 226, 246, 283
17:5 182, 191, 199
17:5–6 184
17:6 171, 182
17:7 182, 184, 229
17:7–8 137, 190, 191
17:7–10 184
17:7–11 xxii, 184
17:8 182, 184
17:8–11 191
17:9 182, 184
17:10 184
17:11 126, 138, 183, 184, 192, 230
17:11–12 126
17:12 191, 193
17:12–13 xxii, xxv, xl, 145, 152, 184, 187, 235
17:13 152
17:14 171, 182, 192, 199, 224
17:14–15 188
17:14–18 xxii, xxiii, 184, 192, 193, 203, 206, 249
17:15 136, 161, 182, 192
17:15–16 182, 184
17:16 182, 192
17:16–18 188
17:17 182, 192, 197, 224
17:18 xxv, 152, 183, 184, 187, 193, 207
18 146, 190
18–19 183

18:1 xxi, 142, 163, 183, 197, 200, 201, 203, 204, 217, 245, 263, 265, 269
18:1–19:51 193–208, 194–197
18:1–22:34 243
18:2 197, 200, 204, 205, 244
18:3 197, 204, 205, 255
18:3–6 xxii
18:3–7 200
18:4 171, 197, 205, 244
18:5 179, 197, 205
18:6 136, 197, 205, 224
18:7 xxi, 10, 171, 197, 205, 224, 226, 233, 244, 283
18:8 197, 200, 224, 263
18:8–10 xxii
18:9 110, 197, 205
18:9–10 200
18:10 136, 205, 224, 263
18:11 198, 206, 224
18:11–13 190
18:11–28 xxii, 200, 206
18:12 77, 103
18:12–13 200
18:12–20 144
18:12–19:48 206
18:13 190, 197, 206, 230
18:14 103, 197, 200
18:14–15 198
18:15 xviii, 197
18:15–19 200
18:16 127, 188, 198, 206
18:17 180, 198, 199, 240
18:18 132
18:20 146, 171, 198, 200
18:21 198
18:21–24 144
18:21–28 200
18:22 198, 206
18:24 198, 229
18:25 101, 229
18:25–28 103
18:26 198
18:26–28 198
18:28 109, 127, 171, 189, 198, 206
19 143, 144, 190, 209
19:1 171, 198, 199, 206, 224
19:1–6 198
19:1–9 201
19:1–46 xxii
19:2 171, 198
19:2–7 201
19:4 137, 198, 202
19:5 198, 202
19:6 198, 202
19:7 198, 200, 228
19:8 171, 198, 201, 202
19:9 171, 198, 201, 202, 206
19:10 171, 198, 199, 206, 224
19:10–11 201
19:10–16 201
19:11 138, 199, 230, 231
19:12 199, 201, 230
19:13 199, 201, 232
19:14 199, 201
19:14–17 202
19:15 199, 200, 201, 203, 232
19:15–17 202
19:16 171, 199, 201
19:17 198, 199, 224
19:17–23 201
19:18–19 202
19:18–21 201
19:20 199, 230
19:21 199, 222, 231

19:22 199, 201, 203
19:23 171, 201
19:24 198, 199, 224
19:24–31 201
19:25 126, 199, 231
19:25–26 201
19:26 201, 231
19:27 199, 201
19:28 199, 200, 201, 231
19:29 128, 199, 200, 201
19:30 151, 199, 201, 231
19:31 171
19:32 198, 199, 224
19:32–39 201
19:33 201
19:34 199, 201
19:35 222, 228, 231
19:35–38 201
19:36 200
19:37 231, 263
19:38 199, 200
19:39 171, 200, 20
19:40 198, 200, 224
19:40–48 201
19:41 171, 200, 228
19:41–45 201
19:41–46 144
19:42 200, 230
19:44 230
19:45 200, 230
19:46 200
19:46–47 201
19:47 xxv, xl
19:47–48 200, 206
19:48 xxii, 171, 200, 201
19:49 171, 206, 207
19:49–50 201, 223
19:49–51 203
19:50 200, 206, 264, 281, 283
19:51 xxi, xxv, 171, 200, 203, 207, 221, 224, 226, 246, 254, 269, 283
20 209, 213, 214, 215, 216, 218
20–24 209
20:1 211, 213
20:1–2 211, 216
20:1–3 214
20:1–6 211
20:1–7 xxii
20:1–9 210, 210–218
20:2 211, 213
20:3 210, 211, 216
20:4 211, 213, 217, 254
20:4–6 211, 213, 215
20:5 211, 213, 217
20:6 211, 217
20:7 211, 213, 217, 221, 269
20:7–8 211, 214
20:8 xxv, 161, 211, 213
20:8–9 xxi
20:9 211, 212, 213, 217, 223
21 144, 162, 163, 169, 172, 205, 209, 212, 215, 216, 225, 228, 232, 233
21:1 211, 221, 223, 226, 246, 254
21:1–3 xxi, 223
21:1–6 xxv
21:1–8 225
21:1–42 218–233, 219–221, 223
21:2 171, 201, 226, 263, 269
21:2–3 xxv
21:2–11 221
21:3 223, 225, 227
21:4 223, 225, 227
21:4–7 221

21:4–42 xxii
21:5 221, 222, 223, 224, 227
21:5–6 221
21:5–7 225
21:5–9 224
21:6 212, 221, 223, 224, 227
21:6–7 xxv
21:7 221, 223, 227
21:8 221, 223, 225, 227
21:9 212, 221, 223, 224, 225, 227
21:9–11 212
21:10 221, 223, 225, 227
21:10–12 223
21:11 125, 221
21:11–12 225, 227
21:12 221
21:12–36 212
21:13 212, 222, 225, 227, 228
21:13–16 223
21:13–18 224
21:13–40 225
21:14 212, 228
21:14–15 225
21:15 115, 222, 228
21:16 222, 227, 228, 244
21:16–21 212
21:17 228
21:18 222, 223
21:19 222, 224
21:20 179, 212, 222, 224
21:20–26 229
21:21 222, 269, 270
21:21–22 224, 229
21:22 222, 224, 230
21:22–23 212
21:23 82
21:23–24 224
21:23–25 201
21:24 162, 222, 230
21:24–28 212
21:25 138, 212, 222, 224, 230
21:26 222, 226
21:27 221, 222, 224, 230
21:27–33 230
21:28 199, 230
21:28–29 201, 224
21:29 199, 222, 231
21:30 199, 231
21:30–31 201, 224
21:31 222, 224, 231
21:32 201, 222, 231
21:33 224
21:34 138, 222, 224, 230, 231
21:34–35 224
21:34–40 231
21:34–42 221
21:35 222, 232
21:36 222, 232
21:36–37 222, 232
21:37 161, 232
21:38 162, 232
21:38–39 224
21:39 222, 232
21:40 174, 221, 222, 224
21:41 222, 224, 228
21:41–42 223, 232, 234
21:42 223, 224, 264, 281
21:43 xxv, 235, 255
21:43–44 244
21:43–45 xxi, xxv, xxvi, xl,
209, 223, 233–234,
233–236, 236, 241, 254
21:44 xxvi, 21, 234, 235, 254
21:44–45 234
21:45 235, 236

22 xxi, xxiii, 13, 91, 206,
241, 244, 254, 283
22–24 13, 234
22:1 234, 239, 241, 242, 244
22:1–6 xxi, 242
22:1–8 241
22:1–9 xxv
22:1–34 236–250, 237–239
22:2 xxv, 8, 10, 242, 244, 283
22:2–3 xxvi, 269
22:3 239, 242, 244
22:4 xxv, xxvi, 8, 21, 228,
234, 239, 242, 244, 283
22:4–5 10
22:5 xxv, 239, 242, 244,
255, 256, 277, 283
22:5–6 xxv
22:6 242, 245
22:7 239, 241, 242, 245
22:7–8 242, 244
22:8 239, 242, 245, 269
22:9 228, 239, 240, 241, 242, 263
22:9–11 149, 171, 245
22:9–12 242
22:9–34 xxii, 11, 241
22:10 240, 242, 245
22:10–11 145
22:10–34 xxv
22:11 240, 245
22:11–12 242
22:12 240, 245, 247, 263
22:13 240, 241, 246
22:13–14 242
22:13–15 242
22:13–34 242
22:14 240, 246, 247, 254
22:15 240
22:16 240, 242, 246
22:16–20 242
22:17 161, 240, 246
22:17–18 242
22:18 240, 247, 249
22:19 228, 240, 242, 247
22:20 240, 242, 247, 249
22:21 242, 247, 254
22:21–29 242
22:22 240, 242, 247
22:22–23 249
22:23 240, 242, 248
22:24 242, 248
22:24–25 242
22:24–28 242
22:25 241, 248
22:26 241
22:26–28 242
22:27 249, 255
22:28 241, 249
22:29 241, 242, 249
22:30 240, 241, 242, 249, 254
22:30–34 242
22:31 241, 242, 249, 264
22:31–32 241
22:32 149, 171, 241, 242, 249, 264
22:33 241, 242
22:34 241, 242, 246, 249, 269
23 xxvi, 13, 147, 253,
254, 257, 265, 266, 269
23:1 xxvi, 21, 146, 147,
234, 241, 253, 254, 278
23:1–16 xxi, xxv, 250–257, 251
23:2 17, 90, 217, 252, 254, 263, 270
23:2–24:1 265
23:3 xxvi, 252, 254, 256, 281
23:3–5 253, 265
23:4 xxv, 146, 171, 252, 254

23:4–5 256
23:5 xxv, 152, 252, 254, 255, 256
23:5–13 254
23:6 4, 8, 255, 277
23:6–8 xxv, 253
23:6–13 265
23:7 xxv, 252, 255, 256, 283
23:8 255
23:9 xxvi, 255, 256
23:9–10 253
23:10 256
23:11 xxv, 252, 253, 256
23:11–12 256
23:12 xxv, 252, 256, 265
23:12–13 xxv, 253
23:13 xxv, 152, 252, 254, 256, 265
23:14 xxvi, 252, 256
23:15 xxv, 252, 256
23:15–16 xxvi, 253, 254, 265
23:16 xxv, 83, 252, 256,
265, 270, 283
24 xxv, xxvi, xxix, xxxiv, 13,
89, 91, 95, 265, 266, 267,
268, 269, 277, 278, 279, 282
24:1 xxi, 17, 90, 191, 217,
252, 263, 266, 269
24:1–10 xxvi
24:1–28 xxiii, xxv, 229, 257–
280, 261–262, 283
24:2 263, 265, 268, 270
24:2–13 35, 265, 266, 267, 268, 278
24:3 263, 270
24:4 263, 271, 277
24:5 263, 264, 271
24:6 263, 264
24:7 77, 263, 265, 271, 273
24:8 263, 271, 272
24:8–10 xxv
24:9 264, 272
24:10 264, 272
24:11 xxi, xxv, 97, 264, 272
24:11–13 xxvi
24:12 xxi, 264, 272
24:12–13 xxi, 272
24:13 xxv, 263, 264
24:14 264, 268, 272, 276, 283
24:14–15 265
24:14–16 266
24:14–24 265
24:14–28 19
24:15 xxv, 264, 273, 283
24:16 268, 274, 283
24:17 xxvi, 264, 276
24:17–18 266, 274
24:18 xxvi, 264, 268, 276, 283
24:19 xxvi, 264, 265, 283
24:19–20 265, 266, 268, 274
24:20 xxv, xxvi, 264, 265, 275, 281
24:21 266, 268, 276, 283
24:22 265, 268, 276, 278, 283
24:22–24 266
24:23 xxv, 264, 268, 276
24:24 xxi, xxii, 265, 268, 276, 283
24:25 xxv, 256, 265, 276, 278
24:25–27 266
24:26 90, 265, 277
24:27 265, 268, 276, 278
24:28 171, 266, 278, 281
24:28–31 281
24:29 281, 282
24:29–30 xxii
24:29–32 282
24:29–33 280–281, 280–284
24:30 200, 281, 283

Reference	Page(s)
24:31	xxvi, 131, 171, 217, 281, 282, 283
24:31–32	xxi
24:32	171, 281, 282, 283
24:32–33	xxii, 282
24:33	246, 282, 283

Judges

Reference	Page(s)
1	4, 143, 147, 186, 187, 206, 226, 236
1–3	166, 193
1:1	282
1:1–21	186
1:1–3:6	254
1:5–7	109
1:10	180
1:10–15	xl, 113
1:11	115, 188
1:11–15	170, 180, 186
1:16	137
1:17	137
1:18	34, 149
1:19	183, 188, 235
1:19–35	145
1:19–36	163
1:20	113, 114, 125, 188
1:21	109, 127, 185, 235
1:21–36	105
1:22–26	30, 34
1:23	190
1:27	126, 138, 182, 187, 230
1:27–35	235
1:27–36	xl
1:29	187, 190
1:30	199, 201, 232
1:30–33	206
1:31	128, 151, 199, 201, 231
1:33	201, 227
1:34–36	200, 201
1:35	200, 201, 230
2	153, 193, 253
2–3	163
2:6	281
2:6–10	193, 282, 283, 284
2:6–15	131
2:6–23	253
2:7	281
2:8	281
2:9	281, 283
2:10	281
2:12	270
2:14	83
2:17	270
2:19	270
2:20	8, 83
2:20–23	15
2:21–23	192
3	166
3:1–6	253
3:3	102, 127
3:8	83
3:9–11	188
3:10–11	162
3:14	282
3:20–23	253
3:31	148
4	115, 125, 139
4–5	231
4:2	125
4:7	125, 230
4:11	277
4:13	230
4:17	125
4:23	124
4:24	125
5	113, 125, 139, 172, 206
5:14	191
5:19	138
5:21	230
6:11	61, 277
6:11–16	12
6:19	277
6:22	84
7:8	16
7:23	102
8	162
8–9	229
8:1	243
8:1–3	xxiii
8:14	84
8:15	98
8:16	84
8:22	102
8:31–9:57	267
8:33	267
9	267, 268, 277
9:4	267
9:6	267, 277
9:16	272
9:18	267
9:19	272
9:37	277
9:46	248, 267
9:55	102
10	279
10–11	166
10:6–7	148
10:7	83
10:13	270
10:15–16	273
11	165
11:4–11	217
11:5–11	84
11:12	135
11:13	162
11:19	161, 232
11:20	232
11:23	254
11:26	161, 232
11:33	159, 162
11:35	84
12:1	243
12:1–6	xxiii
12:19–20	243
13–16	148
14:3	57
15:9–13	227
15:18	57
16:23–30	149
17–18	226
17–21	206
18	28, 79, 206, 227
18:2	79
18:5–6	79
18:10	79
18:12	103
18:21	xxi
19	226
19–21	xxiii, 82, 246
19:10–11	127
20	82, 246
20:10	16
20:11–48	102
20:18	81
20:18–48	81
20:23	81
20:26–27	81
20:27	45
20:28	81, 246
20:29	81
20:30–36	81
20:37	81
20:38–41	81
20:42–48	81
21:1	102
21:12	243
21:19	243

Ruth

Reference	Page(s)
2:1	65
2:14	60
3–4	216
4:1–12	84, 217

1 Samuel

Reference	Page(s)
1–2	248
1–4	243
1:3	243
1:18	117
2:17–17	233
2:22	204
2:34	243
4	243
4–6	45
4–7	148
4:1	138, 151
4:3	68
4:3–5	45
4:4	243
4:5–6	70
4:11	243
4:17	243
4:19	243
5:1–9	149
5:8–9	150
6	228
6:20	275
7	115
7:10	115
7:14	150
7:15–17	185
7:16	43
7:16–17	43
8:5	59
8:8	270
9:6–8	173
10:3	277
10:8	43
10:19	270
10:20–21	85
10:26	43
11:3	84, 217
11:11	162, 166
11:14–15	43
12:14–15	8
13–14	148, 229
13:2	43
13:4–15	43
13:5	77
13:6	102
13:15	43
14:3	243
14:6	57
14:16	43
14:22	102
14:23	77
14:31	230
14:33–35	92
14:42	85
14:47	162, 166
15:1–9	xxxiv
15:3	86
15:7	146, 149
15:9–10	86
15:12–33	43

Ref	Page	Ref	Page	Ref	Page
15:34	43	7:9	12	2:1–9	253
16	xxiii	7:11	21, 234	2:3	13, 244
16:4	84, 217	8	147, 148	2:3–4	8
16:5	46	8:1	148	2:8	162, 232
17–19	148	8:3–12	148	2:26	229
17:2	102	8:4	128	2:27	243
17:4	130	8:10–11	8	3	229
17:17	60	8:10–12	162	3:4–5	100
17:19–25	102	8:12	162	3:7	168
17:26	46, 57	9:4–5	156, 162	3:8	273
17:36	57	10	147, 148	3:10	249
17:37	12	10–12	166	3:15	45, 92
17:52	150	10:1–19	148	4:9	228
18:5	249	10:6–14	136, 163	4:10	137, 191
22:1	137	10:8	243	4:11	122, 126, 182
22:6	277	10:12	5	4:12	138, 230
22:10	16	11:1	162	4:13	162, 169, 232
22:24	23	11:15	243	4:14	162, 232
22:31	273	12:26	165	4:39	200
23:1–6	148	12:26–29	162	5:1	11
23:5	276	13:8–14	243	5:4	149
23:22	101	13:25	245	5:15–24	151
24:5	232	13:37–38	148	5:18	234
24:6–7	148	13:37–15:8	136	5:27	191
25	170	14:1–11	216	5:32	22, 146
25:18	60	14:7	17	6:19	45
26:1	43	14:15	57	8	84, 94
26:19	270	14:17	21	8:1	45
27	148	15	171	8:6	45
27–29	148	15:7–12	xxiv	8:12–13	117
27:1–7	150	15:12–15	243	8:14–21	105
27:8	136, 145, 148	15:21	243	8:17–18	168
27:9	149	15:21–37	190	8:23	33
29:1	138, 151	15:24	45	8:24–25	8
29:6	168	16:5–14	xxiv	8:53	10
30	147	16:15–17:23	190	8:56	10, 22, 234
30:14	170	16:18	102	8:56–57	8
30:27	228	17:4	84	8:64	92
30:28	228	17:14	102	8:65	11, 147, 148, 152
30:30	137, 198	17:24	102, 162	9:4–7	8
31	148	17:24–27	232	9:6	270
31:1–7	138	17:27	156, 162	9:9	270
31:4	57	17:28	60	9:11–14	151
31:13	277	18:4	249	9:15–17	119, 138, 190, 229
		18:18	277	9:15–22	191
2 Samuel		19:33	162, 232	9:16	113, 181
1:18	110	19:40	174, 245	9:17	230
1:20	57	20:1–22	xxiv	9:19	148, 152
2	232	20:24	191	9:20–21	100, 190
2:1–3	xxiv	21:1–4	100	9:25	92
2:1–4	171	21:15–22	148	10:2	168
2:8	162, 199	21:18–22	130	11	175, 256
2:8–9	185	21:20–22	150	11:1–8	130, 166
2:9	144	22:41	118	11:4	270
2:12	162	23:1–7	253	11:6	173
2:29	162	23:8–17	148	11:9–13	8
3:3	136, 148, 163	23:9	102	11:10	270
3:17	84	23:13	137	11:31–39	8
3:36	249	23:30	283	11:33	166
4:1	197	24:1	83	12:1	229
4:2	103	24:2–8	11	12:25	229
5	147	24:5	161	12:25–29	267
5:3	84	24:5–6	11	12:31	39
5:6	109, 127	24:6	28	13	173
5:6–10	114, 190	24:6–7	151	14:3	98
5:8	127	24:7	127	14:7–11	8
5:11	151	24:15	11	14:9	270
5:17–25	148	24:16	127	14:17	191
5:25	190, 229	24:16–17	61	14:17–16:23	139
6	45	24:18	127	14:23	277
6:2	103	24:25	92	14:25–27	xxiv
6:7	83			15:22	229
6:15	70	*1 Kings*		15:27	230
6:17–18	92	1:2–16	150	16:4	277
7:1	22, 234	2:1–4	8	16:15–17	230

16:31	130	23:25	13	23:25	22		
16:34	66, 70, 71	23:26	83	24:23	222		
17:17–24	173	23:26–27	253	25:5	70		
18:17–40	19	23:27	84	26:29	16		
18:31–32	92	23:29–30	138	26:29–32	226		
18:40	230	24:2	166	27:1	16		
20:26–30	151	24:14	65	27:16–22	172		
20:30–43	130	25	xx, 147	27:29	133		
21	153	25:27–30	xxv, 23, 62	28:2	21		
21:3	12			28:18	228		
22	232	*1 Chronicles*		28:20	6		
		2:1–2	172				
2 Kings		2:7	76	*2 Chronicles*			
1:4–8	173	3:2	148	1:3	10		
1:9–16	173	4–8	223	7:8	11		
2:9–15	7	4:11	173	11:8	150		
2:15	21	4:28–33	201	11:10	230		
3:2	277	4:30	198	11:13–15	226		
3:10	84	4:31	198	13:11	244		
4:25	11	4:32	198	14:5	22		
5:17	270	5:11	161	14:12	77		
6:5	84	5:16	133	15:15	22		
6:15	84	5:27–6:66	223	19:5–11	16		
6:22	264	6	162, 222, 225	19:11	5, 16		
8:28–29	232	6:34	10	20:20	8		
9:1–14	232	6:39	199, 221, 223, 225	20:26	xxxi		
9:27	230	6:39–66	223	20:30	22		
10:11	110	6:39–40	223	23:6	244		
10:26–27	277	6:39–41	225	24:6	10		
10:31	13	6:40–41	223	24:20	8		
10:31	161	6:40–45	215	25:13	230		
11:8	168	6:42	222, 223	26:11	16		
13:3	83	6:42–44	223	28:18	230		
13:14–19	151	6:43	115, 222	30:16	173		
13:25	151	6:45	222, 223, 224, 225	31:21	8		
14:6	13	6:46	221, 224, 225	32:7	6		
14:11	228	6:46–48	225	33:15–16	273		
14:13	228	6:46–50	224	34:13	16		
14:25	11	6:47	221, 224	35:17	60		
15:10	230	6:48	224, 225				
15:14	191	6:49	224	*Ezra*			
15:14–16	139	6:50	221, 224, 225	2:23	229		
15:20	65	6:51	179, 221, 224	2:25	103		
15:29	231	6:52–54	224	2:26	229		
17:7–20	8	6:53	222	2:43–58	100		
17:10	277	6:54–80	221	3:2	173		
17:13	13	6:55	222, 224	3:11–13	70		
17:17	270	6:56	136, 222, 224	6:19	60		
17:34	13	6:57	199	9:1–10:44	105		
17:35	270	6:57–58	224	10:1	90		
17:37	13, 270	6:58	199, 222	10:10–12	19		
17:38	270	6:59–60	224				
18:4	277	6:60	222	*Nehemiah*			
18:6–7	8	6:61	222, 224	1:7–8	10		
18:12	10	6:62	222, 224	7:2	273		
19:4	46	6:63–64	222, 224	7:27	229		
19:12–13	84	6:64	161	7:29	103		
19:26	46	6:65–66	224	7:30	229		
19:27	168	7:20–29	206	7:46–60	100		
19:35	61	7:29	126, 182	8:2	90		
19:42–44	102	7:30–40	190	8:2–6	19		
21:1–16	253	8:33	199	9:7	273		
21:2–15	8	9:39	199	9:14	10		
21:8	10, 13	11:32	283	9:22	161, 232		
21:11	13	12:25–38	172	9:28	22		
22:11–20	8	13:5	11, 145, 148	10:30	10		
22:17	270	13:6	103	11:27	181		
23:1–3	19	20:4	161	11:28	198		
23:4	277	22:9	22	11:29	231		
23:8	226, 229	22:13	6, 8	11:30	137		
23:13	166	22:18	22	11:31	229		
23:21–23	57	23:4	16	11:32	229		
23:24	13	23:14	173	12:29	229		
23:24–25	179	23:19	222				

Esther		6:7	17	7:14	243
1:9	249	8:5	101	7:18	270
1:21	249	8:12	101	9:4	58
2:4	249	12:25	248	9:24–25	58
		13:14	13	10:10	46
Job		15:5	101	11:10	270
3:13	21	16:33	171	11:22–23	229
3:26	21	18:9	197	12:16	255
5:13	101	19:25	101	13:10	270
12:4	273	22:29	270	14:13	84
31:28	278	24:10	197	16:11	270
33:5	270	30:9	278	16:13	270
39:26	132			18:18	12
41:2	270	**Song of Songs**		19:4	270
		2:1	133	19:13	270
Psalms		7:5	232	20:16	70
1:2	8			22:9	270
1:3	8	**Isaiah**		23:36	46
7:18	42	1:29	277	25:6	270
9:2	42	2:13	136	26:6	243
15:2	273	5:3	272	26:9	243
18:24	273	6:9–10	274	29:27	229
18:31	273	7	10	32:6–7	216
18:41	118	8:16	13	32:7–9	229
18:47	46	10:29	229	32:29	270
19:8	273	10:30	229	35:15	270
23:2	21	11:2	21	40:14	166
26:7	42	11:20	21	41:5	229
27:14	6	13:7	79, 197	41:10	166
31:25	6	14:3	21	41:15	166
33:3	70	14:7	21	42:11	281
33:12	273	15:2	135	42:17	111
33:19	59	15:4	135, 161, 232	44:3	270
37:18	273	15:5	109	44:5	270
40:6	42	16:8–9	135, 161, 232	44:8	270
41:12	39	16:9	232	44:14	111
42:3	46	19:1	79	44:15	270
47:5	273	19:19	277	45:3	21
56:14	59	23:3	145	48:2	159, 161, 232
60:8	162, 229	26:13	255	48:3	109
78:60	204, 243	28:12	21	48:8	161
83:4	101	32:18	21	48:19	161
83:8	146	33:9	133, 135	48:21	161, 232
83:10	125	35:2	133	48:32	232
84:3	46	37:28	168	48:34	109, 161, 232
84:12	273	40–55	33	48:35	161
86:20	42	41:8–9	273	48:45	232
90:1	173	43:6	132, 146	49:1–2	17
95:11	22	43:10	273	49:2–3	162
97:5	47	44:1–2	273	49:3	159, 232
98:1	42	49:7	273	49:7–22	175
101:2	273	51:23	118	49:23	248
101:6	273	57:5	277		
105:26	10	59:13	278	**Lamentations**	
106:22	42	63	175	1:3	22
106:28	161	63:11	10	2:22	111
106:30	246	63:14	21, 22		
108:8	162, 229	63:18	17	**Ezekiel**	
111:4	42	65:10	133	1:9	245
114:7	47	66:1	21	1:12	245
116:7	21			4:14	84
121:8	168	**Jeremiah**		4:16	248
132:8	21	1:1	220	6:18	277
132:14	21	1:6	84	7:26	12
135:4	273	1:16	270	9:8	84
135:11	35	2:18	145	11:13	84
136:19–20	35	2:27	277	12:18	248
137:7	175	3:6	277	20:28	277
		3:16	45	21:12	79
Proverbs		4:10	84	21:25	162
1:4	101	5:7	255	25:5	162
1:8	13	5:12	278	25:9	162
4:4	13	7:6	270	25:13	146
4:11	13	7:9	270	26:11	277
		7:12	243	27:9	146

27:15	272	5:8	77	*Nahum*	
43–47	272	6:9	229	2:11	79
44–48	228	8	13		
45	153	8:3	276	*Habakkuk*	
45:21	56	9:10	161	2:19	277
47:8	145	10:1–2	277		
48	248	10:5	77	*Zephaniah*	
48:1–29	127			1:5	255
48:31–35	172	*Joel*		1:16	70
		4:4	145		
Daniel				*Haggai*	
3:5	70	*Amos*		1:1	63
3:7	70	1:14	70, 162	1:12	63
3:10	70	2:2	70	2:2	63
3:15	70	3:1–2	274	2:4	5, 63
6:21	46	4:1	136	2:11–13	12
6:27	46	4:4–5	243		
8:11	61	5:10	273	*Zechariah*	
9:11	10	6:13	156, 162, 165	3	63
12:13	21	6:14	11	4:14	47
		7:7	247	6:5	47
Hosea				6:8	21
1:7	264	*Micah*		9:14	132
2:1	46	1:15	137	10:1	4
3:1	270	2:2	12	14:10	229
3:4	277	4:13	47		
4	13	5:12	277	*Malachi*	
4:2	77	6:4	263	3:10	39
4:6	12	6:5	30, 44	3:14	244
4:13	277	6:15	17	3:22	10
4:15	77				

B. Old Testament Apocrypha and Pseudepigrapha

1 Esdras
5:19　　　　103

C. The New Testament

Matthew		*1 Corinthians*		*James*	
1:5–6	35	9:12	233	2:25	35
10:10	233	9:14	233		

D. Orders and Tractates in Mishnaic Literature

Baba Batra 14b, 15a　　　　xxviii